DYNAMIC EPISTEMIC LOGIC

SYNTHESE LIBRARY

STUDIES IN EPISTEMOLOGY,

LOGIC, METHODOLOGY, AND PHILOSOPHY OF SCIENCE

VOLUME 337

DYNAMIC EPISTEMIC LOGIC

by

Hans van Ditmarsch

University of Otago
New Zealand

Wiebe van der Hoek

University of Liverpool
United Kingdom

Barteld Kooi

University of Groningen
The Netherlands

Springer

A C.I.P. Catalogue record for this book is available from the Library of Congress.

ISBN 978-1-4020-5838-7 (HB)
ISBN 978-1-4020-5839-4 (e-book)

Published by Springer,
P.O. Box 17, 3300 AA Dordrecht, The Netherlands.

www.springer.com

Printed on acid-free paper

Contents

Preface

This is both a textbook and a monograph on *dynamic epistemic logic*. Dynamic epistemic logic is the logic of knowledge and change. The book consists of chapters:

1. Introduction
2. Epistemic Logic
3. Belief Revision
4. Public Announcements
5. Epistemic Actions
6. Action Models
7. Completeness
8. Expressivity

A common pattern in individual chapters is to introduce a logic by sections on structures, syntax, semantics, axiomatisation, applications, and notes. The structures are the same for almost all the logics discussed, namely multi-agent Kripke models. So the reader will not see these being reintroduced all the time. For most of the logics we present Hilbert-style axiomatisations. The somewhat substantial technical material involved in the completeness proofs for such axiomatisations has been addressed in a separate chapter, 'Completeness'. Examples for all concepts and logics introduced are found in running text and also as separate sections with applications, often analysing well-known logical puzzles and games in detail. The 'notes' sections give an overview of the historical record for the logic. That information is therefore omitted from other sections. Apart from examples, the running text also contains exercises. Selected answers to exercises from all chapters are found together at the back of the book.

A sweeping outline of the chapterwise content of this book is the following. Chapter 1, 'Introduction', explains why this book is about logic, about knowledge, and about change of knowledge; it also contains an overview of related topics that are considered out of focus and therefore not further mentioned in detail, such as temporal epistemic logic. Chapter 2, 'Epistemic logic', is an overview of and introduction into multi-agent epistemic logic—the logic of knowledge—including modal operators for groups, such as general and common knowledge. This may serve as a general introduction to those unfamiliar with the area, but with sufficient general knowledge of logic. Chapter 3, 'Belief revision', is a fairly detailed presentation on how to model change in a logical setting, both within and without the epistemic logical framework. This relates our modal approach to the area in artificial intelligence that is also named 'belief revision'. Unlike other chapters, it does not mainly model knowledge but also pays detailed attention to belief. Chapter 4, 'Public announcements', is a comprehensive introduction into the logic of knowledge with dynamic operators for truthful public announcements. Many interesting applications are presented in this chapter. Chapter 5, 'Epistemic actions', introduces a generalisation of public announcement logic to more complex epistemic actions; a different perspective on modelling epistemic actions is independently presented in Chapter 6, 'Action models'. 'Completeness' gives details on the completeness proof for the logics introduced in the Chapters 2, 4 and 6. Chapter 8, 'Expressivity', discusses various results on the expressive power of the logics presented. As is to be expected—but with some surprises—the expressive power increases with the complexity of the logical language and corresponding semantics.

There are various ways in which a semester course can be based upon the book. All chapters are self-contained, so that one or more can be skipped if necessary. The core chapters are 2, 4, and 5. Another core path consists of Chapters 2, 4, and 6, in which case one should skip Section 6.8 that compares the approach of Chapter 5 with that of Chapter 6. Advanced classes, where familiarity with epistemic logic is assumed, will prefer to skip Chapter 2. A course focusing on technical logical aspects may consist of all the Chapters 2, 4, 5, 6, 7, and 8, whereas a course focusing on systems modelling will typically skip the Chapters 7 and 8. Chapter 1 may be helpful for motivation to any audience. Chapter 3 is indispensable to an audience with an artificial intelligence or philosophical background.

The companion website to the book `http://www.csc.liv.ac.uk/~del` contains slide presentations, more answers to exercises, an overview of errata, sample exams, updated bibliographies, and other matters of educational or academic interest.

Acknowledgements

The plans for this book started with mutually encouraging contacts between Wiebe van der Hoek and Floor Oosting. We thank Floor Oosting for her encouragement throughout the project. Johan van Benthem has always been in the background, both as an advisor and continuously forwarding us potential users and lecturers. We owe him much.

Input from many students of various graduate semester courses or summerschool courses have greatly helped. We thank the participants to ESSLLI Vienna, ESSLLI Edinburgh, the Logic and Automated Reasoning summerschool in Canberra, and the ILLC Master of Logic program. We are very grateful to many colleagues who provided us with input, in particular to those who read a pre-final version in detail before we handed it over to the publisher. We also thank the anonymous reviewer for the useful comments on our manuscript before it went to print. An incomplete list of people whom we owe thanks consists of, apart from those already mentioned: Thomas Ågotnes, Philippe Balbiani, Alexandru Baltag, Stefano Borgo, Elizabeth Coppock, Jan van Eijck, Jelle Gerbrandy, Paul Gochet, Andreas Herzig, Samson de Jager, Larry Moss, Eric Pacuit, Floris Roelofsen, Ji Ruan, Thomas Schneider, David Steiner, Peter Timmerman, Yde Venema, Rineke Verbrugge, and Mike Wooldridge.

Hans van Ditmarsch acknowledges support from the Netherlands Organisation for Scientific Research enabling a visit to the Netherlands in 2004, and support from the Science Division of the University of Otago freeing him for research time to complete this publication.

Dunedin, Liverpool, Groningen
October 2006

Hans van Ditmarsch
Wiebe van der Hoek
Barteld Kooi

1

Introduction

This chapter differs a little in spirit and style from the other chapters: for one thing, while in the other chapters we postpone the discussion of relevant sources in the literature to the end, the aim of this chapter naturally invites us to mention contributors to 'the field' while we try to put the work of this book in context within other, similar and less related, approaches.

So then, what is this book about? The book provides a *logical* approach to *change of information*. Our approach is *logical* in the sense that we are interested in *reasoning* about change of information and we distinguish *valid* from *invalid* reasoning. We do so by providing a logical toolbox: we specify a number of formal languages which we can use to formalise reasoning, give axiomatisations for several logics and provide them with semantics. Moreover we present a number of technical results about these formal systems.

Before we discuss change of information, let us first be clear on what we mean by *information*. We regard information as something that is relative to a subject who has a certain perspective on the world, called an *agent*, and the kind of information we have in mind is meaningful as a whole, not just loose bits and pieces. This makes us call it *knowledge* and, to a lesser extent, *belief*. This conception of information is due to the fields known as *epistemic* and *doxastic logic* (which stem from the Greek words for knowledge and belief: ἐπιστήμη and δόξα, respectively.)

Finally, the kind of *change* of information that is the focus of this book is change due to *communication*. One of the characteristics of communication is that it does not change the bare facts of the world, but only information that agents may have. Hence, the issue of information change due to changes of facts, has mostly been left out of consideration. Since communication involves more than one agent, we also focus on *multi-agent* aspects of change of information. *Dynamic epistemic logic* is the field which studies this kind of information change using epistemic logic as a background theory.

This book provides answers to all of the following questions. How is it possible that two persons are both ignorant about a specific fact, i.e., they neither know *whether* it is true, and that, by revealing this ignorance to each other, the ignorance disappears? And how do we model such a situation? How do we explain the phenomenon that simply announcing a certain proposition makes it untrue? How is it possible that making repeatedly the 'same' announcement still can have a different effect on the knowledge of the agents involved, every time the announcement is being made? How do we explain that, even when some statement is announced and this is a 'common experience' in the group (i.e., everybody in a group notices that the announcement is being made, and this on itself is being noticed by everybody, etc.), that then afterwards the statement does not have to be 'commonly known'?

Let us now briefly give an overview of epistemic and dynamic epistemic logic, embed our work in a broader context, and also discuss some of the other approaches to information change, some of which this book builds further upon, but most of which we will *not* further address.

1.1 Epistemic and Doxastic Logic

The clearest source which our work and that of many others builds upon is Hintikka's book *Knowledge and Belief: An Introduction to the Logic of the Two Notions* [99]. Combining his mathematical skills with the directional aerial for ideas of von Wright on modal logic, Hintikka composed a manuscript that was one of the first to give a clear semantics to the notions of knowledge and belief. This not only ended an era of attempts in philosophy to have the means to formally discuss these notions, it also marked the start of a prosperous half-century of further developments in epistemics, often from surprisingly new angles.

The subtitle *An Introduction to the Logic of the Two Notions* indicates the further focus to the publications in which we also situate our book: the account is a logical one. Von Wright [195] was one of the first who gave a—mainly syntactic—formal account of reasoning about knowledge in terms of modal logic. The early 1960s was the era when *possible world semantics* emerged, of which some first traces can be found in Carnap's work [34], which was picked up and enriched with the notion of *accessibility* between worlds by Hintikka [98], and further shaped by Kripke [121]. (For a more detailed historical account, see [36].) These semantic insights proved to be very fruitful to interpret notions as diverse as epistemic, doxastic, temporal, deontic, dynamic, and those regarding provability. It was the era in which modal logic rapidly evolved into a main tool for reasoning in all kinds of disciplines.

The idea of possible world semantics for knowledge and belief is to think of the information that an agent has in terms of the *possible worlds* that are *consistent* with the information of that agent. These possible worlds are said to be *accessible* for the agent, and knowledge or belief can be defined in terms of this. An agent knows or believes that something is the case, if and only if it is the case in all the worlds that are accessible to the agent. This semantics for epistemic logic allows us to formalise reasoning about knowledge and belief.

Moreover, the semantics provides a concise way to represent the information of an agent, and it easily allows one to add more agents, such that it also represents the information that the agents have about each other, so-called *higher-order information.*

1.2 Dynamic Epistemic Logic

Information is communicated, so knowledge and belief are by no means static. Not surprisingly, many logicians have taken this into account. In the context of epistemic logic, there are many different approaches. Dynamic epistemic logic is an umbrella term for a number of extensions of epistemic logic with dynamic operators that enable us to formalise reasoning about information change. It came forth from developments in formal linguistics, computer science, and philosophical logic.

The development of dynamic epistemic logic was partly inspired by Groenendijk and Stokhof's work on information change in the semantics of linguistics and philosophy of language, which resulted in their semantics of dynamic interpretation [81]. The view that discourse is a process and that the meaning of an utterance can best be interpreted as a 'cognitive program' that changes the information states of the participants in a discourse, has been quite influential in formal linguistics [156]. In this view 'meaning' is not explicated in terms of *truth conditions*, but rather in terms of *update conditions*, which describe the information change that an utterance gives rise to, as is also stated in [191], where Veltman uses this *update semantics* to analyse default reasoning. In these dynamic approaches to linguistics one can for example explain the difference in meaning between "John left. Mary started to cry." and "Mary started to cry. John left." The difference in meaning is due to the order in which the information is processed.

Another development that led to dynamic epistemic logic is the development of *dynamic modal logic*. It developed strongly in the early 1980s, as a specification language to reason about the correctness and behaviour of computer programs, and in general: aspects of numerical computation. The main proponents are Harel, Kozen and Tiuryn, [92, 93], Pratt [169], Halpern with several co-authors (with Ben Ari and Pnueli '[17], with Reif [90] and with Berman and Tiuryn [28]), Parikh [161] and Goldblatt [79]. The logic contains formulas of the form $[\pi]\varphi$, which are read as 'successfully executing program π yields a φ state'. From there, we arrive at dynamic epistemic logic by firstly enriching the programs in such a way that they describe information change, instead of the (numerical) state variable change that was intended by Harel and others. Secondly, the language has to contain *epistemic* operators as well, in order to reason about both information and its change.

Communication ('the process of sharing information', according to Wikipedia) is an obvious source for changing one's information state. Having been studied by philosophers and linguistics, in both pragmatics and semantics, formalisations focus on describing preconditions and postconditions of utterances, conditions that refer to the mental state of the speaker and the hearer. Also here, computer scientists formalised important parts of communication, especially on (the hardness of) achieving knowledge in a distributed environment. We mention three papers from the mid-1980s that were very influential, also for the approach followed here: Halpern and Moses [88] used an interpreted systems approach to show that common knowledge is in many cases hard to achieve, Parikh and Ramanujam [164] introduced their history-based semantics to reason about the evolution of knowledge overruns of a protocol, and Chandy and Misra [35] gave a characterisation of the minimum information flow necessary for a process to 'learn' specific facts about the system.

Further inspiration came from *belief revision*. This is a branch of philosophical logic that deals with the dynamics of the information. This approach originates in a paper by Alchourrón, Gärdenfors, and Makinson, [3], which triggered a stream of research in the "AGM-paradigm". Issues are the difference between revision and update (i.e., informational and factual change), dealing with iterated revision, and specific properties of revision. However, in belief revision the operators that describe information change are not taken to be dynamic operators in the sense of dynamic modal logic.

The first step towards making dynamic logic epistemic was made in the late 1980s. A suggestion to apply dynamic modal logic to model *information* change was made by van Benthem in the Proceedings of the 1987 Logic Colloquium [19, pp. 366–370]. The suggestion was to use dynamic operators to describe *factual* change—in other words, unlike in dynamic logic where we typically think of variables as numerical variables, we now think of variables as propositional variables. Van Benthem also suggested that 'theory change operators' from belief revision can be reinterpreted as dynamic modal operators. Van Benthem's suggestions were further developed in [20, 176, 110, 21]. In the late 1990s this inspired Segerberg and collaborators to put theory change operators in the language [132, 185, 184, 133]. This approach is known as DDL, or 'dynamic doxastic logic'. It is discussed together with belief revision in Chapter 3.

The first steps towards making epistemic logic dynamic were made by Plaza in 1989 [168] (the proceedings of a symposium that from our current perspective seems obscure), an obligatory reference for any researcher active in the area; and, independently, by Gerbrandy and Groeneveld in 1997, in the Journal of Logic, Language, and Information [77]. In [168], Plaza defines a logic for *public announcements*. His results are similar to those by Gerbrandy and Groeneveld in [77]. Plaza's operator is actually not a dynamic modal operator but a binary propositional connective. Gerbrandy and Groeneveld's paper is seen as a milestone in the 'update semantics' history of public announcement logic, with precursors found in [60, 123, 82, 191] and also relating to [19]. Public announcement logic is treated in great detail in Chapter 4.

The next step in the development was to model more complex actions than public announcements, such as card showing actions, where different agents have different perspectives on the action (one agent can see something is going on while the others know exactly what is happening). Different approaches were developed by Baltag, Moss, and Solecki, by Gerbrandy, by the authors of this book, and by others [11, 12, 75, 131, 43, 10, 49, 175]. This took place from the late 1990s onward. Two of these general frameworks of *epistemic actions* are the major topics of Chapter 5 (Epistemic actions) and Chapter 6 (Action models). They present somewhat different, compatible, viewpoints on epistemic actions.

Recent further developments that are beyond the scope of this book include the incorporation of factual change into languages that express epistemic change, for example found in recent work by van Benthem, van Eijck, and Kooi [26] (mirroring similar differences between belief update and belief revision in the AGM tradition), preference-based modelling of belief revision with dynamic modal operators by Aucher [4], by van Ditmarsch [48], and by van Benthem and Liu [27], and various proposals to integrate dynamic epistemic logics with 'AI-flavoured' semantics that model actions and change of actions, such as situation calculus, as in work by Levesque and Lakemeyer, and by Demolombe [125, 41].

Now let us put dynamic epistemic logic in a somewhat broader perspective.

1.3 Information, Belief, and Knowledge

There are many theories of information, like epistemology, philosophy of science, probability theory, statistics, game theory, information theory, situation theory, computer science, and artificial intelligence. Each seems to focus on a different aspect of information. Let us take a brief look at some of the theories about information, such that it becomes clear just how rich a concept information is and on which of these aspects dynamic epistemic logic focuses.

The oldest field that deals with questions regarding knowledge is *epistemology*, a branch of philosophy. It has focussed on the justification of coining certain information as knowledge since Plato's *Theaetetus*, a dialogue in which Socrates, Theodorus, and Theaetetus try to define what knowledge is. People are often deceived or simply mistaken, and claim to have knowledge nonetheless. What then are necessary and sufficient conditions to say that something is knowledge, and how does one come to know something? In Plato's *Meno*, Socrates and Meno discuss the nature of *virtue*, which again brings them to the notion of knowledge. Are they the same? Is it necessary to know what is good, in order to be virtuous? Socrates maintains in this discussion that everything that can be known, can be taught and acquisition of knowledge is a process of remembering what happened in the past. The focus of epistemology is on propositional knowledge (knowing that something is true), rather than procedural knowledge (knowing how to perform a certain task), or knowledge in the sense that one knows someone or something. Epistemic logic is exclusively concerned with propositional knowledge. However epistemic logic is not so much concerned with the question how one can justify that something is knowledge, but what one can infer from something being knowledge. Its focus is on reasoning about knowledge, rather than the nature of knowledge.

Another philosophical discipline that looks at information and information change from a methodological viewpoint is *philosophy of science*, which revolves around questions regarding the nature of science. Scientific theories represent a body of knowledge produced by a scientific community. Questions regarding the justification of such knowledge are fueled by the development of science. Scientific theories are often extended or replaced by new ones when the old theory makes predictions that contradict new evidence, or when the old theory does not explain certain phenomena adequately. Philosophy of science is not only concerned with the question how scientific knowledge can be justified, but also how the development of this knowledge can be justified. This kind of information change is studied in the area of belief revision, that was originally intended to describe theory change. However, just as in the case of epistemology, we are not so much concerned with the question how such information change is justified, but with reasoning about information change. Moreover we are mainly interested in *deductive* reasoning, i.e., the question which inferences are *logically valid*, whereas in science there is a much broader notion reasoning encompassing inductive and abductive reasoning.

Probability theory and *statistics* are branches of mathematics that deal with information. Their origins can be traced back to the desire to understand gambling games, whose outcome is uncertain, but where it is clear what the possible outcomes are and how the outcome comes about. In a more general setting one can also be uncertain about how the process works, and only have knowledge of it by a limited number of observations. A salient way to deal with new information in probability theory is *conditioning* according to Bayes' law which enables one to adjust one's probabilities *given some new evidence*. So, just like dynamic epistemic logic, probability theory and statistics are also concerned with reasoning about information and its change, but the model of information that is used is more quantitative than the model that is used in epistemic logic. Still, the similarities are such that nothing prevents one to give a logical account of probability theory: for a comprehensive and contemporary approach we refer to Halpern's [85]. There are also probabilistic versions of dynamic epistemic logic, developed by van Benthem [24] and by Kooi [115].

There are many logical approaches of which the main motivation lies in the desire to represent the available information in a more sophisticated way than just indicating whether the relevant information (knowledge, belief) is there, or not. These logics are often said to enable 'reasoning about uncertainty'. Apart from probabilistic logic [85], we mention knowledge representation in fuzzy logic (which is exactly the title of Zadeh's [196]), possibilistic logic, mainly developed by Dubois and Prade (e.g., their monograph [55]), and many-valued approaches (see Gottwald's monograph [80]). Here, we will only be concerned with non-probabilistic issues regarding information, and represent information merely with the use of possible worlds.

Game theory, which started as a branch of economics, is a scientific theory about interacting agents which tries to answer the question how one should act in strategic situations involving more than one agent, i.e., games. The first mathematical formalisation of game theory is by von Neumann and Morgenstern [157] (a modern introduction can be found in [158]). In game theory there are two distinctions when it comes to information: *perfect* versus *imperfect information*, and *complete* versus *incomplete information*. In games of perfect information the players are completely informed about the state of the game. In games of imperfect information each player only has partial information. Both games of perfect and imperfect information are games of complete information. Games of incomplete information are games where the players are not sure about the structure of the game or are not sure about the preferences of the other players. In short, information plays an important role in game theory, just as in dynamic epistemic logic. In game theory the focus is on the *actions* that rational players should perform in a multi-agent context. In dynamic epistemic logic the focus is also on multi-agent situations, but here the focus is on reasoning about the information rather than on actions. However, many of the examples to which we will apply dynamic epistemic logic are game-like situations.

The first scientific theory that explicitly mentions information is *information theory*. Originally developed by Shannon in [186], it deals with quantitative questions about information. How much information does a message contain? How much information can be communicated? How can information be sent efficiently? Information theory was generalised by Kolmogorov in [113] to what is now known as Kolmogorov complexity, which focuses on the computational resources needed to describe something. For a modern introduction to information theory and Kolmogorov complexity see [37] and [130], respectively. The aspect of information that these theories focus on, is the representation of information as bits such that they can be stored and manipulated by machines. In dynamic epistemic logic we abstract from problems of how to store information and how to communicate information. We simply assume that it happens and start our investigations from there.

A theory that addresses from a philosophical point of view the fundamental issue how information is stored and how it can be communicated, is *situation theory*. This research program, initiated by Barwise and Perry [16], deals with the question what information actually *is* and how it is possible at all that information is *passed* on. How can one thing carry information about another? This is explained in terms of situations that are related by *constraints*. Situation theory mainly deals with the intentional aspects of information: information is about something. How is this so? These issues are not touched upon by dynamic epistemic logic.

Computer science is obviously involved with storing and manipulating information. Theories of information and knowledge play an increasingly important role in this area, e.g., *knowledge representation* is part of the computer science curriculum as a rule. Since computers or processes communicate with each other, it is natural to think of them as multi-agent systems, and to represent what they know before and after sending certain messages. In security and authentication protocols it is of vital importance to demonstrate that some parties stay *ignorant* about the contents of certain messages. Indeed epistemic logic has been applied to this area by Fagin, Halpern, Moses, and Vardi [62], and we also deal with examples from this area (see also Example 2.3 regarding the *alternating bit protocol* in the next chapter).

In the area of *programming* (within computer science) there is awareness that knowledge of the 'processing unit' is important. This is especially apparent in the case of an 'if then else' construct, where, depending on the truth of a condition, the program is supposed to follow a certain branch. However, a program line like `IF no_traffic_left AND no_traffic_right THEN DO cross_road` is hard to execute for a robot: the program better refer to its *knowledge* than to the state of the world, as in `IF KNOW(no_traffic_right) AND ...` Halpern and Fagin [61] proposed to enrich the programming paradigm with *knowledge-based protocols*, or *knowledge-based programs* as they were later called, which should enable such epistemic constructs. Although as of yet there are no knowledge-based programming languages, writing a specification in such a language makes the programmer aware at which places he has to make sure that certain information is available (in the case of the robot-example, the robot might want to perform a sense action, before entering the if-construct). Relevant studies are most notably by Vardi about implementing knowledge-based programs [190], and by van der Meyden on the computational complexity of automatically synthesizing executable programs from knowledge-based programs [145].

This brings us close to other logical approaches to information change similar to dynamic epistemic logic. Formal approaches to information can roughly be divided in two categories. In the first, one is 'only' able to distinguish what is part of the information from what is not. This 'information set' can be described on a meta-level, as in the already mentioned paradigm of belief revision, and as in Moore's auto-epistemic logic [153], or explicitly in the object language. Apart from the epistemic and doxastic logics that we build upon in this book, examples are logic programming approaches (see for instance the survey paper of Damásio and Pereira, [39] and Gelfond's paper [73] on logic programming and incomplete information) which typically deal with two kinds of negation: one to indicate that the negation of a proposition is in the information set, the other representing that the proposition is not included in the information, or that the proposition is unknown.

Perhaps the most prominent contribution to reasoning about information change are the publications by (many combinations of) Fagin, Halpern, Moses, and Vardi from the 1980s onward. Their book *Reasoning About Knowledge* [62] is a culmination of many papers on the subject. Whereas one might find many objections to one of the widely accepted logics for knowledge (see Chapter 2), the *interpreted systems* model of Fagin, Halpern, Moses, and Vardi provides a semantics of that logic that is *computationally grounded*. By identifying an agent's access in the possible world semantics with what he can observe, the properties of knowledge follow in a natural way.

The notion of a *run* (a sequence of state transitions) in an interpreted system elegantly facilitates reasoning about dynamic aspects of knowledge. This resulted in publications on the notion of *knowledge in distributed computing* by Parikh and Ramanujam [164] and of *knowledge and time*, including work on axiomatisation by Halpern, van der Meyden, and Vardi [87, 143], and on model checking [69, 171]. There is a recent surge of interest in model checking dynamics of knowledge in specific scenarios [147, 50]; and we should not fail to mention the dynamic epistemic model checker DEMO by van Eijck [57]—because of the close relation to the logics in this book, DEMO is in fact presented in some detail in Section 6.7.

In artificial intelligence (AI) it is well accepted that a serious theory of planning takes into account what is known by the executing agent; notably after Moore's work [152] (this is *R.C.* Moore, not to be confused with *G.E.* Moore, to whom we owe the 'Moore-sentences' playing a crucial role in Chapter 4). Moore used a formalism that combined aspects of both epistemic logic and dynamic logic [93] to capture what needs to be known in order to carry out a plan. He introduced the notion of *epistemic precondition* of an action, which refers to the knowledge that is needed to successfully perform it—the paradigm example is that of knowing the code of a safe, in order to be able to open it. Moore's work was also influential in making a proper distinction between knowledge *de dicto* (I know that there is a code that is needed to open the safe) and knowledge *de re* (there is a code that I know to open the safe). For a survey of the many formalisms that have subsequently been developed in a similar spirit, we refer to Wooldridge's [194].

In AI the representation of knowledge has always been a major issue of research. Knowledge bases, expert systems, logic programs: they all are a means to represent some structured information, and much research on for instance non-monotonic reasoning was motivated by the kind of issues involving the subscription of a knowledge set. Modelling the *subject* (who has the information) as well became a significant issue with the rise of the area of *intelligent agents*. This is very much a part of AI nowadays; one of today's most popular textbooks in AI, Russell and Norvig's [177], is built upon the intelligent agent metaphor. Agents, in this sense, are software components about which one reasons on a high level. The *Belief, Desire, and Intentions* paradigm, which was first formalised by Rao and Georgeff [172] inspired many frameworks and architectures that, apart from an informational attitude, also model motivational and emotional attitudes. The area of multi-agent systems provides a nice case for one of the main focuses in the book, namely that it is challenging to model situations in which the attitudes of one agent involve attitudes of other agents (which involve ...). Indeed, the ability to reason about *higher-order information* distinguishes epistemic logic from many other approaches to information.

Rao and Georgeff's work [172] can be seen as an attempt to formalise work on intentions by the philosopher Bratman [32]. It is fair to say that also the work on representing knowledge and belief in game theory, computer science, planning, AI, and agent theories goes back to work in philosophy. Philosophy also brings the motivational and informational attitudes together, since philosophers often refer to knowledge as 'intentional information': information that has a purpose, or use.

The *situation calculus* was initiated in the late 1960's by McCarthy and Hayes [142]. Later milestones are the development of the programming language Golog and variants of it [126]. Situation calculus is used for describing how actions and other events affect the world, and can be located somewhere between computer science and AI. Only recently has the representation of knowledge become a main issue in the situation calculus [124]. The situation calculus comes with its own knowledge-based programs, as in Reiter's [173, Chapter 11]. An important issue here is to guarantee that at run-time of a knowledge-based program it is guaranteed that the necessary knowledge will be provided, and that the process always can 'break a tie'. Sardiña therefore proposes to treat plans in the situation calculus as *epistemically feasible* programs: programs for which the executing agent, at every stage of execution, by virtue of what it knew initially and the subsequent readings of his sensors, always *knows* what step to take next ...' [181].

Another approach in logic to the dynamics of epistemics and doxastics is due to Moss and Parikh [155] and also undertaken by Georgatos [74] and Heinemann [95], inspired by the work of Vickers [192]. They give a 'topological semantics' for knowledge and also have a topological interpretation of information change in so-called subset models or treelike spaces. There are two modalities: one for knowledge and one for effort. It is left open exactly what this effort is, but it can lead to information change. This approach is further developed in [38] and [159]. In [159] it is generalised to the multi-agent case and here, 'effort' is interpreted as consulting the knowledge base of a certain agent.

This book can by no means deal with all approaches to modelling knowledge, belief, or information, not even if we would restrict ourselves to logical approaches, and the same applies to change of information: we can by no means be complete, nor do we intend to be. In fact, if our reader is in search for a specific formalism to model his or her specific 'information change scenario', then it is well possible that another approach than the one propagated in this book much better fulfils these needs.

We hope this chapter has made clear how dynamic epistemic logic fits in the broader scientific background. Each chapter concludes with a notes section, which guides the reader to the literature relevant to the topic of that chapter.

2

Epistemic Logic

2.1 Introduction

In this chapter we introduce the basic epistemic logic, to which we add a dynamic component in consecutive chapters. Epistemic logic, as it is conceived today, is very much influenced by the development of modal logic, and, in particular, by its Kripke semantics. We will emphasise the intuitive appeal of this semantics in this chapter and, indeed, throughout the book, since also the dynamics of epistemics will fruitfully utilise them.

The logical system *S5* is by far the most popular and accepted epistemic logic, and we will without further ado present it in this chapter, as a basis for the rest of the book. We do this first for agents in a group each with their own individual knowledge (Section 2.2), and then look at group notions of knowledge (Section 2.3), most notably that of common knowledge. On the fly, we give several examples and exercises.

Most, if not all of the material covered here belongs to the 'core of folklore in epistemic logic', therefore, the emphasis is on semantics and concepts, rather than on proofs of theorems.

Having presented the basic material, we then in Section 2.4 comment upon how the material in this chapter carries over to the notion of belief, rather than knowledge, and, finally, a section called 'Notes' (Section 2.5), collects the bibliographical and other meta-information regarding this chapter.

2.2 Basic System: *S5*

We now present the basic system for knowledge for a group of agents. Doing so, we follow a traditional outline, presenting the language, semantics, and axiomatisation in subsequent subsections.

2.2.1 Language

The basic language for knowledge is based on a countable set of atomic propositions P and a finite set of (names for) agents, A. Atomic propositions $p, q, \ldots$ describe some state of affairs in 'the actual world', or in a game, for example. In the following, p is an arbitrary atomic proposition from P, and a denotes an arbitrary agent from A.

Definition 2.1 (Basic epistemic language) Let P be a set of atomic propositions, and A a set of agent-symbols. The language $\mathcal{L}_K$, the language for multi-agent epistemic logic, is generated by the following BNF:

$$\varphi \ ::= \ p \mid \neg\varphi \mid (\varphi \wedge \varphi) \mid K_a\varphi \qquad \Box$$

This BNF-notation says that atoms are formulas, and one can build complex formulas from formulas using negation '$\neg$', conjunction '$\wedge$' and knowledge operators 'K_a'. Examples of formulas that can be generated using this definition are $(p \wedge \neg K_a K_a(p \wedge K_a \neg p))$ and $\neg K_a \neg(p \wedge K_a(q \wedge \neg K_a r))$. Here, p is an atom from P and a is an agent name from A. Other typical elements that we will use for atoms are q, r, and also p', q', r', $\ldots p''$, ... Other variables for agents will be b, c and a', b', ... In examples, we will also use other symbols for the agents, like S for Sender, R for receiver, etc. Throughout the book, we will use a number of 'standard abbreviations and conventions', like $(\varphi \vee \psi) = \neg(\neg\varphi \wedge \neg\psi)$, the symbol $\top$ as an abbreviation for $p \vee \neg p$ (for an arbitrary $p \in P$) and $\bot$ denoting $\neg\top$. Moreover, $(\varphi \to \psi) = (\neg\varphi \vee \psi)$, and $(\varphi \leftrightarrow \psi)$ is a shorthand for the conjunction of the implication in both directions. We omit outermost parenthesis if doing so does not lead to confusion.

For every agent a, $K_a\varphi$ is interpreted as "agent a knows (that) φ". Note that the epistemic language is a rather simple extension of that of propositional logic: we just add a unary operator for every agent. Here, an agent may be a human being, a player in a game, a robot, a machine, or simply a 'process'. We also introduce some epistemic definitions. The fact that a does not know that $\neg\varphi$ ($\neg K_a \neg\varphi$) is sometimes also pronounced as: "φ is consistent with a's knowledge", or, "the agent considers it possible that φ" (cf. also Section 2.2.2). We write $\hat{K}_a\varphi$ for this: $\hat{K}_a\varphi = \neg K_a \neg\varphi$. For any group B of agents from A, "Everybody in B knows φ", written $E_B\varphi$, is defined as the conjunction of all individuals in B knowing φ. Thus, we add an E_B operator for every $B \subseteq A$:

$$E_B\varphi = \bigwedge_{b \in B} K_b\varphi$$

Analogously to $\hat{K}$, we define $\hat{E}_B\varphi$ as $\neg E_B \neg\varphi$. Using the definition of E_B, this unravels to $\bigvee_{b \in B} \hat{K}_b\varphi$: "at least one individual in the group B considers φ a possibility".

Hence, examples of well-formed formulas are $p \wedge \neg K_a p$ ("p is true but agent a does not know it") and $\neg K_b K_c p \wedge \neg K_b \neg K_c p$ (saying that "agent b does not know *whether* agent c knows p). Another example is $K_a(p \to E_B p)$ ("agent a knows, that if p is true, everybody in B will know it").

Exercise 2.2 We have three agents, say a (Anne), b (Bill), and c (Cath). We furthermore have two atoms, p ("Anne has a sister") and q ("Anne has a brother"). Translate the following expressicns in our formal language:

1. If Anne had a sister, she would know it.
2. Bill knows that Anne knows whether she has a sister.
3. Cath knows that if Anne has a sibling, it is a sister.
4. Anne considers it possible that Bill does not know that Anne has a sister.
5. Everybody in the group of three knows that Anne does not have a sibling if she does not know to have one.
6. Anne knows that if there is anybody who does not know that she has a sister, it must be Bill. □

We will often refer to $K_a, K_b, \ldots, \hat{K}_a, \hat{K}_b \ldots, E_B, \hat{E}_B$ as *epistemic operators*, or sometimes, and more generally, as *modal operators*. For any modal operator X, we define $X^0\varphi$ to be equal to φ, and $X^{n+1}\varphi$ to be $XX^n\varphi$. We will also apply this convention to sequences of formulas. Hence, for instance $E_A^2\varphi$ means that everybody knows that everybody knows φ, and $(K_a\hat{K}_b)^2\varphi$ says that a knows that b considers it possible that a knows that b considers it possible that φ.

To demonstrate the usefulness of a language in which we allow iterations of individual epistemic operators, we now look at a simple *protocol specification* using epistemic operators. The derivation and correctness proofs of such protocols were a main motivation for computer scientists to study epistemic logic.

Example 2.3 (Alternating bit protocol) There are two processors, let us say a 'Sender S' and a 'Receiver R', although this terminology is a little bit misleading, since both parties can send messages to each other. The goal is for S to read a tape $X = \langle x_0, x_1, \ldots \rangle$, and to send all the inputs it has read to R over a communication channel. R in turn writes down everything it receives on an output tape Y. Unfortunately the channel is not trustworthy, i.e., there is no guarantee that all messages arrive. On the other hand, *some* messages will not get lost, or more precisely: if you repeat sending a certain message long enough, it will eventually arrive. This property is called *fairness*. Now the question is whether one can write a protocol (or a program) that satisfies the following two constraints, provided that fairness holds:

- *safety:* at any moment, Y is a prefix of X;
- *liveness:* every x_i will eventually be written as y_i on Y.

Hence, safety expresses that R will only write a correct initial part of the tape X into Y. This is easily achieved by allowing R to never write anything, but the liveness property says that R cannot linger on forever: every bit of X should eventually appear in Y.

In the protocol below, the construct 'send msg until ψ' means that the message msg is repeatedly sent, until the Boolean ψ has become true. The test $K_R(x_i)$ intuitively means that Receiver knows that the i-th element of X is equal to x_i: more precisely, it is true if Receiver receives a bit b and the last bit he has written is x_{i-1}. The other Booleans, like $K_S K_R(x_i)$ are supposed to express that S has received the message "$K_R(x_i)$".

PROTOCOL FOR S:

$S1$ i :=0
$S2$ while true do
$S3$ begin read x_i;
$S4$ send x_i until $K_S K_R(x_i)$;
$S5$ send "$K_S K_R(x_i)$" until $K_S K_R K_S K_R(x_i)$
$S6$ i := i + 1
$S7$ end

PROTOCOL FOR R:

$R2$ when $K_R(x_0)$ set i :=0
Necwhile true do
$R3$ begin write x_i;
$R4$ send "$K_R(x_i)$" until $K_R K_S K_R(x_i)$;
$R5$ send "$K_R K_S K_R(x_i)$" until $K_R(x_{i+1})$
$R6$ i := i + 1
$R7$ end

An important aspect of the protocol is that Sender at line $S5$ does not continue reading X and does not yet add 1 to the counter i. We will show why this is crucial for guaranteeing safety. For, suppose that the lines $S5$ and $R5$ would be absent, and that instead line $R4$ would read as follows:

$R4'$ send "$K_R(x_i)$" until $K_R(x_{i+1})$;

Suppose also, as an example, that $X = \langle a, a, b, \dots \rangle$. Sender starts by reading x_0, an a, and sends it to R. We know that an instance of that a will arrive at a certain moment, and so by line $R3$ it will be written on Y. Receiver then acts as it should and sends an acknowledgement ($R4'$) that will also arrive eventually, thus Sender continues with $S6$ followed by $S3$: once again it reads an a and sends it to Receiver. The latter will eventually receive an instance of that a, but will not know how to interpret it: "is this symbol a a repetition of the previous one, because Sender does not know that I know what x_0 is, or is this a the next element of the input tape, x_1"? This would clearly endanger safety.

One can show that knowledge of depth four is sufficient and necessary to comply with the specification. As a final remark on the protocol, it be noted that most programming languages do not refer to epistemic notions. So in general a protocol like the one described above still needs to be transformed into 'a real program'. It is indeed possible to rewrite this protocol without using any knowledge operators. The result is known as the 'alternating bit protocol' (see notes for references). □

We now give an example where some typical reasoning about ignorance, and iterations of everybody's knowledge, are at stake.

Example 2.4 (Consecutive numbers) Two agents, a (Anne) and b (Bill) are facing each other. They see a number on each other's head, and those numbers are consecutive numbers n and $n+1$ for a certain $n \in \mathbb{N}$. They both know this, and they know that they know it, etc. However, they do not have any other a priori knowledge about their own number. Let us assume we have 'atoms' a_n and b_n, for every $n \in \mathbb{N}$, expressing that the number on Anne's head equals n, and that on Bill's head reads n, respectively.

Suppose that in fact a_3 and b_2 are true. Assuming that the agents only see each other's number and that it is common knowledge that the numbers are consecutive, we now have the following (if you find it hard to see why these statements are true, move on and collect some technical tools first, and then try to do Exercise 2.10):

1. $K_a b_2$
   Anne can see b's number.
   For the same reason, we have $K_b a_3$.
2. $K_a(a_1 \vee a_3)$
   expressing that Anne knows that her number is either 1 or 3.
   Similarly, we of course have $K_b(b_2 \vee b_4)$.
3. $K_a K_b(b_0 \vee b_2 \vee b_4)$
   This follows from the previous item.
   Similarity induces that we also have $K_b K_a(a_1 \vee a_3 \vee a_5)$
4. $K_a K_b K_a(b_0 \vee b_2 \vee b_4)$
   If you find it hard to see this, wait until we have explained a formal semantics for this situation, in Section 2.2.2.
   In a similar vein, we have $K_b K_a K_b(a_1 \vee a_3 \vee a_5)$

The above sequence of truths for the real state characterised by $(a_3 \wedge b_2)$ has a number of intriguing consequences for iterated knowledge concerning a and b. This is easier to see if we also enumerate a number of 'epistemic possibilities' for the agents. Let us suppose that the aim of this scenario is, for both Anne and Bill, to find out the number on their head. For this, we introduce win_a for "Anne knows the number on her head", and similarly, win_b.

5. $\hat{K}_a a_1 \wedge \hat{K}_a a_3$
   Anne considers it possible that her number is 1, but she also considers it possible that she is wearing 3.
   Similarly, we obtain $\hat{K}_b b_2 \wedge \hat{K}_a b_4$

6. $K_a(\neg \mathsf{win_a} \wedge \neg \mathsf{win_b})$
   Note that only if one of the numbers is 0, can somebody know her or his number: anyone who sees 0 knows to have 1. Anne considers two situations possible: one in which $a_1 \wedge b_2$ holds, and another in which $a_3 \wedge b_2$ is true. In neither of those situations is an agent wearing 0, so that Anne knows there is no winner.
   Similarly, we have $K_b(\neg \mathsf{win_a} \wedge \neg \mathsf{win_b})$
7. $E_{\{a,b\}} \neg a_5 \wedge \neg E_{\{a,b\}} E_{\{a,b\}} \neg a_5$
   Anne and Bill know that Anne does not have 5 (because Bill knows she has a 3, and Anne knows she has either 1 or 3). However, not everybody knows that everybody knows this, since we have $\hat{K}_b \hat{K}_a a_5$: Bill thinks it possible that the situation is such that Anne has 3 and Bill 4, in which case Anne would see Bill's 4, and considers it possible that she has 5! Once again, clear semantics may help in verifying these properties: see Section 2.2.2, especially Exercise 2.10.
8. $E_{\{a,b\}}(\neg \mathsf{win_a} \wedge \neg \mathsf{win_b}) \wedge \neg E_{\{a,b\}} E_{\{a,b\}}(\neg \mathsf{win_a} \wedge \neg \mathsf{win_b})$
   Although everybody knows that neither of the agents can win (this follows from item 6), it is not the case that this very fact is known by everybody! To see the latter, note that a thinks it possible that she wears 1 and b 2, in which case b would consider it possible that a's number is 1 and his 0, in which case a would know her number: $\hat{K}_a \hat{K}_b (a_1 \wedge K_a a_1)$. □

It is worthwhile to notice that, in Example 2.4 $\neg E_{\{a,b\}} E_{\{a,b\}} \neg a_5$ holds in the state characterised by $(a_3 \wedge b_2)$ since $\hat{K}_b \hat{K}_a a_5$ is true. We recall a generalised version of this insight in the following exercise, since it will be useful later on.

Exercise 2.5 Let $B = \{b_1, \ldots, b_m\}$ be a group of m agents. Argue that $E_B^n \varphi$ is false if and only if there is a sequence of agents names $a^1, a^2, \ldots a^n$ $(a^i \in B, i \leq n)$ such that $\hat{K}_{a^1} \hat{K}_{a^2} \ldots \hat{K}_{a^n} \neg \varphi$ holds. Note that it is well possible that $n > m$: some agents can reappear in the sequence. □

2.2.2 Semantics

Now let us move to a formal treatment of the logics of knowledge for individual agents within a group. Crucial in the approach to epistemic logic is the use of its *semantics* which uses a special case of Kripke models. In such a model, two notions are of main importance: that of *state* and that of *indistinguishability*. We explain these using a very simple example. We call it the GLO-scenario, named after Groningen, Liverpool, and Otago. Suppose we have one agent, say b, who lives in Groningen. For some reason, he builds a theory about the weather conditions in both Groningen and Liverpool: in Groningen it is either sunny (denoted by the atom g), or not ($\neg g$). Likewise for Liverpool: sunny (l) or not ($\neg l$). If for the moment we identify a 'state' with a possible state of the world, then, a priori, we have 4 such states: $\langle g, l \rangle$, in which it is both sunny

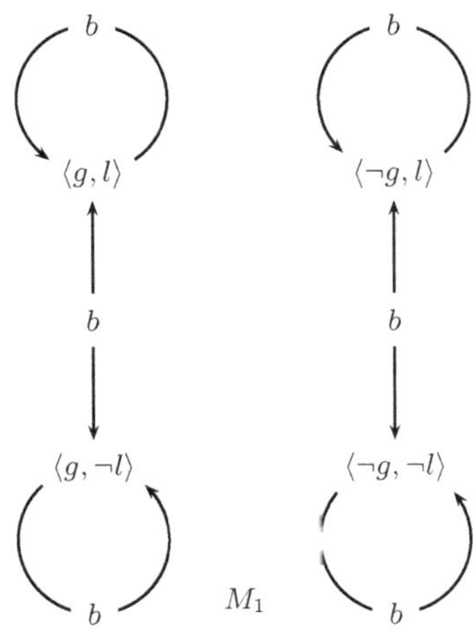

Figure 2.1. Kripke model M_1, representing a GLO scenario.

in Groningen and in Liverpool, $\langle g, \neg l \rangle$ in which the weather in Groningen is again sunny but not in Liverpool, etc. Since b is situated in Groningen, we can assume that he is aware of the weather in Groningen, but not of that in Liverpool. In other words: he cannot distinguish state $\langle g, l \rangle$ from $\langle g, \neg l \rangle$, neither can he tell the difference between $\langle \neg g, l \rangle$ and $\langle \neg g, \neg l \rangle$.

This situation is represented in the Kripke model M_1 of Figure 2.1, where indistinguishability of agent b is represented by an arrow labelled with b. The points in this model are called states, which are in this case indeed states of the world. An arrow labelled with an agent b going from state s to t, is read as: 'given that the state is s, as far as b's information goes, it might as well be t', or 'in state s, agent b considers it possible that the state in fact is t', or, in the case of the models we will mostly consider, 'agent b cannot distinguish state s from state t'. The latter description refers to an equivalence relation (cf. Definition 2.13): no agent is supposed to distinguish s from itself; if t is indistinguishable from s then so is s from t and, finally, if s and t are the same for agent b, and so are t and u, then b cannot tell the difference between s and u. Note that the accessibility relation in model M_1 of Figure 2.1 is indeed an equivalence relation.

Definition 2.6 Given a countable set of atomic propositions P and a finite set of agents A, a *Kripke model* is a structure $M = \langle S, R^A, V^P \rangle$, where

- S is a set of states. The set S is also called the domain $\mathcal{D}(M)$ of M.
- R^A is a function, yielding for every $a \in A$ an accessibility relation $R^A(a) \subseteq S \times S$. We will often write R_a rather than $R^A(a)$ and freely mix a prefix notation ($R_a st$) with an infix notation ($sR_a t$).
- $V^P : P \to 2^S$ is a valuation function that for every $p \in P$ yields the set $V^P(p) \subseteq S$ of states in which p is true.

We will often suppress explicit reference to the sets of P and A, and represent a model as $M = \langle S, R, V\rangle$. In such a case, we may also write V_p rather than $V(p)$, for any atom p and the valuation V.

If we know that all the relations R_a in M are equivalence relations, we call M an *epistemic model*. In that case, we write $\sim_a$ rather than R_a, and we represent the model as $M = \langle S, \sim, V\rangle$. □

We will interpret formulas in states. Note that in M_1 of Figure 2.1, the names of the states strongly suggest the valuation V_1 of M_1: we for instance have $\langle g, \neg l\rangle \in V_1(g)$ and $\langle g, \neg l\rangle \notin V_1(l)$. As to the epistemic formulas, in M_1, we want to be able to say that if the state of the world is $\langle g, l\rangle$, i.e., both Groningen and Liverpool show sunny weather, then agent b *knows* it is sunny in Groningen, (since all the states he considers possible, $\langle g, l\rangle$ and $\langle g, \neg l\rangle$ verify this), but he does not know that it is sunny in Liverpool (since he cannot rule out that the real state of the world is $\langle g, \neg l\rangle$, in which case it is not sunny in Liverpool). In short, given the model M_1 and the state $\langle g, l\rangle$, we expect $K_b g \wedge \neg K_b l$ to hold in that state.

Definition 2.7 Epistemic formulas are interpreted on pairs (M, s) consisting of a Kripke model $M = \langle S, R, V\rangle$ and a state $s \in S$. Whenever we write (M, s), we assume that $s \in \mathcal{D}(M)$. Slightly abusing terminology, we will sometimes also refer to (M, s) as a *state*. If M is an epistemic model (see Definition 2.6), (M, s) is also called an *epistemic state*. We will often write M, s rather than (M, s). Such a pair will often be referred to as a *pointed model*.

Now, given a model $M = \langle S, R, V\rangle$ we define that formula φ is true in (M, s), also written as $M, s \models \varphi$, as follows:

$$
\begin{array}{ll}
M, s \models p & \text{iff } s \in V(p) \\
M, s \models (\varphi \wedge \psi) & \text{iff } M, s \models \varphi \text{ and } M, s \models \psi \\
M, s \models \neg\varphi & \text{iff not } M, s \models \varphi \\
M, s \models K_a\varphi & \text{iff for all } t \text{ such that } R_a st, M, t \models \varphi
\end{array}
$$

Instead of 'not $M, s \models \varphi$' we also write '$M, s \not\models \varphi$'. The clause for K_a is also phrased as 'K_a is the necessity operator with respect to R_a'. Note that the dual $\hat{K}_a$ obtains the following truth condition, for which it is also dubbed 'a possibility operator with respect to R_a':

$$M, s \models \hat{K}_a\varphi \text{ iff there is a } t \text{ such that } R_a st \text{ and } M, t \models \varphi \tag{2.1}$$

When $M, s \models \varphi$ for all $s \in \mathcal{D}(M)$, we write $M \models \varphi$ and say that φ is true in M. If $M \models \varphi$ for all models M in a certain class $\mathcal{X}$ (like, for instance, all epistemic models), we say that φ is valid in $\mathcal{X}$ and write $\mathcal{X} \models \varphi$. If $M \models \varphi$ for all Kripke models M, we say that φ is valid, and write $\models \varphi$ or $\mathcal{K} \models \varphi$, where $\mathcal{K}$ is the set of all Kripke models. We use $\not\models$ to deny any of such claims, for instance $M \not\models \varphi$ says that φ is not true in M, meaning that there is some state $s \in \mathcal{D}(M)$ that falsifies it, i.e., for which $M, s \models \neg\varphi$.

If for formula φ there is a state (M, s) such that $(M, s) \models \varphi$, we say that φ is *satisfied* in (M, s), and, if M belongs to a class of models $\mathcal{X}$, we then say that φ is satisfiable in $\mathcal{X}$. □

The keypoint in the truth definition is that an agent a is said to know an assertion φ in a state (M, s) if and only if that assertion is true in all the states he considers possible, given s. Going back to Figure 2.1, we have $M_1, \langle g, l\rangle \models K_b g \wedge \neg K_b l \wedge \neg K_b \neg l$: agent b knows *that* it is sunny in Groningen, but does not know *whether* it is sunny in Liverpool, he does not know that l, nor that $\neg l$.

Kripke semantics makes our epistemic logic *intensional*, in the sense that we give up the property of *extensionality*, which dictates that in any formula, one can always substitute subformulas for different, but equivalent ones. To see that we indeed got rid of extensionality, note that, in Figure 2.1 we have $M_1, \langle g, l\rangle \models (g \wedge l) \wedge (K_b g \wedge \neg K_b l)$ (saying that g and l have the same truth value, but still one can know one without knowing the other).

A second feature of Kripke semantics to note at this point is that it gives us a natural way to interpret arbitrary nested knowledge formulas. For instance, not only does b not know in $\langle g, l\rangle$ that l ($M_1, \langle g, l\rangle \models \neg K_b l$), he knows about his ignorance! (i.e., $M_1, \langle g, l\rangle \models K_b \neg K_b l$.)

Exercise 2.8 M_1 is the model of Figure 2.1.

1. Formalise the following claims:
    a) In state $\langle g, l\rangle$, agent b considers it possible that it is sunny in Groningen, and also that it is sunny in Liverpool, and also that it is not sunny in Liverpool.
    b) In state $\langle \neg g, l\rangle$, agent b knows it is not sunny in Groningen, although he does not know it is sunny in Liverpool.
    c) In state $\langle g, l\rangle$, agent b knows both that he knows that it is sunny in Groningen and that he does not know that it is sunny in Liverpool.
    d) In model M_1, it is true that agent b knows whether it is sunny in Groningen, but he does not know whether it is sunny in Liverpool.
    e) In any model, any agent knows that any fact or its negation holds.
    f) It is not a validity that an agent always knows either a fact, or that he knows its negation.
2. Verify the following:
    a) $M_1, \langle g, l\rangle \models \hat{K}_b g \wedge \hat{K}_b l \wedge \hat{K}_b \neg l$
    b) $M_1, \langle \neg g, l\rangle \models K_b \neg g \wedge \neg K_b l$
    c) $M_1, \langle g, l\rangle \models K_b(K_b g \wedge \neg K_b l)$
    d) $M_1 \models (K_b g \vee K_b \neg g) \wedge (\neg K_b l \wedge \neg K_b \neg l)$
    e) $\models K_a(\varphi \vee \neg\varphi)$
    f) $\not\models K_a\varphi \vee K_a \neg\varphi$ □

We already observed that M_1 of Figure 2.1 is in fact an epistemic model $M_1 = \langle S, \sim, V\rangle$. Since such models will be so prominent in this book, we economise on their representation in figures by representing the equivalence

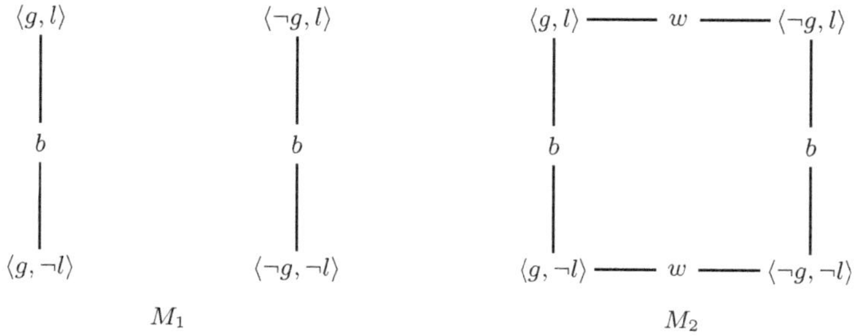

Figure 2.2. Two GLO scenarios.

relations by lines, rather than by arrows. Moreover, we will leave out all reflexive arrows. See model M_1 of Figure 2.2, which is a more economical representation of the model M_1 of Figure 2.1.

One of the ways to make the model M_1 of Figure 2.2 a real multi-agent model is illustrated by the model M_2 in that figure. It represents the situation in which a second agent, w, is situated in Liverpool and knows about the weather there. Note that now we have for instance

$$M_2, \langle g, l \rangle \models K_b g \land \neg K_b l \land \neg K_w g \land K_w l$$

Indeed, we even have $M_2 \models (K_b g \lor K_b \neg g) \land (K_w l \lor K_w \neg l)$: whatever the state of the world is, agent b knows whether the sun shines in Groningen, and w knows the weather condition in Liverpool.

But the model M_2 models much more than that: not only does b know the weather conditions in Groningen, and w those in Liverpool, but, apparently, this is also known by both of them! For instance, we can verify (2.2), which says that, in $M_2, \langle g, l \rangle$, agent w does not know whether it is sunny in Groningen, but w *does* know that b knows whether it is sunny there.

$$M_2, \langle g, l \rangle \models \neg K_w g \land \neg K_w \neg g \land K_w (K_b g \lor K_b \neg g) \tag{2.2}$$

This is verified as follows. First of all, we have $M_2, \langle g, l \rangle \models \neg K_w g$, since, in state $\langle g, l \rangle$, agent w considers $\langle \neg g, l \rangle$ to be the real world, in which g is false, hence he does not know g. More formally, since $\langle g, l \rangle R_w \langle \neg g, l \rangle$ and $M_2, \langle \neg g, l \rangle \models \neg g$, we have $M_2, \langle g, l \rangle \models \neg K_w g$. Given $\langle g, l \rangle$, agent w also considers $\langle g, l \rangle$ itself as a possibility, so not in all the states that w considers possible, $\neg g$ is true. Hence, $M_2, \langle g, l \rangle \models \neg K_w \neg g$. All the states that w considers possible in $\langle g, l \rangle$, are $\langle g, l \rangle$ and $\langle \neg g, l \rangle$. In the first, we have $K_b g$, in the second, $K_b \neg g$. So, in all the states that w considers possible given $\langle g, l \rangle$, we have $K_b g \lor K_b \neg g$. In other words, $M_2, \langle g, l \rangle \models K_w (K_b g \lor K_b \neg g)$.

Exercise 2.9 summarises some multi-agent properties of model M_2: it is important, for the reader to appreciate the remainder of this book, that he or she is sure to be able to do that exercise!

Exercise 2.9 Let M_2 be as above. Verify that:

1. $M_2, \langle g, l \rangle \models g \wedge \hat{K}_w K_b \neg g$
   Although g is true in $\langle g, l \rangle$, agent w considers it possible that b knows $\neg g$!
2. $M_2, \langle g, l \rangle \models (g \wedge l) \wedge \hat{K}_b \hat{K}_w (\neg g \wedge \neg l)$
   Although $(g \wedge l)$ is true at $\langle g, l \rangle$, agent b considers it possible that w considers it possible that $\neg g \wedge \neg l$
3. $M_2 \models K_w(g \rightarrow K_b g)$
   Everywhere in the model, it holds that w knows that, whenever it is sunny in Groningen, b knows it. □

We end the *GLO* story with two remarks regarding 'states' and valuations. In the two models we have considered so far (M_1 and M_2), the notion of epistemic state and valuation coincided. In general, this need not be the case. First of all, not every possible valuation (a possible state of the world) needs to be present in a(n) (epistemic) model. Suppose that we enrich our language with an atom o, denoting whether it is sunny in Otago, New Zealand. Then, obviously, the valuation that would denote the state in which $g \wedge l \wedge o$ is true for instance would not appear in any model, since a background theory, based on geographical insights, ensures that o can never be true at the same time with g or with l. Secondly, in general it is possible that one and the same valuation, or one and the same possible world, can represent different epistemic states.

Let us, rather than enrich the set of propositions in our *GLO* example, enrich the set of agents with an agent h who, as a matter of fact, happens to live in Otago. Suppose the world is in such a state that g and l are true. Moreover, we make the same assumptions about b and w as we did earlier: b knows about g, and w knows about l, and all this is known by each agent. See model M_2 of Figure 2.3, which is exactly the same epistemic model as M_2 of Figure 2.2.

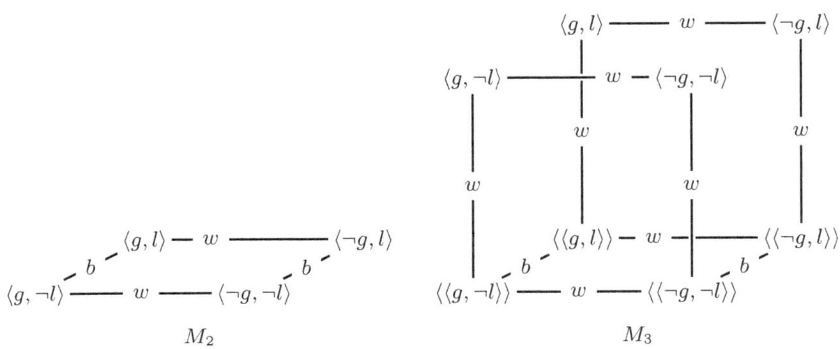

Figure 2.3. GLO scenarios, one with multiple occurrences of the same valuation.

This book is about the dynamics of epistemics, of which a first example will now be given. It is night-time in Otago, but since the three agents are involved in writing a book, this fact does not stop h from calling his European co-authors. He first calls w. They have some social talk (w tells h that the sun is shining in Liverpool) and they discuss matters of the book. Then h tells w truthfully what he is going to do next: call b and report what h and w have discussed so far. The poor w does not have a clue whether this also means that h will reveal the weather condition of Liverpool (l) to b. Hence, w considers two epistemic states possible that have the same valuation: in one of them, we have $g \wedge l \wedge \neg K_b l$ and in the other, $g \wedge l \wedge K_b l$. The first state corresponds with the state $\langle\langle g, l\rangle\rangle$ in model M_3 of Figure 2.3, and which is exactly at the position $\langle g, l\rangle$ of model M_2, the second with $\langle g, l\rangle$ 'just above' the previous one in the figure. In model M_2 every two states $\langle x, y\rangle$ and $\langle\langle x, y\rangle\rangle$ have the same valuation, although they are not the same states! Given the fact that one in general has different states with the same valuation, it is not a good idea to name a state after its valuation, as we have done in M_1 and M_2. As an aside, we have not modelled h's knowledge in model M_3.

Note, in passing, that we applied another economic principle in representing epistemic models, in M_3 of Figure 2.3: although, by transitivity of such models, there should be a connecting line between $\langle g, l\rangle$ and *both* occurrences of $\langle \neg g, l\rangle$, we leave out one of them in our drawing, relying on the reader's ability to 'complete the transitive closure' of our representation.

What exactly does the epistemic state $M_3, \langle\langle g, l\rangle\rangle$ describe? Well, it is the situation in which h did *not* tell b about l (since b still considers a state possible in which $\neg l$), but in which both b and w know that h might have informed b about the truth value of l. Note for instance that we have that b knows that w does not know whether b knows l: we have

$$M_3, \langle\langle g, l\rangle\rangle \models l \wedge \neg K_b l \wedge K_b(\neg K_w K_b l \wedge \neg K_w \neg K_b l) \tag{2.3}$$

(2.3) expresses that, although l holds, b does not know this, but b knows that w neither knows that b knows that l, nor that b does not know that l.

Exercise 2.10 (Modelling consecutive numbers) Read again the description of the Consecutive Numbers example, Example 2.4. Check the truth definition for E_B at Definition 2.30.

1. Draw the appropriate model for it. Omit reflexive arrows. Call the model M and denote the factual state as $\langle 3, 2\rangle$.
2. Show that $M, \langle 1, 0\rangle \models K_a a_1 \wedge \mathsf{win_a}$
3. What are the states in which an agent can win the game? What is the difference between them, in terms of epistemic properties, given that the real state is $\langle 3, 2\rangle$?
4. Verify the statements 1–8 of Example 2.4 in state $M, \langle 3, 2\rangle$. □

How appropriate are Kripke models to represent knowledge? A possible answer has it that they incorporate too strong properties. This is sometimes referred to as *logical omniscience*; it is technically summarised in the following proposition.

Proposition 2.11 Let φ, ψ be formulas in $\mathcal{L}_K$, and let K_a be an epistemic operator for $a \in A$. Let $\mathcal{K}$ be the set of all Kripke models, and $\mathcal{S}5$ the set of Kripke models in which the accessibility relation is an equivalence (see Definition 2.13). Then the following hold:

- $\mathcal{K} \models K_a\varphi \wedge K_a(\varphi \rightarrow \psi) \rightarrow K_a\psi$ *LO*1
- $\mathcal{K} \models \varphi \Rightarrow \models K_a\varphi$ *LO*2
- $\mathcal{K} \models \varphi \rightarrow \psi \Rightarrow \models K_a\varphi \rightarrow K_a\psi$ *LO*3
- $\mathcal{K} \models \varphi \leftrightarrow \psi \Rightarrow \models K_a\varphi \leftrightarrow K_a\psi$ *LO*4
- $\mathcal{K} \models (K_a\varphi \wedge K_a\psi) \rightarrow K_a(\varphi \wedge \psi)$ *LO*5
- $\mathcal{K} \models K_a\varphi \rightarrow K_a(\varphi \vee \psi)$ *LO*6
- $\mathcal{S}5 \models \neg(K_a\varphi \wedge K_a\neg\varphi)$ *LO*7

□

The fact that the above properties hold in all Kripke models is referred to as the problem of *logical omniscience* since they express that agents are omniscient, perfect logical reasoners. For example, *LO*1 says that knowledge is closed under consequences. *LO*2 expresses that agents know all ($\mathcal{S}5$-)validities. *LO*3-*LO*6 all assume that the agent is able to make logical deductions with respect to his knowledge, and, on top of that, *LO*7 ensures that his knowledge is internally consistent. The properties of Proposition 2.11 reflect *idealised* notions of knowledge, that do not necessarily hold for human beings. For example, many people do not know all tautologies of propositional logic, so *LO*2 does not hold for them. We will see how, in many systems, the properties of Proposition 2.11 are nevertheless acceptable. If the properties mentioned here are unacceptable for a certain application, a possible world approach to knowledge is probably not the best option: all listed properties are valid in all Kripke models, except for *LO*7, which is only true on *serial* models (see Definition 2.13).

The popularity of Kripke semantics reaches far further than the area of epistemics. Depending on the intended interpretation of the modal operator, one can freely write, rather than K_a, other symbols for these operators. Interpretations that are very common (and hence are supposed to satisfy the properties of Proposition 2.11) are 'φ is believed' $B_a\varphi$, or 'φ is always the case' ($\Box\varphi$), 'φ is a desire' ($D_a\varphi$), 'φ is obligatory' ($\bigcirc\varphi$), 'φ is provable' ($\Box\varphi$), or 'φ is a result of executing program π' ($[\pi]\varphi$).

All this does not mean that these notions have exactly the same logic, or properties. Rather, opting to model a specific operator using the Kripke semantics of Definition 2.7, Proposition 2.11 gives some minimal properties of it. One of the main features of Kripke semantics is that one can, in a modular fashion, put additional constraints on the accessibility relation, to obtain some extra modal validities. As a simple example, if in the model M the accessibility relation R_a is reflexive (i.e., $\forall s R_a ss$), then M satisfies $K_a\varphi \rightarrow \varphi$ (see Exercise 2.12). Hence, if $\mathcal{T}$ is the class of all reflexive models, i.e., $\mathcal{T} = \{M = \langle S, R, V\rangle \mid \text{ every } R_a \text{ is reflexive}\}$, then $\mathcal{T} \models K_a\varphi \rightarrow \varphi$.

Exercise 2.12 Show, that if $M = \langle S, R, V \rangle$ is such that R_a is reflexive, then M satisfies the truth axiom: $M \models K_a\varphi \to \varphi$. □

We now define some classes of models that are of crucial importance in epistemic logic.

Definition 2.13 Recall that R stands for a family of accessibility relations, one R_a for each $a \in A$.

1. The class of all Kripke models is sometimes denoted $\mathcal{K}$. Hence, $\mathcal{K} \models \varphi$ coincides with $\models \varphi$.
2. R_a is said to be *serial* if for all s there is a t such that $R_a st$
   The class of serial Kripke models $\{M = \langle S, R, V \rangle \mid$ every R_a is serial$\}$ is denoted by $\mathcal{KD}$.
3. R_a is said to be *reflexive* if for all s, $R_a ss$
   The class of reflexive Kripke models $\{M = \langle S, R, V \rangle \mid$ every R_a is reflexive$\}$ is denoted by $\mathcal{T}$.
4. R_a is *transitive* if for all s, t, u, if $R_a st$ and $R_a tu$ then $R_a su$
   The class of transitive Kripke models is denoted by $\mathcal{K}4$.
   The class of reflexive transitive models is denoted by $\mathcal{S}4$.
5. R_a is *Euclidean* if for all s, t, and u, if $R_a st$ and $R_a su$ then $R_a tu$
   The class of transitive Euclidean models is denoted by $\mathcal{K}45$.
   The class of serial transitive Euclidean models is denoted by $\mathcal{KD}45$.
6. R_a is an *equivalence relation* if R_a is reflexive, transitive, and symmetric (for all s, t, if $R_a st$ then $R_a ts$). Equivalently, R_a is an equivalence relation if R_a is reflexive, transitive and Euclidean.
   The class of Kripke models with equivalence relations is denoted by $\mathcal{S}5$.□

These classes of models will be motivated shortly, but, as said before, the main emphasis in this book will be on $\mathcal{S}5$.

How much can two epistemic states M, s and M', s' differ without affecting the knowledge of any agent? In other words, how expressive is our epistemic language $\mathcal{L}_K$, to which granularity can it distinguish models from each other? We address the issue of expressivity of several languages introduced in this book in Chapter 8, but now present a basic underlying notion and result.

Definition 2.14 (Bisimulation) Let two models $M = \langle S, R, V \rangle$ and $M' = \langle S', R', V' \rangle$ be given. A non-empty relation $\mathfrak{R} \subseteq S \times S'$ is a bisimulation iff for all $s \in S$ and $s' \in S'$ with $(s, s') \in \mathfrak{R}$:

atoms $s \in V(p)$ iff $s' \in V'(p)$ for all $p \in P$
forth for all $a \in A$ and all $t \in S$, if $(s, t) \in R_a$, then there is a $t' \in S'$ such that $(s', t') \in R'_a$ and $(t, t') \in \mathfrak{R}$
back for all $a \in A$ and all $t' \in S'$, if $(s', t') \in R'_a$, then there is a $t \in S$ such that $(s, t) \in R_a$ and $(t, t') \in \mathfrak{R}$

We write $(M, s) \leftrightarrows (M', s')$, iff there is a bisimulation between M and M' linking s and s'. Then we call (M, s) and (M', s') bisimilar. □

Obviously, for M, s and M', s' to bisimulate each other, the **atoms**-clause guarantees that there is agreement on objective formulas (not only between s and s', but recursively in all states that can be reached), the **forth**-clause preserves ignorance formulas going from M, s to M', s', and the **back**-clause preserves knowledge. This is made more precise in the (proof of) the following theorem, which says that the epistemic language $\mathcal{L}_K$ cannot distinguish bisimilar models. We write $(M, s) \equiv_{\mathcal{L}_K} (M', s')$ if and only if $(M, s) \models \varphi$ iff $(M', s') \models \varphi$ for all formulas $\varphi \in \mathcal{L}_K$.

Theorem 2.15 For all pointed models (M, s) and (M', s'), if $(M, s) \leftrightarroweq (M', s')$, then $(M, s) \equiv_{\mathcal{L}_K} (M', s')$. □

Proof We proceed by induction on φ.

Base case Suppose $(M, s) \leftrightarroweq (M', s')$. By **atoms**, it must be the case that $(M, s) \models p$ if and only if $(M', s') \models p$ for all $p \in P$

Induction hypothesis For all pointed models (M, s) and (M', s'), if we have that $(M, s) \leftrightarroweq (M', s')$, then it follows that $(M, s) \models \varphi$ if and only if $(M', s') \models \varphi$.

Induction step

negation Suppose that $(M, s) \models \neg\varphi$. By the semantics this is the case if and only if $(M, s) \not\models \varphi$. By the induction hypothesis this is equivalent to $(M', s') \not\models \varphi$, which is the case if and only if $(M', s') \models \neg\varphi$.

conjunction Suppose that $(M, s) \models \varphi_1 \wedge \varphi_2$, with, by the induction hypothesis, the theorem proven for φ_1 and φ_2. By the semantics the conjunction $\varphi_1 \wedge \varphi_2$ is true in (M, s) if and only if $(M, s) \models \varphi_1$ and $(M, s) \models \varphi_2$. By the induction hypothesis this is equivalent to $(M', s') \models \varphi_1$ and $(M', s') \models \varphi_2$. By the semantics this is the case if and only if $(M', s') \models \varphi_1 \wedge \varphi_2$.

individual epistemic operator Suppose $(M, s) \models K_a\varphi$. Take an arbitrary t' such that $(s', t') \in R'_a$. By **back** there is a $t \in S$ such that $(s, t) \in R_a$ and $(t, t') \in \mathfrak{R}$. Therefore, by the induction hypothesis $(M, t) \models \varphi$ if and only if $(M', t') \models \varphi$. Since $(M, s) \models K_a\varphi$, by the semantics $(M, t) \models \varphi$. Therefore $(M', t') \models \varphi$. Given that t' was arbitrary, $(M', t') \models \varphi$ for all t' such that $(s', t') \in R'_a$. Therefore by the semantics $(M', s') \models K_a\varphi$.

The other way around is analogous, but then **forth** is used. □

So, having a bisimulation is *sufficient* for two states to verify the same formulas, and hence to represent the same knowledge. In Chapter 8 we will see that it is not *necessary*, however. Note that the proof given above did not depend on R or R' being reflexive, transitive, or Euclidean. So indeed it also holds for other modal logics than *S5*.

2.2.3 Axiomatisation

A logic is a set of formulas. One way to characterise them is semantically: take a set of formulas that is valid in a class of models. An *axiomatisation*

all instantiations of propositional tautologies	
$K_a(\varphi \rightarrow \psi) \rightarrow (K_a\varphi \rightarrow K_a\psi)$	distribution of K_a over $\rightarrow$
From φ and $\varphi \rightarrow \psi$, infer ψ	modus ponens
From φ, infer $K_a\varphi$	necessitation of K_a

Table 2.1. The basic modal system **K**.

is a syntactic way to specify a logic: it tries to give a core set of formulas (the axioms) and inference rules, from which all other formulas in the logic are derivable. The first axiomatisation **K** we present gives the axioms of a minimal modal logic: it happens to capture the validities of the semantic class $\mathcal{K}$, i.e., the class of *all* Kripke models. We assume that the modal operators K_a that appear in any axiomatisation are ranging over a set of agents A, which we will not always explicitly mention.

Definition 2.16 The basic epistemic logic **K**, where we have an operator K_a for every $a \in A$, is comprised of all instances of propositional tautologies, the K axiom, and the derivation rules Modus Ponens (MP) and Necessitation (Nec), as given in Table 2.1. □

These axioms and rules define the weakest multi-modal logic **K**, for a set of agents A. The distribution axiom is sometimes also called the axiom K. In formal proofs, we will sometimes refer to the first axiom as $Prop$, and to the two inference rules as MP and Nec, respectively. A modal operator satisfying axiom K and inference rule necessitation is called a *normal* modal operator. All systems that we study in this book will be extensions of **K**. Note that the φ in the first axiom about instantiations of propositional tautologies does not have to be in the propositional *language*: examples of formulas that we obtain by $Prop$ are not only $p \vee \neg p$ and $p \rightarrow (q \rightarrow p)$ but also $K_a\hat{K}_b\neg q \vee \neg K_a\hat{K}_b\neg q$ and $K_ap \rightarrow (K_b(p \vee \hat{K}_bp) \rightarrow K_ap)$. Also note that the necessitation rule does not tell us that φ *implies* $K_a\varphi$: it merely states that for any theorem φ that can be derived in this system, we get another one for free, i.e., $K_a\varphi$. Admittedly, we have not yet made precise what it means to be a theorem of an axiomatisation.

Definition 2.17 Let **X** be an arbitrary axiomatisation with axioms Ax_1, $Ax_2, \ldots, Ax_n$ and rules $Ru_1, Ru_2, \ldots Ru_k$, where each rule $Ru_j (j \leq k)$ is of the form "From $\varphi_1, \ldots \varphi_{j_{ar}}$ infer φ_j". We call j_{ar} the *arity* of the rule. Then, a *derivation* for φ within **X** is a finite sequence $\varphi_1, \ldots \varphi_m$ of formulas such that:

1. $\varphi_m = \varphi$;
2. every φ_i in the sequence is
   a) either an instance of one of the axioms $Ax_1, Ax_2, \ldots Ax_n$
   b) or else the result of the application of one of the rules $Ru_j (j \leq k)$ to j_{ar} formulas in the sequence that appear before φ_i.

If there is a derivation for φ in **X** we write $\vdash_{\mathbf{X}} \varphi$, or, if the system **X** is clear form the context, we just write $\vdash \varphi$. We then also say that φ is a *theorem* of **X**, or that **X** proves φ. □

In Table 2.1 and Definition 2.17 we sloppily used the terms *axiom* and *formula* interchangeably, or, more precisely, we use the same meta-variables $\varphi, \psi, \ldots$, for both. Strictly speaking, a formula should not contain such variables. For instance, the *formula* $K_a(p \to q) \to (K_a p \to K_a q)$ is an instance, and hence, derivable in one step, from the axiom *scheme* K. This sloppiness is almost always harmless. In fact, it makes it easy to for instance define that two axioms A and B are *equivalent* with respect to an axiomatisation $\mathbf{X}$. For any system $\mathbf{X}$ and axiom φ, let $\mathbf{X}+\varphi$ denote the axiom system that has axiom φ added to those of $\mathbf{X}$, and the same rules as $\mathbf{X}$. Moreover, let $\mathbf{X} - \varphi$ denote the axiom system $\mathbf{X}$, but without the axiom φ. Then, two axioms A and B are equivalent with respect to $\mathbf{X}$ if $\vdash_{(\mathbf{X}-A)+B} A$ and $\vdash_{(\mathbf{X}-B)+A} B$.

The following exercise establishes two simple facts about this minimal modal logic $\mathbf{K}$:

Exercise 2.18 Let $\vdash \varphi$ stand for $\vdash_{\mathbf{K}} \varphi$.

1. Show that the rule of *Hypothetical Syllogism* (HS) is derivable: $\vdash \varphi \to \chi, \vdash \chi \to \psi \Rightarrow \ \vdash \varphi \to \psi$
2. Show $\vdash \varphi \to \psi \Rightarrow \vdash K_a\varphi \to K_a\psi$.
3. Show that, given $\mathbf{K}$, the distribution axiom is equivalent to K' $(K_a\varphi \wedge K_a(\varphi \to \psi)) \to K_a\psi)$ and also to K'' $K_a(\varphi \wedge \psi) \to (K_a\varphi \wedge K_a\psi)$
4. Show that $\vdash (K_a\varphi \wedge K_a\psi) \to K_a(\varphi \wedge \psi)$. □

The properties of logical omniscience $LO1 - LO6$ that we gave in Proposition 2.11 are also derivable in $\mathbf{K}$. Although these properties indicate that the notion of knowledge that we are formalising is quite strong and overidealised, at the same time there appear to be other properties of knowledge that are often desirable or natural, and which are not theorems in $\mathbf{K}$, like $K_a\varphi \to \varphi$: what is known, must be true. We will follow standard practice in computer science and embrace (a number of) the additional axioms given in Table 2.2.

The truth-axiom will also be referred to as axiom T and expresses that knowledge is *veridical*: whatever one claims to know, must be true. In other words, it not only inconsistent to say 'I know it is Tuesday, although in fact it is Wednesday', but this also applies when referring to knowledge of a third person, i.e., it makes no sense to claim 'although Bob knows that Ann holds an Ace of spades, it is in fact a Queen of hearts'.

The other two axioms specify so-called *introspective agents*: an agent not only knows what he knows (positive introspection), but also, he knows what he does not know (negative introspection). These axioms will also be denoted

$K_a\varphi \to \varphi$	truth
$K_a\varphi \to K_aK_a\varphi$	positive introspection
$\neg K_a\varphi \to K_a\neg K_a\varphi$	negative introspection

Table 2.2. Axioms for knowledge.

by axiom 4 and axiom 5, respectively. For human agents especially 5 seems an unrealistically strong assumption, but for artificial agents, negative introspection often makes sense. In particular, when in the underlying semantics access for agents is interpreted as indistinguishability, both types of introspection come for free.

A special case of this is provided by the so-called *interpreted systems*, one of the main paradigms for epistemic logic in computer science. Here, the idea is that every agent, or processor, has a *local view* of the system, which is characterised by the value of the local variables. A process a cannot distinguish two global states s and t, if the assignment to a's values are the same, in s and t. One easily verifies that under this definition of access for agent a, knowledge verifies all properties of Table 2.2.

We can now define some of the main axiomatic systems in this book. Recall that $\mathbf{X} + \varphi$ denotes the axiom system that has axiom φ added to those of $\mathbf{X}$, and the same rules as $\mathbf{X}$.

Definition 2.19 We define the following axiom systems: see Figure 2.4. □

Exercise 2.20 Consider the following axiom B: $\varphi \to K_a \hat{K}_a \varphi$.
Show that axiom 5 and B are equivalent with respect to $\mathbf{K} + T + 4$, i.e., show that $\vdash_{\mathbf{K}+T+4+5} B$ and $\vdash_{\mathbf{K}+T+4+B} 5$. □

Although the focus in this book is on **S5**, we end this section by showing a nice kind of 'modularity' in adding axioms to the minimal modal logic **K**. Recall that a logic is a set of formulas, and we have now seen two ways to characterise a logic: as a set of *validities* of a class of models, and as a set of *derivables* of an axiom system. The following theorem is folklore in modal logic: for completeness of **S5** see also Theorem 7.7 of Chapter 7.

Theorem 2.21

1. (Soundness and completeness)
   Axiom system **K** is sound and complete with respect to the semantic class $\mathcal{K}$, i.e., for every formula φ, we have $\vdash_{\mathbf{K}} \varphi$ iff $\mathcal{K} \models \varphi$.
   The same holds for **T** w.r.t. $\mathcal{T}$, for **S4** w.t.t. $\mathcal{S}4$ and, finally, for **S5** w.r.t. $\mathcal{S}5$.
2. (Finite models and decidability)
   Each of the systems mentioned above has the finite model property: any φ is satisfiable in a class $\mathcal{X}$ if and only if it is satisfiable in a finite model of that class.

T	=	$\mathbf{K} + T$
S4	=	$\mathbf{T} + 4$
S5	=	$\mathbf{S4} + 5$

Figure 2.4. Some basic axiom systems.

Moreover, all the systems mentioned are *decidable*: for any class $\mathcal{X}$ mentioned, there exists a decision procedure that determines, in a finite amount of time, for any φ, whether it is satisfiable in $\mathcal{X}$ or not. □

We also define a notion of *derivability from premises*, which gives rise to *strong completeness*.

Definition 2.22 Let $\Box$ be an arbitrary modal operator. An inference rule Ru is called a *necessitation rule for* $\Box$ if it is of the form "From φ, infer $\Box\varphi$". Let again $\mathbf{X}$ be an arbitrary axiomatisation with axioms Ax_1, Ax_2, ..., Ax_n and rules $Ru_1, Ru_2, \dots Ru_k$, where each rule $Ru_j (j \leq k)$ is of the form "From $\varphi_1, \dots \varphi_{j_{ar}}$ infer φ_j". Define the *closure under necessitation rules* of $\mathbf{X}$ as the smallest set $Cl_{Nec}(\mathbf{X}) \supseteq \{Ax_1, \dots, Ax_n\}$ such that for any $\psi \in Cl_{Nec}(\mathbf{X})$, and necessitation rule for $\Box$, also $\Box\psi \in Cl_{Nec}(\mathbf{X})$. Let $\Gamma \cup \{\varphi\}$ be a set of formulas. A *derivation for* φ *from* Γ is a finite sequence $\varphi_1, \dots \varphi_m$ of formulas such that:

1. $\varphi_m = \varphi$;
2. every φ_i in the sequence is
   a) either an instance of one of the schemes in $Cl_{Nec}(\mathbf{X})$
   b) or a member of Γ
   c) or else the result of the application of one of the rules $Ru_j (j \leq k)$ which is not a necessitation rules to j_{ar} formulas in the sequence that appear before φ_i.

If there is a derivation from Γ for φ in $\mathbf{X}$ we write $\Gamma \vdash_{\mathbf{X}} \varphi$, or, if the system $\mathbf{X}$ is clear form the context, we just write $\Gamma \vdash \varphi$. We then also say that φ is *derivable* in $\mathbf{X}$ from the premises Γ.

Given a class of models $\mathcal{C}$, we say that $\mathbf{X}$ is *strongly complete* with respect to $\mathbf{X}$, if for any Γ and φ, we have

$$\Gamma \vdash \varphi \text{ only if (for all } M \in \mathcal{C}, s \in M: \; M, s \models \Gamma \text{ implies } M, s \models \varphi)$$

If the 'only if' is replaced by 'if', we say that $\mathbf{X}$ is *strongly sound* with respect to $\mathcal{C}$. □

So, $\Gamma \vdash_{\mathbf{X}} \varphi$ holds, if there is a proof of φ using the premises in Γ, but without applying necessitation to them. This constraint guarantees that premises are 'local', or 'private', i.e., not necessarily known to everyone. For instance, without this constraint, we would have $\{K_a p, -K_b p\} \vdash_{\mathbf{S5}} \bot$, since allowing necessitation to the first premise would yield $K_b K_a p$ $(*)$. Then, a necessitation step of axiom T gives $K_b(K_a p \rightarrow p)$, which, together with $(*)$ and the distribution of K_b over $\rightarrow$ gives $K_b p$, which is inconsistent with the second premise.

Theorem 2.23 Axiom system $\mathbf{K}$ is strongly sound and strongly complete with respect to the semantic class $\mathcal{K}$. The same holds for $\mathbf{T}$ w.r.t. $\mathcal{T}$, for $\mathbf{S4}$ w.t.t. $\mathcal{S}4$ and, finally, for $\mathbf{S5}$ w.r.t. $\mathcal{S}5$. □

2.3 Group Notions of Knowledge

The notion of 'everybody knows' (or, general knowledge, as it is sometimes called) was already defined in the previous section (page 12). In this section, we introduce some other notions of group knowledge for multiple agent systems. The main emphasis will be on *common knowledge*, a notion that is important throughout this book.

2.3.1 Language

If one adds the definition of general knowledge to **S5**, the prominent epistemic logic, it is easy to see that this notion of everybody knowing inherits veridicality from K, but, if there is more than one agent in A, the same is not true for the introspection properties. And, indeed, lack of positive introspection for the whole group makes sense: if the agents b and w both hear on the radio that it is sunny in Otago (o), we have $E_{\{b,w\}}o$, but not necessarily $E_{\{b,w\}}E_{\{b,w\}}o$: agent b cannot just assume that w heard this announcement as well (see also Example 2.4, item 7). For a similar reason, negative introspection does not (and should not) automatically carry over to E-knowledge: if w missed out on the radio programme announcing o, we have $\neg E_{\{b,w\}}o$, but how could b infer this? This would be needed to conclude $E_{\{b,w\}}\neg E_{\{b,w\}}o$.

Hence, although it is easy to prove in **S5** that for every $n \geq 1$, $K_a^n\varphi$ is equivalent to $K_a\varphi$, for E_B-knowledge, all iterations $E_B^m\varphi$ and E_B^n are in principle different ($m \neq n$). A limiting, and as we shall see, intriguing notion here is *Common Knowledge*, which intuitively captures the infinite conjunction

$$C_B\varphi = \bigwedge_{n=0}^{\infty} E_B^n\varphi$$

The logic of knowledge with common knowledge is denoted $S5C$. Common knowledge is a very strong notion, and hence can in general only be obtained for *weak* formulas φ (sometimes $C_B\varphi$ is dubbed 'any fool knows φ'). One can intuitively grasp the fact that the number of iterations of the E-operator makes a real difference in practice.

Example 2.24 (Saint Nicholas) Suppose that p stands for "Saint Nicholas does not exist" (on December 5, according to tradition in several countries, Saint Nicholas is supposed to visit homes and to bring presents. Children generally start to disbelieve in his existence when they are around six years old, but for various reasons many children like to pretend to believe in him a little longer. Of course, nobody is supposed to reveal the secret on the family evening itself).

Let F be the family gathering together on this evening, and let a, b and c represent different members of F. Imagine how the family's celebration of Saint Nicholas' Eve would look like if $K_ap \wedge \neg E_Fp$ holds (in which case a will absolutely not make any comment suggesting the visitor in his Saint's dressing and the white beard is in fact the family's neighbour– note that $\neg E_F p$ implies $\hat{K}_a \neg E_F p$, if knowledge is veridical).

Now compare this to the situation where $E_F p \wedge \neg E_F E_F p$ holds (again, if $\neg K_a K_b p$, family member a will not make any public comment upon Saint Nicholas' non-existence, even though everybody knows the saint does not exist), or an evening in which $E_F E_F p \wedge \neg E_F E_F E_F p$ holds. In the latter case, we might for instance have $\neg K_a K_b K_a p$. In that case, a might without danger reveal his disbelief: since a knows that everybody knows p already, he might wish not to look childish by demonstrating to b that a indeed also belongs to the group of adults 'who know'. However, a might also opt to try and exploit $\hat{K}_a \hat{K}_b \hat{K}_a \neg p$, and challenge b not to reveal to a the wisdom that Saint Nicholas does not exist. Similarly, in case that $E_F E_F p \wedge \neg K_a K_b K_c p$, member a might try to resolve possible complications by informing b that $K_c p$, however a might instead choose to exploit the possible situation that $\hat{K}_b \hat{K}_c \neg p$, and try to bring b in a complex situation in which b has to make an effort not to reveal the secret p to c. This would imply some possible entertainment for a (since $K_a K_c p$) which will in fact not occur (since $K_b K_c p$). □

Another way to grasp the notion of common knowledge is to realise in which situations $C\varphi$ does *not* hold for a group. This is the case as long as someone, on the grounds of their knowledge, considers it a possibility that someone considers it a possibility that someone ... that φ does not hold (see also Exercise 2.37 and the remark above it). The following example illustrates such a situation.

Example 2.25 (Alco at the conference) Alco is one of a group B of visitors at a conference in Barcelona, where at a certain point during the afternoon he becomes bored and decides, in fact as the only member of B, to lounge in the hotel bar. While he is enjoying himself there, an important practical announcement φ is made in the lecture room. Of course at that moment $C_B\varphi$ does not hold, nor even $E_B\varphi$. But now suppose that in the bar the announcement comes through by way of an intercom connected to the lecture room. Then we do have $E_B\varphi$, but not $C_B\varphi$; after all, the other visitors of the conference do not know that Alco knows φ.

After hearing φ, Alco leaves the hotel for some sightseeing in the city. At that moment someone in the lecture room worriedly asks whether Alco knows φ, upon which the programme chair reassures her, and thereby anybody else present in the conference room, that this is indeed the case, because of the intercom. Of course at that moment, $C_B\varphi$ still does not hold! □

Now we are ready to give the definition of the full language of epistemic logic, including common knowledge.

Definition 2.26 (Language $\mathcal{L}_{KC}$ with common knowledge) Let P be a set of atomic propositions, and A a set of agent-symbols. We use $a, b, c, \ldots$ as variables over A, and B as a variable over coalitions of agents, i.e., subsets of A. The language $\mathcal{L}_{KC}$, the language for multi-agent epistemic logic with common knowledge, is generated by the following BNF:

$$\varphi \ ::= \ p \mid \neg\varphi \mid (\varphi \wedge \varphi) \mid K_a\varphi \mid C_B\varphi$$

For 'small' groups of agents B, we will sometimes write $C_a\varphi, C_{ab}\varphi, C_{abc}\varphi$, ..., rather than $C_{\{a\}}\varphi, C_{\{a,b\}}\varphi, C_{\{a,b,c\}}\varphi, \ldots$. Similarly for general knowledge, $E_B\varphi$. □

Thus, $\mathcal{L}_{KC}$ extends $\mathcal{L}_K$ with a notion of common knowledge, for every group.

Example 2.27 (Byzantine generals) Imagine two allied generals, a and b, standing on two mountain summits, with their enemy in the valley between them[1]. It is generally known that a and b together can easily defeat the enemy, but if only one of them attacks, he will certainly lose the battle.

General a sends a messenger to b with the message m (= "I propose that we attack on the first day of the next month at 8 PM sharp"). It is not guaranteed, however, that the messenger will arrive. Suppose that the messenger does reach the other summit and delivers the message to b. Then $K_b m$ holds, and even $K_b K_a m$. Will it be a good idea to attack? Certainly not, because a wants to know for certain that b will attack as well, and he does not know that yet. Thus, b sends the messenger back with an 'okay' message. Suppose the messenger survives again. Then $K_a K_b K_a m$ holds. Will the generals attack now? Definitely not, because b does not know whether his 'okay' has arrived, so $K_b K_a K_b m$ does not hold, and common knowledge of m has not yet been established.

In general, for every $n \geq 0$, one can show the following by induction. Recall that $(K_a K_b)^n$ is the obvious abbreviation for $2n$ knowledge operators K_a and K_b in alternation, starting with K_a.

odd rounds After the messenger has safely brought $2n + 1$ such messages (mostly acknowledgements), $K_b(K_a K_b)^n m$ is true, but $(K_a K_b)^{n+1} m$ is not.

even rounds After the messenger has safely brought $2n + 2$ such messages, one can show the following: $(K_a K_b)^{n+1} m$ is true, but $K_b(K_a K_b)^{n+1} m$ is not.

Thus, common knowledge will never be established in this way, using a messenger. Moreover one can prove that in order to start a coordinated attack, common knowledge of m *is* necessary. □

[1] Maybe this example from the theoretical computer scientists' folklore is not politically very correct, but one can imagine more peaceful variants in which synchronisation is of vital importance, e.g., two robots that have to carry a heavy container together.

Before we move on to semantics, let us spend one paragraph on another prominent notion of group knowledge, a notion that will not play an important role in this book, though. *Implicit* or *distributed knowledge* also helps to understand processes within a group of people or collaborating agents. Distributed knowledge is the knowledge that is implicitly present in a group, and which could become explicit if someone would pull all their knowledge together. For instance, it is possible that no agent knows the assertion ψ, while at the same time the distributed knowledge $D_{ab}\psi$ may be derived from $K_a\varphi \wedge K_b(\varphi \rightarrow \psi)$. An example of distributed knowledge in a group is, for instance, the fact whether two members of that group have the same birthday. Distributed knowledge is a rather weak notion, but can be obtained of rather strong facts. Distributed knowledge is sometimes referred to as 'the wise man knows'.

2.3.2 Semantics

The semantics for our modal language $\mathcal{L}_{KC}$ can be obtained without adding additional features to our epistemic models $M = \langle S, \sim, V \rangle$ as defined in Definition 2.6. Recall that E_B has been discussed in Section 2.2.1 and can be defined within $\mathcal{L}_{KC}$. Let us also consider an operator D_B that models distributed knowledge in the group B. The language $\mathcal{L}_{KCD}$ extends $\mathcal{L}_K$ with this operator. The operators E_B, D_B and C_B are all necessity operators, and the accessibility relation that we need for each of them can be defined in terms of the relations $R_a (a \in A)$.

Definition 2.28 Let S be a set, and $R_b (b \in B)$ be a set of relations on it. Recall that a relation R_b is nothing but a *set* $\{(x, y) \mid R_b xy\}$.

- Let $R_{E_B} = \bigcup_{b \in B} R_b$.
- Let $R_{D_B} = \bigcap_{b \in B} R_b$.
- The *transitive closure* of a relation R is the smallest relation R^+ such that:
  1. $R \subseteq R^+$;
  2. for all x, y, and z, if $(R^+xy \& R^+yz)$ then R^+xz

  If we moreover demand that for all x, R^+xx, we obtain the *reflexive transitive closure* of R, which we denote with R^*. □

Note that R^*xy if y is *reachable* from x using only R-steps. More precisely, we have the following:

Remark

1. If R is reflexive, then $R^+ = R^*$.
2. R^+xy iff either $x = y$ and Rxy or else for some $n > 1$ there is a sequence $x_1, x_2, \ldots x_n$ such that $x_1 = x, x_n = y$ and for all $i < n$, Rx_ix_{i+1}. □

Definition 2.30 Let, given a set P of atoms and A of agents, $M = \langle S, \sim, V \rangle$ be an epistemic model, and $B \subseteq A$. The truth definition of $(M, s) \models \varphi$, with $\varphi \in \mathcal{L}_{KCD}$ is an extension of Definition 2.7 with the following clauses:

- $(M, s) \models E_B\varphi$ iff for all $t, R_{E_B}st$ implies $(M, t) \models \varphi$.
- $(M, s) \models D_B\varphi$ iff for all $t, R_{D_B}st$ implies $(M, t) \models \varphi$.
- $(M, s) \models C_B\varphi$ iff for all $t, R^*_{E_B}st$ implies $(M, t) \models \varphi$.

For $R^*_{E_B}$ we will also write R_{C_B}, or even R_B. Note that, if R_a is an equivalence relation, then $R_a = R^*_a$. □

Thus, everybody in B knows φ in s, if every agent $b \in B$ only considers states possible, from s, in which φ is true. Phrased negatively, $E_B\varphi$ does not hold as long as there is one agent who considers a state possible in which φ is false. And, φ is distributed knowledge in s if φ is true in every state that is considered a possible alternative to s by *every agent* in B. The idea being, that if one agent considers t a possibility, given s, but another does not, the latter could 'inform' the first that he need not consider t. Finally, φ is common knowledge of B in s, if φ is true in every state that is reachable from s, using any accessibility of any agent in B as a step. Again, put negatively, φ is *not* commonly known by B in s, if some agent in B considers it possible that some agent in B considers it possible that ... some agent in B considers it possible that φ is false.

Concerning the relation between the types of knowledge presented, one may observe that we have, if $a \in B$:

$$C_B\varphi \Rightarrow E_B\varphi \Rightarrow K_a\varphi \Rightarrow D_B\varphi \Rightarrow \varphi$$

which makes precise that common knowledge is a strong notion (which is easiest attained for weak φ, like tautologies), and distributed knowledge is weak (obtainable about strong statements, 'closest to the true ones').

Since the truth definition of $E_B\varphi$ should follow from its syntactic definition as given on page 12, and from now on we will rarely consider distributed knowledge, we define $\mathcal{S}5\mathcal{C}$ as the class of models in $\mathcal{S}5$ for which we have a truth definition for common knowledge:

Definition 2.31 The class of epistemic models $\mathcal{S}5\mathcal{C}$ will be $\mathcal{S}5$ with the truth definition for $C_B\varphi$, $(B \subseteq A)$, as given in Definition 2.30. □

Example 2.32 (Common knowledge in consecutive numbers) Consider the consecutive numbers example again (Example 2.4, the solution to Exercise 2.10, and, specifically, the model M from Figure A.1). Given that the actual numbers are $\langle 3, 2\rangle$, Bill obviously does not have a 4, although this is not clear for everyone: $M, \langle 3, 2\rangle \models \neg b_4 \wedge \neg E_{ab}\neg b_4$ (since $\neg K_b\neg b_4$ holds here). Also, although everybody knows that Anne does not have a 5, not everybody knows that everybody knows this: $M, \langle 3, 2\rangle \models E_{ab}\neg a_5 \wedge \neg E_{ab}E_{ab}\neg a_5$ (since $\langle 3, 2\rangle \sim_b \langle 3, 4\rangle$ and $\langle 3, 4\rangle \sim_a \langle 5, 4\rangle$ and $M, \langle 5, 4\rangle \models a_5$). We can continue and observe that $M, \langle 3, 2\rangle \models E_{ab}E_{ab}\neg b_6 \wedge \neg E_{ab}E_{ab}E_{ab}\neg b_6$.
The reader should be convinced now that, even though Anne sees a 2 on Bill's head, and Bill notices the 3 on Anne's head, it is not common knowledge between Anne and Bill that Anne's number is not 1235! (Bill considers it

possible he has a 4 in which case Ann considers it possible she has a 5 in which case Bill cannot rule out he has a 6 in which case ....) It *is* common knowledge between them though, given $\langle 3, 2 \rangle$, that Bill's number is not 1235! (Since both agents only consider worlds possible in which Bill's number is even.) As a validity:

$$M \models (a_3 \land b_2) \rightarrow (\neg C_{ab} \neg a_{1235} \land C_{ab} \neg b_{1235}) \quad \square$$

We give one final example concerning the semantics of common knowledge, in this chapter. It is a stronger version of the Byzantine generals, since its assumptions are weaker.

Example 2.33 (Possible delay) Two parties, S and R, know that their communication channel is trustworthy, but with one small catch: when a message *Msg* is sent at time t, it either arrives immediately, or at time $t + \epsilon$. This catch is common knowledge between S and R. Now S sends a message to R at time t_0. When will it be common knowledge between S and R that *Msg* has been delivered? Surprisingly, the answer is: "Never!"

Let us model this as follows. Write m for: *Msg* has been delivered, and let a state $\langle s_i, d_j \rangle$ be the state in which *Msg* has been sent at time t_i, and delivered at time t_j. So, it is commonly known that the difference between i and j is either 0 or ϵ. Assume that in the 'real' state Msg was sent at $i = 0$. For any time point $t_0 + k \cdot \epsilon$ $(k \in \mathbb{N})$, let M_k be the epistemic model representing the knowledge after k steps. Thus, $M_k, \langle s_0, d_0 \rangle$ represents the epistemic state in which there was no delay in delivery of *Msg* and in which k time steps have passed, and $M_k, \langle s_0, d_1 \rangle$ stands for the situation in which the message was sent at t_0, delivered after one delay ϵ, and after which k steps of epsilon have passed after t_0. It is important to realise that

$$M_k, \langle s_i, d_j \rangle \models m \text{ iff } j \leq k$$

If we assume that *Msg* is delivered immediately, and we investigate the situation at t_0, we get the model M_0 of Figure 2.5, with the real state $\langle s_0, d_0 \rangle$. In this state, m is true, even R knows it (since the states that R considers possible, given $\langle s_0, d_0 \rangle$, are $\langle s_0, d_0 \rangle$ and $\langle s_{-1}, d_0 \rangle$ (R knows *Msg* has been delivered, but he holds it for possible that this took ϵ delay, i.e., that it was sent at s_{-1}). In $\langle s_0, d_0 \rangle$, agent S does *not* know m: he considers it possible that this takes a delay and that the real state is $\langle s_0, d_1 \rangle$. So, we conclude that $M_0, \langle s_0, d_0 \rangle \models \neg C_{SR} m$.

All the states in which m is true are those in the upper oval, in Figure 2.5. Note that we have not specified a beginning of time, in fact the 'upper half' can be finite, or even consist only of $\langle s_0, d_0 \rangle$.

Let us now wait one ϵ, and obtain model M_1 of Figure 2.6. Of course, $\langle s_0, d_0 \rangle$ is still a description of the actual state: we assumed that the message was sent at time 0, and immediately delivered. The states $\langle s_0, d_1 \rangle$ and $\langle s_1, d_1 \rangle$ now also verify m: since we are at time 1, and delivery in those states is at 1,

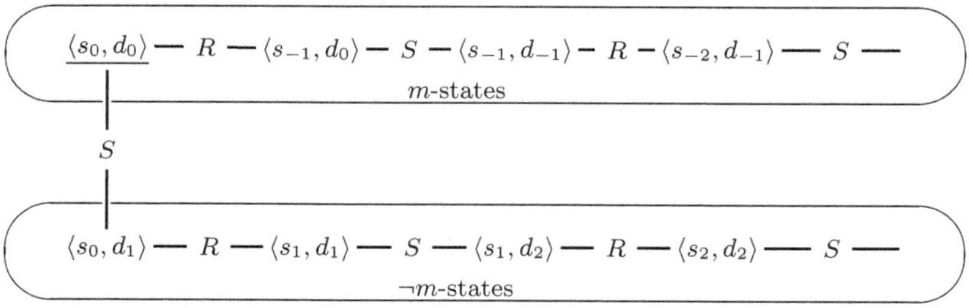

Figure 2.5. No delay, M_0.

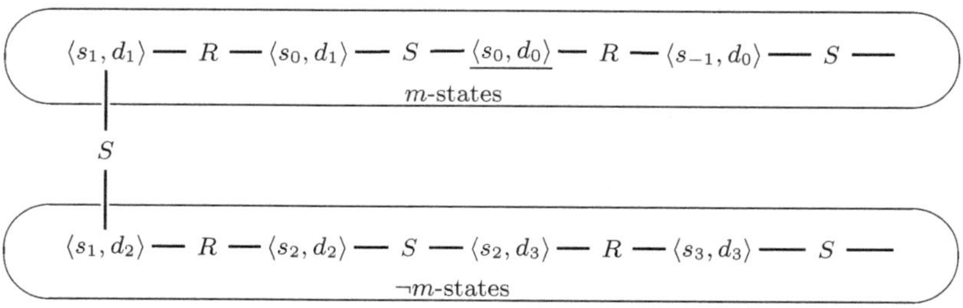

Figure 2.6. No delay, M_1.

these two states get 'promoted' to the 'upper oval' of the model. See Figure 2.6. We have $M_1, \langle s_0, d_0 \rangle \models E_{SR}E_{SR}m$, but $M_1, \langle s_0, d_0 \rangle \models \neg E_{SR}E_{SR}E_{SR}m$: given $\langle s_0, d_0 \rangle$, sender S holds it possible that *Msg* was sent at 0 and delivered with delay ($\langle s_0, d_1 \rangle$), a state in which R holds it for possible that the message arrived at time 1 without delay ($\langle s_1, d_1 \rangle$), a situation in which S should be prepared to accept that the message is sent at time 1 *with* delay ($\langle s_1, d_2 \rangle$). All in all, we conclude $M_1, \langle s_0, d_0 \rangle \models \neg C_{SR}m$.

From all this, it should be clear that, no matter how many units k of ϵ we wait, we will get a model M_k in which the state $\langle s_0, d_0 \rangle$ is 'shifted' $k + 2$ positions to the right, and the 'first' state down left the model M_k would be $\langle s_k, d_{k+1} \rangle$. In this state, at time k, delivery has not taken place, i.e., m is false, and, since $\langle s_k, d_{k+1} \rangle$ is $R_{C_{SR}}$-accessible from $\langle s_0, d_0 \rangle$, we have $M_k, \langle s_0, d_0 \rangle \models \neg C_{SR}m$ □

Exercise 2.34 What consequences would it have if the above guarantee would hold the way we send e-mail using the Internet? □

$C_B(\varphi \to \psi) \to (C_B\varphi \to C_B\psi)$	distribution of C_B over $\to$
$C_B\varphi \to (\varphi \land E_B C_B\varphi)$	mix
$C_B(\varphi \to E_B\varphi) \to (\varphi \to C_B\varphi)$	induction of common knowledge
From φ, infer $C_B\varphi$	necessitation of C_B

Table 2.3. Axioms of the epistemic system **S5C**.

2.3.3 Axiomatisation

The following definition establishes the axiomatisation of $\mathcal{S}5\mathcal{C}$.

Definition 2.35 Let A be a given set of agents, and let B be an arbitrary subset of it. Then the axiom system **S5C** consists of all the axioms and rules of **S5**, plus the axioms and derivation rule of Table 2.3. □

Axiom 'mix' implies that common knowledge is veridical. It also ensures all finite restrictions of the 'definition' of common knowledge given on page 31: one can show that this axiom and the definition of E_B ensure that, for every $k \in \mathbb{N}$, we have $\vdash C_B\varphi \to E_B^k\varphi$. The distribution axiom and the necessitation rule ensure that C_B is a normal modal operator. The induction axiom explains how one can derive that φ is common knowledge: by deriving φ itself together with common knowledge about $\varphi \to E\varphi$. We think that proving its soundness may help in understanding it.

Example 2.36 We show that the induction axiom is valid in the class of $\mathcal{S}5\mathcal{C}$-models. So, let M be an arbitrary $\mathcal{S}5\mathcal{C}$ model, then we have to prove that in any s, $(M,s) \models C_B(\varphi \to E_B\varphi) \to (\varphi \to C_B\varphi)$. To do so, assume that $(M,s) \models C_B(\varphi \to E_B\varphi)$ (1). This means that $(M,t) \models \varphi \to E_B\varphi$ for all t for which $R^*_{E_B}st$ (2). In order to prove the consequent of the induction axiom, suppose $(M,s) \models \varphi$ (3). Our task is now to show $(M,s) \models C_B\varphi$, which by Remark 2.29 is equivalent to saying: (4) for all n such that $R^n_{E_B}st$, we have $(M,t) \models \varphi$. And, indeed, the latter is done with induction over n. The basic case ($n = 0$) requires us to establish that for all t for which $R^0_{E_B}st$, i.e., for $t = s$, that $(M,t) \models \varphi$, which is immediate from (3). So, now suppose claim (4) is true for n. Take any t that is $n+1$ R_{E_B}-steps away from s, i.e. for which $R^{n+1}_{E_B}st$. Then there must be a state u for which $R^n_{E_B}su$ and $R^1_{E_B}ut$. The induction hypothesis guarantees that $(M,u) \models \varphi$, and from (1) we derive $(M,u) \models \varphi \to E_B\varphi$. This implies that $(M,u) \models E_B\varphi$, and hence, since $R^1_{E_B}ut$, also $(M,t) \models \varphi$, which completes the proof. □

The following exercise asks for some derivations in **S5C**. The first item establishes positive introspection of common knowledge, the second negative introspection. The third and fourth items demonstrate that an agent in B can never have any uncertainty about the common knowledge of B: $C_B\varphi$ holds if and only if some agent in B knows that it holds. Item 5 of Exercise 2.37 demonstrates that any depth of mutual knowledge of members in B about

φ follows from φ being common knowledge within B. Note that, by using contraposition, as soon as we have, for some chain of agents $a_1, a_2, \ldots, a_n \in B$ we can establish that $\hat{K}_{a_1}\hat{K}_{a_2}\cdots\hat{K}_{a_n}\neg\varphi$, then φ cannot be common knowledge in B. Finally the last item of Exercise 2.37 guarantees that common knowledge is preserved under subgroups.

Exercise 2.37 Let $a \in B \subseteq A$. Show that the following are derivable, in **S5C**:

1. $C_B\varphi \leftrightarrow C_BC_B\varphi$
2. $\neg C_B\varphi \leftrightarrow C_B\neg C_B\varphi$
3. $C_B\varphi \leftrightarrow K_aC_B\varphi$
4. $\neg C_B\varphi \leftrightarrow K_a\neg C_B\varphi$
5. $C_B\varphi \to K_{a_1}K_{a_2}\ldots K_{a_n}\varphi$, where every $a_i \in B (i \leq n)$
6. $C_B\varphi \to C_{B'}\varphi$ iff $B' \subseteq B$

Theorem 2.38 (Soundness and completeness) Compare. Theorem 7.19 For all $\varphi \in \mathcal{L}_{KC}$, we have $\vdash_{\mathbf{S5C}} \varphi$ iff $\mathcal{S}5\mathcal{C} \models \varphi$. □

2.4 Logics for Belief

Although there are many different logics for belief, it is generally well accepted that the main difference between knowledge and belief is that the latter does not comply with axiom T: whereas it does not make sense to say 'John knows today it is Tuesday, although it is Wednesday', it seems perfectly reasonable to remark 'John believes today is Tuesday, although in fact it is Wednesday'. So for beliefs (which we refer to using B_a) the property T, $B_a\varphi \to \varphi$, may fail.

Conversely, given a doxastic notion (i.e., belief) one may wonder what needs to be added to make it epistemic (i.e., knowledge). Obviously, for belief to become knowledge, it has to be true, but it is widely acknowledged that some additional criterion has to be met (suppose two supporters of opposite sport teams both believe that 'their' team will win the final; it would be not immediately clear that we should coin one of these attitudes 'knowledge'). In Plato's dialogue *Theaetetus*, Socrates discusses several theories of what knowledge is, one being that knowledge is true belief 'that has been given an account of'. Although in the end rejected by Socrates, philosophers have embraced for a long time the related claim that 'knowledge is true, justified belief'. A paper by Gettier, *Is Justified True Belief Knowledge?*, marked an end to this widely accepted definition of belief and sparked a lively and interesting discussion in the philosophical literature. Here, we will refrain from such deliberations.

From a technical point of view, to recover some kind of reasoning abilities of agents, it is often assumed that, although believed sentences need not be

all instantiations of propositional tautologies	
$K_a(\varphi \to \psi) \to (K_a\varphi \to K_a\psi)$	distribution of K_a over $\to$
$\neg B_a\bot$	consistent beliefs
$B_a\varphi \to B_aB_a\varphi$	positive introspection
$\neg B_a\varphi \to B_a\neg B_a\varphi$	negative introspection
From φ and $\varphi \to \psi$ infer ψ	modus ponens
From φ infer $B_a\varphi$	necessitation of belief

Table 2.4. Axioms for the belief system **KD45**.

true, they should at least be *internally consistent*. In other words, for belief, T is replaced by the weaker axiom D: $\neg B_a\bot$. This is the same as adding an axiom D' : $B_a\varphi \to \neg B_a\neg\varphi$ (see Exercise 2.39): for any φ that the agent accepts to believe, he cannot also believe its opposite $\neg\varphi$ at the same time. For the other axioms, it is not so straightforward to pick a most obvious or even most popular choice, although belief systems with positive and negative introspection are quite common. Let us summarise the axioms of the belief system **KD45**, obtained in this way, in Table 2.4.

Exercise 2.39 Given that the axiom D' is $B_a\varphi \to \neg B_a\neg\varphi$, show that indeed axiom D and D' are equivalent with respect to **K**. □

The next two exercises show that, firstly, the system for belief is indeed weaker than that of knowledge, and secondly, how one can derive *Moore's principle* (2.4) in it. Moore's principle states that a rational agent (say, one whose beliefs are consistent), will not believe, at the same time, for any φ, that it is true while he does not believe it. This principle will play a main role in the next chapter's attempt to relate belief revision to dynamic epistemic logic, and it will also be a source of many paradoxical situations in both fields, as will become clear in the next chapters.

$$\neg B_a\bot \to \neg B_a(\varphi \wedge \neg B_a\varphi) \tag{2.4}$$

Exercise 2.40 Show that, indeed, T is stronger than the axiom D. That is, show that, $\vdash_{\mathbf{K}+T} D$, but not $\vdash_{\mathbf{K}+D} T$. For the latter, use that $\vdash_{\mathbf{K}+D} \varphi$ iff $KD \models \varphi$, where KD is the set of all serial Kripke models. □

Exercise 2.41 Show that Moore's principle (2.4) is derivable in $KD45$, by showing that even $\neg B_a(\varphi \wedge \neg B_a\varphi)$ has a derivation. □

We mention the following result.

Theorem 2.42 Axiom system **KD45** is sound and complete with respect to the semantic class $\mathcal{KD}45$, i.e., for every formula φ, we have $\vdash_{\mathbf{KD45}} \varphi$ iff $\mathcal{KD}45 \models \varphi$. □

Of course, it may be interesting to study frameworks in which *both* knowledge and belief occur. Although $K_a\varphi \to B_a\varphi$ is an accepted principle relating the two (fuelled by the claim 'knowledge is justified, true belief'), it is not immediately clear which other interaction properties to accept, like for instance $K_a\varphi \rightarrow B_aK_a\varphi$. Also, one can, as with knowledge, define group notions of belief, where in the case of belief common belief is usually interpreted with respect to the transitive closure (note: not the reflexive transitive closure) of the union of the individual accessibility relations.

2.5 Notes

Hintikka, most notably through [99], is broadly acknowledged as the father of modern epistemic logic, although Hintikka himself thinks that von Wright deserves this credit.[2] Modern epistemic logic started to flourish after modal logic (with its roots in Aristotle) was formalised and given a possible world semantics. It is hard to track down the exact origins of this semantics, but it is widely known as Kripke semantics, after Kripke, who devoted a number of early papers to the semantics of modal logic (see [120]). A contemporary and thorough standard work in modal logic is the monograph [29] by Blackburn, de Rijke and Venema, to which we refer the reader for a deeper analysis and for further references on this subject.

From the late 1970s, epistemic logic in the sense it is treated in this chapter became subject of study or applied in the areas of artificial intelligence (witnessed by Moore's early work [152] on reasoning about actions and knowledge), philosophy (see Hintikka's [100]), and game theory. Regarding the latter, Aumann is one of the most prominent to mention. His [5] gives one of the first formalisations of common knowledge, a notion that was already informally discussed in 1969 by Lewis in [128]. And in Aumann's survey paper [6] on interactive epistemology the reader will immediately recognise the system $\mathcal{S}5$. Together with Brandenburger, Aumann argued in [7] that knowledge is crucial for game theoretic solutions. For a contemporary and modal logical treatment of the latter, see also de Bruin's thesis [33].

In the 1980s, computer scientists became interested in epistemic logic. In fact, the field matured a lot by a large stream of publications around Fagin, Halpern, Moses, and Vardi. Their important textbook *Reasoning about Knowledge* [62] which appeared in 1995, is in fact a survey of many papers co-authored by (subsets of) them over a period of more than ten years. We refer to [62] for more references. Their emphasis on *interpreted systems* as an underlying model for their framework makes the **S5** axioms easy to digest, and this semantics also facilitates reasoning about knowledge during *computation*

[2] Hintikka referred to von Wright as the founder of modern epistemic logic in his invited talk at the PhiLog conference *Dimensions in Epistemic Logic*, Roskilde, Denmark, May 2002. In the volume [96] dedicated to this event Hintikka [101] refers to von Wright's [195] as the thrust of epistemic logic (which was practiced already in the Middle Ages, see [30]) 'to the awareness of contemporary philosophers'.

runs in a natural way. Their work also generated lots of (complexity) results on knowledge and time, we also mention the work of van der Meyden (e.g., [143]) in this respect. The textbook [148] on epistemic logic by Meyer and van der Hoek also appeared in 1995. There, the emphasis is more on 'classical Kripke-world semantics', and the book discusses various notions of belief, and non-classical reasoning. All the theorems mentioned and the proofs omitted in this chapter can be found in [62, 148].

In the 1990s, the paradigm of *agents* re-enforced the computer science community's interest in modal logical approaches to notions like knowledge and belief. We here only mention the influential BDI ('Belief, Desires, and Intentions') framework, as developed by Rao and Georgeff [172]. For a more extensive survey on modal logics for rational agents, see van der Hoek and Wooldridge's [105] and the references therein. Recently, we see a growing interest in epistemic knowledge by researchers in computer science, agent theory and games. Such a multi-disciplinary stance was much influenced by the TARK [188] and LOFT [136] conferences: we refer to their proceedings for further references.

Regarding Example 2.3, the proof that knowledge of depth four is sufficient and necessary to comply with the protocol can be found in Halpern and Zuck's [91], which gives a thorough knowledge-based analyses of the so-called sequence-transmission problem. Meyer and van der Hoek [148] give a detailed description of how to transfer the solution given here into the 'alternating bit protocol', in which all explicit references to knowledge have been removed. The aim of this example is to show how a knowledge-based specification can help to find a solution: the alternating bit protocol itself was known before epistemic logicians thought about this kind of problems (see Bartlett, Scantlebury, and Wilkinson's analyses [13] of 1969). For a simulation of the protocol, the reader be referred to `http://www.ai.rug.nl/mas/protocol/`.

Although [148] gives a rather ad-hoc procedure to eliminate the epistemic operators from the specification, there is a stream of research in *knowledge-based programs* (first defined by Kurki-Suonio [122]) that tries to systematically determine which kind of program can 'count as' a knowledge-based program: see the work by Halpern [84], Vardi [190], or their joint work with Fagin and Moses [63]. Example 2.3 in fact analyses a *Knowledge-based protocol*, a term that was introduced in 1989 by Halpern and Fagin [86], and which is still popular in analysing for instance protocols for the Internet (see Stulp and Verbrugge's [187] for an example).

Our running example of consecutive numbers is one of the many and popular puzzles trying to explain common knowledge, like the muddy children puzzle (see Chapter 4). The original source of the consecutive number example is not known to us, but the earliest reference we found to a variant of this puzzle is in Littlewood's [135] from 1953. A recent analysis of the problem using *Interactive Discovery Systems* can be found in Parikh's [162], with references to Littlewood and to van Emde Boas, Groenendijk, and Stokhof's [60]. Littlewood's version presented in [31], which is an extended rewriting of [135], reads as follows:

> The following will probably not stand up to close analysis, but given a little goodwill is entertaining.
> There is an indefinite supply of cards marked 1 and 2 on opposite sides, and of card marked 2 and 3, 3 and 4, and so on. A card is drawn at random by a referee and held between the players A, B so that each sees one side only. Either player may veto the round, but if it is played the player seeing the higher number wins. The point now is that every round is vetoed. If A sees a 1 the other side is 2 and he must veto. If he sees a 2 the other side is 1 or 3: if 1 then B must veto; if he does not veto then A must. And so on by induction.

The notion of bisimulation is a focal point in expressivity results of modal logic, and was independently discovered in areas as diverse as computer science, philosophical logic, and set theory. In computer science it plays a fundamental role in the analysis of when two automata 'behave the same'. In this context, the notion of bisimulation was developed through a number of co-inspired papers by Park [165] and Milner [150]. Van Benthem introduced [18] p-morphisms (essentially bisimulations) in his correspondence theory for modal logic, and finally, Forti and Honsell developed their notion of bisimulation for their work [65] on non-well founded sets. A nice and short overview of the origins of bisimulation is given in Sangiorgi's [180].

The issue of logical omniscience was already mentioned in [99] and quite extensively discussed in the monographs [62] and [148], with several solutions mentioned. Further references are found there.

Completeness proofs for the logics presented here can be found in many textbooks. A standard reference for techniques in modal logic is Blackburn, de Rijke, and Venema's [29]. Strong completeness and the role of applying necessitation to the premises is discussed in papers by van der Hoek and Meyer [106] and by Parikh [163]

The problem of the Byzantine generals was formalised already in 1980 by Pease, Shostak, and Lamport [166]. A survey of this problem is provided by Fischer's [64]. The formalisation of the 'possible delay' problem, (Example 2.33), is taken from [62], although their treatment is in the setting of interpreted systems. Our semantic analysis is inspired by van der Hoek and Verbrugge [104].

The famous paper 'Is Justified True Belief Knowledge?' by Gettier [78] is a good example of a clear challenge of one definition of belief, and has many successors in the philosophical literature. Kraus and Lehmann [119] were among the first who looked at logics that combined knowledge and belief defined in a possible worlds framework. Van der Hoek [102] gives a semantic analysis of 'how many' interaction axioms (like the mentioned $K_a\varphi \rightarrow B_aK_a\varphi$) one can assume without the two notions of knowledge and belief collapsing to one and the same thing.

3

Belief Revision

3.1 Introduction

Now that we have presented a theory of multi-agent knowledge in Chapter 2, a natural next step is to study how an agent's epistemic attitude can *change* over time. We have in fact already seen that such changes are important: for instance in the Consecutive Numbers puzzle (Example 2.4), the information state of each agent changes as a result of an announcement by any of the agents (note that even the first announcement of a ("I don't know the numbers" $= \varphi$) changes *his* information state: after uttering φ, we have that a knows that b knows that φ ($K_a K_b \varphi$: in fact we even have $K_a K_b K_a K_b \varphi$, etc.)).

Modelling such kinds of information change is exactly what this book is about! Before plunging in the full intricacies of changes of mutual knowledge in a multi-agent setting, in this chapter we will first lay out how one of the first theories regarding the change of beliefs formalises intuitions for changing one's information. This chapter differs from other chapters in the sense that, to make the connection with the existing literature on information change as seamless as possible, the main informational attitude that we mention is that of *belief*. This is because the mainstream of research in formal information change has been coined *belief revision*. The reader should keep in mind though that if we use the term 'belief' in this chapter, it might either refer to a technical **KD45**-like notion, or to a less well-defined doxastic or even an epistemic attitude.

There are many dimensions and parameters along which one can relate approaches to belief revision. For instance, does the agent only update his beliefs or knowledge about a world, or can the world itself also change? The setting in which only the information about the world is allowed to change is often dubbed *belief revision*, whereas, if we reason about new information about a changing world, this is often called *update*. In this chapter our main emphasis is on belief revision, which models the change of information during for instance communication.

Another important parameter to classify approaches to belief revision is the choice of the object language. In the 'classical' approach, the object language is *purely propositional*, and the changes of information or beliefs are presented on a meta-level. Obviously, when one wants to represent the change of knowledge in a multi-agent scenario (like that of the consecutive numbers as introduced in Example 2.4) one needs a richer object language, which gives an account of what certain agents know or believe (of other agents). Making the object language contain the full epistemic language of, say, Section 2.2.1, will be our concern in the following chapters of this book.

This chapter is organised as follows. Section 3.2 gives an overview of a standard account to information change, to wit the AGM-approach to belief revision. We will briefly discuss the AGM-postulates for the types of belief change called expansion, contraction, and revision. In Section 3.3 we discuss a possible worlds approach to deal with this paradigm. Section 3.4 can be conceived of as a motivation of the remainder of this book: it shows why an extension of the AGM-paradigm to the cases where we allow for higher order beliefs, possibly of more than one agent, are not straightforward. Readers familiar with 'classical belief revision theory' may prefer to immediately jump to Section 3.4.

3.2 The AGM-approach

It is commonly accepted that the current interest in the dynamics of beliefs is very much influenced by a contribution of C.E. Alchourrón, P. Gärdenfors, and D. Makinson. It lead to a now prominent paradigm in belief revision, called after the authors, i.e., AGM. Where Alchourrón's original motivation concerned the revision of norms, Gärdenfors' interest was to model *theory revision*, the idea being that a (scientific) theory in general has a tendency to only make the smallest necessary changes when it has to explain phenomena that were not yet accounted for. So an underlying principle here is that of *minimal change* (of the theory).

Moving to the area of belief revision (where a belief set $\mathcal{K}$ is a set of propositional formulas), AGM distinguishes three kinds of change, given a belief set $\mathcal{K}$ and some new information φ. In an *expansion* of $\mathcal{K}$ with φ, the resulting belief set $\mathcal{K} \oplus \varphi$ is one that accepts φ: the evidence is added to the beliefs, possibly yielding inconsistency. It is important to notice that the deliberation about the status of φ is not part of this process: in an expansion, the assumption is that φ has passed the test of acceptance. A *contraction* of $\mathcal{K}$ with φ, denoted by $\mathcal{K} \ominus \varphi$, yields a set of beliefs from which φ is removed, or, more precisely, from which φ does not follow. Finally, a *revision* of $\mathcal{K}$ with φ, denoted $\mathcal{K} \circledast \varphi$, is the result of incorporating new information φ, which in the most interesting case is contradictory with $\mathcal{K}$, into a new, consistent belief set that contains φ and for the rest is 'similar' to $\mathcal{K}$. Using what is known as the *Levi-identity*, revision can be expressed in terms of the other two operations:

$$\mathcal{K} \circledast \varphi \equiv (\mathcal{K} \ominus \neg\varphi) \oplus \varphi \tag{3.1}$$

In other words, in order to revise a belief set with new (contradictory) information φ, one first makes space for φ by deleting everything that contradicts it (that is, $\neg\varphi$), after which one can safely add φ.

Let us agree on a language for the AGM-setting.

Definition 3.1 We define $\mathcal{L}_0$ to be the set of propositional formulas, generated by some set of atoms P, and the classical connectives. Let $Cn(\cdot)$ be the *classical consequence operator*, i.e., $Cn(\Sigma) = \{\sigma \in \mathcal{L}_0 \mid \Sigma \vdash \sigma\}$. A *belief set* $\mathcal{K}$ is a set of propositional formulas closed under $Cn(\cdot)$, i.e., $Cn(\mathcal{K}) = \mathcal{K}$. We denote the unique inconsistent belief set, consisting of all propositional formulas, by $\mathcal{K}_\perp$. Moreover, unless stated otherwise, φ, ψ and χ denote propositional formulas in this chapter, representing new information. □

Having fixed the language of beliefs to be purely propositional, reasoning about change is done on a meta-level, describing the behaviour of each type of change by means of some postulates. Such postulates play the role of desirable properties for the operators at hand, inspired by general intuition about theory change or information change. As we will see, by means of representation theorems, one then tries to characterise sets of postulates by choosing an appropriate underlying mathematical model for the operators.

Coming up with a set of postulates in the case of expansion might seem a bit as an overkill, since expansion has a unique and simple characterisation (Theorem 3.2). However, we include them in order to have a uniform approach for all the operators, and, moreover, the postulates for expansion still make some interesting properties of belief expansion explicit.

3.2.1 Expansion

Recall that $\oplus$ models expansion: the idea of $\mathcal{K}\oplus\varphi$ being that it is the resulting belief set once we accept φ as new information in the situation that our current belief set is $\mathcal{K}$. The behaviour of expansion is assumed to be in accordance with the postulates of Table 3.1.

Postulate ($\mathcal{K} \oplus 1$) guarantees that the result of an expansion is a belief set: this facilitates performing repeated expansions, and, as we will require this constraint of all operations, it also enables us to write down requirements like the Levi identity (3.1) or commutativity of $\oplus$ (see below). The second postulate for $\oplus$, *success*, expresses what expansion is all about: once we have decided to accept φ as new information, it should be incorporated in our beliefs.

The other postulates all refer to some kind of *minimal change*, or *informational economy*, or *rationality.* To be more precise, ($\mathcal{K} \oplus 3$) says that, when one decides to add information to one's beliefs, one need not throw away any beliefs, but keep all from the old belief set (this could be considered a *minimal type of change* – don't remove anything unnecessarily). One can show

$(\mathcal{K} \oplus 1)$ $\mathcal{K} \oplus \varphi$ is a belief set	*type*
$(\mathcal{K} \oplus 2)$ $\varphi \in \mathcal{K} \oplus \varphi$	*success*
$(\mathcal{K} \oplus 3)$ $\mathcal{K} \subseteq \mathcal{K} \oplus \varphi$	*expansion*
$(\mathcal{K} \oplus 4)$ If $\varphi \in \mathcal{K}$ then $\mathcal{K} = \mathcal{K} \oplus \varphi$	*minimal action*
$(\mathcal{K} \oplus 5)$ For all $\mathcal{H}$, if $\mathcal{K} \subseteq \mathcal{H}$ then $\mathcal{K} \oplus \varphi \subseteq \mathcal{H} \oplus \varphi$	*monotony*
$(\mathcal{K} \oplus 6)$ $\mathcal{K} \oplus \varphi$ is the smallest set satisfying $(\mathcal{K} \oplus 1) - (\mathcal{K} \oplus 5)$	*minimal change*

Table 3.1. The Postulates for Expansion.

(Exercise 3.4) that $(\mathcal{K} \oplus 1), (\mathcal{K} \oplus 2)$ and $(\mathcal{K} \oplus 3)$ guarantee minimality 'from below': nothing should be given up when expanding. In other words, postulates $(\mathcal{K} \oplus 1), (\mathcal{K} \oplus 2)$ and $(\mathcal{K} \oplus 3)$ guarantee

$$Cn(\mathcal{K} \cup \{\varphi\}) \subseteq \mathcal{K} \oplus \varphi \tag{3.2}$$

The postulate *minimal action*, i.e. $(\mathcal{K} \oplus 4)$, minimizes the circumstances under which to change the belief set $\mathcal{K}$ when we accept information φ: namely only if φ is not already there (in $\mathcal{K}$, that is). Postulate $(\mathcal{K} \oplus 6)$ is obviously about *minimal change*: once we have accepted that an expansion corresponds to addition $(\mathcal{K} \oplus 3)$, we should not add more than absolutely necessary. One easily shows (Exercise 3.5), that under the assumption of all the other postulates, $(\mathcal{K} \oplus 6)$ is equivalent to

$$\mathcal{K} \oplus \varphi \subseteq Cn(\mathcal{K} \cup \{\varphi\}) \tag{3.3}$$

Finally, we give $(\mathcal{K} \oplus 5)$ for historical reasons, it is, similar to $(\mathcal{K} \oplus 4)$, derivable from the others, though (see Exercise 3.8).

Accepting the postulates for expansion, a natural question now is whether there exist operations that satisfy them.

Theorem 3.2 A function $\oplus$ satisfies $(\mathcal{K} \oplus 1) - (\mathcal{K} \oplus 6)$ iff $\mathcal{K} \oplus \varphi = Cn(\mathcal{K} \cup \{\varphi\})$ □

Theorem 3.2 is a representation theorem for expansion: the postulates allow for an explicit definition of $\oplus$. Moreover, this definition happens to uniquely define $\oplus$. We will shortly see that this is not the case for contraction and revision.

Using Theorem 3.2, we can immediately derive a number of properties of expansion (see Table 3.2), some even involving connectives (although none of the postulates explicitly refers to them).

Exercise 3.3 Prove the properties of Table 3.2 □

Exercise 3.4 Let $\oplus$ satisfy $(\mathcal{K} \oplus 1) - (\mathcal{K} \oplus 3)$.
Show: $Cn(\mathcal{K} \cup \{\varphi\}) \subseteq \mathcal{K} \oplus \varphi$. □

If $\vdash \varphi \leftrightarrow \psi$, then $\mathcal{K} \oplus \varphi = \mathcal{K} \oplus \psi$	*extensionality*
$(\mathcal{K} \oplus \varphi) \oplus \psi = \mathcal{K} \oplus (\varphi \wedge \psi)$	*conjunction*
$(\mathcal{K} \oplus \varphi) \oplus \psi = (\mathcal{K} \oplus \psi) \oplus \varphi$	*commutativity*
$(\mathcal{K} \cap \mathcal{H}) \oplus \varphi = (\mathcal{K} \oplus \varphi) \cap (\mathcal{H} \oplus \varphi)$	*distributivity*

Table 3.2. Some derived properties of expansion.

Exercise 3.5 Let $\oplus$ satisfy $(\mathcal{K} \oplus 1) - (\mathcal{K} \oplus 5)$.
Show: $\mathcal{K} \oplus \varphi \subseteq Cn(\mathcal{K} \cup \{\varphi\})$ iff $\oplus$ satisfies $(\mathcal{K} \oplus 6)$. □

Formally, if an operator $\oplus$ satisfies $(\mathcal{K} \oplus 6)$, it also, by definition, satisfies $(\mathcal{K} \oplus 1) - (\mathcal{K} \oplus 5)$. In order to be able to compare the postulates in an interesting way, let us therefore define a relativised version of $(\mathcal{K} \oplus 6)$.

Definition 3.6 Given a set of postulates $(\mathcal{K} \oplus i_1), \ldots, (\mathcal{K} \oplus i_k)$, we define a minimal change postulate $(\mathcal{K} \oplus min)^{\{i_1,\ldots,i_k\}}$, as follows:

$(\mathcal{K} \oplus min)^{\{i_1,\ldots,i_k\}} \mathcal{K} \oplus \varphi$ is the smallest set satisfying $(\mathcal{K} \oplus i_1), \ldots, (\mathcal{K} \oplus i_k)$
□

We now can formulate a dependency between some postulates for expansion: the proof of the next theorem is left as an exercise.

Theorem 3.7

1. Let $\oplus$ satisfy $(\mathcal{K} \oplus 1), (\mathcal{K} \oplus 2), (\mathcal{K} \oplus 3)$ and $(\mathcal{K} \oplus min)^{\{1,2,3\}}$.
   Then $\oplus$ also satisfies $(\mathcal{K} \oplus 4)$.
2. Let $\oplus$ satisfy $(\mathcal{K} \oplus 1) - (\mathcal{K} \oplus 3)$ and $(\mathcal{K} \oplus min)^{\{1,2,3\}}$.
   Then $\oplus$ also satisfies $(\mathcal{K} \oplus 5)$. □

Proof See Exercise 3.8 □

Exercise 3.8 Prove Theorem 3.7. □

3.2.2 Contraction

We will write $\mathcal{K} \ominus \varphi$ for the belief set that results when φ is given up as a belief. This is not as straightforward as an expansion: Suppose an agent's belief set is $\mathcal{K} = Cn(\{p, q, r\})$. Also, suppose this agent wants to contract p from $\mathcal{K}$. Note that removing p and then closing off under consequence does not give the desired result, since $Cn(\mathcal{K} \setminus \{p\}) = \mathcal{K}$! (To see this, note that $(r \rightarrow p) \in Cn(\mathcal{K}) \setminus \{p\}$.) Furthermore, suppose, given $\mathcal{K}$, that the agent needs to contract $p \wedge q$. Obviously, there seems no reason to give up r, but regarding p and q it is sufficient (and under the regime of minimality it even

$(\mathcal{K} \ominus 1)$ $\mathcal{K} \ominus \varphi$ is a belief set	*type*
$(\mathcal{K} \ominus 2)$ $\mathcal{K} \ominus \varphi \subseteq \mathcal{K}$	*contraction*
$(\mathcal{K} \ominus 3)$ If $\varphi \notin \mathcal{K}$ then $\mathcal{K} = \mathcal{K} \ominus \varphi$	*minimal action*
$(\mathcal{K} \ominus 4)$ If $\not\vdash \varphi$ then $\varphi \notin \mathcal{K} \ominus \varphi$	*success*
$(\mathcal{K} \ominus 5)$ If $\varphi \in \mathcal{K}$ then $\mathcal{K} \subseteq (\mathcal{K} \ominus \varphi) \oplus \varphi$	*recovery*
$(\mathcal{K} \ominus 6)$ If $\vdash \varphi \leftrightarrow \psi$ then $\mathcal{K} \ominus \varphi = \mathcal{K} \ominus \psi$	*extensionality*
$(\mathcal{K} \ominus 7)$ $((\mathcal{K} \ominus \varphi) \cap (\mathcal{K} \ominus \psi)) \subseteq \mathcal{K} \ominus (\varphi \wedge \psi)$	*min-conjunction*
$(\mathcal{K} \ominus 8)$ If $\varphi \notin \mathcal{K} \ominus (\varphi \wedge \psi)$ then $\mathcal{K} \ominus (\varphi \wedge \psi) \subseteq \mathcal{K} \ominus \varphi$	*max-conjunction*

Table 3.3. The Postulates for Contraction.

seems favourable) to only give up one of those atoms, but it is not clear which one. Here is where the notion of *entrenchment* enters the picture: the more an agent is entrenched to a fact, the less willing he is to give it up. So, apart from representing the agent's beliefs, we also need to keep track of the *reasons* for his specific beliefs.

The underlying assumptions for the postulates of $\ominus$ (see Table 3.3) are, that the result of a contraction is unique (so that indeed, in the example of contracting with $p \wedge q$, a choice has to be made), and that we remain faithful to the principle of informational economy.

The postulates $(\mathcal{K} \ominus 1) - (\mathcal{K} \ominus 6)$ form a basic system for contraction, and can be motivated in a similar way as the postulates for expansion: $(\mathcal{K} \ominus 1)$ determines the type of $\ominus$: the result is a belief set (rather than for instance an empty set, or 'error', or a set of belief sets). Postulate $(\mathcal{K} \ominus 2)$ specifies that, when contracting, nothing should be added to the belief set; $(\mathcal{K} \ominus 3)$ is similar to $(\mathcal{K} \oplus 4)$ and stipulates that nothing should be done if the desired aim is already fulfilled, and $(\mathcal{K} \ominus 6)$ says that the result of a contraction should not depend on the syntactic presentation of the sentence we want to contract with. Finally, *recovery*, or $(\mathcal{K} \ominus 5)$, gives a connection between expansion and contraction: Suppose you believe φ, and also ψ. Then, if you give up the belief φ, it might be that you are forced to give up ψ as well, but (by the principle of minimal change) only if necessary. This implies that, as soon you decide to add φ again, ψ should be accepted as well! As the solution to Exercise 3.9 shows, from $(\mathcal{K} \oplus 3), (\mathcal{K} \ominus 3)$ and $(\mathcal{K} \ominus 5)$ we derive

$$(\mathcal{K} \ominus 5'): \quad \mathcal{K} \subseteq (\mathcal{K} \ominus \varphi) \oplus \varphi \tag{3.4}$$

Exercise 3.9 Let $\ominus$ satisfy $(\mathcal{K} \ominus 1) - (\mathcal{K} \ominus 5)$, and let $\oplus$ satisfy $(\mathcal{K} \oplus 3)$. Show:
$\mathcal{K} \subseteq (\mathcal{K} \ominus \varphi) \oplus \varphi$. □

Of course, by $(\mathcal{K} \ominus 1)$, one cannot contract successfully with a tautology, since 'the smallest' belief set is $Cn(\emptyset)$, the set of all classical tautologies, which is not the empty set: an agent cannot believe nothing. Therefore, it might have been more appropriate to have coined ($\mathcal{K} \ominus 4$) *conditional success*. Minimality then suggests that $\mathcal{K} \ominus \top = \mathcal{K}$, which, assuming the postulates for expansion, indeed is the case, as demonstrated by Exercise 3.10.

Exercise 3.10 Show that the postulates for contraction and expansion guarantee that $\mathcal{K} \ominus \top = \mathcal{K}$. How many (and which) postulates are needed? □

The postulates ($\mathcal{K} \ominus 7$) and ($\mathcal{K} \ominus 8$) give constraints on the behaviour of $\ominus$ when contracting with a conjunction. A first property that needs investigation is whether, when contracting with $\varphi \wedge \psi$, we might as well contract with both independently, and then retain only what is in both results: should the equality $\mathcal{K} \ominus (\varphi \wedge \psi) = \mathcal{K} \ominus \varphi \cap \mathcal{K} \ominus \psi$ (*) hold? By minimality, $\subseteq$ should not hold in general: if one has to give up $\varphi \wedge \psi$, it is not clear that one should always give up both φ and ψ: If I believe that (a weak) student John passed a particular exam (φ), and also that (a good) student Peter passed that exam (ψ), and then I find out that they did not both pass, I might be inclined to only give up φ.

Note that the $\supseteq$-direction of (*) is in fact ($\mathcal{K} \ominus 7$): It gives a minimal criterion on the contents of $\mathcal{K} \ominus (\varphi \wedge \psi)$, namely that everything that is retained after giving up φ and after giving up ψ should also stay in $\mathcal{K} \ominus (\varphi \wedge \psi)$. This is again motivated by a minimality principle: Suppose a particular belief χ survives, *no matter* whether I contract $\mathcal{K}$ with φ or with ψ. Then χ should also survive if I 'only' contract with the stronger formula $\varphi \wedge \psi$, the idea being that it is 'easier' to give up a logically strong formula than it is to give up a weak one.

The latter does not mean however that we have $\vdash \varphi \rightarrow \psi \Rightarrow \mathcal{K} \ominus \psi \subseteq \mathcal{K} \ominus \varphi$, in fact in general we do not even have $\mathcal{K} \ominus \varphi \subseteq \mathcal{K} \ominus (\varphi \wedge \psi)$ (**). As a witness, suppose I believe that student Peter is slightly better than student John. Also, I believe that both pass the exam (φ for Peter, and ψ for John). Now suppose further I have to give up φ. It is well possible that I stick to my belief that ψ, which, would we have (**), gives $\psi \in \mathcal{K} \ominus (\varphi \wedge \psi)$, which is absurd: if I have to admit that not all students passed, I start eliminating the weakest.

Finally, ($\mathcal{K} \ominus 8$) gives a maximum criterion on the contents of $\mathcal{K} \ominus (\varphi \wedge \psi)$. This postulate is best motivated as follows. First, one might expect that we have: If $\varphi \notin \mathcal{K} \ominus (\varphi \wedge \psi)$ then $\mathcal{K} \ominus (\varphi \wedge \psi) = \mathcal{K} \ominus \varphi$. For, if φ is already given up when giving up $\varphi \wedge \psi$, postulate *success* is fulfilled and there is no need to remove more, or less, to obtain $\mathcal{K} \ominus (\varphi \wedge \psi)$. In the case of the previous example, if I believe that Peter is a better student than John, then giving up the belief that both Peter and John passed the exam is the same as giving up the belief that John passed it. However, I might instead have a firm belief that Peter and John are equally good students, in which case we would not have $\mathcal{K} \ominus (\varphi \wedge \psi) = \mathcal{K} \ominus \varphi$. The following 'factorisation' gives our motivation for ($\mathcal{K} \ominus 7$) and ($\mathcal{K} \ominus 8$):

Theorem 3.11 Let $\ominus$ satisfy $(\mathcal{K} \ominus 1) - (\mathcal{K} \ominus 6)$. Then $\ominus$ satisfies $(\mathcal{K} \ominus 7)$ and $(\mathcal{K} \ominus 8)$ iff we have, for any φ and ψ, either (i), (ii) or (iii):

(i) $\mathcal{K} \ominus (\varphi \wedge \psi) = \mathcal{K} \ominus \varphi$
(ii) $\mathcal{K} \ominus (\varphi \wedge \psi) = \mathcal{K} \ominus \psi$
(iii) $\mathcal{K} \ominus (\varphi \wedge \psi) = \mathcal{K} \ominus \varphi \cap \mathcal{K} \ominus \psi$ □

Proof See Exercise 3.12. □

A result like Theorem 3.11 is usually explained using the notion of *entrenchment*: the agent either is more entrenched to ψ than to φ (in which case item (i) of the theorem applies), or the other way around (case (ii)) or he is equally entrenched to both (iii).

Exercise 3.12 Prove Theorem 3.11. Hint: see also Section 3.6. □

3.2.3 Revision

The most studied form of belief change is that of revision. The idea of a revision $\mathcal{K} \circledast \varphi$ is that the agent, having accepted φ to be incorporated in his beliefs, wants to sensibly change his beliefs in such a way that (1) his beliefs remain consistent (if φ and $\mathcal{K}$ are), (2) that as a result he believes φ, and (3) that he keeps believing 'as much as possible' as he already did, and (4) adopts as 'few as possible' new beliefs. The postulates for revision are given in Table 3.4: recall that $\mathcal{K}_\perp$ is the inconsistent belief set, i.e., the whole language.

Just like the postulates $(\mathcal{K} \ominus 1) - (\mathcal{K} \ominus 6)$ make up a basic system for contraction, the first six postulates $(\mathcal{K} \circledast 1) - (\mathcal{K} \circledast 6)$ yield a basic system for revision. Postulates $(\mathcal{K} \circledast 1)$ and $(\mathcal{K} \circledast 2)$ have a motivation analogous to the *type* and *success* postulates for the other operators, and the same holds for *extensionality*. Postulate $(\mathcal{K} \circledast 3)$ guarantees that when revising with φ, we do not add anything more than when we would expand with φ (the latter already

$(\mathcal{K} \circledast 1)$ $\mathcal{K} \circledast \varphi$ is a belief set	*type*
$(\mathcal{K} \circledast 2)$ $\varphi \in \mathcal{K} \circledast \varphi$	*success*
$(\mathcal{K} \circledast 3)$ $\mathcal{K} \circledast \varphi \subseteq \mathcal{K} \oplus \varphi$	*upper bound*
$(\mathcal{K} \circledast 4)$ If $\neg\varphi \notin \mathcal{K}$ then $\mathcal{K} \oplus \varphi \subseteq \mathcal{K} \circledast \varphi$	*lower bound*
$(\mathcal{K} \circledast 5)$ $\mathcal{K} \circledast \varphi = \mathcal{K}_\perp$ iff $\vdash \neg\varphi$	*triviality*
$(\mathcal{K} \circledast 6)$ If $\vdash \varphi \leftrightarrow \psi$ then $\mathcal{K} \circledast \varphi = \mathcal{K} \circledast \psi$	*extensionality*
$(\mathcal{K} \circledast 7)$ $\mathcal{K} \circledast (\varphi \wedge \psi) \subseteq (\mathcal{K} \circledast \varphi) \oplus \psi$	*iterated*$(\mathcal{K} \circledast 3)$
$(\mathcal{K} \circledast 8)$ If $\neg\psi \notin \mathcal{K} \circledast \varphi$ then $(\mathcal{K} \circledast \varphi) \oplus \psi \subseteq \mathcal{K} \circledast (\varphi \wedge \psi)$	*iterated*$(\mathcal{K} \circledast 4)$

Table 3.4. The Postulates for Revision.

being a 'minimal way' to add φ). According to $(\mathcal{K} \circledast 4)$ and $(\mathcal{K} \circledast 3)$, if φ is consistent with $\mathcal{K}$, revision and expansion with φ are the same. Although it does not look like it in the first instance, $(\mathcal{K} \circledast 4)$ is again related to minimality: it says we should not throw away formulas from $\mathcal{K}$ unnecessarily, when revising with φ. Without it the naive revision function of Definition 3.14 would qualify as a revision operator, in the sense that it would satisfy the remaining basic postulates. Postulate $(\mathcal{K} \circledast 5)$ guarantees that we only are forced to accept an inconsistent belief set if the new information is inconsistent. (Note that the 'if' direction follows from the first two postulates.)

If the new information φ is consistent with what is believed, revision causes no problem at all: Suppose $\circledast$ satisfies all the basic postulates $(\mathcal{K} \circledast 1)-(\mathcal{K} \circledast 6)$. Then: if $\neg\varphi \notin \mathcal{K}$, then $\mathcal{K} \circledast \varphi = \mathcal{K} \oplus \varphi$. This is immediate, since we have $\mathcal{K} \circledast \varphi \subseteq \mathcal{K} \oplus \varphi$ as postulate $(\mathcal{K} \circledast 3)$, whereas the other direction is $(\mathcal{K} \circledast 4)$.

One can now also prove the following *preservation* principle for revision, which says that, if you initially do not believe the opposite of the new information, there is no need to give up anything, when adopting the new information:

$$\text{if } \neg\varphi \notin \mathcal{K} \text{ then } \mathcal{K} \subseteq \mathcal{K} \circledast \varphi \tag{3.5}$$

$(\mathcal{K} \circledast 7)$ and $(\mathcal{K} \circledast 8)$ are meant to generalise $(\mathcal{K} \circledast 3)$ and $(\mathcal{K} \circledast 4)$ in the case of iterated revision. Together they imply the following: if $\psi \notin \mathcal{K} \circledast \varphi$, then revising with $\varphi \wedge \psi$ is the same as first revising with φ, and then expanding with ψ. Indeed, $(\mathcal{K} \circledast 3)$ and $(\mathcal{K} \circledast 4)$ follow from $(\mathcal{K} \circledast 7)$ and $(\mathcal{K} \circledast 8)$, if we make a natural and weak assumption about $\mathcal{K} \circledast \top$, namely that $\mathcal{K} \circledast \top = \mathcal{K}$. For the exact formulation, we refer to Exercise 3.13.

Exercise 3.13 Suppose that $\circledast$ satisfies $(\mathcal{K} \circledast 1)$, $(\mathcal{K} \circledast 2)$ and $(\mathcal{K} \circledast 5)$ - $(\mathcal{K} \circledast 8)$.

1. Show that, if $\circledast$ moreover satisfies $(\mathcal{K} \circledast 3)$ and $(\mathcal{K} \circledast 4)$, it also satisfies $\mathcal{K} \circledast \top = \mathcal{K}$ for any $\mathcal{K} \neq \mathcal{K}_\perp$.
2. Suppose that $\circledast$ satisfies, on top of the 6 given postulates, also $\mathcal{K} \circledast \top = \mathcal{K}$, for any $\mathcal{K} \neq \mathcal{K}_\perp$. Show that it then satisfies $(\mathcal{K} \circledast 3)$ and $(\mathcal{K} \circledast 4)$. □

In Section 3.2.4 we will see examples of belief revision functions. Here, we give a partial example. The following operator $\circledast_n$ models a 'revision' which decides to forget everything that is already believed, once information is encountered that is not in line with the current beliefs.

Definition 3.14 Let the naive revision function $\circledast_n$ be defined as follows:

$$\mathcal{K} \circledast_n \varphi = \begin{cases} \mathcal{K} & \text{if } \varphi \in \mathcal{K} \\ Cn(\varphi) & \text{else} \end{cases}$$ □

Exercise 3.15 Determine which of the postulates for revision hold for $\circledast_n$, and which do not. □

Recall from (3.1) how the Levi identity $\mathcal{K} \circledast \varphi \equiv (\mathcal{K} \ominus \neg\varphi) \oplus \varphi$ defines revision with new information as the process of first contracting with its negation, and then expanding with it. One might wonder whether, if Tables 3.3 and 3.1 give minimality conditions for contraction and expansion, respectively, the Levi identity yields a revision function that adheres to the principles given in Table 3.4. The answer appears to be positive, both for the basic sets of postulates, and for the ones concerning iteration and conjunction:

Theorem 3.16 Suppose we have a contraction function $\ominus$ that satisfies $(\mathcal{K} \ominus 1) - (\mathcal{K} \ominus 4)$ and $(\mathcal{K} \ominus 6)$, and an expansion function $\oplus$ that satisfies $(\mathcal{K} \oplus 1) - (\mathcal{K} \oplus 6)$. Then:

1. If $\circledast$ is defined as in (3.1), it satisfies $(\mathcal{K} \circledast 1) - (\mathcal{K} \circledast 6)$
2. a) If $\ominus$ moreover satisfies $(\mathcal{K} \ominus 7)$, then $\circledast$ satisfies $(\mathcal{K} \circledast 7)$
   b) If $\ominus$ moreover satisfies $(\mathcal{K} \ominus 8)$, then $\circledast$ satisfies $(\mathcal{K} \circledast 8)$ □

3.2.4 Characterisation Results

Theorem 3.2 gives a characterisation result for expansion: it offers in fact a unique description of the procedure to expand a belief set in a way that complies with the postulates for expansion. We know from Theorem 3.16, that if we also understand what a contraction function should look like, we are done, since revision can be defined in terms of expansion and contraction.

So, suppose that $\varphi \in \mathcal{K}$ and the agent wants to contract with φ (the case in which $\varphi \notin \mathcal{K}$ is trivial, due to $(\mathcal{K} \ominus 3)$). Let us also suppose that φ is not a tautology (if it is, by Exercise 3.10, we are again in a trivial case). For a contraction $\mathcal{K} \ominus \varphi$ then, we are interested in subsets $\mathcal{K}'$ of $\mathcal{K}$ that no longer contain φ, but which are such that they are the result of removing as little as possible from $\mathcal{K}$ as needed. The latter can be rephrased as: if, in going from $\mathcal{K}$ to $\mathcal{K}'$ we remove any formula ψ, it is because otherwise φ would still be entailed. The following definition tries to capture this kind of $\mathcal{K}'$:

Definition 3.17 A belief set $\mathcal{K}'$ is a maximal belief set of $\mathcal{K}$ that fails to imply φ iff the following holds:

1. $\mathcal{K}' \subseteq \mathcal{K}$
2. $\mathcal{K}' \not\vdash \varphi$
3. If $\psi \in \mathcal{K}$ but $\psi \notin \mathcal{K}'$, then $\psi \to \varphi \in \mathcal{K}'$.

The set of all maximal belief sets that fail to imply φ is denoted by $\mathcal{K} \perp \varphi$. Moreover, $M(\mathcal{K}) = \bigcup\{\mathcal{K} \perp \varphi \mid \varphi \in \mathcal{L}_0\}$ is the set of all maximal belief sets of $\mathcal{K}$ that fail to imply some formula φ. □

Example 3.18 Suppose we only have three atoms p, q and r, and $\mathcal{K} = Cn(\{p, q, r\})$. Then $\mathcal{K} \perp (p \wedge q)$ is given by

$$\begin{aligned}\mathcal{K} \perp (p \wedge q) = \{&Cn(\{p, r\}),\ Cn(\{q, r\}),\\ &Cn(\{p, q \leftrightarrow r\}),\ Cn(\{q, p \leftrightarrow r\}),\\ &Cn(\{p \leftrightarrow q, q \leftrightarrow r\}),\ Cn(\{p \leftrightarrow q, r\})\}\end{aligned} \tag{3.6}$$

□

Good candidates for $\mathcal{K} \ominus \varphi$ can be found among $\mathcal{K} \perp \varphi$ if the latter set is non-empty (note that $\mathcal{K} \perp \varphi = \emptyset$ iff $\vdash \varphi$): by definition, they are belief sets (hence, satisfy ($\mathcal{K} \ominus 1$)), by clause 1 of Definition 3.17 they satisfy ($\mathcal{K} \ominus 2$), while clause 2 guarantees *success* (($\mathcal{K} \ominus 4$)). The postulates ($\mathcal{K} \ominus 3$) and ($\mathcal{K} \ominus 5$) are also satisfied (see Exercise 3.22). Regarding ($\mathcal{K} \ominus 6$), we have to be careful to choose the same elements from 'the same' sets $\mathcal{K} \perp \varphi$ and $\mathcal{K} \perp \psi$ if φ and ψ are equivalent. Therefore, we will base any contraction $\ominus$ on a fixed *selection function* S, which, given a set $\mathcal{K} \perp \varphi$, selects a subset of it when $\mathcal{K} \perp \varphi \neq \emptyset$, otherwise $S(\mathcal{K} \perp \varphi) = \{\mathcal{K}\}$.

Definition 3.19 Let S be a selection function as described above. A *partial meet contraction function* $\ominus_{pm}$ is defined as:

$$\mathcal{K} \ominus_{pm} \varphi = \begin{cases} \bigcap S(\mathcal{K} \perp \varphi) \text{ whenever } \mathcal{K} \perp \varphi \neq \emptyset \\ \mathcal{K} \text{ otherwise} \end{cases}$$ □

So a partial meet contraction function selects some sets that just do not entail φ, and intersects them. In case $\mathcal{K} \perp \varphi$ is empty, the contraction yields $\mathcal{K}$, and in case $\varphi \notin \mathcal{K}$, we indeed get $\mathcal{K} \ominus \varphi = \mathcal{K}$. These cases are dealt with in Exercise 3.20.

Exercise 3.20 Show the following, for any φ and $\mathcal{K}$:

1. $\mathcal{K} \perp \varphi = \emptyset$ iff $\vdash \varphi$
2. $\mathcal{K} \perp \varphi = \{\mathcal{K}\}$ iff $\varphi \notin \mathcal{K}$
3. if $\vdash \varphi \leftrightarrow \psi$ then $\mathcal{K} \perp \varphi = \mathcal{K} \perp \psi$.

Now let $\ominus$ be a partial meet contraction. Show that the items above guarantee that:

1. If $\vdash \varphi$, then $\mathcal{K} \ominus \varphi = \mathcal{K}$
2. If $\varphi \notin \mathcal{K}$, then $\mathcal{K} \ominus \varphi = \mathcal{K}$ (postulate ($\mathcal{K} \in 3$)).
3. if $\vdash \varphi \leftrightarrow \psi$ then $\mathcal{K} \ominus \varphi = \mathcal{K} \ominus \psi$. □

We will now briefly discuss two extreme cases of partial meet contraction. First, S could be such that it picks exactly one element (if possible). This is called a *maxichoice contraction*, and here denoted by $\ominus_{mc}$. In the scenario of Example 3.18, where $\mathcal{K} = Cn(\{p, q, r\})$, each contraction $\mathcal{K} \ominus_{mc} (p \wedge q)$ would give a 'maximal result': adding anything that is in $Cn(\{p, q, r\})$ but not in the belief set selected from $\mathcal{K} \perp (p \wedge q)$, to that belief set, would give $(p \wedge q) \in \mathcal{K} \ominus_{mc} (p \wedge q)$ again.

Proposition 3.21 The maxichoice contraction function $\ominus_{mc}$ satisfies the basic postulates for contraction, i.e., ($\mathcal{K} \ominus 1$) – ($\mathcal{K} \ominus 6$). □

Proof See Exercise 3.22. □

Exercise 3.22 Prove Proposition 3.21. □

The maxichoice contraction function might be considered to be (too) arbitrary: in the case of Example 3.18, ($\mathcal{K} = Cn(\{p, q, r\})$), we would have that $\mathcal{K} \ominus p \wedge q$ would pick some arbitrary element from $\mathcal{K} \perp (p \wedge q)$. If the agent is more entrenched to p, he might pick $Cn(\{p,r\})$, if he is most entrenched to q, the new belief set is $Cn(\{q,r\})$ (we have not introduced the notion of entrenchment formally, it is supposed to indicate which beliefs the agent is more 'attached to' than others. In fact, one could use the above criterion as a working definition: an agent is more entrenched to φ than to ψ if, when having to contract with $\varphi \wedge \psi$, he would give up ψ easier than φ).

But what if, in the example, his most entrenched belief is $p \leftrightarrow q$? We would expect him to give up p as well as q, when he has to contract with $p \wedge q$.

The *full meet contraction* function $\ominus_{fm}$ predicts that, indeed, in this example both p and q will be given up: it is based on the selection function that uses all sets from $\mathcal{K} \perp \varphi$, i.e., $S(\mathcal{K} \perp \varphi) = (\mathcal{K} \perp \varphi)$ (if this set is non-empty). This is the second example of a partial meet contraction. However, whereas the maxichoice contraction made too arbitrary choices, and left the resulting belief set too big, full meet contraction does the opposite, and chooses a smallest result (both p and q are given up). Indeed, one can show that the revision defined by the Levi-identity would yield the naive revision function of Definition 3.14!

Proposition 3.23 Let $\ominus_{fm}$ be the full meet contraction, and define revision using the Levi identity: $\mathcal{K} \circledast \varphi = (\mathcal{K} \ominus_{fm} \neg\varphi) \oplus \varphi$. Show that $\circledast$ is the naive revision $\circledast_n$ of Definition 3.14. □

Proof See Exercise 3.24. □

Exercise 3.24 Prove Proposition 3.23. □

What is the relevance of partial meet contractions? If we accept the basic postulates for contraction, they are all we have!

Theorem 3.25 A contraction function $\ominus$ satisfies the postulates $(\mathcal{K} \ominus 1)$ – $(\mathcal{K} \ominus 6)$ iff it can be generated by a partial meet contraction function. □

Theorem 3.25 gives a nice and precise characterisation of *general* contractions: they should be based on *some* selection of the maximal subsets of the belief that do not imply the fact to be contracted. However, in a *specific* context (like in our example) it still does not tell us *how* to make that selection. Let us go back to Example 3.18. Suppose our agent decides for a contraction function $\ominus'$ for which $\mathcal{K} \ominus' p = Cn(\{q,r\})$ and $\mathcal{K} \ominus' q = Cn(\{p,r\})$. It indicates that he is less entrenched to $p \leftrightarrow q$ than to either p or to q. So we would expect that at least one of the two atoms survives in $\mathcal{K} \ominus' (p \wedge q)$. But this is not guaranteed by partial meet contractions (i.e., it is well possible that $\mathcal{K} \ominus' (p \wedge q) = Cn(\{r\})$), in fact we did not specify *anything* in terms of entrenchments yet.

If we want to discriminate between members of $\mathcal{K} \perp \varphi$, we need a relation $\leq$ on $M(\mathcal{K})$ (this means that the order does not depend on the particular formula we contract with). Let us now say that a selection function S is a *marking-off identity* for $\leq$, (or, for short, S marks off $\leq$) if it 'marks off' exactly the $\leq$-best elements:

$$S(\mathcal{K} \perp \varphi) = \{\mathcal{K}' \in (\mathcal{K} \perp \varphi) : \mathcal{K}'' \leq \mathcal{K}' \text{ for all } \mathcal{K}'' \in (\mathcal{K} \perp \varphi)\} \tag{3.7}$$

One can show that if the contraction $\ominus'$ mentioned above indeed satisfies $\mathcal{K} \ominus' (p \wedge q) = Cn(\{r\})$, it cannot be generated by a selection function that marks off some relation. To see this, first note that $\ominus'$ does not satisfy ($\mathcal{K} \ominus 7$): we have that $(p \vee q) \in (\mathcal{K} \ominus' p) \cap (\mathcal{K} \ominus' q)$, but $p \vee q \notin \mathcal{K} \ominus' (p \wedge q)$. But we also have the following general fact: any contraction generated by a marking-off selection function satisfies ($\mathcal{K} \ominus 7$), see Exercise 3.26.

Exercise 3.26 Let $\ominus$ be a contraction that is based on a selection function S that marks off some binary relation $\leq$ on $M(\mathcal{K})$. Show: $\ominus$ satisfies ($\mathcal{K} \ominus 7$). Hint: show first that, for any φ and ψ, we have $\mathcal{K} \perp (\varphi \wedge \psi) \subseteq (\mathcal{K} \perp \varphi) \cup (\mathcal{K} \perp \psi)$.□

Before we state the final characterisation result of this section, note that thus far, we have not assumed any property of $\leq$ that would make it look like a preference relation. The most common property of preference relations is transitivity.

Theorem 3.27 A contraction function is based on a selection function that is a marking-off identity of a transitive relation iff the contraction function satisfies ($\mathcal{K} \ominus 1$) – ($\mathcal{K} \ominus 8$). □

3.3 Possible Worlds Semantics for Information Change

Since we give a possible worlds interpretation of belief, it is appropriate, in this book, to give a semantic treatment of belief revision in terms of possible worlds. A truth definition of belief (cf. Definition 2.7) reads as follows:

$$M, w \models B_i \varphi \text{ iff } \forall v (R_i wv \Rightarrow M, v \models \varphi) \tag{3.8}$$

Now, the guiding principle behind a possible worlds semantics for belief revision is, that *the more worlds an agent considers possible, the less he believes, and vice versa.* Extreme cases in the context of belief would be that: (*i*) the agent considers *no world possible*, which models the fact that he *believes everything*, including all literals p and $\neg p$; (*ii*) the agent considers *one world possible*, in which case he is omniscient with respect to this world: he *believes everything there is to say about that world* (in particular, he either believes φ or else $\neg\varphi$, for every φ); and (*iii*) the agent does not rule out any world, i.e., considers *all worlds possible*, in which case he *believes nothing*, except for tautologies, like $\varphi \vee \neg\varphi$. Note that in our current setting, the extreme cases are indeed (*i*) and (*iii*), since belief sets can be inconsistent.

In the case where 'only' propositional formulas are believed, we can assume that a possible world coincides with a valuation, and syntactically represent such a world as a maximal consistent set of propositional formulas. Let us, given a world w, write w_0 for its corresponding maximal consistent set: $\mathsf{w}_0 = \{\varphi \in \mathcal{L}_0 \mid w \models \varphi\}$. We will call w_0 the *(propositional) theory of* w, and, conversely, say that the valuation w is the *(unique) model for* w_0. With $[\![\varphi]\!]_0$ we will denote φ's propositional extension: $[\![\varphi]\!]_0 = \{w \mid w \models \varphi\}$. The extension of a belief set $\mathcal{K}$ is $[\![\mathcal{K}]\!]_0 = \bigcap_{\varphi \in \mathcal{K}} [\![\varphi]\!]_0$. Finally, we denote the set of *all* possible valuations by $\mathcal{V}$.

A belief set $\mathcal{K}_w$ of an agent, given a Kripke model M and state w, can then be thought of as

$$\mathcal{K}_w = \{\varphi \in \mathcal{L}_0 \mid M, w \models B\varphi\} = \bigcap_{Rwv} \mathsf{v}_0 \tag{3.9}$$

Conversely, given an agent's beliefs $\mathcal{K}_w$ at w, we can construct the set of worlds $R(w)$ that he apparently considers possible in w:

$$R(w)_{\mathcal{K}} = \{v \in \mathcal{V} \mid v \models \mathcal{K}_w\} \tag{3.10}$$

Now, given Theorem 3.2 it is obvious what an expansion should semantically look like: since $\mathcal{K} \oplus \varphi$ is simply an *addition* of φ, yielding $Cn(\mathcal{K} \cup \varphi)$, semantically this means we have to *restrict* the set of possible worlds (this process is often called *relativisation*):

Definition 3.28 Given a Kripke model M, world w and accessibility relation R, the *relativisation* of R to $[\![\varphi]\!]_0$ yields a model M', world $w' = w$, and access R', where $R' = R \cap (W \times [\![\varphi]\!]_0)$. We also write $(M, w) \underline{\oplus} [\![\varphi]\!]_0$ for (M', w').□

The following lemma justifies Definition 3.28: it says that adding information φ to an agent's beliefs semantically boils down to relativising the worlds he considers possible to those satisfying φ:

Lemma 3.29 Let $\mathcal{K}_w$ be an agent's belief set at w. Then:

$$\psi \in \mathcal{K}_w \oplus \varphi \text{ iff } (M, w) \underline{\oplus} [\![\varphi]\!]_0 \models B\psi \qquad \Box$$

How about contraction? Extending the analogous of Lemma 3.29, we expect that an agent that wants to contract with φ should *add* some worlds to those he considers possible, to wit, some worlds in which φ is false. The question, of course is, *which* worlds? The semantical counterpart of an entrenchment relation (see also (3.7)) is often referred to as a *system of spheres*, which models so-called *fall-back* theories relative to the agent's current theories.

To capture this, a system of spheres for $R(w)$ in a model M with domain W is a set $Sphe(R(w))$ of spheres $Sp \supseteq R(w)$ that are linearly ordered by $\supseteq$, and contains the maximum W and the minimum $R(w)$, and, for all φ, if some $S \in Sphe(R(w))$ intersects with $[\![\varphi]\!]_0$, then there is a $\subseteq$-smallest $S' \in Sphe(R(w))$ that intersects with $[\![\varphi]\!]_0$. See Figure 3.1. Intuitively, the spheres S that are 'closest' to those worlds $R(w)$ that the agents currently thinks possible, represent the sets of worlds he would 'fall back' upon, were he to give up some of his beliefs.

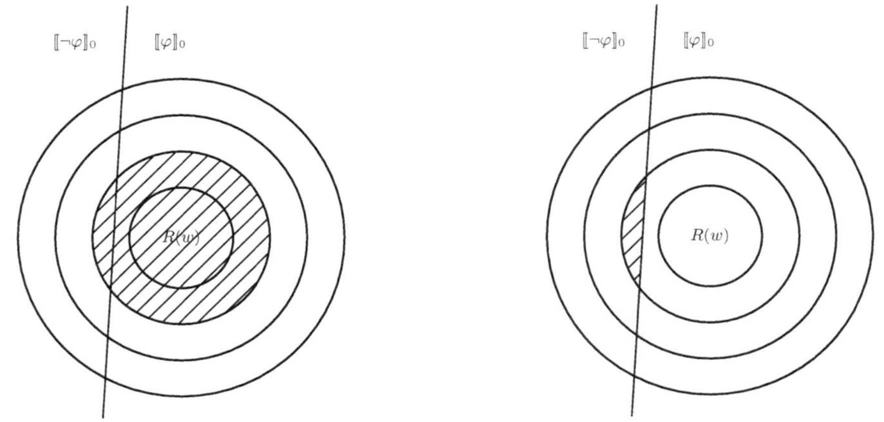

Figure 3.1. A system of spheres around $R(w)$. In both figures, $R(w)$ is the inner sphere, and $[\![\neg\varphi]\!]_0$ and $[\![\varphi]\!]_0$ are separated by a vertical line. In the figure on the left, the shaded area denotes the worlds that correspond to a contraction with $[\![\neg\varphi]\!]_0$ ('close' to $R(w)$, but allowing some $\neg\varphi$-worlds), in the figure on the right, the shaded area covers the worlds that correspond with a revision with $\neg\varphi$ ('close' to $R(w)$, but only $\neg\varphi$-worlds).

Contraction can now easily be defined: given the current set $R(w)$ of alternatives for our agent, if he wants to give up believing φ this means that $R(w) \cap [\![\neg\varphi]\!]_0$ should not be empty: if it is, the agent falls back, i.e., enlarges his set of accessible worlds to the first sphere $Sp \supseteq R(w)$ that has a non-empty intersection with $[\![\neg\varphi]\!]_0$. See Figure 3.1, where in the left model, the shaded area consists of the worlds that form the expanded set of $R(w)$, so that φ is not believed anymore.

Definition 3.30 Given a Kripke model M, world w and accessibility relation R, and a system of spheres $Sphe(R(w))$ around $R(w)$, the semantic contraction $(M, w) \ominus [\![\varphi]\!]_0$ is defined as M', w', with $w' = w$, and $M' = \langle W, R' \rangle$, where $R'(w) = S$, with $S = min\{S' \in Sphe(R(w)) \mid S' \cap [\![\neg\varphi]\!]_0 \neq \emptyset\}$, and for all $v \neq w$, $R'(v) = R(v)$. □

If we agree on this, the semantic counterpart of revision is dictated by the Levi identity: an agent that wants to revise with φ first 'goes to' the first sphere S that intersects with $[\![\neg\varphi]\!]_0$, and then 'throws away' from that S all those worlds that still satisfy φ. Again, see Figure 3.1, where the marked area in the right model gives those worlds that are considered possible after a revision with $\neg\varphi$.

For completeness reasons, we also provide a semantic definition for $\circledast$:

Definition 3.31 Given a Kripke model M, world w and accessibility relation R, and a system of spheres $Sphe(R(w))$ around $R(w)$, let $\ominus$ be given as in Definition 3.30. Then $(M, w) \circledast [\![\varphi]\!]_0$ is defined as $\langle W, R'' \rangle, w'$, where $R''(w'') = R'(w') \cap [\![\varphi]\!]_0$ and $(M, w) \ominus [\![\neg\varphi]\!]_0 = \langle W, R' \rangle, w'$ and $w'' = w'$. □

3.4 Paradoxes of Introspective Belief Change

When applying the ideas of belief revision to the epistemic logic setting of Chapter 2, the main idea, in the semantics, is the following. Uncertainty of an agent at state s 'corresponds' to the agent considering a lot of alternative states possible: ignorance of agent a is represented by the operator $\hat{B}_a$: the more different states a considers possible in s, the more $\hat{B}_a\varphi$ formulas will hold in s, the less $B_a\varphi$ formulas will be true in s. This principle suggests that gaining new beliefs should semantically correspond with eliminating access to worlds, while giving up beliefs in s should allow the agent to consider worlds possible that were inaccessible before.

Example 3.32 Consider a simple example, depicted in Figure 3.2. In the model M to the left, we have an $S5$-agent a who is not sure whether p is true or not (assume p is only true in 1). In principle, we can associate two belief sets with the agent, $\mathcal{K}_0$ and $\mathcal{K}_1$, where $\mathcal{K}_i = \{\varphi \in \mathcal{L}_0 \mid M, i \models B\varphi\}$ $(i = 0, 1)$. If p is the only atom in the language, then the agent's only possible belief set in Figure 3.2 is $\mathcal{K}_0 = \mathcal{K}_1 = \{\varphi \in \mathcal{L}_0 \mid \mathbf{S5} \vdash \varphi\}$. In other words, the agent is fully ignorant.

Suppose p is true (i.e., 1 is our real state). Then, a revision with p leads us to the state 1 in the model on the right hand side of Figure 3.2, and as a result, the agent indeed believes p. A revision with p would have given the same result.

It is important to realise again that *all* the information that is explicitly formalised in the approach so far, is *objective* information, i.e., there is no reference to the agent's beliefs, other than in a meta-language, when we refer to his belief set. In this section, we will consider how to lift that restriction, i.e., we look at richer logical systems. These enrichments can present themselves in a variety of ways:

1. update with factual information φ, but allow the agent to have introspective capabilities (in $\mathcal{K}$);
2. allow both the information and the beliefs of the agent to refer to his beliefs;
3. have a multi-agent language where one agent can reason about beliefs held by another agent
4. revise in a fully fledged, multi-agent language, including the notion of common knowledge, and on top of that, in the object language, operators that refer to different kinds of belief change.

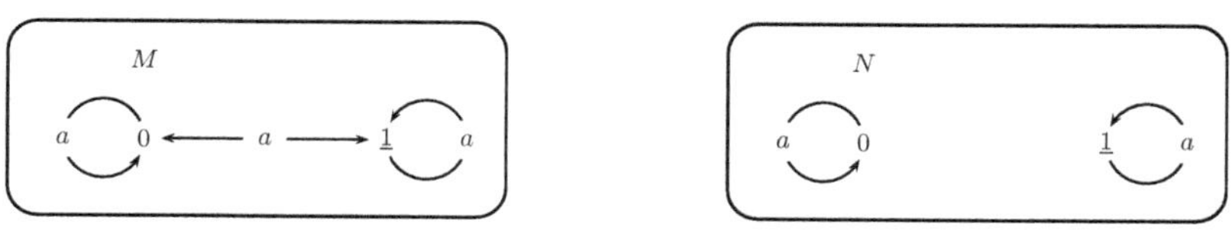

Figure 3.2. Revision: agent a changes his mind.

No matter whether we deal with knowledge or beliefs, representing them somehow in the object language for information change enforces us to rethink the whole program of belief revision, since now we are dealing with introspective agents (see Section 3.6 for a reference of the following quote):

> When an introspective agent learns more about the world (and himself) then the reality that he holds beliefs about undergoes change. But then his introspective (higher-order) beliefs have to be adjusted accordingly.

We will now give some examples that show what kind of problems one encounters when trying to propose a belief revision framework for introspective agents.

Static Belief Sets

This argument is placed in variety **1**, mentioned above: we only need to have higher order beliefs in the belief set. So let us suppose we have one agent, whose belief adheres to the system **KD45**. We point out, that for such an agent, although it might be possible to change his mind, it is impossible to only *gain* beliefs, or, conversely, to only *give up* some of his beliefs. To see this, recall that a belief set now is closed under **KD45**-consequences: think of it as a set $\mathcal{K}_w$ as in (3.9), but now in a richer language, with more allowed inferences, and with the constraint that w is a world *in a $\mathcal{KD}45$-model.*

Now suppose we have two of such belief sets $\mathcal{K}_1$ and $\mathcal{K}_2$, and suppose that one is strictly included in the other, say $\mathcal{K}_1 \subset \mathcal{K}_2$. Then there is some φ in $\mathcal{K}_2$, that is not in $\mathcal{K}_1$. By positive introspection, we have $B\varphi \in \mathcal{K}_2$, and, by negative introspection, $\neg B\varphi \in \mathcal{K}_1$. Since $\mathcal{K}_1 \subset \mathcal{K}_2$, we also have $\neg B\varphi \in \mathcal{K}_2$. Belief sets are still closed under propositional consequence, so that we conclude $\bot \in \mathcal{K}_2$, which contradicts the fact that the beliefs satisfy axiom D, which says that beliefs are consistent!

Paradox of Serious Possibility

Here is a belief revision consequence of the previous insight. Let us again assume that beliefs can be about **KD45**-beliefs, although we do not need such an assumption about the new information, so suppose $\varphi \in \mathcal{L}_0$. Let us also assume $\not\vdash \neg\varphi$, so that, by the *triviality* postulate ($\mathcal{K} \circledast 5$), we have that $\mathcal{K} \circledast \varphi$ is consistent. Suppose the agent has no opinion about φ: he neither believes φ nor $\neg\varphi$. By negative introspection, we hence have both $\neg B\varphi, \neg B\neg\varphi \in \mathcal{K}$.

Now we can see what happens if the agent were to learn φ. By the *success* postulate ($\mathcal{K} \circledast 2$) and positive introspection, we have $B\varphi \in \mathcal{K} \circledast \varphi$. By *preservation* (3.5), we have that $\neg B\varphi$ persists in $\mathcal{K}$ in this revision, giving again an inconsistent belief set.

Moore's Principle

Let us move on to an example in which the agent both has higher order beliefs in his belief set, and in which he also can revise with belief formulas. Recall that *Moore's principle* (2.4) is a higher order property of beliefs: it is derivable in **KD45**, and says that you cannot at the same time believe both a formula and it being disbelieved, given that your beliefs are consistent: $\neg B\bot \rightarrow \neg B(\varphi \wedge \neg B\varphi)$. In fact, since **KD45** does not allow for beliefs to be inconsistent, we know from Exercise 2.41 that we even have $\neg B(\varphi \wedge \neg B\varphi)$ as a **KD45**-validity.

Now let φ be a (**KD45**-)consistent formula, that is not ($\mathcal{KD}45$-)valid. It is easy to see that then $\varphi \wedge \neg B\varphi$ is satisfiable: no agent is forced to believe any contingent formula. So suppose $\varphi \wedge \neg B\varphi$ holds, and that our agent discovers that, although φ is not believed by him, it turns out to be true. Since we know by Moore's principle that the agent moreover does not believe $\varphi \wedge \neg B\varphi$, we can apply *preservation* (3.5) and accept that the revision of $\mathcal{K}$ with $\varphi \wedge \neg B\varphi$ is just an expansion: $\mathcal{K} \oplus (\varphi \wedge \neg B\varphi)$. By *success* for $\oplus$, the formula $(\varphi \wedge \neg B\varphi)$ should as a result of this expansion be believed: $B(\varphi \wedge \neg B\varphi)$. We have now obtained an inconsistent set (since $\neg B(\varphi \wedge \neg B\varphi)$ is derivable in **KD45**), only by revising a consistent belief set with a consistent formula!

Effect on Third Parties

Let us move to scenario **3**, where we have multiple agents. Let us also assume that the belief set of each agent incorporates beliefs of the other agents. Add a second agent b to Example 3.32 (see Figure 3.3). If we assume that p is true, then initially (that is, in 1), neither a nor b do believe p, and this is common belief between the two agents. Suppose again that a revises with p, transforming $M, 1$ into $M', 1$. But note that in $M', 1$ also b has learnt something, i.e., that a believes whether p!

We are not saying that this is absurd (for instance, it might well be that agent b notices that a finds out whether p, without b getting to know information about p), but it *is* suspicious that b does change his beliefs if we *only specified a belief change for* a! (It might for instance be the case that a revises with p because, while b is not aware of this, a remembers some events from which undoubtedly p follows.)

It is clear that, in order to properly reason about this kind of scenarios, we *need* a language enabling reasoning about each other's information, and

Figure 3.3. Revision: agent a changes his mind. What does b notice?

also a language that can explicitly state what kind of event it is that makes a change his mind, thereby making precise what b notices about this. And, indeed, this is exactly the enterprise that this book is going to undertake in subsequent chapters.

The Importance of Ignorance

Imagine the following scenario:

> Two agents a and b both are ignorant about a fact p. They meet and b asks a: 'do you know whether p?' To which the first agent answers, *truthfully*: 'yes, p'.

Does this make sense? Yes, but obviously in order to explain it, we need to address higher order information about p. Here is a less abstract version of the story:

> Professor a is programme chair of a conference on Changing Beliefs. It is not allowed to submit more than one paper to this conference, a rule all authors of papers did abide to (although the belief that this rule makes sense is gradually changing, but this is besides the point here). Our programme chair a likes to have all decisions about submitted papers out of the way before the weekend, since on Saturday he is due to travel to attend a workshop on Applying Belief Change. Fortunately, although there appears not to be enough time to notify all authors, just before he leaves for the workshop, his reliable secretary assures him that she has informed all authors of rejected papers, by personally giving them a call and informing them about the sad news concerning their paper. Freed from this burden, Professor a is just in time for the opening reception of the workshop, where he meets the brilliant Dr. b. The programme chair remembers that b submitted a paper to Changing Beliefs, but to his own embarrassment he must admit that he honestly cannot remember whether it was accepted or not. Fortunately, he does not have to demonstrate his ignorance to b, because b's question 'Do you know whether my paper has been accepted?' does make a reason as follows: a is sure that would b's paper have been rejected, b would have had that information, in which case b had not shown his ignorance to a. So, instantaneously, a updates his belief with the fact that b's paper is accepted, and he now can answer truthfully with respect to this new revised belief set.

Rather than giving a semantic account, let us try to formalise this scenario in the AGM paradigm, generalised to multi-agents, where information can be higher-order (we are in variety **3** above). Agent a has initially a belief set $\mathcal{K}^a$ in which p (b's paper is accepted) is not present, but instead, apart from $\neg B_a p$ and $\neg B_a \neg p$, we have $\neg B_b p \in \mathcal{K}^a$ (nobody has been notified about acceptance, yet) and $(\neg p \leftrightarrow B_b\neg p) \in \mathcal{K}^a$ (if the paper would have been rejected, b would have been informed, and vice versa). Now, we can interpret b's question as new information; $\neg B_b p \wedge \neg B_b \neg p$ $(= \alpha)$. This is consistent with $\mathcal{K}^a$, so $\mathcal{K}^a \circledast \alpha = \mathcal{K}^a \oplus \alpha$, in particular, $\neg B_b \neg p \in \mathcal{K}^a \circledast \alpha$, from which a can, using $(\neg p \leftrightarrow B_b \neg p) \in \mathcal{K}^a$ and hence $(\neg p \leftrightarrow B_b \neg p) \in \mathcal{K}^a \circledast \alpha$, conclude p.

Unsuccessful Revision

Here is an example of, we think, an intriguing phenomenon. We assume multiple agents, and belief sets with full mutual beliefs, and also doxastic information to revise with (variety **3**). Recall the Consecutive Numbers scenario from Example 2.4. (Recall that we do not draw any of the reflexive arrows, moreover, to be consistent with the examples in this chapter, we will refer to the agents' information as belief, but one might also call it knowledge.) Two agents, a and b, both have a number on their head, the difference between them exactly 1. No agent can see his own number, and this all is common belief. Now let us suppose the numbers are 2 for a, and 1 for b. In other words, we are in state $(2, 1)$ of the first model of Figure 3.4.

Let us use φ for the fact that both a and b do not believe their own numbers correctly: $\varphi = \neg B_a a_2 \wedge \neg B_b b_1$. Note that we have $M, (2, 1) \models \varphi$, and, since M is in fact an $\mathcal{S}5$-model, $\neg\varphi \notin \mathcal{K}^a_{(2,1)}$: agent a considers φ perfectly compatible with his beliefs. Now suppose somebody would mention φ to both agents. This would mean that a now can rule out that $(0, 1)$ is the real situation, because that is the world in which $B_b b_1$ holds. Semantically, we would 'move to' state $(2', 1')$ in Figure 3.4. But then, a would conclude that $\neg\varphi$, since the only world in which b has a 1 without believing that, is when a has a 2 and b a 1. In other words: $M', (2', 1') \models B_a \neg\varphi$.

Summarising, we are in a situation with a consistent belief set $\mathcal{K}^a_{(2,1)}$, in which our agent a has to revise with a formula φ, true in $(2, 1)$, with the requirement that $\neg\varphi \in \mathcal{K}^a_{(2,1)} \circledast \varphi$. Obviously, a cannot stick to the *success* postulate $(\mathcal{K} \circledast 2)$! This is already a problem for expansion, since by the fact that $\neg\varphi \notin \mathcal{K}^a_{(2,1)}$, we would expect $\mathcal{K}^a_{(2,1)} \circledast \varphi = \mathcal{K}^a_{(2,1)} \oplus \varphi$. This implies that our agent a should 'expand' in such a way that $\neg\varphi \in \mathcal{K}^a_{(2,1)} \oplus \varphi$, which seems a hard action to perform.

We have as yet not given a scenario in variety 4 yet, where apart from doxastic or epistemic operators in the object language, there is also a way to

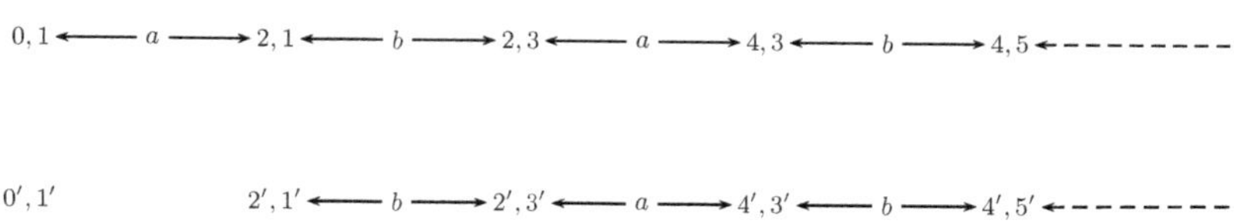

Figure 3.4. Revision with a true Statement.

represent the *change* itself in that language. We do this in the next section: it can be seen as a connection between the areas of belief revision, and that of dynamic epistemic logic.

3.5 Dynamic Doxastic Logic

Consider the Consecutive Number scenario again (introduced in Example 2.4 and also discussed in Section 3.4). If agent b would hear that after a revises with φ, denoting that a knows the two numbers, then b would also know them! However, to represent this in b's beliefs, we have to directly refer to (the effect) of certain revisions.

Dynamic logic is a suitable formalism to reason about actions, and it has also been (and will be, in this book) put to work to reasoning about doxastic or epistemic actions, like the belief change actions discussed in this chapter.

The atomic actions in dynamic doxastic logic are $\oplus$, $\ominus$ and $\circledast$. So let us add operators $[\oplus\cdot]$, $[\ominus\cdot]$ and $[\circledast\cdot]$ to the language, with the intended reading of for instance $[\oplus\varphi]\psi$ that after expansion with φ, ψ holds. Then, one can already neatly express general properties of belief change operators. Let $\odot$ be an arbitrary operator for belief change (say $\odot$ is one of $\oplus, \ominus, \circledast$). Then the laws depicted in Table 3.5 all hold for the belief change operators of Section 3.2. Which is not say that they always *should:* in fact there have been several proposals to make revision *relational* and give up *partial functionality*. Furthermore, *objective persistence* is not true in actions like 'watching' and arguably an activity like *learning* does not necessarily abide to *idempotence*. The point here is that we now can at least express such properties in one and the same object language.

$\psi \leftrightarrow [\odot\varphi]\psi$	$\psi \in \mathcal{L}_0$	*objective persistence*
$\langle\odot\varphi\rangle\psi \rightarrow [\odot\varphi]\psi$		*partial functionality*
$[\odot\varphi] \rightarrow [\odot\varphi][\odot\varphi]\psi$		*idempotence*

Table 3.5. Some laws for belief change.

It becomes even more interesting if we can refer to beliefs in the language, so that we can directly express all the postulates discussed so far. Such a language is indeed the object of study in dynamic doxastic logic.

$$\begin{aligned} \varphi &:= p \mid \neg\varphi \mid \varphi \wedge \varphi \mid B_a\varphi \mid [\alpha]\varphi \\ \alpha &:= \oplus_a\varphi \mid \ominus_a\varphi \mid \circledast_a\varphi \end{aligned}$$

A postulate like *success* for revision becomes now simply $[\circledast_a\varphi]\varphi$, and Moore's principle (2.4) is $\neg B_a\bot \rightarrow \neg B_a(\varphi \wedge \neg B_a\varphi)$. Note that in a multi-agent setting we can also express interesting properties like $B_i((\varphi \leftrightarrow \psi) \wedge$

$[\circledast_j\varphi]B_j\chi \wedge [\circledast_j\psi]\neg B_j\chi)$ expressing that, although i believes that φ and ψ are equivalent, he does not believe that j revision with either of them has the same effect. To express, in the Consecutive Number scenario, that agent b would notice that after a revises with φ, a knows the two numbers, then b would also know them, we could write $[\oplus_b[\oplus_a\varphi]B_a\neg\varphi]B_b\neg\varphi$.

If we want to stay close to the AGM-postulates, then we should restrict our dynamic doxastic language:

Definition 3.33 We define the language $\mathcal{L}_{B[]}$, with typical element φ, in terms of the propositional language $\mathcal{L}_0$, with typical element φ_0, as follows:

$$\begin{array}{lll} \varphi_0 & := & p \mid \neg\varphi_0 \mid \varphi_0 \wedge \varphi_0 \\ \varphi & := & \varphi_0 \mid \neg\varphi \mid \varphi \wedge \varphi \mid B\varphi_0 \mid [\oplus\varphi_0]\varphi \mid [\ominus\varphi_0]\varphi \end{array}$$ □

Example 3.34 We briefly discuss some properties and axioms of a possible basic system for dynamic doxastic logic, **DDL**, they are summarised in Figure 3.6. (We will not give a full definition, but refer the reader to Section 3.6 for further reference.)

Since we can define $\circledast$ by using the Levi-identity, we only give the axioms for $\oplus$ and $\ominus$ and define $[\circledast\varphi]\psi \leftrightarrow [\ominus\neg\varphi][\oplus\varphi]\psi$. To focus on the AGM postulates for contraction, the basic **DDL**-system does not assume any properties for the belief-operator B, other than it being a normal modal operator. Moreover, in light of the discussion in the previous section, the basic system is defined only over a limited language $\mathcal{L}_{B[]}$.

First of all, in the basic system **DDL** we assume that all the modal operators $B, [\oplus\psi]$, and $[\ominus\psi]$ are *normal modal operators*, in the sense that they satisfy Necessitation and Modus Ponens. We also assume the properties of objective persistence, functionality, and idempotence, for $\oplus$ and $\ominus$. Further, for the belief change operators $\oplus$ and $\ominus$ the modal counterpart of *extensionality* is called *congruence*. For expansion, in Table 3.6 we furthermore give the modal counterpart *modal*($\mathcal{K} \oplus 4$) of the *success* postulate, and what we call a Ramsey axiom for expansion, saying that ψ is believed after expansion with φ, if and only if $\varphi \rightarrow \psi$ is already believed initially. We have listed the *contraction* axiom in Table 3.6 as the modal version of ($\mathcal{K} \ominus 2$). □

Of course, the aim of having a language for **DDL** is not just to mimic the AGM postulates. In fact, not even every postulate *can* directly be

$\vdash \varphi \leftrightarrow \psi \Rightarrow \vdash [\odot\varphi]\chi \leftrightarrow [\odot\psi]\chi$	congruence, $\odot \in \{\oplus, \ominus\}$
$B\varphi \rightarrow (\chi \leftrightarrow [\oplus\varphi]\chi)$	modal ($\mathcal{K} \oplus 4$)
$[\oplus\varphi]B\psi \leftrightarrow B(\varphi \rightarrow \psi)$	Ramsey (expansion)
$[\ominus\varphi]B\chi \rightarrow B\chi$	*modal* ($\mathcal{K} \ominus 2$)
$B\varphi \rightarrow (B\chi \rightarrow [\ominus\varphi][\oplus\varphi]\chi)$	*modal recovery*

Table 3.6. Some properties of a basic modal logic **DDL** for AGM-style belief change.

'axiomatised', like for instance *monotony* for expansion or *success* for contraction. To cope with the latter, one might adapt the system, and for instance say that a contraction is only possible for formulas that are not a tautology. This would also effect postulate *type* for $\ominus$, but, since we argued that belief sets should be richer than classically closed sets anyway, we will not pursue that route here, but instead look at generalisations from the next chapter on.

One final motivation for even richer languages is in place here. Recall that the 'Effect on Third Parties' scenario of page 60. Here the new information is p, but this is only revealed to agent a. But this means that we in fact need a richer structure in the action descriptions themselves: a structure that gives epistemic information about *who* exactly is aware of *what* in the change described by the action. The transition of Figure 3.3 would be best described by something like

$$\oplus_a p \text{ `and' } \oplus_{a,b} (\oplus_a p \text{`or' } \oplus_a \neg p)$$

expressing that a expands with p, and both agents 'commonly' expand with the fact that a either expands with p or with $\neg p$. This granularity is not available in **DDL**: Chapter 5 is devoted to precisely describe this kind of actions.

3.6 Notes

As with many topics of this book, belief revision grew out from research interests in both computer science and philosophy. In the late 1970's, computer scientists developped more and more sophisticated databases, and ways to update them. Doyle's *truth maintenance systems* [54] were very influential. Around the same time, but more in a philosophical context, a number of publications by Levi [127] and by Harper [94] posed issues and a basic framework for *rational belief change*. . The pioneering work that put belief revision firmly on the logical agenda is that of Alchourrón, Gärdenfors, and Makinson [3], using postulates to characterise belief revision and contraction. Our treatment in Section 3.2 is mainly based upon [3], but also on Gärdenfors' [71], where postulates for expansion are added. One direction for Exercise 3.12 is can be found in [3, Observation 6.5], the other direction is in [71, Appendix A].

The system of spheres that semantically gives an account of contraction and revision (Section 3.3) is accredited to Grove [83]. It is inspired by the sphere semantics that Lewis gave for counterfactuals [129]. Although Grove presents a sphere semantics for revision only, our corresponding semantics for contraction can be directly 'read off' from it.

The quote in Section 3.4 is taken from a paper by Lindström and Rabinowicz [132], two authors who have published also several papers on dynamic doxastic logic. The publications on the latter topic more or less started off with van Benthem's contribution to the Proceedings of the 1987

Logic Colloquium [19, pp. 366–370], and the proceedings of a workshop organised by Fuhrmann and Morreau on 'the Logic of Change' in 1989 [68], and are since then influenced heavily by a paper of de Rijke [176] and several papers by Segerberg [183, 182] (see also our short discussion on page 4). Segerberg generalized the system of spheres to what he calls 'hypertheories' to give a semantic account of **DDL**. Section 3.5 above is loosely based on [182].

Belief revision is still an active area of research. Some important issues are for instance the difference between belief revision and updates. Katsuno and Mendelzon [112] were among the first to point out the difference; a convincing modal account of it is given in Ryan, Schobbens, and Rodrigues's [178]. Darwiche and Pearl [40] address *iterated belief revision*, the paper realizes that to cater for iterations, a revising agent should not only adapt his beliefs, but also his entrenchments. Van der Hoek and de Rijke [103] studied contractions in a multi-agent context. Readers who are interested to learn more about belief revision, are advised to visit `www.beliefrevision.org`.

4

Public Announcements

4.1 Introduction

If I truthfully say 'a kowhai tree has yellow flowers' to a group of friends, that fact is then commonly known among them. This indeed works for propositions about *facts*, such as in the example, but it is a mistaken intuition that whatever you announce is thereafter commonly known: it does not hold for certain *epistemic* propositions.

Example 4.1 (Buy or sell?) Consider two stockbrokers Anne and Bill, having a little break in a Wall Street bar. A messenger comes in and delivers a letter to Anne. On the envelope is written "urgently requested data on United Agents". Anne opens and reads the letter, which informs her of the fact that United Agents is doing well, such that she intends to buy a portfolio of stocks of that company, immediately. Anne now says to Bill: "Guess you don't know it yet, but United Agents is doing well." □

Even if we assume that Anne only speaks the truth, and that her conjecture about Bill is correct, Anne is in fact saying two things, namely both "it is true that United Agents is doing well" and "it is true that Bill does not know that United Agents is doing well". As a consequence of the first, Bill now knows that United Agents is doing well. He is therefore no longer ignorant of that fact. Therefore, "Bill does not know that United Agents is doing well" is now false. In other words: Anne has announced something which becomes false because of the announcement. This is called an unsuccessful update. Apparently, announcements are like footsteps in a flowing river of information. They merely refer to a specific moment in time, to a specific information state, and the information state may change because of the the announcement that makes an observation about it.

What is a convenient logical language to describe knowledge and announcements? The phenomenon of unsuccessful updates rules out an appealing straightforward option of a 'static' nature. Namely, if announcements always became common knowledge, one could have modelled them 'indirectly' by referring to their pre- and postcondition: the precondition is the announcement formula, and the postcondition common knowledge of that formula. But, as we have seen, sometimes announced formulas become false, and in general something other than the announcement may become common knowledge. The relation between the announcement and its postcondition is not straightforward. Therefore, the 'meaning' of an announcement is hard to grasp in a *static* way. An operator in the language that expresses the 'act' of announcing is to be preferred; and we can conveniently grasp its meaning in a *dynamic* way. By 'dynamic' we mean, that the statement is not given meaning relative to a (static) information state, but relative to a (dynamic) *transformation* of one information state into another information state. Such a binary relation between information states can be captured by a dynamic modal operator. To our basic multi-agent logical language we add such dynamic modal operators for announcements. This chapter deals with the thus obtained public announcement logic.

We start with looking at our warming-up example in more detail. The Sections 'Syntax', 'Semantics', and 'Axiomatisation' present the logic. The completeness proof is deferred to Chapter 7. 'Muddy Children', 'Sum and Product', and 'Russian Cards' present logical puzzles.

4.2 Examples

'Buy or sell?' continued Let us reconsider Example 4.1 where Anne (a) and Bill (b) ponder the big company's performance, but now in more detail. Let p stand for 'United Agents is doing well'. The information state after Anne has opened the letter can be described as follows: United Agents is doing well, Anne knows this, and Anne and Bill commonly know that Anne knows *whether* United Agents is doing well. This information state is represented by the epistemic state below, and to be explicit once more, we draw all access between states.

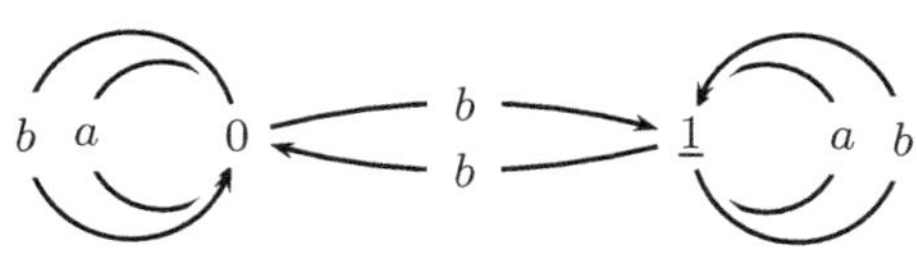

In the figure, 0 is the name of the state where p is false, and 1 is the name of the state where p is true. All relations are equivalence relations. We therefore prefer the visualisation where reflexivity and symmetry are assumed, so that states that are the same for an agent need to be linked only. Transitivity is also assumed. A link between states can also have more than one label. See Chapter 2 where these conventions were introduced. In this case, we get

0 ——— b ——— $\underline{1}$

We assume that Anne only makes truthful announcements, and only public announcements. Because the announcement is *truthful*, the formula of the announcement must be true on the moment of utterance, in the actual state. That the announcement is *public*, means that Bill can hear what Anne is saying, that Anne knows that Bill can hear her, etc., ad infinitum. We can also say that it is common knowledge (for Anne and Bill) that Anne is making the announcement. From 'truthful' and 'public' together it follows that states where the announcement formula is false are excluded from the public eye as a result of the announcement. It is now commonly known that these states are no longer possible. Among the remaining states, that include the actual state, there is no reason to make any further epistemic distinctions that were not already there.

It follows that the result of a public announcement is the restriction of the epistemic state to those states where the announcement is true, and that all access is kept between these remaining states. The formula of the announcement in Example 4.1 is $p \wedge \neg K_b p$. The formula $p \wedge \neg K_b p$ only holds in state 1 where p holds and not in state 0 where p does not hold. Applied to the current epistemic state, the restriction therefore results in the epistemic state

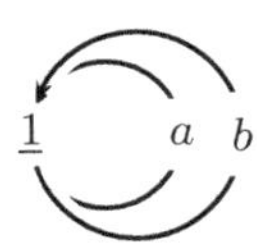

In this state it is common knowledge that p. In our preferred visualisation we get

$\underline{1}$

In the epistemic state before the announcement, $\neg K_b p$ was true, and after the announcement $K_b p$ is true, which follows from the truth of $C_{ab} p$. In the epistemic state before the announcement, the announced formula $p \wedge \neg K_b p$ was of course true. After its announcement, its negation has become true. Note that $\neg(p \wedge \neg K_b p)$ is equivalent to $\neg p \vee K_b p$ which follows by weakening from $K_b p$.

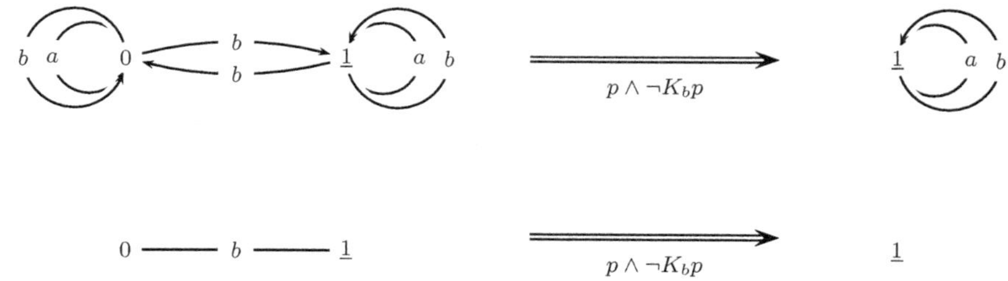

Figure 4.1. Buy or Sell?

Figure 4.1 contains an overview of the visualisations and transitions in this example. Before the formal introduction of the language and its semantics, we first continue with other examples of announcements, in a different setting.

Example 4.2 (Three player card game) Anne, Bill, and Cath have each drawn one card from a stack of three cards 0, 1, and 2. This is all commonly known. In fact, Anne has drawn card 0, Bill card 1, and Cath card 2. Anne now says "I do not have card 1". □

Write 012 for the deal of cards where Anne holds 0, Bill holds card 1, and Cath holds card 2. The deck of cards is commonly known. Players can only see their own card, and that other players also hold one card. They therefore know their own card and that the cards of the other players must be different from their own. In other words: deals 012 and 021 are the same for Anne, whereas deals 012 and 210 are the same for Bill, etc. There are, in total, six different deals of cards over agents. Together with the induced equivalence relation by knowing your own card, and the actual deal of cards, we get the epistemic state $(Hexa, 012)$:

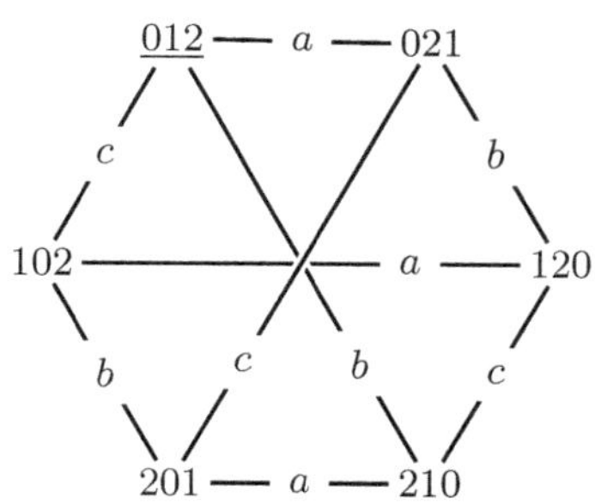

Facts are described by atoms such as 0_a for 'Anne holds card 0'. Let us have a look at some epistemic formulas too. In this epistemic state, it holds that 'Anne knows that Bill doesn't know her card' which is formally $K_a\neg(K_b0_a \vee K_b1_a \vee K_b2_a)$. It also holds that 'Anne considers it possible that Bill holds card 2 whereas actually Bill holds card 1' which is formally $1_b \wedge \hat{K}_a 2_b$.

We also have that 'It is commonly known that each player holds (at most) one card' described by $C_{abc}((0_a \rightarrow (\neg 1_a \wedge \neg 2_a)) \wedge \ldots)$. Anne's announcement "I do not have card 1" corresponds to the formula $\neg 1_a$. This announcement restricts the model to those states in which the formula is true, i.e., to the four states 012, 021, 201, and 210 where she does not hold card 1. As said, the new accessibility relations are the old ones restricted to the new domain.

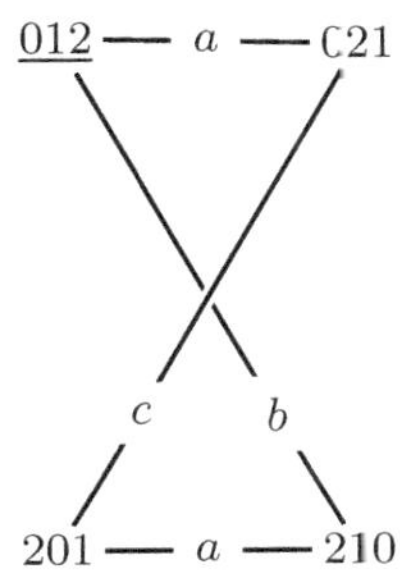

In this epistemic state, it holds that Cath knows that Anne holds 0—described by $K_c 0_a$—even though Anne does not know that Cath knows that—described by $\neg K_a K_c 0_a$—whereas Bill still does not know Anne's card—described by $\neg(K_b 0_a \vee K_b 1_a \vee K_b 2_a)$. More specifically, Bill does not know that Anne holds card 0: $\neg K_b 0_a$. Yet other informative announcements can be made in this epistemic state:

Example 4.3 (Bill does not know Anne's card) In the epistemic state resulting from Anne's announcement "I do not have card 1", Bill says "I still do not know your card". □

The announcement formula $\neg(K_b 0_a \vee K_b 1_a \vee K_b 2_a)$ only holds in b-equivalence classes where Bill has an alternative card for Anne to consider, so, in this case, in the class $\{012, 210\}$. The announcement therefore results in the epistemic state

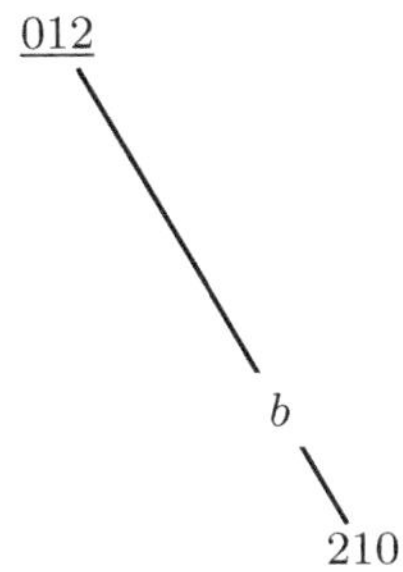

We can see that the announcement was informative for Anne, as she now knows Bill's card. Still, Bill does not know hers. If Anne were proudly to

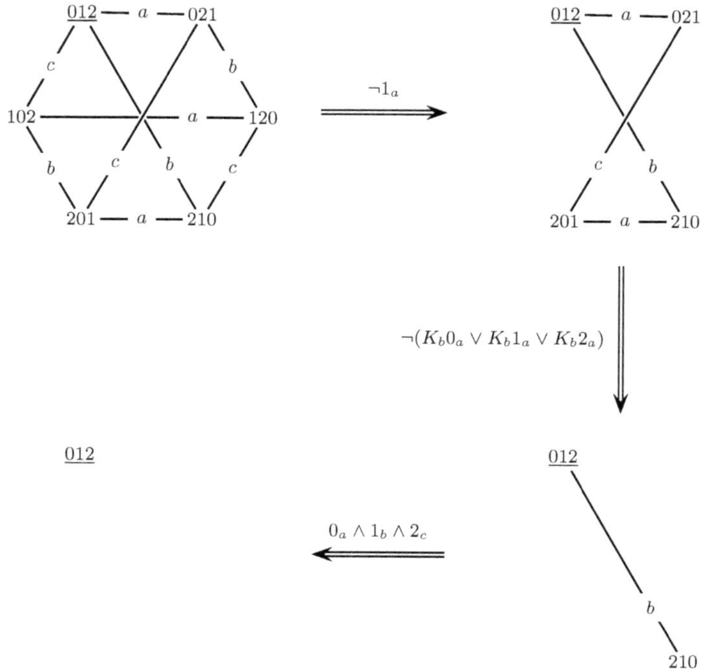

Figure 4.2. The result of three subsequent announcements of card players. The top left figure visualises Anne, Bill, and Cath holding cards 0, 1, and 2, respectively.

announce that she now knows Bill's card, that would not make a difference, as $K_a0_b \vee K_a1_b \vee K_a2_b$ holds in both 012 and 210: this was already commonly known to all players. In other words, the *same* epistemic state results from this announcement. If instead she announces that she now knows that the card deal is 012, no further informative public announcements can be made.

012

An overview of the information changes in this 'cards' example is found in Figure 4.2. We now formally introduce the language and its semantics.

4.3 Syntax

Definition 4.4 (Logical languages $\mathcal{L}_{K[]}(A,P)$ and $\mathcal{L}_{KC[]}(A,P)$) Given are a finite set of agents A and a countable set of atoms P. The language $\mathcal{L}_{KC[]}(A,P)$ (or, when the set of agents and atoms are clear or not relevant, $\mathcal{L}_{KC[]}$), is inductively defined by the BNF

$$\varphi \ ::= \ p \mid \neg\varphi \mid (\varphi \wedge \varphi) \mid K_a\varphi \mid C_B\varphi \mid [\varphi]\varphi$$

where $a \in A$, $B \subseteq A$, and $p \in P$. Without common knowledge, we get the logical language $\mathcal{L}_{K[]}(A, P)$, or $\mathcal{L}_{K[]}$. Its BNF is

$$\varphi \ ::= \ p \mid \neg\varphi \mid (\varphi \wedge \varphi) \mid K_a\varphi \mid [\varphi]\varphi$$ □

The new construct in the language is $[\varphi]\psi$—note that, as usual, in the BNF form $[\varphi]\varphi$ we only express the *type* of the formulas, which is the same for the announcement formula and the one following it, whereas the more common mathematical way to express this is as an inductive construct $[\varphi]\psi$ that is formed from two arbitrary and possibly different formulas φ and ψ. Formula $[\varphi]\psi$ stands for 'after announcement of φ, it holds that ψ'. Alternatively, we may sometimes say 'after *update* with φ, it holds that ψ'—note that 'update' is a more general term also used for other dynamic phenomena. For 'announcement', always read 'public and truthful announcement'. Strictly speaking, as $[\varphi]$ is a $\Box$-type modal operator, formula $[\varphi]\psi$ means 'after *every* announcement of φ, it holds that ψ', but because announcements are partial functions, this is the same as 'after announcement of φ, it holds that ψ'. The dual of $[\varphi]$ is $\langle\varphi\rangle$. Formula $\langle\varphi\rangle\psi$ therefore stands for 'after *some* truthful public announcement of φ, it holds that ψ'. Unlike the $\Box$-form, this formulation assumes that φ can indeed be truthfully announced—but here we are anticipating the semantics of announcements.

Example 4.5 Anne's announcement '(United Agents is doing well and) You don't know that United Agents is doing well' in Example 4.1 was formalised as $p \wedge \neg K_b p$. That it is an unsuccessful update, or in other words, that it becomes false when it is announced, can be described as $\langle p \wedge \neg K_b p\rangle\neg(p \wedge \neg K_b p)$. This description uses the diamond-form of the announcement to express that an unsuccessful update can indeed be truthfully announced. □

Example 4.6 In the 'three cards' Example 4.2, Anne's announcement 'I do not have card 1' was described by $\neg 1_a$. Bill's subsequent announcement 'I do not know your card' was described by $\neg(K_b 0_a \vee K_b 1_a \vee K_b 2_a)$, and Anne's subsequent announcement 'The card deal is 012' was described by $0_a \wedge 1_b \wedge 2_c$. After this sequence of three announcements, Bill finally gets to know Anne's card: $K_b 0_a \vee K_b 1_a \vee K_b 2_a$. See also Figure 4.2. This sequence of three announcements plus postcondition is described by

$$[\neg 1_a][\neg(K_b 0_a \vee K_b 1_a \vee K_b 2_a)][0_a \wedge 1_b \wedge 2_c](K_b 0_a \vee K_b 1_a \vee K_b 2_a)$$

If the third announcement had instead been Anne saying 'I now know your card' (described by $K_a 0_b \vee K_a 1_b \vee K_a 2_b$), Bill would not have learnt Anne's card:

$$[\neg 1_a][\neg(K_b 0_a \vee K_b 1_a \vee K_b 2_a)][K_a 0_b \vee K_a 1_b \vee K_a 2_b]\neg(K_b 0_a \vee K_b 1_a \vee K_b 2_a)$$

□

For theoretical reasons—related to expressive power, and completeness—the language $\mathcal{L}_{K[]}$, *without* common knowledge operators, is of special interest. Otherwise, we tend to think of the logic for the language $\mathcal{L}_{KC[]}$ as *the* 'public announcement logic', in other words, public announcement logic is the logic *with* common knowledge operators.

4.4 Semantics

The effect of the public announcement of φ is the restriction of the epistemic state to all (factual) states where φ holds, including access between states. So, 'announce φ' can be seen as an epistemic state transformer, with a corresponding dynamic modal operator $[\varphi]$. We need to add a clause for the interpretation of such dynamic operators to the semantics. We remind the reader that we write V_p for $V(p)$, $\sim_a$ for $\sim(a)$, $\sim_B$ for $(\bigcup_{a \in B} \sim_a)^*$, and $[\![\varphi]\!]_M$ for $\{s \in \mathcal{D}(M) \mid M, s \models \varphi\}$.

Definition 4.7 (Semantics of the logic of announcements) Given is an epistemic model $M = \langle S, \sim, V \rangle$ for agents A and atoms P.

$$
\begin{array}{lll}
M, s \models p & \text{iff} & s \in V_p \\
M, s \models \neg\varphi & \text{iff} & M, s \not\models \varphi \\
M, s \models \varphi \wedge \psi & \text{iff} & M, s \models \varphi \text{ and } M, s \models \psi \\
M, s \models K_a\varphi & \text{iff} & \text{for all } t \in S : s \sim_a t \text{ implies } M, t \models \varphi \\
M, s \models C_B\varphi & \text{iff} & \text{for all } t \in S : s \sim_B t \text{ implies } M, t \models \varphi \\
M, s \models [\varphi]\psi & \text{iff} & M, s \models \varphi \text{ implies } M|\varphi, s \models \psi
\end{array}
$$

where $M|\varphi = \langle S', \sim', V' \rangle$ is defined as follows:

$$
\begin{array}{ll}
S' & = [\![\varphi]\!]_M \\
\sim'_a & = \sim_a \cap ([\![\varphi]\!]_M \times [\![\varphi]\!]_M) \\
V'_p & = V_p \cap [\![\varphi]\!]_M
\end{array}
$$

□

The dual of $[\varphi]$ is $\langle\varphi\rangle$:

$$M, s \models \langle\varphi\rangle\psi \quad \text{iff} \quad M, s \models \varphi \text{ and } M|\varphi, s \models \psi$$

The set of all valid public announcement principles in the language $\mathcal{L}_{K[]}$ without common knowledge is denoted PA, whereas the set of validities in the full language $\mathcal{L}_{KC[]}$ is denoted PAC.

Some knowledge changes that are induced by Anne's announcement in the 'three cards' Example 4.2 that she does not have card 1, see also Figure 4.2, are computed in detail below, to give an example of the interpretation of announcements. For a different and more visual example, see Figure 4.3, wherein we picture the result of Bill's subsequent announcement 'I do not know Anne's card'.

Example 4.8 Let $(\mathit{Hexa}, 012)$ be the epistemic state for card deal 012. In that epistemic state it is true that, after Anne says that she does not have card 1, Cath knows that Anne holds card 0; formally $\mathit{Hexa}, 012 \models [\neg 1_a]K_c 0_a$:

We have that $\mathit{Hexa}, 012 \models [\neg 1_a]K_c 0_a$ iff ($\mathit{Hexa}, 012 \models \neg 1_a$ implies $\mathit{Hexa}|\neg 1_a, 012 \models K_c 0_a$). Concerning the antecedent, $\mathit{Hexa}, 012 \models \neg 1_a$ iff

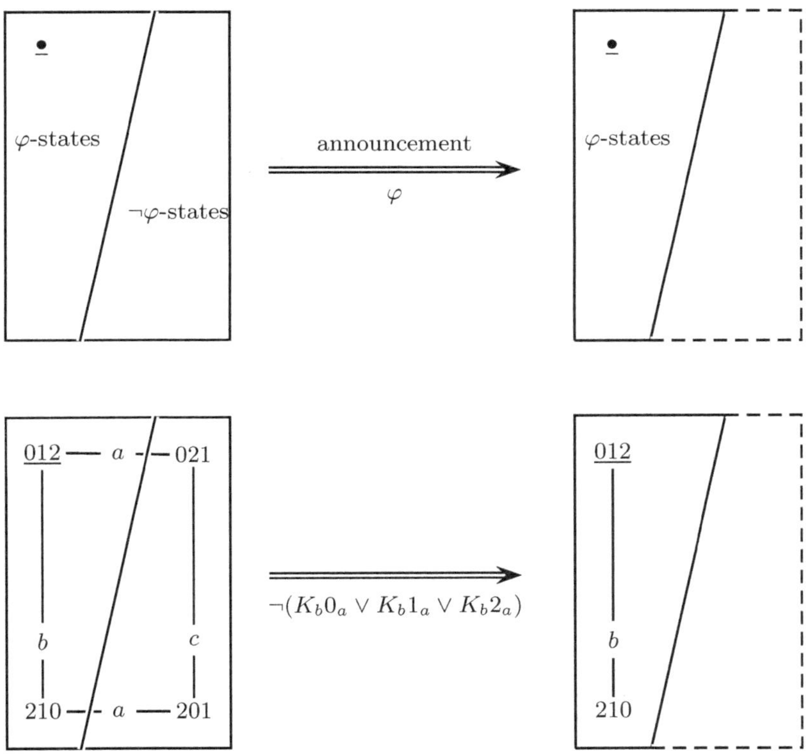

$$
\begin{array}{|l||l|}
S = \{012, 021, 201, 210\} & S' = \{012, 210\} \\
\sim_b = \{(012, 012), (012, 210), \dots\} & \sim'_b = \sim_b \cap \{012, 210\}^2 = \dots, \\
\sim_a = \dots, \sim_c = \dots & \sim'_a = \dots, \sim'_c = \dots \\
V_{0_a} = \{012, 021\}, & V'_{0_a} = V_{0_a} \cap \{012, 210\} = \{012\}, \\
V_{1_a} = \emptyset, \dots & V'_{1_a} = V_{1_a} \cap \{012, 210\} = \emptyset, \dots
\end{array}
$$

Figure 4.3. Visualisation of the semantics of an announcement. From top to bottom: the abstract semantics of an announcement, the effect of Bill announcing 'I do not know your card, Anne', and the formal representation of the two corresponding epistemic states. The middle left figure pictures the same epistemic state $(\mathit{Hexa}|\neg 1_a, 012)$ as 'the one with crossed legs' top right in Figure 4.2. We have merely flipped 210—a—201 in the current visualisation, for our convenience.

$Hexa, 012 \not\models 1_a$. This is the case iff $012 \notin V_{1_a} (= \{102, 120\})$, and the latter is true.

It remains to show that $Hexa|\neg 1_a, 012 \models K_c 0_a$. This is equivalent to 'for all $s \in \mathcal{D}(Hexa|\neg 1_a)$: $012 \sim_c s$ implies $Hexa|\neg 1_a, s \models 0_a$. Only state 012 itself is c-accessible from 012 in {012, 021, 210, 201 }. Therefore, the condition is fulfilled if $Hexa|\neg 1_a, 012 \models 0_a$. This is so, because $012 \in V_{0_a} = \{012, 021\}$.

In epistemic state ($Hexa$, 012) it is also true that, after Anne says that she does not have card 1, Bill does not know that Anne holds card 0; formally $Hexa, 012 \models [\neg 1_a]\neg K_b 0_a$:

We have that $Hexa, 012 \models [\neg 1_a]\neg K_b 0_a$ iff ($Hexa, 012 \models \neg 1_a$ implies $Hexa|\neg 1_a, 012 \models \neg K_b 0_a$). The premiss is satisfied as before. For the conclusion, $Hexa|\neg 1_a, 012 \models \neg K_b 0_a$ iff $Hexa|\neg 1_a, 012 \not\models K_b 0_a$ iff there is a state s such that $012 \sim_b s$ and $Hexa|\neg 1_a, s \not\models 0_a$. State $210 = s$ satisfies that: $012 \sim_b 210$ and $Hexa|\neg 1_a, 210 \not\models 0_a$, because $210 \notin V_{0_a} = \{012, 021\}$. □

Exercise 4.9 After Anne has said that she does not have card 1, she considers it possible that Bill now knows her card: $[\neg 1_a]\hat{K}_a K_b 0_a$. If Bill has 2 and learns that Anne does not have 1, Bill knows that Anne has 0. But, of course, Bill has 1, and 'does not learn very much.' Also, after Anne has said that she does not have card 1, Cath—who has 2—knows that Bill has 1 and that Bill therefore is still uncertain about Anne's card: $[\neg 1_a]K_c \neg K_b 0_a$. Finally, when Anne says that she does not have card 1, and then Bill says that he does not know Anne's card, and then Anne says that the card deal is 012, it has become common knowledge what the card deal is. Make these observations precise by showing all of the following:

- $Hexa, 012 \models [\neg 1_a]\hat{K}_a K_b 0_a$
- $Hexa, 012 \models [\neg 1_a]K_c \neg K_b 0_a$
- $Hexa, 012 \models [\neg 1_a][\neg(K_b 0_a \vee K_b 1_a \vee K_b 2_a)][0_a \wedge 1_b \wedge 2_c]C_{abc}(0_a \wedge 1_b \wedge 2_c)$□

Revelation So far, all announcements were made by an agent that was also modelled in the system. We can also imagine an announcement as a 'public event' that does not involve an agent. Such an event publicly 'reveals' the truth of the announced formula. Therefore, announcements have also been called 'revelations'—announcements by the divine agent, that are obviously true without questioning. In fact, when modelling announcements made by agents occurring in the model, we have overlooked one important aspect: when agent a announces φ, it actually announces $K_a\varphi$—I know that φ, and in a given epistemic state $K_a\varphi$ may be more informative than φ. For example, consider the four-state epistemic model in the top-right corner of Figure 4.2. In state 021 of this model, there is a difference between *Bill* saying "Anne has card 0" and a 'revelation' in the above sense of "Anne has card 0". The former—given that Bill is speaking the truth—is an announcement of $K_b 0_a$ which only holds in state 021 of the model, so it results in the singleton model 021 where all agents have full knowledge of the card deal. Note that in state 012 of the model 0_a is true but Bill does not know that, so $K_b 0_a$ is false.

But a revelation "Anne has card 0" is indeed 'only' the announcement of 0_a which holds in states 012 *and* 021 of the model, and results in epistemic state $\underline{012}$——a——021 where Anne still does not know the card deal.

In multi-agent systems the divine agent can be modelled as the 'insider' agent whose access on the domain is the identity, in which case we have that $\varphi \leftrightarrow K_{\mathsf{insider}}\varphi$ is valid (on $\mathcal{S}5$). Otherwise, when an agent says φ, this is an announcement of $K_a\varphi$, and we do not have that $K_a\varphi \leftrightarrow \varphi$. See Section 4.12 on the Russian Cards problem for such matters.

4.5 Principles of Public Announcement Logic

This section presents various principles of public announcement logic, more precisely, ways in which the logical structure of pre- and postconditions interacts with an announcement.

If an announcement can be executed, there is only one way to do it. Also, it cannot always be executed. In other words, announcements are *partial functions.*

Proposition 4.10 (Announcements are functional) It is valid that

$$\langle\varphi\rangle\psi \rightarrow [\varphi]\psi$$

□

Proof Let M and s be arbitrary. We then have that $M, s \models \langle\varphi\rangle\psi$ iff ($M, s \models \varphi$ and $M|\varphi, s \models \psi$). The last (propositionally) implies ($M, s \models \varphi$ implies $M|\varphi, s \models \psi$) which is by definition $M, s \models [\varphi]\psi$. □

Proposition 4.11 (Announcements are partial) Schema $\langle\varphi\rangle\top$ is invalid. □

Proof In an epistemic state where φ is false, $\langle\varphi\rangle\top$ is false as well. (In other words: *truthful* public announcements can only be made if they are indeed true.) □

The setting in Proposition 4.11 is not the only way in which the partiality of announcements comes to the fore. This will also show from the interaction between announcement and negation, and from the interaction between announcement and knowledge.

Proposition 4.12 (Public announcement and negation) $[\varphi]\neg\psi \leftrightarrow (\varphi \rightarrow \neg[\varphi]\psi)$ is valid. □

In other words: $[\varphi]\neg\psi$ can be true for two reasons; the first reason is that φ cannot be announced. The other reason is that, after the announcement was truthfully made, ψ is false (note that $\neg[\varphi]\psi$ is equivalent to $\langle\varphi\rangle\neg\psi$). The proof is left as an exercise to the reader. The various ways in which announcement and knowledge interact will be addressed separately, later.

Proposition 4.13 All of the following are equivalent:

- $\varphi \rightarrow [\varphi]\psi$
- $\varphi \rightarrow \langle\varphi\rangle\psi$
- $[\varphi]\psi$ □

Proof As an example, we show that $\varphi \rightarrow [\varphi]\psi$ is equivalent to $[\varphi]\psi$. Let M and s be an arbitrary model and state, respectively. Then—in great detail:

$M, s \models \varphi \rightarrow [\varphi]\psi$
$\Leftrightarrow$
$M, s \models \varphi$ implies $M, s \models [\varphi]\psi$
$\Leftrightarrow$
$M, s \models \varphi$ implies ($M, s \models \varphi$ implies $M|\varphi, s \models \psi$)
$\Leftrightarrow$
($M, s \models \varphi$ and $M, s \models \varphi$) implies $M|\varphi, s \models \psi$
$\Leftrightarrow$
$M, s \models \varphi$ implies $M|\varphi, s \models \psi$
$\Leftrightarrow$
$M, s \models [\varphi]\psi$ □

Proposition 4.14 All of the following are equivalent:

- $\langle\varphi\rangle\psi$
- $\varphi \wedge \langle\varphi\rangle\psi$
- $\varphi \wedge [\varphi]\psi$ □

The proof of Proposition 4.14 is left as an exercise.

Exercise 4.15 Show that the converse of Proposition 4.10 does not hold. (Hint: choose an announcement formula φ that is false in a given epistemic state.) □

Exercise 4.16 Prove the other equivalences of Proposition 4.13, and prove the equivalences of Proposition 4.14. (The proof above shows more detail than is normally required.) □

Instead of first saying 'φ' and then saying 'ψ' you may as well have said for the first time 'φ and after that ψ'. This is expressed in the following proposition.

Proposition 4.17 (Public announcement composition)
$[\varphi \wedge [\varphi]\psi]\chi$ is equivalent to $[\varphi][\psi]\chi$. □

Proof For arbitrary M, s:

$s \in M|(\varphi \wedge [\varphi]\psi)$
$\Leftrightarrow$
$M, s \models \varphi \wedge [\varphi]\psi$

$\Leftrightarrow$
$M, s \models \varphi$ and $(\ M, s \models \varphi$ implies $M|\varphi, s \models \psi\ )$
$\Leftrightarrow$
$s \in M|\varphi$ and $M|\varphi, s \models \psi$
$\Leftrightarrow$
$s \in (M|\varphi)|\psi$ □

This property turns out to be a useful feature for analysing announcements that are made with specific intentions: those intentions tend to be postconditions ψ that supposedly hold after the announcement. So if an agent a says φ with the intention of achieving ψ, this corresponds to the announcement $K_a\varphi \wedge [K_a\varphi]K_a\psi$. Section 4.12 will give more concrete examples. The validity $[\varphi \wedge [\varphi]\psi]\chi \leftrightarrow [\varphi][\psi]\chi$ is in the axiomatisation. It is the only way to reduce the number of announcements in a formula, and therefore an essential step when deriving theorems involving two or more announcements.

How does knowledge change as the result of an announcement? The relation between announcements and *individual* knowledge is still fairly simple. Let us start by showing that an announcement *does* make a difference: $[\varphi]K_a\psi$ is not equivalent to $K_a[\varphi]\psi$. This is because the epistemic state transformation that interprets an announcement is a partial function. A simple counterexample of $[\varphi]K_a\psi \leftrightarrow K_a[\varphi]\psi$ is the following. First note that in $(Hexa, 012)$ it is true that after every announcement of 'Anne holds card 1', Cath knows that Anne holds card 0. This is because that announcement cannot take place in that epistemic state. In other words, we have that

$$Hexa, 012 \models [1_a]K_c0_a$$

On the other hand, it is false that Cath knows that after the announcement of Anne that she holds card 1 (which she can imagine to take place), Cath knows that Anne holds card 0. Instead, Cath then knows that Anne holds card 1! So we have

$$Hexa, 012 \not\models K_c[1_a]0_a$$

We now have shown that

$$\not\models [\varphi]K_a\psi \leftrightarrow K_a[\varphi]\psi$$

An equivalence holds if we make $[\varphi]K_a\psi$ conditional to the executability of the announcement, thus expressing partiality.

Proposition 4.18 (Public announcement and knowledge)
$[\varphi]K_a\psi$ is equivalent to $\varphi \rightarrow K_a[\varphi]\psi$. □

Proof
$M, s \models \varphi \rightarrow K_a[\varphi]\psi$
$\Leftrightarrow$
$M, s \models \varphi$ implies $M, s \models K_a[\varphi]\psi$

$\Leftrightarrow$
$M, s \models \varphi$ implies (for all $t \in M : s \sim_a t$ implies $M, t \models [\varphi]\psi$)
$\Leftrightarrow$
$M, s \models \varphi$ implies (for all $t \in M : s \sim_a t$ implies ($M, t \models \varphi$ implies $M|\varphi, t \models \psi$))
$\Leftrightarrow$
$M, s \models \varphi$ implies (for all $t \in M$: $M, t \models \varphi$ and $s \sim_a t$ implies $M|\varphi, t \models \psi$)
$\Leftrightarrow$
$M, s \models \varphi$ implies (for all $t \in M|\varphi, s \sim_a t$ implies $M|\varphi, t \models \psi$)
$\Leftrightarrow$
$M, s \models \varphi$ implies $M|\varphi, s \models K_a\psi$
$\Leftrightarrow$
$M, s \models [\varphi]K_a\psi$ □

The interaction between announcement and knowledge can be formulated in various other ways. Their equivalence can be shown by using the equivalence of $\varphi \rightarrow [\varphi]\psi$ to $[\varphi]\psi$, see Proposition 4.13. One or the other may appeal most to the intuitions of the reader.

Proposition 4.19 All valid are:

- $[\varphi]K_a\psi \leftrightarrow (\varphi \rightarrow K_a[\varphi]\psi)$ (Proposition 4.18)
- $\langle\varphi\rangle K_a\psi \leftrightarrow (\varphi \wedge K_a(\varphi \rightarrow \langle\varphi\rangle\psi))$
- $\langle\varphi\rangle \hat{K}_a\psi \leftrightarrow (\varphi \wedge \hat{K}_a\langle\varphi\rangle\psi)$ □

For an example, we prove the third by use of the first.

Proof
$M, s \models \langle\varphi\rangle\hat{K}_a\psi$
$\Leftrightarrow$ duality of modal operators
$M, s \models \neg[\varphi]K_a\neg\psi$
$\Leftrightarrow$ by Proposition 4.18
$M, s \models \neg(\varphi \rightarrow K_a[\varphi]\neg\psi)$
$\Leftrightarrow$ propositional
$M, s \models \varphi \wedge \neg K_a[\varphi]\neg\psi$
$\Leftrightarrow$ duality
$M, s \models \varphi \wedge \hat{K}_a\langle\varphi\rangle\psi$

Therefore, $M, s \models \langle\varphi\rangle\hat{K}_a\psi \leftrightarrow (\varphi \wedge \hat{K}_a\langle\varphi\rangle\psi)$. As this was for an arbitrary model and state, it follows that $\langle\varphi\rangle\hat{K}_a\psi \leftrightarrow (\varphi \wedge \hat{K}_a\langle\varphi\rangle\psi)$ is valid. □

Exercise 4.20 Show the second equivalence in Proposition 4.19. □

Exercise 4.21 Investigate whether it is true in the two-state epistemic state of Example 4.1 that $\langle p \wedge \neg K_b p\rangle\hat{K}_a\hat{K}_b\neg p$. □

For all operators except common knowledge we find equivalences similar to the ones we have already seen. Together they are

Proposition 4.22

$$\begin{array}{ll} [\varphi]p & \leftrightarrow (\varphi \rightarrow p) \\ [\varphi](\psi \wedge \chi) & \leftrightarrow ([\varphi]\psi \wedge [\varphi]\chi) \\ [\varphi](\psi \rightarrow \chi) & \leftrightarrow ([\varphi]\psi \rightarrow [\varphi]\chi) \\ [\varphi]\neg\psi & \leftrightarrow (\varphi \rightarrow \neg[\varphi]\psi) \\ [\varphi]K_a\psi & \leftrightarrow (\varphi \rightarrow K_a[\varphi]\psi) \\ [\varphi][\psi]\chi & \leftrightarrow [\varphi \wedge [\varphi]\psi]\chi \end{array}$$

□

Simple proofs are left to the reader. Note the surprising equivalence for the case $\rightarrow$. Together, these validities conveniently provide us with a 'rewrite system' that allows us to eliminate announcements, one by one, from a formula in the language $\mathcal{L}_{K[]}$, resulting in an equivalent formula in the language $\mathcal{L}_K$, without announcements. In other words, in the logic *PA* 'announcements are not really necessary', in a theoretical sense. This will also be useful towards proving completeness. Chapters 7 and 8 present these matters in detail.

In a *practical sense*, having announcements is of course quite useful: it may be counterintuitive to specify dynamic phenomena in a language without announcements, and the descriptions may become rather lengthy. Remember your average first course in logic: a propositional logical formula is equivalent to a formula that only uses the 'Sheffer Stroke' (or NAND). But from the perspective of readability it is usually considered a bad idea to have formulas only using that single connective.

When we add common knowledge to the language, life becomes harder. The relation between announcement and common knowledge, that will be addressed in a separate section, cannot be expressed in an equivalence, but only in a rule. In particular—as we already emphasised—announcing φ does not make it common knowledge.

Exercise 4.23 Prove the validities in Proposition 4.22. □

Exercise 4.24 Given that $\rightarrow$ is defined from $\neg$ and $\wedge$ in our inductively defined language, what is $[\varphi](\psi \rightarrow \chi)$ equivalent to, and how does this outcome relate to the validity $[\varphi](\psi \rightarrow \chi) \leftrightarrow ([\varphi]\psi \rightarrow [\varphi]\chi)$ that was established in Proposition 4.22? What principle would one 'normally' expect for a 'necessity'-type modal operator? □

Exercise 4.25 Show that $\langle\varphi\rangle\neg\psi \leftrightarrow (\varphi \wedge -\langle\varphi\rangle\psi)$ is valid. □

4.6 Announcement and Common Knowledge

A straightforward generalisation of $[\varphi]K_a\psi \leftrightarrow (\varphi \rightarrow K_a[\varphi]\psi)$, the principle relating announcement and individual knowledge, is $[\varphi]C_A\psi \leftrightarrow (\varphi \rightarrow C_A[\varphi]\psi)$, but this formula scheme is invalid. Consider the instance

$\underline{11} — a — 01 — b — 10 \quad \Longrightarrow \quad \underline{11} \qquad 10$

Figure 4.4. After the announcement of p, q is common knowledge. But it is not common knowledge that after announcing p, q is true.

$[p]C_{ab}q \leftrightarrow (p \rightarrow C_{ab}[p]q)$ of the supposed principle. We show that the left side of this equivalence is true, and the right side false, in state 11 of the model M on the left in Figure 4.4. In this model, let 01 the name for the state where p is false and q is true, etc.
We have that $M, 11 \models [p]C_{ab}q$ because $M|p, 11 \models C_{ab}q$. The model $M|p$ is pictured on the right in Figure 4.4. It consists of two disconnected states. Obviously, $M|p, 11 \models C_{ab}q$, because $M|p, 11 \models q$ and 11 is now the only reachable state from 11. On the other hand, we have that $M, 11 \not\models p \rightarrow C_{ab}[p]q$, because $M, 11 \models p$ but $M, 11 \not\models C_{ab}[p]q$. The last is, because $11 \sim_{ab} 10$ in M (because $11 \sim_a 01$ and $01 \sim_b 10$), and $M, 10 \not\models [p]q$. When evaluating q in $M|p$, we are now in its *other* disconnected part, where q is false: $M|p$, $10 \not\models q$.

Fortunately there is a way to get common knowledge after an announcement. The principle for announcement and common knowledge will also be a derivation rule in the axiomatisation to be presented later.

Proposition 4.26 (Public announcement and common knowledge)
If $\chi \rightarrow [\varphi]\psi$ and $(\chi \wedge \varphi) \rightarrow E_B\chi$ are valid, then $\chi \rightarrow [\varphi]C_B\psi$ is valid. □

Proof Let M and s be arbitrary and suppose that $M, s \models \chi$. We have to prove that $M, s \models [\varphi]C_B\psi$. Therefore, suppose $M, s \models \varphi$, and let t be in the domain of $M|\varphi$ such that $s \sim_B t$, i.e., we have a path from s to t for agents in B, of arbitrary finite length. We now have to prove that $M|\varphi, t \models \psi$. We prove this by induction on the length of that path.

If the length of the path is 0, then $s = t$, and $M|\varphi, s \models \psi$ follows from the assumption $M, s \models \chi$ and the validity of $\chi \rightarrow [\varphi]\psi$. Now suppose the length of the path is $n+1$ for some $n \in \mathbb{N}$, with—for $a \in B$ and $u \in M|\varphi$—$s \sim_a u \sim_B t$. From $M, s \models \chi$ and $M, s \models \varphi$, from the validity of $(\chi \wedge \varphi) \rightarrow E_B\chi$, and from $s \sim_a u$ (we were given that $u \in M|\varphi$, therefore u is also in the domain of M), it follows that $M, u \models \chi$. Because u is in the domain of $M|\varphi$, we have $M, u \models \varphi$. We now apply the induction hypothesis on the length n path such that $u \sim_B t$. Therefore $M|\varphi, t \models \psi$. □

The soundness of the principle of announcement and common knowledge is depicted in Figure 4.5. The following informal explanation also drawing on that visual information may help to grasp the intuition behind it.

First, note that $\chi \rightarrow [\varphi]\psi$ is equivalent to $\chi \rightarrow (\varphi \rightarrow [\varphi]\psi)$ which is equivalent to $(\chi \wedge \varphi) \rightarrow [\varphi]\psi$. This first premiss of 'announcement and common knowledge' therefore says that, given an arbitrary state in the domain where

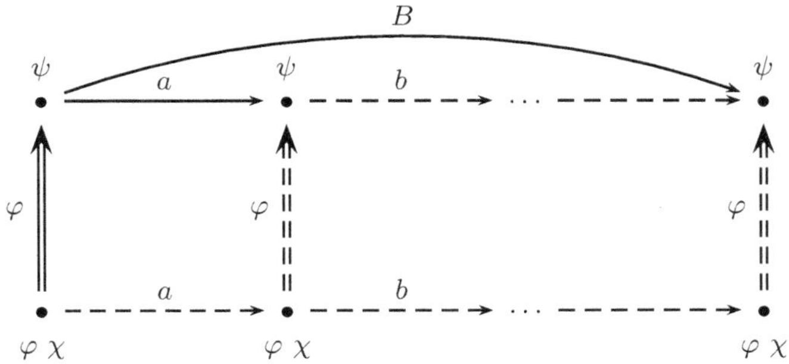

Figure 4.5. Visualisation of the principle relating common knowledge and announcement.

χ and φ hold, if we restrict the domain to the φ-states—in other words, if we do a φ-step, then ψ holds in the resulting epistemic state. The second premiss of 'announcement and common knowledge' says that, given an arbitrary state in the domain where χ and φ hold, if we do an arbitrary a-step in the domain, then we always reach an epistemic state where χ holds. For the conclusion, note that $\chi \rightarrow [\varphi]C_B\psi$ is equivalent to $(\chi \wedge \varphi) \rightarrow [\varphi]C_B\psi$. The conclusion of 'common knowledge and announcement' therefore says that, given an arbitrary state in the domain where χ and φ hold, if we do a φ-step followed by a B-path, we always reach a ψ-state. The induction uses, that if we do a φ-step followed by an a-step, the diagram 'can be completed', because the premisses ensure that we can reach a state so that we can, instead, do the a-step first, followed by the φ-step.

Corollary 4.27 Let the premisses for the 'announcement and common knowledge' rule be satisfied. Then every B-path in the model $M|\varphi$ runs along ψ-states. □

In other words: every B-path in M that runs along φ-states (i.e., such that in every state along that path φ is satisfied) also runs along $[\varphi]\psi$-states. In view of such observations, in Chapter 7 we call such paths $B\varphi$-paths .

The following Corollary will be useful in Section 4.7.

Corollary 4.28 $[\varphi]\psi$ is valid iff $[\varphi]C_B\psi$ is valid. □

Proof From right to left is obvious. From left to right follows when taking $\chi = \top$ in Proposition 4.26. □

Exercise 4.29 An alternative formulation of 'announcement and common knowledge' is:

If $(\chi \wedge \varphi) \rightarrow [\varphi]\psi \wedge E_B\chi$ is valid, then $(\chi \wedge \varphi) \rightarrow [\varphi]C_B\psi$ is valid.

Show that this is equivalent to 'announcement and common knowledge'. (Hint: use the validity $[\varphi']\varphi'' \leftrightarrow (\varphi' \rightarrow [\varphi']\varphi''))$. □

Exercise 4.30 If $\chi \to [\varphi]\psi$ is valid, then $\chi \to [\varphi]C_B\psi$ may not be valid. Give an example. □

4.7 Unsuccessful Updates

Let us recapitulate once more our deceptive communicative expectations. If an agent truthfully announces φ to a group of agents, it appears *on first sight* to be the case that he 'makes φ common knowledge'. In other words, if φ holds, then after announcing that, $C_A\varphi$ holds, i.e.: $\varphi \to [\varphi]C_A\varphi$ is valid. As we have already seen at the beginning of this chapter, this expectation is unwarranted, because the truth of epistemic parts of the formula may be influenced by its announcement. But sometimes the expectation *is* warranted: formulas that always become common knowledge after being announced, will be called *successful*. Let us see what the possibilities are.

After announcing φ, φ sometimes remains true and sometimes becomes false, and this depends both on the formula *and* on the epistemic state. We illustrate this by announcements in the epistemic state of introductory Example 4.1, where from two agents Anne and Bill, Anne knows the truth about p but Bill does not. This epistemic state can be formally defined as $(L, 1)$, where model L has domain $\{0, 1\}$, accessibility relation for agent a is $\sim_a = \{(0,0),(1,1)\}$ or the identity on the domain, accessibility relation for agent b is $\sim_b = \{(0,0),(1,1),(0,1),(1,0)\}$ or the universal relation on the domain, and valuation $V_p = \{1\}$.

If in this epistemic state $(L, 1)$ Anne says, truthfully: "I know that United Agents is doing well", then after this announcement K_ap, it *remains true* that K_ap:

$$L, 1 \models [K_ap]K_ap$$

This is, because in L the formula K_ap is true in state 1 only, so that the model $L|K_ap$ consists of the singleton state 1, with reflexive access for a and b. It also becomes common knowledge that Anne knows p: we have

$$L, 1 \models [K_ap]C_{ab}K_ap$$

and a fortiori

$$L, 1 \models K_ap \to [K_ap]C_{ab}K_ap$$

Indeed, this formula can easily be shown to be valid

$$\models K_ap \to [K_ap]C_{ab}K_ap$$

Instead, in epistemic state $(L, 1)$ Anne could have said to Bill, just as in Example 4.1: "You don't know that United Agents is doing well". Using the conversational implicature that that fact is true, this is an announcement of $K_a(p \land \neg K_bp)$. (This time we express explicitly that Anne knows what she

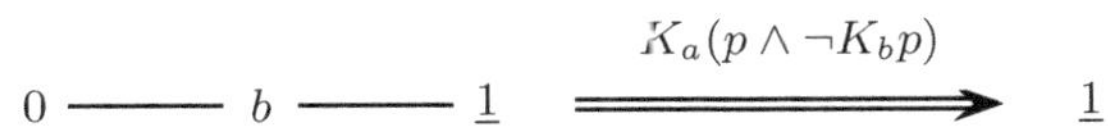

Figure 4.6. A simple unsuccessful update: Anne says to Bill "(p is true and) you don't know that p."

says—the result is the same as for $p \wedge \neg K_b p$.) It also only succeeds in state 1. After it, Bill knows that p, from $K_b p$ follows $\neg p \vee K_b p$, which is equivalent to $\neg(p \wedge \neg K_b p)$, therefore $K_a(p \wedge \neg K_b p)$ is *no longer* true

$$L, 1 \models [K_a(p \wedge \neg K_b p)]\neg K_a(p \wedge \neg K_b p)$$

and so it is certainly not commonly known, so that

$$\not\models K_a(p \wedge \neg K_b p) \rightarrow [K_a(p \wedge \neg K_b p)]C_{ab}K_a(p \wedge \neg K_b p)$$

The epistemic state transition induced by this update is visualised (once more) in Figure 4.6.

Incidentally, $[K_a(p \wedge \neg K_b p)]\neg K_a(p \wedge \neg K_b p)$ is even valid, but that seems to be less essential than that we have found an epistemic state $(L, 1)$ wherein the formula $K_a(p \wedge \neg K_b p)$ is true and becomes false after its announcement.

Definition 4.31 (Successful and unsuccessful formulas and updates) Given a formula $\varphi \in \mathcal{L}_{KC[]}$ and an epistemic state (M, s) with $M \in \mathcal{S}5$.

- φ is a *successful formula* iff $[\varphi]\varphi$ is valid.
- φ is an *unsuccessful formula* iff it is not successful.
- φ is a *successful update* in (M, s) if $M, s \models \langle\varphi\rangle\varphi$
- φ is an *unsuccessful update* in (M, s) iff $M, s \models \langle\varphi\rangle\neg\varphi$

In the definitions, the switch between the 'box' and the 'diamond' versions of announcement may puzzle the reader. In the definition of a successful *formula* we really need the 'box'-form: clearly $\langle\varphi\rangle\varphi$ is invalid for all φ except tautologies. But in the definition of a successful *update* we really need the 'diamond'-form: clearly, whenever the announcement formula is false in an epistemic state, $[\varphi]\neg\varphi$ would therefore be true. That would not capture the intuitive meaning of an unsuccessful update, because that is formally represented as a feature of an epistemic state transition. We must therefore assume that the announcement formula can indeed be truthfully announced.

Updates with true successful formulas are always successful, but sometimes updates with unsuccessful formulas are successful. By 'always' ('sometimes') we mean 'in all (some) epistemic states'. The truth of the first will be obvious: if a successful formula φ is true in an epistemic state (M, s), then $\varphi \wedge [\varphi]\varphi$ which is equivalent to $\langle\varphi\rangle\varphi$ is also true in that state, so it is also a successful update. One can actually distinguish different degrees of 'success', that also nicely match somewhat tentative distinctions made in the literature. For example, one can say that φ is *individually unsuccessful* in (M, s) iff $M, s \models \langle\varphi\rangle K_a\neg\varphi$.

The following Proposition states that at least for validities such distinctions do not matter. It is an instance of Corollary 4.28 for $B = A$ and $\psi = \varphi$.

Proposition 4.32 Let $\varphi \in \mathcal{L}_{KC[]}$. Then $[\varphi]\varphi$ is valid if and only if $[\varphi]C_A\varphi$ is valid. □

However, note that $[\varphi]\varphi$ is *not* logically equivalent to $[\varphi]C_A\varphi$. Using Proposition 4.13 that states the logical equivalence of $[\varphi]\psi$ and $\varphi \rightarrow [\varphi]\psi$ we further obtain that.

Proposition 4.33 $[\varphi]\varphi$ is valid if and only if $\varphi \rightarrow [\varphi]C_A\varphi$ is valid. □

This makes precise that the successful formulas 'do what we want them to do': if true, they become common knowledge when announced.

It is not clear what fragment of the logical language consists of the successful formulas. There is no obvious inductive definition. When φ and ψ are successful, $\neg\varphi$, $\varphi \wedge \psi$, $\varphi \rightarrow \psi$, or $[\varphi]\psi$ may be unsuccessful.

Example 4.34 Formula $p \wedge \neg K_a p$ is unsuccessful, but both p and $\neg K_a p$ are successful. This can be shown as follows:

For p it is trivial. For $\neg K_a p$ it is not. Let M, s be arbitrary. We have to prove that $M, s \models [\neg K_a p]\neg K_a p$, in other words, that $M, s \models \neg K_a p$ implies $M|\neg K_a p, s \models \neg K_a p$. Let $M, s \models \neg K_a p$. Then there must be a $t \sim_a s$ such that $M, t \models \neg p$, and therefore also $M, t \models \neg K_a p$, and therefore $t \in M|\neg K_a p$. From $s \sim_a t$ in $M|\neg K_a p$ and $M|\neg K_a p, t \models \neg p$ follows $M|\neg K_a p, s \models \neg K_a p$.□

Exercise 4.35 Give a formula φ such that φ is successful but $\neg\varphi$ is not successful. Give formulas φ, ψ such that φ and ψ are successful but $\varphi \rightarrow \psi$ is not successful. Give formulas φ, ψ such that φ and ψ are successful but $[\varphi]\psi$ is not successful. □

There are some results concerning successful fragments. First, *public knowledge formulas* are successful:

Proposition 4.36 (Public knowledge updates are successful) Let $\varphi \in \mathcal{L}_{KC[]}(A, P)$. Then $[C_A\varphi]C_A\varphi$ is valid. □

Proof Let $M = \langle S, \sim, V\rangle$ and $s \in S$ be arbitrary. The set $[s]_{\sim_A}$ denotes the $\sim_A$-equivalence class of s—below, we write $M|[s]_{\sim_A}$ for the model restriction of M to $[s]_{\sim_A}$.

We first show that, for arbitrary ψ: $M, s \models \psi$ iff $M|[s]_{\sim_A}, s \models \psi$ (1). We then show that, if $M, s \models C_A\varphi$, then $[s]_{\sim_A} \subseteq [\![C_A\varphi]\!]_M$ (2). Together, it follows that $M, s \models C_A\varphi$ iff $M|[s]_{\sim_A}, s \models C_A\varphi$, and that $M|[s]_{\sim_A}, s \models C_A\varphi$ implies $M|C_A\varphi, s \models C_A\varphi$. By definition, "$M, s \models C_A\varphi$ implies $M|C_A\varphi, s \models C_A\varphi$" equals $M, s \models [C_A\varphi]C_A\varphi$.

(1) Observe that M is bisimilar to $M|[s]_{\sim_A}$ via the bisimulation relation $\mathfrak{R} \subseteq [s]_{\sim_A} \times S$ defined as $(t, t) \in \mathfrak{R}$ for all $t \in [s]_{\sim_A}$. Subject to this bisimulation, we have that $(M, s) \leftrightarroweq (M|[s]_{\sim_A}, s)$. This is merely a special case of invariance under generated submodel constructions.

(2) Assume that $M, s \models C_A\varphi$. Let $s \sim_A t$. Using the validity $C_A\varphi \rightarrow C_AC_A\varphi$, we also have $M, t \models C_A\varphi$. In other words: $[s]_{\sim_A} \subseteq [\![C_A\varphi]\!]_M$. □

Although $[C_A\varphi]C_A\varphi$ is valid, this is not the case for arbitrary $B \subseteq A$. Consider the standard example $(L, 1)$ where Anne can distinguish between p and $\neg p$ but Bill cannot. We then have that $[C_B\varphi]C_B\varphi$ is false in this model for $B = \{a\}$ and $\varphi = p \wedge \neg K_b p$.

By announcing a public knowledge formula, no accessible states are deleted from the model. Obviously the truth of formulas can only change by an announcement if their truth value depends on states that are deleted by the announcement. We will now show that formulas from the following fragment $\mathcal{L}^0_{KC[]}(A, P)$ (of the logical language $\mathcal{L}_{KC[]}(A, P)$) of the *preserved formulas*, with inductive definition

$$\varphi ::= p \mid \neg p \mid \varphi \wedge \varphi \mid \varphi \vee \varphi \mid K_a\varphi \mid C_B\varphi \mid [\neg\varphi]\varphi$$

are truth preserving under 'deleting states'. From this, it then follows that the fragment is successful. Instead of 'deleting states', we say that we restrict ourselves to a *submodel* : a restriction of a model to a subset of the domain, with the obvious restriction of access and valuation to that subset.

Proposition 4.37 (Preservation) Fragment $\mathcal{L}^0_{KC[]}(A, P)$ is preserved under submodels. □

Proof By induction on $\mathcal{L}^0_{KC[]}(A, P)$. The case for propositional variables, conjunction, and disjunction is straightforward.

Let $M = \langle S, \sim, V\rangle$ be given and let $M' = \langle S', \sim', V'\rangle$ be a submodel of it. Suppose $s \in S'$. Suppose $M, s \models K_a\varphi$. Let $s' \in S'$ and $s \sim_a s'$. Then $M, s' \models \varphi$. Therefore, by the induction hypothesis, $M', s' \models \varphi$. Therefore $M', s \models K_a\varphi$. The case for $C_B\varphi$ is analogous.

Suppose $M, s \models [\neg\varphi]\psi$. Suppose, towards a contradiction, that $M', s \not\models [\neg\varphi]\psi$. Therefore, by the semantics, $M', s \models \neg\varphi$ and $M'|\neg\varphi, s \not\models \psi$. Therefore, by using the contrapositive of the induction hypothesis, also $M, s \models \neg\varphi$. Moreover $M'|\neg\varphi$ is a submodel of $M|\neg\varphi$, because a state $t \in S'$ only survives if $M', t \models \neg\varphi$, therefore by the induction hypothesis $M, t \models \neg\varphi$. So $[\![\neg\varphi]\!]_{M'} \subseteq [\![\neg\varphi]\!]_M$. But from $M, s \models [\neg\varphi]\psi$ (which we assumed) and $M, s \models \neg\varphi$ follows $M|\neg\varphi, s \models \psi$, therefore by the induction hypothesis also $M'|\neg\varphi, s \models \psi$. This contradicts our earlier assumption. Therefore $M', s \models [\neg\varphi]\psi$. □

Corollary 4.38 Let $\varphi \in \mathcal{L}^0_{KC[]}(A, P)$ and $\psi \in \mathcal{L}_{KC[]}(A, P)$. Then $\varphi \rightarrow [\psi]\varphi$ is valid. □

This follows immediately from Proposition 4.37, because restriction to ψ-states is a restriction to a submodel.

Corollary 4.39 Let $\varphi \in \mathcal{L}^0_{KC[]}(A, P)$. Then $\varphi \rightarrow [\varphi]\varphi$ is valid. □

In particular, restriction to the φ-states themselves is a restriction to a submodel.

Corollary 4.40 (Preserved formulas are successful)
Let $\varphi \in \mathcal{L}^0_{KC[]}(A, P)$. Then $[\varphi]\varphi$ is valid. □

This follows from Corollary 4.39 and Proposition 4.13.

Some successful formulas are not preserved, such as $\neg K_a p$, see above. There are more successful than preserved formulas, because the entailed requirement that $\varphi \rightarrow [\psi]\varphi$ is valid *for arbitrary* ψ is much stronger than the requirement that $\varphi \rightarrow [\varphi]\varphi$ is valid. In the last case we are only looking at the very specific submodel resulting from the announcement of *that* formula, not at arbitrary submodels.

A last 'partial' result states the obvious that

Proposition 4.41 Inconsistent formulas are successful. □

Exercise 4.42 In $(\mathit{Hexa}, 012)$, Anne says to Bill: "(I hold card 0 and) You don't know that I hold card 0". Show that this is an unsuccessful update. In the resulting epistemic state Bill says to Anne: "But (I hold card 1 and) you don't know that I hold card 1". Show that that is also an unsuccessful update. □

Exercise 4.43 In $(\mathit{Hexa}, 012)$, an outsider says to the players: "It is general but not common knowledge that neither 201 nor 120 is the actual deal." Show that this is an unsuccessful update. □

4.8 Axiomatisation

We present both a Hilbert-style axiomatisation **PA** for the logic *PA* of public announcements without common knowledge operators, and an extension **PAC** of that axiomatisation for the logic *PAC* of public announcements (with common knowledge operators). For the basic definitions and an introduction in axiomatisations, see Chapter 2.

4.8.1 Public Announcement Logic without Common Knowledge

Definition 4.44 (Axiomatisation PA)
Given are a set of agents A and a set of atoms P, as usual. Table 4.1 presents the axiomatisation **PA** (or **PA**(A, P), over the language $\mathcal{L}_{K[]}(A, P)$); $a \in A$ and $p \in P$. □

Example 4.45 We show in **PA** that $\vdash [p]K_a p$. By the justification 'propositional' we mean that the step requires (one or more) tautologies and applications of modus ponens—and that we therefore refrain from showing that in cumbersome detail.

all instantiations of propositional tautologies	
$K_a(\varphi \to \psi) \to (K_a\varphi \to K_a\psi)$	distribution of K_a over $\to$
$K_a\varphi \to \varphi$	truth
$K_a\varphi \to K_aK_a\varphi$	positive introspection
$\neg K_a\varphi \to K_a\neg K_a\varphi$	negative introspection
$[\varphi]p \leftrightarrow (\varphi \to p)$	atomic permanence
$[\varphi]\neg\psi \leftrightarrow (\varphi \to \neg[\varphi]\psi)$	announcement and negation
$[\varphi](\psi \wedge \chi) \leftrightarrow ([\varphi]\psi \wedge [\varphi]\chi)$	announcement and conjunction
$[\varphi]K_a\psi \leftrightarrow (\varphi \to K_a[\varphi]\psi)$	announcement and knowledge
$[\varphi][\psi]\chi \leftrightarrow [\varphi \wedge [\varphi]\psi]\chi$	announcement composition
From φ and $\varphi \to \psi$, infer ψ	modus ponens
From φ, infer $K_a\varphi$	necessitation of K_a

Table 4.1. The axiomatisation **PA**.

1	$p \to p$	tautology
2	$[p]p \leftrightarrow (p \to p)$	atomic permanence
3	$[p]p$	1,2, propositional
4	$K_a[p]p$	3, necessitation
5	$p \to K_a[p]p$	4, propositional
6	$[p]K_ap \leftrightarrow (p \to K_a[p]p)$	announcement and knowledge
7	$[p]K_ap$	5,6, propositional

□

The following proposition lists some desirable properties of the axiomatisation—the proofs are left as an exercise to the reader.

Proposition 4.46 Some properties of **PA** are:

1. *Substitution of equals*
   If $\vdash \psi \leftrightarrow \chi$, then $\vdash \varphi(p/\psi) \leftrightarrow \varphi(p/\chi)$.
2. *Partial functionality*
   $\vdash (\varphi \to [\varphi]\psi) \leftrightarrow [\varphi]\psi$
3. *Public announcement and implication*
   $\vdash [\varphi](\psi \to \chi) \leftrightarrow ([\varphi]\psi \to [\varphi]\chi)$ □

Exercise 4.47 Prove that the schema $\langle\varphi\rangle\psi \to [\varphi]\psi$ is derivable in **PA**. (This is easy.) □

Exercise 4.48 Prove Proposition 4.46.1. (Use induction on the formula φ.) □

Exercise 4.49 Prove Proposition 4.46.2. (Use induction on the formula ψ. It requires frequent applications of Proposition 4.46.1.) □

Exercise 4.50 Prove Proposition 4.46.3. (Use the equivalence 'by definition' of $\varphi \to \psi$ and $\neg(\varphi \wedge \neg\psi)$.) □

Theorem 4.51 The axiomatisation **PA**(A, P) is sound and complete. □

To prove soundness and completeness of the axiomatisation **PA** for the logic *PA*, we need to show that for arbitrary formulas $\varphi \in \mathcal{L}_{K[]}$: $\models \varphi$ iff $\vdash \varphi$. The soundness of all axioms involving announcements was already established in previous sections. The soundness of the derivation rule 'necessitation of announcement' is left as an exercise to the reader. The completeness of this axiomatisation is shown in Chapter 7.

Exercise 4.52 Prove that the derivation rule 'necessitation of announcement', "from φ follows $[\psi]\varphi$", is sound. □

4.8.2 Public Announcement Logic

The axiomatisation for public announcement logic *PAC* with common knowledge is more complex than that for public announcement logic *PA* without common knowledge. The axiomatisation **PAC** (over the language $\mathcal{L}_{KC[]}$) consists of **PA** plus additional axioms and rules involving common knowledge. For the convenience of the reader, we present the axiomatisation in its entirety. The additional rules and axioms are at the end. In these rules and axioms, $B \subseteq A$.

Definition 4.53 (Axiomatisation PAC)
The axiomatisation **PAC** (or **PAC**(A, P)) is defined in Table 4.2. □

all instantiations of propositional tautologies	
$K_a(\varphi \to \psi) \to (K_a\varphi \to K_a\psi)$	distribution of K_a over $\to$
$K_a\varphi \to \varphi$	truth
$K_a\varphi \to K_aK_a\varphi$	positive introspection
$\neg K_a\varphi \to K_a\neg K_a\varphi$	negative introspection
$[\varphi]p \leftrightarrow (\varphi \to p)$	atomic permanence
$[\varphi]\neg\psi \leftrightarrow (\varphi \to \neg[\varphi]\psi)$	announcement and negation
$[\varphi](\psi \wedge \chi) \leftrightarrow ([\varphi]\psi \wedge [\varphi]\chi)$	announcement and conjunction
$[\varphi]K_a\psi \leftrightarrow (\varphi \to K_a[\varphi]\psi)$	announcement and knowledge
$[\varphi][\psi]\chi \leftrightarrow [\varphi \wedge [\varphi]\psi]\chi$	announcement composition
$C_B(\varphi \to \psi) \to (C_B\varphi \to C_B\psi)$	distribution of C_B over $\to$
$C_B\varphi \to (\varphi \wedge E_BC_B\varphi)$	mix of common knowledge
$C_B(\varphi \to E_B\varphi) \to (\varphi \to C_B\varphi)$	induction of common knowledge
From φ and $\varphi \to \psi$, infer ψ	modus ponens
From φ, infer $K_a\varphi$	necessitation of K_a
From φ, infer $C_B\varphi$	necessitation of C_B
From φ, infer $[\psi]\varphi$	necessitation of $[\psi]$
From $\chi \to [\varphi]\psi$ and $\chi \wedge \varphi \to E_B\chi$, infer $\chi \to [\varphi]C_B\psi$	announcement and common knowledge

Table 4.2. The axiomatisation **PAC**.

The induction axiom was already part of the axiomatisation **S5C** for the logic $S5C$. Induction is derivable from **PAC** *minus* that axiom (see Exercise 4.55), but because we prefer to see **PAC** as an *extension* of **S5C**, we have retained it in **PAC**. We continue with an example derivation in **PAC**.

Example 4.54 After the announcement that some atomic proposition is false, this is commonly known. Formally: $\vdash [\neg p]C_A\neg p$.

1. $\neg p \rightarrow \neg(\neg p \rightarrow p)$	tautology
2. $[\neg p]p \leftrightarrow (\neg p \rightarrow p)$	atomic permanence
3. $\neg p \rightarrow \neg[\neg p]p$	1,2, propositional
4. $[\neg p]\neg p \leftrightarrow (\neg p \rightarrow \neg[\neg p]p)$	announcement and negation
5. $[\neg p]\neg p$	3, 4, propositional
6. $\top \rightarrow [\neg p]\neg p$	5, propositional (weakening)
7. $\top$	tautology
8. $K_a\top$	7, necessitation
9. $\top \wedge \neg p \rightarrow K_a\top$	8, propositional (weakening)
10. $\top \wedge \neg p \rightarrow E_A\top$	9 for all $a \in A$, propositional
11. $\top \rightarrow [\neg p]C_A\neg p$	10, 6, announcement and common knowledge
12. $[\neg p]C_A\neg p$	11, propositional □

Exercise 4.55 Show that 'induction', $C_B(\varphi \rightarrow E_B\varphi) \rightarrow \varphi \rightarrow C_B\varphi$, is derivable in **PAC** *without* induction. □

Exercise 4.56 Show that $[C_A\varphi]C_A\varphi$ is derivable in **PAC**. (Use induction on φ.) □

Proposition 4.46 also holds for **PAC**. This requires one more inductive case in the proofs of items 1 and 2, respectively, of the Proposition. We leave it as an exercise.

Exercise 4.57 Prove the generalisations of Proposition 4.46. □

Exercise 4.58 Show that $\vdash [\varphi]\psi$ iff $\vdash [\varphi]C_B\psi$. □

Theorem 4.59 The axiomatisation **PAC**(A, P) is sound and complete. □

For soundness it only remains to show that rule 'announcement and common knowledge' is validity preserving. This was already done in Proposition 4.26. A detailed completeness proof for **PAC** is found in Chapter 7.

4.9 Knowledge and Belief

There are alternative semantics for announcements if they may be not truthful or not public. The treatment of private and other non-public announcements is complex and will also receive attention in the coming chapters. For now,

Figure 4.7. A weaker form of announcement.

suppose announcements are not necessarily truthful, but merely that they are believed (to be true) by all agents. From an observer's or meta-perspective we then have no reason to remove any states from the domain where the announcement is false. But your average gullible agent 'of course' accepts the announcement as the truth: whatever the state of the world, after the announcement the agent should believe that it *was* true. This can be achieved if we generalise our perspective from that of models where all accessibility relations are equivalence relations to that of arbitrary accessibility relations. As in previous chapters whenever we had a more general modal perspective, we therefore write $R(s,t)$ instead of $s \sim t$. The result of an announcement is now, unlike above, that the domain of the epistemic state remains unchanged, and that for every state and for every agent, any state where the announcement is true and that is accessible from that state for that agent, remains accessible. Technically—let R' be access in the resulting epistemic state:

$$R'(s,t) \quad \text{iff} \quad (\ R(s,t) \text{ and } M,t \models \varphi\ )$$

In Example 4.1, where Anne tells Bill the result of the United Agents stocks, this would lead to the transition in Figure 4.7.

Note that in this case, where the actual state is 1, both agents still end up commonly believing that p. If 0 had been the actual state, we would have to assume that Anne was falsely informed in the letter that she received, and that she did not even consider that possibility (nor Bill). Or, alternatively, that the announcement was not by Anne to Bill ("You do not know that United Agents is doing well") but by an outsider to both: "Bill does not know that United Agents is doing well". This semantics for public announcement is suitable for the *introspective* agents introduced in Chapter 2. The corresponding reduction axiom for 'introspective announcement' is—it is of course more proper to write B_a instead of K_a here

$$[\varphi]B_a\psi \leftrightarrow B_a(\varphi \to [\varphi]\psi)$$

Now compare this with the reduction axiom for *truthful* announcement

$$[\varphi]K_a\psi \leftrightarrow (\varphi \to K_a[\varphi]\psi)$$

of Section 4.5! Note that the latter can *not* be seen as a special case of the former, namely for knowledge, because the semantics of truthful announcement is different from the semantics of introspective announcement.

The remaining sections present logical puzzles in detail.

4.10 Muddy Children

Example 4.60 (Muddy Children) A group of children has been playing outside and are called back into the house by their father. The children gather round him. As one may imagine, some of them have become dirty from the play and in particular: they may have mud on their forehead. Children can only see whether other children are muddy, and not if there is any mud on their own forehead. All this is commonly known, and the children are, obviously, perfect logicians. Father now says: "At least one of you has mud on his or her forehead." And then: "Will those who know whether they are muddy please step forward." If nobody steps forward, father keeps repeating the request. Prove that, if m of n children are muddy, the muddy children will step forward after father has made his request m times. □

The Muddy Children puzzle is a classic example of unsuccessful updates: from the 'announcement' that nobody knows whether he or she is muddy, the muddy children may learn that they are muddy. Of course, 'not stepping forward' is not a public announcement in the sense of an utterance. It is more a 'public truthful *event*'. That merely reveals the true nature of the dynamic objects we are considering: information changing actions. Father's request to step forward—that is an utterance but *not* an information changing announcement—should be seen as the facilitator of that event, or as a signal synchronising the information change.

To give the general idea of the analysis using public announcement logic, we look at the special case of three children Anne, Bill, and Cath (a, b, and c). Suppose that Anne and Bill are muddy, and that Cath is not muddy. After two requests from Father the muddy children know that they are muddy and will step forward. Informally their knowledge can be explained as follows.

Suppose you are Anne. Then you see that Bill is muddy and Cath is not. Now Father says that at least one child is muddy. Now if you were *not* muddy, Bill cannot see anyone who is muddy, and therefore he would infer that he is muddy. Father now asks those children who know whether they are muddy to step forward, and none step forward. You conclude that Bill did not know that he was muddy. Therefore, the tentative hypothesis that you are not muddy is incorrect, and as there are only two possibilities, you must therefore be muddy yourself. Therefore, the next time the father asks you to step forward if you know whether you are muddy, you step forward.

The situation is the same for Bill. Therefore he steps forward too after the second request.

We can represent the initial situation of the (three) muddy children problem with a cube. Each of the three children can be muddy or not. For this we introduce three atomic propositions m_a, m_b, m_c. Therefore there are eight possible states. We call the model for three children *Cube*. See the top-left corner of Figure 4.8. The states are labelled xyz, where $x, y, z \in \{0, 1\}$, where

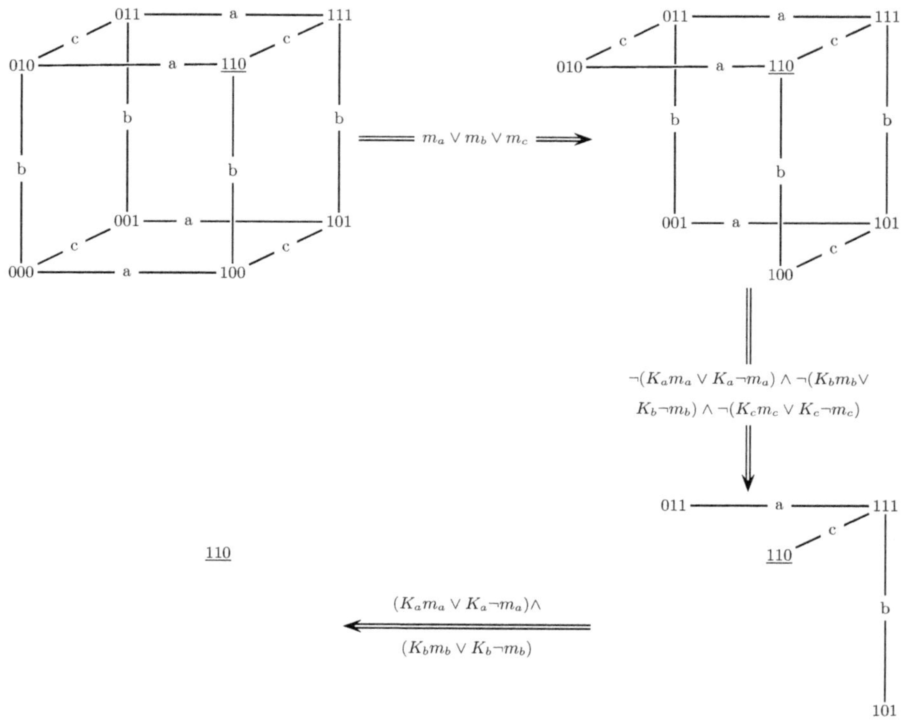

Figure 4.8. The top-left corner depicts the epistemic state where Anne and Bill are muddy, and Cath is not. The first transition depicts the effect of the announcement that at least one child is muddy. The second transition depicts the effect of no child stepping forward, i.e., an announcement that nobody knows whether (s)he is muddy. This is an unsuccessful update. The last transition depicts the result of Anne and Bill stepping forward, because they both know whether (that) they are muddy.

$x = 1$ means that Anne is muddy, and $y = 0$ means that Bill is not muddy, etc. In state 110, for instance, a and b are muddy, but c is not. Let us assume that 110 is the actual state. Although it is the case in 110 that everybody knows there is at least one muddy child this is *not* common knowledge. For example, a considers it possible that b considers it possible that no child is muddy. Formally, we have that $\mathit{Cube}, 110 \models E_{abc}(m_1 \vee m_2 \vee m_3)$, but that $\mathit{Cube}, 110 \models \neg C_{abc}(m_1 \vee m_2 \vee m_3)$, because $110 \sim_a 010 \sim_b 000$ and $\mathit{Cube}, 000 \models \neg(m_1 \vee m_2 \vee m_3)$.

Father's announcement that at least one of the children is muddy is an announcement of the formula $m_a \vee m_b \vee m_c$. Let us abbreviate this formula with muddy:

$$\mathsf{muddy} = m_1 \vee m_2 \vee m_3$$

The formula muddy is false in the state 000, therefore by the semantics of public announcements we get a new model where this state has been eliminated, and the accessibility relations are adapted accordingly. See the top-right corner of Figure 4.8. One can simply check that $\mathit{Cube}|\mathsf{muddy}, 110 \models C_{abc}\mathsf{muddy}$. Therefore this is a successful update in $(\mathit{Cube}, 110)$. After the announcement that at least one child is muddy, at least one child is muddy.

The epistemic state we have thus acquired, has a special feature. When one focuses on the states where exactly one child is muddy, one sees that each of these states is indistinguishable from another state for only two of the children. That means that one child knows what the actual state would be if there were only one muddy child. In particular, the child who knows what the actual state would be, knows it is muddy. For instance:

$$\mathit{Cube}|\mathsf{muddy}, 100 \models K_a m_a$$

Now the father asks those children who know whether they are muddy to step forward. When no one steps forward, this means that no child knows whether it is muddy. The formula that expresses that at least one child knows whether it is muddy, is $\mathsf{knowmuddy}$ (unlike 'knowing that φ', $K\varphi$, 'knowing whether φ' is described by $K\varphi \vee K\neg\varphi$).

$$\mathsf{knowmuddy} = (K_a m_a \vee K_a \neg m_a) \vee (K_b m_b \vee K_b \neg m_b) \vee (K_c m_c \vee K_c \neg m_c)$$

When none of the children step forward, this corresponds to the 'announcement' of $\neg\mathsf{knowmuddy}$. Consequently, those states where exactly one child is muddy are eliminated by this announcement. We get the bottom-right epistemic state shown in Figure 4.8.

The announcement that none of the children know whether they are muddy yields a situation where Anne and Bill know that they are muddy. Before the announcement, Anne knows that if she is not muddy, then Bill learns that he is muddy, and Bill knows that if he is not muddy, then Anne learns that she is muddy. By observing that none of the children know, Anne and Bill can infer that they must be muddy themselves. From $K_b m_b$ follows $K_b m_b \vee K_b \neg m_b$, from which follows $\mathsf{knowmuddy}$. Therefore $\neg\mathsf{knowmuddy}$ is false, therefore $\neg\mathsf{knowmuddy}$ is an unsuccessful update in $(\mathit{Cube}|\mathsf{muddy}, 110)$. :

$$\mathit{Cube}|\mathsf{muddy}, 110 \models \langle\neg\mathsf{knowmuddy}\rangle\mathsf{knowmuddy}$$

In the epistemic state $(\mathit{Cube}|\mathsf{muddy}|\neg\mathsf{knowmuddy}, 110)$ it is not merely the case that $\mathsf{knowmuddy}$ is true (at least one of Anne, Bill, and Cath know whether they are muddy), but Anne and Bill both know whether they are muddy (because they both know *that* they are muddy). The transition induced by this 'announcement' of $(K_a m_a \vee K_a \neg m_a) \wedge (K_b m_b \vee K_b \neg m_b)$ results in the model in the bottom-left corner of Figure 4.8. In this singleton epistemic state there is full knowledge of the state of the world.

If all three children had been muddy, $\neg\mathsf{knowmuddy}$ would have been a *successful* update in epistemic state $(\mathit{Cube}|\mathsf{muddy}, 111)$:

$$\mathit{Cube}|\mathsf{muddy}, 111 \models \langle\neg\mathsf{knowmuddy}\rangle\neg\mathsf{knowmuddy}$$

This is because in that state of the model, even at the bottom-right of Figure 4.8, every child still considers it possible that it is not muddy. Of course, in that case father's third request reveals an unsuccessful update:

$$Cube|\mathsf{muddy}|\neg\mathsf{knowmuddy}, 111 \models \langle\neg\mathsf{knowmuddy}\rangle\mathsf{knowmuddy}$$

Exercise 4.61 Prove that for the general situation of n children of which m are muddy, after m requests of father asking the muddy children to step forward, the muddy children will step forward. □

Exercise 4.62 Suppose Father's first utterance was not 'At least one of you is muddy' but 'Anne is muddy'. What will now happen after Father's request, and after his repeated request? □

4.11 Sum and Product

Example 4.63 (Sum and Product) *A says to S and P: "I have chosen two natural numbers x and y such that $1 < x < y$ and $x + y \leq 100$. I am now going to announce their sum $s = x + y$ to S only, and their product $p = x \cdot y$ to P only. The content of these announcements remains a secret." He acts accordingly. The following conversation between S and P then takes place:*

1. *P says: "I don't know the numbers."*
2. *S: "I knew that."*
3. *P: "Now I know the numbers."*
4. *S: "Now I know them too."*

Determine the numbers x and y. □

Without giving away the solution, we will make some remarks about the problem from a semantic epistemic viewpoint. It is clear that the puzzle can be solved by starting with an epistemic model consisting of points (x, y) with $2 \leq x < y \leq 98$. The two accessibility relations are quite obvious as well:

$$\begin{array}{lll}(x,y) \sim_S (x',y') & \text{iff} & x + y = x' + y' \\ (x,y) \sim_P (x',y') & \text{iff} & x \cdot y = x' \cdot y'\end{array}$$

Now, according to the first statement by P, we may remove all points that are only $\sim_P$-accessible to themselves; and the answer by S allows us to remove all points—in the original model—that are $\sim_S$-accessible to such points that are only $\sim_P$-accessible to themselves. Continuing like this, the one possible answer is derived.

Interestingly enough, if the lower and/or upper bounds of the numbers x and y are relaxed, it may not be the case anymore that there is a single possible answer. It is even so, that other pairs (x, y) with $2 \leq x < y \leq 98$

may then give rise to the first two lines in the conversation above. Worse than that, for some other bounds on these numbers there is again a unique solution in the 2–98 range—so the same conversation may take place—but one that is different from the solution when it is known at the outset that $2 \leq x < y \leq 98$.

For a modelling in public announcement logic, let x and y stay as well for the atomic propositions 'the first number is x' and 'the second number is y' respectively. We then have that 'S knows the numbers' is described by the formula $\bigwedge_{2\leq x<y\leq 98}((x \wedge y) \rightarrow K_S(x \wedge y))$, and '$P$ knows the numbers' by $\bigwedge_{2\leq x<y\leq 98}((x \wedge y) \rightarrow K_P(x \wedge y))$.

Another interesting consideration is to determine which points are reachable ($\{S, P\}$-accessible) from each other for the epistemic models modelling the stages in the conversation. This allows one to compute the common knowledge among S and P at any stage. For the first moment described in the puzzle, just before the conversation starts, all points (x, y) with $x + y \geq 7$ are reachable from each other. As there are no solutions for $x + y < 7$ (try it!), this means that at the starting point of the problem, even if the two agents have quite strong distributed knowledge, only one thing is common knowledge, namely that $x + y \geq 7$.

Exercise 4.64 Determine the unique solution of the 'Sum and Product'-problem, for the given bounds. □

Exercise 4.65 Describe all four announcements in public announcement logic. □

Exercise 4.66 Show that announcement 2 is an unsuccessful update. Show that the sequence of all four announcements, when seen as a single announcement by using composition, is an unsuccessful update. □

4.12 Russian Cards

Example 4.67 From a pack of seven known cards $0, 1, 2, 3, 4, 5, 6$ Anne and Bill each draw three cards and Cath gets the remaining card. How can Anne and Bill openly inform each other about their cards, without Cath learning for any of their cards who holds it?

Without loss of generality, suppose that Anne draws $\{0, 1, 2\}$, that Bill draws $\{3, 4, 5\}$, and Cath 6. Any sequence of public announcements is allowed. □

All announcements must be public and truthful. First, consider what Anne may and may not say. Suppose she says "I have 0 or 5". Anne cannot distinguish that announcement from "I have 0 or 6". From that, Cath would learn that Anne has 0. Lost. So Anne is not likely to say that.

Suppose, instead, Anne says "I have 0 or 1 or 5". Cath can have at most one of these three cards. Therefore she remains uncertain about the ownership of the other two. But how to continue? And can we explore such statements systematically? Because she might as well have said something like "I have 0 or 1 or two out of 2, 3, 4, and if I hold 6 then Bill holds 4 or 5, unless ..."

First, a word on the structures underlying our reasoning about this problem. Given a stack of known cards and some players, the players blindly draw some cards from the stack. In a state where cards are dealt in that way, but where no game actions of whatever kind have been done, it is commonly known what the cards are, that they are all different, how many cards each player holds, and that players only know their own cards. From the last it follows that two deals are *the same for an agent*, if he holds the same cards in both, and if all players hold the same number of cards in both. This induces an equivalence relation on deals. In model *Hexa* from Example 4.2 each player gets a single card. Now, two players have three cards instead.

The general perspective is a *card deal* d that we see as a function that assigns *cards* Q to *players* (*agents*) A. The *size* $\sharp d$ of a deal of cards d lists for each player how many cards he holds. Two deals $d, e \in (Q \to A)$ are indistinguishable ('the same') for a player $a \in A$ if $\sharp d = \sharp e$ and $d^{-1}(a) = e^{-1}(a)$. For the deal where Anne holds $0, 1, 2$, Bill holds $3, 4, 5$, and Cath holds 6, we informally write 012.345.6, etc.

For a given deal d, an epistemic state represents the knowledge that players have about each other, specifically, that the players *only* know their own cards. Its domain consists of all deals where the players hold the same number of cards as in d, i.e., all deals of size $\sharp d$. The accessibility relations for the players are of course precisely those induced by the indistinguishability between deals given above. Facts about card ownership are written as q_a for 'card q is held by player a'. The valuation of a state in the domain corresponds to the card deal that the state stands for, $d \in V_{q_a}$ iff player a holds card q in deal d.

The specific epistemic model for the deal 012.345.6 that we investigate we call *Russian*, so that epistemic state $(Russian, 012.345.6)$ formally encodes the knowledge of the players Anne, Bill and Cath (a, b, c) in this card deal. It consists of $\binom{7}{3}\binom{4}{3}\binom{1}{1} = 140$ deals. The description δ^d of card deal d sums up the valuation, e.g.,

$$\delta^{012.345.6} = 0_a \wedge 1_a \wedge 2_a \wedge \neg 3_a \wedge ... \wedge \neg 0_b \wedge ... \wedge \neg 5_c \wedge 6_c$$

The description δ^d_a of the hand of player a is the restriction of the description of the deal to all atoms 'about that player', e.g., Anne's hand $\{0, 1, 2\}$ is described by

$$\delta_a^{012.345.6} = 0_a \wedge 1_a \wedge 2_a \wedge \neg 3_a \wedge \neg 4_a \wedge \neg 5_a \wedge \neg 6_a$$

For $\delta_a^{012.345.6}$ we also write 012_a, etc. Some typical formulas satisfied in the epistemic state $(Russian, 012.345.6)$ are: $K_a 0_a$ for: 'Anne knows that she holds card 0'; $K_b \neg K_a 3_b$ for: 'Bill knows that Anne doesn't know that he holds card 3'; and $C_{abc} \bigvee_{d \in \mathcal{D}(Russian)} K_a \delta_a^d$ for: 'it is common knowledge that Anne knows her own hand of cards'.

After a sequence of announcements that is a solution of the Russian Cards problem, it should hold that Anne knows Bill's cards, Bill knows Anne's cards, and Cath does not know any of Anne's or Bill's cards. So, at first sight, the following postconditions are sufficient:

Definition 4.68 Given a card deal d, in the epistemic state (D, d) where the problem is solved it must hold that:

$$\begin{array}{l} \mathsf{aknowsbs} = \bigwedge_{e \in \mathcal{D}(D)} (\delta_b^e \rightarrow K_a \delta_b^e) \\ \mathsf{bknowsas} = \bigwedge_{e \in \mathcal{D}(D)} (\delta_a^e \rightarrow K_b \delta_a^e) \\ \mathsf{cignorant} = \bigwedge_{q \in Q} \bigwedge_{n=a,b} \neg K_c q_n \end{array}$$

□

We will now consider whether and how some specific protocols satisfy these conditions. First consider:

Example 4.69 Anne says: "I have $\{0, 1, 2\}$, or Bill has $\{0, 1, 2\}$," and Bill says: "I have $\{3, 4, 5\}$, or Anne has $\{3, 4, 5\}$." □

Update of $(Russian, 012.345.6)$ with $012_a \vee 012_b$ results in an epistemic state that consists of eight card deals (see Figure 4.9), and where $\mathsf{cignorant}$ holds but not common knowledge of it. Subsequent update with $345_a \vee 345_b$ results in an epistemic state consisting of the two deals 012.345.6 and 345.012.6, that are the same for Cath and different for Anne and Bill, so that common knowledge of $\mathsf{cignorant}$, $\mathsf{aknowsbs}$ and $\mathsf{bknowsas}$ holds. However, this is not a fair treatment of the information:

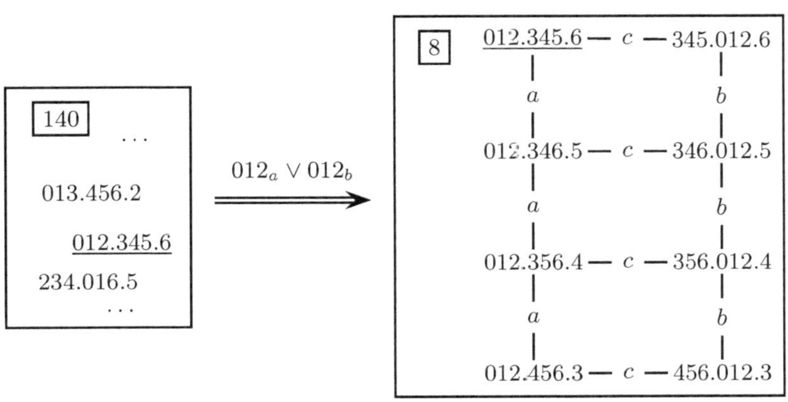

Figure 4.9. After Anne says: "I have 012 or Bill has 012", it may appear that the eight-deal epistemic state on the right results. But actually, that would be the result of an 'insider' revealing that "Anne has 012 or Bill has 012". Because Anne knows that her announcement is true, its meaning is not $012_a \vee 012_b$ but $K_a(012_a \vee 012_b)$, and a four-deal epistemic state instead results, wherein Cath knows the card deal.

A merely truthful public announcement of φ by an agent a would indeed correspond to an update with φ, but an announcement based on a's information corresponds to an update with $K_a\varphi$. If Anne's announcements had been made by an *insider* i, a virtual player who can look in everybody's cards, or differently said, a player whose accessibility on the epistemic state is the identity relation, the update would indeed have been φ, because in this case φ is equivalent to $K_i\varphi$. But Anne knows *less* than an insider, and therefore her announcements are *more* informative. Typically, φ can be true but not known by Anne, so $K_a\varphi$ holds in fewer worlds of the current epistemic state than φ.

As it is common knowledge that Anne initially does not know any of Bill's cards, she can only truthfully announce "I have $\{0,1,2\}$, or Bill has $\{0,1,2\}$" if she actually holds $\{0,1,2\}$. We can see this as follows.

Suppose, for example, that Anne's hand had been $\{3,4,6\}$ instead. Then the disjunction $012_a \vee 012_b$ must be true, given that 012_a is false, because 012_b is true: Bill has $\{0,1,2\}$. If Anne had held $\{3,4,6\}$, she could not have *known* 012_b to be true in the state where she only knows her own cards. Therefore, she could not have announced $012_a \vee 012_b$ if she held $\{3,4,6\}$. Similarly for the three other deals in which Anne does not hold 012, including the deal 345.012.6 that is the alternative for Cath given actual deal 012.345.6.

In other words: an update with $K_a(012_a \vee 012_b)$ in $(\mathit{Russian}, 012.345.6)$ already restricts *Russian* to those four worlds where Anne's hand is 012. These are the deals 012.345.6, 012.346.5, 012.356.4, 012.456.3, that are all different for Bill and for Cath. After that update, Cath knows all of Anne's cards, so cignorant is definitely false. Formally, the difference between the two updates can be expressed as:

$$\mathit{Russian}, 012.345.6 \models [012_a \vee 012_b]\mathsf{cignorant}$$
$$\mathit{Russian}, 012.345.6 \not\models [K_a(012_a \vee 012_b)]\mathsf{cignorant}$$

After update with $K_a(012_a \vee 012_b)$, a further update with $K_b(345_a \vee 345_b)$ results in a singleton epistemic state where it is common knowledge that 012.345.6 is the deal of cards.

It is rather obvious that players' announcements should be based on their information. We now move to the less obvious:

Example 4.70 Anne says: "I don't have 6," and Bill says: "Neither have I." □

After the first announcement cignorant holds, and $\binom{6}{3}\binom{4}{3} = 80$ card deals remain. After Bill's announcement aknowsbs and bknowsas hold as well, and again all three are even commonly known, and 20 card deals remain. What is wrong here? In the initial epistemic state, Anne cannot distinguish actual deal 012.345.6 from deal 012.346.4. If 012.346.4 had been the deal, after Anne's announcement Cath would have known the owner of one of the cards not held by itself, so cignorant fails again. So even though for the actual deal 012.345.6 postcondition cignorant holds after Anne's announcement, Anne does not know that. Formally:

$$Russian, 012.345.6 \models [K_a \neg 6_a]\text{cignorant}$$
$$Russian, 012.345.6 \not\models [K_a \neg 6_a]K_a\text{cignorant}$$

It may even be less obvious why the following is also not a solution:

Example 4.71 Anne says: "I have $\{0,1,2\}$, or I don't have any of these cards," and Bill says: "I have $\{3,4,5\}$, or I don't have any of these cards." □

After an update of $(Russian, 012.345.6)$ with $(K_a\text{first} =)\ K_a(012_a \vee (\neg 0_a \wedge \neg 1_a \wedge \neg 2_a))$ we reach an epistemic state that consists of 20 card deals. See Figure 4.10.

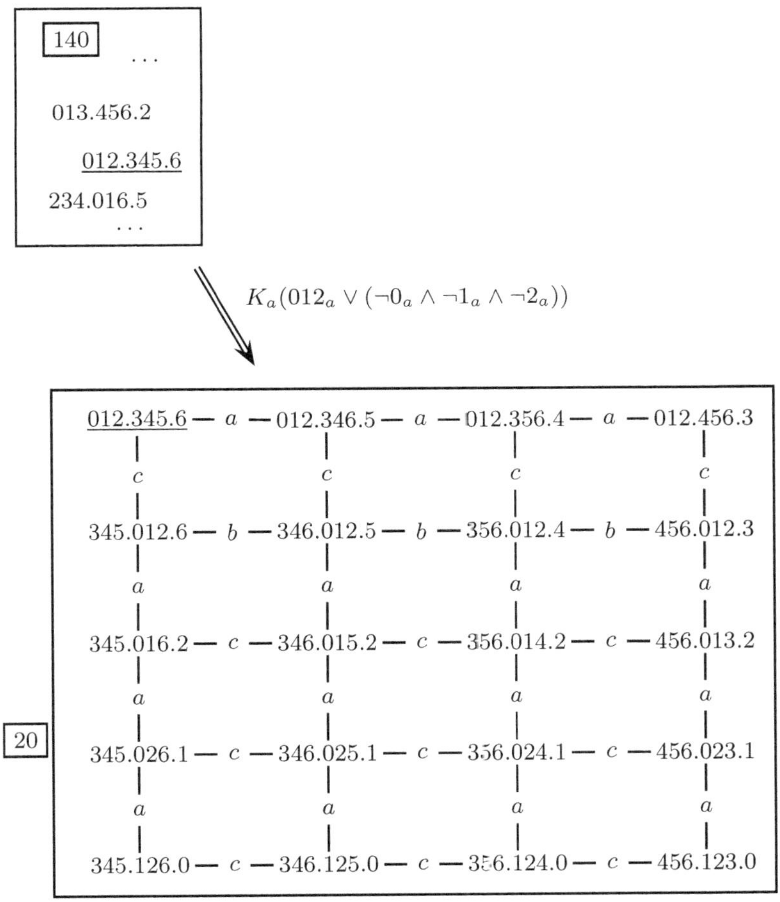

Figure 4.10. Anne says: "I have $\{0,1,2\}$ or I have none of these cards."

By a further update with $K_b(345_b \vee (\neg 3_b \wedge \neg 4_b \wedge \neg 5_b))$ we again reach the epistemic state that consists of deals 012.345.6 and 345.012.6 that are the same for Cath and different for Anne and Bill. Example 4.70 can be said to be 'unsafe' in the sense that another execution of the apparently underlying protocol (namely Anne saying: "I don't have 4") would have resulted in Cath learning her cards. Instead, in the protocol underlying Example 4.71, Anne's announcement seems 'safe' in that respect: no other execution of the protocol would have resulted in Cath learning any of her cards. Therefore, indeed, Anne *knows* that Cath is ignorant of her cards after her announcement. However, Cath does not know *that*, and, surprisingly, Cath can derive factual knowledge from that ignorance. Cath rightfully assumes that Anne would not dare make an unsafe communication: Anne wants to know that after her announcement Cath does not know any of her cards. Therefore, the update corresponding to first is not just $K_a\mathsf{first}$ but $K_a\mathsf{first} \wedge [K_a\mathsf{first}]K_a\mathsf{cignorant}$: "I know that first, and that after having said that, Cath doesn't know my cards."

For Cath, only deal 345.012.6 is the same as 012.345.6 after update with $K_a\mathsf{first}$. If the deal had been 345.012.6, Anne could have imagined it to have been, e.g., 345.016.2. In that case it would have been informative for Cath when Anne had announced first: Cath would have known that Anne does not have 0, 1, and 2: so $\mathsf{cignorant}$ is not true. We now can wind up the argument: because $\mathsf{cignorant}$ does not hold after announcement of $K_a\mathsf{first}$ in deal 345.016.2 of the restricted model, $K_a\mathsf{cignorant}$ does not hold after announcement of $K_a\mathsf{first}$, in 345.012.6, therefore $K_a\mathsf{first} \wedge [K_a\mathsf{first}]K_a\mathsf{cignorant}$ does not hold in deal 345.012.6 of the initial epistemic state, so updating with that formula results in deal 345.012.6 of *Russian* being deleted. But as this was the only alternative for Cath in that model, Cath now knows that the deal is 012.345.6, so Cath knows all of Anne's cards! Formally:

$$\begin{array}{l} \mathit{Russian}, 012.345.6 \models [K_a\mathsf{first}]\mathsf{cignorant} \\ \mathit{Russian}, 012.345.6 \models [K_a\mathsf{first}]K_a\mathsf{cignorant} \\ \mathit{Russian}, 012.345.6 \not\models [K_a\mathsf{first}]K_cK_a\mathsf{cignorant} \\ \mathit{Russian}, 012.345.6 \models [K_a\mathsf{first} \wedge [K_a\mathsf{first}]K_a\mathsf{cignorant}]\neg\mathsf{cignorant} \end{array}$$

and therefore as well, just to make the unsuccessful update stand out:

$$\mathit{Russian}|K_a\mathsf{first}, 012.345.6 \models \langle K_a\mathsf{cignorant}\rangle\neg K_a\mathsf{cignorant}$$

In other words: Cath does not learn Anne's cards from the mere fact that her announcement is based on her information. Instead, Cath learns Anne's cards from her intention to prevent Cath learning her cards. Without that intention, Cath would not have learnt Anne's cards. This is an interesting new type of unsuccessful update.

If, instead, Anne's intention is to guarantee $C_{abc}\mathsf{cignorant}$, it is no longer possible that this unintentionally provides factual information to Cath, in other words, the unsuccessful update just described can then no longer occur. This is because updates with publicly known information are always successful:

$M, s \models [K_a\varphi \wedge [K_a\varphi]C_{abc}\mathsf{cignorant}]C_{abc}\mathsf{cignorant}$
$\Leftrightarrow$ announcement composition
$M, s \models [K_a\varphi][C_{abc}\mathsf{cignorant}]C_{abc}\mathsf{cignorant}$
$\Leftarrow$
$M|K_a\varphi, s \models [C_{abc}\mathsf{cignorant}]C_{abc}\mathsf{cignorant}$
$\Leftrightarrow$ Proposition 4.36
true

To summarise our results, if Anne says φ with the intention of solving the Russian Cards problem, this is not just an announcement of φ, but actually an announcement of $K_a\varphi \wedge [K_a\varphi]C_{abc}\mathsf{cignorant}$. This is called a *safe announcement*. It will be clear, that a solution to the problem consists of a sequence of such safe announcements. If it is common knowledge after such a sequence that Anne and Bill know each other's hand of cards, i.e., $C_{abc}\mathsf{aknowsbs}$ and $C_{abc}\mathsf{bknowsas}$ are true, then we have indeed a solution. A somewhat weaker requirement seems to be sufficient, namely that (only) Anne and Bill and not necessarily Cath have that common knowledge ($C_{ab}\mathsf{aknowsbs}$ and $C_{ab}\mathsf{bknowsas}$), but we will overlook those details here.

A few more things are relevant to observe. First, on domains of card deals all announcements are equivalent to 'one of the following card deals is actually the case'. This is, because the effect of an announcement is a restriction of the domain, and that domain consists of a finite number of all different card deals. But beyond that, all announcements by the agents in question are equivalent to 'I hold one of the following hands of cards'. This is, because a player a's announcement of φ means, as we have seen, at least $K_a\varphi$, and the denotation of that is a finite number of a-equivalence classes in the domain of card deals, where, given the structure of the initial model, each such class is characterised by a hand of cards. This greatly simplifies the search for solutions of the Russian Cards problem. Finally, given that the domain is finite, only a finite number of informative announcements can be made. An *informative* announcement is quite simply one wherein a player announces that at least one from his commonly known set of hands is not his actual hand. It can be easily seen that uninformative announcements serve no role in protocols to solve the cards problem.

We continue with some example solutions, by way of exercises:

Exercise 4.72 (A five hand solution) Assume deal of cards 012.345.6. Show that the following is a solution: Anne announces: "I have one of $\{012, 034, 056, 135, 246\}$," and Bill announces "Cath has card 6." □

Exercise 4.73 (A six hand solution) Assume deal of cards 012.345.6. Show that the following is a solution: Anne announces: "I have one of $\{012, 034, 056, 135, 146, 236\}$," and Bill announces "Cath has card 6." □

Exercise 4.74 (A seven hand solution) Assume deal of cards 012.345.6. Show that the following is a solution: Anne announces: "I have one of $\{012, 034, 056, 135, 146, 236, 245\}$," and Bill announces "Cath has card 6." □

Exercise 4.75 Show that no solution consists of less than five hands. □

Exercise 4.76 Anne announces: "The sum of my cards modulo 7 is 3," and Bill announces "Cath has card 6." Show this is also a solution. What if the actual deal of cards had not been 012.345.6? □

A final exercise makes clear that the last word has not yet been said on such cryptography for ideal agents:

Exercise 4.77 Assume deal of cards 012.345.6. Anne now adds one other hand, namely 245, to the five-hand solution in Exercise 4.72. Anne announces: "I have one of $\{012, 034, 056, 135, 245, 246\}$," and Bill announces "Cath has card 6." Are the announcements safe? Show that it is not common knowledge that Bill has learnt Anne's cards. What is known instead? □

This sequence is *only* a solution of 'length two' to the Russian Cards problem on the assumption that it is not common knowledge that the solution will have length two. Because, if that is common knowledge, Cath would, after all, learn that Anne holds 0. Analysis of the underlying protocol and of up to three more announcements reveals that, after all, this does not provide a new solution to the problem.

4.13 Notes

Public announcements The logic *PA* of multi-agent epistemic logic with public announcements and without common knowledge has been formulated and axiomatised by Plaza [168], and, independently, for the somewhat more general case of introspective agents, by Gerbrandy and Groeneveld [77]. In [168], public announcement is seen as a binary operation $+$, such that $\varphi + \psi$ is equivalent to $\langle\varphi\rangle\psi$.[1]

The axiomatisation of the logic $\mathcal{L}_{KC[]}$ of public announcements *with* common knowledge has been established by Baltag, Moss, and Solecki [11], see also [12, 10]; the completeness of **PAC** is a special case of the completeness of their more general logic of action models—see also Chapter 6. A simplified, direct completeness proof for **PAC**, by Kooi, is presented in Chapter 7.

[1] In the expression $[\varphi]\psi$ we introduced $[\cdot]$, in Definition 4.7, as a *unary* operator on $\mathcal{L}_{KC[]}$ formulas, with a formula φ as input and a dynamic modal operator $[\varphi]$ as output. But a different viewpoint is to think of a public announcement as a *binary* operator on formulas: $[\cdot]\cdot : \mathcal{L}_{KC[]} \times \mathcal{L}_{KC[]} \rightarrow \mathcal{L}_{KC[]}$, so that we have that $([\cdot]\cdot)(\varphi, \psi) = [\varphi]\psi$. That would be an unusual notation for a binary operator, and one might instead prefer prefix or infix notation, such as the mentioned $\varphi + \psi$ for $\langle\varphi\rangle\psi$, in Plaza. The viewpoint of an announcement as a binary operation on formulas does not generalise to more complex updates or epistemic actions, where the program being executed cannot be identified with a formula.

Precursors of public announcement logic There are a fair number of precursors of these results. There is (i) a prior line of research in dynamic modal approaches to semantics, not necessarily also epistemic, and (ii) a prior line of research in meta-level descriptions of epistemic change, not necessarily on the object level as in dynamic modal approaches—partly also addressed in Chapter 3 and in the introductory Chapter 1. We will discuss (i) in some detail.

An approach roughly known as 'dynamic semantics' or 'update semantics' was followed in van Emde Boas, Groenendijk, and Stokhof [60], Landman [123], Groeneveld [82], and Veltman [191]. There are strong relations between that and more *PDL*-motivated work by de Rijke [176], and Jaspars [110]. As background literature to various dynamic features we recommend van Benthem [21, 20]. More motivated by runs in interpreted systems is van Linder, van der Hoek, and Meyer [131]. All these approaches use dynamic modal operators for information change, but (1) typically not (except [131]) in a multi-modal language that also has epistemic operators, (2) typically not for more than one agent, and (3) not necessarily such that the effects of announcements or updates are defined given the update formula and the current information state: the *PDL*-related and interpreted system related approaches *presuppose* a transition relation between information states, such as for atomic actions in *PDL*.

We outline, somewhat arbitrarily, some features of these approaches. Groeneveld's approach [82] is typical for dynamic semantics in that is has formulas $[\varphi]_a\psi$ to express that after an update of agent a's information with φ, ψ is true. His work was later merged with that of Gerbrandy, resulting in the seminal [77]. De Rijke [176] defines theory change operators $[+\varphi]$ and $[*\varphi]$ with a dynamic interpretation that link an enriched dynamic modal language to AGM-type theory revision [3], as already presented in Chapter 3. In functionality, it is not dissimilar from Jaspars [110] φ-addition (i.e., expansion) operators $[\varphi]_u$ and φ-retraction (i.e., contraction) operators $[\varphi]_d$, called updates and downdates by Jaspars. Van Linder, van der Hoek, and Meyer [131] use a setting that combines dynamic effects with knowledge and belief, but to interpret their (various) action operators they assume an explicit transition relation as part of the Kripke structure interpreting such descriptions.

As somewhat parallel developments to [75] we also mention Lomuscio and Ryan [137]. They do not define dynamic modal operators in the language, but they define epistemic state transformers that clearly correspond to the interpretation of such operators: $M * \varphi$ is the result of refining epistemic model M with a formula φ, etc. Their semantics for updates is only an *approximation* of public announcement logic, as the operation is only defined for *finite* (approximations of) models.

For the other line of research leading up to public announcement logic, namely in meta-level descriptions of epistemic change, a comprehensive overview is beyond the scope of these notes. For an example, we refer to the work of Fagin, Halpern, Vardi, and Moses [62], and that of van der Meyden [146].

Semantics of public announcement The semantics of public announcement in Definition 4.7 is actually slightly imprecise. Consider what happens if in the phrase

$$M, s \models [\varphi]\psi \text{ iff } M, s \models \varphi \text{ implies } M|\varphi, s \models \psi$$

the formula φ is false in M, s. In that case, $M|\varphi, s \models \psi$ is undefined, because s is now not part of the domain of the model $M|\varphi$. Apparently, we 'informally' use that an implication 'left implies right' in the meta-language is not just true when 'left is false or right is true' in the standard binary sense, where both left and right are defined, but also when left is false even when right is undefined. An alternative definition of the semantics of public announcement, that does not have that informality, is

$$M, s \models [\varphi]\psi \text{ iff for all } (M', s') \text{ such that } (M, s)[\![\varphi]\!](M', s') : (M', s') \models \psi$$

where $(M, s)[\![\varphi]\!](M', s')$ iff $M' = M|\varphi$ and $s = s'$. This is the standard form of a binary relation (between epistemic states). The interpretation of more general epistemic actions will have this form as well.

Theory of public announcement logic The logic *PAC* is not a normal modal logic, as it is not closed under uniform substitution of propositional variables. For example, even though $[p]p$ is a theorem, $[p \wedge \neg K_a p](p \wedge \neg K_a p)$ is obviously not. This also makes it quite clear that 'announcement' is *undefinable* in the language $\mathcal{L}_K$ without announcements: $[\varphi]\psi$ is not equivalent to some $\chi(\varphi, \psi) \in \mathcal{L}_K$, i.e., to some formula constructed with propositional and individual epistemic operators from occurrences of φ and ψ. Because announcement can be seen as a binary operation on formulas, this was a relevant consideration at the inception of this logic by Plaza [168].

For completeness issues, see Chapter 7, and for expressivity results, see Chapter 8. The logic *PA* is compact and strongly complete [12]. (Given $\Sigma \models \varphi$ we also have $\Sigma \vdash \varphi$, and as all proofs are finite only a finite subset $\Sigma' \subseteq \Sigma$ can have been used in the proof. But then also $\Sigma' \models \varphi$.) For complexity issues, we refer to Halpern and Moses [89]—note that every $\mathcal{L}_{K[]}$ formula is logically equivalent to a $\mathcal{L}_K$ formula—and to the recent results obtained by Lutz in [138]. The logic *PAC* is not strongly complete (nor compact). This is due to the infinitary character of the common knowledge operators, similarly to related 'problems' for *PDL*. For various theoretical issues, see [12] and the standard reference volumes [29, 118, 89].

Unsuccessful updates The term 'unsuccessful update' was coined by Gerbrandy [75]. Van Benthem [23] formulated and proved Proposition 4.37, that the fragment $\mathcal{L}^0_{KC[]}$ is preserved under submodels, for a similar fragment, namely without common knowledge and without any announcement operators. However, also the converse held for that fragment, i.e., if a formula of the language is preserved under submodels, then it is in the fragment. It is unknown whether this also holds for $\mathcal{L}^0_{KC[]}$. The result formulated in Proposition 4.37 is also rather like a result of Gerbrandy [75, pp.100–101]. He proved, for a slightly different notion of (successful) updates, and a language without common knowledge, that formulas are successful if epistemic formulas do not occur within the scope of an odd number of negations. Proposition 4.36 was established by van Ditmarsch [47]. A syntactic characterisation of the successful formulas has, as far as we know, not been found. That inconsistent formulas are unsuccessful (Proposition 4.41) was observed by Ji Ruan, Wiebe van der Hoek, and Gabriel Sandu. Two investigations on unsuccessful updates are to appear in the journal Synthese: [51] reflects the presentation given in this chapter, and Gerbrandy's [76] is similar to [75].

The notion of unsuccessful update is of course a (negative) derivative from the 'success postulate' in belief revision (Chapter 3). It can also be seen as a dynamic generalisation of one particular type of Moore-sentence, namely $p \wedge \neg Kp$. This sentence cannot be believed, or known, after its announcement. Hintikka's 'Knowledge and belief' [99, p.64] provides a list of excellent references on this topic, of which the most proper first backreference is Moore's "A reply to my critics", a chapter in the 'Library of Living Philosophers' volume dedicated to him, wherein Moore writes

> I went to the pictures last Tuesday, but I don't believe that I did' is a perfectly absurd thing to say, although *what* is asserted is something which is perfectly possibly logically. [151, p.543]

The further development of this notion firstly puts Moore-sentences in a *multi-agent* perspective of announcements of the form 'p is true and *you* don't believe that', and secondly puts Moore-sentences in a *dynamic* perspective of the unsuccessful update that cannot be believed after being announced.

Muddy Children The Muddy Children puzzle is one of the best known puzzles that involve knowledge. It is known that versions of this puzzle were circulating in the fifties. The earliest source that we know (1956—recently found by Verbrugge and van Ditmarsch) is a 'coloured hat' version of this puzzle, by van Tilburg [189]. This is one of 626 so-called 'Breinbrouwsels' (Brain Brews) that appeared as mathematical entertainment in the weekly (Dutch language) journal 'Katholieke Illustratie', from 1954 to 1965. Another early source of the puzzle (1958) is a puzzle book by Gamow and Stern [70]. They present what is known as the 'cheating wives' version. A version with cheating husbands rather than wives can be found in Moses, Dolev, and Halpern [154]. Another version features wise men, see McCarthy [141]. The version that is most popular today involves muddy children. It was introduced in Barwise [14]. The introduction to epistemic logic by Fagin *et al.* [62] is largely based on a wonderful exploration of this muddy children problem, and it also plays a major part in Meyer and van der Hoek's [148]. Parikh [163] analyses what happens if even one child does not reason perfectly and fails to respond properly.

The first analysis of this problem with epistemic logic was presented in [154], where the dynamics was modelled on the meta-level rather than in the logical language. The first object level treatment of this problem using public announcement logic was by [168]. An analysis of the problem using dynamic epistemic logic can be found in [75].

Sum and Product The Sum and Product riddle was first presented by Freudenthal in [66, 67]. It then later surfaced again in McCarthy [141]—who was unaware at that time of the origin of this problem (personal communication). Versions of the problem—different announcements, different ranges for the numbers—elicited much discussion since its inception in Freudenthal [66]. This includes [72, 179, 109] and a website maintained by Sillke that contains many other references: `www.mathematic.uni-bielefeld.de/~sillke/PUZZLES/logic_sum_product`. More geared towards an epistemic logical audience are [141, 168, 160, 144, 104]. McCarthy [141] models the problem elegantly in modal logic, for processing in the (first-order) logic theorem prover FOL. This includes an off-hand 'avant la lettre' introduction of what clearly corresponds to the essential concept of common knowledge: what Sum and Product commonly know is crucial to a clear understanding of the problem. Plaza [168] models the problem in public announcement logic. The results on common knowledge in Sum and Product are by Panti [160]; these are actually for a variant of the puzzle where the upper bound of 99 is given as a fact but not as common knowledge. Van der Meyden [144] suggests a solution in temporal epistemic logic.

Russian Cards The Russian Cards problem was originally presented at the Moscow Mathematics Olympiad in 2000, suggested by A. Shapovalov. The intended solution was that Anne announces the sum of her cards modulo 7, and that Bill then announces Cath's card. The jury was puzzled by 'non-solutions' of the form "I have hand 012 or Bill has hand 012", as discussed in Section 4.12. See Makarychevs' piece in the Mathematical Intelligencer [139]. Alexander Shen, Moscow, has been very helpful with inside information on the history of this riddle. Publications on this problem include van Ditmarsch [47], and Atkinson and collaborators [1]—there is a relation to certain problems in cryptography and block design.

5

Epistemic Actions

5.1 Introduction

The previous chapter dealt with public announcements. There are various more complex 'updates', or, as we call them, epistemic actions. This chapter introduces a language and logic for epistemic actions. Public announcements are epistemic actions that convey the same information for all agents. They result in a restriction of the domain of the model and therefore in a restriction of the corresponding accessibility relations. More complex epistemic actions convey different information to different agents. They may result in the refinement of accessibility relations while the domain of the model remains unchanged, and they may even result in the enlargement of the domain of the model (and its structure), even when the complexity is measured by the number of non-bisimilar states. We start with a motivating example. Reconsider Example 4.1 on page 67 of the previous chapter 'public announcements'.

Example 5.1 (Buy or sell?) Consider two stockbrokers Anne and Bill, having a little break in a Wall Street bar, sitting at a table. A messenger comes in and delivers a letter to Anne. On the envelope is written "urgently requested data on United Agents". □

As before, we model this as an epistemic state for one atom p, describing 'the letter contains the information that United Agents is doing well', so that $\neg p$ stands for United Agents *not* doing well. And it is reasonable to assume that both Anne (a) and Bill (b) know what information on United Agents is due, as this was announced by the messenger in their presence. In other words: a and b are both uncertain about the value of p, and this is common knowledge. In fact, p is true. Unlike before, where we assumed Anne had read the letter, we start with the initial situation where both Anne and Bill are ignorant. The epistemic model for this we call *Letter*. Figure 5.1 presents the epistemic state $(Letter, 1)$.

In Figure 5.1 we choose mnemonically convenient names 0 and 1 for states where p is false and true, respectively. In Example 4.1 we assumed that the

0 —— a, b —— $\underline{1}$

Figure 5.1. Epistemic state $(Letter, 1)$ modelling the situation where Anne and Bill are ignorant about atom p that is in fact true.

letter-reading was not aloud, and with Bill watching Anne. Also we did not formally model that action. This time we will model the action, and also add some more variation. Consider the following scenarios. Except for the parts between brackets, of which only one or no agent is aware, Anne and Bill commonly know that these actions are taking place.

Example 5.2 (tell) Anne reads the letter aloud. United Agents is doing well. □

Example 5.3 (read) Bill sees that Anne reads the letter. (United Agents is doing well.) □

Example 5.4 (mayread) Bill leaves the table and orders a drink at the bar so that Anne may have read the letter while he was away. (She does not read the letter.) (United Agents is doing well.) □

Example 5.5 (bothmayread) Bill orders a drink at the bar while Anne goes to the bathroom. Each may have read the letter while the other was away from the table. (Both read the letter.) (United Agents is doing well.) □

After execution of the action tell it is common knowledge that p: in the resulting epistemic state $C_{ab}p$ holds. This is not the case when the action is read, but still, some common knowledge is obtained there, namely $C_{ab}(K_a p \vee K_a \neg p)$: it is commonly known that Anne knows the contents of the letter, irrespective of it being p or $\neg p$. This is yet different in the third action, mayread; after that action, Bill does not even know if Anne knows p or knows $\neg p$: $\neg K_b(K_a p \vee K_a \neg p)$. Still, Bill has learnt something: he now considers it possible that Anne knows p, or knows $\neg p$. For Bill, action mayread involves actual choice for Anne: whatever the truth about p, she may have learnt it, or not. In the case of bothmayread both $\neg K_b(K_a p \vee K_a \neg p)$ and $\neg K_a(K_b p \vee K_b \neg p)$ are postconditions. Each agent has a choice, from the perspective of the other agent. Actually, *both* agents learn p, so that p is generally known: $E_{ab}p$, but they are ignorant of each other's knowledge: $\neg E_{ab}E_{ab}p$ (from which follows, in particular, that p is not common knowledge: $\neg C_{ab}p$), and *that* is commonly known to them: $C_{ab}\neg E_{ab}E_{ab}p$. The state transitions induced by each of these actions are shown in Figure 5.2.[1]

From these actions, we can only model the tell action in public announcement logic: it is public announcement of p. In public announcement logic 'after

[1] In Example 4.1 the action read was implicit. Therefore, the two-point model in Figure 5.2 resulting from that action is the same as the two-point model in Figure 4.1 in which public announcements take place.

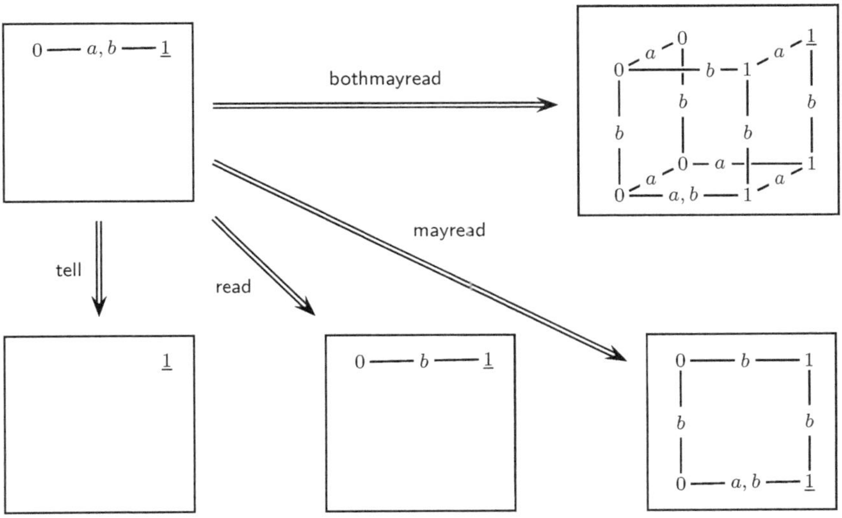

Figure 5.2. Epistemic states resulting from the execution of the four example actions. The top left figure represents $(Letter, 1)$. Points of epistemic states are underlined. Assume transitivity of access. For mayread and bothmayread only one of more executions is shown.

public announcement of φ, it holds that ψ' was described as $[\varphi]\psi$. In epistemic action logic this will be described as

$$[L_A?\varphi]\psi$$

Here, L stands for 'learning'. This is a dynamic counterpart of static common knowledge. We can paraphrase $[L_A?\varphi]\psi$ by: after the group A learns φ, it holds that ψ. One might also say: after it is common knowledge that the action 'that φ' takes place, it holds that ψ.

A simple example of an action involving learning by subgroups strictly smaller than the public, is the read action. It is described as

$$L_{ab}(!L_a?p \cup L_a?\neg p)$$

This stands for 'Agents a and b learn that a learns the truth about fact p, and actually agent a learns that p'; or, in yet other words 'Anne and Bill learn that Anne learns that p or that Anne learns that $\neg p$, and actually (this is the role of the exclamation mark in front of that alternative) Anne learns that p. In this case, the action results in a refinement of agent a's accessibility relations (corresponding to her increased knowledge). Although such knowledge refinement is related to non-deterministic choice, in this case Anne has no choice: either p or $\neg p$ is true, but not both.

In the mayread action instead, Anne has a choice from Bill's point of view. This action will be described by

$$L_{ab}(L_a?p \cup L_a?\neg p \cup \,!?\top)$$

which stands for 'Agents a and b learn that a *may* learn the truth about fact p, although actually nothing happens'. Or, in yet other words: 'Agents a and b learn that either a learns the truth about fact p, or not; and actually she does not'. Actions involving choice may increase the complexity of the epistemic state, as measured in the number of non-bisimilar states. This is indeed the case here: we go from two to four states, as one may check in Figure 5.2.

The bothmayread action is a more complex scenario also involving non-deterministic choice. It will be explained in detail after the formal introduction of the action language and its semantics.

A relational language for epistemic actions is introduced in Section 5.2. The semantics for this language is given in Section 5.3. This section contains subsections on valid principles for the logic. We do not give an axiomatisation for the logic—there are some difficulties with a principle relating knowledge and epistemic actions, summarily addressed near the end of Section 5.3. Sections 5.4 and 5.5 model multi-agent system features in the epistemic action logics: 'card game states', and 'spreading gossip', respectively.

5.2 Syntax

To the language $\mathcal{L}_{KC}$ for multi-agent epistemic logic with common knowledge for a set A of agents and a set P of atomic propositions, we add dynamic modal operators for programs that are called epistemic actions or just actions. Actions may change the knowledge of the agents involved, but do not change facts.

Definition 5.6 (Formulas, actions, group) The language $\mathcal{L}_!(A, P)$ is the union of the *formulas* $\mathcal{L}_!^{\mathrm{stat}}(A, P)$ and the *actions* $\mathcal{L}_!^{\mathrm{act}}(A, P)$, defined by

$$\varphi ::= p \mid \neg\varphi \mid (\varphi \wedge \varphi) \mid K_a\varphi \mid C_B\varphi \mid [\alpha]\psi$$

$$\alpha ::= ?\varphi \mid L_B\beta \mid (\alpha \,!\, \alpha) \mid (\alpha \;¡\; \alpha) \mid (\alpha \;;\; \beta') \mid (\alpha \cup \alpha)$$

where $p \in P$, $a \in A$, $B \subseteq A$, and $\psi \in \mathcal{L}_!^{\mathrm{stat}}(gr(\alpha), P)$, $\beta \in \mathcal{L}_!^{\mathrm{act}}(B, P)$, and $\beta' \in \mathcal{L}_!^{\mathrm{act}}(gr(\alpha), P)$. The *group* $gr(\alpha)$ of an action α is defined as: $gr(?\varphi) = \emptyset$, $gr(L_B\alpha) = B$, $gr(\alpha \,!\, \alpha') = gr(\alpha)$, $gr(\alpha \;¡\; \alpha') = gr(\alpha')$, $gr(\alpha \;;\; \alpha') = gr(\alpha')$, and $gr(\alpha \cup \alpha') = gr(\alpha) \cap gr(\alpha')$. □

As usual, we omit the parameters P and/or A unless this might cause ambiguity. So instead of $\mathcal{L}_!(A, P)$ we write $\mathcal{L}_!(A)$ or even $\mathcal{L}_!$. Unlike before, the parameter A is now often essential, and will in that case have to remain explicit. The dual of $[\alpha]$ is $\langle\alpha\rangle$. We omit parentheses from formula and action expressions unless ambiguity results.

Action $?\varphi$ is a *test*. Operator L_B is called *learning*, and the construct $L_B?\varphi$ is pronounced as 'group B learn that φ'. Action $(\alpha \; ! \; \alpha')$ is called *(left) local choice*, and $(\alpha \; ¡ \; \alpha')$ is called *(right) local choice*. Action $(\alpha \; ; \; \alpha')$ is *sequential execution*—'first α, then α'', and action $(\alpha \cup \alpha')$ is *non-deterministic choice* between α and α'.

In epistemic action logic, 'the set of agents' occurring in formulas and in structures is a constantly changing parameter. The notion of *group gr* keeps track of the agents occurring in learning operators in actions. The constructs $[\alpha]\psi$, $L_B\beta$, and $(\alpha \; ; \; \beta')$ in the definition, wherein the group of an action is used as a constraint, guarantee that in an epistemic state for agents B that is the result of action execution, formulas containing modal operators for agents not in B are not in the language. This also explains the possibly puzzling clause $gr(\alpha \; ; \; \alpha') = gr(\alpha')$: the group of α' is by definition the smaller of $gr(\alpha)$ and $gr(\alpha')$.

Local choice $(\alpha \; ! \; \alpha')$ may be seen as 'from α and α', choose the first,' and local choice $\alpha \; ¡ \; \alpha'$ as 'from α and α', choose the second'. Given that, why bother having those constructs? We need them, because the semantics of a learning operator that binds an action containing local choice operations, is defined in terms of those operators. We will see that in $L_B(\alpha \; ! \; \alpha')$, everybody in B but not in learning operators occurring in α, α', is unaware of the choice for α. That choice is therefore 'local'. The operations '!' and '¡' are dual; $\alpha \; ! \; \alpha'$ means the same as $\alpha' \; ¡ \; \alpha$. Typically, we prove local choice properties for '!' only, and not for '¡'.

Instead of $(\alpha \; ! \; \alpha')$ we generally write $(!\alpha \cup \alpha')$. This expresses more clearly that given choice between α and α', the agents involved in those actions choose α, whereas that choice remains invisible to the agents that learn about these alternatives but are not involved. Similarly, instead of $(\alpha \; ¡ \; \alpha')$ we generally write $(\alpha \cup \; !\alpha')$. There is a simple relation between 'local choice' and 'non-deterministic choice', but before we explain that, a few examples.

Example 5.7 The action read where Bill sees that Anne reads the letter is described as $L_{ab}(L_a?p \; ! \; L_a?\neg p)$, also written as $L_{ab}(!L_a?p \cup L_a?\neg p)$. It can be paraphrased as follows: 'Anne and Bill learn that either Anne learns that United Agents is doing well or that Anne learns that United Agents is not doing well; and actually Anne learns that United Agents is doing well.' The part $(L_a?p \; ! \; L_a?\neg p)$ means that the first from alternatives $L_a?p$ and $L_a?\neg p$ is chosen, but that agent b is unaware of that choice. □

Example 5.8 The descriptions in $\mathcal{L}_!^{\text{act}}(\{a, b\}, \{p\})$ of the actions in the introduction are (including read again):

tell	$L_{ab}?p$
read	$L_{ab}(!L_a?p \cup L_a?\neg p)$
mayread	$L_{ab}(L_a?p \cup L_a?\neg p \cup \; !?\top)$
bothmayread	$L_{ab}(!L_a?p \cup L_a?\neg p \cup \; ?\top) \; ; \; L_{ab}(!L_b?p \cup L_b?\neg p \cup \; ?\top)$

In the last two actions, instead of $?\top$ (for 'nothing happens') we may as well write $(?p\cup ?\neg p)$. We abused the language somewhat in those actions: 'from several actions, choose the first' is a natural and obvious generalisation of local choice. A description $L_{ab}(L_a?p \cup L_a?\neg p\cup\; !?\top)$ is formally one of the following three

$$\begin{array}{l} L_{ab}(L_a?p \;¡\; (L_a?\neg p \;¡\; ?\top)) \\ L_{ab}((L_a?p \;¡\; L_a?\neg p) \;¡\; ?\top) \\ L_{ab}((L_a?p \;!\; L_a?\neg p) \;¡\; ?\top) \end{array}$$

□

A non-deterministic action contains $\cup$ operators and may have more than one execution in a given epistemic state. In terms of relations between epistemic states: the relation is not functional. The only difference between an action with $\cup$ and one where this has been replaced by '!' or '¡' is, in terms of its interpretation, a restriction on that relation that makes it (more) functional.

Definition 5.9 (Type of an action) The *type*

$$\alpha_\cup$$

of action α is the result of substituting '$\cup$' for all occurrences of '!' and '¡' in α, except when under the scope of '?'. If $\alpha_\cup = \beta_\cup$ we say that α and β are the same type of action. An *instance* of an action α is the result of substituting either '!' or '¡' for all occurrences of '$\cup$' in α, except, again, when under the scope of '?'. For an arbitrary instance of an action α we write

$$\alpha_!$$

Let $\sim_!$ be the least congruence relation on actions such that $(\alpha \,!\, \alpha') \sim_! (\alpha \;¡\; \alpha')$. If $\alpha \sim_! \beta$, then α and β are *comparable.* An $\mathcal{L}_!$ action is *deterministic* iff it does not contain $\cup$ operators, except when under the scope of '?'. □

In other words, if $\alpha \sim_! \beta$, then α and β are the same except for swaps of '!' for '¡' and vice versa. All instances of an action are comparable among each other, all instances of an action are deterministic, and the type of an action is itself an action. Local choice (nor other) operators in the scope of a test operator '?' do not matter: tests occurring in action descriptions represent *preconditions* for action execution; whatever is tested, is irrelevant from that perspective.

Example 5.10 The type $\mathsf{read}_\cup$ of the action read is $L_{ab}(L_a?p \cup L_a?\neg p)$. □

The action $\mathsf{read}_\cup$ is different from read, because another instance (and therefore possible execution) of $\mathsf{read}_\cup$ is $L_{ab}(L_a?p \;¡\; L_a?\neg p)$, also written as $L_{ab}(L_a?p\cup\; !L_a?\neg p)$. Actions $L_{ab}(!L_a?p \cup L_a?\neg p)$ and $L_{ab}(L_a?p\cup\; !L_a?\neg p)$ are *comparable*, i.e., $L_{ab}(!L_a?p \cup L_a?\neg p) \sim_! L_{ab}(L_a?p\cup\; !L_a?\neg p)$.

Example 5.11 The types of the actions in the introduction are:

$\mathsf{tell}_\cup$	$L_{ab}?p$
$\mathsf{read}_\cup$	$L_{ab}(L_a?p \cup L_a?\neg p)$
$\mathsf{mayread}_\cup$	$L_{ab}(L_a?p \cup L_a?\neg p \cup\ ?^{-})$
$\mathsf{bothmayread}_\cup$	$L_{ab}(L_a?p \cup L_a?\neg p \cup\ ?^{-})\ ;\ L_{ab}(L_b?p \cup L_b?\neg p \cup\ ?\top)$ □

The action mayread is one of three of that type, and bothmayread one of 9. If we are more formal, this amounts to one of 4, and 16, respectively. The difference is easily explained. With $L_{ab}((L_a?p\ \text{¡}\ L_a?\neg p)\ \text{¡}\ ?\top)$ as the chosen precision of mayread, that action has the same type as the other instance $L_{ab}((L_a?p\ !\ L_a?\neg p)\ \text{¡}\ ?\top)$. But both are precisions of mayread, wherein the choice between the first two alternatives is invisible.

There is a certain symmetry in action descriptions that appears broken in tell. If we had described tell as $(!L_{ab}?p \cup L_{ab}?\neg p)$ instead of $L_{ab}?p$, its type would have been $(L_{ab}?p \cup L_{ab}?\neg p)$. That description expresses that Anne tells the truth about p, whatever it is: a description that is independent from the actual state, so to speak. So why the shorter description? In an action $(!L_{ab}?p \cup L_{ab}?\neg p)$, the choice expressed in ! is visible 'only to the agents involved in the choice options and not to others': but in this case there are no other agents, so there is no point in using that description.

5.3 Semantics

5.3.1 Basic Definitions

The language $\mathcal{L}_!(A, P)$ is interpreted in multi-agent epistemic states. For an introduction to and overview of the structures relevant to this semantics, see Chapter 2. For the class of epistemic models for agents A and atoms P we write $\mathcal{S}5(A, P)$, for the class of epistemic states we write $\bullet\mathcal{S}5(A, P)$. In this chapter we often combine models for different groups of agents. If M is a multi-agent epistemic model for agents A, we write $gr(M) = A$ and say 'the group of model M is A', and, given some state s in the domain of M, similarly, $gr((M, s)) = A$. For the class of all epistemic models for subsets of agents A and atoms P we write $\mathcal{S}5(\subseteq A, P)$, and similarly for epistemic states. We abuse the language and write $M \in \mathcal{S}5(A, P)$ for an arbitrary epistemic model M in class $\mathcal{S}5(A, P)$, etc.

A peculiarity of this setting is that a model for the *empty* set of agents is an $S5$ model, i.e., an epistemic model. This is, because for each agent $a \in \emptyset$, the accessibility relation R_a associated with that agent (namely: none) is an equivalence relation. Note the difference between an *empty* accessibility relation $R_a = \emptyset$ and the *absence* of an accessibility relation for a given agent. A model with an empty accessibility relation for a given agent is not an $S5$ model, because access is not reflexive for that agent.

The semantics of $\mathcal{L}_!(A, P)$ has a clause for the interpretation of dynamic modal formulas of form $[\alpha]\varphi$, where α is an action and φ a formula. In public announcement logic this was $[\psi]\varphi$, for *two* arbitrary formulas, but now we have a whole range of epistemic actions, not just public announcement.

As was indicated in the introduction earlier, sometimes the domain of an epistemic state is enlarged due to an epistemic action. The question is where those extra states come from? And once we have acquired them, how do we determine which are indistinguishable for an agent? And how do we determine the valuation for these states? The idea is the following. If the agents in a group *learn* that an action α takes place, we consider the epistemic states that result from executing α or comparable actions. These *epistemic states* are taken to be the *factual states* in the model that results from executing learning α. We obtain extra states by having actions with non-deterministic choice. The accessibility relation is then determined by the internal structure of the epistemic states that are taken to be factual states. In order to accommodate this, we need a notion of equivalence between epistemic states. We therefore lift equivalence of factual states in an epistemic state, to equivalence of epistemic states. This notion will be used in Definition 5.13 of action interpretation.

Definition 5.12 (Equivalence of epistemic states) Let $M, M' \in \mathcal{S}5(\subseteq A)$, $s \in M$, $s' \in M'$, and $a \in A$. Then

$$(M,s) \sim_a (M',s') \text{ iff } \begin{array}{l} a \notin gr(M) \cup gr(M') \text{ or} \\ M = M' \text{ and } s \sim_a s' \text{ or} \\ \text{there is a } t \in M : (M,t) \leftrightarroweq (M',s') \text{ and } s \sim_a t \end{array} \quad \square$$

In other words: if an agent does not occur in either epistemic state, the epistemic states are the same from that agent's point of view; otherwise, they are the same if the points of those epistemic states are the same for that agent, modulo bisimilarity (see Definition 2.14 of bisimilarity $\leftrightarroweq$ on page 24 in Chapter 2). Note that we choose to overload the notation $\sim_a$: it applies equally to factual states and epistemic states. Exercise 5.16 demonstrates what happens when the bisimilarity clause is removed. From the above definition one can immediately observe[2] that for all $a \in gr(M) \cup gr(M')$:

$$\text{If } (M,s) \sim_a (M',s'), \text{ then } gr(M) = gr(M')$$

Definition 5.13 (Semantics of formulas and actions) Let $M = \langle S, \sim, V\rangle \in \mathcal{S}5(A, P)$ and $s \in S$. The semantics of $\mathcal{L}_!^{\text{stat}}(A, P)$ formulas and $\mathcal{L}_!^{\text{act}}(A, P)$ actions is defined by double induction.

---

[2] Definition 5.12 gives three ways to achieve $(M, s) \sim_a (M', s')$. The case $a \notin gr(M) \cup gr(M')$ is ruled out by the assumption. The case $M = M'$ makes $gr(M) = gr(M')$ trivial. In the remaining case M is bisimilar to M', so that $gr(M) = gr(M')$ is also trivial.

$$\begin{array}{lll}
M,s \models p & \text{iff} & s \in V_p \\
M,s \models \neg\varphi & \text{iff} & M,s \not\models \varphi \\
M,s \models \varphi \wedge \psi & \text{iff} & M,s \models \varphi \text{ and } M,s \models \psi \\
M,s \models K_a\varphi & \text{iff} & \text{for all } s' \in S : s \sim_a s' \text{ implies } M,s' \models \varphi \\
M,s \models C_B\varphi & \text{iff} & \text{for all } s' \in S : s \sim_B s' \text{ implies } M,s' \models \varphi \\
M,s \models [\alpha]\varphi & \text{iff} & \text{for all } M',s' : \\
 & & (M,s)[\![\alpha]\!](M',s') \text{ implies } M',s' \models \varphi
\end{array}$$

$$\begin{array}{lll}
(M,s)[\![?\varphi]\!](M',s') & \text{iff} & M' = \langle [\![\varphi]\!]_M, \emptyset, V|[\![\varphi]\!]_M\rangle \text{ and } s = s' \\
(M,s)[\![L_B\alpha]\!](M',s') & \text{iff} & M' = \langle S', \sim', V'\rangle \text{ and } (M,s)[\![\alpha]\!]s' \text{ (see below)} \\
[\![\alpha \,;\, \alpha']\!] & = & [\![\alpha]\!] \circ [\![\alpha']\!] \\
[\![\alpha \cup \alpha']\!] & = & [\![\alpha]\!] \cup [\![\alpha']\!] \\
[\![\alpha \,!\, \alpha']\!] & = & [\![\alpha]\!]
\end{array}$$

In the clause for $[\alpha]\varphi$, $(M',s') \in \bullet\mathcal{S}5(\subseteq A,P)$. In the clause for $?\varphi$, $(V|[\![\varphi]\!]_M)_p = V_p \cap [\![\varphi]\!]_M$. In the clause for $L_B\alpha$, $(M',s') \in \bullet\mathcal{S}5(B,P)$ such that

$$S' = \{(M'',s'') \mid \text{there is a } t \in S : (M,t)[\![\alpha_\cup]\!](M'',s'')\} ;$$

if $(M,s)[\![\alpha_\cup]\!](M_1'',s'')$ and $(M,t)[\![\alpha_\cup]\!](M_2'',t'')$, then for all $a \in B$

$$(M_1'',s'') \sim_a' (M_2'',t'') \quad \text{iff} \quad s \sim_a t \text{ and } (M_1'',s'') \sim_a (M_2'',t'')$$

where the rightmost $\sim_a$ is equivalence of epistemic states; and for an arbitrary atom p and state (M'',u) (with valuation V'') in the domain of M':

$$(M'',s'') \in V_p' \quad \text{iff} \quad s'' \in V_p''$$

We call all the validities under this semantics the logic EA.. □

The notion $\langle\alpha\rangle$ is dual to $[\alpha]$ and is defined as

$$M,s \models \langle\alpha\rangle\varphi \quad \text{iff} \quad \text{there is a } (M',t) : (M,s)[\![\alpha]\!](M',t) \text{ and } M',t \models \varphi$$

A test results in an epistemic state without access for any agent. This is appropriate: knowledge changes as the result of 'learning'; therefore, before we encounter a learn operator we cannot say anything at all about the knowledge of the agents in the resulting epistemic state: no access. (Note that 'no access' is different from 'empty access'—see the explanation at the beginning of this subsection.) In other words, the computation of agents' knowledge is postponed until, working one's way upward from subactions that are tests, L operators are encountered in the action description.

To execute an action $L_B\alpha$ in an epistemic state (M,s), we do not just have to execute the (proper part of the) *actual* action α in the *actual* epistemic state (M,s), but also any *other* action of the same type of α in any *other* epistemic state (M,t) with the same underlying model M. The resulting set of epistemic states is the domain of the epistemic state that results from executing $L_B\alpha$ in (M, s). In other words: these epistemic states represent factual states. Such factual states cannot be distinguished from each other by an agent $a \in B$ iff their origins are indistinguishable, and if they are also indistinguishable as epistemic states. (In fact, if the agent occurs in those epistemic states, the first follows from the last. See Lemma 5.17, later.)

The semantics of learning is the raison d'être for local choice operators. Even though $[\![\beta \ ! \ \beta']\!] = [\![\beta]\!]$, so that—from a more abstract perspective—$[\![\beta \ ! \ \beta']\!]$ is computed from $[\![\beta]\!]$ *only*, $[\![L_B(\beta \ ! \ \beta')]\!]$ is computed from both $[\![\beta]\!]$ *and* $[\![\beta']\!]$. That is because the semantics of $[\![L_B(\beta \ ! \ \beta')]\!]$ is defined in terms of $[\![(\beta \ ! \ \beta')_\cup]\!]$, which is $[\![\beta_\cup \cup \beta'_\cup]\!]$, which is $[\![\beta_\cup]\!] \cup [\![\beta'_\cup]\!]$: a function of $[\![\beta]\!]$ *and* $[\![\beta']\!]$.

The semantics is complex because epistemic states serve as factual states. It is important to realise that this is merely a complex *naming device*. What counts in the model that results from a learning action, is the valuation of atoms on the domain and the access between states of the domain—whatever the names of such states.

If the interpretation of epistemic action α in epistemic state (M, s) is not empty, we say that α is *executable* in (M, s). If the interpretation is functional as well, write $(M, s)[\![\alpha]\!]$ for the unique (M', s') such that $(M, s)[\![\alpha]\!](M', s')$. Various properties of this semantics can be more conveniently formulated for actions whose interpretation is always functional. For those, see Section 5.3.4. First, an elaborate example of the semantics.

5.3.2 Example of Epistemic Action Semantics

The interpretation of the action $\mathsf{read} = L_{ab}(!L_a?p \cup L_a?\neg p)$ in epistemic state $(\mathit{Letter}, 1)$ (see Example 5.3 and Figure 5.2) is defined in terms of the interpretation of its type $(L_a?p \cup L_a?\neg p)$ on $(\mathit{Letter}, 1)$ and $(\mathit{Letter}, 0)$. To interpret $(L_a?p \cup L_a?\neg p)$ on $(\mathit{Letter}, 1)$ we may either interpret $L_a?p$ or $L_a?\neg p$. Only the first can be executed. The interpretation of $L_a?p$ on $(\mathit{Letter}, 1)$ is defined in terms of the interpretation of $?p$ on any epistemic state (Letter, x) where $?p$ can be executed, i.e. where p holds, that is on $(\mathit{Letter}, 1)$ only. Epistemic state $(\mathit{Letter}, 1)[\![?p]\!]$ is the singleton epistemic state consisting of factual state 1 without access, and where p is true. This epistemic state is therefore the single factual state in the domain of $(\mathit{Letter}, 1)[\![L_a?p]\!]$. Because the epistemic state that it stands for lacks access for a, and because $1 \sim_a 1$ in *Letter* (or quite simply because $\sim_a$ is an equivalence relation for all agents in the group of the model, currently $\{a\}$), that factual state has reflexive access for a:

$$(\mathit{Letter}, 1)[\![?p]\!] \sim_a (\mathit{Letter}, 1)[\![?p]\!]$$

In the next and final stage of the interpretation, where we construct the effect of L_{ab}, note that (as factual states)

$$(\mathit{Letter}, 1)[\![L_a?p]\!] \sim_b (\mathit{Letter}, 0)[\![L_a?\neg p]\!]$$

because agent b does not occur in those epistemic states and $1 \sim_b 1$ in *Letter*, but that

$$(Letter, 1)[\![L_a?p]\!] \not\sim_a (Letter, 0)[\![L_a?\neg p]\!]$$

because a does occur in both epistemic states and $(Letter, 1)[\![L_a?p]\!]$ is not bisimilar to $(Letter, 0)[\![L_a?\neg p]\!]$. As in the previous step of the construction, p is true in $(Letter, 1)[\![L_a?p]\!]$ and false in $(Letter, 0)[\![L_a?\neg p]\!]$. Finally, the epistemic state $(Letter, 1)[\![L_a?p]\!]$ is also the point of the resulting model. See Figure 5.3 for an overview of these computations.

Exercise 5.14 Compute the interpretation of tell $= L_{ab}?p$ on $(Letter, 1)$ (see Example 5.8). □

Exercise 5.15 The action bothmayread (see Example 5.8) is described as $L_{ab}(!L_a?p \cup L_a?\neg p \cup\ ?\top)\ ;\ L_{ab}(!L_b?p \cup L_b?\neg p \cup\ ?\top)$. Compute the result of executing the second part of this action, $L_{ab}(!L_b?p \cup L_b?\neg p \cup\ ?\top)$, in the epistemic state $(Letter, 1)[\![L_{ab}(!L_a?p \cup L_a?-p \cup\ ?\top)]\!]$ resulting from executing its first part. □

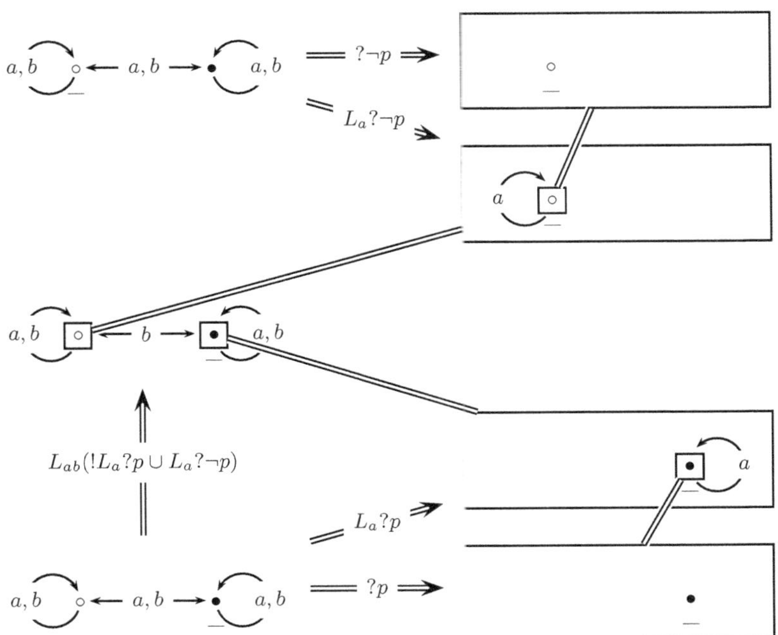

Figure 5.3. Details of the interpretation of action read in $(Letter, 1)$. All access is visualised. Atom p holds in • states, and does not hold in ∘ states. Linked boxes are identical. See also Figure 5.2.

Exercise 5.16 In the second clause of Definition 5.12, bisimilarity to an $\sim_a$-equal epistemic state is a sufficient condition for $\sim_a$-equivalence of epistemic states. Without the bisimilarity 'relaxation', not enough epistemic states would be 'the same'.

Consider the epistemic state $(Letter, 1)$. Show that without the bisimilarity condition, agent b can distinguish the effects of action

$$L_{ab}(!(L_{ab}L_{ab}?q \ ; \ L_{ab}(!L_a?p \cup L_a?\neg p)) \cup (L_{ab}?q \ ; \ L_{ab}(L_a?p\cup \ !L_a?\neg p)))$$

from those of action

$$L_{ab}((L_{ab}L_{ab}?q \ ; \ L_{ab}(!L_a?p \cup L_a?\neg p))\cup!(L_{ab}?q \ ; \ L_{ab}(L_a?p\cup \ !L_a?\neg p)))$$

Explain also why this is undesirable. □

5.3.3 Semantic Properties

Lemma 5.17 Suppose that $(M,s)[\![\alpha]\!](M',s')$ and $(M,t)[\![\beta]\!](M'',t'')$, and that $a \in gr(M') \cup gr(M'')$. If $(M',s') \sim_a (M'',t'')$, then $s \sim_a t$. □

Proof Equivalence of $(M',s') \sim_a (M'',t'')$ is established by equivalence of the points of those epistemic states, modulo bisimilarity. But the *only* place where access between factual states, such as points, is ever constructed in the semantics of actions, is in the clause for 'learning'. In that part of the semantics, access can only be established if the 'origins' of those states are already the same, i.e., if $s \sim_a t$. □

The more intuitive contrapositive formulation of this Lemma says, that if an agent can distinguish states from each other, they will never become the same. In a temporal epistemic context this is known as the property of *perfect recall.*

Proposition 5.18 (Action algebra) Let $\alpha, \alpha', \alpha'' \in \mathcal{L}_!^{\mathrm{act}}(A)$. Then:

- $[\![(\alpha \cup \alpha') \cup \alpha'']\!] = [\![\alpha \cup (\alpha' \cup \alpha'')]\!]$
- $[\![(\alpha \ ; \ \alpha') \ ; \ \alpha'']\!] = [\![\alpha \ ; \ (\alpha' \ ; \ \alpha'')]\!]$
- $[\![(\alpha \cup \alpha') \ ; \ \alpha'']\!] = [\![(\alpha \ ; \ \alpha'') \cup (\alpha' \ ; \ \alpha'')]\!]$
- $[\![L_B\alpha]\!] = [\![L_B L_B\alpha]\!]$ □

Proof The first three properties are proved by simple relational algebra. We show the third, the rest is similar: $[\![(\alpha\cup\alpha') \ ; \ \alpha'']\!] = [\![\alpha\cup\alpha']\!]\circ[\![\alpha'']\!] = ([\![\alpha]\!]\cup[\![\alpha']\!])\circ [\![\alpha'']\!] = ([\![\alpha]\!]\circ[\![\alpha'']\!])\cup([\![\alpha']\!]\circ[\![\alpha'']\!]) = [\![\alpha \ ; \ \alpha'']\!]\cup[\![\alpha' \ ; \ \alpha'']\!] = [\![(\alpha \ ; \ \alpha'')\cup(\alpha' \ ; \ \alpha'')]\!]$.

Concerning $[\![L_B\alpha]\!] = [\![L_B L_B\alpha]\!]$, this immediately follows from the semantics of actions: consider the computation of $L_B L_B\alpha$. Let (M,s) be arbitrary. We have that α is executable iff $L_B\alpha$ is executable, that (therefore) the number of epistemic states (M',s') such that $(M,s)[\![\alpha_\cup]\!](M',s')$ equals the number of states (M'', s'') with $(M, s)[\![L_B\alpha_\cup]\!](M'', s'')$—namely, each s'' in the latter corresponds to a (M', s') in the former. Note also that $(L_B\alpha)_\cup = L_B\alpha_\cup$. Therefore the domain an epistemic state resulting from executing $L_BL_B\alpha$ equals the domain of such an epistemic state resulting from executing $L_B\alpha$. Obviously, the valuation does not change either.

In the domain of the first, two factual states are the same for agent a ($\sim_a$) if their s, t origins in M are the same for that agent *and* if they are the same as epistemic states. But these epistemic states in the domain (of an epistemic state resulting from executing $L_BL_B\alpha$), that are the results of executing actions of type $L_B\alpha_\cup$, are the same for a if *their* points (resulting from executions of $\alpha_\cup$) are the same for that agent, i.e., if they are the same for a in the domain of the epistemic state resulting from executing $L_B\alpha$. □

Exercise 5.19 Prove the first two items of Proposition 5.18. □

The two main theorems of interest are that bisimilarity of epistemic states implies their modal equivalence, and that action execution preserves bisimilarity of epistemic states. We prove them *together* by simultaneous induction.

Theorem 5.20 (Bisimilarity implies modal equivalence)
Let $\varphi \in \mathcal{L}_!^{\text{stat}}(A)$. Let $(M, s), (M', s') \in \bullet\mathcal{S}5(A)$. If $(M, s) \leftrightarrows (M, s')$, then $(M, s) \models \varphi$ iff $(M', s') \models \varphi$. □

Proof By induction on the structure of φ. The proof is standard, except for the clause $\varphi = [\alpha]\psi$ that we therefore present in detail.

Assume $(M, s) \models [\alpha]\psi$. We have to prove $(M', s') \models [\alpha]\psi$. Let (N', t') be arbitrary such that $(M', s')[\![\alpha]\!](N', t')$. By simultaneous induction hypothesis (Theorem 5.21) it follows from $(M', s')[\![\alpha]\!](N', t')$ and $(M, s) \leftrightarrows (M', s')$ that there is a (N, t) such that $(N, t) \leftrightarrows (N', t')$ and $(M, s)[\![\alpha]\!](N, t)$. From $(M, s)[\![\alpha]\!](N, t)$ and $(M, s) \models [\alpha]\psi$ (given) follows that $(N, t) \models \psi$. From $(N, t) \leftrightarrows (N', t')$ and $(N, t) \models \psi$ it follows that $(N', t') \models \psi$. From the last and $(M', s')[\![\alpha]\!](N', t')$ it follows that $(M', s') \models [\alpha]\psi$. □

Theorem 5.21 (Action execution preserves bisimilarity)
Let $\alpha \in \mathcal{L}_!^{\text{act}}(A)$ and $(M, s), (M', s') \in \bullet\mathcal{S}5(A)$. If $(M, s) \leftrightarrows (M', s')$ and there is a $(N, t) \in \bullet\mathcal{S}5(\subseteq A)$ such that $(M, s)[\![\alpha]\!](N, t)$, then there is a $(N', t') \in \bullet\mathcal{S}5(\subseteq A)$ such that $(M', s')[\![\alpha]\!](N', t')$ and $(N, t) \leftrightarrows (N', t')$. □

Proof By induction on the structure of α, or, more accurately, by induction on the *complexity* of α defined as: α is more complex than any of its structural parts and $L_B\alpha$ is more complex than $\alpha_\cup$.

Case $?\varphi$: Suppose $\mathfrak{R} : (M, s) \leftrightarrows (M', s')$. By simultaneous induction (Theorem 5.20) it follows from $(M, s) \leftrightarrows (M', s')$ and $(M, s) \models \varphi$ that $(M', s') \models \varphi$. Define, for all $t \in (M, s)[\![?\varphi]\!]$, $u \in (M', s')[\![?\varphi]\!]$: $\mathfrak{R}^{?\varphi}(t, u)$ iff $\mathfrak{R}(t, u)$. Then $\mathfrak{R}^{?\varphi} : (M, s)[\![?\varphi]\!] \leftrightarrows (M', s')[\![?\varphi]\!]$, because (Points:) $\mathfrak{R}^{?\varphi}(s, s')$, (Back and Forth:) both epistemic states have empty access, and (Valuation:) $\mathfrak{R}^{?\varphi}(t, u)$ implies $\mathfrak{R}(t, u)$. In other words: $(M', s')[\![?\varphi]\!]$ is the required (N', t').

Case $L_B\alpha$: Suppose $\mathfrak{R} : (M,s) \leftrightarroweq (M',s')$ and $(M,s)[\![L_B\alpha]\!](N,t)$. Let $(N'',t'') \in (N,t)$ be arbitrary (i.e., the former is an epistemic state that is a factual state in the domain of the latter). Then there is a $u \in (M,s)$ such that $(M,u)[\![\alpha_\cup]\!](N'',t'')$. Because $u \in (M,s)$ and $\mathfrak{R} : (M,s) \leftrightarroweq (M',s')$, there is a $u' \in (M',s')$ such that $\mathfrak{R}(u,u')$ and obviously we also have that $\mathfrak{R} : (M,u) \leftrightarroweq (M',u')$ (the domain of an epistemic state is the domain of its underlying model). By induction, using that the complexity of $\alpha_\cup$ is smaller than that of $L_B\alpha$, there is a (N''',t''') such that $(M',u')[\![\alpha_\cup]\!](N''',t''')$ and $(N'',t'') \leftrightarroweq (N''',t''')$.

Now define (N',t') as follows: its domain consists of worlds (N''',t''') constructed according to the procedure just outlined; accessibility between such worlds is accessibility between those worlds as sets of epistemic states, and valuation corresponds to those in the bisimilar worlds of (N,t). Finally, the point of (N',t') is the result of executing α in (M',s') that is bisimilar to the point of (N,t). The accessibility on (N',t') corresponds to that on (N,t): if $(N_1,t_1) \sim_a (N_2,t_2)$, $(N_1,t_1) \leftrightarroweq (N_1',t_1')$, and $(N_2,t_2) \leftrightarroweq (N_2',t_2')$, then $(N_1',t_1') \sim_a (N_1',t_1')$. Therefore $(M',s')[\![L_B\alpha]\!](N',t')$ and $(N,t) \leftrightarroweq (N',t')$.

Case $\alpha\ ;\ \beta$: Suppose $(M,s) \leftrightarroweq (M',s')$ and $(M,s)[\![\alpha\ ;\ \beta]\!](N,t)$. Note that $[\![\alpha\ ;\ \beta]\!] = [\![\alpha]\!] \circ [\![\beta]\!]$. Let (N_1,t_1) be such that $(M,s)[\![\alpha]\!](N_1,t_1)$ and that $(N_1, t_1)[\![\beta]\!](N,t)$. By induction we have a (N_1',t_1') such that $(M',s')[\![\alpha]\!](N_1',t_1')$ and $(N_1,t_1) \leftrightarroweq (N_1',t_1')$. Again, by induction, we have a (N',t') such that $(N_1',t_1')[\![\beta]\!](N',t')$ and $(N,t) \leftrightarroweq (N',t')$. But then also $(M',s')[\![\alpha\ ;\ \beta]\!](N',t')$.

Case $\alpha \cup \beta$: Suppose $(M,s) \leftrightarroweq (M',s')$ and $(M,s)[\![\alpha \cup \beta]\!](N,t)$. Then either $(M,s)[\![\alpha]\!](N,t)$ or $(M,s)[\![\beta]\!](N,t)$. If $(M,s)[\![\alpha]\!](N,t)$, then by induction there is a (N',t') such that $(M',s')[\![\alpha]\!](N',t')$ and $(N,t) \leftrightarroweq (N',t')$. Therefore, also $(M',s')[\![\alpha \cup \beta]\!](N',t')$. Similarly if $(M,s)[\![\beta]\!](N,t)$.

Cases $\alpha\ !\ \beta$ and α ¡ β are similar to $\alpha \cup \beta$ but even simpler. □

5.3.4 Deterministic and Non-deterministic Actions

Actions may have more than one execution in a given epistemic state. Although the action mayread only has a single execution in a given epistemic state, the type $L_{ab}(L_a?p \cup L_a?\neg p \cup\ ?\top)$ of mayread always has *two* executions. When p is true, Anne can either read the letter, or not. In the first case the corresponding action instance is $L_{ab}(!L_a?p \cup L_a?\neg p \cup\ ?\top)$, in the other case it is $L_{ab}(L_a?p \cup L_a?\neg p \cup\ !?\top)$, i.e., mayread itself. The only source of non-determinism in the language is the non-deterministic action operator $\cup$. It turns out that this operator is superfluous in a rather strong sense: the language with $\cup$ is just as expressive as the language without; for details, see Proposition 8.56 in Chapter 8 on expressivity. This is useful, because properties of the logic and proofs in the logic may be more conveniently formulated or proved in the language without $\cup$. In this subsection we prove some elementary properties of deterministic and non-deterministic actions. A trivial observation is that

Proposition 5.22 Deterministic actions have a (partial) functional interpretation. □

For non-deterministic actions we have the following validity:

Proposition 5.23 Valid is $[\alpha \cup \alpha']\varphi \leftrightarrow ([\alpha]\varphi \wedge [\alpha']\varphi)$. □

A conceptually more intuitive formulation of the above is $\langle \alpha \cup \beta \rangle \varphi \leftrightarrow (\langle \alpha \rangle \varphi \vee \langle \beta \rangle \varphi)$. The proof of Proposition 5.23 is obvious when seen in this dual form, as $[\![\alpha \cup \beta]\!] = [\![\alpha]\!] \cup [\![\beta]\!]$. A stronger but also fairly obvious result holds as well: The interpretation of an action is equal to non-deterministic choice between all its instances:

Proposition 5.24
Let $\alpha \in \mathcal{L}_!^{\mathrm{act}}$. Then $[\![\alpha]\!] = \bigcup_{\alpha_!} [\![\alpha_!]\!]$. □

Proof Note that $\alpha_!$ means an arbitrary instance of α, so that $\bigcup_{\alpha_!}$ is the union for all instances of α. The proof is by induction on the structure of α. The two cases of interest are $\alpha \cup \alpha'$ and $L_B\alpha$:

Case $\alpha \cup \alpha'$:
By definition, $[\![\alpha \cup \alpha']\!]$ equals $[\![\alpha]\!] \cup [\![\alpha']\!]$. By applying the inductive hypothesis to α and α', $[\![\alpha]\!] \cup [\![\alpha']\!]$ equals $\bigcup_{\alpha_!} [\![\alpha_!]\!] \cup \bigcup_{\alpha'_!} [\![\alpha'_!]\!]$. Again by definition, this is equal to $[\![\bigcup_{\alpha_!} \alpha_!]\!] \cup [\![\bigcup_{\alpha'_!} \alpha'_!]\!]$, which is equal to $[\![\bigcup_{\alpha_!} \alpha_! \cup \bigcup_{\alpha'_!} \alpha'_!]\!]$, which is $[\![\bigcup_{(\alpha \cup \alpha)_!} (\alpha \cup \alpha')_!]\!]$. The last equals $\bigcup_{(\alpha \cup \alpha)_!} [\![(\alpha \cup \alpha')_!]\!]$.

Case $L_B\alpha$:
Let M and $s \in \mathcal{D}(M)$ be arbitrary. Suppose $(M, s)[\![L_B\alpha]\!](M', s')$ and $M', s' \models \varphi$. By definition (of the semantics of actions) the point s' of (M', s') is an epistemic state such that $(M, s)[\![\alpha]\!]s'$ By induction, there must be a instance $\alpha_!$ of α such that $(M, s)[\![\alpha_!]\!]s'$. By the semantics of 'learning', we now immediately have $(M, s)[\![L_B\alpha_!]\!](M', s')$ for some instance $L_B\alpha_!$ of $L_B\alpha$.
The other direction is trivial. □

Proposition 5.24 can also be expressed as the validity

$$\langle \alpha \rangle \varphi \leftrightarrow \bigvee_{\alpha_!} \langle \alpha_! \rangle \varphi \ ,$$

or its dual form

$$[\alpha]\varphi \leftrightarrow \bigwedge_{\alpha_!} [\alpha_!]\varphi \ .$$

Execution of deterministic actions of group B results in epistemic states of group B. This validates the overload of the gr operator for both actions and structures:

Proposition 5.25 Given $M \in \mathcal{S}5(A)$, $s \in \mathcal{D}(M)$, and $\alpha \in \mathcal{L}_!^{\mathrm{act}}(A)$. Suppose α is deterministic and executable in (M, s). Then $gr((M, s)[\![\alpha]\!]) = gr(\alpha)$. □

Proof By induction on action structure.

Case '$?\varphi$': By definition of gr, $gr((M,s)[\![?\varphi]\!]) = \emptyset = gr(?\varphi)$.

Case 'L': By definition of gr, $gr((M,s)[\![L_B\alpha]\!]) = B = gr(L_B\alpha)$.

Case ';': By definition of action semantics, $(M,s)[\![\alpha\ ;\ \beta]\!] = ((M,s)[\![\alpha]\!])[\![\beta]\!]$. By definition of gr, $gr(\alpha\ ;\ \beta) = gr(\beta)$. By inductive hypothesis, we have that $gr(((M,s)[\![\alpha]\!])[\![\beta]\!]) = gr(\beta)$.

Case '!': By definition of gr, $gr((M,s)[\![\alpha\ !\ \beta]\!]) = gr((M,s)[\![\alpha]\!])$. By inductive hypothesis, $gr((M,s)[\![\alpha]\!]) = gr(\alpha)$, and also by definition of gr, the last equals $gr(\alpha\ !\ \beta)$.

Case '¡' is as case '!'. □

Exercise 5.26 Show that Proposition 5.25 does not hold for all $\mathcal{L}_!^{\mathrm{act}}$ actions. □

For deterministic actions α, Theorem 5.21 can be formulated more succinctly:

Corollary 5.27 Let $(M,s), (M',s') \in \bullet\mathcal{S}5(A)$, and let $\alpha \in \mathcal{L}_!^{\mathrm{act}}(A)$ be a deterministic action that is executable in (M,s). If $(M,s) \leftrightarrows (M',s')$, then $(M,s)[\![\alpha]\!] \leftrightarrows (M',s')[\![\alpha]\!]$. □

5.3.5 Valid Properties of the Logic

This subsection lists some relevant validities of the logic *EA*. We remind the reader that such validities are candidate axioms for a proof system for *EA*, but that we do not give (nor have) a complete axiomatisation. The matter will be addressed at the end of this subsection.

Public announcements can only be executed when true. Similarly, more complex epistemic actions are sometimes executable, and sometimes not. A direct way to express that an epistemic action α is executable in an epistemic state (M,s) is to require that $M, s \models \langle\alpha\rangle\top$: this expresses that *some* epistemic state can be reached. Alternatively, one can express the condition of executability as the *precondition* of an epistemic action. In the case of a public announcement, the precondition is the announcement formula. For arbitrary epistemic actions, the notion is somewhat more complex but fairly straightforward.

Definition 5.28 (Precondition) The precondition $\mathsf{pre} : \mathcal{L}_!^{\mathrm{act}} \to \mathcal{L}_!^{\mathrm{stat}}$ of an epistemic action is inductively defined as

$$\begin{aligned}
\mathsf{pre}(?\varphi) &= \varphi \\
\mathsf{pre}(\alpha\ ;\ \beta) &= \mathsf{pre}(\alpha) \wedge \langle\alpha\rangle\mathsf{pre}(\beta) \\
\mathsf{pre}(\alpha \cup \beta) &= \mathsf{pre}(\alpha) \vee \mathsf{pre}(\beta) \\
\mathsf{pre}(\alpha\ !\ \beta) &= \mathsf{pre}(\alpha) \\
\mathsf{pre}(L_B\alpha) &= \mathsf{pre}(\alpha)
\end{aligned}$$

□

One can now prove that $\models \mathsf{pre}(\alpha) \leftrightarrow \langle\alpha\rangle\top$. The notion of precondition will make it easier to compare the properties in the following proposition with the axioms in the proof system for the action model logic in Chapter 6.

Exercise 5.29 Show that $\models \mathsf{pre}(\alpha) \leftrightarrow \langle\alpha\rangle\top$. □

Proposition 5.30 All of the following are valid:

- $[?\varphi]\psi \leftrightarrow (\varphi \rightarrow \psi)$
- $[\alpha\ ;\ \alpha']\varphi \leftrightarrow [\alpha][\alpha']\varphi$
- $[\alpha \cup \alpha']\varphi \leftrightarrow ([\alpha]\varphi \wedge [\alpha']\varphi)$
- $[\alpha\ !\ \alpha']\varphi \leftrightarrow [\alpha]\varphi$
- $[\alpha]p \leftrightarrow (\mathsf{pre}(\alpha) \rightarrow p)$
- $[\alpha]\neg\varphi \leftrightarrow (\mathsf{pre}(\alpha) \rightarrow \neg[\alpha]\varphi)$ □

Proof We prove two, one has been proved as Proposition 5.23, and the remaining are left to the reader.

$\models [?\varphi]\psi \leftrightarrow (\varphi \rightarrow \psi)$

Note that in $[?\varphi]\psi \leftrightarrow (\varphi \rightarrow \psi)$, ψ is a propositional formula ($\psi \in \mathcal{L}_!^{\mathrm{stat}}(\emptyset, P)$), because $gr(?\varphi) = \emptyset$. (In Definition 5.6 of the syntax of actions and formulas, see the restriction on ψ in the clause $[\alpha]\psi$.) The truth of propositional formulas is unaffected by action execution.

Suppose $M, s \models [?\varphi]\psi$ and $M, s \models \varphi$. Then $(M, s)[\![?\varphi]\!] \models \psi$. Because $\psi \in \mathcal{L}_!^{\mathrm{stat}}(\emptyset, P)$, also $M, s \models \psi$. Therefore $M, s \models \varphi \rightarrow \psi$.

Suppose $M, s \models \varphi \rightarrow \psi$. If $M, s \not\models \varphi$, then $M, s \models [?\varphi]\psi$ trivially holds. Otherwise, from $M, s \models \varphi$ and $M, s \models \varphi \rightarrow \psi$ follows $M, s \models \psi$. Because $\psi \in \mathcal{L}_!^{\mathrm{stat}}(\emptyset, P)$, and because (since $M, s \models \varphi$) $(M, s)[\![?\varphi]\!]$ exists, also $(M, s)[\![?\varphi]\!] \models \psi$. Therefore, as well, $(M, s) \models [?\varphi]\psi$.

$\models [\alpha]p \leftrightarrow (\mathsf{pre}(\alpha) \rightarrow p)$

Suppose $M, s \models [\alpha]p$, and assume that $M, s \models \mathsf{pre}(\alpha)$. Let M', s' be such that $(M, s)[\![\alpha]\!](M', s')$. From $M, s \models [\alpha]p$ and $(M, s)[\![\alpha]\!](M', s')$ follows $M', s' \models p$. As epistemic actions do not change the valuation of atoms, $M, s \models p$.

For the converse direction, note that $M, s \not\models \mathsf{pre}(\alpha)$ trivially implies $M, s \models [\alpha]p$. Else, $M, s \models \mathsf{pre}(\alpha)$ implies $M, s \models \langle\alpha\rangle\top$—and whenever α can be executed, atoms do not change their value. □

Exercise 5.31 Prove the remaining cases of Proposition 5.30. □

This brings us to the formulation of a principle relating actions and knowledge. For public announcements the principle was $[\varphi]K_a\psi \leftrightarrow (\varphi \rightarrow K_a[\varphi]\psi)$. This principle no longer holds when we replace an announcement φ by an arbitrary action α, because not all agents may have full access to the postconditions of the action α! A typical example is the action read where Anne reads the letter containing p while Bill watches her: $L_{ab}(!L_a?p \cup L_a?\neg p)$.

After execution of this action Anne knows that p is true: $K_a p$. As read is a deterministic action, this is therefore true after *every* execution of the action: $[\mathsf{read}]K_a p$. And Bill knows that too: he considers it possible that p is false and that p is true; in the first case $[\mathsf{read}]K_a p$ is trivially true, in the second case it is true by the argument above. Therefore Bill *knows* that $[\mathsf{read}]K_a p$ is true, in other words $K_b[\mathsf{read}]K_a p$ is true. But on the other hand, it is not the case that after read's execution Bill knows that Anne knows p: $[\mathsf{read}]K_b K_a p$ is false. So, $[\alpha]K_a\psi \leftrightarrow (\mathsf{pre}(\alpha) \rightarrow K_a[\alpha]\psi)$ does not hold for arbitrary epistemic actions.

We need a generalisation of this principle that takes into account that some agents may not know what action is actually taking place. Consider again the action read. Bill cannot distinguish that action from the action $L_{ab}(L_a?p\cup\ !L_a?\neg p)$ where Anne learns $\neg p$ instead. Whatever Bill *knows* after the action read, should therefore also be true if in fact the other action had taken place. In case of these two actions there is no 'interesting' postcondition. But suppose the actions had been $\mathsf{this} = L_{ab}(!L_a?(q \wedge p) \cup L_a?(q \wedge \neg p))$ and $\mathsf{that} = L_{ab}(L_a?(q \wedge p)\cup\ !L_a?(q \wedge \neg p))$ instead. After both actions q is true. In other words: q is true after this, but also after any other action that Bill cannot distinguish from this, namely that. He therefore *knows* that after executing either action, q is true: $K_b[\mathsf{this}]q$ and $K_b[\mathsf{that}]q$, which we temptingly write as $\bigwedge_{\beta\sim_b \mathsf{this}} K_b[\beta]q$. This is sufficient to conclude that $[\mathsf{this}]K_b q$. The general principle on 'actions and knowledge' should then be

$$[\alpha]K_a\varphi \leftrightarrow (\mathsf{pre}(\alpha) \rightarrow \bigwedge_{\beta\sim_a\alpha} K_a[\beta]\varphi)$$

Unfortunately, we do not know of a *general* notion of the syntactic action accessibility $\beta \sim_a \alpha$. A similar problem occurs for a principle relating actions and common knowledge. In Chapter 6 another language for epistemic actions is introduced. In that logic the notion of accessibility between actions is a primitive. The principle relating actions and knowledge is then indeed precisely the principle that we describe above. For that logic we provide an axiomatisation.

We hope that the attention that we have given to the logic *EA* in this textbook, is sufficiently validated because it is (or at least, it seems to us) a convenient and flexible specification language for multi-agent system dynamics, properly backed up by a formal semantics—even though we have not provided a complete axiomatisation. We conclude this chapter with two in-depth investigations of such multi-agent systems.

5.4 Card Game Actions

We describe epistemic states involving players holding cards and exchanging information about their cards and their knowledge, including what they know about other players. First we model the actions of players picking up dealt cards. Then we model various actions in the situation where three players each know their own card. This is the setting of Example 4.2 in Chapter 4. For one of these actions, namely, the show action wherein Anne shows her card to Bill, we once more perform the semantic computation in great detail, to illustrate the semantics of actions. This subsection is followed by a short subsection on 'knowledge games' such as Cluedo. Finally comes yet another cards setting, now involving only two players.

5.4.1 Dealing and Picking Up Cards

Suppose there are three players Anne, Bill and Cath (a, b, c) and three cards 0, 1, and 2. Proposition 0_a expresses that Anne holds card 0, as before, etc. There are six possible deals of three cards over three players. This time we consider the model where the cards have been dealt but where the players have not picked up their card yet. A player's card is simply in front of that player on the table, facedown. Therefore, none of the three players can distinguish any deal from any other deal: their access on the domain of six deals is simply the universal relation; all deals are the same to them. This is the top-left model in Figure 5.4. Suppose the actual deal is 012 (Anne holds 0, Bill holds 1, and Cath holds 2). In this 'initial epistemic state' the following actions take place:

Example 5.32

- pickup_a: Anne picks up her card and looks at it. It is card 0.
- pickup_b: Bill picks up his card and looks at it. It is card 1.
- pickup_c: Cath picks up her card and looks at it. It is card 2. □

When Anne picks up her card, neither Bill nor Cath know which card that is. Publicly is only known that it must be one of the three possible cards 0, 1, 2. Therefore, the action needs a description where all agents learn that Anne learns one of three alternatives, and where the actual alternative is that she picks up card 0. Of course, Bill's and Cath's subsequent actions are quite similar. The descriptions in $\mathcal{L}_!^{\text{act}}$ of these actions are, therefore:

Example 5.33

- $\mathsf{pickup}_a = L_{abc}(!L_a?0_a \cup L_a?1_a \cup L_a?2_a)$
- $\mathsf{pickup}_b = L_{abc}(L_b?0_b \cup\, !L_b?1_b \cup L_b?2_b)$
- $\mathsf{pickup}_c = L_{abc}(L_c?0_c \cup L_c?1_c \cup\, !L_c?2_c)$ □

The resulting models are visualised in Figure 5.4. The final model is, of course, the model *Hexa* where each player only knows his own card.

5.4.2 Game Actions in Hexa

We proceed from the epistemic state $(Hexa, 012)$ where each player only knows his own card, and where the actual deal of cards is that Anne holds 0, Bill holds

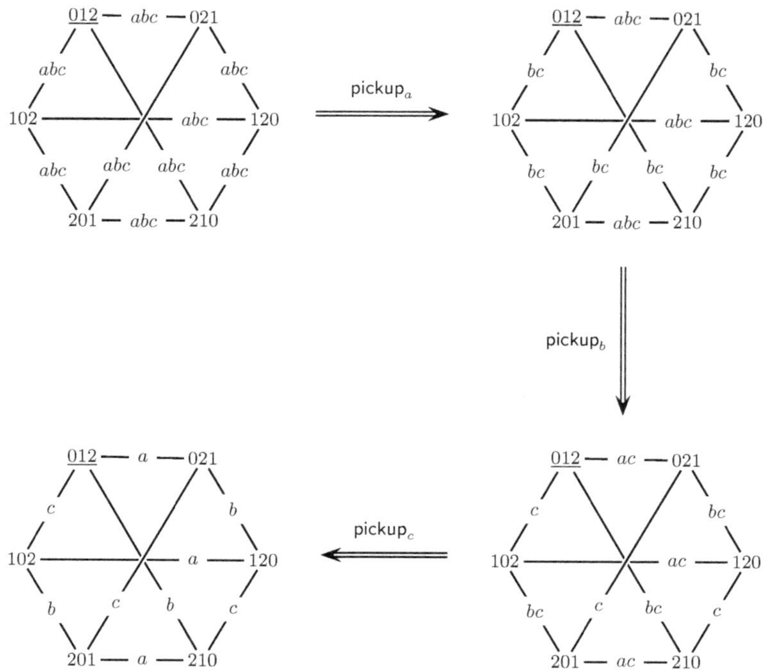

Figure 5.4. Three cards have been dealt over three players. The actual deal is 012: Anne holds 0, Bill holds 1, and Cath holds 2. This is pictured in the top-left corner. Anne now picks up her card (0). Then Bill picks up his card (1). Finally, Cath picks up her card (2). These three transitions are pictured. In fact, in all but the last model there are more links between states in the visualisation than strictly necessary—but the pictured transitions become more elegant that way.

1, and Cath holds 2. That each player only knows his own card induces for each player an equivalence relation on the domain.[3] We can imagine various actions to take place:

Example 5.34 (table) Anne puts card 0 (face up) on the table. □

Example 5.35 (show) Anne shows (only) Bill card 0. Cath cannot see the face of the shown card, but notices that a card is being shown. □

Example 5.36 (whisper) Bill asks Anne to tell him a card that she (Anne) does not have. Anne whispers in Bill's ear "I do not have card 2." Cath notices that the question is answered, but cannot hear the answer. □

[3] We can also see the model as an interpreted system for three agents, where each agent only knows his own local state, where each agent has three local state values—and where additionally there is some interdependence between global states, namely, that the value of your local state cannot be the value of the local state of another agent.

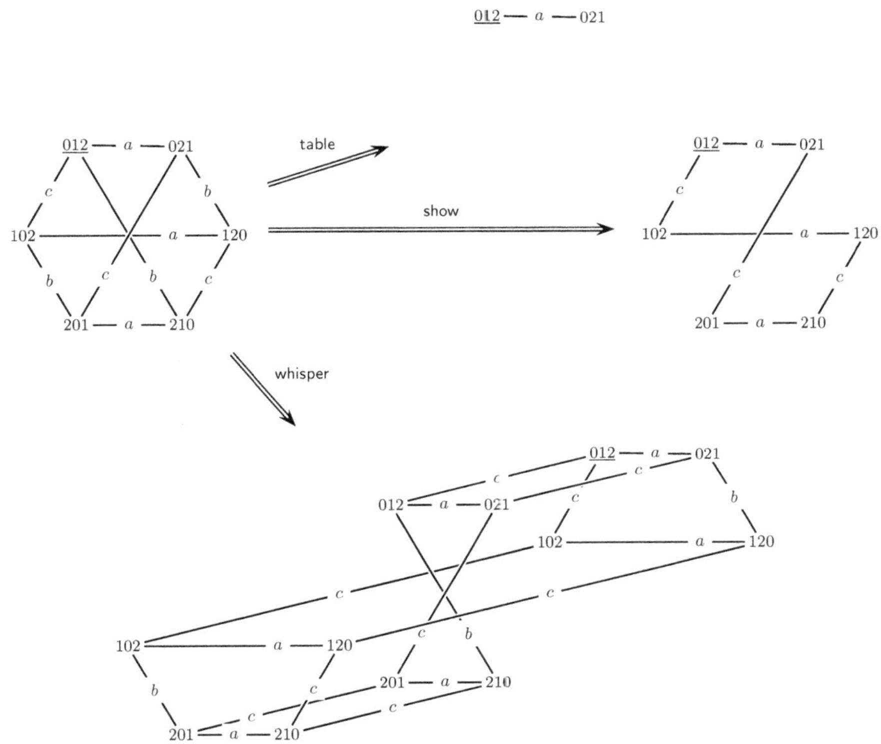

Figure 5.5. The results of executing table, show, and whisper in the state $(\mathit{Hexa}, 012)$ where Anne holds 0, Bill holds 1, and Cath holds 2. The points of the states are underlined. States are named by the deals that characterise them. Assume reflexivity and transitivity of access. The structures resulting from show and whisper are explained in great detail in the text.

We assume that only. the truth is told. In show and whisper, we assume that it is publicly known what Cath can and cannot see or hear.

Figure 5.5 pictures. $(\mathit{Hexa}, 012)$ and the epistemic states that result from executing the three actions. The action table is yet another appearance of a 'public announcement' and it therefore suffices to eliminate the states from the domain where Anne does not hold card 0. We can restrict access and valuation correspondingly, as it is publicly known that eliminated deals are no longer accessible. In show we cannot eliminate any state. After this action, e.g., Anne can imagine that Cath can imagine that Anne has shown card 0, but also that Anne has shown card 1, or card 2. However, some *links* between states have now been severed: whatever the actual deal of cards, Bill cannot consider any other deal after the execution of show. In whisper Anne can *choose* whether to whisper "not 1" or "not 2". The resulting epistemic state has therefore twice as many states as the current epistemic state. This is because for each deal of cards there are now two possible actions that can be executed.

We can paraphrase some more of the structure of the actions. In table, all three players learn that Anne holds card 0, where 'learning' is the dynamic equivalent of 'common knowledge'. Note that there is also a slight but interesting difference between Anne publicly *showing* card 0 to the other players and Anne *saying* that she holds card 0: the first is obviously the public announcement of 0_a whereas the second is more properly the public announcement of $K_a 0_a$, even though we have typically also described that as 0_a.

In the show action, Anne and Bill learn that Anne holds 0, whereas the group consisting of Anne, Bill and Cath learns that Anne and Bill learn which card Anne holds, or, in other words: that either Anne and Bill learn that Anne holds 0, or that Anne and Bill learn that Anne holds 1, or that Anne and Bill learn that Anne holds 2. The choice made by subgroup $\{a, b\}$ from the three alternatives is *local*, i.e., known to them only, because it is hidden from Cath. This is expressed by the 'local choice' operators '!' and '¡'. In fact, Cath knows that Anne can only possibly show card 0 or card 1, and not card 2, as Cath holds card 2 herself. But what counts is that this is not *publicly* known: Bill does not know (before the action takes place) that Cath knows that Anne cannot show card 2. The paraphrase describes the *publicly known* alternatives, and therefore all three.

The whisper action is paraphrased quite similar to the show action, namely as: "Anne and Bill learn that Anne does not hold card 2, and Anne, Bill, and Cath learn that Anne and Bill learn that Anne does not hold card 0, or that Anne and Bill learn that Anne does not hold card 1, or that Anne and Bill learn that Anne does not hold card 2". In the description of this action we also need the local choice operator.

In case of confusion when modelling an action: always first describe the type of an action, and only then the specific instance you want. From the description 'Anne whispers a card that she does not hold into Bill's ear' it is more immediately clear that no specific card can be excluded.

Example 5.37 The description of the actions table, show, and whisper in $\mathcal{L}_!(\{a, b, c\}, \{0_a, 1_a, 2_a, 0_b, \dots\})$ is:

$$\begin{aligned} \text{table} &= L_{abc}?0_a \\ \text{show} &= L_{abc}(!L_{ab}?0_a \cup L_{ab}?1_a \cup L_{ab}?2_a) \\ \text{whisper} &= L_{abc}(L_{ab}?\neg 0_a \cup L_{ab}?\neg 1_a \cup\, !L_{ab}?\neg 2_a) \end{aligned}$$

□

As we assume associativity of $\cup$ in these descriptions, and as local choice between alternatives that have been ruled out is irrelevant, the description $L_{abc}(!L_{ab}?0_a \cup L_{ab}?1_a \cup L_{ab}?2_a)$ is formally one of

$$\begin{gathered} L_{abc}(L_{ab}?0_a \;!\; (L_{ab}?1_a \;!\; L_{ab}?2_a)) \\ L_{abc}(L_{ab}?0_a \;!\; (L_{ab}?1_a \;¡\; L_{ab}?2_a)) \\ L_{abc}((L_{ab}?0_a \;!\; L_{ab}?1_a) \;!\; L_{ab}?2_a) \end{gathered}$$

Example 5.38 The types $\mathsf{table}_\cup$, $\mathsf{show}_\cup$, and $\mathsf{whisper}_\cup$ of these actions are

$$\begin{aligned}\mathsf{table}_\cup &= L_{abc}?0_a \\ \mathsf{show}_\cup &= L_{abc}(L_{ab}?0_a \cup L_{ab}?1_a \cup L_{ab}?2_a) \\ \mathsf{whisper}_\cup &= L_{abc}(L_{ab}?\neg 0_a \cup L_{ab}?\neg 1_a \cup L_{ab}?\neg 2_a)\end{aligned}$$

□

Apparently, there are three actions of type $\mathsf{show}_\cup$ and three actions of type $\mathsf{whisper}_\cup$, representing Anne showing card 0, card 1, and card 2; and Anne whispering that she does not hold card 0, card 1, and card 2, respectively. There are four actions of that type in the more formal description, as the two actions of form $(x \mathbin{!} (y \mathbin{!} z))$ and $(x \mathbin{!} (y \mathbin{¡} z))$ are indistinguishable when written as $(!x \cup y \cup z)$.

Note that the table action $L_{abc}?0_a$ is, obviously, the same as its type. But instead we could have chosen to model that action as $(!L_{abc}?0_a \cup L_{abc}?1_a \cup L_{abc}?2_a)$, in which case its type would have been $(L_{abc}?0_a \cup L_{abc}?1_a \cup L_{abc}?2_a)$. That more properly describes the action "Anne puts her card face up on the table (whatever the card is)".

We continue with details on how to compute the interpretation of these card show actions in the model *Hexa*. To compute the interpretation of show is requested in Exercise 5.39, following immediately below. It is also instructive to actually compute the interpretation of table and see the semantics of public announcements reappear, even though the semantic computations are different. Observations on the computation of $\mathsf{whisper}$ follow after Exercise 5.39.

Exercise 5.39 Compute the interpretation of the show action in $(Hexa, 012)$ in detail. This exercise has a detailed answer. We recommend the reader to pay careful attention to this exercise. □

In the case of the action $\mathsf{whisper}$ $(L_{abc}(L_{ab}?\neg 0_a \cup L_{ab}?\neg 1_a \cup\, !L_{ab}?\neg 2_a))$, where Anne whispers into Bill's ear that she does not have card 2, Cath does not know what Anne has whispered, and should therefore not be able to distinguish in the resulting epistemic state $(Hexa, 012)[\![\mathsf{whisper}]\!]$ the state resulting from whispering "not 0" from the states resulting from "not 1" and "not 2". This is indeed the case. Consider access in $(Hexa, 012)[\![\mathsf{whisper}]\!]$ in Figure 5.5 (page 129). As before, we have named the states by the deals characterising their valuations, to improve readability. The state 012 'in front' in the picture is the epistemic state $(Hexa, 012)[\![L_{ab}?\neg 1_a]\!]$ and the state 012 'at the back' (that is also the point of the resulting structure) is the epistemic state $(Hexa, 012)[\![L_{ab}?\neg 2_a]\!]$. They cannot be distinguished from one another by Cath, because she does not occur in the groups of either epistemic state (so that they are indistinguishable from one another as epistemic states), and because, obviously, $012 \sim_c 012$ in *Hexa*.

In the 'back 012', that corresponds to the answer 'not 2', Bill knows that Anne holds 0. In the 'front 012', that corresponds to the answer 'not 1', Bill still considers 210 to be an alternative, so Bill does not know the card of Anne.

In both the 'back' and the 'front' 012, neither Anne nor Cath know whether Bill knows Anne's card.

But not just the 'front 012' and 'back 012' are indistinguishable for Cath. She also cannot distinguish the 'back 012' from the 'back 102' and the 'back 102' from the 'front 102'. Because of transitivity she cannot distinguish between any of those four: {back 102, back 102, front 012, back 012} is one of her equivalence classes, namely, the one that corresponds to Cath holding card 2.

In different words, Cath considers it possible that Anne holds card 0 and told Bill that she does not hold card 2, but she also considers it possible that Anne holds card 1 and told Bill that she does not hold card 0 (even though Anne actually holds card 0).

5.4.3 Knowledge Games

Actions such as showing and telling other agents about your card(s), occur in many card games. Such games can therefore with reason be called *knowledge games*. Of particular interest are the card games where the *only* actions are epistemic actions. In that case, the goal of the game is to be the first to know (or guess rightly) the deal of cards, or a less specific property such as the whereabouts of specific cards. In *Hexa*, "Bill knows the deal of cards" can be described as $\mathsf{win}_b = K_b\delta^{012} \vee K_b\delta^{021} \vee \ldots$. Here δ^{ijk} is the atomic description of world (deal) ijk, e.g., $\delta^{012} = 0_a \wedge \neg 0_b \wedge \neg 0_c \wedge \neg 1_a \wedge 1_b \wedge \neg 1_c \wedge \neg 2_a \wedge \neg 2_b \wedge 2_c$. The action of Bill winning is therefore described as the public announcement of that knowledge: $L_{abc}?\mathsf{win}_b$.

If the goal of the game is to be the first to guess the deal of cards, and if players are perfectly rational, then ending one's move and passing to the next player also amounts to an action, namely, (publicly) announcing that you do not yet have enough knowledge to win. This action is described as, for the case of Bill, $L_{abc}?\neg\mathsf{win}_b$. In the epistemic state $(Hexa, 012)[\![\mathsf{whisper}]\!]$, Bill knows the card deal. But saying so is still informative for the other players. For example, before Bill said so, Cath still considered it possible that Bill did not know the card deal. If Anne had whispered 'I do not have card 1' instead of 'I do not have card 2', indeed Bill would not have learnt the card deal. Implicitly 'moving on' in that game state amounts to such an implicit declaration $L_{abc}?\neg\mathsf{win}_b$ of not being able to win.

This talk about winning and losing makes more sense for a 'real' knowledge game. The 'murder detection game' Cluedo is an example. The game consists of 21 cards and is played by six players. There is also a game board to play with, but a fair and already most interesting abstraction of Cluedo is to model it as a card game only. Each player has three cards and there are three cards on the table. The first player to guess those cards wins the game. The following actions are possible in Cluedo (and *only* those actions): showing (only to the requesting player) one of three requested cards (of different types, namely, a murder suspect card, a weapon card, and a room card), confirming that you do not hold any of three requested cards (by public announcement), 'ending your move', i.e., announcing that you cannot win, and 'ending the game', i.e., correctly guessing the murder cards. Because each player now holds three cards, the action of showing a card may now involve real choice, such as we have already seen in the case of the somewhat artificial whisper action (*not* legal in Cluedo!). A play of the game Cluedo can therefore be seen as a sequence of different game actions that can all be described as epistemic actions in $\mathcal{L}_!^{\text{act}}$, so in that sense it is represented by a single $\mathcal{L}_!^{\text{act}}$ action.

5.4.4 Different Cards

Two players a, b (Anne, Bill) face three cards p, q, r lying face-down in two stacks on the table. Let p^2 be the atom describing 'card p is in the stack with two cards', so that $\neg p^2$ stands for that 'card p is the single-card stack'. Consider the following two actions:

Example 5.40

- independent
  Anne draws a card from the two-cards stack, looks at it, returns it, and then Bill draws a card from the two-cards stack and looks at it.
- dependent
  Anne draws a card from the two-cards stack, and then Bill takes the remaining card from that stack. They both look at their card. □

Action independent has nine different executions. Action dependent has only six different executions. It is more constrained, because the cards that Anne and Bill draw must be different in dependent, whereas they may be the same in independent.

Action independent is described by the sequence

$$L_{ab}(L_a?p^2 \cup L_a?q^2 \cup L_a?r^2) \ ; \ L_{ab}(L_b?p^2 \cup L_b?q^2 \cup L_b?r^2)$$

Action dependent can also be described as a sequence of two actions, in which case we have to express implicitly that the second card is different from the first. Because the card that Bill draws is different from the card that Anne has just drawn, Anne does not know which is the card that Bill draws. In other words, from the two cards on the stack, it must be the card that she does not know. We get:

$$\begin{array}{l} L_{ab}(L_a?p^2 \cup L_a?q^2 \cup L_a?r^2) \ ; \\ L_{ab}(L_b?(p^2 \wedge \neg K_a p^2) \cup L_b?(q^2 \wedge \neg K_a q^2) \cup L_b?(r^2 \wedge \neg K_a r^2)) \end{array}$$

For example, $L_b?(p^2 \wedge \neg K_a p^2)$ expresses that Bill only learns that card p is on the two-card stack when player a has not learnt that already.

5.5 Spreading Gossip

Example 5.41 Six friends each know a secret. They call each other. In each call they exchange all the secrets that they currently know of. How many calls are needed to spread all the news? □

We first present the solution of the riddle and related combinatorics, and after that we model it in dynamic epistemic logic.

It can be shown that for a number of n friends with $n \geq 4$, the minimum sufficient number of calls is $2n - 4$. The correct answer for six friends is therefore 'eight calls'. A general procedure for communicating n secrets in $2n - 4$ calls, for $n \geq 4$, is as follows:

Assume that both the secrets and the agents are numbered $1, 2, \ldots, n$—there is no reason to distinguish agents from secrets, just as we previously distinguished players from cards. Let ab mean 'agent a calls agent b and they tell each other all their secrets'. For $n = 4$, a sequence of length $2 \cdot 4 - 4 = 4$ is $12, 34, 13, 24$. For $n > 4$ we proceed as follows. *First* make $n - 4$ calls from agent 1 to the agents over 4. This is the call sequence $15, 16, ..., 1n$. *Then*, let agents 1 to 4 make calls as in the case of $n = 4$. That is the call sequence $12, 34, 13, 24$. *Finally*, repeat the first part of the procedure. So we close with another sequence $15, 16, ..., 1n$. The first part of the procedure makes the secrets of 5 to n known to 1. The second part of the procedure makes all secrets known to $1, 2, 3, 4$. The last part of the procedure makes all secrets known to the agents 5 to n.

For six agents, the resulting sequence is $15, 16, 12, 34, 13, 24, 15, 16$. There are also (non-trivially different) other ways to communicate all secrets in eight calls to all six agents. A different sequence is $12, 34, 56, 13, 45, 16, 24, 35$. Table 5.1 shows in detail how the secrets are spread over the agents by this other sequence. We name this call sequence six. Note that in the first, general, procedure some calls occur twice, for example calls 15 and 16 occur twice, whereas in six all calls are different.

call	*between*	1	2	3	4	5	6
1	12	12	12	3	4	5	6
2	34	12	12	34	34	5	6
3	56	12	12	34	34	56	56
4	13	1234	12	1234	34	56	56
5	45	1234	12	1234	3456	3456	56
6	16	123456	12	1234	3456	3456	123456
7	24	123456	123456	1234	123456	3456	123456
8	35	123456	123456	123456	123456	123456	123456

Table 5.1. The protocol six, a minimal sequence for communicating six secrets.

This curious interest for the *minimum* number of calls seems to be more fuelled by a bunch of academics aiming for efficient communication, than by a group of friends wishing to *prolong* the pleasure of such gossip as much as possible. What is the *maximum* number of calls where each time something new is learnt? (Subject to the 'rule' that all shared information is always exchanged.) For n secrets this is $\binom{n}{2}$. For $n = 6$ the maximum is obtained in the call sequence $12, 13, 14, 15, 16, 23, 24, 25, 26, 34, 35, 36, 45, 46, 56$. Fifteen all different calls! In general: agent 1 calls all other agents, agent 2 calls all other agents except agent 1, etc. $\Sigma_1^{n-1} = \frac{1}{2} \cdot n \cdot (n-1)$. The maximum number of *informative* calls between agents is therefore also the maximum number of *different* calls between 2 from n persons. This is not obvious, because not every sequence of informative calls consists of all different calls, and not every sequence of all different calls consists of all informative calls.

Exercise 5.42 Show that not every sequence of informative calls consists of all different calls, and not every sequence of all different calls consists of all informative calls. □

Thus far we have described this system from the viewpoint of an observer that is registering all calls. The telephone company, so to speak. If we describe it from the viewpoint of the callers themselves, i.e., as a multi-agent system, other aspects enter the arena as well. What sort of epistemic action is such a telephone call? Are the secrets generally or publicly known after the communications? Answers to such questions depend on further assumptions about the communications protocol and other 'background knowledge'. To simplify matters, we assume that all communication is faultless, that it is common knowledge that at the outset there are six friends each having one secret, and that always all secrets are exchanged in a call. If no further assumptions are made, after an effective call sequence (where 'effective' means: after which all secrets are exchanged) the secrets are generally known, but they are not commonly known. For example, after six, agent 3 knows that agent 5 knows all secrets, but (s)he does not know this for any other agent. For example, he has no reason to assume that the 35 call was the last in the sequence of eight calls, and that the 24 call had already taken place. Some knowledge of the protocol used to communicate the secrets *may* make a difference. In fact it is a bit unclear how much makes enough of a difference, and this might merit further investigation: e.g., note that on the one hand 35, 16, and 24 can be swapped arbitrarily while guaranteeing general knowledge of the secret, but that on the other hand the number of secrets known by 3 and 5 prior to the moment of the 35 call (four and four) is different from the numbers for 1 and 6, and 2 and 4 (four and two)—information that may reveal part of the executed protocol and therefore knowledge about other agents' information state.

If the agents know that a length 8 protocol is executed, *and* if time is synchronised, then the secrets are commonly known after execution of the protocol. But without either of these, it becomes problematic again. Suppose that time is synchronised but that the length of the protocol is unknown. By agreeing on a protocol 'keep calling until you have established that all other agents know all secrets'—this obviously includes non-informative calls—general knowledge of general knowledge of the secrets can be established, but again, this falls short of common knowledge.

Exercise 5.43 Give a protocol that achieves general knowledge of general knowledge of the secrets, for six agents. □

In the remainder we assume that everybody knows which calls have been made and to whom, but that the secrets that have been exchanged in a call are unknown. After that, the secrets are common knowledge at the completion of the protocol. A more realistic setting for this scenario is where the six agents are seated around a table, where all have a card with their secret written on it. A 'call' now corresponds to two persons showing each other their cards, and both adding the secrets that are new to them on their own card. The other players notice which two players show each other their cards, but not what is written on those cards.

Exercise 5.44 In the two example protocols, no agent learns the *source* of all secrets. But there are protocols where an agent does learn that. Give an example. Prove also that at most one agent knows the source of all secrets. (We also conjecture that after a minimal call sequence no agent knows the source of all secrets.) □

We now proceed to describe the call sequence six as a $\mathcal{L}_!$ epistemic action. We keep naming the six agents $1, 2, 3, 4, 5, 6$ but call the secrets (the value of six propositions) $p_1, \dots, p_6$. The initial epistemic state is one in which each agent only knows 'his own' secret, in other words, it is an interpreted system where agents only know their own local state. The action "agent a and agent b learn each others' secrets" can be paraphrased as "all agents learn that agent a and agent b learn each others' secrets" and this can be further specified as "for each p_n (of all six atomic propositions) all agents learn that a and b learn whether a knows p_n, and all agents learn that a and b learn whether b knows p_n". Formally, the (type of this) action is call_{ab}, defined as the sequence

$$\mathsf{call}_{ab}(p_1) \ ; \ \dots \ ; \ \mathsf{call}_{ab}(p_6)$$

where $\mathsf{call}_{ab}(p_n)$ is defined as:

$$\begin{aligned}\mathsf{call}_{ab}(p_n) = L_{123456}(\ & (L_{ab}?K_a p_n \cup L_{ab}?K_a \neg p_n \cup L_{ab}?\neg(K_a p_n \vee K_a \neg p_n)) \\ & ; \\ & (L_{ab}?K_b p_n \cup L_{ab}?K_b \neg p_n \cup L_{ab}?\neg(K_b p_n \vee K_b \neg p_n)) \\ &)\end{aligned}$$

It will now be clear that the type of action describing the six protocol is

$$\mathsf{call}_{12} \ ; \ \mathsf{call}_{34} \ ; \ \mathsf{call}_{56} \ ; \ \mathsf{call}_{13} \ ; \ \mathsf{call}_{45} \ ; \ \mathsf{call}_{16} \ ; \ \mathsf{call}_{24} \ ; \ \mathsf{call}_{35}$$

For a more concrete example, given the actual distribution of secrets where p_4 is false, in call call_{16} of six agent 6 learns from agent 1 that the value of the secret p_4 is 0. This happens in the part $\mathsf{call}_{16}(p_4)$ of call call_{16}, which is described as:

$$L_{123456}(L_{16}?K_1p_4 \cup !L_{16}?K_1\neg p_4 \cup L_{16}?\neg(K_1p_4 \cup K_1\neg p_4)) \ ; \ \ldots$$

The exclamation mark, or local choice operator, points to the choice known by 1 and 6, but not (publicly known) by the remaining agents, as agent 2 does not yet know the value of p_4 at this stage.

5.6 Notes

Epistemic action logic The history of this logic is mainly the academic birth of van Ditmarsch. It achieved the goal to generalise the dynamic epistemic logic of public announcements by Plaza [168], Gerbrandy [75], and Baltag, Moss, and Solecki [11], which was described in detail in the Notes of Chapter 4. Van Ditmarsch' efforts to generalise the 'card show' action of Example 5.35 played a major part in the development of this framework. The relational action semantics of Section 5.3 found its way to the community in van Ditmarsch' publications [42, 43, 46]. Later developments on this logic (see below) include shared work with van der Hoek and Kooi.

Alternative syntax Alternatively to the primitives of the language $\mathcal{L}_!^{\mathrm{act}}$ one can stipulate a clause $L_B(\alpha, \alpha')$, meaning $L_B(\alpha \ ! \ \alpha')$, and remove the clauses for local choice. The difference seems to be 'syntactic sugar' with some conceptual consequences: by doing this, the notion of the 'type of an action' disappears. Instead of modelling 'Anne reads the content of the letter in the presence of Bill' as an action type $L_{ab}(L_a?p \cup L_a?\neg p)$, with two instances $L_{ab}(!L_a?p \cup L_a?\neg p)$ and $L_{ab}(L_a?p \cup \ !L_a?\neg p)$, we would now have two deterministic actions $L_{ab}(L_a?p, L_a?\neg p)$ and $L_{ab}(L_a?\neg p, L_a?p)$, respectively, and the former action type $L_{ab}(L_a?p \cup L_a?\neg p)$ then corresponds to non-deterministic choice between those two: $L_{ab}(L_a?p, L_a?\neg p) \cup L_{ab}(L_a?\neg p, L_a?p)$. A similar approach to the language is followed, for a more general setting, by Economou in [56].

Concurrent epistemic action logic Concurrent epistemic action logic was proposed by van Ditmarsch in [45] and a proof system for this logic was proposed by van Ditmarsch, van der Hoek, and Kooi in [49]. The completeness proof in [49] was—in retrospect—based on a flawed notion of 'syntactic accessibility between actions'. We have chosen not to include a detailed treatment of this material. The treatment of concurrency for dynamic operators in [45, 49] is similar to that in the logic cPDL—for 'concurrent propositional dynamic logic'—proposed by Peleg [167] and also mentioned in, e.g., Goldblatt [79] and Harel *et al.* [93]. This treatment of concurrency is known as 'true concurrency': the result of executing an action $\alpha \cap \beta$ is the *set* of the results from executing just α and just β. For epistemic states, this means that execution of a concurrent action consisting of two parts each resulting in an epistemic state, results in a set of two epistemic states. The modelling solution is to see the corresponding state-transforming relation no longer as a relation between epistemic states, but as a relation between an epistemic state and a set of epistemic states.

Such 'true concurrency' is an alternative to another approach to concurrency, namely intersection concurrency. The dynamic logic IPDL (intersection PDL) is briefly presented in [93], for a detailed analysis see [8]. In that case, we take the intersection of the respective binary relations that are the interpretation of the two 'intersection-concurrent' actions. For an intersection concurrency sort of epistemic action, see the logic ALL in Kooi's Ph.D. thesis [114]. Versions of unpublished manuscripts by Baltag also contained that feature.

For an example of a concurrent action description in the setting of concurrent epistemic action logic in [45], consider again the action bothmayread, where both Anne and Bill may have read the letter (learnt the truth about p). It is described in this language as

$$\begin{aligned} L_{ab}(\ &(L_a?p \cap L_b?p) \cup (L_a?\neg p \cap L_b?\neg p) \\ &\cup L_a?p \cup L_a?\neg p \cup L_b?p \cup L_b?\neg p \cup\ ?\top\ ) \end{aligned}$$

Executing the part $(L_a?\neg p \cap L_b?\neg p)$ of this action indeed results in a set of two epistemic states. The effect of the L_{ab} operator binding this subaction and other subactions, results after all in the single epistemic state that we are already familiar with (see Figure 5.2). The *set of epistemic states* resulting from executing $(L_a?\neg p \cap L_b?\neg p)$ functions as a (single) *factual state* in the domain of the epistemic state resulting from executing the entire action. For details, see [45, 49].

Playing cards The results on modelling card games have previously appeared in publications by van Ditmarsch, and by Renardel de Lavalette [43, 44, 46, 174].

Spreading gossip The riddle on spreading gossip formed part of the 1999 Dutch Science Quiz. The original version (in Dutch), of which we presented a gender-neutral translation, was

"Zes vriendinnen hebben ieder 'n roddel. Ze bellen elkaar. In elk gesprek wisselen ze alle roddels uit die ze op dat moment kennen. Hoeveel gesprekken zijn er minimaal nodig om iedereen op de hoogte te brengen van alle zes de roddels?"

The answer options in the (multiple choice) quiz were 7, 8, and 9. The answer was, of course, 8. In the aftermath of that science quiz—partly reported in the Dutch media—academics generalised the answer. The given procedure for communicating n secrets (for $n \geq 4$) in $2n - 4$ calls was suggested by Renardel de Lavalette. Hurkens [108] proved (independently) that this is also the minimum. The observations on general and common knowledge and on how to model the spreading of gossip in epistemic logic are partly found in van Ditmarsch's Ph.D. thesis [43].

6

Action Models

6.1 Introduction

In this chapter we introduce the 'action model' approach to describing epistemic actions. This chapter does not presume familiarity with the previous chapter, that was also on epistemic actions (see the Preface for motivation). In the current section we informally introduce action models. Action models are semantic objects that can also be seen as epistemic actions. The action models are defined in Section 6.2, the action model language $\mathcal{L}_{KC\otimes}$ is presented in Section 6.3, and its semantics in Section 6.4. Section 6.5 shows that action model execution preserves bisimulation, and addresses a notion of 'sameness of actions' called 'action emulation'. Section 6.6 presents a proof system for the action model language—we focus on the intuitions behind the different validities (that are mainly also axioms in the proof system), the completeness will only be addressed in Chapter 7. Section 6.7 presents a proof tool that is available for action model logic. This is the epistemic model checker DEMO. In Section 6.8 we address the relation between $\mathcal{L}_{!}^{\mathrm{act}}$ 'relational actions' and $\mathcal{L}_{KC\otimes}^{\mathrm{act}}$ 'action models'—that section therefore *does* after all presume familiarity with the previous chapter. In Section 6.9 we pay some attention to modelling 'private actions', that address change of belief instead of (merely) change of knowledge.

Chapter 4 dealt with public announcements. Public announcements are epistemic actions that convey the same information for all agents. They result in a restriction of the model and therefore in a restriction of the corresponding accessibility relations. More complex epistemic actions convey different information to different agents. They may result in the refinement of accessibility relations while the domain of the model remains unchanged, and they may result in the enlargement of the domain of the model (and its structure). For an example of a more complex epistemic action, we consider the scenario in Example 4.1[1] once again:

[1] Example 4.1 is found on page 67, see also Example 5.1 on page 109.

Example 6.1 (Buy or Sell?) Consider two stockbrokers Anne and Bill, having a little break in a Wall Street bar, sitting at a table. A messenger comes in and delivers a letter to Anne. On the envelope is written "urgently requested data on United Agents". Anne opens and reads the letter in the presence of Bill. (United Agents is doing well.) □

The scenario is modelled as an epistemic state for one atom p, describing 'the letter contains the information that United Agents is doing well', so that $\neg p$ stands for United Agents *not* doing well. We may assume that both Anne (a) and Bill (b) know *what* information on United Agents is due, as this was announced by the messenger in their presence. In other words: a and b are both uncertain about the value of p, and this is common knowledge. When Anne opens and reads the letter, this results in her knowing that p, but not in Bill knowing p. However, in the resulting state we expect Bill to know that Anne knows whether p, as he observed her opening the letter. Also, we expect Anne to know that Bill knows that, that Bill knows that Anne knows that he knows that, etc. The state transition induced by this epistemic action is depicted in Figure 6.1. In this figure, we have chosen mnemonically convenient names 0 and 1 for states where p is false and true, respectively. The action of Anne reading the letter will be represented as an action model $(\mathsf{Read}, \mathsf{p})$, that therefore labels the transition. Note that after $(\mathsf{Read}, \mathsf{p})$, formula $C_{ab}(K_a p \vee K_a \neg p)$ is valid in the model: it is commonly known that Anne knows the contents of the letter, irrespective of it being p or $\neg p$. Bill considers it possible that Anne knows p, described by $K_a p$, and also considers it possible that she knows that p is false, described by $K_a \neg p$. In the actual state 1, Anne now knows that p: $K_a p$ is true.

From Bill's point of view, Anne could be learning that p, and Anne could be learning that $\neg p$. But he cannot distinguish between those two actions. Anne's point of view is different: either she learns p, so that learning $\neg p$ is an impossibility, or she learns $\neg p$, so that learning p is an impossibility. Anne also knows that Bill cannot distinguish between her learning p and her learning $\neg p$. In fact, it is common knowledge to Anne and Bill, that Bill cannot distinguish between the two actions but that Anne can. Let us tentatively call these actions p and np. Action p has precondition p, for which we write $\mathsf{pre}(\mathsf{p}) = p$, and action np has precondition $\neg p$, for which we write $\mathsf{pre}(\mathsf{np}) = \neg p$. We have, to convenience the reader, again chosen for mnemonically suggestive names. These preconditions need not be literals but can be any formula—so a straight identification with valuations is out of the question. The observations

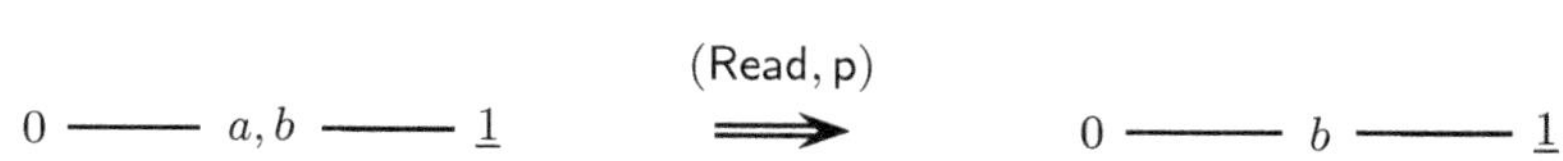

Figure 6.1. Anne reads the letter containing p in the presence of Bill.

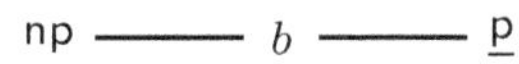

Figure 6.2. The action model (Read, p).

on indistinguishability induce a partition on this set of possible actions {p, np}. The partition for Anne is {p}, {np}, and the partition for Bill is {p, np}. In other words, Anne's partition corresponds to the identity, she can distinguish 'everything', and Bill's to the universal relation, he can distinguish nothing. Also, because of the given that Anne really learns p, action p 'stands out'. To describe 'the entire action', a straight identification with the preconditions of p or np is not sufficient, e.g., the first would then not be different from the action where Anne *announces* the contents of the letter, which also has precondition p. We really appear to need p and np in relation to each other. It has been visualised in Figure 6.2.

Note that both points are reflexive for Anne and Bill; therefore we see no access for Anne, as her access is the identity. The actual action p with precondition p is given special status by underlining it, i.e., by 'pointing' to it. As our description, or depiction, of this action is a structure that resembles a Kripke model, we call it an *action model*. The relation of p and np to each other, plus their preconditions, is also *sufficient* to describe an epistemic action—which means that we can forget about any *internal* structure of p and np, so these are 'just names'. Because of that, we prefer to call them *action points* and not actions. This pointed structure (Read, p) represents the actual epistemic action. It is called an *action model*.

We now replace in Figure 6.1 the label (Read, p) by its visualisation in Figure 6.2. The result is depicted in Figure 6.3.

There is a simple and conceptually appealing way in which we can relate the structure of the initial epistemic state and the structure of the action model, to the structure of the resulting epistemic state. Let us start by an example first. Bill cannot distinguish state 0 where p is false from state 1 where p is true. He also cannot distinguish action np where Anne learns $\neg p$ from action p where Anne learns p. Given that he cannot distinguish two states, and two actions, it seems reasonable to suggest that if one action is executed in one state, and the other action in the other state, he also cannot distinguish the *resulting* states. The state named 0 in the resulting epistemic state is the result of executing action np in the state also named 0

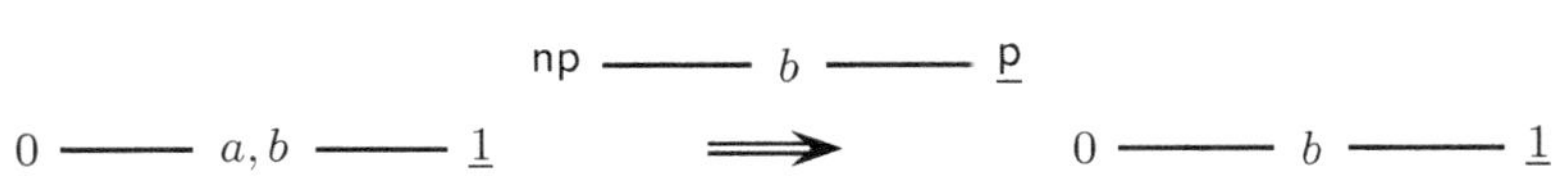

Figure 6.3. Anne reads the letter containing p in the presence of Bill. The picture labelling the state transition is an action model (Read, p).

in the initial epistemic state, and similarly, the state named 1 in the resulting epistemic state is the result of executing action p in the state also named 1 in the initial epistemic state. And indeed, Bill cannot distinguish 0 and 1 in the resulting epistemic state! On the other hand, Anne *can* distinguish 0 and 1 in the resulting epistemic state. But we now have a simple explanation for that: even though she initially could not distinguish 0 and 1, she can distinguish action np from action p. 'Obviously', if she can distinguish two actions, she can also distinguish the *results* from those actions! A different way of saying this, is that agents do not *forget* the consequences of their actions. This is also known as 'perfect recall'.

We now represent factual states in the resulting model as pairs consisting of 'name of the factual state in the initial model' and 'name of the action executed in that factual state in the initial model'. Note that this is so far an *implicit* way to express that agents do not forget how they act—what names factual states have, is irrelevant. What counts is which facts are true in those states and how they relate to other states. Concerning *facts*: the same facts are true in the resulting epistemic state as in the original epistemic state, as our actions are purely epistemic. Concerning *relations*: we then have, that pairs $(0, \mathsf{np})$ and $(1, \mathsf{p})$ in the resulting model are the same for Bill, notation $(0, \mathsf{np}) \sim_b (1, \mathsf{p})$, because both states 0 and 1 were indistinguishable for Bill but also actions np and p, formally: because $0 \sim_b 1$ and $\mathsf{np} \sim_b \mathsf{p}$. The general definition 'two states are indistinguishable for an agent if and only if they resulted from two indistinguishable actions executed in two already indistinguishable states' is formalised by (for an arbitrary agent a):

$$(s, \mathsf{s}) \sim_a (t, \mathsf{t}) \quad \text{iff} \quad s \sim_a t \text{ and } \mathsf{s} \sim_a \mathsf{t}$$

Actually, we ignored the word 'executed' in the previous sentence: this can be explained by only allowing (s, s) pairs such that s can be executed in s. The condition for that, is that the precondition of s is true in state s of the initial epistemic model M, i.e., $M, s \models \mathsf{pre}(\mathsf{s})$.

The construction we explained can be seen as the computation of a 'restricted modal product' of an epistemic state and an action model. A modal product of two modal structures is formed by taking the cartesian product of their domains, and apart from that, performing some computations on the remaining information encoded in these structures, namely, in this case precisely as above. The product is 'restricted', because we do not take the full cartesian product but only allow (s, s) pairs where s can be executed in s. As the actions are epistemic only, there is no reason to change the value of facts (as already mentioned), therefore the valuations of facts in pairs (s, s) are the valuations of facts in the first in that pair, which is the original state s. The designated point of the resulting structure is, obviously, the pair consisting of the designated points of the original structures. In the case of the model $(\mathit{Letter}, 1)$ depicted as $0 \text{—} a, b \text{—} \underline{1}$ and the action model $(\mathsf{Read}, \mathsf{p})$ depicted as $\mathsf{np} \text{—} b \text{—} \underline{\mathsf{p}}$, the result of computing their restricted modal product is shown in Figure 6.4.

Figure 6.4. Anne reads the letter containing p in the presence of Bill, seen as the computation of a restricted modal product. Compare to Figure 6.3 that depicts the same epistemic state transition differently.

Even though the cartesian product consists of four points, the restricted modal product consists of two only, namely $(0, \mathsf{np})$ and $(1, \mathsf{p})$. This is because, respectively, $Letter, 0 \models \neg p$ and $Letter, 1 \models p$; or in precondition notation: $Letter, 0 \models \mathsf{pre}(\mathsf{np})$ and $Letter, 1 \models \mathsf{pre}(\mathsf{p})$. We have that $(0, \mathsf{np}) \not\sim_a (1, \mathsf{p})$, because $\mathsf{np} \not\sim_a \mathsf{p}$—so it is not the case that both $0 \sim_a 1$ *and* $\mathsf{np} \sim_a \mathsf{p}$, required to establish equivalence for a of the pairs.

So far, we have overlooked one salient detail in our informal explanations. The action model $(\mathsf{Read}, \mathsf{p})$ visualised as np—b—$\underline{\mathsf{p}}$ has a domain, and accessibility relations for each agent... So it must be a semantic object! On the other hand, the preconditions of these 'domain' objects are formulas (that might as well be complex, epistemic formulas), so a so-called action *model* therefore is nothing but some *operator* with these formulas as arguments, thus constructing a more complex ... formula. So it must be a syntactic object! The short answer to this is that an action model, such as $(\mathsf{Read}, \mathsf{p})$, can be seen as *both*. It can be seen as syntax, because pointed frames underlying models can be enumerated and can be given names. It can be seen as semantics, because formulas can be interpreted as 'semantic propositions', i.e., functions from pointed Kripke structures to 'true' and 'false'. We switch from one to the other perspective as it pleases us—just as we use a both for agents, as in $\sim_a$, and for agent names, as in K_a. The reader not satisfied with this succinct explanation is suggested to read the following subsections before continuing with the formal introduction of action model logic in the subsequent sections. Others are suggested to skip those subsections and to continue with Section 6.2 on page 149. This completes the informal introduction on action model logic.

6.1.1 Syntax or Semantics?

In a setting of epistemic logic it is not surprising to see equivalence relations partitioning some domain of objects. But there are two surprising differences with how we have so far used such equivalence relations (or, more general, accessibility relations). *First*, the alternatives in the domain of an action model do not stand for factual states of the world, in other words for 'static objects', but they stand for possible actions, i.e., 'dynamic objects'. *Second*, the domain objects appear not to be semantic, but syntactic: preconditions of actions are formulas in the logical language! Relational structures such as Kripke models are from the realm of *semantics*, that tends, in logic, to be strictly separated from the realm of *syntax* or logical language. But, we just have to say this again, action models appear not to be partitioning *semantic* objects, but *syntactic* objects: the preconditions associated with domain objects are *formulas*. The first difference is something that makes logicians happy: "Right, so we have a dynamic counterpart of a static object that we already know quite well." And we will see that in other ways it also combines well with the 'static' epistemic states that we already have. But the second difference, to the contrary, is something that makes logicians unhappy: "Pfui! One must keep syntax and semantics strictly separated, or the world will fall apart." The solution is surprisingly simple (and in the line of similar solutions for dynamic logics incorporating automata):

If we give names to Kripke-frames, we can see action models as syntactic objects. If we represent formulas by semantic propositions, we can see action models as semantic objects. We then simply state that the meaning of the first is the second: 'syntactic' action models are interpreted as their corresponding 'semantic' action models.

6.1.2 Action Models as Syntactic Objects

Naming frames We can think of action models as syntactic objects if we give them names. We can then refer in the language to frames by these names. If we choose the names 'canonically', such that the structure of a name corresponds to the structure of the action model named, then we may 'par abus de langage' subsequently *identify* these names with the action models. That identification is not dissimilar from how we identify an agent name a in the language, as in $K_a\varphi$, with the real agent a for whom access is defined in an epistemic model, as in R_a or $\sim_a$. The crucial point is that not the action *models* themselves are named, but the *frames* underlying them. The preconditions of the points in an action model can be seen as arguments for that (frame) function name. If the action model contains n points, there are n arguments, so the frame name is then an n-ary function.

Enumerating frames Throughout this book, the set of agents A for which a Kripke structure is defined, is required to be finite. Also, we only allow *finite* action models, for a reason related to the proof system. (In neither case is finiteness a *requirement* for enumerability—it just makes it easier to enumerate.) The elements of the domain are called action points. Assume an countable supply of action points $\{\mathsf{s}_1, \mathsf{s}_2, ...\}$. The finite pointed Kripke frames for a given set of agents A can now easily be enumerated. Let us do this for the *epistemic* frames for the set of agents $\{a, b\}$—i.e., we restrict ourselves to accessibility relations that are equivalence relations, for each agent. Note that by definition there are no frames with empty domain.

Given domain $\{\mathsf{s}_1\}$, there is one singleton pointed frame, namely, with universal access for all agents.

Given domain $\{\mathsf{s}_1, \mathsf{s}_2\}$, there is one more singleton pointed frame (namely, with domain $\{\mathsf{s}_2\}$, with universal access for all agents), and there are eight two-element pointed frames (we use the familiar visualisation assuming reflexivity for both agents):

$$\mathsf{s}_1 \qquad\qquad \underline{\mathsf{s}_2}$$
$$\mathsf{s}_1 \text{ —— } a \text{ —— } \underline{\mathsf{s}_2}$$
$$\mathsf{s}_1 \text{ —— } b \text{ —— } \underline{\mathsf{s}_2}$$
$$\mathsf{s}_1 \text{ — } a, b \text{ — } \underline{\mathsf{s}_2}$$
$$\mathsf{s}_2 \qquad\qquad \underline{\mathsf{s}_1}$$
$$\mathsf{s}_2 \text{ —— } a \text{ —— } \underline{\mathsf{s}_1}$$
$$\mathsf{s}_2 \text{ —— } b \text{ —— } \underline{\mathsf{s}_1}$$
$$\mathsf{s}_2 \text{ — } a, b \text{ — } \underline{\mathsf{s}_1}$$

Given domain $\{\mathsf{s}_1, \mathsf{s}_2, \mathsf{s}_3\}$, there is one more singleton pointed frame (namely, with domain $\{\mathsf{s}_3\}$, with universal access for all agents), there are sixteen more two-element pointed frames, and there are already a whole lot of three-element frames to take into account: per agent four different partitions, and three possible points of the structure, which makes $4 \times 4 \times 3 = 48$ pointed frames.

We thus continue for four point domains, five point domains, ad infinitum. At some stage in the enumeration, we will find the pointed frame np—b—$\underline{\mathsf{p}}$ underlying $(\mathsf{Read}, \mathsf{p})$, as action points np and p will occur somewhere in the list of action points. Alternatively, we could think of introducing action point domains on the fly and in that sense we have already found it in the enumeration, namely, as s_1—b—$\underline{\mathsf{s}_2}$ above (strictly speaking, we are only interested in enumerating isomorphism classes of pointed frames).

Given that the set of pointed frames is enumerable, the set of names for such frames is also enumerable. One then could of course choose to let $\mathsf{framename}_1, \mathsf{framename}_2, \ldots$ correspond to the above list of pointed frames, such that $\mathsf{framename}_1$ is the name for singleton frame $\underline{\mathsf{s}_1}$, $\mathsf{framename}_2$ is the name for singleton frame $\underline{\mathsf{s}_2}$, etc. For some $n \in \mathbb{N}$ in this enumeration, $\mathsf{framename}_n$ is then the name for the pointed frame np—b—$\underline{\mathsf{p}}$, let us say for $n = 353319$. We can see the preconditions of the action points in the action model $(\mathsf{Read}, \mathsf{p})$ as arguments of $\mathsf{framename}_{353319}$, in the order in which np and p occur in the enumeration of action points. If np comes before p, the action model is fully represented by the description $\mathsf{framename}_{353319}(\neg p, p)$.

A more obvious way than the cumbersome list $\mathsf{framename}_1, \mathsf{framename}_2, \ldots$ to name frames is to choose names that mirror the structures they name ('canonical' names). For example, let putting a line over a structure (or structural element) indicate that it names the structure. We get a list of names starting with $\overline{\underline{s_1}}$, $\overline{\underline{s_2}}$, ..., instead of $\underline{s_1}$, $\underline{s_2}$, ... And we can stop worrying about the order of preconditions as arguments of framenames: we now write $\mathsf{pre}(\overline{\mathsf{p}}) = p$, etc. The practice of choosing names resembling the semantic objects they name is not unfamiliar. For example, agents $a, b, c, \ldots$ are often named $\mathsf{a}, \mathsf{b}, \mathsf{c}, \ldots$. In Chapter 2 we even identified agents $a, b, c, \ldots$ with their names, that were therefore also written as $a, b, c, \ldots$! Similarly, it is only a small step to allow frames to name themselves. This explains how we can introduce semantic objects such as pointed frames in the language.

6.1.3 Action Models as Semantic Objects

Semantic propositions We can also see action models as semantic objects. For that, we replace the preconditions of action points, that are formulas in the logical language, by what are commonly known as (semantic) *propositions*, that can be seen as functions operating on Kripke structures. Actually, we already introduced such propositions when defining $[\![\varphi]\!]_M$ as the subset of the domain of an epistemic model M, where φ is true. Thus, $[\![\varphi]\!]$ can be seen as a function from epistemic models to subsets of their domains: a clearly semantic object. (Alternatively we could see $[\![\varphi]\!]$ as a function from epistemic states to $\{0, 1\}$.) In other words, $[\![\varphi]\!]$ is a semantic object, that we call a (semantic) *proposition*.

For example, instead of saying that in action model $(\mathsf{Read}, \mathsf{p})$ the precondition of action point p is p, we could alternatively associate with p a *semantic* precondition $[\![p]\!]$. This proposition maps the domain $\{0, 1\}$ of the epistemic model *Letter* to the subset $\{1\}$. It applies to any epistemic model defined for a set of atoms that includes p.

Such propositions $[\![\varphi]\!]$ need to be properly inductively defined, but this is very well possible: $[\![p]\!]$ is a function from epistemic models to subsets of their domains as above, given $[\![\varphi]\!]$ and $[\![\psi]\!]$, $[\![\varphi \wedge \psi]\!]_M = [\![\varphi]\!]_M \cap [\![\psi]\!]_M$. Also for other connectives and modal operators, including $[\alpha]\varphi$. (See the Notes section for references to more details.)

We suggestively write $[\![\mathsf{pre}]\!]$ for the semantic precondition function, so that, for example in the action model $(\mathsf{Read}, \mathsf{p})$, $[\![\mathsf{pre}]\!](\mathsf{p}) = [\![p]\!]$ and we call the action model with semantic precondition $[\![\mathsf{pre}]\!]$: $(\mathsf{Read}^{[\![]\!]}, \mathsf{p})$. (A representation $[\![(\mathsf{Read}, \mathsf{p})]\!]$ would be infelicitous in this case, as we typically see an expression $[\![\alpha]\!]$ for actions α as a binary relation between epistemic states, which is obviously not intended here.)

6.1.4 Concluding

Having defined syntactic correspondents for action models, where frames are described by their names, and semantic correspondents for action models, where precondition formulas are interpreted as (semantic) propositions, we can finally give a proper semantics for action models: an action model description is interpreted as its corresponding action model with propositions as preconditions. As an example, $\mathsf{framename}_{353319}(\neg p, p)$ is interpreted as $(\mathsf{Read}^{[\![]\!]}, \mathsf{p})$.

6.2 Action Models

We successively define action models, the language of action model logic, and the semantics of action model logic. In this section we define action models.

Definition 6.2 (Action model) Let $\mathcal{L}$ be *any* logical language for given parameters agents A and atoms P. An $S5$ action model M is a structure $\langle \mathsf{S}, \sim, \mathsf{pre} \rangle$ such that S is a domain of *action points*, such that for each $a \in A$, $\sim_a$ is an equivalence relation on S, and such that $\mathsf{pre} : \mathsf{S} \rightarrow \mathcal{L}$ is a preconditions function that assigns a *precondition* $\mathsf{pre}(\mathsf{s}) \in \mathcal{L}$ to each $\mathsf{s} \in \mathsf{S}$. A *pointed $S5$ action model* is a structure (M, s) with $\mathsf{s} \in \mathsf{S}$. □

As all structures in our presentation carry equivalence relations, we normally drop the '$S5$' in '$S5$ action model' and 'pointed $S5$ action model'. Further, 'par abus de langage', a pointed action model is also called an action model (as this usage is too ingrained in the literature). Examples will be given in the following sections.

6.3 Syntax of Action Model Logic

Definition 6.3 (Language of action model logic) Given are agents A and atoms P. The language of action model logic $\mathcal{L}_{KC\otimes}(A, P)$ is the union of the *formulas* $\varphi \in \mathcal{L}^{\mathrm{stat}}_{KC\otimes}(A, P)$ (or, when no confusion arises, $\mathcal{L}^{\mathrm{stat}}_{KC\otimes}$) and the *actions* (or *epistemic actions*) $\alpha \in \mathcal{L}^{\mathrm{act}}_{KC\otimes}(A, P)$ defined by

$$\varphi ::= p \mid \neg\varphi \mid (\varphi \wedge \varphi) \mid K_a\varphi \mid C_B\varphi \mid [\alpha]\varphi$$
$$\alpha ::= (\mathsf{M}, \mathsf{s}) \mid (\alpha \cup \alpha)$$

where $p \in P$, $a \in A$, $B \subseteq A$, and (M, s) a pointed action model with (1) a *finite* domain S and (2) such that for all $\mathsf{t} \in \mathsf{S}$, the precondition $\mathsf{pre}(\mathsf{t})$ is a $\mathcal{L}^{\mathrm{stat}}_{KC\otimes}(A, P)$-formula that has already been constructed in a previous stage of the inductively defined hierarchy. □

As usual, $\langle\alpha\rangle\varphi$ is defined by notational abbreviation as $\neg[\alpha]\neg\varphi$. We also use the notational abbreviation M for $\bigcup_{\mathsf{s}\in\mathsf{S}}(\mathsf{M}, \mathsf{s})$.

Restriction (1) is due to the requirements of the axiomatisation for the language, which will only become clear later, and also because operators in the language are not allowed to have an infinite number of arguments. Restriction (2) is obvious for an inductively defined set. Strictly, we have to think of the pointed frame underlying (M, s) as a *name* for that frame, and of the precondition function pre associated with M as the way to construct inductively a more complex expression of type 'epistemic action' from that framename and from arguments that are simpler, already defined, expressions of type 'formula'. The arity of that framename is then of course the number of actions in the domain S of M. We choose to ignore the difference, just as we ignore the difference between agent *names* a in modal operators K_a and *actual* agents a in the equivalence relations $\sim_a$ that interpret these operators. The reader not satisfied by this explanation is referred to Subsection 6.1.1 and beyond, of the introductory Section 6.1.

Exercise 6.4 Show that epistemic action $(\mathsf{Read}, \mathsf{p})$ from the introduction is a well-formed epistemic action in the language $\mathcal{L}^{\mathrm{act}}_{KC\otimes}(\{a, b\}, \{p\})$. □

Example 6.5 (skip and crash) Given a set of agents A and a set of atoms P, the epistemic action skip or $\mathbf{1}$ is defined as $(\langle\{\mathsf{s}\}, \sim, \mathsf{pre}\rangle, \mathsf{s})$ with $\mathsf{pre}(\mathsf{s}) = \top$, and $\mathsf{s} \sim_a \mathsf{s}$ for all $a \in A$.

Similarly, the epistemic action crash or $\mathbf{0}$ is defined as $(\langle\{\mathsf{s}\}, \sim, \mathsf{pre}\rangle, \mathsf{s})$ with $\mathsf{pre}(\mathsf{s}) = \bot$, and $\mathsf{s} \sim_a \mathsf{s}$ for all $a \in A$. This also applies to but does not require $A = \emptyset$.[2] □

Example 6.6 (Public announcement) The action model $\mathsf{pub}(\varphi)$, for 'truthful public announcement of φ', is defined as $(\langle\{\mathsf{pub}\}, \sim, \mathsf{pre}\rangle, \mathsf{pub})$ such that $\mathsf{pre}(\mathsf{pub}) = \varphi$, and $\mathsf{pub} \sim_a \mathsf{pub}$ for all $a \in A$. This corresponds to public announcement as in Chapter 4. (In Exercise 6.14, later, we will *prove* that $\mathsf{pub}(\varphi)$ corresponds to public announcement of φ.) □

Another *syntactic* construct is the composition of two action models.

Definition 6.7 (Composition of action models) Let $\mathsf{M} = \langle \mathsf{S}, \sim, \mathsf{pre}\rangle$ and $\mathsf{M}' = \langle \mathsf{S}', \sim', \mathsf{pre}'\rangle$ be two action models in $\mathcal{L}^{\mathrm{act}}_{KC\otimes}(A, P)$. Then their *composition* $(\mathsf{M} \; ; \; \mathsf{M}')$ is the action model $\langle \mathsf{S}'', \sim'', \mathsf{pre}''\rangle$ such that

$$\begin{array}{lcl} \mathsf{S}'' & = & \mathsf{S} \times \mathsf{S}' \\ (\mathsf{s}, \mathsf{s}') \sim''_a (\mathsf{t}, \mathsf{t}') & \text{iff} & \mathsf{s} \sim_a \mathsf{t} \text{ and } \mathsf{s}' \sim'_a \mathsf{t}' \\ \mathsf{pre}''((\mathsf{s}, \mathsf{s}')) & = & \langle \mathsf{M}, \mathsf{s}\rangle \mathsf{pre}'(\mathsf{s}') \end{array}$$
□

The definition of composition extends in the obvious way to pointed action models: given two pointed action models (M, t) and $(\mathsf{M}', \mathsf{t}')$ as above, their composition $(\mathsf{M}, \mathsf{t}) \; ; \; (\mathsf{M}', \mathsf{t}')$ is the pointed action model $(\mathsf{M}'', (\mathsf{t}, \mathsf{t}'))$, with M'' defined as above. Note that $\mathsf{pre}''((\mathsf{t}, \mathsf{t}')) = \langle \mathsf{M}, \mathsf{t}\rangle \mathsf{pre}'(\mathsf{t}')$.

A composition $(\langle \mathsf{S}'', \sim'', \mathsf{pre}''\rangle, \mathsf{s}'')$ is by definition an epistemic action in the language $\mathcal{L}^{\mathrm{act}}_{KC\otimes}(A, P)$—at least, allowing complex domain names such as pairs $(\mathsf{s}, \mathsf{s}')$—but in the worst case found *three* inductive levels higher up than the maximum of the levels where (M, s) and $(\mathsf{M}', \mathsf{s}')$ are situated in the inductive hierarchy:

---

[2] The set of atoms P cannot be empty, as $\top$ and $\bot$ are defined as $p \vee \neg p$ and $p \wedge \neg p$, respectively.

A precondition $\langle \mathsf{M}, \mathsf{s} \rangle \mathsf{pre}(\mathsf{s}')$ associated with M'' is formally $\neg[\mathsf{M}, \mathsf{s}]\neg\mathsf{pre}(\mathsf{s}')$. Assume that (M, s) is found as an action on level i, and that $\mathsf{pre}(\mathsf{s}')$ is found as a formula on level j. Then $\neg\mathsf{pre}(\mathsf{s}')$ can be constructed on level $j+1$; so that $[\mathsf{M}, \mathsf{s}]\neg\mathsf{pre}(\mathsf{s}')$ can found one level higher than the maximum of $j+1$ and i which in the worst case is $\mathsf{max}(i, j) + 2$. Therefore $\neg[\mathsf{M}, \mathsf{s}]\neg\mathsf{pre}(\mathsf{s}')$ may only be constructed on level $\mathsf{max}(i, j) + 3$.

The intuitive meaning of action model composition is indeed semantic composition. This will be explained in the next section.

6.4 Semantics of Action Model Logic

Definition 6.8 (Semantics of formulas and actions) Given are epistemic state (M, s) with $M = \langle S, \sim, V \rangle$, action model $\mathsf{M} = \langle \mathsf{S}, \sim, \mathsf{pre} \rangle$, and $\varphi \in \mathcal{L}^{\mathrm{stat}}_{KC\otimes}(A, P)$ and $\alpha \in \mathcal{L}^{\mathrm{act}}_{KC\otimes}(A, P)$.

$$
\begin{array}{lll}
M, s \models p & \text{iff} & s \in V_p \\
M, s \models \neg\varphi & \text{iff} & M, s \not\models \varphi \\
M, s \models \varphi \wedge \psi & \text{iff} & M, s \models \varphi \text{ and } M, s \models \psi \\
M, s \models K_a\varphi & \text{iff} & \text{for all } s' \in S : s \sim_a s' \text{ implies } M, s' \models \varphi \\
M, s \models C_B\varphi & \text{iff} & \text{for all } s' \in S : s \sim_B s' \text{ implies } M, s' \models \varphi \\
M, s \models [\alpha]\varphi & \text{iff} & \text{for all } M', s' : \\
& & (M, s)[\![\alpha]\!](M', s') \text{ implies } M', s' \models \varphi
\end{array}
$$

$$
\begin{array}{lll}
(M, s)[\![\mathsf{M}, \mathsf{s}]\!](M', s') & \text{iff} & M, s \models \mathsf{pre}(\mathsf{s}) \text{ and } (M', s') = (M \otimes \mathsf{M}, (s, \mathsf{s})) \\
[\![\alpha \cup \alpha']\!] & = & [\![\alpha]\!] \cup [\![\alpha']\!]
\end{array}
$$

In the clause for the interpretation of action models, $M' = (M \otimes \mathsf{M})$ is a restricted modal product of an epistemic model and an action model, defined as $M' = \langle S', \sim', V' \rangle$ with

$$
\begin{array}{lll}
S' & = & \{(s, \mathsf{s}) \mid s \in S, \mathsf{s} \in \mathsf{S}, \text{ and } M, s \models \mathsf{pre}(\mathsf{s})\} \\
(s, \mathsf{s}) \sim'_a (t, \mathsf{t}) & \text{iff} & s \sim_a t \text{ and } \mathsf{s} \sim_a \mathsf{t} \\
(s, \mathsf{s}) \in V'_p & \text{iff} & s \in V_p
\end{array}
$$

The set of valid formulas from $\mathcal{L}^{\mathrm{stat}}_{KC\otimes}$ without common knowledge under the above semantics will be denoted the *action model validities*, or AM. The set of validities from the full language $\mathcal{L}^{\mathrm{stat}}_{KC\otimes}$ is AMC. □

We can now link the syntactic composition of action models to the intuitive meaning of relational composition.

Proposition 6.9 Let $(\mathsf{M}, \mathsf{s}), (\mathsf{M}', \mathsf{s}') \in \mathcal{L}^{\mathrm{act}}_{KC\otimes}(A, P)$, and $\varphi \in \mathcal{L}^{\mathrm{stat}}_{KC\otimes}(A, P)$. Then $[(\mathsf{M}, \mathsf{s}) \ ; \ (\mathsf{M}', \mathsf{s}')]\varphi$ is equivalent to $[\mathsf{M}, \mathsf{s}][\mathsf{M}', \mathsf{s}']\varphi$. □

Proof Let M, t be arbitrary. We have to show that $M, t \models [(\mathsf{M}, \mathsf{s}) \ ; \ (\mathsf{M}', \mathsf{s}')]\varphi$ if and only if $M, t \models [\mathsf{M}, \mathsf{s}][\mathsf{M}', \mathsf{s}']\varphi$. It suffices to show that $M \otimes (\mathsf{M} \ ; \ \mathsf{M}')$ is isomorphic to $(M \otimes \mathsf{M}) \otimes \mathsf{M}'$.

Let $(t, (\mathsf{s}, \mathsf{s}')) \in \mathcal{D}(M \otimes (\mathsf{M}\ ;\ \mathsf{M}'))$. We then have that $M, t \models \mathsf{pre}''((\mathsf{s}, \mathsf{s}'))$, i.e., $M, t \models \langle \mathsf{M}, \mathsf{s}\rangle \mathsf{pre}'(\mathsf{s}')$. The latter is equivalent to $M, t \models \mathsf{pre}(\mathsf{s}) \wedge [\mathsf{M}, \mathsf{s}]\mathsf{pre}'(\mathsf{s}')$, i.e., $M, t \models \mathsf{pre}(\mathsf{s})$ and $M, t \models [\mathsf{M}, \mathsf{s}]\mathsf{pre}'(\mathsf{s}')$. From $M, t \models \mathsf{pre}(\mathsf{s})$ follows that $(t, \mathsf{s}) \in \mathcal{D}(M \otimes \mathsf{M})$, and from that and $M, t \models [\mathsf{M}, \mathsf{s}]\mathsf{pre}'(\mathsf{s}')$ follows that $((t, \mathsf{s}), \mathsf{s}') \in \mathcal{D}((M \otimes \mathsf{M}) \otimes \mathsf{M}')$. The argument runs both ways.

Concerning accessibility, $(t, (\mathsf{s}, \mathsf{s}')) \sim_a (t_1, (\mathsf{s}_1, \mathsf{s}_1'))$ iff ($t \sim_a t_1$ and $\mathsf{s} \sim_a \mathsf{s}_1$ and $\mathsf{s}' \sim_a \mathsf{s}_1'$) iff $((t, \mathsf{s}), \mathsf{s}') \sim_a ((t_1, \mathsf{s}_1), \mathsf{s}_1')$.

The valuation of facts in triples $(t, (\mathsf{s}, \mathsf{s}'))$ corresponds to that in t. And the same holds for triples $((t, \mathsf{s}), \mathsf{s}')$. □

The *relational composition* $[\![\mathsf{M}, \mathsf{s}]\!] \circ [\![\mathsf{M}', \mathsf{s}']\!]$ of two action models is standardly defined as: $(M, s)([\![\mathsf{M}, \mathsf{s}]\!] \circ [\![\mathsf{M}', \mathsf{s}']\!])(M', s')$ if and only if there is a (M'', s'') such that $(M, s)[\![\mathsf{M}, \mathsf{s}]\!](M'', s'')$ and $(M'', s'')[\![\mathsf{M}', \mathsf{s}']\!](M', s')$. In other words, $M, s \models [\mathsf{M}, \mathsf{s}][\mathsf{M}', \mathsf{s}']\varphi$ if and only if there is a (M', s') such that $(M, s)([\![\mathsf{M}, \mathsf{s}]\!] \circ [\![\mathsf{M}', \mathsf{s}']\!])(M', s')$ and $M', s' \models \varphi$. Therefore, another way of expressing Proposition 6.9 is that $[\![\mathsf{M}, \mathsf{s}]\!] \circ [\![\mathsf{M}', \mathsf{s}']\!]$ equals $[\![(\mathsf{M}, \mathsf{s})\ ;\ (\mathsf{M}', \mathsf{s}')]\!]$.

Because of the following propositions (of which the proof is left to the reader) we need not be concerned about the composition of non-deterministic epistemic actions, and therefore can use the $;$ operator *ad libitum* in action expressions.

Proposition 6.10 Let $\alpha, \beta, \gamma \in \mathcal{L}^{\mathrm{act}}_{KC\otimes}(A, P)$. Then $((\alpha \cup \beta)\ ;\ \gamma)$ equals $((\alpha\ ;\ \gamma) \cup (\beta\ ;\ \gamma))$; and also $(\alpha\ ;\ (\beta \cup \gamma))$ equals $((\alpha\ ;\ \beta) \cup (\alpha\ ;\ \gamma))$. □

Proposition 6.11 Let $\alpha, \beta \in \mathcal{L}^{\mathrm{act}}_{KC\otimes}(A, P)$. Then $[\alpha \cup \beta]\varphi$ is equivalent to $[\alpha]\varphi \wedge [\beta]\varphi$. □

From Propositions 6.10 and 6.11 follows immediately that all expressions $[\alpha]\varphi$ are equivalent to some conjunction $\bigwedge[\mathsf{M}, \mathsf{s}]\varphi$. This can also be used to show that the action model language without non-deterministic choice is just as expressive. (See Chapter 8 for a related discussion on non-determinism in epistemic action logic.)

Exercise 6.12 Prove Propositions 6.10 and 6.11. □

We continue with examples illustrating the semantics, and a number of exercises. First, the reader may want to reconsider the introductory Example 6.1, where, given the epistemic state (*Letter*, 1) where both Anne and Bill do not know p, and where p is true, Anne reads the letter containing p, in the presence of Bill. This was the action model $(\mathsf{Read}, \mathsf{p})$, depicted as np—b—$\underline{\mathsf{p}}$, with $\mathsf{pre}(\mathsf{p}) = p$ and $\mathsf{pre}(\mathsf{np}) = \neg p$. Its execution was depicted in Figure 6.4 on page 145. This can easily be seen as corresponding to the formal semantics in Definition 6.8. Some examples of formulas involving actions are

- After Anne reads the letter containing p, Anne knows that p:
  $[\mathsf{Read}, \mathsf{p}]K_a p$
- After Anne reads the letter containing p, Bill does not know that Anne knows that p:
  $[\mathsf{Read}, \mathsf{p}]\neg K_b K_a p$

- After Anne reads the letter containing p, Anne and Bill commonly know that Anne knows whether p:
  $[\mathsf{Read}, \mathsf{p}]C_{ab}(K_a p \vee K_a \neg p)$

More complex ways of letter reading (that were also modelled in Chapter 5) can also be modelled as action models:

Example 6.13 (mayread) Given is the epistemic state $(\mathit{Letter}, 1)$ where both Anne and Bill do not know p, and where p is true. Consider the action wherein Anne *may read* the letter, i.e., Bill has left the table for a while, and when back, suspects Anne of having read the letter. In fact, Anne did *not* read the letter. In this case, from Bill's perspective one of three alternatives may come to pass, that he cannot distinguish: Anne reads the letter and it contains p, Anne reads the letter and it contains $\neg p$, and Anne does not read the letter. The last can be said to have a precondition $\top$ (or $p \vee \neg p$), as it always succeeds. Obviously, Anne can distinguish between all three actions.

An action model for this action consists of three action points, somewhat suggestively named p, np, and t, with preconditions $\mathsf{pre}(\mathsf{p}) = p$, $\mathsf{pre}(\mathsf{np}) = \neg p$, $\mathsf{pre}(\mathsf{t}) = \top$. The partition for Anne on this domain is the identity, as she can distinguish all these actions. The partition for Bill on this domain is the universal relation, as he cannot distinguish any of the three actions. The actually executed alternative is t. This action model is called $(\mathsf{Mayread}, \mathsf{t})$. The execution of this action is depicted in Figure 6.5.

The new epistemic state consists of four states. Action point np can be executed in state 0 where p is false, as $\mathit{Letter}, 0 \models \mathsf{pre}(\mathsf{np})$. Action point p can be executed in state 1 where p is true, as $\mathit{Letter}, 1 \models \mathsf{pre}(\mathsf{p})$. Action point t can be executed in state 0 where p is false, but also in state 1 where p is true, as its precondition $\top$ is satisfied in any state. The valuation (V') of p in the four new states $(0, \mathsf{np})$, $(1, \mathsf{p})$, $(0, \mathsf{t})$, and $(1, \mathsf{t})$ remains as it was before, i.e., $V'_p = \{(1, \mathsf{p}), (1, \mathsf{t})\}$. Concerning access, we have that $(0, \mathsf{t}) \sim_a (1, \mathsf{t})$ because $0 \sim_a 1$ and $\mathsf{t} \sim_a \mathsf{t}$ (as all access is reflexive). Similarly, for b.

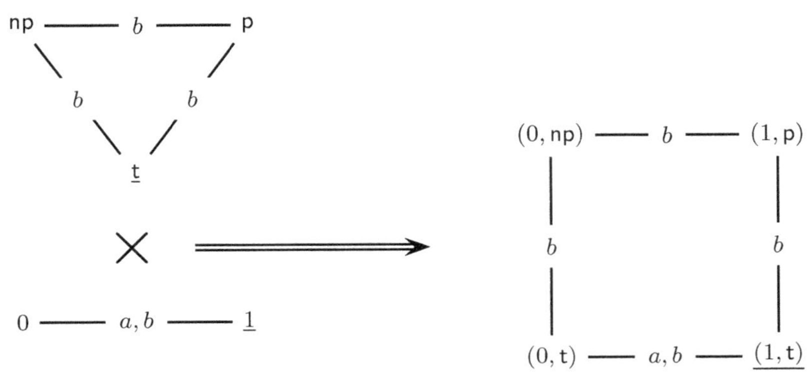

Figure 6.5. Anne may have read the letter—the action model $(\mathsf{Mayread}, \mathsf{t})$.

The action $\mathsf{Mayread}$, i.e., $(\mathsf{Mayread}, \mathsf{p}) \cup (\mathsf{Mayread}, \mathsf{np}) \cup (\mathsf{Mayread}, \mathsf{t})$, is a properly non-deterministic action. When p is true, it has two different executions, and when p is false, it also has two different executions. Examples of formulas involving action models $(\mathsf{Mayread}, \mathsf{t})$ and $\mathsf{Mayread}$ are

- After $(\mathsf{Mayread}, \mathsf{t})$, Anne does not know whether p, but Bill considers that possible: $[\mathsf{Mayread}, \mathsf{t}](\neg(K_a p \vee K_a \neg p) \wedge \hat{K}_b(K_a p \vee K_a \neg p))$
- When p is true, Anne may know that after $\mathsf{Mayread}$, but it is also conceivable that she does not—at least she *cannot* know that p is false: $p \rightarrow (\langle \mathsf{Mayread} \rangle K_a p \wedge \langle \mathsf{Mayread} \rangle \neg K_a p \wedge \neg \langle \mathsf{Mayread} \rangle K_a \neg p)$

For an example, we confirm by semantic computation that $\mathit{Letter}, 1 \models [\mathsf{Mayread}, \mathsf{t}](\neg(K_a p \vee K_a \neg p) \wedge \hat{K}_b(K_a p \vee K_a \neg p))$. This is true, if and only if (applying Definition 6.8) for all (M', s'): $(\mathit{Letter}, 1)[\![\mathsf{Mayread}, \mathsf{t}]\!](M', s')$ implies $M', s' \models \neg(K_a p \vee K_a \neg p) \wedge \hat{K}_b(K_a p \vee K_a \neg p)$. The model (M', s') is the model $(\mathit{Letter} \otimes \mathsf{Mayread}, (1, \mathsf{t}))$ constructed in Figure 6.5. It remains to check that $(\mathit{Letter} \otimes \mathsf{Mayread}, (1, \mathsf{t})) \models \neg(K_a p \vee K_a \neg p) \wedge \hat{K}_b(K_a p \vee K_a \neg p)$, in other words, that both $(\mathit{Letter} \otimes \mathsf{Mayread}, (1, \mathsf{t})) \models \neg(K_a p \vee K_a \neg p)$ and $(\mathit{Letter} \otimes \mathsf{Mayread}, (1, \mathsf{t})) \models \hat{K}_b(K_a p \vee K_a \neg p)$. The last is, because (e.g.) in $(\mathit{Letter} \otimes \mathsf{Mayread})$ state $(0, \mathsf{np})$ is b-accessible from $(1, \mathsf{t})$ and because $(\mathit{Letter} \otimes \mathsf{Mayread}, (0, \mathsf{np})) \models K_a p \vee K_a \neg p$, because $(\mathit{Letter} \otimes \mathsf{Mayread}, (0, \mathsf{np})) \models K_a \neg p$, because $(0, \mathsf{np})$ is a singleton a-class and $(\mathit{Letter} \otimes \mathsf{Mayread}, (0, \mathsf{np})) \models \neg p$, because $(0, \mathsf{np}) \notin V_p$. Etc. □

Exercise 6.14 (skip, crash, public announcement) Show all of the following (assume given set of agents A and atoms P):

- $\varphi \rightarrow [\mathsf{skip}]\varphi$ is valid.
- $[\mathsf{crash}]\bot$ is valid.
- $[\mathsf{pub}(\varphi)]\psi$ is equivalent to $[\varphi]\psi$—where the last is public announcement according to Chapter 4.

The first says that the skip action does not 'do' anything, that it is just a 'tick of the clock', so to speak. The second says that the crash action cannot be executed. Note that the skip action can also be seen as the public announcement of the formula $\top$ ('true'). □

Exercise 6.15 (Action model for bothmayread) Give an action model for the epistemic action $\mathsf{bothmayread}$ in Chapter 5 (Example 5.5 on page 110) where both Anne and Bill consider it possible that the other may have read the letter, and where, actually, both read the letter. □

Example 6.16 (Action composition) Given the epistemic state $(\mathit{Letter}, 1)$ where both Anne and Bill do not know p, and where p is true, first Anne reads the letter—this is the action model $(\mathsf{Read}, \mathsf{p})$ already modelled in the introduction—and then Bill reads the letter. This is the action model

$(\mathsf{Read}_b, \mathsf{pb})$ where Read_b is defined as $\langle\{\mathsf{npb}, \mathsf{pb}\}, \sim, \mathsf{pre}\rangle$ such that $\sim_b$ is the identity and $\sim_a$ the universal relation, and with $\mathsf{pre}(\mathsf{pb}) = p$ and $\mathsf{pre}(\mathsf{npb}) = \neg p$. First, we compute the composition of Read and Read_b:

The domain of action model Read ; Read_b is the cartesian product of the domains of Read and Read_b, which is $\{(\mathsf{np}, \mathsf{npb}), (\mathsf{np}, \mathsf{pb}), (\mathsf{p}, \mathsf{npb}), (\mathsf{p}, \mathsf{pb})\}$. The partition for Anne on this domain is $\{(\mathsf{np}, \mathsf{npb}), (\mathsf{np}, \mathsf{pb})\}$, $\{(\mathsf{p}, \mathsf{npb}), (\mathsf{p}, \mathsf{pb})\}$. The partition for Bill on this domain is $\{(\mathsf{np}, \mathsf{npb}), (\mathsf{p}, \mathsf{npb})\}$, $\{(\mathsf{np}, \mathsf{pb}), (\mathsf{p}, \mathsf{pb})\}$. For example $(\mathsf{np}, \mathsf{npb}) \sim_a (\mathsf{np}, \mathsf{pb})$ because, obviously, $\mathsf{np} \sim_a \mathsf{np}$ and, as Anne does not know whether Bill learns p or learns $\neg p$ *based on the action model structure only*, $\mathsf{npb} \sim_a \mathsf{pb}$. In fact she *knows* that Bill can only learn p, as she already knows p. How to explain the difference? We have not computed the preconditions of the four action points so far, and this will solve that puzzling observation. First, $\mathsf{pre}((\mathsf{np}, \mathsf{npb})) = \langle \mathsf{Read}, \mathsf{np}\rangle \mathsf{pre}(\mathsf{npb})$. Note that $\langle \mathsf{Read}, \mathsf{np}\rangle \mathsf{pre}(\mathsf{npb})$ is equivalent to $\mathsf{pre}(\mathsf{np}) \wedge [\mathsf{Read}, \mathsf{np}]\mathsf{pre}(\mathsf{npb})$ which is $\neg p \wedge [\mathsf{Read}, \mathsf{np}]\neg p$ which given the persistence of atomic information amounts to the same as precondition $\neg p$. Next, we compute $\mathsf{pre}((\mathsf{np}, \mathsf{pb}))$. Using the same simplifications, we end up with a precondition $\neg p \wedge [\mathsf{Read}, \mathsf{np}]p$ which amounts to a precondition $\neg p \wedge p$, i.e, $\bot$! Similarly, $\mathsf{pre}(\mathsf{p}, \mathsf{npb}) = \bot$, and $\mathsf{pre}(\mathsf{p}, \mathsf{pb}) = p$. Concluding, from, e.g., Anne's perspective: even though her partition on the domain is $\{(\mathsf{np}, \mathsf{npb}), (\mathsf{np}, \mathsf{pb})\}$, $\{(\mathsf{p}, \mathsf{npb}), (\mathsf{p}, \mathsf{pb})\}$, only one of the first two action points can ever be executed, and also only one of the second two action points; and something similar holds for Bill.[3] The point of the action model is the pair $(\mathsf{p}, \mathsf{pb})$: both Anne and Bill really learn that p.

If we now execute this composed action model in $(\mathit{Letter}, 1)$, a two-point epistemic state results consisting of two states $(0, (\mathsf{np}, \mathsf{npb}))$ and $(1, (\mathsf{p}, \mathsf{pb}))$, with identity access for Anne and Bill, and the second as the actual state. In that state Anne and Bill have common knowledge of p. If we first execute 'Anne reads the letter' and then 'Bill reads the letter', the result is a isomorphic but with states named $((0, \mathsf{np}), \mathsf{npb})$ and $((1, \mathsf{p}), \mathsf{pb})$, respectively. □

Exercise 6.17 (Action composition) Given, again, the epistemic state $(\mathit{Letter}, 1)$ where both Anne and Bill do not know p, and where p is true, first Anne may read the letter—this is the action model $(\mathsf{Mayread}, \mathsf{p})$ already modelled in Example 6.13, and then Bill may read the letter.

Give an action model for the epistemic action 'Bill may read the letter'. Compute the composition of $(\mathsf{Mayread}, \mathsf{p})$ with that action model (this is an action model consisting of nine action points), and execute the composition in the epistemic state $(\mathit{Letter}, 1)$. As well, execute the action model for 'Bill may read the letter' in the epistemic state resulting from the execution of $(\mathsf{Mayread}, \mathsf{p})$.

Compare both results. □

---

[3] So, 'effectively', the composition is a two-point action model with identity access for Anne and Bill. In what sense are these models 'the same'? This will be addressed in Section 6.5, next.

Exercise 6.18 (Card showing actions) Give action model descriptions for the actions table, show, whisper in the context of three players each holding a card, as modelled by *Hexa*. Also, execute these actions in the epistemic model $(Hexa, 012)$. (See Section 5.4 in Chapter 5.) □

Exercise 6.19 Give an action model description for a player picking up his/her cards, as in Figure 5.4 on page 128. □

In Definition 6.2 of action models, *infinite* action models (i.e., with a domain of infinite size) were not ruled out. A consideration may be whether there are 'reasonable' actions that need such an infinite description, but that are ruled out by the subsequent Definition 6.3 of the language of action model logic, as herein a restriction is made to finite models.

Candidates are found in the context of the 'epistemic riddle' concerning consecutive numbers presented in Example 2.4 in Chapter 2. We consider the version where agents only know their own number, instead of only the number of the other agent:

> Anne and Bill will each be told a natural number. Their numbers are one apart. All this is commonly known to Anne and Bill. Now they are being told the numbers. Anne is being told "4", and Bill "3".

The atomic propositions i_a and i_b needed for an analysis expressed that some natural number is (or will be) associated with Anne, or Bill, respectively. In Chapter 2 we focused on what Anne and Bill know in the model resulting from this scenario, and on how various subsequent public announcements affect their knowledge. But the various actions by the 'announcer' (the announcer need not be modelled) in this scenario can also be modelled as epistemic actions, even though, obviously, not all as public announcements. The actions are

- You will be told a natural number.
- Your numbers are one apart.
- To Anne: Your number is 4.
- To Bill: Your number is 3.

The first can be modelled as an action model with $\mathbb{N} \times \mathbb{N}$ action points (i, j) with preconditions $\mathsf{pre}(i, j) = i_a \wedge j_b$. Anne and Bill have universal access on this cartesian product. This action more or less 'addresses the issue' and in that sense *introduces* ownership of numbers as the facts that we will be talking about, so it may be questioned if this is a reasonable action. For another example, the messenger delivering a letter to Anne could then as well be seen as introducing one of all conceivable facts q, with the fact p describing the state of affairs at United Agents only one of those. But also the other, more intuitively acceptable actions, need an infinite action model description.

The second action can be seen as a public announcement of an infinitely long formula $\bigvee_{i \in \mathbb{N}}(i_a \wedge (i+1)_b) \vee ((i+1)_a \wedge i_b)$—but we do not allow infinitely long formulas, so alternatively we have an infinitely large action model with action points $(i, i+1)$ and $(i+1, i)$ (where formula $i_a \wedge (i+1)_b$ is true in point $(i, i+1)$, and formula $(i+1)_a \wedge i_b$ is true in point $(i+1, i)$), all indistinguishable for Anne and Bill.

The action where Anne is told that her number is 4, again needs an infinite action model. This consists of $\mathbb{N}$ alternatives i with precondition $\mathsf{pre}(i) = i_a$ representing that Anne will be told the number i, and with designated point 4, as Anne is actually told the number 4. Again, Bill cannot distinguish between any of those. The last action where Bill is told number 3 is similar to that where Anne is told her number, so this has an infinite action model as well.

Exercise 6.20 We now repeat the above for $\mathcal{L}_{KC\otimes}$ action models, with the exception of the first action. Suppose it is given that the numbers are not larger than 5, so that we starting with an epistemic model **66** consisting of 6×6 states (with designated point $(4, 3)$). Give action models for the actions

- Your numbers are one apart.
- To Anne: Your number is 4.
- To Bill: Your number is 3.

and also execute them in epistemic state $(\mathbf{66}, (4, 3))$. Next, continue the scenario with the conversation starting with Anne saying "I don't know your number", following by Bill saying "I don't know your number", etc, until one of the agents achieves knowledge. Model those actions as public announcements and execute them in the current epistemic states. How often will Anne and Bill make their announcements under these finite restrictions? What model results? □

6.5 Bisimilarity and Action Emulation

If we execute the same action in two given bisimilar epistemic states, then surely the result should be bisimilar again. This is indeed the case. But given that the action models themselves *also* have structure, we can go beyond such observations. The obvious notion of bisimilarity for action models is as for epistemic states, but with the requirement that points have corresponding *valuations* replaced by the requirement that points have corresponding *preconditions*. We then indeed have that if two bisimilar action models are executed in the same epistemic state, then the resulting epistemic states are bisimilar. It turns out, however, that this requirement for action sameness is too strong: if we *merely* want to guarantee that the resulting epistemic states are bisimilar given two executed actions, then a weaker notion of sameness is already sufficient. Instead of a bisimulation between action models, we require something that is called an *emulation*.

For example, consider on the one hand action model $\langle \{\mathsf{t}\}, \sim, \mathsf{pre} \rangle$ that is reflexive for all agents and with $\mathsf{pre}(\mathsf{t}) = \top$, and on the other hand action model $\langle \{\mathsf{p}, \mathsf{np}\}, \sim', \mathsf{pre}' \rangle$ such that no agent can distinguish between p and np, and with $\mathsf{pre}'(\mathsf{p}) = p$ and $\mathsf{pre}'(\mathsf{np}) = \neg p$. Note that the second is not pointed, so it is actually an epistemic action that is non-deterministic choice between two pointed action models.

These two action models are not bisimilar in the above sense, because the precondition $\top$ of the first cannot be matched by either precondition p or $\neg p$ of the other action model. But, obviously, in any model wherein either can be executed, the other can be executed too, and with bisimilar (and indeed isomorphic) results. The notion of emulation can express that these two action models are similar enough to always result in bisimilar epistemic states.

We continue with a more formal introduction of these matters.

Proposition 6.21 (Preservation of bisimilarity) Given epistemic states (M, s) and (M', s') such that $(M, s) \leftrightarroweq (M', s')$. Let (M, s) with $\mathsf{M} = \langle \mathsf{S}, \sim, \mathsf{pre} \rangle$ be executable in (M, s). Then $(M \otimes \mathsf{M}, (s, \mathsf{s})) \leftrightarroweq (M' \otimes \mathsf{M}, (s', \mathsf{s}))$. □

Proof Note that (M, s) is also executable in (M', s'), as $M, s \models \mathsf{pre}(\mathsf{s})$ and $(M, s) \leftrightarroweq (M', s')$ implies $M', s' \models \mathsf{pre}(\mathsf{s})$. Let $\mathfrak{R} : (M, s) \leftrightarroweq (M', s')$ be a bisimulation between the given epistemic states. The required bisimulation $\mathfrak{R}'$ between the resulting epistemic states is defined as, for arbitrary pairs (t, t) and (t', t'):

$$\mathfrak{R}'((t, \mathsf{t}), (t', \mathsf{t}')) \quad \text{iff} \quad \mathfrak{R}(t, t') \text{ and } \mathsf{t} = \mathsf{t}'$$

□

Definition 6.22 (Bisimulation of actions) Given are action models (M, u) with $\mathsf{M} = \langle \mathsf{S}, \sim, \mathsf{pre} \rangle$, and $(\mathsf{M}', \mathsf{u}')$ with $\mathsf{M}' = \langle \mathsf{S}', \sim', \mathsf{pre}' \rangle$. A *bisimulation* between (M, u) and $(\mathsf{M}', \mathsf{u}')$ is a relation $\mathfrak{R} \subseteq (\mathsf{S} \times \mathsf{S}')$ such that $\mathfrak{R}(\mathsf{u}, \mathsf{u}')$ and such that the following three conditions are met for each agent a (for arbitrary action points):

Forth If $\mathfrak{R}(\mathsf{s}, \mathsf{s}')$ and $\mathsf{s} \sim_a \mathsf{t}$, then there is an $\mathsf{t}' \in \mathsf{S}'$ such that $\mathfrak{R}(\mathsf{t}, \mathsf{t}')$ and $\mathsf{s}' \sim'_a \mathsf{t}'$.

Back If $\mathfrak{R}(\mathsf{s}, \mathsf{s}')$ and $\mathsf{s}' \sim'_a \mathsf{t}'$, then there is an $\mathsf{t} \in \mathsf{S}$ such that $\mathfrak{R}(\mathsf{t}, \mathsf{t}')$ and $\mathsf{s} \sim_a \mathsf{t}$.

Pre If $\mathfrak{R}(\mathsf{s}, \mathsf{s}')$, then $\mathsf{pre}(\mathsf{s})$ is equivalent to $\mathsf{pre}(\mathsf{s}')$.

A relation $\mathfrak{R}$ is a *total bisimulation* between M and M' iff for each $\mathsf{s} \in \mathsf{S}$ there is an $\mathsf{s}' \in \mathsf{S}'$ such that $\mathfrak{R}$ is a bisimulation between (M, s) and $(\mathsf{M}', \mathsf{s}')$, and vice versa. □

As usual we write $(\mathsf{M}, \mathsf{s}) \leftrightarroweq (\mathsf{M}', \mathsf{s}')$ if such a bisimulation exists; or $\mathfrak{R} : (\mathsf{M}, \mathsf{s}) \leftrightarroweq (\mathsf{M}', \mathsf{s}')$, to make the bisimulation explicit.

Proposition 6.23 (Action execution preserves action bisimilarity) Given two action models such that $(\mathsf{M}, \mathsf{s}) \leftrightarroweq (\mathsf{M}', \mathsf{s}')$ and an epistemic state (M, s) such that (M, s) is executable in (M, s). Then $(M \otimes \mathsf{M}, (s, \mathsf{s})) \leftrightarroweq (M \otimes \mathsf{M}', (s, \mathsf{s}'))$. □

Proof Let $\mathfrak{R}$ be a bisimulation $\mathfrak{R} : (\mathsf{M}, \mathsf{s}) \leftrightarroweq (\mathsf{M}', \mathsf{s}')$. Note that $(\mathsf{M}', \mathsf{s}')$ is also executable in (M, s), because from $\mathfrak{R}(\mathsf{s}, \mathsf{s}')$ follows $\models \mathsf{pre}'(\mathsf{s}') \leftrightarrow \mathsf{pre}(\mathsf{s})$; and from $\models \mathsf{pre}'(\mathsf{s}') \leftrightarrow \mathsf{pre}(\mathsf{s})$ and $M, s \models \mathsf{pre}(\mathsf{s})$ follows $M, s \models \mathsf{pre}'(\mathsf{s}')$. The required bisimulation $\mathfrak{R}'$ between the resulting epistemic states is defined, for arbitrary pairs (t, t) and (t', t'), as

$$\mathfrak{R}'((t,\mathsf{t}),(t',\mathsf{t}')) \text{ iff } t = t' \ \& \ \mathfrak{R}(\mathsf{t},\mathsf{t}')$$ □

Corollary 6.24
If $(M, s) \leftrightarrows (M', s')$ and $(\mathsf{M},\mathsf{s}) \leftrightarrows (\mathsf{M}',\mathsf{s}')$, then $(M \otimes \mathsf{M}, (s, \mathsf{s})) \leftrightarrows (M' \otimes \mathsf{M}', (s', \mathsf{s}'))$. □

The now following notion of action emulation captures a weaker form of structural similarity, that however is also sufficient to guarantee bisimilarity of epistemic states resulting from action execution.

Definition 6.25 (Action emulation) Given are pointed action models (M, u) with $\mathsf{M} = \langle \mathsf{S}, \sim, \mathsf{pre} \rangle$, and $(\mathsf{M}', \mathsf{u}')$ with $\mathsf{M}' = \langle \mathsf{S}', \sim', \mathsf{pre}' \rangle$. An *emulation* between (M, u) and $(\mathsf{M}', \mathsf{u}')$ is a relation $\mathfrak{E} \subseteq (\mathsf{S} \times \mathsf{S}')$ such that $\mathfrak{E}(\mathsf{u}, \mathsf{u}')$ and the following three conditions are met for each agent a (for arbitrary action points):

Forth If $\mathfrak{E}(\mathsf{s}, \mathsf{s}')$ and $\mathsf{s} \sim_a \mathsf{t}$, then there are $\mathsf{t}'_1, ...\mathsf{t}'_n \in \mathsf{S}'$ such that for all $i = 1, ..., n$, $\mathfrak{E}(\mathsf{t}, \mathsf{t}'_i)$ and $\mathsf{s}' \sim'_a \mathsf{t}'_i$, and such that $\mathsf{pre}(\mathsf{t}) \models \mathsf{pre}'(\mathsf{t}'_1) \vee \ldots \mathsf{pre}'(\mathsf{t}'_n)$.

Back If $\mathfrak{E}(\mathsf{s}, \mathsf{s}')$ and $\mathsf{s}' \sim'_a \mathsf{t}'$, then there are $\mathsf{t}_1, ...\mathsf{t}_n \in \mathsf{S}$ such that for all $i = 1, ..., n$, $\mathfrak{E}(\mathsf{t}_i, \mathsf{t}')$ and $\mathsf{s} \sim_a \mathsf{t}_i$, and such that $\mathsf{pre}'(\mathsf{t}') \models \mathsf{pre}(\mathsf{t}_1) \vee \ldots \mathsf{pre}(\mathsf{t}_n)$.

Pre If $\mathfrak{E}(\mathsf{s}, \mathsf{s}')$, then $\mathsf{pre}(\mathsf{s}) \wedge \mathsf{pre}'(\mathsf{s}')$ is consistent.

A *total emulation* $\mathfrak{E} : \mathsf{M} \rightleftarrows \mathsf{M}'$ is an emulation such that for each $\mathsf{s} \in \mathsf{S}$ there is a $\mathsf{s}' \in \mathsf{S}'$ with $\mathfrak{E}(\mathsf{s}, \mathsf{s}')$ and vice versa. □

In the definition above, it is **essential** that the accessibility relations are *reflexive* (as they are equivalence relations). This ensures that the entailment requirements in the forth and back conditions also hold in the designated points of the structures.[4]

We can paraphrase the difference between action bisimulation and action emulation as follows. Two bisimilar actions s, s' must have logically *equivalent* preconditions—i.e., $\models \mathsf{pre}(\mathsf{s}) \leftrightarrow \mathsf{pre}'(\mathsf{s}')$—but in the case of two emulous actions it may be that one precondition only *entails* the other, i.e., $\models \mathsf{pre}(\mathsf{s}) \rightarrow \mathsf{pre}'(\mathsf{s}')$ but $\not\models \mathsf{pre}'(\mathsf{s}') \rightarrow \mathsf{pre}(\mathsf{s})$. In that case, formula $\mathsf{pre}'(\mathsf{s}')$ is strictly weaker than $\mathsf{pre}(\mathsf{s})$. This does not hurt if we can make up for the difference by finding sufficient emulous 'alternatives' $\mathsf{t}_1, \ldots, \mathsf{t}_n$ (including s) to s such that even

[4] We suggest that an alternative definition of action emulation is feasible that incorporates the 'extra' conditions in back and forth directly in the **Pre** part, and has 'standard' **Back** and **Forth** instead, as follows:

Forth If $\mathfrak{E}(\mathsf{s}, \mathsf{s}')$ and $\mathsf{s} \sim_a \mathsf{t}$, then there is a t' such that $\mathfrak{E}(\mathsf{t}, \mathsf{t}')$ and $\mathsf{s}' \sim'_a \mathsf{t}'$.

Back If $\mathfrak{E}(\mathsf{s}, \mathsf{s}')$ and $\mathsf{s}' \sim'_a \mathsf{t}'$, then there is a t such that $\mathfrak{E}(\mathsf{t}, \mathsf{t}')$ and $\mathsf{s} \sim_a \mathsf{t}$.

Pre If $\mathfrak{E}(\mathsf{s}, \mathsf{s}')$, then there are $\mathsf{s}'_1, ...\mathsf{s}'_n \in \mathsf{S}'$ including s' such that for all $i = 1, ..., n$, $\mathfrak{E}(\mathsf{s}, \mathsf{s}'_i)$ and $\mathsf{pre}(\mathsf{s}) \models \mathsf{pre}'(\mathsf{s}'_1) \vee \ldots \mathsf{pre}'(\mathsf{s}'_n)$; and there are $\mathsf{s}_1, ...\mathsf{s}_n \in \mathsf{S}$ including s such that for all $i = 1, ..., n$, $\mathfrak{E}(\mathsf{s}_i, \mathsf{s}')$ and $\mathsf{pre}'(\mathsf{s}') \models \mathsf{pre}(\mathsf{s}_1) \vee \ldots \mathsf{pre}(\mathsf{s}_n)$.

Such a definition is more like other variations on standard bisimulation.

though $\not\models \mathsf{pre}(\mathsf{s}') \rightarrow \mathsf{pre}(\mathsf{s})$, after all $\models \mathsf{pre}(\mathsf{s}') \rightarrow \mathsf{pre}(\mathsf{t}_1)\vee\ldots\vee\mathsf{pre}(\mathsf{t}_n)$. This corresponds to the 'back' requirement in the definition. In the other case, namely where $\mathsf{pre}(\mathsf{s})$ is strictly weaker than $\mathsf{pre}'(\mathsf{s}')$, we need the 'forth' requirement.

Example 6.26 Consider the introductory example action models: $\mathsf{one} = \langle\{\mathsf{t}\}, \sim, \mathsf{pre}\rangle$ that is reflexive for all agents and with $\mathsf{pre}(\mathsf{t}) = \top$, and action model $\mathsf{two} = \langle\{\mathsf{p}, \mathsf{np}\}, \sim', \mathsf{pre}'\rangle$ such that no agent can distinguish between p and np, and with $\mathsf{pre}'(\mathsf{p}) = p$ and $\mathsf{pre}'(\mathsf{np}) = \neg p$. The relation $\mathfrak{E}$ between these action models consists of two pairs:

$$\mathfrak{E} = \{(\mathsf{t}, \mathsf{p}), (\mathsf{t}, \mathsf{np})\}$$

We confirm that this relation is an emulation by checking the three requirements in the definition.

Forth First, consider $\mathfrak{E}(\mathsf{t}, \mathsf{p})$. For any agent a, only t itself is $\sim_a$-accessible from t. The requirement amounts to checking that, given $\mathfrak{E}(\mathsf{t}, \mathsf{p})$, we can find sufficient actions such that $\mathsf{pre}(\mathsf{t}) \models \mathsf{pre}'(\mathsf{p}) \vee \ldots$. This is indeed the case, because we also have that $\mathfrak{E}(\mathsf{t}, \mathsf{np})$ and $\mathsf{pre}(\mathsf{t}) \models \mathsf{pre}'(\mathsf{p}) \vee \mathsf{pre}'(\mathsf{np})$, because indeed $\top \models p \vee \neg p$. Similarly for the case $\mathfrak{E}(\mathsf{t}, \mathsf{np})$.

Back Consider again $\mathfrak{E}(\mathsf{t}, \mathsf{p})$. We then have that $\mathsf{p} \sim_a \mathsf{p}$ and $\mathsf{p} \sim_a \mathsf{np}$. In both cases, (obviously) choose t as the the required action point in the other action model. In the first case, somewhat trivially, $p \models \top$, i.e., $\mathsf{pre}'(\mathsf{p}) \models \mathsf{pre}(\mathsf{t})$, and in the second case $\neg p \models \top$, i.e., $\mathsf{pre}'(\mathsf{np}) \models \mathsf{pre}(\mathsf{t})$.

Pre Formula $\mathsf{pre}(\mathsf{t}) \wedge \mathsf{pre}'(\mathsf{p}) = \top \wedge p$ is consistent. Formula $\mathsf{pre}(\mathsf{t}) \wedge \mathsf{pre}'(\mathsf{np}) = \top \wedge \neg p$ is also consistent. □

Exercise 6.27 Consider one agent only. Show that the following four action models are emulous. The preconditions of action points are indicated below their names. Assume transitivity of access, as usual.

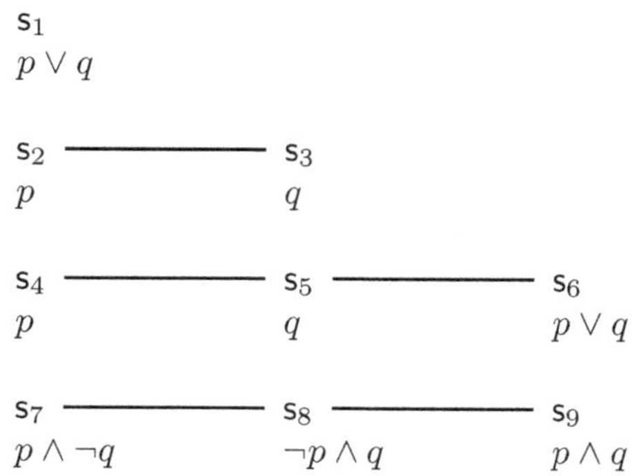

□

Exercise 6.28 Consider Example 6.16 on page 154 again. Show that the action model (Read ; Read_b) and the one without the two action points with $\perp$-preconditions, are emulous. See also Footnote 3 on page 155. □

Proposition 6.29 (Bisimilar actions are emulous) A bisimulation $\mathfrak{R} : (\mathsf{M}, \mathsf{s}) \leftrightarroweq (\mathsf{M}', \mathsf{s}')$ is also an emulation. □

Proof Obvious. The required *set* of action points in 'forth' consists of the *single* action point given by the bisimulation, and for such a pair $(\mathsf{t}, \mathsf{t}') \in \mathfrak{R}$, the bisimulation condition $\models \mathsf{pre}(\mathsf{t}) \leftrightarrow \mathsf{pre}'(\mathsf{t}')$ implies $\mathsf{pre}(\mathsf{t}) \models \mathsf{pre}'(\mathsf{t}')$. Similarly, for 'back'. □

Proposition 6.30 (Emulation guarantees bisimilarity) Given an epistemic model M and action models $\mathsf{M} \rightleftarrows \mathsf{M}'$. Then $(M \otimes \mathsf{M}) \leftrightarroweq (M \otimes \mathsf{M}')$. □

Proof As usual, assume $\mathsf{M} = \langle \mathsf{S}, \sim, \mathsf{pre} \rangle$ and $\mathsf{M}' = \langle \mathsf{S}', \sim', \mathsf{pre}' \rangle$. We show that $\mathfrak{R} : (M \otimes \mathsf{M}) \leftrightarroweq (M \otimes \mathsf{M}')$ for $\mathfrak{R}$ defined as

$$\mathfrak{R}((s, \mathsf{s}), (s', \mathsf{s}')) \text{ iff } \quad s = s' \text{ and } \mathfrak{E}(\mathsf{s}, \mathsf{s}')$$

is a total bisimulation between $(M \otimes \mathsf{M})$ and $(M \otimes \mathsf{M}')$.

Forth Let $(s, \mathsf{s}) \sim_a (t, \mathsf{t})$ and $\mathfrak{R}((s, \mathsf{s}), (s', \mathsf{s}'))$. From $\mathsf{s} \sim_a \mathsf{t}$ and $\mathfrak{E}(\mathsf{s}, \mathsf{s}')$ follows that there are $\mathsf{t}'_1, \dots, \mathsf{t}'_n$ such that $\mathfrak{E}(\mathsf{t}, \mathsf{t}'_1), \dots, \mathfrak{E}(\mathsf{t}, \mathsf{t}'_n)$, and $\mathsf{s}' \sim'_a \mathsf{t}'_1, \dots, \mathsf{s}' \sim'_a \mathsf{t}'_n$, and $\mathsf{pre}(\mathsf{t}) \models \mathsf{pre}'(\mathsf{t}'_1) \vee \dots \vee \mathsf{pre}'(\mathsf{t}'_n)$. From the last and $M, t \models \mathsf{pre}(\mathsf{t})$ follows that for some $i = 1, \dots, n$ it holds that $M, t \models \mathsf{pre}'(\mathsf{t}'_i)$. Therefore $\mathfrak{E}(\mathsf{t}, \mathsf{t}'_i)$, so that we now have, by definition, $\mathfrak{R}((t, \mathsf{t}), (t, \mathsf{t}'_i))$.

Back Similar to forth.

Valuation Given that $\mathfrak{R}((s, \mathsf{s}), (s', \mathsf{s}'))$ it follows that $s = s'$. The valuation of facts does not change after action execution, i.e., $(s, \mathsf{s}) \in V_p$ iff $s \in V_p$ iff $(s, \mathsf{s}') \in V_p$.[5] □

It can be shown that for action models with propositional preconditions, action emulation fully characterises the effect of action execution. In other words, not just Proposition 6.30 holds, but also 'the opposite': *if* the execution of two 'propositional' action models in an epistemic model results in bisimilar epistemic models, *then* there must be an emulation relating them. We do not give a proof (see the Notes for a reference). For non-propositional preconditions, these matters are more complex.

Example 6.31 Consider the two emulous action models one and two of Example 6.26, for a set of agents $\{a, b\}$, and the epistemic model M for Anne and Bill such that Bill is uncertain about the truth of p but Anne knows whether p. The result of executing one and two, respectively, in that model is shown in Figure 6.6. It will be obvious that $M \otimes \mathsf{one} \leftrightarroweq M \otimes \mathsf{two}$. □

[5] The obvious 'pointed' version of Proposition 6.30 does not hold. Given an epistemic state (M, s) and action models $(\mathsf{M}, \mathsf{s}) \rightleftarrows (\mathsf{M}', \mathsf{s}')$ and such that (M, s) is executable in (M, s), then $(M \otimes \mathsf{M}, (s, \mathsf{s}))$ may *not* be bisimilar to $(M \otimes \mathsf{M}', (s, \mathsf{s}'))$. This is because $\mathsf{pre}'(\mathsf{s}')$ may not be true in (M, s)—although there must be a $\mathsf{s}'_i \in \mathsf{S}'$ among the 'alternatives' for s' with $\mathsf{pre}(\mathsf{s}) \models \mathsf{pre}'(\mathsf{s}') \vee \dots \vee \mathsf{pre}'(\mathsf{s}'_n) \vee \dots$, such that this s'_n fulfils the role required for $(M \otimes \mathsf{M}, (s, \mathsf{s})) \leftrightarroweq (M \otimes \mathsf{M}', (s, \mathsf{s}'_n))$.

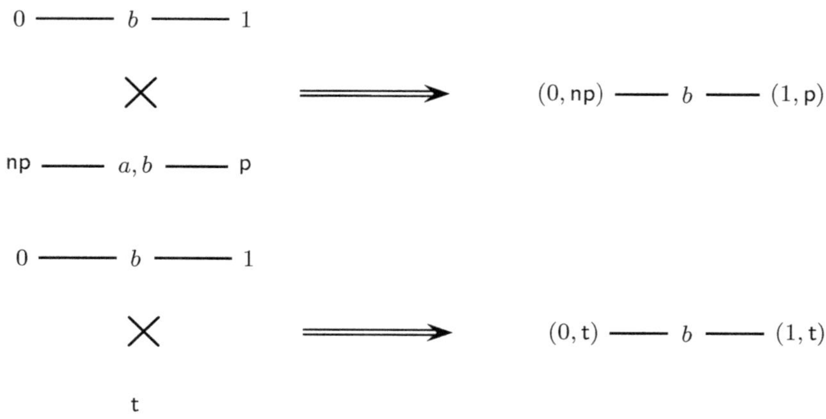

Figure 6.6. Emulous actions result in bisimilar epistemic models.

6.6 Validities and Axiomatisation

The principles of action model logic resemble those for public announcement logic, but there are also differences. A major difference between the two logics is that epistemic actions may be non-deterministic (so that, in other words, $\langle\alpha\rangle\varphi \rightarrow [\alpha]\varphi$ is invalid). The principle of non-determinism, $[\alpha \cup \beta]\varphi \leftrightarrow [\alpha]\varphi \wedge [\beta]\varphi$, has already been stated as Proposition 6.11, where we also mentioned that all expressions $[\alpha]\varphi$ are equivalent to some conjunction $\bigwedge[\mathsf{M}, \mathsf{s}]\varphi$. This justifies that we can formulate all principles in terms of pointed action models only.

To start with, just like public announcement logic, epistemic actions do not change the value of atomic propositions. (Proofs are often elementary and are left to the reader.)

Proposition 6.32 (Atomic permanence) $[\mathsf{M}, \mathsf{s}]p \leftrightarrow (\mathsf{pre}(\mathsf{s}) \rightarrow p)$ is valid. □

Action model logic has also in common with public announcement logic that action interpretation is a *partial* relation, i.e., actions are not always executable. This is for example expressed in the principle of 'action and negation'.

Proposition 6.33 (Action and negation) $[\mathsf{M}, \mathsf{s}]\neg\varphi \leftrightarrow (\mathsf{pre}(\mathsf{s}) \rightarrow \neg[\mathsf{M}, \mathsf{s}]\varphi)$ is valid. □

The principle 'action and conjunction' is just what we expect for a dynamic modal operator.

Proposition 6.34 (Action and conjunction) $[\mathsf{M}, \mathsf{s}](\varphi \wedge \psi) \leftrightarrow ([\mathsf{M}, \mathsf{s}]\varphi \wedge [\mathsf{M}, \mathsf{s}]\psi)$ is valid. □

Exercise 6.35 Prove the soundness of the principles 'atomic permanence', 'action and negation', and 'action and conjunction' in the above propositions. □

The **PAC** principle relating knowledge and announcements was $[\varphi]K_a\psi \leftrightarrow (\varphi \rightarrow K_a[\varphi]\psi)$. A *very* similar principle cannot be for action model logic, because actions may look different for different agents. For example, in the setting of *Hexa*, Cath knows that Bill knows that Anne holds card 0 after Anne shows card 0 to Bill. But it is not the case that after Anne shows card 0 to Bill, Cath knows that Bill knows that Anne holds card 0! Let $(\mathsf{Show}, \mathbf{0})$ be that action model, so that $\mathsf{pre}(\mathsf{Show}, \mathbf{0}) = 0_a$, then we have that

$$(Hexa, 012) \models \mathsf{pre}(\mathsf{Show}, \mathbf{0}) \rightarrow K_c[\mathsf{Show}, \mathbf{0}]K_b 0_a$$

but also

$$(Hexa, 012) \not\models [\mathsf{Show}, \mathbf{0}]K_c K_b 0_a$$

What sort of formulas *does* Cath know after this action $(\mathsf{Show}, \mathbf{0})$? If a formula is true not just after that action, but also after the alternative actions that she cannot be (publicly) known to distinguish from $(\mathsf{Show}, \mathbf{0})$, namely Anne showing card 1, or Anne showing card 2, only *then* can she be guaranteed to know it after $(\mathsf{Show}, \mathbf{0})$. This is expressed in the principle 'action and knowledge'. The principle is visualised as well, in Figure 6.7.

Proposition 6.36 (Action and knowledge)
$[\mathsf{M}, \mathsf{s}]K_a\varphi \leftrightarrow (\mathsf{pre}(\mathsf{s}) \rightarrow \bigwedge_{\mathsf{s} \sim_a \mathsf{t}} K_a[\mathsf{M}, \mathsf{t}]\varphi)$ is valid. □

Proof We prove the dual form of the proposition which reads (implicitly replacing φ by $\neg\varphi$)

$$(\mathsf{pre}(\mathsf{s}) \wedge \bigvee_{\mathsf{s} \sim_a \mathsf{t}} \hat{K}_a \langle \mathsf{M}, \mathsf{t} \rangle \varphi) \leftrightarrow \langle \mathsf{M}, \mathsf{s} \rangle \hat{K}_a \varphi$$

Let $M = \langle S, \sim, V \rangle$ and $\mathsf{M} = \langle \mathsf{S}, \sim, \mathsf{pre} \rangle$.

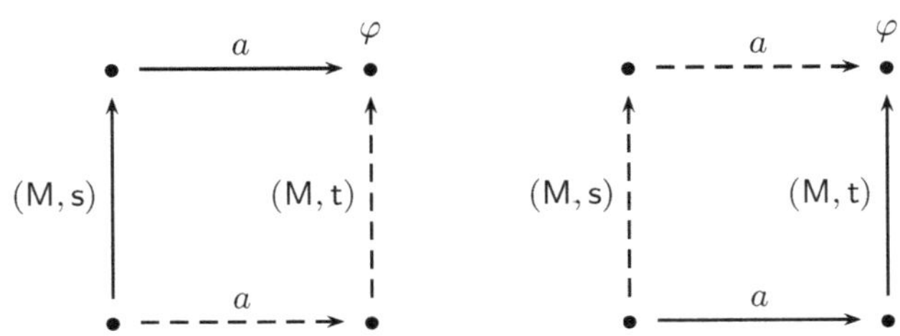

Figure 6.7. The principle of knowledge and action. The dashed lines in the left diagram can be established because $\langle \mathsf{M}, \mathsf{s} \rangle \hat{K}_a \varphi$ implies $\mathsf{pre}(\mathsf{s}) \wedge \bigvee_{\mathsf{s} \sim_a \mathsf{t}} \hat{K}_a \langle \mathsf{M}, \mathsf{t} \rangle \varphi$. The dashed lines in the right diagram can be established because $\mathsf{pre}(\mathsf{s}) \wedge \bigvee_{\mathsf{s} \sim_a \mathsf{t}} \hat{K}_a \langle \mathsf{M}, \mathsf{t} \rangle \varphi$ implies $\langle \mathsf{M}, \mathsf{s} \rangle \hat{K}_a \varphi$.

Assume that $M, s \models \mathsf{pre}(\mathsf{s})$ and that there is a $\mathsf{t} \in \mathsf{S}$ such that $\mathsf{s} \sim_a \mathsf{t}$ and $M, s \models \hat{K}_a \langle \mathsf{M}, \mathsf{t} \rangle \varphi$. From $M, s \models \mathsf{pre}(\mathsf{s})$ follows that $(s, \mathsf{s}) \in M \otimes \mathsf{M}$. From $M, s \models \hat{K}_a \langle \mathsf{M}, \mathsf{t} \rangle \varphi$ follows that there is a $t \in S$ such that $s \sim_a t$ and $M, t \models \langle \mathsf{M}, \mathsf{t} \rangle \varphi$. From $M, t \models \langle \mathsf{M}, \mathsf{t} \rangle \varphi$ follows that $M, t \models \mathsf{pre}(\mathsf{t})$, so that $(t, \mathsf{t}) \in M \otimes \mathsf{M}$; and also that $(M \otimes \mathsf{M}, (t, \mathsf{t})) \models \varphi$. From $s \sim_a t$ and $\mathsf{s} \sim_a \mathsf{t}$ follows $(s, \mathsf{s}) \sim_a (t, \mathsf{t})$. From $(s, \mathsf{s}) \sim_a (t, \mathsf{t})$ and $(M \otimes \mathsf{M}, (t, \mathsf{t})) \models \varphi$ follows $(M \otimes \mathsf{M}, (s, \mathsf{s})) \models \hat{K}_a \varphi$, i.e., $M, s \models \langle \mathsf{M}, \mathsf{s} \rangle \hat{K}_a \varphi$.

Now assume that $M, s \models \langle \mathsf{M}, \mathsf{s} \rangle \hat{K}_a \varphi$. Obviously, it follows that $M, s \models \mathsf{pre}(\mathsf{s})$. Also, $M, s \models \langle \mathsf{M}, \mathsf{s} \rangle \hat{K}_a \varphi$ implies that $(M \otimes \mathsf{M}, (s, \mathsf{s})) \models \hat{K}_a \varphi$, i.e., there is a $(t, \mathsf{t}) \in (S \times \mathsf{S})$ such that $(s, \mathsf{s}) \sim_a (t, \mathsf{t})$ and $(M \otimes \mathsf{M}, (t, \mathsf{t})) \models \varphi$. From $(s, \mathsf{s}) \sim_a (t, \mathsf{t})$ follows $s \sim_a t$ and $\mathsf{s} \sim_a \mathsf{t}$. From $(M \otimes \mathsf{M}, (t, \mathsf{t})) \models \varphi$ follows $(M, t) \models \langle \mathsf{M}, \mathsf{t} \rangle \varphi$. From $s \sim_a t$ and $(M, t) \models \langle \mathsf{M}, \mathsf{t} \rangle \varphi$ follows $(M, s) \models \hat{K}_a \langle \mathsf{M}, \mathsf{t} \rangle \varphi$. As t was just some action point with $\mathsf{s} \sim_a \mathsf{t}$, we now have $(M, s) \models \bigvee_{\mathsf{s} \sim_a \mathsf{t}} \hat{K}_a \langle \mathsf{M}, \mathsf{t} \rangle \varphi$. □

A rather involved rule prescribes how common knowledge can be derived after executing a $\mathcal{L}_{KC\otimes}$ action. We show its soundness. The rule plays a major part in the completeness proof. Chapter 7 will provide more insight on the intuitions behind this rule. The reader may already wish to peek at Figure 7.1 on page 198 that illustrates the conditions for a formula of the form $[\mathsf{M}, \mathsf{s}] C_B \varphi$ to be true.

Proposition 6.37 (Action and common knowledge) Given action model (M, s), and formulas χ_{t} for all $\mathsf{t} \sim_B \mathsf{s}$. If for all $a \in B$ and $\mathsf{u} \sim_a \mathsf{t}$: $\models \chi_{\mathsf{t}} \rightarrow [\mathsf{M}, \mathsf{t}] \varphi$ and $\models (\chi_{\mathsf{t}} \wedge \mathsf{pre}(\mathsf{t})) \rightarrow K_a \chi_{\mathsf{u}}$, then $\models \chi_{\mathsf{s}} \rightarrow [\mathsf{M}, \mathsf{s}] C_B \varphi$. □

Proof Given (M, s) with $\mathsf{M} = \langle \mathsf{S}, \sim, \mathsf{pre} \rangle$, and formulas χ_{t} for all $\mathsf{t} \in \mathsf{S}$ such that $\mathsf{t} \sim_B \mathsf{s}$. For arbitrary $a \in B$ and $\mathsf{t}, \mathsf{u} \in \mathsf{S}$ such that $\mathsf{s} \sim_B \mathsf{t}$ and $\mathsf{t} \sim_a \mathsf{u}$, we may assume that $\models \chi_{\mathsf{t}} \rightarrow [\mathsf{M}, \mathsf{t}] \varphi$ and that $\models (\chi_{\mathsf{t}} \wedge \mathsf{pre}(\mathsf{t})) \rightarrow K_a \chi_{\mathsf{u}}$. (Note that also $\mathsf{s} \sim_B \mathsf{u}$, as $a \in B$.)

We now have to show that $\models \chi_{\mathsf{s}} \rightarrow [\mathsf{M}, \mathsf{s}] C_B \varphi$. Assume an arbitrary epistemic state (M, s) such that $M, s \models \chi_{\mathsf{s}}$. First, note that χ_{s} *exists*, as $\mathsf{s} \sim_B \mathsf{s}$. Further, assume that $M, s \models \mathsf{pre}(\mathsf{s})$. We then have to prove that $(M \otimes \mathsf{M}, (s, \mathsf{s})) \models C_B \varphi$. Assume an arbitrary state (u, u) in $M \otimes \mathsf{M}$. We now show that $(M \otimes \mathsf{M}, (u, \mathsf{u})) \models \varphi$ by induction on the length of the path in $M \otimes \mathsf{M}$ leading from (s, s) to (u, u). We do this by proving the *stronger* statement that for an arbitrary path to (u, u): $(M \otimes \mathsf{M}, (u, \mathsf{u})) \models \varphi$ and $M, u \models \chi_{\mathsf{u}}$. The case $n = 0$ immediately follows from the validity of $\models \chi_{\mathsf{t}} \rightarrow [\mathsf{M}, \mathsf{t}] \varphi$ for the case $\mathsf{t} = \mathsf{s}$, applied to epistemic state M, s; and from the assumptions $M, s \models \chi_{\mathsf{s}}$ and $M, s \models \mathsf{pre}(\mathsf{s})$. Next, suppose the length of the path is $n+1$. Then we have a state (t, t) such that $(s, \mathsf{s}) \sim_B (t, \mathsf{t}) \sim_a (u, \mathsf{u})$. From the proof assumptions follows that there are χ_t, χ_t as stipulated. The length of the $\sim_B$ path from (s, s) to (t, t) is n, so from the induction hypothesis we may conclude that $M \otimes \mathsf{M}, (t, \mathsf{t}) \models \varphi$ and $M, t \models \chi_{\mathsf{t}}$. Note that $M \otimes \mathsf{M}, (t, \mathsf{t}) \models \varphi$ also implies $M, t \models \mathsf{pre}(\mathsf{t})$. From $M, t \models \chi_{\mathsf{t}}$, $M, t \models \mathsf{pre}(\mathsf{t})$, $\mathsf{t} \sim_a \mathsf{u}$, and from the assumed validity $\models (\chi_{\mathsf{t}} \wedge \mathsf{pre}(\mathsf{t})) \rightarrow K_a \chi_{\mathsf{u}}$, follows that $M, t \models K_a \chi_{\mathsf{u}}$. From $M, t \models K_a \chi_{\mathsf{u}}$

all instantiations of propositional tautologies	
$K_a(\varphi \rightarrow \psi) \rightarrow (K_a\varphi \rightarrow K_a\psi)$	distribution of K_a over $\rightarrow$
$K_a\varphi \rightarrow \varphi$	truth
$K_a\varphi \rightarrow K_aK_a\varphi$	positive introspection
$\neg K_a\varphi \rightarrow K_a\neg K_a\varphi$	negative introspection
$[\mathsf{M}, \mathsf{s}]p \leftrightarrow (\mathsf{pre}(\mathsf{s}) \rightarrow p)$	atomic permanence
$[\mathsf{M}, \mathsf{s}]\neg\varphi \leftrightarrow (\mathsf{pre}(\mathsf{s}) \rightarrow \neg[\mathsf{M}, \mathsf{s}]\varphi)$	action and negation
$[\mathsf{M}, \mathsf{s}](\varphi \wedge \psi) \leftrightarrow ([\mathsf{M}, \mathsf{s}]\varphi \wedge [\mathsf{M}, \mathsf{s}]\psi)$	action and conjunction
$[\mathsf{M}, \mathsf{s}]K_a\varphi \leftrightarrow (\mathsf{pre}(\mathsf{s}) \rightarrow \bigwedge_{\mathsf{s}\sim_a\mathsf{t}} K_a[\mathsf{M}, \mathsf{t}]\varphi)$	action and knowledge
$[\mathsf{M}, \mathsf{s}][\mathsf{M}', \mathsf{s}']\varphi \leftrightarrow [(\mathsf{M}, \mathsf{s}); (\mathsf{M}', \mathsf{s}')]\varphi$	action composition
$[\alpha \cup \beta]\varphi \leftrightarrow [\alpha]\varphi \wedge [\beta]\varphi$	non-deterministic choice
$C_B(\varphi \rightarrow \psi) \rightarrow (C_B\varphi \rightarrow C_B\psi)$	distribution of C_B over $\rightarrow$
$C_B\varphi \rightarrow (\varphi \wedge E_BC_B\varphi)$	mix
$C_B(\varphi \rightarrow E_B\varphi) \rightarrow (\varphi \rightarrow C_B\varphi)$	induction axiom
From φ and $\varphi \rightarrow \psi$, infer ψ	modus ponens
From φ, infer $K_a\varphi$	necessitation of K_a
From φ, infer $C_B\varphi$	necessitation of C_B
From φ, infer $[\mathsf{M}, \mathsf{s}]\varphi$	necessitation of (M, s)
Given (M, s), and χ_t for all $\mathsf{t} \sim_B \mathsf{s}$. If for all $a \in B$ and $\mathsf{u} \sim_a \mathsf{t}$: $\chi_\mathsf{t} \rightarrow [\mathsf{M}, \mathsf{t}]\varphi$ and $(\chi_\mathsf{t} \wedge \mathsf{pre}(\mathsf{t})) \rightarrow K_a\chi_\mathsf{u}$, then $\chi_\mathsf{s} \rightarrow [\mathsf{M}, \mathsf{s}]C_B\varphi$.	action and comm. knowl.

Table 6.1. The proof system **AMC**.

and $t \sim_a u$ follows $M, u \models \chi_\mathsf{u}$. Now we use the *other* validity $\models \chi_\mathsf{t} \rightarrow [\mathsf{M}, \mathsf{t}]\varphi$ again, for instantiation $\mathsf{t} = \mathsf{u}$, and also using that $(u, \mathsf{u}) \in (M \otimes \mathsf{M})$ so that $M, u \models \mathsf{pre}(\mathsf{u})$, and we derive $(M \otimes \mathsf{M}, (u, \mathsf{u})) \models \varphi$. □

Table 6.1 contains the entire proof system **AMC** for action model logic. All 'new' axioms have now been introduced as valid principles. Note that the principle for action composition was already established in Proposition 6.9. The completeness of **AMC** will be shown in Chapter 7. We end this section with an example derivation in **AMC**.

Example 6.38 After Anne reads the letter containing p, she knows p. This can also be derived in the proof system **AMC**: $\vdash [\mathsf{Read}, \mathsf{p}]K_ap$.

1	$p \rightarrow p$	tautology
2	$[\mathsf{Read}, \mathsf{p}]p \leftrightarrow (p \rightarrow p)$	$\mathsf{pre}(\mathsf{p}) = p$, atomic permanence
3	$[\mathsf{Read}, \mathsf{p}]p$	1, 2, propositional
4	$K_a[\mathsf{Read}, \mathsf{p}]p$	3, necessitation of K_a
5	$p \rightarrow K_a[\mathsf{Read}, \mathsf{p}]p$	4, weakening
6	$[\mathsf{Read}, \mathsf{p}]K_ap \leftrightarrow (p \rightarrow \bigwedge_{\mathsf{p}\sim_a\mathsf{s}} K_a[\mathsf{Read}, \mathsf{s}]p)$	$[\mathsf{p}]_{\sim_a} = \{\mathsf{p}\}$, action and knowledge
7	$[\mathsf{Read}, \mathsf{p}]K_ap$	5, 6, propositional

Exercise 6.39 Give derivations of

- $\vdash_{\mathbf{AMC}} [\mathsf{Read}, \mathsf{p}]K_b(K_a p \vee K_a \neg p)$
- $\vdash_{\mathbf{AMC}} [\mathsf{Read}](K_a p \vee K_a \neg p)$
- $\vdash_{\mathbf{AMC}} [\mathsf{Read}]C_{ab}(K_a p \vee K_a \neg p)$ □

6.7 Epistemic Model Checking

Although a complete axiomatisation for the logic may help us to determine whether some formula is a theorem of the logic and thus a validity, this is in itself not much help in finding a derivation that does the job. And then we are not even talking about automated theorem proving. This area seems still under development for multi-agent epistemic logic. Although there are automated theorem provers for multi-agent epistemic logic without common knowledge, there are none, as far as we know, for common knowledge logics or even more complex dynamic epistemic logics. The presence of infinitary modal operators such as common knowledge causes proof search problems. These operators do not allow for straight reduction rules that remove the operator under consideration. Instead, we have axioms such as, e.g., 'use of common knowledge' $C_B\varphi \leftrightarrow \varphi \wedge E_B C_B \varphi$, where the C-operator occurs on both the right-hand and the left-hand side. There is progress in semi-analytic calculi that perform proof search subject to restrictions on formulas that occur in the search (see the Notes section). Typically the restriction is relative to a finite set of formulas, a 'closure set' or Fischer-Ladner closure as used in Chapter 7, that is constructed from the to be derived formula. But efficient proof tools seem not yet available.

An alternative to checking by means of automated theorem proving whether some formula is a consequence of a theory (or other set of formulas), is to check whether the formula is true in a model (or models) that incorporates sufficient features of that theory (or those formulas). In this area of epistemic model checking progress *has* been made for logics with infinitary operators. In a given finite epistemic model the accessibility relation interpreting, for example, a common knowledge operator is just another (finite) set of pairs, computable from the accessibility relations of the individual agents in the group that commonly knows. This satisfactorily addresses an aspect that is problematic in theorem proving.

To model the *dynamics* in such an epistemic model checker, the same ways are open that were already outlined in the introductory Chapter 1. Currently available epistemic model checkers tend to model dynamic features in a *temporal* epistemic setting, where unlike in dynamic epistemic logic, wherein time is implicit, the results of actions are modelled by explicit representation of time. Recently, a truly *dynamic* epistemic model checker has become available. It allows specifications in the action model logic introduced in this chapter. We shortly introduce this model checker DEMO and show some elementary interaction with DEMO by way of the familiar examples in the chapter. (For references see the Notes section.)

DEMO stands for Dynamic Epistemic MOdelling. It allows for the specification and graphical display of epistemic models *and* action models, and for formula evaluation in epistemic states, including epistemic states specified as (possibly iterated) restricted modal products. So we can verify postconditions of the effect of subsequent action executions in given epistemic models. DEMO is written in de programming language Haskell. Its code implements a reduction of action model logic *AMC* to *PDL*. We give no details, but refer to the notes. The DEMO specification of the familiar epistemic state $(Letter, 1)$ for Anne and Bill not being able to determine the truth of a fact p is as follows:

```
letter :: EpistM
letter = (Pmod [0 1] val acc [1])
  where
  val = [(0,[]),(1,[P 0])]
  acc = [(a,0,0),(a,0,1),(a,1,0),(a,1,1),(b,0,0),(b,0,1),
         (b,1,0),(b,1,1)]
```

Expression `letter :: EpistM` tells us that the semantic object being defined is an epistemic model (and not an action model). The list `(Pmod [0 1] val acc [1])` specifies that this a a pointed structure `Pmod`, consisting of two elements `[0 1]` (domain objects are standardly numbered starting from 0), with a valuation `val` and with accessibility relation `acc` as outlined in the next part of the definition. The fifth argument `1` specifies that state 1 is the point of the structure. The valuation `val` is summed up as, per state, a list of facts true in that state (so not, as we do, for each atomic proposition a list of states where it is true). Note that `(0,[])` specifies that p is *false* (i.e., absent) in state 0. Defining equivalence relations as sets of pairs is rather cumbersome, but in DEMO there is no way around it; `(a,0,0)` stands for $(0,0) \in R_a$, or $R_a(0,0)$, etc. Fortunately, apart from the graphical display (that we do not illustrate) DEMO also contains a more succinct way to represent $S5$ models:

```
DEMO > showM letter
==> [1]
[0,1]
(1,p)
(a,[[0,1]])
(b,[[0,1]])
```

In the last, the *name* `p` stands for the *proposition* `Prop(P 0)`. Also, it is customary in DEMO that the index 0 with a proposition is suppressed. Therefore, it says `p` and not `p0`. Equivalence relations are now displayed as partitions on the domain. Please overlook all this syntactic sugar and allow us to continue with the specification of the action model (Read, p) with Read $= \langle\{\mathsf{p},\mathsf{np}\},\sim,\mathsf{pre}\rangle$ with pre(p) $= p$ and pre(np) $= \neg p$, and $\sim_a$ the identity and $\sim_b$ the universal relation, wherein Anne reads the contents of the letter and it contains p.

```
read :: PoAM
read = (Pmod [0,1] pre acc [1])
  where
  pre = [(0,Neg p),(1,p)]
  acc = [(a,0,0),(a,1,1),(b,0,0),(b,0,1),(b,1,0),(b,1,1)]
```

The expression `PoAM` stands for 'pointed action model'. The action point p is now named 1 and the action point np is now named 0. This action model more conveniently shows as:

```
DEMO > showM read
==> [1]
[0,1]
(0,-p)(1,p)
(a,[[0],[1]])
(b,[[0,1]])
```

We can now refer to the restricted modal product (*Letter* $\otimes$ Read) as follows in a very direct way.

```
DEMO > showM (upd letter read)
==> [1]
[0,1]
(1,p)
(a,[[0],[1]])
(b,[[0,1]])
```

This is the epistemic state where Bill knows that Anne knows the truth about p. States are not represented by $(state, action)$ pairs, as in Section 6.4, but they are, after each update, renumbered starting from 0. The construct `(upd letter read)` stands for the epistemic state that results from executing action model `read` in epistemic state `letter`; `upd` stands for 'update'. We can also check postconditions in the resulting state. For example

```
DEMO > isTrue (upd letter read) (K a p)
True
DEMO > isTrue (upd letter read)
           (CK [a,b] Disj[K a p, K a (Neg p)])
True
```

Expression `K a p` stands for $K_a p$, i.e., 'Anne knows that p'; and `CK [a,b] Disj[K a p, K a (Neg p)]` for $C_{ab}(K_a p \vee K_a \neg p)$, 'Anne and Bill commonly know that Anne knows whether p.'

As a final example we show the code for the epistemic state $(Hexa, 012)$ for three players each holding a card, such that Anne holds 0, Bill holds 1, and Cath holds 2. Cards 0, 1, and 2 are now represented by P, Q, and R respectively, and an atomic fact like 'Anne holds card 0' by `P 1`, all for reasons of syntax restrictions.

We also represent the action model for Anne showing her card 0 to Bill, without Cath seeing which card that is, and an obvious postcondition of that show action. In both cases we only show the 'displayed', not the defined, version. See also Exercise 6.18 and Section 5.4 of the previous chapter.

```
DEMO > showM hexa
==> 0
[0,1,2,3,4,5]
(0,[p1,q2,r3])(1,[p1,r2,q3])(2,[q1,p2,r3])(3,[q1,r2,p3])
   (4,[r1,p2,q3])(5,[r1,q2,p3])
(a,[[0,1],[2,3],[4,5]])
(b,[[0,5],[1,3],[2,4]])
(c,[[0,2],[1,4],[3,5]])
```

The action model `show` represents Anne showing her card 0 (p) to Bill. Note that `p1` (Anne holds card 0) is the precondition for the point 0 of this action model consisting of three states 0, 1, and 2.

```
DEMO > showM show
==> 0
[0,1,2]
(0,p1)(1,q1)(2,r1)
(a,[[0],[1],[2]])
(b,[[0],[1],[2]])
(c,[[0,1,2]])
```

Some obvious postconditions are that Bill now knows that Anne holds card 0: $K_b 0_a$ (where `p1` stands for 0_a), and that Anne, Bill and Cath commonly know that Anne and Bill commonly know Anne's card: $C_{abc}(C_{ab}0_a \vee C_{ab}1_a \vee C_{ab}2_a)$.

```
DEMO > isTrue (upd hexa show) (K b p1)
True
DEMO > isTrue (upd hexa show) (CK [a,b,c]
            Disj[CK [a,b] p1, CK [a,b] q1, CK [a,b] r1])
True
```

DEMO has various 'shorthands' and alternative ways to express common action models. The `show` action can alternatively be modelled using a `reveal` template, that expresses that one of a finite number of alternatives is revealed to a subgroup without the remaining agents knowing which alternative. Another common shorthand is the `pub` template for public announcement.

6.8 Relational Actions and Action Models

In this section we compare the epistemic action logic EA, of the previous chapter, with the action model logic AMC. Let us consider once more the action wherein Anne *may* learn that United Agents is doing well by opening and reading the letter, but where she actually doesn't read it, so remains ignorant. In Chapter 5 we described this action in the language $\mathcal{L}_!^{\mathrm{act}}$ as

$$\mathsf{mayread} = L_{ab}(L_a?p \cup L_a?\neg p \cup\ !?\top)$$

In other words: Anne and Bill learn that Anne learns that p, or that Anne learns that $\neg p$, or that 'nothing happens', and actually nothing happens. In this action language the interpretation of an epistemic action is a binary relation between epistemic states that is computed from similar relations but that interpret its subactions; therefore we call it a *relational* action language, as opposed to the action model language for epistemic actions in this chapter. The type of the action $\mathsf{mayread}$ is

$$L_{ab}(L_a?p \cup L_a?\neg p \cup\ ?\top)$$

(without the exclamation mark indicating local choice, known only to Anne) and there are three actions of that type, namely,

$$\begin{array}{l} L_{ab}(!L_a?p \cup L_a?\neg p \cup\ ?\top) \\ L_{ab}(L_a?p \cup\ !L_a?\neg p \cup\ ?\top) \\ L_{ab}(L_a?p \cup L_a?\neg p \cup\ !?\top) \end{array}$$

The preconditions of these actions are, respectively, p, $\neg p$, and $\top$. Bill cannot tell which of those actions actually takes place: they are all the same to him. Whereas Anne can distinguish all three actions. If she learns p, she can distinguish that from the action wherein she learns $\neg p$, and obviously as well from the action wherein she does not read the letter. In Section 5.3.5 it was suggested that this induces a syntactic accessibility among epistemic actions, e.g., that

$$L_{ab}(!L_a?p \cup L_a?\neg p \cup\ ?\top) \sim_b L_{ab}(L_a?p \cup\ !L_a?\neg p \cup\ ?\top)$$

We visualise this access among the three $\mathcal{L}_!$ actions in Figure 6.8. As usual, reflexivity is assumed, so this also expresses that Anne can distinguish all three actions. And, also as usual, the actual action $L_{ab}(L_a?p \cup L_a?\neg p \cup\ !?\top)$ is underlined.

If we consider in Figure 6.8 the labels of the points as arbitrary names, we might as well replace them by any other names, as long as the preconditions of the points remain the same. For example, we may replace them by labels p, np, and t with preconditions p, $\neg p$, and $\top$, respectively. We thus get Figure 6.9. This is the action model $(\mathsf{Mayread}, \mathsf{t})$, already introduced in Example 6.13!

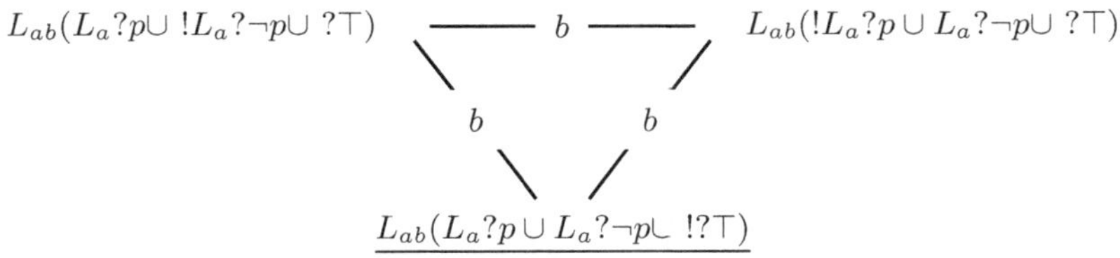

Figure 6.8. Relation between three $\mathcal{L}_!$ actions.

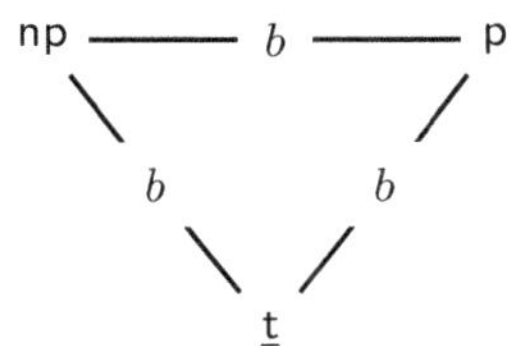

Figure 6.9. The action model (Mayread, t) resembles the structure in Figure 6.8.

In all fairness, the labels of the points in Figure 6.8 are of course *not* just names but epistemic actions. But it is interesting to observe that we might have done a similar trick with the three *epistemic actions* (Mayread, p), (Mayread, np), and (Mayread, t) by the much simpler expedient of lifting the notion of accessibility between points in a structure to accessibility between pointed structures. For example, (Mayread, p) $\sim_b$ (Mayread, np), because p $\sim_b$ np in Mayread. The result is captured in Figure 6.10. This is relevant to observe, because we may now turn the table around and quote Figure 6.10 as the proper correspondent of Figure 6.8, thus justifying the 'normal' action model represented in Figure 6.9.

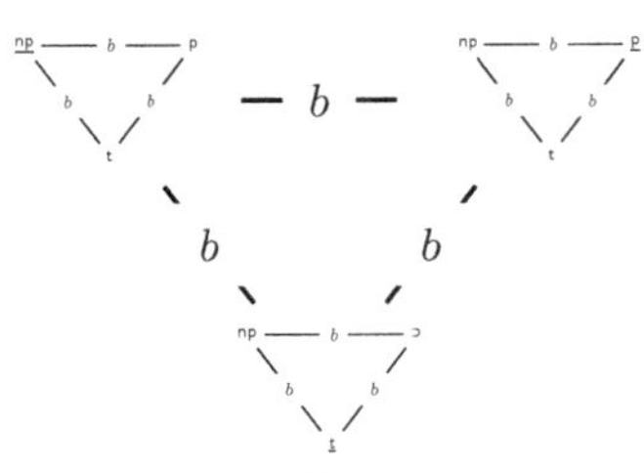

Figure 6.10. A structure with action models as points, obtained by 'lifting' accessibility relations in (Mayread, p).

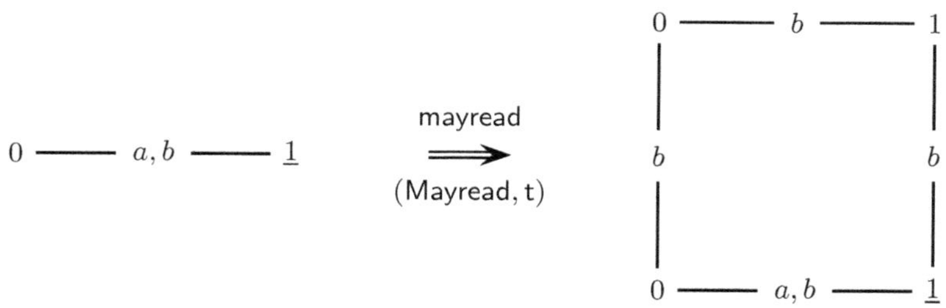

Figure 6.11. The result of the action 'Anne may read the letter' (and she actually does not read it).

In either case, the state transition induced by the execution of the action in epistemic state $(Letter, 1)$ is the one depicted in Figure 6.11. In the figure, we have suggestively named the states in the resulting model after the facts that are true in those states. In fact, the actual state after execution of $\mathsf{mayread}$ is named $(Letter, 1)[\![?\top]\!]$ (and where p is true) whereas the actual state after execution of $(\mathsf{Mayread}, \mathsf{t})$ is named $(1, \mathsf{t})$ (and where p is true).

This is just an example translating a $\mathcal{L}_!$ action into a $\mathcal{L}_{KC\otimes}$ action model. The method does not apply to arbitrary $\mathcal{L}_!$ actions, because we do not know a notion of syntactic access among $\mathcal{L}_!$ actions that exactly corresponds to the notion of semantic access—and the last is required.

Vice versa, given an action model, we can construct a $\mathcal{L}_{!\cap}$ action—this is the language of epistemic actions *with concurrency* only addressed in the Notes section of Chapter 5. For an example, see the Notes section of this chapter. This method applies to *arbitrary* $(S5)$ $\mathcal{L}_{KC\otimes}$ action models. Without concurrency we do not know of such a general method, but some obvious correspondences exist for special cases. We close this subsection with an example of such a correspondence.

Example 6.40 Consider the case where a subgroup B of all agents A is told which of n alternatives described by propositions $\varphi_1, \ldots, \varphi_n$ is actually the case, but such that the remaining agents do not know which from these alternatives that is. Let φ_i be the actually told proposition. In $\mathcal{L}_{KC\otimes}$ this is described as a pointed action model visualised as (with the preconditions below the unnamed action points)

In other words: the agents in B have identity access on the model, but the agents in $A \backslash B$ have universal access on the model, and the designated action point is the one with precondition φ_i.

In $\mathcal{L}_!$ the type of the obvious corresponding action is

$$L_A(L_B?\varphi_1 \cup \ldots \cup L_B?\varphi_n)$$

and the action itself is the one with alternative $L_B?\varphi_i$ selected, abbreviated as

$$L_A(L_B?\varphi_1 \cup \ldots !L_B?\varphi_i \ldots \cup L_B?\varphi_n)$$ □

Exercise 6.41 Consider again Exercise 6.20. Also using the $\mathcal{L}_!^{act}$ 'template' as in Example 6.40, give action descriptions in $\mathcal{L}_!^{act}$ of:

- You will be told a natural number not larger than 5.
- Your numbers are one apart.
- To Anne: Your number is 4.
- To Bill: Your number is 3. □

6.9 Private Announcements

In this section we pay attention to modelling private (truthful) announcements, that transform an epistemic state into a *belief* state, where agents not involved in private announcements lose their access to the actual world. Or in different words: agents that are unaware of the private announcement therefore have false beliefs about the actual state of the world, namely, they believe that what they knew *before* the action, is still true. The proper general notion of action model is as follows—and is of course similar to the general notion of Kripke model, except with preconditions instead of valuations.

Definition 6.42 (Action model for belief) Let $\mathcal{L}$ be a logical language for given parameters agents A and atoms P. An action model M is a structure $\langle \mathsf{S}, \mathsf{R}, \mathsf{pre} \rangle$ such that S is a domain of *action points*, such that for each $a \in A$, R_a is an accessibility relation on S, and such that $\mathsf{pre} : \mathsf{S} \rightarrow \mathcal{L}$ is a preconditions function that assigns a *precondition* $\mathsf{pre}(\mathsf{s}) \in \mathcal{L}$ to each $\mathsf{s} \in \mathsf{S}$. A *pointed action model* is a structure (M, s) with $\mathsf{s} \in \mathsf{S}$. □

One also has to adjust various other definitions, namely those of action model language, action model execution, and action model composition. We hope that the adjustments will be obvious to the reader.

The 'typical' action that needs such a more general action model is the 'private announcement to a subgroup' mentioned above. Let subgroup B of the public A learn that φ is true, without the remaining agents realising (or even suspecting) that. The action model for that is pictured in Figure 6.12.

Example 6.43 Consider the epistemic state $(\mathit{Letter}, 1)$ where Anne and Bill are uncertain about the truth of p. The epistemic action that Anne learns p without Bill noticing that, consists of two action points p and t, with

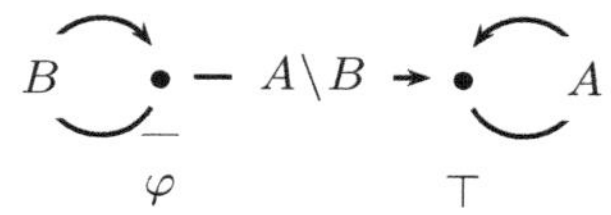

Figure 6.12. Subgroup B learn that φ without the remaining agents noticing that. Preconditions are below unnamed action points.

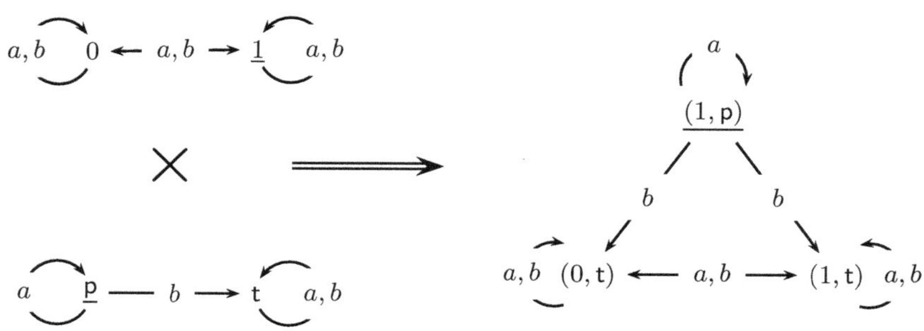

Figure 6.13. Anne learns p without Bill noticing that.

preconditions p and $\top$, and p actually happens. The model and its execution are pictured in Figure 6.13. Obviously, we now have drawn all access explicitly, also in the model *Letter*. We leave the details of the computation to the reader.

Exercise 6.44 Consider the epistemic state $(Hexa, 012)$ where Anne, Bill, and Cath hold cards 0, 1, and 2, respectively. Model and execute the action where Anne shows her card to Bill *without Cath noticing that.* Model and execute the action where Anne shows her card to Bill, with Anne and Bill (commonly) thinking that Cath does not notice that, but where actually Cath *does* notice it (but still, unfortunately, cannot see which card is being shown). Compare this to Exercise 6.18. □

6.10 Notes

Action models The action model framework has been developed by Baltag, Solecki, and Moss, and has appeared in various forms [11, 12, 9, 10]. The final form of their semantics is probably Baltag and Moss's [10]. Van Ditmarsch explored similar ideas, partly influenced by Baltag's ideas, in [42, 43, 44]—in his 'approach', action model points consist of (any) subsets of the domain of the epistemic model in which they are executed (so that bisimilarity of epistemic models is not preserved under action execution).

There are several differences between our presentation of the original ideas by Baltag *et al.* and the seminal presentation of their ideas in [10]. We summarily point out some differences.

Action models in [10] may have more than one point (designated object). (In fact, pointed (multi- or not) action models are called *program models* in [10, pp.27–28].) A multi-pointed action model with n points can be considered a non-deterministic action choosing between n single-pointed alternatives. In [10] non-determinism is modelled as the direct sum of action models[10, p.201], not as the union of induced relations between epistemic states.

The difference between formulas and (semantic) propositions in the introduction is 'taken all the way' in [10]. In that respect, their action models are purely semantic objects with 'semantic' propositions (which they call *epistemic propositions*, see [10, p.176]) as preconditions, not formulas in the logical language. The relation between action models and their descriptions in the logical language is by the intermediation of *action signatures*. (The counterparts of pointed action models in the logical language are called basic actions [10, p.208].) These are placeholders for either precondition propositions or precondition formulas. Unlike frames, they carry a list of *ordered* designated points as well. The proof system they give for action model logic is always relative to such a signature.

In [10], the crash action has an action model with an empty domain. Instead, we have modelled crash as a singleton action model with precondition $\bot$. This appeared to be preferable given that Kripke structures 'typically' are required to have non-empty domains [29].

Emulation The notion of action bisimulation was proposed by Baltag and Moss in [10]. The notion of action emulation was proposed by van Eijck and Ruan in [59]. This promising notion seems still under development and has not appeared in final form.

Theorem proving and model checking Automated theorem provers for epistemic logics include the Logics Workbench, developed in Bern [97]. Proof calculi investigating common knowledge logics include [111, 134, 2]—the mentioned semi-analytic cut relative to the Fischer-Ladner closure is used in [2].

Current epistemic model checkers include MCK, by Gammie and van der Meyden [69], DEMO, by van Eijck [58], and MCMAS, by Raimondi and Lomuscio [170]. MCK and MCMAS require temporal epistemic specifications (and the interpreted systems architecture). The model checker DEMO has been applied in [52].

Action model descriptions in concurrent epistemic action logic We give an application of the general construction found in an unpublished manuscript by van Ditmarsch. Consider an action point in the model $(\mathsf{Mayread}, \mathsf{t})$. For example, the action point p with precondition p. We can associate different $\mathcal{L}_!$ action constructs with that, from different points of view. From an 'objective' point of view, a test $?p$ has to succeed there. The agents, instead, are individually learning in which equivalence class (for actions) they live. From the point of view of Anne, who can distinguish that action from both others, she is learning that p, which is described by $L_a?p$. (In this case, Anne's perspective is the same as the objective precondition, but this is a mere consequence from her not having an alternative action to consider.) From the point of view of Bill, who cannot distinguish that action from both others, he is learning that $p \vee \neg p \vee \top$, which is described by $L_b?(p \vee \neg p \vee \top)$ which is equivalent with $L_b?\top$. As we need all these perspectives at the same time, this can be described by the $\mathcal{L}_{!\cap}$ action $?p \cap L_a?p \cap L_b?\top$. Given that we do this for all three atomic actions, we get

$$\begin{array}{l} ?p \cap L_a?p \cap L_b?\top \\ ?\neg p \cap L_a?\neg p \cap L_b?\top \\ ?\top \cap L_a?\top \cap L_b?\top \end{array}$$

As these options are learnt by the agents together, the resulting $\mathcal{L}_{!\cap}$ description is therefore

$$L_{ab}((?p \cap L_a?p \cap L_b?\top) \cup (?\neg p \cap L_a?\neg p \cap L_b?\top) \cup\, !(?\top \cap L_a?\top \cap L_b?\top))$$

This description indeed induces the same relation as $L_{ab}(L_a?p \cup L_a?\neg p \cup\, !?\top)$.

7

Completeness

7.1 Introduction

One can think of a logic simply as a set of formulas. The formulas in the set are the "good ones" and the formulas outside the set are the "bad ones". There are various ways of specifying such a set of formulas. Two standard ways of doing this is by *semantics* on the one hand, and by a *proof system* on the other hand. Given that one tries to capture the same set with the semantics and the proof system, one would like these to characterise the same set of formulas. If all deducible formulas are valid according to the semantics, then the proof system is called *sound* with respect to the semantics ($\vdash \varphi$ implies $\models \varphi$). A proof system is *complete* with respect to certain semantics iff every formula that is valid according to the semantics is deducible in the proof system ($\models \varphi$ implies $\vdash \varphi$). Often it is easy to show that a proof system is sound, and we have shown the soundness of the proof systems in this book when they were introduced. Completeness is usually much harder to prove. This chapter is dedicated to showing completeness of some of the proof systems that we have seen thus far.

Completeness is often proved by contraposition. Rather than show that every valid formula is deducible, one shows that if a formula is not deducible, then there is a state in which the formula is not true. Usually this is done by constructing one large model where every consistent formula is true somewhere (the *canonical model*). This approach can also be taken for the basic system of epistemic logic *S5*. Completeness for *S5* is shown in Section 7.2. Constructing one model for all consistent formulas does not work when common knowledge is added to the language. In that case a model is constructed for only a finite fragment of the language. Completeness for *S5C* is shown in Section 7.3. Sometimes it is not necessary to construct a canonical model for a logic. Public announcement logic without common knowledge is just as expressive as *S5*, i.e., for any formula in $\mathcal{L}_{K[]}$ we can find a formula in $\mathcal{L}_K$ that is equivalent to it (and trivially the converse also holds). These formulas can be found in a systematic way via a translation that uses the axioms for the interaction of public announcements with other logical operators. By the axioms we find that every formula is provably equivalent to its translation. In this way completeness for public announcement logic without common knowledge follows from completeness for *S5*. This is shown in Section 7.4. We combine ideas from the completeness proof for *S5C* and the completeness proof for *PA* in the completeness proof for *PAC*. So we construct a model for only a finite fragment of the language, while we fully exploit the axioms that describe the interaction between announcements and other logical operators. Completeness for public announcement logic with common knowledge is shown in Section 7.5. This sort of exercise is repeated in a generalised form for the logic of action models without and with common knowledge is Sections 7.6 and 7.7. In Section 7.8 we introduce relativised common knowledge, which allows an easy completeness proof for a logic with both common knowledge and public announcement operators. Notes and references are provided in Section 7.9.

7.2 *S5*: The Basic Case

In this section we prove completeness for the basic system for epistemic logic: *S5*. The proof system **S5** is shown in Table 7.1. We construct a model where every consistent formula is true in some state. In a model a state determines the truth value of every formula in the language. The analogue of a state in proof theoretic terms is a maximal consistent set of formulas.

Definition 7.1 (Maximal consistent) Let $\Gamma \subseteq \mathcal{L}_K$. Γ is maximal consistent iff

1. Γ is consistent: $\Gamma \nvdash \bot$
2. Γ is maximal: there is no $\Gamma' \subseteq \mathcal{L}_K$ such that $\Gamma \subset \Gamma'$ and $\Gamma' \nvdash \bot$. □

These maximal consistent sets are used as the set of states in the canonical model. What we will show below is that proof theory and semantics coincide, i.e., a formula is an element of a maximal consistent set iff that formula is true in the state of the model, when that maximal consistent set is taken

all instantiations of propositional tautologies	
$K_a(\varphi \to \psi) \to (K_a\varphi \to K_a\psi)$	distribution of K_a over $\to$
$K_a\varphi \to \varphi$	truth
$K_a\varphi \to K_aK_a\varphi$	positive introspection
$\neg K_a\varphi \to K_a\neg K_a\varphi$	negative introspection
From φ and $\varphi \to \psi$, infer ψ	modus ponens
From φ, infer $K_a\varphi$	necessitation of K_a

Table 7.1. The proof system **S5**.

as the state. This is known as the Truth Lemma. In order to arrange this we must choose both the valuation of propositional variables and the accessibility relations for the agents in accordance with these maximal consistent sets.

Definition 7.2 (Canonical model) The canonical model $M^c = \langle S^c, \sim^c, V^c\rangle$ is defined as follows

- $S^c = \{\Gamma \mid \Gamma \text{ is maximal consistent}\}$
- $\Gamma \sim_a^c \Delta$ iff $\{K_a\varphi \mid K_a\varphi \in \Gamma\} = \{K_a\varphi \mid K_a\varphi \in \Delta\}$
- $V_p^c = \{\Gamma \in S^c \mid p \in \Gamma\}$ □

In order to show that every consistent formula is true at some state in the canonical model, it must be the case that every consistent formula is an element of a maximal consistent set. The following Lemma shows that this is the case for any consistent set of formulas.

Lemma 7.3 (Lindenbaum) Every consistent set of formulas is a subset of a maximal consistent set of formulas. □

Proof Let Δ be a consistent set of formulas. Take some enumeration of $\mathcal{L}_K$ (note that this exists given that the set of atomic propositions is countable and the set of agents is finite). Let φ_n be the n-th formula in this enumeration. Now consider the following sequence of sets of formulas.

$$\begin{aligned} \Gamma_0 &= \Delta \\ \Gamma_{n+1} &= \begin{cases} \Gamma_n \cup \{\varphi_{n+1}\} & \text{if } \Gamma_n \cup \{\varphi_{n+1}\} \text{ is consistent} \\ \Gamma_n & \text{otherwise} \end{cases} \end{aligned}$$

Let $\Gamma = \bigcup_{n\in\mathbb{N}} \Gamma_n$. It is clear that $\Delta \subseteq \Gamma$. We now show that Γ is both consistent and maximal. To see that Γ is consistent, first observe by induction on n that every Γ_n is consistent. By assumption Γ_0 is consistent. It is easy to see that if Γ_n is consistent, then Γ_{n+1} is consistent. Since derivations only use finitely many formulas, Γ is also consistent.

To see that Γ is maximal, take an arbitrary formula φ_n such that $\varphi_n \notin \Gamma$. Then $\varphi_n \notin \Gamma_n$ too. Therefore $\Gamma_n \cup \{\varphi_n\}$ is inconsistent and so is $\Gamma \cup \{\varphi_n\}$. Since φ_n was arbitrary there is no Γ' such that $\Gamma \subset \Gamma'$ and Γ' is consistent.□

When we prove the Truth Lemma we will use the following properties of maximal consistent sets.

Lemma 7.4 If Γ and Δ are maximal consistent sets, then

1. Γ is deductively closed,
2. $\varphi \in \Gamma$ iff $\neg\varphi \notin \Gamma$,
3. $(\varphi \wedge \psi) \in \Gamma$ iff $\varphi \in \Gamma$ and $\psi \in \Gamma$,
4. $\Gamma \sim_a^c \Delta$ iff $\{K_a\varphi \mid K_a\varphi \in \Gamma\} \subseteq \Delta$,
5. $\{K_a\varphi \mid K_a\varphi \in \Gamma\} \vdash \psi$ iff $\{K_a\varphi \mid K_a\varphi \in \Gamma\} \vdash K_a\psi$. □

Proof Suppose Γ and Δ are maximal consistent sets.

1. Suppose $\Gamma \vdash \varphi$. Then $\Gamma \cup \{\varphi\}$ is also consistent. Therefore, by maximality, $\varphi \in \Gamma$.
2. From left to right. Suppose $\varphi \in \Gamma$. By consistency $\neg\varphi \notin \Gamma$.
   From right to left. Suppose $\neg\varphi \notin \Gamma$. By maximality $\Gamma \cup \{\neg\varphi\} \vdash \bot$. But then $\Gamma \vdash \varphi$. Therefore $\varphi \in \Gamma$, because Γ is deductively closed (this lemma, item 1).
3. $(\varphi \wedge \psi) \in \Gamma$ is equivalent to $\varphi \in \Gamma$ and $\psi \in \Gamma$ because Γ is deductively closed (this lemma, item 1).
4. From left to right it follows immediately from the definition of $\sim^c$.
   From right to left suppose that $\{K_a\varphi \mid K_a\varphi \in \Gamma\} \subseteq \Delta$. Suppose that $K_a\varphi \in \Delta$. Therefore, by item 2 of this lemma, $\neg K_a\varphi \notin \Delta$, and so $K_a\neg K_a\varphi \notin \Delta$. Therefore, by our assumption and the definition of $\sim^c_a$, $K_a\neg K_a\varphi \notin \Gamma$, and so by negative introspection $\neg K_a\varphi \notin \Gamma$. Consequently, by item 2 of this lemma, $K_a\varphi \in \Gamma$.
5. From right to left follows straightforwardly from $\vdash K_a\psi \rightarrow \psi$.
   From left to right. Suppose that $\{K_a\varphi \mid K_a\varphi \in \Gamma\} \vdash \psi$. Therefore, there is a finite subset $\Gamma' \subseteq \{K_a\varphi \mid K_a\varphi \in \Gamma\}$ such that $\vdash \bigwedge\Gamma' \rightarrow \psi$. Therefore by necessitation and distribution $\vdash K_a \bigwedge\Gamma' \rightarrow K_a\psi$ (see Exercise 2.18, item 2). Therefore $\vdash \bigwedge\{K_a\chi \mid \chi \in \Gamma'\} \rightarrow K_a\psi$ (see Exercise 2.18, item 4). Since $\vdash K_a\varphi \rightarrow K_aK_a\varphi$, $\{K_a\varphi \mid \varphi \in \Gamma\} \vdash \bigwedge\{K_a\chi \mid \chi \in \Gamma'\}$. Therefore, $\{K_a\varphi \mid K_a\varphi \in \Gamma\} \vdash K_a\psi$. □

With all these properties we are ready to prove the Truth Lemma.

Lemma 7.5 (Truth) For every $\varphi \in \mathcal{L}_K$ and every maximal consistent set Γ:

$$\varphi \in \Gamma \text{ iff } (M^c, \Gamma) \models \varphi$$ □

Proof By induction on φ.

Base case Suppose φ is a propositional variable p. Then by the definition of V^c, $p \in \Gamma$ iff $\Gamma \in V^c_p$, which by the semantics is equivalent to $(M^c, \Gamma) \models p$.

Induction hypothesis For every maximal consistent set Γ and for given φ and ψ it is the case that $\varphi \in \Gamma$ iff $(M^c, \Gamma) \models \varphi$, and $\psi \in \Gamma$ iff $(M^c, \Gamma) \models \psi$

Induction step We distinguish the following cases:

the case for $\neg\varphi$**:** $\neg\varphi \in \Gamma$ is equivalent to $\varphi \notin \Gamma$ by item 2 of Lemma 7.4. By the induction hypothesis this is equivalent to $(M^c, \Gamma) \not\models \varphi$, which by the semantics is equivalent to $(M^c, \Gamma) \models \neg\varphi$.

the case for $\varphi \wedge \psi$**:** $(\varphi \wedge \psi) \in \Gamma$ is equivalent to $\varphi \in \Gamma$ and $\psi \in \Gamma$ by item 3 of Lemma 7.4. By the induction hypothesis this is equivalent to $(M^c, \Gamma) \models \varphi$ and $(M^c, \Gamma) \models \psi$, which by the semantics is equivalent to $(M^c, \Gamma) \models \varphi \wedge \psi$.

the case for $K_a\varphi$**:** From left to right. Suppose $K_a\varphi \in \Gamma$. Take an arbitrary maximal consistent set Δ. Suppose that $\Gamma \sim^c_a \Delta$. So $K_a\varphi \in \Delta$ by the definition of $\sim^c_a$. Since $\vdash K_a\varphi \rightarrow \varphi$, and Δ is deductively closed, it must be the case that $\varphi \in \Delta$. By the induction hypothesis this is equivalent to $(M^c, \Delta) \models \varphi$. Since Δ was arbitrary, $(M^c, \Delta) \models \varphi$ for all Δ such that $\Gamma \sim_a^c \Delta$. By the semantics this is equivalent to $(M^c, \Gamma) \models K_a\varphi$.

From right to left. Suppose $(M^c, \Gamma) \models K_a\varphi$. Therefore $(M^c, \Delta) \models \varphi$ for all Δ such that $\Gamma \sim_a^c \Delta$. Now we show that $\{K_a\chi \mid K_a\chi \in \Gamma\} \vdash \varphi$. Suppose towards a contradiction that the set

$$\Lambda = \{\neg\varphi\} \cup \{K_a\chi \mid K_a\chi \in \Gamma\}$$

is consistent. By the Lindenbaum Lemma, Λ is a subset of a maximal consistent set Θ. It is clear that $\{K_a\chi \mid K_a\chi \in \Gamma\} \subseteq \Theta$. Therefore, by item 4 of Lemma 7.4, $\Gamma \sim_a^c \Theta$. Since $\neg\varphi \in \Lambda$ and Θ is maximal consistent, $\varphi \notin \Theta$. By the induction hypothesis this is equivalent to $(M^c, \Theta) \not\models \varphi$. This contradicts our assumption. Therefore $\{K_a\chi \mid K_a\chi \in \Gamma\} \vdash \varphi$. By item 5 of Lemma 7.4 this implies that $\Gamma \vdash K_a\varphi$. Therefore $K_a\varphi \in \Gamma$. □

We must also show that the canonical model satisfies the restrictions that we posed for models of *S5*, namely, that the accessibility relations are equivalence relations. This was expressed by the truth axiom and the axioms for positive and negative introspection. Remember that these corresponded to frame properties. Now we are dealing with a model, but this model also satisfies the properties expressed by these axioms.

Lemma 7.6 (Canonicity) The canonical model is reflexive, transitive, and Euclidean. □

Proof This follows straightforwardly from the definition of $\sim_a^c$. □

Now the completeness proof is easy.

Theorem 7.7 (Completeness) For every $\varphi \in \mathcal{L}_K$

$$\models \varphi \text{ implies } \vdash \varphi$$ □

Proof By contraposition. Suppose $\not\vdash \varphi$. Then $\{\neg\varphi\}$ is a consistent set. By the Lindenbaum Lemma $\{\neg\varphi\}$ is a subset of a maximal consistent set Γ. By the Truth Lemma $(M^c, \Gamma) \models \neg\varphi$. Therefore $\not\models \varphi$. □

Due to our compact notation it seems that Lemma 7.6 is superfluous. However it is crucial that the canonical model is an *S5* model. The theorem does not mention the class of models or the proof system explicitly, but if we do, it reads: for every $\varphi \in \mathcal{L}_K$

$$S5 \models \varphi \text{ implies } \mathbf{S5} \vdash \varphi$$

So the canonical model has to be an *S5* model. Because we often omit the class of models and the proof system, Theorem 7.7, Theorem 7.19, Theorem 7.26, Theorem 7.36, and Theorem 7.52 look almost the same, but they are about different proof systems.

all instantiations of propositional tautologies	
$K_a(\varphi \to \psi) \to (K_a\varphi \to K_a\psi)$	distribution of K_a over $\to$
$K_a\varphi \to \varphi$	truth
$K_a\varphi \to K_aK_a\varphi$	positive introspection
$\neg K_a\varphi \to K_a\neg K_a\varphi$	negative introspection
$C_B(\varphi \to \psi) \to (C_B\varphi \to C_B\psi)$	distribution of C_B over $\to$
$C_B\varphi \to (\varphi \wedge E_BC_B\varphi)$	mix
$C_B(\varphi \to E_B\varphi) \to (\varphi \to C_B\varphi)$	induction axiom
From φ and $\varphi \to \psi$, infer ψ	modus ponens
From φ, infer $K_a\varphi$	necessitation of K_a
From φ, infer $C_B\varphi$	necessitation of C_B

Table 7.2. The proof system **S5C**.

7.3 *S5C*: Dealing with Non-compactness

In this section we prove completeness for *S5C*. The proof system **S5C** is given in Table 7.2. Note that *S5C* is not compact if there are at least two agents. Take the set

$$\Lambda = \{E_B^n p \mid n \in \mathbb{N}\} \cup \{\neg C_B p\}$$

where E_B^n is an abbreviation for a sequence of n E_B operators (see page 13). B should consist of at least two agents. Every finite subset of Λ is satisfiable, but Λ is not. This indicates one of the difficulties in trying to construct a canonical model for *S5* with infinite maximal consistent sets, since we cannot guarantee that the union of countably many consistent sets is satisfiable, which is the whole idea of a canonical model. Therefore we construct a finite model for only a finite fragment of the language, depending on the formula we are interested in. This fragment is known as the *closure* of a formula.

Definition 7.8 (Closure) Let $cl : \mathcal{L}_{KC} \to \wp(\mathcal{L}_{KC})$, be the function such that for every $\varphi \in \mathcal{L}_{KC}$, $cl(\varphi)$ is the smallest set such that:

1. $\varphi \in cl(\varphi)$,
2. if $\psi \in cl(\varphi)$, then $Sub(\psi) \subseteq cl(\varphi)$ (where $Sub(\psi)$ is the set of subformulas of ψ),
3. if $\psi \in cl(\varphi)$ and ψ is not a negation, then $\neg\psi \in cl(\varphi)$,
4. if $C_B\psi \in cl(\varphi)$, then $\{K_aC_B\psi \mid a \in B\} \subseteq cl(\varphi)$. □

We construct a canonical model for this fragment only. This model will be finite since this fragment is finite.

Lemma 7.9 $cl(\varphi)$ is finite for all formulas $\varphi \in \mathcal{L}_{KC}$. □

Proof By induction on φ.

Base case If φ is a propositional variable p, then the closure of φ is $\{p, \neg p\}$, which is finite.

Induction hypothesis $cl(\varphi)$ and $cl(\psi)$ are finite.

Induction step We distinguish the following cases:

the case for $\neg\varphi$: The closure of $\neg\varphi$ is the set $\{\neg\varphi\} \cup cl(\varphi)$. As $cl(\varphi)$ is finite by the induction hypothesis, this set is finite.

the case for $(\varphi \wedge \psi)$: The closure of $(\varphi \wedge \psi)$ is the set $\{(\varphi \wedge \psi), \neg(\varphi \wedge \psi)\} \cup cl(\varphi) \cup cl(\psi)$. As $cl(\varphi)$ and $cl(\psi)$ are finite by the induction hypothesis, this set is finite.

the case for $K_a\varphi$: The closure of $K_a\varphi$ is the set $\{K_a\varphi, \neg K_a\varphi\} \cup cl(\varphi)$. As $cl(\varphi)$ is finite by the induction hypothesis, this set is finite.

the case for $C_B\varphi$: The closure of $C_B\varphi$ is the following union: $cl(\varphi) \cup \{C_B\varphi, \neg C_B\varphi\} \cup \{K_aC_B\varphi, \neg K_aC_B\varphi \mid a \in B\}$. As $cl(\varphi)$ is finite by the induction hypothesis, this set is finite. □

We will now consider consistent sets that are maximal for such a closure, rather than for the whole language.

Definition 7.10 (Maximal consistent in Φ) Let $\Phi \subseteq \mathcal{L}_{KC}$ be the closure of some formula. Γ is maximal consistent in Φ iff

1. $\Gamma \subseteq \Phi$
2. Γ is consistent: $\Gamma \nvdash \bot$
3. Γ is maximal in Φ: there is no $\Gamma' \subseteq \Phi$ such that $\Gamma \subset \Gamma'$ and $\Gamma' \nvdash \bot$. □

These maximal consistent sets in Φ are taken as states in the canonical model for Φ. Since these sets are finite, the conjunction over such a set is a finite formula. Let $\underline{\Gamma} = \bigwedge \Gamma$. The valuation and the accessibility relations are defined as in the case of *S5*.

Definition 7.11 (Canonical model for Φ) Let Φ be the closure of some formula. The canonical model $M^c = (S^c, \sim^c, V^c)$ for Φ is defined as follows

- $S^c = \{\Gamma \mid \Gamma \text{ is maximal consistent in } \Phi\}$
- $\Gamma \sim_a^c \Delta$ iff $\{K_a\varphi \mid K_a\varphi \in \Gamma\} = \{K_a\varphi \mid K_a\varphi \in \Delta\}$
- $V_p^c = \{\Gamma \in S^c \mid p \in \Gamma\}$ □

The analogue of the Lindenbaum Lemma now becomes rather trivial since Φ is finite. But we still need to show it.

Lemma 7.12 (Lindenbaum) Let Φ be the closure of some formula. Every consistent subset of Φ is a subset of a maximal consistent set in Φ. □

Proof Let $\Delta \subseteq \Phi$ be a consistent set of formulas. Let $|\Phi| = n$. Let φ_k be the k-th formula in an enumeration of Φ. Now consider the following sequence of sets of formulas.

$$\begin{aligned} \Gamma_0 &= \Delta \\ \Gamma_{k+1} &= \begin{cases} \Gamma_k \cup \{\varphi_{k+1}\} & \text{if } \Gamma_k \cup \{\varphi_{k+1}\} \text{ is consistent} \\ \Gamma_k & \text{otherwise} \end{cases} \end{aligned}$$

It is clear that $\Delta \subseteq \Gamma_n$. We now show that Γ_n is both consistent and maximal in Φ. To see that Γ_n is consistent, first observe by induction on k that every Γ_k is consistent. So Γ_n is consistent.

To see that Γ_n is maximal in Φ take an arbitrary formula $\varphi_k \in \Phi$ such that $\varphi_k \notin \Gamma_n$. Therefore $\Gamma_{k-1} \cup \{\varphi_k\}$ is inconsistent and so is $\Gamma_n \cup \{\varphi_k\}$. Since φ_k was arbitrary there is no $\Gamma' \subseteq \Phi$ such that $\Gamma_n \subset \Gamma'$ and Γ' is consistent. □

The semantics of $C_B\varphi$ uses the reflexive transitive closure of the union of the accessibility relations of members of B. One way to look at this reflexive transitive closure is to view it as all paths in the model labelled by agents in B. This turns out to be a very convenient notion to use in our proofs.

Definition 7.13 (Paths) A B-path from Γ is a sequence $\Gamma_0, \ldots, \Gamma_n$ of maximal consistent sets in Φ such that for all k (where $0 \leq k < n$) there is an agent $a \in B$ such that $\Gamma_k \sim_a^c \Gamma_{k+1}$ and $\Gamma_0 = \Gamma$.

A φ-path is a sequence $\Gamma_0, \ldots, \Gamma_n$ of maximal consistent sets in Φ such that for all k (where $0 \leq k \leq n$) $\varphi \in \Gamma_k$.

We take the length of a path $\Gamma_0, \ldots, \Gamma_n$ to be n. □

Most of the properties we used in the proof for completeness of *S5* are, in slightly adapted form, also true for *S5* with common knowledge, namely restricted to the closure Φ. But we will also need an extra property for formulas of the form $C_B\varphi$, which we focus on in the proof.

Lemma 7.14 Let Φ be the closure of some formula. Let $M^c = (S^c, \sim^c, V^c)$ be the canonical model for Φ. If Γ and Δ are maximal consistent sets in Φ, then

1. Γ is deductively closed in Φ (for all formulas $\varphi \in \Phi$, if $\vdash \underline{\Gamma} \rightarrow \varphi$, then $\varphi \in \Gamma$),
2. if $\neg\varphi \in \Phi$, then $\varphi \in \Gamma$ iff $\neg\varphi \notin \Gamma$,
3. if $(\varphi \wedge \psi) \in \Phi$, then $(\varphi \wedge \psi) \in \Gamma$ iff $\varphi \in \Gamma$ and $\psi \in \Gamma$,
4. if $\underline{\Gamma} \wedge \hat{K}_a\underline{\Delta}$ is consistent, then $\Gamma \sim_a^c \Delta$,
5. if $K_a\psi \in \Phi$, then $\{K_a\varphi \mid K_a\varphi \in \Gamma\} \vdash \psi$ iff $\{K_a\varphi \mid K_a\varphi \in \Gamma\} \vdash K_a\psi$,
6. if $C_B\varphi \in \Phi$, then $C_B\varphi \in \Gamma$ iff every B-path from Γ is a φ-path. □

Proof 1–5 See exercise 7.15.

6. From left to right. We proceed by induction on the length of the B-path, but we load the induction (we prove something stronger). We show that if $C_B\varphi \in \Gamma$, then every B-path is a φ-path *and* a $C_B\varphi$-path. Suppose that $C_B\varphi \in \Gamma$.

   Base case Suppose the length of the B-path is 0, i.e. $\Gamma = \Gamma_0 = \Gamma_n$. Since $\vdash C_B\varphi \rightarrow \varphi$, both $C_B\varphi \in \Phi$ and $\varphi \in \Phi$, and Γ is deductively closed in Φ, both $C_B\varphi$ and $\varphi \in \Gamma$.

   Induction hypothesis If $C_B\varphi \in \Gamma$, then every B-path of length n is a φ-path and a $C_B\varphi$-path.

   Induction step Take a B-path of length $n+1$ from Γ. By the induction hypothesis $C_B\varphi \in \Gamma_n$. Let a be the agent in B such that $\Gamma_n \sim_a^c \Gamma_{n+1}$. Since $\vdash C_B\varphi \rightarrow E_BC_B\varphi$ and $\vdash E_BC_B\varphi \rightarrow K_aC_B\varphi$, it must be the case that $K_aC_B\varphi \in \Gamma_{n+1}$ by the definition of $\sim_a^c$ and the fact that $K_aC_B\varphi \in \Phi$, because $C_B\varphi \in \Phi$. By similar reasoning as in the base case, $C_B\varphi \in \Gamma_{n+1}$ and $\varphi \in \Gamma_{n+1}$ too.

So we are done with the proof from left to right.

From right to left. Suppose that every B-path from Γ is a φ-path. Let $S_{B,\varphi}$ be the set of all maximal consistent sets Δ in Φ such that every B-path from Δ is a φ-path. Now consider the formula

$$\chi = \bigvee_{\Delta \in S_{B,\varphi}} \underline{\Delta}$$

We prove the following

$$\vdash \underline{\Gamma} \to \chi \quad \text{(a)}$$
$$\vdash \chi \to \varphi \quad \text{(b)}$$
$$\vdash \chi \to E_B\chi \quad \text{(c)}$$

From these it follows that $C_B\varphi \in \Gamma$. Because from (c) it follows by necessitation that $\vdash C_B(\chi \to E_B\chi)$. By the induction axiom this implies that $\vdash \chi \to C_B\chi$. By (a) this implies that $\vdash \underline{\Gamma} \to C_B\chi$. By (b) and necessitation and distribution for C_B this implies that $\vdash \underline{\Gamma} \to C_B\varphi$. Therefore $C_B\varphi \in \Gamma$.

a) $\Gamma \vdash \chi$, because $\underline{\Gamma}$ is one of the disjuncts of χ.
b) Note that $\varphi \in \Delta$ if Δ is in $S_{B,\varphi}$. Therefore φ is a conjunct of every disjunct of χ. Therefore $\vdash \chi \to \varphi$.
c) Suppose toward a contradiction that $\chi \wedge \neg E_B\chi$ is consistent. Since χ is a disjunction there must be a disjunct $\underline{\Delta}$ such that $\underline{\Delta} \wedge \neg E_B\chi$ is consistent. By similar reasoning there must be an $a \in B$ such that $\underline{\Delta} \wedge \hat{K}_a\neg\chi$ is consistent. Since $\vdash \bigvee\{\underline{\Delta} \mid \Delta \in S^c\}$ (see exercise 7.16), it is the case that $\underline{\Delta} \wedge \hat{K}_a \bigvee_{\Theta \in (S^c \setminus S_{B,\varphi})} \underline{\Theta}$ is consistent. Then, by modal reasoning, $\underline{\Delta} \wedge \bigvee_{\Theta \in (S^c \setminus S_{B,\varphi})} \hat{K}_a\underline{\Theta}$ is consistent. Therefore there must be a $\Theta \notin S_{B,\varphi}$ which is maximal consistent in Φ, such that $\underline{\Delta} \wedge \hat{K}_a\underline{\Theta}$ is consistent. But then by (4) of this Lemma, $\Delta \sim_a^c \Theta$. Since Θ is not in $S_{B,\varphi}$, there must be a B-path from Θ which is not a φ-path. But then there is a B-path from Δ which is not a φ-path. This contradicts that $\Delta \in S_{B,\varphi}$, which it is because $\underline{\Delta}$ is one of χ's disjuncts. Therefore $\vdash \chi \to E_B\chi$. □

Exercise 7.15 Prove 1–5 of Lemma 7.14. □

Exercise 7.16 Show that $\vdash \bigvee\{\underline{\Gamma} \mid \Gamma \text{ is maximal consistent in } cl(\varphi)\}$. □

Now we are ready to prove the Truth Lemma.

Lemma 7.17 (Truth) Let Φ be the closure of some formula. Let $M^c = (S^c, \sim^c, V^c)$ be the canonical model for Φ. For all $\Gamma \in S^c$, and all $\varphi \in \Phi$:

$$\varphi \in \Gamma \text{ iff } (M^c, \Gamma) \models \varphi$$

□

Proof Suppose $\varphi \in \Phi$. We now continue by induction on φ.

Base case The base case is like the base case in the proof of Lemma 7.5.

Induction hypothesis For every maximal consistent set Γ it is the case that $\varphi \in \Gamma$ iff $(M^c, \Gamma) \models \varphi$.

Induction step The case for negation, conjunction, and individual epistemic operators are like those cases in the proof of Lemma 7.5. There is one extra case:

the case for $C_B\varphi$: Suppose that $C_B\varphi \in \Gamma$. From item 6 of Lemma 7.14 it follows that this is the case iff every B-path from Γ is a φ-path. By the induction hypothesis this is the case iff every B-path is a path along which φ is true. By the semantics this is equivalent to $(M^c, \Gamma) \models C_B\varphi$. □

The canonical model for any closure satisfies all the properties we require of the accessibility relations for the agents.

Lemma 7.18 (Canonicity) Let Φ be the closure of some formula. The canonical model for Φ is reflexive, transitive, and Euclidean. □

Proof This follows straightforwardly from the definition of $\sim_a^c$. □

Now it is easy to show completeness.

Theorem 7.19 (Completeness) For every $\varphi \in \mathcal{L}_{KC}$

$$\models \varphi \text{ implies } \vdash \varphi$$ □

Proof By contraposition. Suppose $\not\vdash \varphi$. Therefore $\{\neg\varphi\}$ is a consistent set. By the Lindenbaum Lemma $\{\neg\varphi\}$ is a subset of some Γ which is maximal consistent in $cl(\neg\varphi)$. Let M^c be the canonical model for $cl(\neg\varphi)$. By the Truth Lemma $(M^c, \Gamma) \models \neg\varphi$. Therefore $\not\models \varphi$. □

7.4 *PA*: Completeness by Translation

The completeness proof for public announcement logic without common knowledge is quite different from the completeness proofs we have seen so far. The proof system **PA** is given in Table 7.3. When one looks closely at the axioms for this logic, one notices that what is the case after an announcement can be expressed by saying what is the case before the announcement. The following translation captures this observation.

Definition 7.20 (Translation) The translation $t : \mathcal{L}_{K[]} \to \mathcal{L}_K$ is defined as follows:

$$\begin{array}{ll} t(p) & = p \\ t(\neg\varphi) & = \neg t(\varphi) \end{array}$$

all instantiations of propositional tautologies	
$K_a(\varphi \rightarrow \psi) \rightarrow (K_a\varphi \rightarrow K_a\psi)$	distribution of K_a over $\rightarrow$
$K_a\varphi \rightarrow \varphi$	truth
$K_a\varphi \rightarrow K_aK_a\varphi$	positive introspection
$\neg K_a\varphi \rightarrow K_a\neg K_a\varphi$	negative introspection
$[\varphi]p \leftrightarrow (\varphi \rightarrow p)$	atomic permanence
$[\varphi]\neg\psi \leftrightarrow (\varphi \rightarrow \neg[\varphi]\psi)$	announcement and negation
$[\varphi](\psi \wedge \chi) \leftrightarrow ([\varphi]\psi \wedge [\varphi]\chi)$	announcement and conjunction
$[\varphi]K_a\psi \leftrightarrow (\varphi \rightarrow K_a[\varphi]\psi)$	announcement and knowledge
$[\varphi][\psi]\chi \leftrightarrow [\varphi \wedge [\varphi]\psi]\chi$	announcement composition
From φ and $\varphi \rightarrow \psi$, infer ψ	modus ponens
From φ, infer $K_a\varphi$	necessitation of K_a

Table 7.3. The proof system **PA**.

$$
\begin{array}{ll}
t(\varphi \wedge \psi) & = t(\varphi) \wedge t(\psi) \\
t(K_a\varphi) & = K_a t(\varphi) \\
t([\varphi]p) & = t(\varphi \rightarrow p) \\
t([\varphi]\neg\psi) & = t(\varphi \rightarrow \neg[\varphi]\psi) \\
t([\varphi](\psi \wedge \chi)) & = t([\varphi]\psi \wedge [\varphi]\chi) \\
t([\varphi]K_a\psi) & = t(\varphi \rightarrow K_a[\varphi]\psi) \\
t([\varphi][\psi]\chi) & = t([\varphi \wedge [\varphi]\psi]\chi)
\end{array}
$$

□

The soundness of the proof system shows that this translation preserves the meaning of a formula. In order to show that every formula is provably equivalent to its translation we will use a trick that will be very useful when we prove completeness for public announcement logic with common knowledge.

Proofs by induction on formulas use the inductive definition of the logical language. In the inductive step one uses the induction hypothesis for subformulas of that formula. It seems however that this use of the induction hypothesis is not enough for the case at hand. For example $\varphi \rightarrow \neg[\varphi]\psi$ is not a subformula of $[\varphi]\neg\psi$, but we would like to apply the induction hypothesis to the former when we are proving the inductive step for the latter. Since the inductive definition of the logical language does not say anything about the order of these formulas we can impose an order on them that suits our purposes best. For this we define the following *complexity measure*.

Definition 7.21 (Complexity) The complexity $c : \mathcal{L}_{K[]} \rightarrow \mathbb{N}$ is defined as follows:

$$
\begin{array}{ll}
c(p) & = 1 \\
c(\neg\varphi) & = 1 + c(\varphi) \\
c(\varphi \wedge \psi) & = 1 + \max(c(\varphi), c(\psi)) \\
c(K_a\varphi) & = 1 + c(\varphi) \\
c([\varphi]\psi) & = (4 + c(\varphi)) \cdot c(\psi)
\end{array}
$$

□

This complexity measure preserves the order prescribed by the inductive definition of the logical language, but it has some additional desirable properties.

In the definition the number 4 appears in the clause for action models. It seems arbitrary, but it is in fact the least natural number that gives us the following properties.

Lemma 7.22 For all φ, ψ, and χ:

1. $c(\psi) \geq c(\varphi)$ if $\varphi \in Sub(\psi)$
2. $c([\varphi]p) > c(\varphi \rightarrow p)$
3. $c([\varphi]\neg\psi) > c(\varphi \rightarrow \neg[\varphi]\psi)$
4. $c([\varphi](\psi \wedge \chi)) > c([\varphi]\psi \wedge [\varphi]\chi)$
5. $c([\varphi]K_a\psi) > c(\varphi \rightarrow K_a[\varphi]\psi)$
6. $c([\varphi][\psi]\chi) > c([\varphi \wedge [\varphi]\psi]\chi)$ □

Exercise 7.23 Prove Lemma 7.22. □

With these properties we can show that every formula is provably equivalent to its translation.

Lemma 7.24 For all formulas $\varphi \in \mathcal{L}_{K[]}$ it is the case that

$$\vdash \varphi \leftrightarrow t(\varphi)$$ □

Proof By induction on $c(\varphi)$.

Base case If φ is a propositional variable p, it is trivial that $\vdash p \leftrightarrow p$.
Induction hypothesis For all φ such that $c(\varphi) \leq n$: $\vdash \varphi \leftrightarrow t(\varphi)$.
Induction step The case for negation, conjunction, and individual epistemic operators follow straightforwardly from the induction hypothesis and Lemma 7.22, item 1.

the case for $[\varphi]p$**:** This case follows straightforwardly from the atomic permanence axiom, item 2 of Lemma 7.22, and the induction hypothesis.

the case for $[\varphi]\neg\psi$**:** This case follows straightforwardly from the announcement and negation axiom, item 3 of Lemma 7.22, and the induction hypothesis.

the case for $[\varphi](\psi \wedge \chi)$**:** This case follows straightforwardly from the announcement and conjunction axiom, item 4 of Lemma 7.22, and the induction hypothesis.

the case for $[\varphi]K_a\psi$**:** This case follows straightforwardly from the announcement and knowledge axiom, item 5 of Lemma 7.22, and the induction hypothesis.

the case for $[\varphi][\psi]\chi$**:** This follows straightforwardly from the announcement composition axiom, item 6 of Lemma 7.22 and the induction hypothesis. □

We can also use induction on the complexity of the formula to show that the translation is indeed a function from $\mathcal{L}_{K[]}$ to $\mathcal{L}_K$.

Exercise 7.25 Show that for all $\varphi \in \mathcal{L}_{K[]}$, it is the case that $t(\varphi) \in \mathcal{L}_K$ by induction on $c(\varphi)$. □

Completeness follows from Lemma 7.24 and Theorem 7.7.

Theorem 7.26 (Completeness) For every $\varphi \in \mathcal{L}_{K[]}$

$$\models \varphi \text{ implies } \vdash \varphi$$ □

Proof Suppose $\models \varphi$. Therefore $\models t(\varphi)$, by the soundness of the proof system and **PA** $\vdash \varphi \leftrightarrow t(\varphi)$ (Lemma 7.24). The formula $t(\varphi)$ does not contain any announcement operators. Therefore **S5** $\vdash t(\varphi)$ by completeness of **S5** (Theorem 7.7). We also have that **PA** $\vdash t(\varphi)$, as **S5** is a subsystem of **PA**. Since **PA** $\vdash \varphi \leftrightarrow t(\varphi)$, it follows that **PA** $\vdash \varphi$. □

7.5 *PAC*: Induction on Complexity

In this section we prove completeness for public announcement logic with common knowledge. The proof system **PAC** is given in Table 7.4.

We will combine the ideas for the proofs of *S5C* and *PA*. Again we construct a canonical model with respect to a finite fragment of the language. The additional clauses follow the axioms for announcements.

all instantiations of propositional tautologies	
$K_a(\varphi \rightarrow \psi) \rightarrow (K_a\varphi \rightarrow K_a\psi)$	distribution of K_a over $\rightarrow$
$K_a\varphi \rightarrow \varphi$	truth
$K_a\varphi \rightarrow K_aK_a\varphi$	positive introspection
$\neg K_a\varphi \rightarrow K_a\neg K_a\varphi$	negative introspection
$[\varphi]p \leftrightarrow (\varphi \rightarrow p)$	atomic permanence
$[\varphi]\neg\psi \leftrightarrow (\varphi \rightarrow \neg[\varphi]\psi)$	announcement and negation
$[\varphi](\psi \wedge \chi) \leftrightarrow ([\varphi]\psi \wedge [\varphi]\chi)$	announcement and conjunction
$[\varphi]K_a\psi \leftrightarrow (\varphi \rightarrow K_a[\varphi]\psi)$	announcement and knowledge
$[\varphi][\psi]\chi \leftrightarrow [\varphi \wedge [\varphi]\psi]\chi$	announcement composition
$C_B(\varphi \rightarrow \psi) \rightarrow (C_B\varphi \rightarrow C_B\psi)$	distribution of C_B over $\rightarrow$
$C_B\varphi \rightarrow (\varphi \wedge E_BC_B\varphi)$	mix of common knowledge
$C_B(\varphi \rightarrow E_B\varphi) \rightarrow (\varphi \rightarrow C_B\varphi)$	induction of common knowledge
From φ and $\varphi \rightarrow \psi$, infer ψ	modus ponens
From φ, infer $K_a\varphi$	necessitation of K_a
From φ, infer $C_B\varphi$	necessitation of C_B
From φ, infer $[\psi]\varphi$	necessitation of $[\psi]$
From $\chi \rightarrow [\varphi]\psi$ and $\chi \wedge \varphi \rightarrow E_B\chi$, infer $\chi \rightarrow [\varphi]C_B\psi$	announcement and common knowledge

Table 7.4. The proof system **PAC**.

Definition 7.27 (Closure) Let $cl : \mathcal{L}_{KC[]} \to \wp(\mathcal{L}_{KC[]})$, such that for every $\varphi \in \mathcal{L}_{KC[]}$, $cl(\varphi)$ is the smallest set such that:

1. $\varphi \in cl(\varphi)$,
2. if $\psi \in cl(\varphi)$, then $Sub(\psi) \subseteq cl(\varphi)$,
3. if $\psi \in cl(\varphi)$ and ψ is not a negation, then $\neg\psi \in cl(\varphi)$,
4. if $C_B\psi \in cl(\varphi)$, then $\{K_a C_B \psi \mid a \in B\} \subseteq cl(\varphi)$,
5. if $[\psi]p \in cl(\varphi)$, then $(\psi \to p) \in cl(\varphi)$,
6. if $[\psi]\neg\chi \in cl(\varphi)$, then $(\psi \to \neg[\psi]\chi) \in cl(\varphi)$,
7. if $[\psi](\chi \wedge \xi) \in cl(\varphi)$, then $([\psi]\chi \wedge [\psi]\xi) \in cl(\varphi)$,
8. if $[\psi]K_a\chi \in cl(\varphi)$, then $(\psi \to K_a[\psi]\chi) \in cl(\varphi)$,
9. if $[\psi]C_B\chi \in cl(\varphi)$, then $[\psi]\chi \in cl(\varphi)$ and $\{K_a[\psi]C_B\chi \mid a \in B\} \subseteq cl(\varphi)$,
10. if $[\psi][\chi]\xi \in cl(\varphi)$, then $[\psi \wedge [\psi]\chi]\xi \in cl(\varphi)$. □

Lemma 7.28 $cl(\varphi)$ is finite for all formulas $\varphi \in \mathcal{L}_{KC[]}$. □

Proof The proof is just like the proof of Lemma 7.9. □

Although the closure is defined differently, many definitions and lemma's work in precisely the same way as in the case for *S5C*. The notions of maximal consistent in Φ and the canonical model for Φ are just as before (see Definition 7.10 and 7.11), and we do not repeat them. Also the Lindenbaum Lemma is proved in the same way as before.

Lemma 7.29 (Lindenbaum) Let Φ be the closure of some formula. Every consistent subset of Φ is a subset of a maximal consistent set in Φ. □

Proof The proof is just like the proof of Lemma 7.12. □

When we look closely at the proof obligations which have not been dealt with before, then there is only one extra case, namely proving the Truth Lemma for formulas of the form $[\varphi]C_B\psi$. Semantically this means that every B-path in the new model (obtained by removing all states where φ does not hold from the old model), runs along ψ-states. That is equivalent to saying that every B-path that is also a φ-path in the old model runs along $[\varphi]\psi$-states. In view of this it is useful to introduce the notion of a B-φ-path.

Definition 7.30 (B-φ-path) A B-φ-path from Γ is a B-path that is also a φ-path. □

The extra property we require of the canonical models concerns formulas of the form $[\varphi]C_B\psi$. This can be stated in terms of paths.

Lemma 7.31 Let Φ be the closure of some formula. Let $M^c = (S^c, \sim^c, V^c)$ be the canonical model for Φ. If Γ and Δ are maximal consistent sets in Φ, then

1. Γ is deductively closed in Φ,
2. if $\neg\varphi \in \Phi$, then $\varphi \in \Gamma$ iff $\neg\varphi \notin \Gamma$,
3. if $(\varphi \wedge \psi) \in \Phi$, then $(\varphi \wedge \psi) \in \Gamma$ iff $\varphi \in \Gamma$ and $\psi \in \Gamma$,

4. if $\underline{\Gamma} \wedge \hat{K}_a \underline{\Delta}$ is consistent, then $\Gamma \sim_a^c \Delta$,
5. if $K_a\psi \in \Phi$, then $\{K_a\varphi \mid K_a\varphi \in \Gamma\} \vdash \psi$ iff $\{K_a\varphi \mid K_a\varphi \in \Gamma\} \vdash K_a\psi$,
6. if $C_B\varphi \in \Phi$, then $C_B\varphi \in \Gamma$ iff every B-path from Γ is a φ-path,
7. if $[\varphi]C_B\psi \in \Phi$, then $[\varphi]C_B\psi \in \Gamma$ iff every B-φ-path from Γ is a $[\varphi]\psi$-path. □

Proof The proofs of 1–6 are similar to the proofs of 1–6 of Lemma 7.14.

7. From left to right. We now continue by induction on the length of the path, but we load the induction. We show that if $[\varphi]C_B\psi \in \Gamma$, then every B-φ-path is a $[\varphi]\psi$-path *and* a $[\varphi]C_B\psi$-path. Suppose $[\varphi]C_B\psi \in \Gamma$.

   Base case Suppose the length of the B-φ-path is 0. Therefore we have to show that if $[\varphi]C_B\psi \in \Gamma_0$, then $[\varphi]\psi \in \Gamma_0$. This can be shown as follows. Observe that $\vdash C_B\psi \rightarrow \psi$. By necessitation and distribution of $[\varphi]$ we have that $\vdash [\varphi]C_B\psi \rightarrow [\varphi]\psi$. Therefore, given clause 9 of Definition 7.27 and that Γ_0 is deductively closed in cl, $[\varphi]\psi \in \Gamma_0$.

   Induction hypothesis Every B-φ-path of length n is both a $[\varphi]\psi$-path and a $[\varphi]C_B\psi$-path.

   Induction step Suppose now that the B-φ path is of length $n+1$, i.e. there is a B-φ-path $\Gamma_0, \ldots \Gamma_n, \Gamma_{n+1}$. Suppose that $\Gamma_n \sim_a^c \Gamma_{n+1}$. By the induction hypothesis we may assume that $[\varphi]C_B\psi \in \Gamma_n$. By the mix axiom we have that $\vdash C_B\psi \rightarrow K_aC_B\psi$. By applying necessitation and distribution of $[\varphi]$ we get $\vdash [\varphi]C_B\psi \rightarrow [\varphi]K_aC_B\psi$. By the axiom for announcements and knowledge $\vdash [\varphi]K_aC_B\psi \rightarrow (\varphi \rightarrow K_a[\varphi]C_B\psi)$. Since $\varphi \in \Gamma_n$, it must be the case that $\Gamma_n \vdash K_a[\varphi]C_B\psi$. Therefore by the definition of $\sim_a^c$, it is the case that $K_a[\varphi]C_B\psi \in \Gamma_{n+1}$, and so $[\varphi]C_B\psi \in \Gamma_{n+1}$. By similar reasoning as in the base case, $[\varphi]\psi \in \Gamma_{n+1}$.

   From right to left. Suppose that every B-φ-path from Γ is a $[\varphi]\psi$-path. Let $S_{B,\varphi,[\varphi]\psi}$ be the set of maximal consistent sets Δ such that every B-φ-path from Δ is a $[\varphi]\psi$-path. Now consider the formula

$$\chi = \bigvee_{\Delta \in S_{B,\varphi,[\varphi]\psi}} \underline{\Delta}$$

   We will show the following

$$\vdash \underline{\Gamma} \rightarrow \chi \tag{a}$$
$$\vdash \chi \rightarrow [\varphi]\psi \tag{b}$$
$$\vdash \chi \wedge \varphi \rightarrow E_B\chi \tag{c}$$

   From these it follows that $[\varphi]C_B\psi \in \Gamma$. By applying the announcement and common knowledge rule to (b) and (c) it follows that $\vdash \chi \rightarrow [\varphi]C_B\psi$. By (a) it follows that $\vdash \underline{\Gamma} \rightarrow [\varphi]C_B\psi$. Therefore $[\varphi]C_B\psi \in \Gamma$.

   a) This follows immediately, because $\Gamma \in S_{B,\varphi,[\varphi]\psi}$, and $\underline{\Gamma}$ is one of χ's disjuncts.

b) Since every B-φ-path is a $[\varphi]\psi$-path for every $\Delta \in S_{B,\varphi,[\varphi]\psi}$ it must be the case that $[\varphi]\psi \in \Delta$. Therefore, $[\varphi]\psi$ is one of the conjuncts in every disjunct of χ. Therefore by propositional reasoning $\chi \rightarrow [\varphi]\psi$.

c) Suppose toward a contradiction that $\chi \wedge \varphi \wedge \neg E_B\chi$ is consistent. Because χ is a disjunction there must be a disjunct $\underline{\Theta}$ such that $\underline{\Theta} \wedge \varphi \wedge \neg E_B\chi$ is consistent. Since $\underline{\Theta} \wedge \varphi$ is consistent and Θ is maximal consistent in Φ and $\varphi \in \Phi$ it must be the case that $\varphi \in \Theta$. So $\underline{\Theta} \wedge \neg E_B\chi$ is consistent. Then there must be an agent a such that $\underline{\Theta} \wedge \hat{K}_a\neg\chi$ is consistent. Since $\vdash \bigvee\{\underline{\Gamma} \mid \Gamma \in S^c\}$, there must be a Ξ in the complement of $S_{B,\varphi,[\varphi]\psi}$ such that $\underline{\Theta} \wedge \hat{K}_a\underline{\Xi}$ is consistent. By item 4 of Lemma 7.31 this is equivalent to $\Theta \sim_a^c \Xi$. But since there is a B-φ-path from Ξ which is not a $[\varphi]\psi$-path and $a \in B$, there is also a B-φ-path from Θ which is not a $[\varphi]\psi$-path. This contradicts that $\Theta \in S_{B,\varphi,[\varphi]\psi}$, but it must be, because $\underline{\Theta}$ is one of χ's disjuncts. Therefore $\vdash \chi \wedge \varphi \rightarrow E_B\chi$. □

In order to prove the Truth Lemma we again need a notion of complexity that allows us to use the induction hypothesis for formulas that are not subformulas of the formula at hand. The following complexity measure is a simple extension of Definition 7.21 with a clause for $C_B\varphi$, and meets all our requirements.

Definition 7.32 (Complexity) The complexity $c : \mathcal{L}_{KC[]} \rightarrow \mathbb{N}$ is defined as follows:

$$\begin{array}{ll} c(p) & = 1 \\ c(\neg\varphi) & = 1 + c(\varphi) \\ c(\varphi \wedge \psi) & = 1 + \max(c(\varphi), c(\psi)) \\ c(K_a\varphi) & = 1 + c(\varphi) \\ c(C_B\varphi) & = 1 + c(\varphi) \\ c([\varphi]\psi) & = (4 + c(\varphi)) \cdot c(\psi) \end{array}$$

□

Lemma 7.33 For all φ, ψ, and χ:

1. $c(\psi) \geq c(\varphi)$ for all $\varphi \in Sub(\psi)$
2. $c([\varphi]p) > c(\varphi \rightarrow p)$
3. $c([\varphi]\neg\psi) > c(\varphi \rightarrow \neg[\varphi]\psi)$
4. $c([\varphi](\psi \wedge \chi) > c([\varphi]\psi \wedge [\varphi]\chi)$
5. $c([\varphi]K_a\psi) > c(\varphi \rightarrow K_a[\varphi]\psi)$
6. $c([\varphi]C_B\psi) > c([\varphi]\psi)$
7. $c([\varphi][\psi]\chi) > c([\varphi \wedge [\varphi]\psi)$

□

Proof The proof is just like the proof of Lemma 7.22. □

Now we are ready to proof the Truth Lemma.

Lemma 7.34 (Truth) Let Φ be the closure for some formula. Let $M^c = (S^c, \sim^c, V^c)$ be the canonical model for Φ. For all $\Gamma \in S^c$, and all $\varphi \in \Phi$:

$$\varphi \in \Gamma \text{ iff } (M^c, \Gamma) \models \varphi$$

□

Proof Suppose $\varphi \in \Phi$. We now continue by induction on $c(\varphi)$.

Base case The base case is just like the base case in the proof of Lemma 7.17.
Induction hypothesis For all φ such that $c(\varphi) \leq n$: $\varphi \in \Gamma$ iff $(M^c, \Gamma) \models \varphi$.
Induction step Suppose $c(\varphi) = n + 1$. The cases for negation, conjunction, individual epistemic operators, and common knowledge operators are just like the proof of Lemma 7.17. When φ is of the form $[\psi]\chi$ we distinguish the following cases:

the case for $[\psi]p$**:** Suppose $[\psi]p \in \Gamma$. Given that $[\psi]p \in \Phi$, $[\psi]p \in \Gamma$ is equivalent to $(\psi \rightarrow p) \in \Gamma$ by the atomic permanence axiom. By item 2 of Lemma 7.33 we can apply the induction hypothesis. Therefore this is equivalent to $(M^c, \Gamma) \models \psi \rightarrow p$. By the semantics this is equivalent to $(M^c, \Gamma) \models [\psi]p$.

the case for $[\psi]\neg\chi$**:** Suppose $[\psi]\neg\chi \in \Gamma$. Given that $[\psi]\neg\chi \in \Phi$, $[\psi]\neg\chi \in \Gamma$ is equivalent to $(\psi \rightarrow \neg[\psi]\chi) \in \Gamma$ by the announcement and negation axiom. By item 3 of Lemma 7.33 we can apply the induction hypothesis. Therefore this is equivalent to $(M^c, \Gamma) \models \psi \rightarrow \neg[\psi]\chi$. By the semantics this is equivalent to $(M^c, \Gamma) \models [\psi]\neg\chi$.

the case for $[\psi](\chi \wedge \xi)$**:** Suppose $[\psi](\chi \wedge \xi) \in \Gamma$. Given that $[\psi](\chi \wedge \xi) \in \Phi$, $[\psi](\chi \wedge \xi) \in \Gamma$ is equivalent to $([\psi]\chi \wedge [\psi]\xi) \in \Gamma$ by the announcement and conjunction axiom. By item 4 of Lemma 7.33 we can apply the induction hypothesis. Therefore this is equivalent to $(M^c, \Gamma) \models [\psi]\chi \wedge [\psi]\xi$. By the semantics this is equivalent to $(M^c, \Gamma) \models [\psi](\chi \wedge \xi)$.

the case for $[\psi]K_a\chi$**:** Suppose $[\psi]K_a\chi \in \Gamma$. Given that $[\psi]K_a\chi \in \Phi$, $[\psi]K_a\chi \in \Gamma$ is equivalent to $(\psi \rightarrow K_a[\psi]\chi) \in \Gamma$ by the announcement and knowledge axiom. By item 5 of Lemma 7.33 we can apply the induction hypothesis. Therefore this is equivalent to $(M^c, \Gamma) \models \psi \rightarrow K_a[\psi]\chi$. By the semantics this is equivalent to $(M^c, \Gamma) \models [\psi]K_a\chi$.

the case for $[\psi]C_B\chi$**:** Suppose $[\psi]C_B\chi \in \Gamma$. Given that $[\psi]C_B\chi \in \Phi$, $[\psi]C_B\chi \in \Gamma$ iff every B-ψ-path from Γ is a $[\psi]\chi$-path by item 6 of Lemma 7.31. By item 6 of Lemma 7.33 we can apply the induction hypothesis. Therefore this is equivalent to every B-ψ-path from Γ is a path along which $[\psi]\chi$ is true. By the semantics, this is equivalent to $(M^c, \Gamma) \models [\psi]C_B\chi$.

the case for $[\psi][\chi]\xi$**:** Suppose $[\psi][\chi]\xi \in \Gamma$. Given that $[\psi][\chi]\xi \in \Phi$, $[\psi][\chi]\xi \in \Gamma$ is equivalent to $[\psi \wedge [\psi]\chi]\xi \in \Gamma$ by the announcement composition axiom. By item 7 of Lemma 7.33 we can apply the induction hypothesis. Therefore this is equivalent to $(M^c, \Gamma) \models [\psi \wedge [\psi]\chi]\xi$. This is equivalent to $(M^c, \Gamma) \models [\psi][\chi]\xi$. □

Again the accessibility relations in the canonical model are all equivalence relations.

Lemma 7.35 (Canonicity) The canonical model is reflexive, transitive, and Euclidean. □

Proof This follows straightforwardly from the definition of $\sim_a^c$. □

Now it is easy to prove the completeness theorem.

Theorem 7.36 (Completeness) For every $\varphi \in \mathcal{L}_{KC[]}$

$$\models \varphi \text{ implies } \vdash \varphi$$ □

Proof By contraposition. Suppose $\not\vdash \varphi$. Therefore $\{\neg\varphi\}$ is a consistent set. By the Lindenbaum Lemma there is a set Γ which is maximal consistent in $cl(\neg\varphi)$ such that $\neg\varphi \in \Gamma$. Let M^c be the canonical model for $cl(\neg\varphi)$. By the Truth Lemma $(M^c, \Gamma) \models \neg\varphi$. Therefore $\not\models \varphi$. □

7.6 *AM*: Translating Action Models

Before we consider the full logic *AMC*, we consider the fragment without common knowledge to which we turn in the next section. The completeness proof for **AM** is just like the completeness proof for **PA**. We provide a translation from formulas that contain action modalities to formulas that do not contain action modalities. This translation follows the axioms of the proof system. The proof system **AM** is given in Table 7.5. The axioms that describe the interaction of action models with other logical operators are very similar to the axioms of **PA** that describe the interaction of public announcements and with other logical operators (see Table 7.3). In fact one can see those axioms of **PA** to be special cases of the ones for **AM**. So again these axioms also provide a translation.

Definition 7.37 (Translation) The translation $t : \mathcal{L}_{K\otimes} \to \mathcal{L}_K$ is defined as follows:

$$\begin{aligned} t(p) &= p \\ t(\neg\varphi) &= \neg t(\varphi) \end{aligned}$$

all instantiations of propositional tautologies	
$K_a(\varphi \to \psi) \to (K_a\varphi \to K_a\psi)$	distribution of K_a over $\to$
$K_a\varphi \to \varphi$	truth
$K_a\varphi \to K_aK_a\varphi$	positive introspection
$\neg K_a\varphi \to K_a\neg K_a\varphi$	negative introspection
$[\mathsf{M},\mathsf{s}]p \leftrightarrow (\mathsf{pre}(\mathsf{s}) \to p)$	atomic permanence
$[\mathsf{M},\mathsf{s}]\neg\varphi \leftrightarrow (\mathsf{pre}(\mathsf{s}) \to \neg[\mathsf{M},\mathsf{s}]\varphi)$	action and negation
$[\mathsf{M},\mathsf{s}](\varphi \wedge \psi) \leftrightarrow ([\mathsf{M},\mathsf{s}]\varphi \wedge [\mathsf{M},\mathsf{s}]\psi)$	action and conjunction
$[\mathsf{M},\mathsf{s}]K_a\varphi \leftrightarrow (\mathsf{pre}(\mathsf{s}) \to \bigwedge_{\mathsf{s}\sim_a\mathsf{t}} K_a[\mathsf{M},\mathsf{t}]\varphi)$	action and knowledge
$[\mathsf{M},\mathsf{s}][\mathsf{M}',\mathsf{s}']\varphi \leftrightarrow [(\mathsf{M},\mathsf{s});(\mathsf{M}',\mathsf{s}')]\varphi$	action composition
$[\alpha \cup \alpha']\varphi \leftrightarrow ([\alpha]\varphi \wedge [\alpha']\varphi)$	non-deterministic choice
From φ and $\varphi \to \psi$, infer ψ	modus ponens
From φ, infer $K_a\varphi$	necessitation of K_a
From φ, infer $[\mathsf{M},\mathsf{s}]\varphi$	necessitation of (M,s)

Table 7.5. The proof system **AM**.

$$\begin{array}{ll} t(\varphi \wedge \psi) & = t(\varphi) \wedge t(\psi) \\ t(K_a\varphi) & = K_a t(\varphi) \\ t([\mathsf{M},\mathsf{s}]p) & = t(\mathsf{pre(s)} \rightarrow p) \\ t([\mathsf{M},\mathsf{s}]\neg\varphi) & = t(\mathsf{pre(s)} \rightarrow \neg[\mathsf{M},\mathsf{s}]\varphi) \\ t([\mathsf{M},\mathsf{s}](\varphi \wedge \psi)) & = t([\mathsf{M},\mathsf{s}]\varphi \wedge [\mathsf{M},\mathsf{s}]\psi) \\ t([\mathsf{M},\mathsf{s}]K_a\varphi) & = t(\mathsf{pre(s)} \rightarrow K_a[\mathsf{M},\mathsf{s}]\varphi) \\ t([\mathsf{M},\mathsf{s}][\mathsf{M}',\mathsf{s}']\varphi) & = t([\mathsf{M},\mathsf{s};\mathsf{M}',\mathsf{s}']\chi) \\ t([\alpha \cup \alpha']\varphi) & = t([\alpha]\varphi) \wedge t([\alpha']\varphi) \end{array}$$ □

By the soundness of the proof system this translation preserves the meaning of a formula. All that is left to be shown is that every formula is also provably equivalent to its translation. In order to show this we will also need a different order on the language so that we can apply the induction hypothesis to formulas that are not subformulas of the formulas at hand. We extend the complexity measure for $\mathcal{L}_{K[]}$ to the language with action models and show that it has the desired properties. We also need to assign complexity to action models. We take this to be the maximum of the complexities of preconditions of the action model.

Definition 7.38 (Complexity) The complexity $c : \mathcal{L}_{K\otimes} \rightarrow \mathbb{N}$ is defined as follows:

$$\begin{array}{ll} c(p) & = 1 \\ c(\neg\varphi) & = 1 + c(\varphi) \\ c(\varphi \wedge \psi) & = 1 + \max(c(\varphi), c(\psi)) \\ c(K_a\varphi) & = 1 + c(\varphi) \\ c([\alpha]\varphi) & = (4 + c(\alpha)) \cdot c(\varphi) \\ c(\mathsf{M},\mathsf{s}) & = \max\{c(\mathsf{pre(t)}) \mid \mathsf{t} \in \mathsf{M}\} \\ c(\alpha \cup \alpha') & = 1 + \max(c(\alpha), c(\alpha')) \end{array}$$ □

We can safely take the maximum of the complexity of the preconditions in the action model, since action models are *finite*. Therefore the complexity of a formula or an action model will always be a natural number. Again the number 4 appears in the clause for action models, because it gives us the following properties.

Lemma 7.39 For all φ, ψ, and χ:

1. $c(\psi) \geq c(\varphi)$ if $\varphi \in Sub(\psi)$
2. $c([\mathsf{M},\mathsf{s}]p) > c(\mathsf{pre(s)} \rightarrow p)$
3. $c([\mathsf{M},\mathsf{s}]\neg\varphi) > c(\mathsf{pre(s)} \rightarrow \neg[\mathsf{M},\mathsf{s}]\varphi)$
4. $c([\mathsf{M},\mathsf{s}](\varphi \wedge \psi)) > c([\mathsf{M},\mathsf{s}]\varphi \wedge [\mathsf{M},\mathsf{s}]\psi)$
5. $c([\mathsf{M},\mathsf{s}]K_a\varphi) > c(\mathsf{pre(s)} \rightarrow K_a[\mathsf{M},\mathsf{s}]\varphi)$
6. $c([\mathsf{M},\mathsf{s}][\mathsf{M}',\mathsf{s}']\varphi) > c([\mathsf{M},\mathsf{s};\mathsf{M}',\mathsf{s}']\varphi)$
7. $c([\alpha \cup \alpha']\varphi) > c([\alpha]\varphi \wedge [\alpha']\varphi)$ □

Proof The proof is very similar to that of Lemma 7.23 □

Now we can prove the lemma that says that every formula is provably equivalent to its translation.

Lemma 7.40 For all formulas $\varphi \in \mathcal{L}_{K\otimes}$ it is the case that

$$\vdash \varphi \leftrightarrow t(\varphi)$$ □

Proof The proof is very similar to the proof of Lemma 7.24 □

Completeness follows automatically.

Theorem 7.41 (Completeness) For every $\varphi \in \mathcal{L}_{K\otimes}$

$$\models \varphi \text{ implies } \vdash \varphi$$ □

Proof Suppose $\models \varphi$. Therefore $\models t(\varphi)$, by the soundness of the proof system and $\mathbf{AM} \vdash \varphi \leftrightarrow t(\varphi)$ (Lemma 7.40). The formula $t(\varphi)$ does not contain any action models. Therefore $\mathbf{S5} \vdash t(\varphi)$ by completeness of **S5** (Theorem 7.7). We also have that $\mathbf{AM} \vdash t(\varphi)$, as **S5** is a subsystem of **AM**. Since $\mathbf{AM} \vdash \varphi \leftrightarrow t(\varphi)$, it follows that $\mathbf{AM} \vdash \varphi$. □

7.7 *AMC*: Generalising the Proof for *PAC*

In this section we prove completeness for *AMC*. The proof system **AMC** is given in Table 7.6. The proof system is a lot like the proof system for *PAC*, but now it deals with more general epistemic actions. Still, the axioms are quite similar.

Definition 7.42 (Closure) Let $cl : \mathcal{L}_{KC\otimes} \rightarrow \wp(\mathcal{L}_{KC\otimes})$, such that for every $\varphi \in \mathcal{L}_{KC\otimes}$, $cl(\varphi)$ is the smallest set such that:

1. $\varphi \in cl(\varphi)$,
2. if $\psi \in cl(\varphi)$, then $Sub(\psi) \subseteq cl(\varphi)$,
3. if $\psi \in cl(\varphi)$ and ψ is not a negation, then $\neg\psi \in cl(\varphi)$,
4. if $C_B\psi \in cl(\varphi)$, then $\{K_a C_B \psi \mid a \in B\} \subseteq cl(\varphi)$,
5. if $[\mathsf{M},\mathsf{s}]p \in cl(\varphi)$, then $(\mathsf{pre}(\mathsf{s}) \rightarrow p) \in cl(\varphi)$,
6. if $[\mathsf{M},\mathsf{s}]\neg\psi \in cl(\varphi)$, then $(\mathsf{pre}(\mathsf{s}) \rightarrow \neg[\mathsf{M},\mathsf{s}]\psi) \in cl(\varphi)$,
7. if $[\mathsf{M},\mathsf{s}](\psi \wedge \chi) \in cl(\varphi)$, then $([\mathsf{M},\mathsf{s}]\psi \wedge [\mathsf{M},\mathsf{s}]\chi) \in cl(\varphi)$,
8. if $[\mathsf{M},\mathsf{s}]K_a\psi \in cl(\varphi)$ and $\mathsf{s} \sim_a \mathsf{t}$, then $(\mathsf{pre}(\mathsf{s}) \rightarrow K_a[\mathsf{M},\mathsf{t}]\psi) \in cl(\varphi)$,
9. if $[\mathsf{M},\mathsf{s}]C_B\psi \in cl(\varphi)$, then $\{[\mathsf{M},\mathsf{t}]\psi \mid \mathsf{s} \sim_B \mathsf{t}\} \subseteq cl(\varphi)$ and $\{K_a[\mathsf{M},\mathsf{t}]C_B\psi \mid a \in B \text{ and } \mathsf{s} \sim_B \mathsf{t}\} \subseteq cl(\varphi)$,
10. if $[\mathsf{M},\mathsf{s}][\mathsf{M}',\mathsf{s}']\psi \in cl(\varphi)$, then $[(\mathsf{M},\mathsf{s});(\mathsf{M}',\mathsf{s}')]\psi \in cl(\varphi)$,
11. if $[\alpha \cup \alpha']\psi \in cl(\varphi)$, then $([\alpha]\psi \wedge [\alpha']\psi) \in cl(\varphi)$. □

Lemma 7.43 $cl(\varphi)$ is finite for all formulas $\varphi \in \mathcal{L}_{KC\otimes}$. □

Proof The proof is just like the proof of Lemma 7.9. Note that action models are finite, and only finitely many of them occur in a formula. □

all instantiations of propositional tautologies	
$K_a(\varphi \to \psi) \to (K_a\varphi \to K_a\psi)$	distribution of K_a over $\to$
$K_a\varphi \to \varphi$	truth
$K_a\varphi \to K_aK_a\varphi$	positive introspection
$\neg K_a\varphi \to K_a\neg K_a\varphi$	negative introspection
$[\mathsf{M},\mathsf{s}]p \leftrightarrow (\mathsf{pre}(\mathsf{s}) \to p)$	atomic permanence
$[\mathsf{M},\mathsf{s}]\neg\varphi \leftrightarrow (\mathsf{pre}(\mathsf{s}) \to \neg[\mathsf{M},\mathsf{s}]\varphi)$	action and negation
$[\mathsf{M},\mathsf{s}](\varphi \wedge \psi) \leftrightarrow ([\mathsf{M},\mathsf{s}]\varphi \wedge [\mathsf{M},\mathsf{s}]\psi)$	action and conjunction
$[\mathsf{M},\mathsf{s}]K_a\varphi \leftrightarrow (\mathsf{pre}(\mathsf{s}) \to \bigwedge_{\mathsf{s}\sim_a\mathsf{t}} K_a[\mathsf{M},\mathsf{t}]\varphi)$	action and knowledge
$[\mathsf{M},\mathsf{s}][\mathsf{M}',\mathsf{s}']\varphi \leftrightarrow [(\mathsf{M},\mathsf{s});(\mathsf{M}',\mathsf{s}')]\varphi$	action composition
$[\alpha \cup \alpha']\varphi \leftrightarrow ([\alpha]\varphi \wedge [\alpha']\varphi)$	non-deterministic choice
$C_B(\varphi \to \psi) \to (C_B\varphi \to C_B\psi)$	distribution of C_B over $\to$
$C_B\varphi \to (\varphi \wedge E_BC_B\varphi)$	mix
$C_B(\varphi \to E_B\varphi) \to (\varphi \to C_B\varphi)$	induction axiom
From φ and $\varphi \to \psi$, infer ψ	modus ponens
From φ, infer $K_a\varphi$	necessitation of K_a
From φ, infer $C_B\varphi$	necessitation of C_B
From φ, infer $[\mathsf{M},\mathsf{s}]\varphi$	necessitation of (M,s)
Let (M,s) be an action model and let a set of formulas χ_t for every t such that $\mathsf{s} \sim_B \mathsf{t}$ be given. From $\chi_\mathsf{t} \to [\mathsf{M},\mathsf{t}]\varphi$ and $(\chi_\mathsf{t} \wedge \mathsf{pre}(\mathsf{t})) \to K_a\chi_\mathsf{u}$ for every $\mathsf{t} \in \mathsf{S}$, $a \in B$ and $\mathsf{t} \sim_a \mathsf{u}$, infer $\chi_\mathsf{s} \to [\mathsf{M},\mathsf{s}]C_B\varphi$.	action and common knowledge

Table 7.6. The proof system **AMC**.

Again, many definitions and lemmas work in precisely the same way as in the case for *S5* with common knowledge. The notions of maximal consistent in Φ and the canonical model for Φ are just as before. Also the Lindenbaum Lemma is proved in the same way as before.

Lemma 7.44 (Lindenbaum) Let Φ be the closure of some formula. Every consistent subset of Φ is a subset of a maximal consistent set in Φ. □

Proof The proof is just like the proof of Lemma 7.12. □

Semantically it is quite clear what it means for a formula of the form $[\mathsf{M},\mathsf{s}]C_B\varphi$ to be true in a state s. It means that every B-path from (s,s) in the resulting model ends in a φ-state. But that means that in the original model, a B-path for which there is a matching B-path $\mathsf{s}_0,\dots \mathsf{s}_n$ in the action model ends in a $[\mathsf{M},\mathsf{s}_n]\varphi$-state. This is shown in Figure 7.1. In view of this, in the proofs we will use the notion of a $B\mathsf{Mst}$-path.

Definition 7.45 (BMst-path) A $B\mathsf{Mst}$-path from Γ is a B-path $\Gamma_0,\dots\Gamma_n$ from Γ such that there is a B-path $\mathsf{s}_0,\dots \mathsf{s}_n$ from s to t in M and for all $k < n$ there is an agent $a \in B$ such that $\Gamma_k \sim_a^c \Gamma_{k+1}$ and $\mathsf{s}_k \sim_a \mathsf{s}_{k+1}$ and for all $k \leq n$ it is the case that $\mathsf{pre}(\mathsf{s}_k) \in \Gamma_k$. □

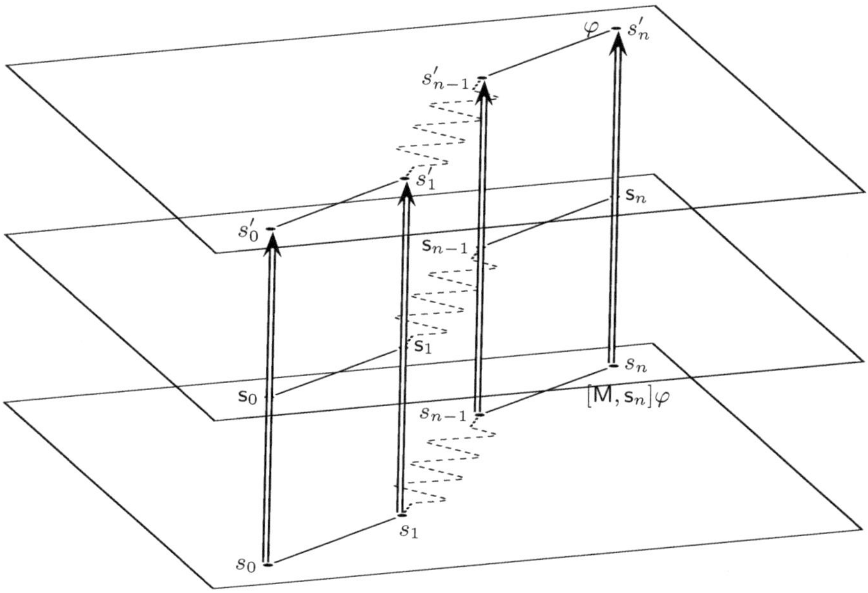

Figure 7.1. This Figure helps to make the semantic intuition for formulas of the form $[\mathsf{M}, \mathsf{s}]C_B\varphi$ clearer. The model below is the original model. The model in the middle is the action model. The top model is the resulting model.

Lemma 7.46 Let Φ be the closure of some formula. Let $M^c = (S^c, \sim^c, V^c)$ be the canonical model for Φ. If Γ and Δ are maximal consistent sets in Φ, then

1. Γ is deductively closed in Φ,
2. if $\neg\varphi \in \Phi$, then $\varphi \in \Gamma$ iff $\neg\varphi \notin \Gamma$,
3. if $(\varphi \wedge \psi) \in \Phi$, then $(\varphi \wedge \psi) \in \Gamma$ iff $\varphi \in \Gamma$ and $\psi \in \Gamma$,
4. if $\underline{\Gamma} \wedge \hat{K}_a\underline{\Delta}$ is consistent, then $\Gamma \sim^c_a \Delta$,
5. if $K_a\psi \in \Phi$, then $\{K_a\varphi \mid K_a\varphi \in \Gamma\} \vdash \psi$ iff $\{K_a\varphi \mid K_a\varphi \in \Gamma\} \vdash K_a\psi$,
6. if $C_B\varphi \in \Phi$, then $C_B\varphi \in \Gamma$ iff every B-path from Γ is a φ-path,
7. if $[\mathsf{M}, \mathsf{s}]C_B\varphi \in \Phi$, then $[\mathsf{M}, \mathsf{s}]C_B\varphi \in \Gamma$ iff for all $\mathsf{t} \in \mathsf{S}$ every $B\mathsf{Mst}$-path from Γ ends in an $[\mathsf{M}, \mathsf{t}]\varphi$-state. □

Proof The proofs of 1 – 6 are similar to the proofs of 1 – 6 of of Lemma 7.31. The proof of 7 is also rather similar to that of the proof of 7 of Lemma 7.31.

7. From left to right. Suppose $[\mathsf{M}, \mathsf{s}]C_B\varphi \in \Gamma$. We now continue by induction on the length of the path, but we load the induction. We show that if $[\mathsf{M}, \mathsf{s}]C_B\varphi \in \Gamma$, then every $B\mathsf{Mst}$-path ends in an $[\mathsf{M}, \mathsf{t}]\varphi$-state which is also an $[\mathsf{M}, \mathsf{t}]C_B\varphi$-state.
   Base case Suppose the length of the path is 0. Therefore we merely need to show that if $[\mathsf{M}, \mathsf{s}]C_B\varphi \in \Gamma_0$, then $[\mathsf{M}, \mathsf{s}]\varphi \in \Gamma_0$. This can

be shown as follows. Observe that $C_B\varphi \rightarrow \varphi$. By necessitation and distribution of $[\mathsf{M},\mathsf{s}]$ we have that $[\mathsf{M},\mathsf{s}]C_B\varphi \rightarrow [\mathsf{M},\mathsf{s}]\varphi$. $[\mathsf{M},\mathsf{s}]\varphi \in \Phi$ by Definition 7.42. Therefore $[\mathsf{M},\mathsf{s}]\varphi \in \Gamma_0$.

Induction hypothesis Every $B\mathsf{Mst}$-path of length n ends in an $[\mathsf{M},\mathsf{t}]\varphi$-state which is also an $[\mathsf{M},\mathsf{t}]C_B\varphi$-state.

Induction step Suppose now that the path is of length $n+1$, i.e., there is a $B\mathsf{Mst}$-path $\Gamma_0,\ldots\Gamma_n,\Gamma_{n+1}$. Therefore there is a $B\mathsf{Msu}$-path for some u from Γ_0 to Γ_n. By the induction hypothesis we may assume that $[\mathsf{M},\mathsf{u}]C_B\varphi \in \Gamma_n$. Since there is a $B\mathsf{Mst}$-path, there is an agent $a \in B$ such that $\Gamma_n \sim_a^c \Gamma_{n+1}$ and $\mathsf{u} \sim_a \mathsf{t}$. By the mix axiom we have that $\vdash C_B\psi \rightarrow K_aC_B\psi$. By applying necessitation and distribution of $[\mathsf{M},\mathsf{u}]$ we get $\vdash [\mathsf{M},\mathsf{u}]C_B\varphi \rightarrow [\mathsf{M},\mathsf{u}]K_aC_B\varphi$. By the axiom for action and knowledge $\vdash [\mathsf{M},\mathsf{u}]K_aC_B\varphi \rightarrow (\mathsf{pre}(\mathsf{u}) \rightarrow K_a[\mathsf{M},\mathsf{t}]C_B\varphi)$. Since $\mathsf{pre}(\mathsf{u}) \in \Gamma_n$, it must be the case that $\Gamma_n \vdash K_a[\mathsf{M},\mathsf{t}]C_B\varphi$. Therefore by the definition of $\sim_a^c$ and Definition 7.42, it is the case that $K_a[\mathsf{M},\mathsf{t}]C_B\varphi \in \Gamma_{n+1}$, and so $[\mathsf{M},\mathsf{t}]C_B\psi \in \Gamma_{n+1}$. And, by similar reasoning as in the base case, $[\mathsf{M},\mathsf{t}]\psi \in \Gamma_{n+1}$.

From right to left. Suppose that every $B\mathsf{Mst}$-path from Γ ends in an $[\mathsf{M},\mathsf{t}]\varphi$-state. Let $S_{B,\mathsf{M},\mathsf{t},\varphi}$ be the set of maximal consistent sets in Φ, Δ such that every $B\mathsf{Mtu}$-path from Δ ends in an $[\mathsf{M},\mathsf{u}]\varphi$-state for all u such that $\mathsf{t} \sim_B \mathsf{u}$. Now consider the formulas

$$\chi_{\mathsf{t}} = \bigvee_{\Delta \in S_{B,\mathsf{M},\mathsf{t},\varphi}} \underline{\Delta}$$

We will show the following

$$\vdash \underline{\Gamma} \rightarrow \chi_{\mathsf{s}} \tag{a}$$

$$\vdash \chi_{\mathsf{t}} \rightarrow [\mathsf{M},\mathsf{t}]\varphi \tag{b}$$

$$\vdash (\chi_{\mathsf{t}} \wedge \mathsf{pre}(\mathsf{t})) \rightarrow K_a\chi_{\mathsf{u}} \text{ if } a \in B \text{ and } \mathsf{t} \sim_a \mathsf{u} \tag{c}$$

From these it follows that $[\mathsf{M},\mathsf{s}]C_B\varphi \in \Gamma$. By applying the action and common knowledge rule to (b) and (c) it follows that $\vdash \chi_{\mathsf{s}} \rightarrow [\mathsf{M},\mathsf{s}]C_B\varphi$. By (a) it follows that $\vdash \underline{\Gamma} \rightarrow [\mathsf{M},\mathsf{s}]C_B\varphi$. Therefore $[\mathsf{M},\mathsf{s}]C_B\varphi \in \Gamma$.

a) This follows immediately, because $\Gamma \in S_{B,\mathsf{M},\mathsf{s},\varphi}$, and $\underline{\Gamma}$ is one of χ_{s}'s disjuncts.
b) Since every $B\mathsf{Mtu}\varphi$-path ends in an $[\mathsf{M},\mathsf{u}]\varphi$-state for every $\Delta \in S_{B,\mathsf{M},\mathsf{t},\varphi}$ it must be the case that the length one $B\mathsf{Mtt}\varphi$-path ends in an $[\mathsf{M},\mathsf{t}]\varphi$-state. Therefore $[\mathsf{M},\mathsf{t}]\varphi \in \Delta$. Therefore, $[\mathsf{M},\mathsf{t}]\varphi$ is one of the conjuncts in every disjunct of χ_{t}. Therefore by propositional reasoning $\chi_{\mathsf{t}} \rightarrow [\mathsf{M},\mathsf{t}]\varphi$.
c) Suppose toward a contradiction that $\chi_{\mathsf{t}} \wedge \mathsf{pre}(\mathsf{t}) \wedge \neg K_a\chi_{\mathsf{u}}$ is consistent. Because χ_{t} is a disjunction there must be a disjunct $\underline{\Theta}$ such that $\underline{\Theta} \wedge \mathsf{pre}(\mathsf{t}) \wedge \neg K_a\chi_{\mathsf{u}}$ is consistent. Since $\underline{\Theta}$ is maximal consistent in Φ and $\mathsf{pre}(\mathsf{t}) \in \Phi$ it must be the case that $\mathsf{pre}(\mathsf{t}) \in \Theta$. So $\underline{\Theta} \wedge \hat{K}_a\neg\chi_{\mathsf{u}}$ is consistent. Since $\vdash \bigvee\{\underline{\Gamma} \mid \Gamma \in S^c\}$, there must be a Ξ in the complement

of $S_{B,\mathsf{M},\mathsf{u},\varphi}$ such that $\underline{\Theta} \wedge \hat{K}_a \Xi$ is consistent. By item 4 of Lemma 7.46 this is equivalent to $\Theta \sim_a^c \Xi$. But since Ξ is not in $S_{B,\mathsf{M},\mathsf{u},\varphi}$ there must be an v such that there is a $B\mathsf{Muv}$-path not ending in an $[\mathsf{M},\mathsf{v}]\varphi$-state from Ξ. But then there is also a $B\mathsf{Mtv}$-path from Θ not ending in an $[\mathsf{M},\mathsf{v}]\varphi$-state. This contradicts that $\Theta \in S_{B,\mathsf{M},\mathsf{t},\varphi}$, but it must be, because $\underline{\Theta}$ is one of χ_t's disjuncts. Therefore $\vdash (\chi_\mathsf{t} \wedge \mathsf{pre}(\mathsf{t})) \to K_a\chi_\mathsf{u}$.□

We extend the complexity measure of Definition 7.38 to the full language of *AMC*. The only extra case is that of common knowledge, which is treated in the same way as individual knowledge.

Definition 7.47 (Complexity) The complexity $c : \mathcal{L}_{KC\otimes} \to \mathbb{N}$ is defined as follows:

$$\begin{array}{ll} c(p) & = 1 \\ c(\neg\varphi) & = 1 + c(\varphi) \\ c(\varphi \wedge \psi) & = 1 + \max(c(\varphi), c(\psi)) \\ c(K_a\varphi) & = 1 + c(\varphi) \\ c(C_B\varphi) & = 1 + c(\varphi) \\ c([\alpha]\varphi) & = (4 + c(\alpha)) \cdot c(\varphi) \\ c(\mathsf{M},\mathsf{s}) & = \max\{c(\mathsf{pre}(\mathsf{t})) \mid \mathsf{t} \in \mathsf{M}\} \\ c(\alpha \cup \alpha') & = 1 + \max(c(\alpha), c(\alpha')) \end{array}$$

□

Lemma 7.48 For all φ, ψ, and χ:

1. $c(\psi) \geq c(\varphi)$ for all $\varphi \in Sub(\psi)$.
2. $c([\mathsf{M},\mathsf{s}]p) > c(\mathsf{pre}(\mathsf{s}) \to p)$
3. $c([\mathsf{M},\mathsf{s}]\neg\varphi) > c(\mathsf{pre}(\mathsf{s}) \to \neg[\mathsf{M},\mathsf{s}]\varphi)$
4. $c([\mathsf{M},\mathsf{s}](\varphi \wedge \psi)) > c([\mathsf{M},\mathsf{s}]\varphi \wedge [\mathsf{M},\mathsf{s}]\varphi)$
5. $c([\mathsf{M},\mathsf{s}]K_a\varphi) > c(\mathsf{pre}(\mathsf{s}) \to K_a[\mathsf{M},\mathsf{t}]\varphi)$ for all $\mathsf{t} \in \mathsf{M}$
6. $c([\mathsf{M},\mathsf{s}]C_B\varphi) > c([\mathsf{M},\mathsf{t}]\varphi)$ for all $\mathsf{t} \in \mathsf{M}$
7. $c([\mathsf{M},\mathsf{s}][\mathsf{M}',\mathsf{s}']\varphi) > c([(\mathsf{M},\mathsf{s});(\mathsf{M}',\mathsf{s}')]\varphi)$
8. $c([\alpha \cup \alpha']\varphi) > c([\alpha]\varphi \wedge [\alpha']\varphi)$ □

Exercise 7.49 Prove Lemma 7.48. □

Lemma 7.50 (Truth) Let Φ be the closure for some formula. Let $M^c = (S^c, \sim^c, V^c)$ be the canonical model for Φ. For all $\Gamma \in S^c$, and all $\varphi \in \Phi$:

$$\varphi \in \Gamma \text{ iff } (M^c, \Gamma) \models \varphi$$

□

Proof The proof is very much like the proof of Lemma 7.34 □

Lemma 7.51 (Canonicity) The canonical model is reflexive, transitive, and Euclidean. □

Proof This follows straightforwardly from the definition of $\sim_a^c$. □

Now it is easy to prove the completeness theorem.

Theorem 7.52 (Completeness) For every $\varphi \in \mathcal{L}_{KC\otimes}$

$$\models \varphi \text{ implies } \vdash \varphi \qquad \square$$

Proof By contraposition. Suppose $\not\vdash \varphi$. Therefore $\{\neg\varphi\}$ is a consistent set. By the Lindenbaum Lemma there is a set Γ which is maximal consistent in $cl(\neg\varphi)$ such that $\neg\varphi \in \Gamma$. Let M^c be the canonical model for $cl(\neg\varphi)$. By the Truth Lemma $(M^c, \Gamma) \models \neg\varphi$. Therefore $\not\models \varphi$. $\square$

7.8 Relativised Common Knowledge

In Sections 7.4 to 7.7 we saw two fairly easy completeness proofs of **PA** and **AM** that used translations, and two quite difficult completeness proofs of **PAC** and **AMC**. This could lead one to suspect that the addition of update modalities to a base epistemic logic without common knowledge leads to an easy completeness proof and that adding update modalities to a base logic with common knowledge precludes an easy completeness proof via translation. This section will introduce a logic that does contain a common knowledge operator *and* allows an easy completeness proof when we add public announcements to the language. The reader not interested in this rather technical excursion can skip this section.

The logic that we introduce below contains a *relativised common knowledge* operator. This is a dyadic operator which is quite like ordinary common knowledge. To understand why this operator allows a completeness proof by translation, we first investigate why such an approach did not work in the case of **PAC**. In the proof of Lemma 7.31 which was used for the completeness proof for **PAC** the crucial property that was to be proved was that given that $[\varphi]C_B\psi$ is in the closure:

$$[\varphi]C_B\psi \in \Gamma \text{ iff every } B\text{-}\varphi\text{-path is a } [\varphi]\psi\text{-path.}$$

The problem for a translation is that what is on the right hand side of the equivalence cannot be expressed without public announcement operators. We cannot say anything about all B-φ-paths in the language of *S5C*. (This claim will be made more precise in the next chapter.) The idea is that with a relativised common knowledge operator we can. In Section 7.8.1 we give the language, semantics and a sound and complete proof system for the epistemic logic with relativised common knowledge. In subsection 7.8.2 we provide the completeness proof for public announcement logic with relativised common knowledge.

7.8.1 Language, Semantics, and Completeness

Our aim is now to define *S5RC*, the validities of relativised common knowledge. The language is defined as follows.

Definition 7.53 Given are a set of agents A and a set of atoms P. The language $\mathcal{L}_{KRC}$ consists of all formulas given by the following BNF:

$$\varphi ::= p \mid \neg\varphi \mid (\varphi \wedge \varphi) \mid K_a\varphi \mid C_B(\varphi, \varphi)$$

where $p \in P$, $a \in A$ and $B \subseteq A$. □

The idea is that $C_B(\varphi, \psi)$ expresses that every B-φ-path is a ψ-path. In this way we can express something about B-φ-paths without public announcements. The exact semantics of this operator are as follows.

Definition 7.54 (Semantics) Given is an epistemic model $M = \langle S, \sim, V\rangle$. The semantics for atoms, negations, conjunctions, and individual operators are as usual.

$$\begin{array}{c}(M, s) \models C_B(\varphi, \psi) \\ \text{iff} \\ (M, t) \models \psi \text{ for all } t \text{ such that } (s, t) \in (\bigcup_{a \in B} \sim_a \cap (S \times [\![\varphi]\!]_M))^+\end{array}$$

where $in(\bigcup_{a\in B} \sim_a \cap(S \times [\![\varphi]\!]_M))^+$ is the *transitive* closure of in $(\bigcup_{a\in B} \sim_a \cap(S \times [\![\varphi]\!]_M))$. Let us call *S5RC* the validities of the language $\mathcal{L}_{KRC}$ under this semantics. □

We use the transitive closure in the definition rather than the *reflexive* transitive closure, because we do not want $C_B(\varphi, \psi)$ to imply that ψ, but merely that $E_B(\varphi \to \psi)$. The operator is quite like ordinary common knowledge. In fact, we can express ordinary common knowledge with relativised common knowledge. The formula $\varphi \wedge C_B(\top, \varphi)$ expresses that every B-$\top$-path is a φ-path. Since every B-path is a B-$\top$-path, it expresses that every B-path is a φ-path, which is to say that φ is ordinary common knowledge. The proof system for epistemic logic with relativised common knowledge is also very much like that of **S5C**.

Definition 7.55 (Proof system) The proof system **S5RC** consists of the axioms and rules of Table 7.7. □

The axioms concerning relativised common knowledge are generalisations of the axioms for ordinary common knowledge (cf. Table 7.2).

Theorem 7.56 The proof system **S5RC** is sound, i.e., if $\vdash \varphi$, then $\models \varphi$. □

Exercise 7.57 Prove Theorem 7.56. □

The structure of the completeness proof for this logic is similar to that for **S5C**. We need to adapt the definition of the closure of a formula, and some of the steps in the proofs are more complicated, but other than that there are little differences.

Definition 7.58 (Closure) Let $cl : \mathcal{L}_{KRC} \to \wp(\mathcal{L}_{KRC})$, be the function such that for every $\varphi \in \mathcal{L}_{KRC}$, $cl(\varphi)$ is the smallest set such that:

all instantiations of propositional tautologies	
$K_a(\varphi \rightarrow \psi) \rightarrow (K_a\varphi \rightarrow K_a\psi)$	distribution of K_a over $\rightarrow$
$K_a\varphi \rightarrow \varphi$	truth
$K_a\varphi \rightarrow K_aK_a\varphi$	positive introspection
$\neg K_a\varphi \rightarrow K_a\neg K_a\varphi$	negative introspection
$C_B(\varphi, \psi \rightarrow \chi) \rightarrow (C_B(\varphi, \psi) \rightarrow C_B(\varphi, \chi))$	distribution of $C_B(\cdot,\cdot)$ over $\rightarrow$
$C_B(\varphi, \psi) \leftrightarrow E_B(\varphi \rightarrow (\psi \wedge C_B(\varphi, \psi)))$	mix of relativised common knowledge
$C_B(\varphi, \psi \rightarrow E_B(\varphi \rightarrow \psi)) \rightarrow (E_B(\varphi \rightarrow \psi) \rightarrow C_B(\varphi, \psi))$	induction of relativised common knowledge
From φ and $\varphi \rightarrow \psi$, infer ψ	modus ponens
From φ, infer $K_a\varphi$	necessitation of K_a
From φ, infer $C_B(\psi, \varphi)$	necessitation of $C_B(\cdot,\cdot)$

Table 7.7. The proof system **S5RC**.

1. $\varphi \in cl(\varphi)$,
2. if $\psi \in cl(\varphi)$, then $Sub(\psi) \subseteq cl(\varphi)$,
3. if $\psi \in cl(\varphi)$ and ψ is not a negation, then $\neg\psi \in cl(\varphi)$,
4. if $C_B(\psi, \chi) \in cl(\varphi)$, then $\{K_a(\psi \rightarrow (\chi \wedge C_B(\psi, \chi))) \mid a \in B\} \subseteq cl(\varphi)$. □

Lemma 7.59 $cl(\varphi)$ is finite for all $\varphi \in \mathcal{L}_{KRC}$. □

Proof The proof is analogous to that of Lemma 7.9 □

The notions of maximal consistency in Φ and the canonical model are the same as before. The Lindenbaum Lemma is also the same as before and we get the same properties of maximal consistent sets as before. The only additional proof obligation is the following lemma.

Lemma 7.60 Let Φ be the closure of some formula. Let $M^c = (S^c, \sim^c, V^c)$ be the canonical model for Φ. Let Γ be a maximal consistent set in Φ. If $C_B(\varphi, \psi) \in \Phi$, then $C_B(\varphi, \psi) \in \Gamma$ iff every B-φ-path from a $\Delta \in S^c$ such that there is an agent $a \in B$ and $\Gamma \sim_a^c \Delta$ is a ψ-path. □

Proof From left to right. Suppose that $C_B(\varphi, \psi) \in \Gamma$. If there are no B-φ-paths from a Δ that is B-reachable from Γ we are done. Otherwise we proceed by induction on the length of the B-φ-path, but we load the induction. We show that if $C_B(\varphi, \psi) \in \Gamma$, then every B-φ-path from a B-reachable state from Γ is a ψ-path and a $C_B(\varphi, \psi)$-path.

Base case Suppose that the length of the B-φ-path is 0, i.e. $\Delta = \Delta_0 = \Delta_n$. Given that there are B-φ-paths from Δ, it must be the case that $\varphi \in \Delta$. Since $\vdash C_B(\varphi, \psi) \rightarrow E_B(\varphi \rightarrow (\psi \wedge C_B(\varphi, \psi)))$ (by the mix axiom) and $\vdash E_B(\varphi \rightarrow (\psi \wedge C_B(\varphi, \psi))) \rightarrow (\varphi \rightarrow (\psi \wedge C_B(\varphi, \psi)))$ and Δ is deductively closed in Φ, we can conclude that $\psi \in \Delta$ and $C_B(\varphi, \psi) \in \Delta$.

Induction hypothesis If $C_B(\varphi, \psi) \in \Gamma$, then every B-φ-path from a B-reachable state from Γ of length n is a ψ-path and a $C_B(\varphi, \psi)$-path.

Induction step Take a B-φ-path of length $n+1$ from Δ. By the induction hypothesis $C_B(\varphi,\psi) \in \Delta_n$. Let a be the agent in B such that $\Gamma_n \sim_a^c \Gamma_{n+1}$. Since $\vdash C_B(\varphi,\psi) \to E_B(\varphi \to (\psi \wedge C_B(\varphi,\psi)))$ and $\vdash E_B(\varphi \to (\psi \wedge C_B(\varphi,\psi))) \to K_a(\varphi \to (\psi \wedge C_B(\varphi,\psi)))$, it must be the case that $\varphi \to (\psi \wedge C_B(\varphi,\psi)) \in \Delta_{n+1}$ by the definition of $\sim_a^c$. Since Δ_{n+1} is part of a B-φ-path, it must be the case that $\varphi \in \Delta_{n+1}$. By similar reasoning as in the base case, $\psi \in \Gamma_{n+1}$ and $C_B(\varphi,\psi) \in \Gamma_{n+1}$.

From right to left. Suppose that every B-φ-path from B-reachable states from Γ is a ψ-path. Let $S_{B,\varphi,\psi}$ be the set of all maximal consistent sets Δ such that every B-φ-path from Δ is a ψ-path. Now consider the formula

$$\chi = \bigvee_{\Delta \in S_{B,\varphi,\psi}} \underline{\Delta}$$

We prove the following

$$\vdash \underline{\Gamma} \to E_B\chi \tag{1}$$
$$\vdash \chi \to (\varphi \to \psi) \tag{2}$$
$$\vdash \chi \to E_B(\varphi \to \chi) \tag{3}$$

From these it follows that $C_B(\varphi,\psi) \in \Gamma$. Because from (3) it follows by necessitation that $\vdash C_B(\varphi, \chi \to E_B(\varphi \to \chi))$. By the induction axiom this implies that $\vdash E_B(\varphi \to \chi) \to C_B(\varphi,\chi)$. By (3) this implies that $\vdash \chi \to C_B(\varphi,\chi)$. By (b) and necessitation and distribution of $C_B(\varphi,\cdot)$ this implies that $\vdash \chi \to C_B(\varphi, \varphi \to \psi)$. By the induction axiom we get $\vdash C(\varphi,\varphi)$, and therefore $\vdash \chi \to C_B(\varphi,\psi)$. By necessitation, (1) and distribution we get $\vdash \underline{\Gamma} \to E_B C_B(\varphi,\psi)$. Therefore, by the truth axiom, $\vdash \underline{\Gamma} \to C_B(\varphi,\psi)$. Therefore $C_B(\varphi,\psi) \in \Gamma$.

1. Suppose towards a contradiction that $\underline{\Gamma} \wedge \neg E_B\chi$ is consistent. That means that $\underline{\Gamma} \wedge \bigvee_{a\in B} \neg K_a\chi$ is consistent. Therefore there is an agent $a \in B$ such that $\underline{\Gamma} \wedge \neg K_a\chi$ is consistent. Therefore $\underline{\Gamma} \wedge \hat{K}_a\neg\chi$ is consistent. Again we can prove that $\vdash \bigvee\{\underline{\Delta} \mid \Delta \in S^c\}$. Let $\overline{\chi}$ be $\bigvee(S^c \setminus S_{B,\varphi,\psi})$. It is clear that $\neg\chi \leftrightarrow \overline{\chi}$. Therefore $\underline{\Gamma} \wedge \hat{K}_a\overline{\chi}$ is consistent. Since $\overline{\chi}$ is a disjunction, there must be a $\Delta \in (S^c \setminus S_{B,\varphi,\psi})$ such that $\underline{\Gamma} \wedge \hat{K}_a\underline{\Delta}$ is consistent. From this we can conclude that $\Gamma \sim_a^c \Delta$. This contradicts the assumption that every B-φ-path from B-reachable states from Γ is a ψ-path, since $\Delta \notin S_{B,\varphi,\psi}$
2. Note that $\vdash \underline{\Delta} \to (\varphi \to \psi)$ if Δ is in $S_{B,\varphi,\psi}$. Therefore $\varphi \to \psi$ follows from every disjunct of χ. Therefore $\vdash \chi \to (\varphi \to \psi)$.
3. Suppose toward a contradiction that $\chi \wedge \neg E_B(\varphi \to \chi)$ is consistent. Since χ is a disjunction there must be a disjunct $\underline{\Delta}$ such that $\underline{\Delta} \wedge \neg E_B(\varphi \to \chi)$ is consistent. By similar reasoning there must be an $a \in B$ such that $\underline{\Delta} \wedge \hat{K}_a(\varphi \wedge \neg\chi)$ is consistent. Since $\vdash \bigvee\{\underline{\Delta} \mid \Delta \in S^c\}$, it is the case that $\underline{\Delta} \wedge \hat{K}_a(\varphi \wedge \bigvee_{\Theta \notin S_{B,\varphi,\psi}} \underline{\Theta})$ is consistent. Then, by modal reasoning, $\underline{\Delta} \wedge \bigvee_{\Theta \notin S_{B,\varphi,\psi}} \hat{K}_a(\varphi \wedge \underline{\Theta})$ is consistent. Therefore there must be a $\Theta \notin S_{B,\varphi,\psi}$

which is maximal consistent in Φ, such that $\underline{\Delta} \wedge \hat{K}_a(\varphi \wedge \underline{\Theta})$ is consistent. But then $\Delta \sim_a^c \Theta$ and $\varphi \in \Theta$. Since Θ is not in $S_{B,\varphi,\psi}$, there must be a B-φ-path from Θ which is not a ψ-path. But then there is a B-φ-path from Δ which is not a ψ-path. This contradicts that $\Delta \in S_{B,\varphi,\psi}$, which it is because $\underline{\Delta}$ is one of χ's disjuncts. Therefore $\vdash \chi \to E_B(\varphi \to \chi)$. □

This is the extra lemma we need for the Truth lemma.

Lemma 7.61 (Truth) Let Φ be the closure of some formula. Let $M^c = (S^c, \sim^c, V^c)$ be the canonical model for Φ. For all $\Gamma \in S^c$, and all $\varphi \in \Phi$:

$$\varphi \in \Gamma \text{ iff } (M^c, \Gamma) \models \varphi$$

□

Proof Suppose $\varphi \in \Phi$. We proceed by induction on φ. The cases for propositional variables, negations, conjunction, and individual epistemic operators are the same as in the proof of Lemma 7.17. Therefore we focus on the case for relativised common knowledge.

Suppose that $C_B(\varphi, \psi) \in \Gamma$. From Lemma 7.60 it follows that this is the case iff every B-φ-path from Γ is a ψ-path. By the induction hypothesis this is the case iff every B-path where φ is true along the path, is a path along which ψ is true as well. By the semantics this is equivalent to $(M^c, \Gamma) \models C_B(\varphi, \psi)$. □

Now completeness follows in the usual way

Theorem 7.62 (Completeness) For every $\varphi \in \mathcal{L}_{KRC}$

$$\models \varphi \text{ implies } \vdash \varphi$$

□

Proof By contraposition. Suppose $\not\vdash \varphi$. Therefore $\{\neg\varphi\}$ is a consistent set. By the Lindenbaum Lemma $\{\neg\varphi\}$ is a subset of some Γ which is maximal consistent in $cl(\neg\varphi)$. Let M^c be the canonical model for $cl(\neg\varphi)$. By the Truth Lemma $(M^c, \Gamma) \models \neg\varphi$. Therefore $\not\models \varphi$. □

7.8.2 Adding Public Announcements

In this section we provide a completeness proof for public announcement logic with relativised common knowledge just like the completeness proof for **PA** and **AM**. First we extend the language $\mathcal{L}_{KRC}$ with announcement operators.

Definition 7.63 Given are a set of agents A and a set of atoms P. The language $\mathcal{L}_{KRC[]}$ consists of all formulas given by the following BNF:

$$\varphi ::= p \mid \neg\varphi \mid (\varphi \wedge \varphi) \mid K_a\varphi \mid C_B(\varphi, \varphi) \mid [\varphi]\varphi$$

where $p \in P$, $a \in A$ and $B \subseteq A$. □

$[\varphi]p \leftrightarrow (\varphi \rightarrow p)$	atomic permanence
$[\varphi]\neg\psi \leftrightarrow (\varphi \rightarrow \neg[\varphi]\psi)$	announcement and negation
$[\varphi](\psi \wedge \chi) \leftrightarrow ([\varphi]\psi \wedge [\varphi]\chi)$	announcement and conjunction
$[\varphi]K_a\psi \leftrightarrow (\varphi \rightarrow K_a[\varphi]\psi)$	announcement and knowledge
$[\varphi]C_B(\psi,\chi) \leftrightarrow (\varphi \rightarrow C(\varphi \wedge [\varphi]\psi, [\varphi]\chi))$	announcement and relativised common knowledge
$[\varphi][\psi]\chi \leftrightarrow [\varphi \wedge [\varphi]\psi]\chi$	announcement composition
From ψ, infer $[\varphi]\psi$	necessitation of $[\varphi]$

Table 7.8. Additional axioms and rules, which, added to those of Definition 7.55, give the system **PARC**.

The semantics of all these operators is simply the combination of the definitions given earlier. For the proof system we need additional axioms that describe the interaction of the announcement operator with the other logical operators, including relativised common knowledge.

Definition 7.64 (Proof system) The proof system **PARC** consists of the axioms and rules from Definition 7.55 together with the axioms and rule of table 7.8. □

Let us focus on the new axiom. Let us first show that it is indeed sound.

Lemma 7.65 $\models [\varphi]C_B(\psi,\chi) \leftrightarrow (\varphi \rightarrow C(\varphi \wedge [\varphi]\psi, [\varphi]\chi))$ □

Proof $(M,s) \models [\varphi]C_B(\psi,\chi)$
$\Leftrightarrow$
$(M,s) \models \varphi$ implies that $(M|\varphi, s) \models C_B(\psi,\chi)$
$\Leftrightarrow$
$(M,s) \models \varphi$ implies that $(M|\varphi, t) \models \chi$ for all t such that $(s,t) \in (\bigcup_{a\in B} \sim'_a \cap [\![\psi]\!]^2_{M|\varphi})^*$
$\Leftrightarrow$
$(M,s) \models \varphi$ implies that $(M,t) \models [\varphi]\chi$ for all t such that $(s,t) \in (\bigcup_{a\in B} \sim_a \cap [\![\varphi \wedge [\varphi]\psi]\!]^2_M)^*$
$\Leftrightarrow$
$(M,s) \models \varphi$ implies that $(M,t) \models C_B(\varphi \wedge [\varphi]\psi, [\varphi]\chi)$
$\Leftrightarrow$
$(M,s) \models \varphi \rightarrow C_B(\varphi \wedge [\varphi]\psi, [\varphi]\chi)$ □

So indeed we can use this equivalence for a translation.

Definition 7.66 (Translation) The translation $t : \mathcal{L}_{KRC[]} \rightarrow \mathcal{L}_{KRC}$ is defined as follows:

$$\begin{array}{ll} t(p) & = p \\ t(\neg\varphi) & = \neg t(\varphi) \\ t(\varphi \wedge \psi) & = t(\varphi) \wedge t(\psi) \\ t(K_a\varphi) & = K_a t(\varphi) \end{array}$$

$$\begin{array}{ll}
t([\varphi]p) & = t(\varphi \rightarrow p) \\
t([\varphi]\neg\psi) & = t(\varphi \rightarrow -[\varphi]\psi) \\
t([\varphi](\psi \wedge \chi)) & = t([\varphi]\psi \wedge [\varphi]\chi) \\
t([\varphi]K_a\psi) & = t(\varphi \rightarrow K_a[\varphi]\psi) \\
t([\varphi]C_a(\psi,\chi)) & = t(\varphi \rightarrow C_a(\varphi \wedge [\varphi]\psi, [\varphi]\chi)) \\
t([\varphi][\psi]\chi) & = t([\varphi \wedge [\varphi]\psi]\chi)
\end{array}$$ □

Lemma 7.65 shows that the extra clause in this translations is also correct. Now we extend the complexity measure for relativised common knowledge. Here we change 4 to 5, to get the right properties.

Definition 7.67 (Complexity) The complexity $c : \mathcal{L}_{KRC[]} \rightarrow \mathbb{N}$ is defined as follows:

$$\begin{array}{ll}
c(p) & = 1 \\
c(\neg\varphi) & = 1 + c(\varphi) \\
c(\varphi \wedge \psi) & = 1 + \max(c(\varphi), c(\psi)) \\
c(K_a\varphi) & = 1 + c(\varphi) \\
c(C_B(\varphi,\psi)) & = 1 + \max(c(\varphi), c(\psi)) \\
c([\varphi]\psi) & = (5 + c(\varphi)) \cdot c(\psi)
\end{array}$$ □

This complexity measure preserves the order prescribed by the inductive definition of the logical language, and gives us the following properties.

Lemma 7.68 For all φ, ψ, and χ:

1. $c(\psi) \geq c(\varphi)$ if $\varphi \in Sub(\psi)$
2. $c([\varphi]p) > c(\varphi \rightarrow p)$
3. $c([\varphi]\neg\psi) > c(\varphi \rightarrow \neg[\varphi]\psi)$
4. $c([\varphi](\psi \wedge \chi) > c([\varphi]\psi \wedge [\varphi]\chi)$
5. $c([\varphi]K_a\psi) > c(\varphi \rightarrow K_a[\varphi]\psi)$
6. $c([\varphi]C_B(\psi,\chi)) > c(\varphi \rightarrow C_B(\varphi \wedge [\varphi]\psi, [\varphi]\chi))$
7. $c([\varphi][\psi]\chi) > c([\varphi \wedge [\varphi]\psi]\chi)$ □

Proof The only real extra case compared to Lemma 7.22 is the case for $[\varphi]C_B(\psi,\chi)$.

Assume that $c(\psi) \geq c(\chi)$ (the case for $c(\chi) \geq c(\psi)$ is similar). Then

$$\begin{aligned}
c([\varphi]C_B(\psi,\chi)) &= (5 + c(\varphi)) \cdot (1 + \max(c(\psi), c(\chi))) \\
&= 5 + c(\varphi) + 5 \cdot \max(c(\psi), c(\chi)) + c(\varphi) \cdot \max(c(\psi), c(\chi)) \\
&= 5 + c(\varphi) + 5 \cdot c(\psi) + c(\varphi) \cdot c(\psi)
\end{aligned}$$

and

$$\begin{aligned}
c(\varphi \rightarrow C_B(\varphi \wedge [\varphi]\psi, [\varphi]\chi)) &= c(\neg(\varphi \wedge \neg C_B(\varphi \wedge [\varphi]\psi, [\varphi]\chi))) \\
&= 1 + 1 + \max(c(\varphi), \\
&\quad 1 + 1 + \max(1 + \max(c(\varphi), \\
&\quad (5 + c(\varphi)) \cdot c(\psi)), (5 + c(\varphi)) \cdot c(\chi))) \\
&= 5 + ((5 + c(\varphi)) \cdot c(\psi)) \\
&= 5 + 5c(\psi) + c(\varphi)c(\psi)
\end{aligned}$$

The latter is less than the former. □

With these properties we can show that every formula is provably equivalent to its translation.

Lemma 7.69 For all formulas $\varphi \in \mathcal{L}_{KRC[]}$ it is the case that

$$\vdash \varphi \leftrightarrow t(\varphi)$$ □

Proof The proof is analogous to that of Lemma 7.24. □

Completeness follows from this lemma and Theorem 7.62.

Theorem 7.70 (Completeness) For every $\varphi \in \mathcal{L}_{KRC[]}$

$$\models \varphi \text{ implies } \vdash \varphi$$ □

Proof Suppose $\models \varphi$. Therefore $\models t(\varphi)$, by the soundness of the proof system and **PARC** $\vdash \varphi \leftrightarrow t(\varphi)$ (Lemma 7.69). The formula $t(\varphi)$ does not contain any announcement operators. Therefore **S5RC** $\vdash t(\varphi)$ by completeness of **S5RC** (Theorem 7.62). We also have that **PARC** $\vdash t(\varphi)$, as **S5RC** is a subsystem of **PARC**. Since **PARC** $\vdash \varphi \leftrightarrow t(\varphi)$, it follows that **PARC** $\vdash \varphi$. □

7.9 Notes

Completeness is one of the main subjects in logic. Logicians want to make sure that the semantical notion of validity coincides with the proof theoretic notion of validity. Usually soundness (proof theoretic validity implies semantic validity) is easy to show, and completeness (semantic validity implies proof theoretic validity) is harder. Much of the logical literature is devoted to completeness proofs. There are many standard techniques and completeness proofs generally have the same template. In their book on modal logic, Blackburn, de Rijke, and Venema provide a general template for completeness proofs for normal modal logics [29]. The completeness proof for **S5** provided in Section 7.2 follows the well-known proof for completeness of a normal modal logic. The only adaption is that the accessibility relations are defined in such a way that it is immediately clear that they are equivalence relations.

The completeness proof for **S5C** is slightly more difficult than the completeness proof for **S5**. Epistemic logic with common knowledge is no longer compact. That means that there are infinite sets of formulas such that every finite subset is satisfiable, but the set as a whole is not satisfiable. This makes it difficult to prove the Lindenbaum Lemma for non-compact logics, but it also makes it difficult to prove the Truth Lemma for formulas with common knowledge. Therefore the canonical model is custom-made to provide a countermodel for a *specific* formula. This situation also arises in the context of PDL. The Kleene star, which expresses arbitrary (finite) iterations of a program, makes PDL non-compact. An easy to read completeness proof is provided by Kozen and Parikh [117]. In textbooks on epistemic logic one can also find completeness proofs for **S5C** [148, 62]. The proof in this chapter is based on notes by Rineke Verbrugge on [148], and is also very much like the proof in [117].

The standard techniques for proving completeness do not directly apply to *PA*, because it is not a normal modal logic. The rule of uniform substitution (from φ, infer $\varphi[\psi/p]$) is not valid due to the fact that the truth value of atoms never changes due to actions, but other formulas can change. Public announcement logic was first introduced by Plaza [168], and so was the technique of proving completeness via a translation. Jelle Gerbrandy proved completeness in this way for the dynamic epistemic logic in his dissertation [75]. It was also used Baltag, Moss, and Solecki [11].

In the work by Baltag, Moss, and Solecki the completeness proof for *AM* and *AMC* was given. The completeness proof for *PAC* is a special case of this general completeness proof, which was presented in this chapter for didactic reasons. The general case is a bit more difficult but the basic idea is the same. The complicated rules — such as the announcement common knowledge rule and the action common knowledge rule — are part of the proof systems, because a reduction from *PAC* to *S5C* is not possible. The idea of viewing updates as a kind of relativisation, proposed by van Benthem [22], led to the idea of using relativised common knowledge to obtain an easy completeness proof for public announcement logic with a common knowledge operator. This was worked out in [116]. Relativised common knowledge will also be discussed in the next chapter when we turn our attention to the expressive power of dynamic epistemic logics.

8

Expressivity

8.1 Introduction

Logic is about inference, and it is especially concerned with the question when an inference is valid. In answering this question one does not look at particular inferences, one rather looks at their abstract logical form by translating the sentences that make up inferences to formulas of a logical language, where only those aspects deemed important for the logical form are represented. In semantics something similar occurs. The models provided by the semantics of a logical language abstract from particular situations, and only those aspects deemed important are represented.

It is interesting to note that different logical languages can be interpreted in the same class of models. For example, the logical languages presented in this book are all interpreted in the same class of Kripke models. This could be regarded as surprising, since one would expect semantics to be tailored to a particular logical language in such a way that all the properties of a model can be expressed in the logical language. In other words, one would expect that models have the same logical theory (i.e., satisfy the same set of formulas) if and only if they are identical. Otherwise the models could be regarded as being too rich. Therefore one would also expect that languages that are interpreted in the same class of models are equally expressive. However this need not be the case.

In a setting where different logical languages are interpreted in the same class of models, a natural question rises: which properties can be expressed with which logical languages, and which cannot be expressed? We are also interested in the question how the various logical languages are related. Given two languages: is one more expressive than another? In this chapter we answer some of these questions about expressive power for the languages treated in this book.

In Section 8.2 several notions of comparative expressive power are introduced. These are illustrated with examples from propositional logic. In Section 8.3 it is shown that the notion of bisimulation does not fit our needs when we want to study expressive power, yet the ideas behind the notion of bisimulation are important for model comparison games for modal logics, which are introduced in Section 8.4. These model comparison games, and extensions of these games are used in the remainder of the chapter. In Section 8.5 the basic epistemic logic is studied. In Section 8.6 it is shown that epistemic logic with common knowledge is more expressive than basic epistemic logic. In Section 8.7 it is shown that public announcements do not add expressive power to basic epistemic logic. In contrast, public announcements do add expressive power to epistemic logic with common knowledge, which is shown in Section 8.8. In Section 8.9 it is shown that non-deterministic choice does not add expressive power to the logic of epistemic actions, nor to action model logic. In Section 8.10 it is shown that action model logic without common knowledge is just as expressive as basic modal logic. In Section 8.11 it is shown that epistemic logic with relativised common knowledge is more expressive than public announcement logic with common knowledge. Notes are provided in Section 8.12

8.2 Basic Concepts

In general one can think of expressive power as follows. A formula of a logical language, which is interpreted in a class of models, expresses an abstract property of the models in which this formula is true. The more properties expressible with the language, the more expressive power the language has. But what does it mean to say that one logical language is more expressive than another? First we define equivalence of formulas, to express that two (different) formulas express the same property of models.

Definition 8.1 (Equivalence) Two formulas φ and ψ are *equivalent* iff they are true in the same states. We denote this as $\varphi \equiv \psi$. □

Now we can define various notions concerning relative expressive power of two logical languages. The symbol $\equiv_{\mathcal{L}}$ was used in Section 2.2 to denote that two states have the same theory in language $\mathcal{L}$. Below we overload the symbol $\equiv$ even. In the definition of equivalence above it is used to denote that two formulas are equivalent. Below we also use it denote that two languages are equally expressive. These notions depend on the semantics, but we assume it is clear which semantics is used.

Definition 8.2 (Expressive power) Let two logical languages $\mathcal{L}_1$ and $\mathcal{L}_2$ that are interpreted in the same class of models be given.

- $\mathcal{L}_2$ is *at least as expressive as* $\mathcal{L}_1$ if and only if for every formula $\varphi_1 \in \mathcal{L}_1$ there is a formula $\varphi_2 \in \mathcal{L}_2$ such that $\varphi_1 \equiv \varphi_2$. This is denoted as $\mathcal{L}_1 \preceq \mathcal{L}_2$.
- $\mathcal{L}_1$ and $\mathcal{L}_2$ are equally expressive if and only if $\mathcal{L}_1 \preceq \mathcal{L}_2$ and $\mathcal{L}_2 \preceq \mathcal{L}_1$. This is denoted as $\mathcal{L}_1 \equiv \mathcal{L}_2$.

- $\mathcal{L}_2$ is more expressive than $\mathcal{L}_1$ if and only if $\mathcal{L}_1 \preceq \mathcal{L}_2$ but $\mathcal{L}_2 \not\equiv \mathcal{L}_1$. This is denoted as $\mathcal{L}_1 \prec \mathcal{L}_2$. □

This is all rather abstract, but it will be more clear if we look at these notions in the familiar setting of propositional logic. In the remainder of this section we will look at the expressive power of several fragments of propositional logic. We only consider classical semantics where the models are valuations that assign a truth value to the propositional variables. We illustrate each of the relations defined in Definition 8.2.

Let a countable set of propositional variables P be given. The language of propositional logic, $\mathcal{L}_{PL}$, is given by the following BNF:

$$\varphi ::= p \mid \neg\varphi \mid (\varphi \wedge \varphi) \mid (\varphi \vee \varphi) \mid (\varphi \rightarrow \varphi) \mid (\varphi \leftrightarrow \varphi)$$

It is well known that all these operators can be expressed by just using negation and conjunction. We used this fact in presenting the logical languages in this book, and introduced the other operators as abbreviations. Another well-known result is that every formula of propositional logic can be translated to a language which contains NAND ($\bar{\wedge}$) as its only logical operator $\mathcal{L}_{\mathrm{NAND}}$:

$$\varphi ::= p \mid (\varphi \,\bar{\wedge}\, \varphi)$$

where the semantics are given by the following truth table:

φ	ψ	$(\varphi \,\bar{\wedge}\, \psi)$
0	0	1
0	1	1
1	0	1
1	1	0

Exercise 8.3 Show that the following equivalences hold.

$$\begin{array}{ll}
\varphi \,\bar{\wedge}\, \psi & \equiv \neg(\varphi \wedge \psi) \\
\neg\varphi & \equiv \varphi \,\bar{\wedge}\, \varphi \\
\varphi \wedge \psi & \equiv (\varphi \,\bar{\wedge}\, \psi) \,\bar{\wedge}\, (\varphi \,\bar{\wedge}\, \psi) \\
\varphi \vee \psi & \equiv (\varphi \,\bar{\wedge}\, \varphi) \,\bar{\wedge}\, (\psi \,\bar{\wedge}\, \psi) \\
\varphi \rightarrow \psi & \equiv \varphi \,\bar{\wedge}\, (\psi \,\bar{\wedge}\, \psi) \\
\varphi \leftrightarrow \psi & \equiv (\varphi \,\bar{\wedge}\, \psi) \,\bar{\wedge}\, (\varphi \,\bar{\wedge}\, \varphi) \,\bar{\wedge}\, (\psi \,\bar{\wedge}\, \psi)
\end{array}$$

□

With these equivalences we can proves the following theorem.

Theorem 8.4 $\mathcal{L}_{PL} \equiv \mathcal{L}_{NAND}$ □

Proof We have to show that $\mathcal{L}_{PL} \preceq \mathcal{L}_{NAND}$ and $\mathcal{L}_{NAND} \preceq \mathcal{L}_{PL}$. To show the latter note the first equivalence of Exercise 8.3. This equivalence alone is not enough. We have to show that every formula in $\mathcal{L}_{NAND}$ is equivalent to some formula in $\mathcal{L}_{PL}$. We can do this by providing a translation function $t : \mathcal{L}_{NAND} \rightarrow \mathcal{L}_{PL}$ which yields the appropriate formula in a systematic way.

$$\begin{aligned} t(p) &= p \\ t(\varphi \barwedge \psi) &= \neg(t(\varphi) \wedge t(\psi)) \end{aligned}$$

Now we can show that $\varphi \equiv t(\varphi)$ for every formula $\varphi \in \mathcal{L}_{NAND}$ by induction on φ using the equivalence above . Since $t(\varphi) \in \mathcal{L}_{PL}$, we conclude that $\mathcal{L}_{NAND} \preceq \mathcal{L}_{PL}$.

To show that $\mathcal{L}_{PL} \preceq \mathcal{L}_{NAND}$ is a little more work. The last five equivalences of Exercise 8.3 point towards the following translation $t : \mathcal{L}_{PL} \rightarrow \mathcal{L}_{\text{NAND}}$

$$\begin{aligned} t(p) &= p \\ t(\neg\varphi) &= t(\varphi) \barwedge t(\varphi) \\ t(\varphi \wedge \psi) &= (t(\varphi) \barwedge t(\psi)) \barwedge (t(\varphi) \barwedge t(\psi)) \\ t(\varphi \vee \psi) &= (t(\varphi) \barwedge t(\varphi)) \barwedge (t(\psi) \barwedge t(\psi)) \\ t(\varphi \rightarrow \psi) &= t(\varphi) \barwedge (t(\psi) \barwedge t(\psi)) \\ t(\varphi \leftrightarrow \psi) &= (t(\varphi) \barwedge t(\psi)) \barwedge (t(\varphi) \barwedge t(\varphi)) \barwedge (t(\psi) \barwedge t(\psi)) \end{aligned}$$

Using the equivalences above we can show that $\varphi \equiv t(\varphi)$ for every formula $\varphi \in \mathcal{L}_{PL}$ by induction on φ. Since $t(\varphi) \in \mathcal{L}_{NAND}$, we conclude that $\mathcal{L}_{PL} \preceq \mathcal{L}_{NAND}$. □

This illustrates one of the important strategies one can employ to show that two logical languages are equally expressive: provide a translation from one language to the other that provides an appropriate equivalent formula in the other language for each formula in the one language, and vice versa.

Now let us take a language that is not as expressive as $\mathcal{L}_{PL}$. Take the language $\mathcal{L}_{\text{even}}$

$$\varphi ::= p \mid (\varphi \triangledown \varphi) \mid (\varphi \leftrightarrow \varphi)$$

where $\triangledown$ (the exclusive disjunction) has the following semantics

φ	ψ	$(\varphi \triangledown \psi)$
0	0	0
0	1	1
1	0	1
1	1	0

It is easily seen that the language of propositional logic is at least as expressive as this language. However, this language is not as expressive as the language of propositional logic. It seems quite expressive, since for example negations can be expressed.

$$\neg\varphi \equiv \varphi \triangledown (\varphi \leftrightarrow \varphi)$$

In order to show that the language of propositional logic is really more expressive than the language under consideration, we have to find a formula of propositional logic, which is not equivalent to any formula in $\mathcal{L}_{\text{even}}$. A formula that fits this purpose turns out to be $p \wedge q$.

Theorem 8.5 $\mathcal{L}_{\text{even}} \prec \mathcal{L}_{PL}$. □

Proof We will show that $p \wedge q$ cannot be expressed with $\mathcal{L}_{\text{even}}$. First we show that all formulas in $\mathcal{L}_{\text{even}}$ share a certain property, which $p \wedge q$ lacks. The property is that in the truth table for a formula $\varphi \in \mathcal{L}_{\text{even}}$ and the truth table is for at least two atoms, then there are an even number of 0's in every column. We show this by induction on φ. It holds for atoms, since these are false in exactly half of the rows, and the number of rows is a positive power of two. Suppose it holds for φ and ψ. Now consider the column for $\varphi \leftrightarrow \psi$. Let

x be the number of rows where φ is 0 and ψ is 0
y be the number of rows where φ is 0 and ψ is 1
z be the number of rows where φ is 1 and ψ is 0

The induction hypothesis says that $x + y$ is even and that $x + z$ is even. Now, if x is even, then both y and z are also even. And, if x is odd, then both y and z are odd. In both cases $y + z$ is even. Therefore the column for $\varphi \leftrightarrow \psi$ contains an even number of 0's. A similar argument applies to formulas of the form $\varphi \nabla \psi$.

Take the formula $p \wedge q$. The truth table for this formula contains a column with three 0's. Therefore for all $\varphi \in \mathcal{L}_{\text{even}}$ it is the case that $p \wedge q \not\equiv \varphi$. Therefore $\mathcal{L}_{\text{even}} \prec \mathcal{L}_{PL}$. □

Exercise 8.6 Consider also the following fragment of propositional logic $\mathcal{L}_{\wedge\vee}$

$$\varphi ::= p \mid (\varphi \wedge \varphi) \mid (\varphi \vee \varphi)$$

Show that it is not the case that $\mathcal{L}_{\wedge\vee} \preceq \mathcal{L}_{\text{even}}$ and that it is not the case that $\mathcal{L}_{\text{even}} \preceq \mathcal{L}_{\wedge\vee}$. □

8.3 Bisimulation

The previous section provided an introduction to the notions involved regarding the issue of expressivity using examples from propositional logic. Now we turn to modal logic. One of the properties of propositional logic is that models of propositional logic have the same theory if and only if they are identical. This is not the case in modal logic. In a sense modal languages are not expressive enough to distinguish two non-identical models, and in some case even two bisimilar models might be indistinguishable. As was shown in Chapter 2, if two models are bisimilar, then they satisfy the same formulas. The converse does not hold. The difficulty is that formulas are finite, but models may be infinite. And even though a theory can capture certain infinitary aspects of a model, it cannot capture the whole model. The problems start with the set of atoms being countably infinite. In Section 8.3.1 two models are provided, which are not bisimilar, although they do have the same theory in a language with countably many atoms. In Section 8.3.2 it is shown that the same can occur when the set of atoms is empty.

8.3.1 Countably Many Atoms

The idea of the models provided in the next definitions is that the difference between the models only becomes apparent by considering the whole set of atoms simultaneously. Consider the following models.

Definition 8.7 Let a countable set of atoms P be given. Assume that there is an enumeration of these such that p_n is the n-th atom in this enumeration. $M^1 = \langle S^1, R^1, V^1 \rangle$, where

- $S^1 = \{s^1\} \cup \mathbb{N}$
- $R^1 = \{s^1\} \times \mathbb{N}$
- $V^1(p_n) = \{n\}$. □

In this model each atom is true in exactly one state $n \in \mathbb{N}$. Moreover all $n \in \mathbb{N}$ are accessible from s^1. Note that this model is not a model for knowledge since the accessibility relation is not reflexive, nor is it a model for belief since the model is not serial either and not Euclidean. Hence we use the more neutral R to indicate the accessibility relation, rather than $\sim$. Nonetheless we will interpret the language $\mathcal{L}_K$ on these kinds of models in this chapter.

Definition 8.8 Let a countable set of atoms P be given. Assume that there is a enumeration of these such that p_n is the n-th atom in this enumeration. $M^2 = \langle S^2, R^2, V^2 \rangle$, where

- $S^2 = \{s^2, \omega\} \cup \mathbb{N}$
- $R^2 = \{s^2\} \times (\mathbb{N} \cup \{\omega\})$
- $V^2(p_n) = \{n\}$ □

This model has one extra state, ω, where no atom is true.

It is clear that (M^1, s^1) and (M^2, s^2) are not bisimilar. This is because **back** is not satisfied: in M^2 the state ω is accessible from s^2, but there is no state agreeing on all atoms with ω accessible from s^1 in M^1.

Surprisingly (M^1, s^1) and (M^2, s^2) do satisfy the same formulas. This can be shown by induction on formulas: clearly s^1 and s^2 satisfy the same atoms, namely none at all. Using the induction hypothesis the cases for negation and conjunction are easy. The only non-trivial case is for individual epistemic operators. Suppose a formula of the form $K\varphi$ could distinguish these two models. Note that each state $n \in \mathbb{N}$ satisfies the same formulas in both models. The only way for this to happen is that $K\varphi$ is true in (M^1, s^1) but false in (M^2, s^2). That means that φ is true in all of $\mathbb{N}$, but false in ω. But φ is finite, so only finitely many atoms occur in φ. Let n be the highest number such that p_n occurs in φ. Clearly $(n+1)$ must agree with ω on φ ($n+1 \models \varphi$ iff $\omega \models \varphi$). But this contradicts that φ is true in all of $\mathbb{N}$. Therefore $(M^1, s^1) \equiv_{\mathcal{L}_K} (M^2, s^2)$.

This illustrates just one of the reasons that the converse of Theorem 2.15 does not hold. But even if we limit the number of atoms to finitely many, there can still be infinitely many different non-equivalent formulas, which makes the same kind of counterexample possible. This is shown in the next section.

8.3.2 Hedgehogs

Consider the following hedgehog model

Definition 8.9 (Hedgehog with finite spines) $H_{fin} = \langle S, R, V \rangle$, where

- $S = \{(n, m) \mid n \in \mathbb{N},\ m \in \mathbb{N} \text{ and } m \leq n\} \cup \{s_{fin}\}$
- $R = \{((n, m), (n, m+1)) \mid m < n\} \cup \{(s_{fin}, (n, 0)) \mid n \in \mathbb{N}\}$
- $V = \emptyset$ □

This model consists of a spine of length n for every $n \in \mathbb{N}$. All these are accessible from the same state s_{fin}. In this model the valuation is empty. Hence the same propositional formulas are true in each state. Compare this model to the following model.

Definition 8.10 (Hedgehog with an infinite spine) $H_{inf} = \langle S, R, V \rangle$, where

- $S = \{(n, m) \mid n \in \mathbb{N},\ m \in \mathbb{N} \text{ and } m \leq n\} \cup \{(\omega, n) \mid n \in \mathbb{N}\} \cup \{s_{inf}\}$
- $R = \{((n, m), (n, m+1)) \mid m < n \text{ or } n = \omega\} \cup \{(s_{inf}, (n, 0)) \mid n \in \mathbb{N} \cup \{\omega\}\}$
- $V = \emptyset$ □

This model has an infinite spine consisting of the (ω, n) states. A picture of H_{fin} and H_{inf} is given in Figure 8.1. Note that (n, m) in H_{fin} is bisimilar to (n, m) in H_{inf} for all n and m. And note that (n, m) is bisimilar to $(n+1, m+1)$ for all n and m in both models.

Exercise 8.11 Consider the following model $M = \langle S, R, V \rangle$

- $S = \mathbb{N} \cup \{\omega\}$
- $R = \{(n, n-1) \mid n \in \mathbb{N} \setminus \{0\}\} \cup (\{\omega\} \times \mathbb{N})$
- $V = \emptyset$

Draw a picture of the model M. Show that $(H_{fin}, s_{fin}) \leftrightarrows (M, \omega)$. □

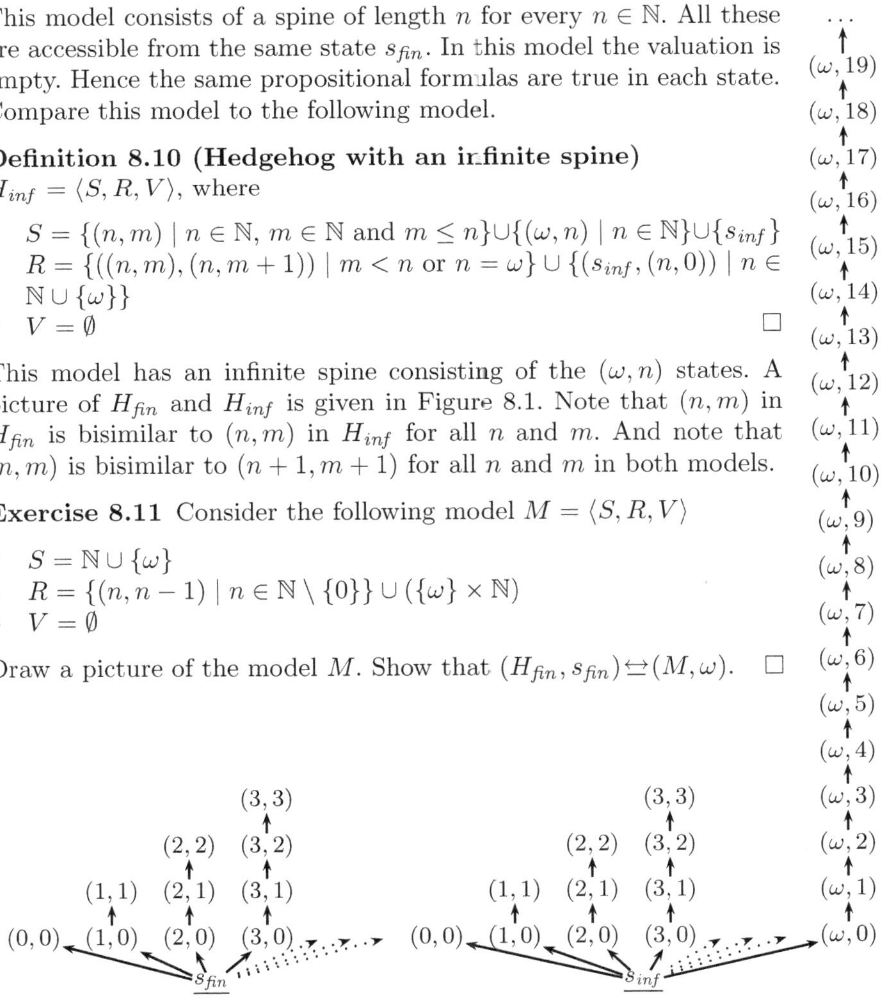

Figure 8.1. Two hedgehogs models. The model on the left has a spine of length n for every $n \in \mathbb{N}$. The model on the right also has a spine of infinite length.

The models shown in figure 8.1 are very much like the models provided in Section 8.3.1 (Definition 8.7 and 8.8). In those models, the atoms provided formulas that were true in exactly one state. In the case of the hedgehogs there is a complex formula that distinguishes every immediate successor of s_{inf} from the others: in state $(n, 0)$ the formula $\hat{K}^n\top \wedge K^{n+1}\bot$ is true, and it is false in all other states $(m, 0)$ (where $m \neq n$). However all these formulas are false in $(\omega, 0)$. That leads to the following theorem.

Theorem 8.12 It is not the case that $(H_{fin}, s_{fin}) \leftrightarrows (H_{inf}, s_{inf})$. □

Proof For every $n \in \mathbb{N}$ there is a formula that distinguishes $(\omega, 0)$ from $(n, 0)$, i.e. the formula $\hat{K}^n\top \wedge K^{n+1}\bot$. Therefore, by Theorem 2.15, none of these are bisimilar. Therefore there is no bisimulation for (H_{fin}, s_{fin}) and (H_{inf}, s_{inf}), because the **back** clause cannot be satisfied. □

The question is whether the difference between these models is large enough for there to be a formula $\varphi \in \mathcal{L}_K$ such that $(H_{fin}, s_{fin}) \models \varphi$ and $(H_{inf}, s_{inf}) \not\models \varphi$. As it turns out, there is no such formula (Theorem 8.15). Although for every finite spine there is a formula distinguishing the infinite spine from it, there is no formula that distinguishes the infinite spine from all finite spines. If such a formula were to exist it would be finite, and the formulas distinguishing finite spines from the infinite spine are of *arbitrary modal depth*.

Definition 8.13 (Modal depth) The modal depth of a formula is given by the following function $d : \mathcal{L}_K \to \mathbb{N}$

$$\begin{array}{ll} d(p) & = 0 \\ d(\neg\varphi) & = d(\varphi) \\ d(\varphi \wedge \psi) & = \max(d(\varphi), d(\psi)) \\ d(K_a\varphi) & = 1 + d(\varphi) \end{array}$$

□

We use this notion to prove the following lemma. In this lemma we use the fact that (n, m) in H_{fin} is bisimilar to (n, m) in H_{inf} for all n and m. Therefore we write $(n, m) \models \varphi$ to indicate that $(H_{fin}, (n, m)) \models \varphi$ and $(H_{inf}, (n, m)) \models \varphi$. We write $(\omega, n) \models \varphi$ for $(H_{inf}, (\omega, n)) \models \varphi$.

Lemma 8.14 For all φ such that $d(\varphi) = n$ it is the case that $(n, 0) \models \varphi$ iff $(\omega, 0) \models \varphi$ and $(m, 0) \models \varphi$ for all $m > n$ □

Proof The base case, and the cases for negation and conjunction, are easy. The only non-trivial case is for formulas of the form $K\varphi$. Let $d(\varphi) = n$. By the induction hypothesis it holds that $(n, 0) \models \varphi$ iff $(\omega, 0) \models \varphi$ and $(m, 0) \models \varphi$ for all $m > n$. For all $k \in ((\mathbb{N}\setminus\{0\}) \cup \{\omega\})$ it holds that $(k, 0) \models K\varphi$ iff $(k, 1) \models \varphi$. Since $(m, 0)$ is bisimilar to $(m+1, 1)$ for all m and $(\omega, 0)$ is bisimilar to $(\omega, 1)$, it must be the case that $(n+1, 1) \models \varphi$ iff $(\omega, 1) \models \varphi$ and $(m+1, 1) \models \varphi$ for all $m > n$. Therefore $(n, 0) \models K\varphi$ iff $(\omega, 0) \models K\varphi$ and $(m, 0) \models K\varphi$ for all $m > n$. □

This lemma leads to the following theorem.

Theorem 8.15 $(H_{fin}, s_{fin}) \equiv_{\mathcal{L}_K} (H_{inf}, s_{inf})$

Proof By induction on φ. The case for atoms, negation and conjunction is straightforward. The only non-trivial case is that of $K\varphi$. It is easy to see that if $(H_{inf}, s_{inf}) \models K\varphi$, then $(H_{fin}, s_{fin}) \models K\varphi$. For the other way around suppose $(H_{fin}, s_{fin}) \models K\varphi$ and $(H_{inf}, s_{inf}) \not\models K\varphi$. The only way for this to occur is if $(\omega, 0) \not\models \varphi$. But then, by Lemma 8.14, $(n, 0) \not\models \varphi$ for that n such that $d(\varphi) = n$. This contradicts that $(H_{fin}, s_{fin}) \models K\varphi$. □

So modal logic cannot distinguish these models. However the models differ to such an extent that they are not bisimilar.

So "being bisimilar" does not correspond with "having the same theory". However, bisimulation is a very significant notion, because it is the right notion for many models. First consider the class of finite models. A model is finite if and only if it consists of only a finite number of states (i.e., $M = \langle S, R, V \rangle$ is finite if and only if $|S| \in \mathbb{N}$).

Theorem 8.16 Let two *finite* models $M = \langle S, R, V \rangle$ and $M' = \langle S', R', V' \rangle$ and two states $s \in S$ and $s' \in S'$ be given. If $(M, s) \equiv_{\mathcal{L}_K} (M', s')$, then $(M, s) \leftrightarroweq (M', s')$. □

Proof Suppose $(M, s) \equiv_{\mathcal{L}_K} (M', s')$. Now let

$$\mathfrak{R} = \{(t, t') \mid (M, t) \equiv_{\mathcal{L}_K} (M', t')\}$$

We will show that $\mathfrak{R}$ is a bisimulation.

atoms Trivial.

forth Suppose $(t, t') \in \mathfrak{R}$ and $(t, u) \in R_a$. Suppose there is no state u' such that $(t', u') \in R'_a$ and $(u, u') \in \mathfrak{R}$. Consequently, for every u' such that $(t', u') \in R'_a$ there is a formula $\varphi_{u'}$ such that $(M', u') \models \varphi_{u'}$ and $(M, u) \not\models \varphi_{u'}$. Now let

$$\varphi = \bigvee_{(t',u') \in R'_a} \varphi_{u'}$$

Since there are only finitely many states, this formula is finite. It is clear that $(M, t) \models \hat{K}_a \neg\varphi$, although $(M', t') \models K_a\varphi$. But this contradicts our initial assumption.

back The proof is analogous to the proof for **forth**. □

The crucial point is that we can assume that φ is a finite formula, which cannot be assumed in the general case. Indeed, φ'_u could be a different formula for each u' such that $(t', u') \in R'_a$. This result can be extended even further.

Exercise 8.17 A model is said to have a *finite degree* iff $\{t \mid (s, t) \in R_a\}$ is finite for every $s \in S$ and $a \in A$, i.e., the set of accessible states is always finite. Consider the class of models of finite degree. Show that there is a model of finite degree which is not a finite model. Show that Theorem 8.16 can be extended to the class of models of finite degree. □

These results suggest that there is something inherently finitary about having the same theory, although these theories themselves are infinite. In the next section the model comparison games are introduced. It is shown that they can be used to find the right model theoretic notion for having the same theory. The games themselves are finite, but there are infinitely many games.

8.4 Games

In Section 8.3 we saw that when two models have the same theory, this does not imply that they are bisimilar. In this section we provide a notion of model equivalence that coincides with having the same theory. This relation is based on characterising model comparison games that provide an equivalence relation on models such that this relation holds iff the models have the same theory.

The idea is the following. A game is played with two models by two players: spoiler and duplicator. Spoiler tries to show that the models are different, whereas duplicator tries to show that the models are the same. However, spoiler only has a finite number of rounds to show that the models are different. If he has not been able to show it by then, duplicator wins the game. One can think of the number of rounds as the depth of the formulas. If duplicator has a winning strategy for a game of every possible number of rounds then the two models have the same theory. But now the converse also holds. If two models have the same theory, then duplicator has a winning strategy for the model comparison game of any length.

Section 8.3.1 and 8.3.2 pointed out that bisimulation does not coincide with having the same theory when infinitely many atoms were considered, and when infinitely many states played a role in the theory. The games are set up in such a way that one looks at a finite part of the model and one can take only finitely many atoms into account.

Definition 8.18 (The $\mathcal{L}_K(P)$ game) Let two models $M = \langle S, R, V \rangle$ and $M' = \langle S', R', V' \rangle$ and two states $s \in S$ and $s' \in S'$ be given. The *n-round $\mathcal{L}_K(P)$ game* between spoiler and duplicator on (M, s) and (M', s') is the following. If $n = 0$ spoiler wins if s and s' differ in their atomic properties for P, else duplicator wins. Otherwise spoiler can initiate one of the following scenarios in each round:

forth-move Spoiler chooses an agent a and a state t such that $(s, t) \in R_a$. Duplicator responds by choosing a state t' such that $(s', t') \in R'_a$. The output of this move is (t, t').

back-move Spoiler chooses an agent a and a state t' such that $(s', t') \in R'_a$. Duplicator responds by choosing a state t such that $(s, t) \in R_a$. The output of this move is (t, t').

If either player cannot perform an action prescribed above (a player cannot choose a successor), that player loses. If the output states differ in their atomic properties for P, spoiler wins the game. The game continues with the new output states. If spoiler has not won after all n rounds, duplicator wins the game. □

One should think of the number of rounds in the game as the *modal depth* of the formulas the players are concerned with. The idea is that spoiler has a winning strategy for the n-round game iff there is a formula φ such that $d(\varphi) \leq n$ and φ is true in one model and false in the other. We can also look at the language $\mathcal{L}_K$ from this perspective and distinguish the language up to each level.

Definition 8.19 The language $\mathcal{L}_K^n$ of formulas of depth less than or equal to n is defined inductively. The language $\mathcal{L}_K^0$ consists of all formulas given by the following BNF:

$$\varphi ::= p \mid \neg\varphi \mid (\varphi \wedge \varphi)$$

The language $\mathcal{L}_K^{n+1}$ consists of all formulas given by the following BNF:

$$\varphi ::= \psi \mid K_a\psi \mid \neg\varphi \mid (\varphi \wedge \varphi)$$

where $\psi \in \mathcal{L}_K^n$. □

Clearly $\mathcal{L}_K^n = \{\varphi \in \mathcal{L}_K \mid d(\varphi) \leq n\}$ and $\mathcal{L}_K = \bigcup_{n \in \mathbb{N}} \mathcal{L}_K^n$. The advantage of looking at $\mathcal{L}_K$ in this way is that we can easily set up proofs with a double induction. Firstly, on the depth n and secondly, on the structure of φ at that depth. The advantage of looking at this hierarchy of languages is that on any level only finitely many different propositions can be expressed: if $[\![\varphi]\!]$ is the class of all models where φ is true, then $\{[\![\varphi]\!] \mid \varphi \in \mathcal{L}_K^n\}$ is finite.

Lemma 8.20 Given a finite set of atoms P. For every n there are only finitely many different propositions up to logical equivalence in $\mathcal{L}_K^n(P)$. □

Proof By induction on n.

Base case For 0, the set $\{[\![\varphi]\!] \mid d(\varphi) \leq 0\}$ contains all Boolean formulas. Since P is finite, this set is also finite up to equivalence .

Induction hypothesis The set $\{[\![\varphi]\!] \mid d(\varphi) \leq n\}$ is finite.

Induction step The set of formulas of depth $n + 1$ consists of formulas of the form $K_a\varphi$, and Boolean combinations thereof. Since the number of agents is finite and $\{[\![\varphi]\!] \mid d(\varphi) \leq n\}$ is finite, this set of formulas is also finite up to equivalence. □

This lemma is crucial in proving the following theorem, which is formulated from duplicator's point of view. Here $(M, s) \equiv_{\mathcal{L}_K^n} (M', s')$ means that these two models have the same theory in $\mathcal{L}_K^n$.

Theorem 8.21 For all $n \in \mathbb{N}$, all models (M, s) and (M', s') and all finite sets of atoms P: duplicator has a winning strategy for the n-round $\mathcal{L}_K(P)$-game on (M, s) and (M', s') iff $(M, s) \equiv_{\mathcal{L}_K^n} (M', s')$. □

Proof By induction on n.

Base case Follows directly from the definition of the game.

Induction hypothesis For all models (M, s) and (M', s') and all finite sets of atoms P: duplicator has a winning strategy for the n-round $\mathcal{L}_K(P)$-game on (M, s) and (M', s') iff $(M, s) \equiv_{\mathcal{L}_K^n} (M', s')$.

Induction step From left to right. Suppose duplicator has a winning strategy for the $n+1$-round game on (M, s). We proceed by induction on $\varphi \in \mathcal{L}_K^{n+1}$.

Base cases Suppose φ is of the form ψ, where $\psi \in \mathcal{L}_K^n$. Then it follows directly from the first induction hypothesis that $(M, s) \models \psi$ iff $(M', s') \models \psi$.

The other base case is where φ is of the form $K_a\psi$, where $\psi \in \mathcal{L}_K^n$. Suppose, without loss of generality, that $(M, s) \models K_a\psi$. Take an arbitrary t' such that $(s', t') \in R'_a$. Since duplicator has a winning strategy, she has a response to every move spoiler can make. So if spoiler chooses t' in a back-move, then there is a t such that $(s, t) \in R_a$ and duplicator has a winning strategy for the remaining n-round subgame on (M, t) and (M', t'). By the induction hypothesis it must be the case that $(M, t) \models \psi$ iff $(M', t') \models \psi$. From the assumption that $(M, s) \models K_a\psi$ and $(s, t) \in R_a$ it follows that $(M, t) \models \psi$. Therefore $(M', t') \models \psi$. Since t' was arbitrary, $(M', t') \models \psi$ for all t' such that $(s', t') \in R'_a$. Therefore $(M', s') \models K_a\psi$.

Induction hypothesis Let φ and ψ be formulas of $\mathcal{L}_K^{n+1}n$, and $(M, s) \models \varphi$ iff $(M', s') \models \varphi$, and $(M, s) \models \psi$ iff $(M', s') \models \psi$.

Induction step

negation Suppose that $(M, s) \models \neg\varphi$. By the semantics this is the case iff $(M, s) \not\models \varphi$. By the second induction hypothesis this is equivalent to $(M', s') \not\models \varphi$, which by the semantics is equivalent to $(M', s') \models \neg\varphi$.

conjunction Suppose that $(M, s) \models \varphi \wedge \psi$. By the semantics this is equivalent to $(M, s) \models \varphi$ and $(M, s) \models \psi$. By the second induction hypothesis this is equivalent to $(M', s') \models \varphi$ and $(M', s') \models \psi$, which by the semantics is equivalent to $(M', s') \models \varphi \wedge \psi$.

Therefore $(M, s) \equiv_{\mathcal{L}_K^{n+1}} (M', s')$.

From right to left. Suppose that $(M, s) \equiv_{\mathcal{L}_K^{n+1}} (M', s')$. We now have to describe duplicator's winning strategy. Suppose, without loss of generality, that spoiler's first move is a forth-move and he chooses a state t such that $(s, t) \in R_a$. We have to show that there is a t' such that $(s', t') \in R'_a$ and $(M, t) \equiv_{\mathcal{L}_K^n} (M', t')$. Because then, by the first induction hypothesis, duplicator has a winning strategy for the remaining subgame. Suppose there is no such t'. That means that for every t' such that $(s', t') \in R'_a$ spoiler has a winning strategy for the remaining subgame. By the first induction hypothesis there is a formula $\varphi_{t'}$ of depth at most n for every

t' with $(s', t') \in R'_a$, such that $(M', t') \models \varphi_{t'}$ and $(M, t) \not\models \varphi_{t'}$. By Lemma 8.20 the set $\{\varphi_{t'} \mid (s', t') \in R'_a\}$ contains only finitely many different non-equivalent formulas. Let f be a function that chooses one formula from each equivalence class $[t']$. Therefore the formula

$$\varphi = \bigvee_{(s',t') \in R'_a} f([t'])$$

is finite. Moreover its depth is at most n. Note that $(M', s') \models K_a\varphi$, but $(M, s) \not\models K_a\varphi$. But $d(K_a\varphi) \leq n + 1$. This contradicts the initial assumption, therefore duplicator has a winning strategy for the $n + 1$-round game. □

So for $\mathcal{L}_K^n$, the model comparison game provides the right model-theoretic notion that coincides with having the same theory. But by looking at all games we also have the right notion for the whole language $\mathcal{L}_K$.

Theorem 8.22 $(M, s) \equiv_{\mathcal{L}_K} (M', s')$ iff for all $n \in \mathbb{N}$ duplicator has a winning strategy for the n-round $\mathcal{L}_K$-game on (M, s) and (M', s'). □

Exercise 8.23 Prove Theorem 8.22. □

This last theorem may be somewhat unexpected. It seems that if duplicator has a winning strategy for every game of finite length, then the models must be bisimilar as well. This is not the case however. Let us illustrate this point with the hedgehog models from Section 8.3.

Consider again the models H_{fin} and H_{inf} (Section 8.3.2). The results about these models imply that duplicator has a winning strategy for the model comparison game for any number of rounds. There is a uniform way of describing the winning strategies for duplicator. The only real choice in the game is the first move. If spoiler chooses a state on any of the finite spines, duplicator can respond by choosing the spine of the same length, and so has a winning strategy. Otherwise, spoiler chooses the first state of the infinite spine and duplicator responds by choosing the spine of length n, where n is the number of rounds in the game. The only way spoiler can win is to force one of the output states to be a blind state, so that in the next round duplicator will not be able to respond. However, by choosing the spine of length n, that will not occur, because this spine is too long.

So one may wonder what the relation is between these games and the notion of bisimulation. This becomes clear when we consider an $\mathcal{L}_K$-game with ω rounds (the first limit ordinal). In that case the notion of bisimulation and there being a winning strategy for duplicator coincide. One can think of the bisimulation relation as indicating duplicator's winning strategy. A pair of linked states is a winning situation for duplicator. And then indeed one sees the close link between the back and forth condition and there being a winning strategy. For suppose (s, s') is a winning situation for duplicator.

Then if spoiler chooses a successor of either of these states, then by back or forth duplicator can find a state such that the output of the move is a pair (t', t') which again is a winning situation.

Now consider the game with ω rounds for the hedgehogs models. Spoiler has a winning strategy for this game. His first move is to choose the first state of the infinite spine. Duplicator responds by choosing the first state of some finite spine; let us say of length n. If spoiler keeps playing on the infinite spine then in round $n+1$ duplicator will not be able to respond. So spoiler has a winning strategy.

In the remainder of this chapter we will extend and apply the results about model comparison games from this section to some of the (dynamic) epistemic logics that were introduced in the previous chapters.

8.5 *S5*

We will use the games introduced in the previous section to investigate the expressive power of the language of epistemic logic.

8.5.1 Single-agent *S5*

Consider the model comparison game for *S5*-models for one agent. These have a special feature.

Theorem 8.24 Duplicator has a winning strategy for the n-round $\mathcal{L}_K$-game on (M, s) and (M', s') for every $n \in \mathbb{N}$ iff duplicator has a winning strategy for the 1-round $\mathcal{L}_K$-game on (M, s) and (M', s'). □

Proof From left to right is trivial. From right to left, suppose that duplicator has a winning strategy for the 1-round $\mathcal{L}_K$ game. That means that s and s' agree on their atomic properties for P. Moreover for any a-accessible state selected in either model, duplicator can respond by picking an a-accessible state in the other model, such that these states agree on atomic properties for P. But since the set of a-accessible states is the same for all states that are a-accessible from the starting state s or s' (they are equivalence classes), the same strategy can be repeated indefinitely. Therefore duplicator has a winning strategy for the n-round $\mathcal{L}_K$-game. □

Exercise 8.25 Show that in the 1-round game where duplicator has a winning strategy on (M, s) and (M', s'), duplicator's strategy generates a bisimulation: $\{(t, t') \mid$ in the winning strategy duplicator responds with t' if spoiler chooses t or duplicator responds with t if spoiler chooses $t'\}$ is a bisimulation.□

Theorem 8.26 $(M, s) \equiv_{\mathcal{L}_K} (M', s')$ iff $(M, s) \equiv_{\mathcal{L}^1_K} (M', s')$. □

Proof Follows straightforwardly from Theorems 8.22 and 8.24. □

Theorem 8.26 suggest that $\mathcal{L}^1_K(\{a\})$ is just as expressive as $\mathcal{L}_K(\{a\})$. This is indeed the case.

Theorem 8.27 $\mathcal{L}_K(\{a\}) \equiv \mathcal{L}_K^1(\{a\})$ □

Proof It is easy to see that $\mathcal{L}_K^1(\{a\}) \preceq \mathcal{L}_K(\{a\})$, since $\mathcal{L}_K^1(\{a\})$ is a sublanguage of $\mathcal{L}_K(\{a\})$.

For the other way around take a formula $\varphi \in \mathcal{L}_K(\{a\})$. Given a model $M = \langle S, \sim, V\rangle \in \mathcal{S}5$ and a state $s \in S$. Let δ_s be $\bigwedge\{p \mid p \in P(\varphi)$ and $(M,s) \models p\}$, where $P(\varphi)$ is the set of atoms occurring in φq. Let $\mathcal{S}5(\varphi)$ be the class of epistemic states that satisfy φ. Now consider the following formula:

$$\psi = \bigvee_{(M,s)\in\mathcal{S}5(\varphi)} \left(\delta_s \wedge \bigwedge_{s\sim_a t} \hat{K}\delta_t \wedge K \bigvee_{s\sim_a t} \delta_t\right)$$

Since $P(\varphi)$ is finite, there are only finitely many different δ_t. But then all the sets referred to in the definition of ψ are finite. So this formula is in $\mathcal{L}_K^1(\{a\})$. All that remains, is to show that $\varphi \equiv \psi$.

Suppose that $(M,s) \models \varphi$. Therefore one of the disjuncts of ψ is true. Therefore $(M,s) \models \psi$.

Suppose $(M,s) \models \psi$. Therefore there is a disjunct of ψ true in (M,s), i.e., there is an (M',s') such that $(M,s) \models \delta_{s'} \wedge \bigwedge_{s'\sim_a' t'} \hat{K}\delta_{t'} \wedge K \bigvee_{s'\sim_a' t'} \delta_{t'}$. But that means that duplicator has a winning strategy for the 1-round $\mathcal{L}_K^1(\{a\})$ game played on (M,s) and (M',s') for the set $P(\varphi)$ (the *finite* set of atoms occurring in φ). But then by Theorem 8.24 duplicator has a winning strategy for the n-round $\mathcal{L}_K$-game on (M,s) and (M',s') for every $n \geq 0$. By Theorem 8.22 $(M,s) \equiv_{\mathcal{L}_K} (M',s')$. Since $(M',s') \models \varphi$, also $(M,s) \models \varphi$. □

8.5.2 Multi-agent *S5*

When more than one agent is considered, it is not the case that every formula is equivalent to a formula of depth at most 1. Indeed, with more than one agent there are infinitely many non-equivalent formulas. We shall show this by modifying the hedgehogs models of Section 8.3.2. First of all note that, contrary to the general modal case, if the $\mathcal{L}_K$-game is played on two *S5* models with empty valuations, duplicator always has a winning strategy.

Exercise 8.28 Let two models $M = \langle S, \sim, V\rangle$ and $M' = \langle S', \sim', V'\rangle$ in $\mathcal{S}5$ be given. Show that if $V = V' = \emptyset$, then $(M,s) \leftrightarroows (M',s')$ for all $s \in S$ and $s' \in S'$. □

Now we modify the hedgehogs for *S5*, by only looking at the spines of the hedgehog.

S5 spines

Consider the models of finite spines.

Definition 8.29 (Finite *S5* spines) $\mathit{Spine}(n) = \langle S, R, V \rangle$, where

- $S = \{m \mid m \in \mathbb{N} \text{ and } m \leq (n+1)\}$
- $R(a) = \{(s,s) \mid s \in S\} \cup$
  $\{(m,k) \mid \min(m,k) \mod 2 = 0 \text{ and } |m-k| = 1\}$
- $R(b) = \{(s,s) \mid s \in S\} \cup$
  $\{(m,k) \mid \min(m,k) \mod 2 = 1 \text{ and } |m-k| = 1\}$
- $V(p) = \{n+1\}$ □

Such a model is very much like a spine of the hedgehog model given in Definition 8.9, but here all the relations are equivalence relations, and the accessibility relation for a links all even states to their successors, and b links all odd states to their successors. The valuation of p indicates the end of a spine. We also consider the model of an infinite spine.

Definition 8.30 (Infinite *S5* spine) $\mathit{Spine}(\omega) = \langle S, R, V \rangle$, where

- $S = \mathbb{N}$
- $R(a) = \{(t,t) \mid t \in S\} \cup$
  $\{(m,k) \mid \min(m,k) \mod 2 = 0 \text{ and } |m-k| = 1\}$
- $R(b) = \{(t,t) \mid t \in S\} \cup$
  $\{(m,k)) \mid \min(m,k) \mod 2 = 1 \text{ and } |m-k| = 1\}$
- $V(p) = \emptyset$ □

A picture of some spine models is given in Figure 8.2. None of the finite spine models are bisimilar to the infinite spine model.

Theorem 8.31 For all $n \in \mathbb{N}$ it is not the case that

$$(\mathit{Spine}(n), 0) \underline{\leftrightarrow} (\mathit{Spine}(\omega), 0)$$ □

Proof For every $n \in \mathbb{N}$ there is a formula that distinguishes $(\mathit{Spine}(\omega), 0)$ from $(\mathit{Spine}(n), 0)$. We can define a φ_n inductively as follows:

$$\begin{aligned} \varphi_0 &= \hat{K}_a p \\ \varphi_1 &= \hat{K}_a \hat{K}_b p \\ \varphi_{n+2} &= \hat{K}_a \hat{K}_b \varphi_n \end{aligned}$$

Observe that $(\mathit{Spine}(n), 0) \models \varphi_n$ and $(\mathit{Spine}(\omega), 0) \not\models \varphi_n$ for every $n \in \mathbb{N}$. Therefore there is no bisimulation for $(\mathit{Spine}(n), 0)$ and $(\mathit{Spine}(\omega), 0)$. □

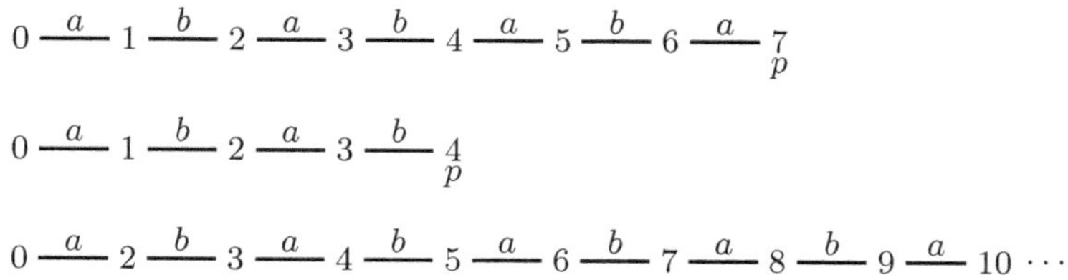

Figure 8.2. Three spine models: *Spine*(6), *Spine*(3) and *Spine*(ω).

However we can use model comparison games to show that up to finite depth the infinite spine satisfies the same formulas as a finite one. If the number of rounds is n then the p-state in *Spine*(n) is just beyond the players' reach.

Theorem 8.32 For every $n \in \mathbb{N}$ it holds that

$$(Spine(n), 0) \equiv_{\mathcal{L}_K^n} (Spine(\omega), 0)$$ □

Proof We prove this theorem using the $\mathcal{L}_K$ game. We show that duplicator has a winning strategy for the n-round $\mathcal{L}_K$-game on $(Spine(n), 0)$ and $(Spine(\omega), 0)$. The only possibility for spoiler to win is to make a forth-move to a p-state, such that duplicator can only reach $\neg p$-states. It is clear that spoiler cannot reach the p-state at the end of *Spine*(n) by alternating a and b forth moves given the number of rounds. So duplicator can keep matching these moves on the infinite spine. Hence for every n duplicator has a winning strategy for the game. Therefore, by Theorem 8.21, $(Spine(n), 0) \equiv_{\mathcal{L}_K^n} (Spine(\omega), 0)$. □

This implies that there is no formula that distinguishes $(Spine(\omega), 0)$ from all the other spine models.

Theorem 8.33 There is no $\varphi \in \mathcal{L}_K$ such that $(Spine(\omega), 0) \notin [\![\varphi]\!]$ and $\{(Spine(n), 0) \mid n \in \mathbb{N}\} \subseteq [\![\varphi]\!]$. □

Proof Suppose there is such a formula φ. Let the depth of φ be n. But then $(Spine(n), 0) \models \varphi$ iff $(Spine(\omega), 0) \models \varphi$, by Theorem 8.32. This contradicts the initial assumption. □

This shows that in multi-agent *S5* the situation as to expressive power is quite similar to the situation in general modal logic.

8.6 *S5C*

Often a new logical language is introduced to be able to capture a concept that the previously available languages were not able to express. Common knowledge is such a concept. In this section we show that common knowledge cannot be expressed in multi-agent *S5*

Theorem 8.34 $\mathcal{L}_K \prec \mathcal{L}_{KC}$ □

Proof It is clear that $\mathcal{L}_K \preceq \mathcal{L}_{KC}$, since $\mathcal{L}_K$ is a sublanguage of $\mathcal{L}_{KC}$. In order to show that $\mathcal{L}_K \not\equiv \mathcal{L}_{KC}$ we have to find a formula $\varphi \in \mathcal{L}_{KC}$ such there is no formula $\psi \in \mathcal{L}_K$ such that $\varphi \equiv \psi$. Consider the following formula:

$$C_{ab}\neg p$$

This formula is false in $(Spine(n), 0)$ for every $n \in \mathbb{N}$ and true in $(Spine(\omega), 0)$. However, by Theorem 8.33, there is no such formula in $\mathcal{L}_K$. □

Still the language cannot distinguish bisimilar models.

Theorem 8.35 For all models (M, s) and (M', s'), if $(M, s) \leftrightarroweq (M', s)$, then $(M, s) \equiv_{\mathcal{L}_{KC}} (M', s')$. □

Proof The only extra case with respect to the proof of Theorem 2.15 in the induction step is that for common knowledge.

Suppose $(M, s) \models C_B\varphi$. Take an arbitrary t' such that $(s', t') \in R'(B)^*$. By repeatedly applying the **back** clause we find a t such that $(s, t) \in R(B)^*$ and $(t, t') \in \mathfrak{R}$. Therefore, by the induction hypothesis, $(M, t) \models \varphi$ if and only if $(M', t') \models \varphi$. Since $(M, s) \models C_B\varphi$, by the semantics, $(M, t) \models \varphi$. Therefore, by the induction hypothesis, $(M', t') \models \varphi$. Given that t' was arbitrary, $(M', t') \models \varphi$ for all t' such that $(s', t') \in R'(B)^*$. Therefore, by the semantics $(M', s') \models C_B\varphi$.

The other way around is analogous, but then **forth** is used. □

In the case of $\mathcal{L}_{KC}$ the converse of this theorem does not hold either. Just as before we need a more fine-grained model-theoretical notion. We obtain this by extending the games introduced in Section 8.4. In model comparison games spoiler tries to show that the models are different; one can view spoiler as looking for a formula to distinguish the models. Therefore, the more formulas in the logical language, the more moves spoiler should be able to make. The $\mathcal{L}_K$-game is extended to the $\mathcal{L}_{KC}$-game by giving spoiler two additional moves.

Definition 8.36 (The $\mathcal{L}_{KC}(P)$ game) Let two models $M = \langle S, R, V \rangle$ and $M' = \langle S', R', V' \rangle$ and two states $s \in S$ and $s' \in S'$ be given. The *n-round $\mathcal{L}_{KC}(P)$ game* between spoiler and duplicator on (M, s) and (M', s') is the following. If $n = 0$ spoiler wins if s and s' differ in their atomic properties for P, else duplicator wins. Otherwise spoiler can initiate one of the following scenarios in each round:

K-forth-move Spoiler chooses an agent a and a state t such that $(s, t) \in R_a$. Duplicator responds by choosing a state t' such that $(s', t') \in R'_a$. The output of this move is (t, t'). The game continues with the new output states.

K-back-move Spoiler chooses an agent a and a state t' such that $(s', t') \in R'_a$. Duplicator responds by choosing a state t such that $(s, t) \in R_a$. The output of this move is (t, t'). The game continues with the new output states.

C-forth-move Spoiler chooses a group B and a state t such that $(s, t) \in R(B)^*$. Duplicator responds by choosing a state t' such that $(s', t') \in R'(B)^*$. The output of this move is (t, t'). The game continues with the new output states.

C-back-move Spoiler chooses a group B and a state t' such that $(s', t') \in R'(B)^*$. Duplicator responds by choosing a state t such that $(s, t) \in R(B)^*$. The output of this move is (t, t'). The game continues with the new output states.

If either player cannot perform an action prescribed above (a player cannot choose a successor), that player loses. If the output states differ in their atomic properties for P, spoiler wins the game. If spoiler has not won after all n rounds, duplicator wins the game. □

Note that the length of the B-paths selected by spoiler and duplicator can differ.

Again we want to show that duplicator has a winning strategy for this game if and only if the models satisfy the same formulas up to the depth of the number of rounds of the game. Therefore, we extend the notion of modal depth to $\mathcal{L}_{KC}$.

Definition 8.37 (Modal depth) The modal depth of a formula is given by the following function $d : \mathcal{L}_{KC} \to \mathbb{N}$

$$\begin{array}{ll} d(p) & = 0 \\ d(\neg\varphi) & = d(\varphi) \\ d(\varphi \wedge \psi) & = \max(d(\varphi), d(\psi)) \\ d(K_a\varphi) & = 1 + d(\varphi) \\ d(C_B\varphi) & = 1 + d(\varphi) \end{array}$$

□

So the common knowledge operator is treated exactly like the individual knowledge operator. Again we view the language as consisting of different sublanguages.

Definition 8.38 The language $\mathcal{L}_{KC}^n$ of formulas of depth n is defined inductively. The language $\mathcal{L}_{KC}^0$ consists of all formulas given by the following BNF:

$$\varphi ::= p \mid \neg\varphi \mid \varphi \wedge \varphi$$

The language $\mathcal{L}_{KC}^{n+1}$ consists of all formulas given by the following BNF:

$$\varphi ::= \psi \mid K_a\psi \mid C_B\psi \mid \neg\varphi \mid \varphi \wedge \varphi$$

where $\psi \in \mathcal{L}_{KC}^n$. □

As before, up to a certain depth only finitely many different propositions can be expressed.

Lemma 8.39 Given a finite set of atoms P. For every n there are only finitely many different propositions up to logical equivalence in $\mathcal{L}_{KC}^n$. □

Exercise 8.40 Prove Lemma 8.39 □

Now we can prove the following theorem.

Theorem 8.41 For all $n \in \mathbb{N}$, all models $M = \langle S, R, V\rangle$ and $M' = \langle S', R', V'\rangle$ and all finite sets of atoms P: duplicator has a winning strategy for the n-round $\mathcal{L}_{KC}(P)$-game on (M, s) and (M', s') iff $(M, s) \equiv_{\mathcal{L}_{KC}^n} (M', s')$. □

Proof The proof is by induction on n. The proof from left to right is by induction on formulas is $\mathcal{L}^n_{KC}$. The only difference with the proof of Theorem 8.21 is that there is an extra base case for formulas of the form $C_B\psi$.

Suppose, without loss of generality, that $(M, s) \models C_B\psi$. Take an arbitrary t' such that $(s', t') \in R'(B)^*$. Since duplicator has a winning strategy, she has a response to every move spoiler can make. So if spoiler chooses t' in a C-back-move for B, then there is a t such that $(s, t) \in R(B)^*$ and duplicator has a winning strategy for the remaining n-round subgame on t and t'. By the induction hypothesis it must be the case that $(M, t) \models \psi$ iff $(M', t') \models \psi$. Since t' was arbitrary, $(M', t') \models \psi$ for all t' such that $(s', t') \in R'(B)^*$. Therefore, by the semantics, $(M', s') \models C_B\psi$. The rest of the proof from left to right is completely analogous.

From right to left. Suppose that $(M, s) \equiv_{\mathcal{L}^{n+1}_{KC}} (M', s')$. We now have to describe duplicator's winning strategy. The case where spoiler's first move is a K-forth-move or K-back-move is analogous to the proof of Theorem 8.21. Otherwise suppose, without loss of generality, that spoiler's first move is a C-forth-move for B and he chooses a t such that $(s, t) \in R(B)^*$. We have to show that there is a t' such that $(s', t') \in R'(B)^*$ and $(M, t) \equiv_{\mathcal{L}^n_{KC}} (M', t')$. Because then, by the induction hypothesis, duplicator has a winning strategy for the remaining subgame. Suppose there is no such t. That means that for every t' such that $(s', t') \in R'(B)^*$ spoiler has a winning strategy for the remaining subgame. By the induction hypothesis there is a formula $\varphi_{t'}$ of depth at most n for every t' such that $(s', t') \in R'(B)^*$, where $(M', t') \models \varphi_{t'}$ and $(M, t) \not\models \varphi_{t'}$. By Lemma 8.39 the set $\{\varphi_{t'} \mid (s')(t') \in R'(B)^*\}$ contains only finitely many different non-equivalent formulas. Let f be a function that chooses one formula from each equivalence class $[t']$. Therefore the formula

$$\varphi = \bigvee_{(s',t') \in R'(B)^*} f([t'])$$

is finite. Moreover its depth is at most n. Note that $(M', s') \models C_B\varphi$, but $(M, s) \not\models C_B\varphi$. But $d(C_B\varphi) \leq n + 1$. This contradicts the initial assumption, therefore duplicator has a winning strategy for the $n + 1$-round game. □

Exercise 8.42 Single-agent *S5C* again presents an special case. Show that $\mathcal{L}_K(\{a\}) \equiv \mathcal{L}_{KC}(\{a\})$. □

Exercise 8.43 Show that $\mathcal{L}_{KC}$ can distinguish the set of models $(\mathit{Spine}(n), 0)$ where n is odd from the set of models $(\mathit{Spine}(n), 0)$ where n is even, and that $\mathcal{L}_K$ cannot. □

8.7 *PA*

In chapter 7 we proved that the proof system **PA** is complete by showing that every formula that contains an announcement operator can be translated to a provably equivalent formula that does not contain any announcement operators. In the light of this chapter we can view this result as saying something about the expressive power of $\mathcal{L}_{K[]}$ with respect to $\mathcal{L}_K$. Since, by soundness of **PA**, the provable equivalence of two formulas implies that they are also semantically equivalent, the result says that $\mathcal{L}_K$ and $\mathcal{L}_{K[]}$ are equally expressive.

Theorem 8.44 $\mathcal{L}_K \equiv \mathcal{L}_{K[]}$ □

Proof It is clear that $\mathcal{L}_K \preceq \mathcal{L}_{K[]}$, since $\mathcal{L}_K$ is a sublanguage of $\mathcal{L}_{K[]}$.

To see that $\mathcal{L}_{K[]} \preceq \mathcal{L}_K$, we use the translation provided in definition 7.20. From Lemma 7.24, together with the soundness of **PA**, it follows that $\varphi \equiv t(\varphi)$ for every $\varphi \in \mathcal{L}_{K[]}$. □

This result is quite surprising since the public announcement operator seems to express something that is not present in epistemic logic. Of course, the translation is not that straightforward, and the length of $t(\varphi)$ may be exponentially longer than the length of φ. So it may be easier to express something with $\mathcal{L}_{K[]}$. In the next section we will see that when public announcements are added to epistemic logic with common knowledge, then they do add expressive power.

8.8 *PAC*

In Chapter 7 it was claimed that *PAC* is more expressive than *S5C*. In this section we are going to show this. In Section 8.5.2 it was shown that *S5C* can distinguish spine-models. So, we will need to look for different models, but we will use some of the same ideas that were present in the spine models. We will try to find models that are different, but spoiler can only show this if there are enough rounds available. In the $\mathcal{L}_K$-game the difference between a finite and the infinite spine-model could only be shown when spoiler had enough rounds at his disposal. In the $\mathcal{L}_{KC}$-game spoiler could take a leap to the end of the finite model, which could not be matched by duplicator. We define a class of models in which such a leap is a bad move for spoiler.

8.8.1 Hairpins

Consider the following hairpin models.

Definition 8.45 $Hairpin(n) = \langle S, \sim, V \rangle$, where

- $S = \{s_m \mid m \leq (n + (n \mod 2))\} \cup \{t_m \mid m \leq (n + (n \mod 2))\} \cup \{u, v\}$
- $s_m \sim_a s_k$ iff $\min(m,k) \mod 2 = 0$ and $|m - k| = 1$
  $t_m \sim_a t_k$ iff $\min(m,k) \mod 2 = 0$ and $|m - k| = 1$
  $u \sim_a v$

- $s_m \sim_b s_k$ iff $\min(m,k) \mod 2 = 1$ and $|m-k| = 1$
  $t_m \sim_b t_k$ iff $\min(m,k) \mod 2 = 1$ and $|m-k| = 1$
  $u \sim_b s_{(n+(n \mod 2))}$
  $v \sim_b t_{(n+(n \mod 2))}$
- $V(p) = \{u\}$ □

One can view a hairpin model as being two spine models joined at the p-state. In order to make sure that the states are alternately linked by a and b, the definition is such that the model contains two extra states if n is odd. Consequently *Hairpin*(n) and *Hairpin*$(n+1)$ are identical if n is odd. The $\mathcal{L}_{KC}$-game will be played in two states of *one* hairpin model. Consider (*Hairpin*$(n), s_0)$ and (*Hairpin*$(n), t_0)$. Firstly, note that a C-move is not useful for spoiler. Such a move for the groups $\{a\}$ and $\{b\}$ boils down to a K-move, and a C-move for the group $\{a, b\}$ can be matched *exactly* by duplicator, since the game is played in the *same* model. Secondly, the p-state cannot be reached by K-moves exclusively, given the number of rounds n, just like the spine models.

Lemma 8.46 For all $n \in \mathbb{N}$ it holds that

$$(\mathit{Hairpin}(n), s_0) \equiv_{\mathcal{L}^n_{KC}} (\mathit{Hairpin}(n), t_0).$$ □

Proof Trivial. □

Lemma 8.47 There is no formula $\varphi \in \mathcal{L}_{KC}$ such that for all $n \in \mathbb{N}$ it is the case that $(\mathit{Hairpin}(n), s_0) \models \varphi$ and $(\mathit{Hairpin}(n), t_0) \not\models \varphi$. □

Proof Suppose there is such a formula. This formula has finite depth m. Therefore, by Lemma 8.46, $(\mathit{Hairpin}(m), s_0) \models \varphi$ and $(\mathit{Hairpin}(m), t_0) \models \varphi$, which contradicts our assumption. □

Now consider the announcement that $\neg p \rightarrow K_a \neg p$. This announcement splits the model in two different parts. In only one of these parts there is a p-state. Therefore, the formula $[\neg p \rightarrow K_a \neg p] C_{ab} \neg p$ is false in *Hairpin*$(n), s_0$, but true in *Hairpin*$(n), t_0$. This is shown in Figure 8.3. This leads to the following theorem.

Theorem 8.48 $\mathcal{L}_{KC} \prec \mathcal{L}_{KC[]}$ □

Proof It is easy to see that $\mathcal{L}_{KC} \preceq \mathcal{L}_{KC[]}$, since $\mathcal{L}_{KC}$ is a sublanguage of $\mathcal{L}_{KC[]}$.

To see that it is not the case that $\mathcal{L}_{KC} \equiv \mathcal{L}_{KC[]}$, consider the formula $[\neg p \rightarrow K_a \neg p] C_{ab} \neg p$. As was shown above, this is false in $(\mathit{Hairpin}(n), s_0)$, but true in $(\mathit{Hairpin}(n), t_0)$ for all $n \in \mathbb{N}$. From Lemma 8.47 it follows that there is no such formula in $\mathcal{L}_{KC}$. Therefore $\mathcal{L}_{KC} \prec \mathcal{L}_{KC[]}$. □

So the language of public announcement logic with common knowledge is really more expressive than the language of epistemic logic with common knowledge. Still the language cannot distinguish bisimilar models, because

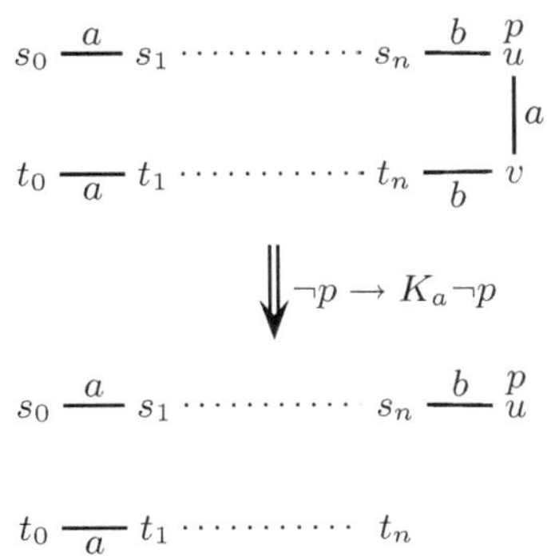

Figure 8.3. A hairpin model before and after a public announcement. In this picture it is assumed that n is even.

public announcements preserve bisimilarity (this is a special case of Proposition 6.21). So if the two models could not be distinguished before the announcement, they cannot be distinguished afterwards. Still the language has more expressive power. If we think about this in terms of model comparison games, it means that spoiler has to have even more power than in the $\mathcal{L}_K$ game. The extra move available to spoiler is called the $[\varphi]$-move.

Definition 8.49 (The $\mathcal{L}_{KC[]}(P)$ game) Let two models $M = \langle S, R, V\rangle$ and $M' = \langle S', R', V'\rangle$ and two states $s \in S$ and $s' \in S'$ be given. The *n-round $\mathcal{L}_{KC[]}(P)$ game* between spoiler and duplicator on (M, s) and (M', s') is the following. If $n = 0$ spoiler wins if s and s' differ in their atomic properties for P, else duplicator wins. Otherwise spoiler can make a K-forth-move, a K-back-move, a C-forth-move, a C-back-move, or he can initiate the following scenario:

$[\varphi]$-move Spoiler chooses a number $r < n$, and sets $T \subseteq S$ and $T' \subseteq S'$, with the current $s \in T$ and likewise $s' \in T'$.

- **Stage 1** Duplicator chooses states $t \in (T \cup T')$, $\bar{t} \in (\overline{T} \cup \overline{T'})$. Then spoiler and duplicator play the r-round game for these states. If duplicator wins this subgame, she wins the n-round game.
- **Stage 2** Otherwise, the game continues in the relativised models $(M|T, s)$ and $(M'|T', s')$ over $(n - r) - 1$ rounds.

If either player cannot perform an action prescribed above, that player loses. If the output states differ in their atomic properties for P, spoiler wins the game. If spoiler has not won after all n rounds, duplicator wins the game. □

So spoiler now has the power to restrict both models. Note that there are no 'back' and 'forth' versions of the $[\varphi]$-move. One should think of the restriction of the model as an announcement with a formula that is true in precisely the states to which the models are restricted. The depth of this formula is at most the number of rounds that spoiler takes for the stage 1 subgame.

As before duplicator has a winning strategy for this game if and only if the models satisfy the same formulas up to the depth of the number of rounds of the game.

Definition 8.50 (Modal depth) The modal depth of a formula is given by the following function $d : \mathcal{L}_{KC[]} \rightarrow \mathbb{N}$

$$\begin{array}{ll} d(p) & = 0 \\ d(\neg\varphi) & = d(\varphi) \\ d(\varphi \wedge \psi) & = \max(d(\varphi), d(\psi)) \\ d(K_a\varphi) & = 1 + d(\varphi) \\ d(C_B\varphi) & = 1 + d(\varphi) \\ d([\varphi]\psi) & = 1 + d(\varphi) + d(\psi) \end{array}$$

□

The announcement operator is quite different from the other logical operators since the depths of the two formulas to which it applies are added. This reflects the two stages of the $[\varphi]$ move.

Definition 8.51 The language $\mathcal{L}^n_{KC[]}$ of formulas of depth n is defined inductively. The language $\mathcal{L}^0_{KC[]}$ consists of all formulas given by the following BNF:

$$\varphi ::= p \mid \neg\varphi \mid \varphi \wedge \varphi$$

The language $\mathcal{L}^{n+1}_{KC[]}$ consists of all formulas given by the following BNF:

$$\varphi ::= \psi \mid K_a\psi \mid C_B\psi \mid [\chi]\xi \mid \neg\varphi \mid \varphi \wedge \varphi$$

where $\psi \in \mathcal{L}^n_{KC[]}$, and there are m and k such that $\chi \in \mathcal{L}^m_{KC[]}$, $\xi \in \mathcal{L}^k_{KC[]}$, and $m + k = n$. □

Again, up to a certain depth there are only finitely many different propositions that can be expressed.

Lemma 8.52 Given a finite set of atoms P. For every n there are only finitely many different propositions up to logical equivalence in $\mathcal{L}^n_{KC[]}$. □

Now we can prove the following theorem.

Theorem 8.53 For all $n \in \mathbb{N}$, all models $M = \langle S, R, V \rangle$ and $M' = \langle S', R', V' \rangle$ and all finite sets of atoms P: duplicator has a winning strategy for the n-round $\mathcal{L}_{KC[]}(P)$ game on (M, s) and (M', s') iff $(M, s) \equiv_{\mathcal{L}^n_{KC[]}} (M', s')$.□

Proof the proof is by induction on n. From left to right, the proof then proceeds by induction on formulas is $\mathcal{L}^n_{KC[]}$. The only difference with the proof of Theorem 8.41 is that there is an extra base case for formulas of the form $[\varphi]\psi$.

Suppose, without loss of generality, that $(M, s) \models [\varphi]\psi$. Suppose φ is false in (M, s). We have supposed that duplicator has a winning strategy for the $n+1$-round game. Therefore duplicator must have a winning strategy for the n-round game. Since $d(\varphi) < d([\varphi]\psi)$, we can apply the induction hypothesis. Therefore $(M', s') \not\models \varphi$, and therefore $(M', s') \models [\varphi]\psi$. Otherwise suppose that spoiler plays a $[\varphi]$-move, and restricts the models in both cases to the states where φ holds (and φ is true in both (M, s) and (M', s')). As the number of rounds spoiler chooses $d(\varphi)$. By the induction hypothesis spoiler will be able to win the stage 1 subgame for every two states duplicator may select by exploiting that states within the restriction satisfy φ and states outside the restriction satisfy $\neg\varphi$. Since duplicator has a winning strategy, it must be that she has a winning strategy for the stage 2 subgame. Since $(M|\varphi, s) \models \psi$, by the induction hypothesis it must be the case that $(M'|\varphi, s') \models \psi$ as well. Therefore $(M', s') \models [\varphi]\psi$.

From right to left. Suppose that $(M, s) \equiv_{\mathcal{L}^{n+1}_{KC[]}} (M', s')$. We have to give duplicator's strategy. The cases where spoiler's first move is a K-move or a C-move are as before. Suppose that spoiler's first move is a $[\varphi]$-move and he chooses sets T and T' and a number $r < (n+1)$. By the induction hypothesis duplicator has a winning strategy for the stage 1 subgame iff there are $t \in T \cup T'$ and $\overline{t} \in (\overline{T} \cup \overline{T'})$ such that they agree on all formulas up to depth r. If such a strategy is available duplicator chooses that strategy. Otherwise the game continues with $n-r$ rounds for $(M|T, s)$ and $(M'|T', s')$. By the induction hypothesis, duplicator has a winning strategy for this game iff $(M|T, s) \equiv_{\mathcal{L}^{n-r}_{KC[]}} (M'|T', s')$. This is indeed the case. To see this take a state $t \in T \cup T'$. For every state $\overline{t} \in \overline{T} \cup \overline{T'}$ there is some formula $\varphi_{t\overline{t}}$ of depth at most r which is true in t but false in t'. By Lemma 8.52 the set $\{\varphi_{t\overline{t}} \mid \overline{t} \in (\overline{T} \cup \overline{T'})\}$ has only finitely many different non-equivalent formulas. Let f be a function that picks one formula from each equivalence class $[\overline{t}]$. Let $\varphi_{t} = \bigvee_{\overline{t} \in (\overline{T} \cup \overline{T'})} f(\overline{t})$. The depth of this formula is also at most r. By similar reasoning the set $\{\varphi_t \mid t \in (T \cup T')\}$ has only finitely many non-equivalent formulas. Let g be a function that picks a formula from each equivalence class $[t]$. Now take $\varphi = \bigvee_{t \in (T \cup T')} g([t])$. This also has depth at most r. Note that this formula is true in every state in $T \cup T'$ and false in every state in $\overline{T} \cup \overline{T'}$. Suppose that $(M|T, s) \not\equiv_{\mathcal{L}^{n-r}_{KC[]}} (M'|T', s')$. Therefore there is some formula ψ of depth at most $n - r$ such that $(M|T, s) \models \psi$ and $(M'|T', s') \not\models \psi$. But then $(M, s) \models [\varphi]\psi$ and $(M', s') \not\models [\varphi]\psi$. Since $d([\varphi]\psi) = n + 1$, this contradicts our initial assumption. Therefore $(M|T, s) \equiv_{\mathcal{L}^{n-r}_{KC[]}} (M'|T', s')$, which implies that duplicator has a winning strategy for the stage 2 subgame by the induction hypothesis. □

8.9 Non-deterministic Choice

In many dynamic epistemic logics the non-deterministic choice operator $\cup$ is used to indicate that an action may be executed in more than one way. In terms of expressive power one might suspect that this operator adds expressive power to those logics. If one thinks of epistemic actions or action models as relations between pointed models, it is clear that with non-deterministic one can define the union of two of those relations. This union might not be otherwise expressible. The question is whether this supposed added expressive power on the level of actions (i.e., relations between models), also means that on the level of formulas (i.e., sets of models) this is also the case. As it turns out non-deterministic choice does not add any expressive power in this regard. This can already be suspected given the axiom for non-deterministic choice:

$$[\alpha \cup \alpha']\varphi \leftrightarrow ([\alpha]\varphi \wedge [\alpha']\varphi)$$

On the right side of the equivalence the non-deterministic choice has been eliminated. This leads to the following theorem.

Theorem 8.54 Let $\mathcal{L}^-_{KC\otimes}$ be the sublanguage $\mathcal{L}_{KC\otimes}$ without non-deterministic choice.

$$\mathcal{L}^-_{KC\otimes} \equiv \mathcal{L}_{KC\otimes} \qquad \square$$

Exercise 8.55 Prove Theorem 8.54 $\square$

Theorem 8.54 follows quite straightforwardly since the non-deterministic choice operator cannot be nested in any complex way. This is quite different in the case of $\mathcal{L}_!$. Here non-deterministic choice operators can be nested within learning operators and so on. This makes it much more difficult to prove that non-deterministic choice does not add any expressive power.

Let us call the language $\mathcal{L}_!$ without $\cup$: $\mathcal{L}^-_!$. Clearly, all actions in $\mathcal{L}^{\text{act-}}_!$ have a functional interpretation. The language with $\cup$ is just as expressive as the language without it. This is expressed in Proposition 8.56.1 – its proof by double induction requires the 'dual' Proposition 8.56.2.

Proposition 8.56

1. $\mathcal{L}^{\text{stat}}_! \equiv \mathcal{L}^{\text{stat-}}_!$.
2. Let $\alpha \in \mathcal{L}^{\text{act}}_!$. For all instances $\alpha_!$ of α that are executable in some $(M, s) \in \bullet\mathcal{S}5$ there is a $\beta \in \mathcal{L}^{\text{act-}}_!$ such that $(M, s)[\![\alpha_!]\!] = (M, s)[\![\beta]\!]$.

Proof The fact that two propositions can only be proved simultaneously is a complication from having a language defined by double induction. Alternatively, we could formulate this as the *single* proposition: "Let $\pi \in \mathcal{L}_!$. If π is a $\mathcal{L}^{\text{stat}}_!$ formula then Proposition 8.56.1 applies and if π is an action then Proposition 8.56.2 applies." We then prove this proposition by ('ordinary') induction on the structure of π. The 'interesting' cases are those where a formula is part of an action, and where an action is part of a formula, i.e., $?\varphi$ and $[\alpha]\varphi$, respectively.

Proposition 8.56.1 is proved by induction on the structure of formulas. From right to left is trivial, as $\mathcal{L}^{\text{stat-}}_! \subseteq \mathcal{L}^{\text{stat}}_!$. From left to right is simple, with the exception of inductive case $[\alpha]\varphi$, where we apply Lemma 5.24 *and* then use the inductive hypothesis for Proposition 8.56.2:

Let $(M,s) \models [\alpha]\varphi$. Then it follows from Lemma 5.24 that $(M,s) \models \bigwedge_{\alpha_!}[\alpha_!]\varphi$. Let $\alpha_!$ be an arbitrary instance of α. If $\alpha_!$ is executable in (M,s), then by using the inductive hypothesis for Proposition 8.56.2 it follows that there is a $\alpha_!^- \in \mathcal{L}_!^{\text{act-}}$ such that $(M,s)[\![\alpha_!]\!] = (M,s)[\![\alpha_!^-]\!]$. From $(M,s)[\![\alpha_!^-]\!] \models \varphi$ and the inductive hypothesis (for Proposition 8.56.1) follows that there is a $\varphi^- \in \mathcal{L}_!^{\text{stat-}}$ such that $(M,s)[\![\alpha_!^-]\!] \models \varphi^-$. So $(M,s) \models [\alpha_!^-]\varphi^-$. As this holds for all $\alpha_!^-$, it follows that $(M,s) \models \bigwedge_{\alpha_!}[\alpha_!^-]\varphi^-$. Formula $\bigwedge_{\alpha_!}[\alpha_!^-]\varphi^-$ is a formula in $\mathcal{L}_!^{\text{stat-}}$.

Proposition 8.56.2 is proved by induction on the structure of actions. The only relevant case to prove is $?\varphi$:

Suppose $?\varphi$ is executable in some (M,s). Then $(M,s) \models \varphi$. By induction, there is a $\varphi^- \in \mathcal{L}_!^{\text{stat-}}$ such that $(M,s) \models \varphi^-$. So the required action is $?\varphi^-$.□

8.10 *AM*

Just as the case for *PA*, we proved in chapter 7 that the proof system *AM* is complete by showing that every formula that contains an action model operator can be translated to a provably equivalent formula that does not contain any such operators. This leads to the following theorem.

Theorem 8.57 $\mathcal{L}_K \equiv \mathcal{L}_{K\otimes}$ □

Proof It is clear that $\mathcal{L}_K \preceq \mathcal{L}_{K\otimes}$, since $\mathcal{L}_K$ is a sublanguage of $\mathcal{L}_{K\otimes}$.

To see that $\mathcal{L}_{K\otimes} \preceq \mathcal{L}_K$, we use the translation provided in definition 7.37. From Lemma 7.40, together with the soundness of **AM**, it follows that $\varphi \equiv t(\varphi)$ for every $\varphi \in \mathcal{L}_{K\otimes}$. □

So it is not only the case that public announcements do not add expressive power to $\mathcal{L}_K$, as was shown in Theorem 8.44, but also action model operators do not add any expressive power to $\mathcal{L}_K$. This also implies that $\mathcal{L}_{KC\otimes}$ cannot distinguish bisimilar models.

8.11 Relativised Common Knowledge

Analogous to the results on expressivity we have seen for *PA* and *AM*, one can show that $\mathcal{L}_{KRC}$ and $\mathcal{L}_{KRC[]}$ are equally expressive.

Theorem 8.58 $\mathcal{L}_{KRC} \equiv \mathcal{L}_{KRC[]}$ □

Exercise 8.59 Prove Theorem 8.58. □

It is also clear that $\mathcal{L}_{KRC}$ is more expressive than $\mathcal{L}_{KC}$, since $\mathcal{L}_{KC[]}$ is more expressive than $\mathcal{L}_{KC}$ and $\mathcal{L}_{KRC}$ is at least as expressive as $\mathcal{L}_{KC[]}$.

Theorem 8.60 $\mathcal{L}_{KRC} \succeq \mathcal{L}_{KC[]}$ □

Proof Using Theorem 8.58 it suffices to show that $\mathcal{L}_{KRC[]} \succeq \mathcal{L}_{KC[]}$. Observe that $C_B\varphi$ is equivalent to $\varphi \wedge C_B(\top, \varphi)$. So, given a formula $\varphi \in \mathcal{L}_{KC[]}$, we can obtain a formula $\psi \in \mathcal{L}_{KRC[]}$ which is equivalent to it, by replacing every occurrence of $C_B\varphi$ by $\varphi \wedge C_B(\top, \varphi)$. □

The remainder of this section is devoted to showing that the converse of this does not hold: we show that $\mathcal{L}_{KRC} \succ \mathcal{L}_{KC[]}$. It is unknown whether this holds for $\mathcal{S}5$, but when we take the general modal case $\mathcal{K}$, it does indeed hold. In order to show that $\mathcal{L}_{KRC}$ is more expressive than $\mathcal{L}_{KC[]}$ we need to find a formula in $\mathcal{L}_{KRC}$ which is not equivalent to any formula in $\mathcal{L}_{KC[]}$. The formula

$$C(p, \neg Kp)$$

fits this purpose. This will be shown in Theorem 8.66.

We can show that this formula cannot be expressed in $\mathcal{L}_{KC[]}$ by using the $\mathcal{L}_{KC[]}$-game. We will show that for every n there are two models such that duplicator has a winning strategy for the n round $\mathcal{L}_{KC[]}$ game game, but $C(p, \neg Kp)$ is true in one of these models and false in the other.

In Definition 8.63 the models that $\mathcal{L}_{KRC}$ can distinguish, but $\mathcal{L}_{KC[]}$ cannot are given. Since the model comparison game for $\mathcal{L}_{KC[]}$ contains the $[\varphi]$-move we also need to prove that the relevant submodels cannot be distinguished by $\mathcal{L}_{KC[]}$. We deal with these submodels first in the next definition and lemma.

Consider the following hourglass models.

Definition 8.61 Let the model $Hourglass(n, m) = \langle S, R, V \rangle$ where $n, m \in \mathbb{N}$ be defined by

- $S = \{s_i \mid 0 \leq i \leq n\} \cup \{t_i \mid 0 \leq i \leq m\} \cup \{u\}$
- $R = \{(s_i, s_{i-1}) \mid 1 \leq i \leq n\} \cup$
  $\{(t_i, t_{i-1}) \mid 1 \leq i \leq m\} \cup$
  $\{(s_i, u) \mid 0 \leq i \leq n\} \cup$
  $\{(t_i, u) \mid 0 \leq i \leq m\} \cup$
  $\{(u, s_n), (u, t_m)\}$
- $V(p) = S \setminus \{u\}$ □

An example of an hourglass model is given in Figure 8.4. The idea is that spoiler cannot distinguish a state in the top line from a state in the bottom line of these models if the lines are long enough. Indeed, apart from u this model consists of two lines. So if spoiler plays K-moves on these lines, duplicator's strategy is the same as for the spines of the hedgehog models from Section 8.3.2. If he moves to u, duplicator also moves to u, and surely duplicator cannot lose the subsequent game in that case. In these models a C-move is very bad for spoiler, since all states are connected by the reflexive transitive closure of R. A $[\varphi]$-move will either yield two spines which are too long, or it will be a smaller hourglass model, which will still be too large, since the $[\varphi]$-move reduces the number of available moves. The lemma below captures this idea.

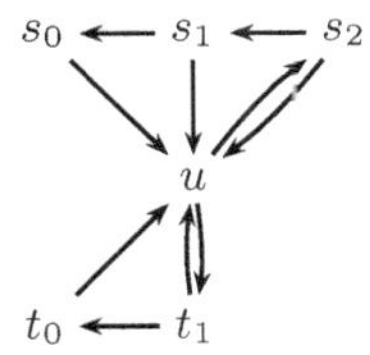

Figure 8.4. A picture of *Hourglass*(2, 1).

Lemma 8.62 For all n, m, i, j, such that $0 \leq i \leq n$ and $0 \leq j \leq m$ it holds that

1. Duplicator has a winning strategy for the $\mathcal{L}_{KC[]}$ game for $(Hourglass(n, m), s_i)$ and $(Hourglass(n, m), s_j)$ with at most $\min(i, j)$ rounds.
2. Duplicator has a winning strategy for the $\mathcal{L}_{KC[]}$ game for $(Hourglass(n, m), t_i)$ and $(Hourglass(n, m), t_j)$ with at most $\min(i, j)$ rounds.
3. Duplicator has a winning strategy for the $\mathcal{L}_{KC[]}$ game for $(Hourglass(n, m), s_i)$ and $(Hourglass(n, m), t_j)$ with at most $\min(i, j)$ rounds. □

Proof We prove 1–3 simultaneously by induction on the number of rounds.

Base case If the number of rounds is 0, then the two states only have to agree on propositional variables. They do agree, since p is true in both.

Induction hypotheses For all n, m, i, j, such that $0 \leq i \leq n$ and $0 \leq j \leq m$ it holds that

1. Duplicator has a winning strategy for the $\mathcal{L}_{KC[]}$ game for $(Hourglass(n, m), s_i)$ and $(Hourglass(n, m), s_j)$ with at most $\min(i, j) = k$ rounds.
2. Duplicator has a winning strategy for the $\mathcal{L}_{KC[]}$ game for $(Hourglass(n, m), t_i)$ and $(Hourglass(n, m), t_j)$ with at most $\min(i, j) = k$ rounds.
3. Duplicator has a winning strategy for the $\mathcal{L}_{KC[]}$ game for $(Hourglass(n, m), s_i)$ and $(Hourglass(n, m), t_j)$ with at most $\min(i, j) = k$ rounds.

Induction step

1. This is trivially true if $i = j$. Otherwise assume without loss of generality that $i < j$. Suppose that $i = k + 1$. There are three different kinds of moves that spoiler can take.

   K-move If spoiler chooses a K-move, he chooses to s_{i-1} (or to s_{j-1}), or to u. In the latter case duplicator responds by also choosing u, and has a winning strategy for the resulting subgame. Otherwise duplicator moves to the s_{j-1} (or s_{i-1}). Duplicator has a winning strategy for the resulting subgame by induction hypothesis 1.

   C-move If spoiler chooses a C-move, he chooses some state in the model. Duplicator responds by choosing the same state, since all the states can be reached by the reflexive transitive closure of the accessibility relation from s_i and from s_j. Duplicator has a winning strategy for the resulting subgame.

[φ]-move Spoiler chooses a number of rounds r and two sets T and T' with $s_i \in T$ and $s_j \in T'$. Since there is only one model, it must be the case that $T = T'$, otherwise duplicator chooses the same state twice in the r-round stage 1 subgame, and has a winning strategy for this subgame. Moreover, for all s_x such that $x \geq r$ it must be the case that $s_x \in T$. Otherwise, duplicator has a winning strategy in the r-round stage 1 subgame by selecting $s_i \in T$ and some $s_y \in \overline{T}$ with $y \geq r$. Induction hypothesis 1 applies to this subgame since $r < i$.
In the stage 2 subgame there are two possibilities. The generated submodel consists of one line, because $u \in \overline{T}$, or the generated submodel is again an hourglass model. In both cases the length of the (top) line is at least $n - r$, and the position of s_i is now at least $i - r$ and the position of s_j is now at least $j - r$. Since the number of rounds is $(i - r) - 1$, either the single line is too long or induction hypothesis 1 applies.

2. Analogous to 1.
3. Analogous to 1 and 2. The cases for the K-move and the C-move are completely analogous, but now in the case for the [φ]-move the fact that for all s_x such that $x \geq r$ it must be the case that $s_x \in T$ and that $t_x \in T$ for all t_x such that $x \geq r$. □

Lastly consider the hourglass models with an appendage. These models are just like hourglass models, but there is one extra state. This state is a *blind state*, i.e., there are no states accessible from it. This extra state enables one to distinguish the top line of the model from the bottom line with the formula $C(p, \neg Kp)$.

Definition 8.63 Let the model *Hourglass*$^+(n, m) = \langle S, R, V \rangle$ where $n, m \in \mathbb{N}$ be defined by

- $S = \{s_i \mid 0 \leq i \leq n\} \cup \{t_i \mid 0 \leq i \leq m\} \cup \{v, u\}$
- $R = \{(s_i, s_{i-1}) \mid 1 \leq i \leq n\} \cup$
  $\{(t_i, t_{i-1}) \mid 1 \leq i \leq m\} \cup$
  $\{(s_i, u) \mid 0 \leq i \leq n\} \cup$
  $\{(t_i, u) \mid 0 \leq i \leq m\} \cup$
  $\{(u, s_n), (u, t_m), (s_0, v)\}$
- $V(p) = S \setminus \{u\}$ □

The picture below represents *Hourglass*$^+(2, 2)$.

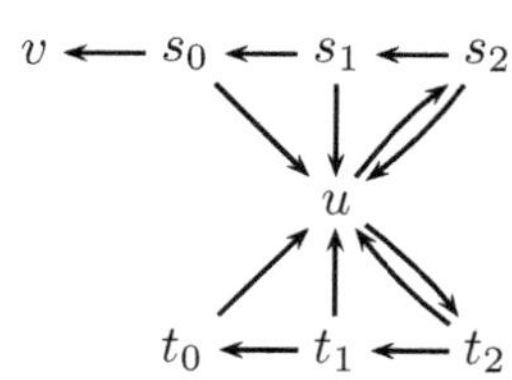

The formula $C(p, \neg Kp)$ is true in every state in the bottom line, but false in the top line, since $\neg Kp$ is not true in state v. However when the $\mathcal{L}_{KC[]}$-game is played spoiler will not be able to win the game if v is farther away than the number of rounds available. Apart from v the model is just like an hourglass. So the only new option for spoiler is to force one of the current states to v, and the other to another state. Then spoiler chooses a K-move and takes a step from the non-v state and duplicator is stuck at v. However if the model is large enough v is too far away. Again a C-move does not help spoiler, because it can be matched exactly by duplicator. Reducing the model with a $[\varphi]$-move will yield either a hourglass (with or without an appendage) or two lines, for which spoiler does not have a winning strategy. The idea leads to the following Lemma.

Lemma 8.64 For all n, m, i, j, such that $0 \leq i \leq n$ and $0 \leq j \leq m$ it holds that

1. Duplicator has a winning strategy for the $\mathcal{L}_{KC[]}$ game for $(\mathit{Hourglass}^+(n, m), s_i)$ and $(\mathit{Hourglass}^+(n, m), s_j)$ with at most $\min(i, j)$ rounds.
2. Duplicator has a winning strategy for the $\mathcal{L}_{KC[]}$ game for $(\mathit{Hourglass}^+(n, m), t_i)$ and $(\mathit{Hourglass}^+(n, m), t_j)$ with at most $\min(i, j)$ rounds.
3. Duplicator has a winning strategy for the $\mathcal{L}_{KC[]}$ game for $(\mathit{Hourglass}^+(n, m), s_i)$ and $(\mathit{Hourglass}^+(n, m), t_j)$ with at most $\min(i, j)$ rounds. □

Proof The proof is analogous to that of Lemma 8.62, except that in this case a $[\varphi]$-move may lead to both an hourglass model and an hourglass model with an appendage. □

The fact that duplicator has a winning strategy for these games means that these models are indistinguishable in $\mathcal{L}_{KC[]}$.

Lemma 8.65 For all $n, m \in \mathbb{N}$ it holds that

$$(\mathit{Hourglass}^+(n, n), s_n) \equiv_{\mathcal{L}^n_{KC[]}} (\mathit{Hourglass}^+(n, n), t_n). \quad \square$$

Proof This follows immediately from Lemma 8.64 and Theorem 8.53. □

This lemma leads to the following theorem.

Theorem 8.66 $\mathcal{L}_{KRC} \succ \mathcal{L}_{KC[]}$. □

Proof Suppose $\mathcal{L}_{KC[]}$ is just as expressive as $\mathcal{L}_{KRC}$. Then there is a formula $\varphi \in \mathcal{L}_{KC[]}$ with $\varphi \equiv C(p, \neg Kp)$. Suppose $d(\varphi) = n$. In that case we would have $(\mathit{Hourglass}^+(n, n), s_n) \not\models \varphi$ and $(\mathit{Hourglass}^+(n, n), t_n) \models \varphi$, contradicting Lemma 8.65. Hence, $\mathcal{L}_{KRC} \succ \mathcal{L}_{KC[]}$. □

8.12 Notes

As was noted in the introduction of this chapter, questions of relative expressive power are interesting for many logics that are interpreted in the same class of models. Some of the results on expressive power of propositional logic presented in Section 8.2 were based on Massey's textbook [140, Chapter 22], where the focus is on functional completeness. However these results are also interesting from the point of view of expressivity.

The idea to use games for comparing models is due to Ehrenfeucht and Fraïssé. Modifying these games for modal logic first seems to be a part of modal logic folklore. It is such an easy adaptation from the case for first-order logic, that no one claims to be the inventor of the game. On the other hand, many authors often do not refer to earlier work when they use such games. The earliest definition of the game known to us is in Kees Doets' dissertation [53]. The game is also given in the context of non-well-founded set theory in [15]. The extension of the game for epistemic logic with common knowledge can be found in [12]. The public announcement move was defined in [116].

The result that in single agent *S5*every formula is equivalent to a formula with modal depth at most 1 is well known in modal logic. It is shown in Hughes and Cresswell [107], which is based on Wajsberg [193] and it was independently shown by Meyer and van der Hoek [148]. It both these approaches the proof is by reducing each formula to a normal form which has modal depth at most 1 by syntactic manipulation. The proof presented in Section 8.5.1 on the other hand uses the semantics of *S5*.

In [168] Plaza introduced $\mathcal{L}_{K[]}$ and provided a sound and complete proof system for it. Plaza showed that $\mathcal{L}_K$ and $\mathcal{L}_{K[]}$ are equally expressive. In [75] it was shown for a more general dynamic epistemic logic (without common knowledge) that it is equally expressive as $\mathcal{L}_K$. The fact that $\mathcal{L}_{KC}$ is more expressive than $\mathcal{L}_K$ is folklore. Baltag, Moss, and Solecki showed, contrary to Plaza's result, that $\mathcal{L}_{KC[]}$ is more expressive than $\mathcal{L}_{KC}$ [12]. In the same paper they also showed that $\mathcal{L}_{K\otimes}$ is equally expressive as $\mathcal{L}_K$. In [116] a complete proof system was provided for $\mathcal{L}_K$ and it was shown that $\mathcal{L}_{KRC}$ and $\mathcal{L}_{KRC[]}$ are equally expressive. It was established that $\mathcal{L}_{KRC}$ is more expressive than $\mathcal{L}_{KC[]}$ in [25] for the $\mathcal{K}$ case. Whether the same is true for *S5* is still an open problem.

In [26] action model logic is translated to propositional dynamic logic, showing that propositional dynamic logic is at least as expressive as action model logic. However if one also allows iteration over action models, then the logic becomes very expressive; it becomes undecidable. This is shown by Miller and Moss [149].

A

Selected Answers to Exercises

Answers to Exercises from Chapter 2

Answer to Exercise 2.5 We give an informal argument using a formal proof concept: that of induction over n. The case $n = 0$ is straightforward ($E_B^0\varphi$ is φ and this is false only if $\neg\varphi$ holds, the latter having an empty sequence of $\hat{K}$-operators.) Let us also consider the case $n = 1$ separately, since we will use it in the induction step. $E_B^1\varphi$ is false, if and only if not everybody from B knows that φ, or, in other words, there is an agent a^1 in B that considers $\neg\varphi$ possible: $\hat{K}_{a^1}\neg\varphi$.

Let us now assume that up to a specific n we know that $E_B^n\varphi$ is false if and only if there is a sequence of agents names $a^1, a^2, \ldots a^n$ $(a^i \in B, i \leq n)$ such that $\hat{K}_{a^1}\hat{K}_{a^2}\ldots\hat{K}_{a^n}\neg\varphi$ holds. Since the a^i's are only variables over names, we might phrase the induction hypothesis alternatively as:

$$\begin{aligned}&E_B^n\varphi \text{ is false iff} \\ \text{there are } a^2, a^3, \ldots a^{n+1} &\text{ such that } \hat{K}_{a^2}\hat{K}_{a^3}\ldots\hat{K}_{a^{n+1}}\neg\varphi \text{ holds}\end{aligned} \tag{A.1}$$

Now consider the case $n+1$. $E_B^{n+1}\varphi$ is false if and only if $E_B E_B^n\varphi$ is false, or, more precisely, if $E_B^1 E_B^n\varphi$ is false. Using our established result for 1 iteration, we have that $E_B^1 E_B^n\varphi$ is false iff for some agent $a^1 \in B$, we have $\hat{K}_a^1\neg E_B^n\varphi$. We now can apply the induction hypothesis (A.1) to $E_B^n\varphi$ to conclude that $E_B^1 E_B^n\varphi$ is false iff for some sequence of agent names $a^1, a^2 \ldots a^{n+1}$ we have $\hat{K}_{a^1}\hat{K}_{a^2}\ldots\hat{K}_{a^{n+1}}\neg\varphi$. □

Answer to Exercise 2.8

1. The formalisation of each item under 1 is the corresponding item under 2 (so 2 (a) formalises 1 (a), etc.).
2. Hint: have first a look at our proof of Equation (2.2) on page 20, or try Exercise 2.9 first. □

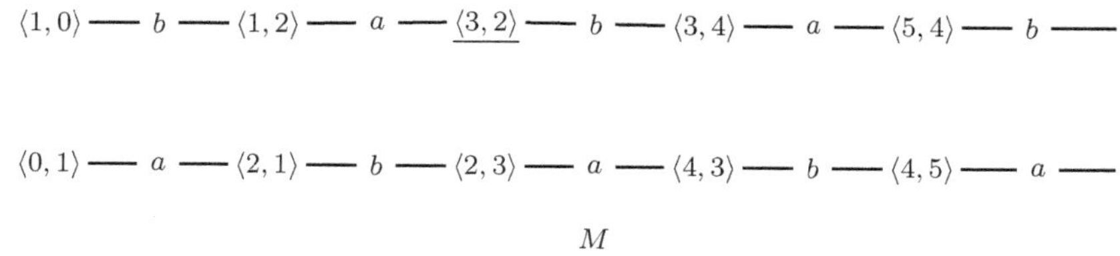

Figure A.1. Modelling Consecutive Numbers.

Answer to Exercise 2.10 Since the accessibility relations are all equivalences, we write $\sim_a$ and $\sim_b$, respectively.

1. See Figure A.1. Note that the model M consists of two disjunctive parts, depending on who wears an odd, and who wears an even number. Once Anne and Bill see the numbers on the other's forehead, they know in 'which part of the model they are'.
2. We show that $M, \langle 1,0\rangle \models K_a a_1 \wedge \mathsf{win_a}$. First of all, note that $\langle 1,0\rangle \sim_a t$ iff $t = \langle 1,0\rangle$: if the state would be $\langle 1,0\rangle$, Anne would see a 0, and exactly know her own number: 1! Hence, we have $M, \langle 1,0\rangle \models K_a a_1$. Since $\mathsf{win_a}$ is defined as a knowing the number on her head, we have the desired property.
3. The previous item demonstrates that $\langle 1,0\rangle$ qualifies for this. By symmetry, we also obtain $\langle 0,1\rangle$, in which Bill can win the game. These are also the only two states in which a player can win the game, since in every other state s, each player considers a state t possible in which his or her own number is different that that in s. When given that $\langle 3,2\rangle$ is the actual state, the two states $\langle 1,0\rangle$ and $\langle 0,1\rangle$ in which an agent can win, differ, in the following respect: $\langle 1,0\rangle$ can be reached, using the agents' access, from the state $\langle 3,2\rangle$, since we have $\langle 3,2\rangle \sim_a \langle 1,2\rangle$ and $\langle 1,2\rangle \sim_b \langle 1,0\rangle$. We can express this in the modal language by saying that in $\langle 3,2\rangle$ it holds that $\hat{K}_a\hat{K}_b(a_1 \wedge b_0)$, and hence $M, \langle 3,2\rangle \models \hat{K}_a\hat{K}_b\mathsf{win_a}$. On the other hand, from $\langle 3,2\rangle$, the state $\langle 0,1\rangle$ is not reachable: $M, \langle 3,2\rangle \models \neg\hat{K}_a\mathsf{win_b} \wedge \neg\hat{K}_b\mathsf{win_b} \wedge \neg\hat{K}_a\hat{K}_b\mathsf{win_b} \wedge \neg\hat{K}_b\hat{K}_a\mathsf{win_b}$. In fact, we have for any n that $M, \langle 3,2\rangle \models \neg\hat{K}_{x_1}\hat{K}_{x_2}\dots\hat{K}_{x_n}\mathsf{win_b}$, $x_i \in \{a,b\}$.
4. We show items 4 and 7 of Example 2.4.
   To start with 4, note that $M, \langle 3,2\rangle \models K_a\varphi$ iff φ is true in both $\langle 3,2\rangle$ and $\langle 1,2\rangle$. In this case, $\varphi = K_b\psi$, and this is true in $\langle 3,2\rangle$ if ψ is true in $\langle 3,2\rangle$ and $\langle 3,4\rangle$, and $K_b\psi$ is true in $\langle 1,2\rangle$ if ψ is true in both $\langle 1,2\rangle$ and $\langle 1,0\rangle$. Hence we have to check whether ψ holds in $\langle 3,2\rangle, \langle 3,4\rangle, \langle 1,2\rangle$ and $\langle 1,0\rangle$. In our case, $\psi = K_a\chi$, so we have to check whether χ holds in all states accessible for a from the four states just mentioned, hence in $\langle 3,2\rangle, \langle 1,2\rangle, \langle 3,4\rangle, \langle 5,4\rangle$ and $\langle 1,0\rangle$ (remember that every state is accessible to itself, for every agent). Now, in our case, $\chi = (b_0 \vee b_2 \vee b_4)$, which is indeed true in those 5 states, so that we have verified $M, \langle 3,2\rangle \models K_aK_bK_a(b_0 \vee b_2 \vee b_4)$.

Regarding item 7, we have to demonstrate both $M, \langle 3,2\rangle \models E_{\{a,b\}}\neg a_5$ and $M, \langle 3,2\rangle \models \neg E_{\{a,b\}}E_{\{a,b\}}\neg a_5$. For the first, note that all the states that a considers possible in $\langle 3,2\rangle$ are $\langle 3,2\rangle$ itself and $\langle 1,2\rangle$. In both of them, $\neg a_5$ holds, hence $M, \langle 3,2\rangle \models K_a\neg a_5$. Similarly, since $\neg a_5$ holds in $\langle 3,2\rangle$ and $\langle 3,4\rangle$, which are all the states t for which $R_b\langle 3,2\rangle t$, we also have $M, \langle 3,2\rangle \models K_b\neg a_5$. The definition of everybody knows ($E_{\{a,b\}}\varphi$ means $K_a\varphi \wedge K_b\varphi$) then yields the desired result. To finally show that $M, \langle 3,2\rangle \models \neg E_{\{a,b\}}E_{\{a,b\}}\neg a_5$, note that $\neg E_{\{a,b\}}E_{\{a,b\}}\neg a_5$ is equivalent to $\neg E_{\{a,b\}}\neg\neg E_{\{a,b\}}\neg a_5$, which, by using the definition of $\hat{E}_{\{a,b\}}$, is equivalent to $\hat{E}_{\{a,b\}}\hat{E}_{\{a,b\}}a_5$. And $M, \langle 3,2\rangle \models \hat{E}_{\{a,b\}}\hat{E}_{\{a,b\}}a_5$ holds since we have all of $R_{E_{\{a,b\}}}\langle 3,2\rangle\langle 3,4\rangle$ and $R_{E_{\{a,b\}}}\langle 3,4\rangle\langle 5,4\rangle$ and $M, \langle 5,4\rangle \models a_5$ (for the definition of $R_{E_{\{a,b\}}}$, go to Definition 2.30). □

Answer to Exercise 2.18

1. Note that, by the axiom of propositional tautologies, we have the following:

$$(\varphi \rightarrow \chi) \rightarrow ((\chi \rightarrow \psi) \rightarrow (\varphi \rightarrow \psi))$$

and then apply Modus Ponens to that and the two antecedents of HS.
2. Suppose that $\vdash \varphi \rightarrow \psi$. By necessitation, we derive $\vdash K_a(\varphi \rightarrow \psi)$. Distribution says that $\vdash K_a(\varphi \rightarrow \psi) \rightarrow (K_a\varphi \rightarrow K_a\psi)$. Applying modus ponens to what we have so far, gives $\vdash K_a\varphi \rightarrow K_a\psi$.
3. The equivalence between K and K' follows from the following instance of *Prop*:
$(\alpha \rightarrow (\beta \rightarrow \gamma)) \leftrightarrow ((\alpha \wedge \beta) \rightarrow \gamma)$.
For K'', from $\vdash (\varphi \wedge \psi) \rightarrow \varphi$ and the the second item of this exercise, we infer $\vdash K_a(\varphi \wedge \psi) \rightarrow K_a\varphi$. Idem for $\vdash K_a(\varphi \wedge \psi) \rightarrow K_a\psi$. The required conclusion now follows by applying modus ponens twice to the following instance of *Prop*:

$$\begin{aligned}&(K_a(\varphi \wedge \psi) \rightarrow K_a\varphi)\\ &\rightarrow ((K_a(\varphi \wedge \psi) \rightarrow K_a\psi) \rightarrow (K_a(\varphi \wedge \psi) \rightarrow (K_a\varphi \wedge K_a\psi)))\end{aligned}$$ □

For the converse, note that K' and hence K' follows from K'' by this instance of *Prop*:
$(K_a(\varphi \wedge \psi) \rightarrow (K_a\varphi \wedge K_a\psi)) \rightarrow (K_a(\varphi \wedge \psi) \rightarrow (K_a\varphi \rightarrow K_a\psi))$
4. Here is a formal proof:

1	$\varphi \rightarrow (\psi \rightarrow (\varphi \wedge \psi))$	*Prop*
2	$K_a\varphi \rightarrow K_a(\psi \rightarrow (\varphi \wedge \psi))$	1, item 2.18.2
3	$(K_a\varphi \wedge K_a\psi) \rightarrow K_a\varphi$	*Prop*
4	$(K_a\varphi \wedge K_a\psi) \rightarrow K_a(\psi \rightarrow (\varphi \wedge \psi))$	$HS, 3, 2$
5	$K_a(\psi \rightarrow (\varphi \wedge \psi)) \rightarrow (K_a\psi \rightarrow K_a(\varphi \wedge \psi))$	K, item 2.18.3
6	$(K_a\varphi \wedge K_a\psi) \rightarrow (K_a\psi \rightarrow K_a(\varphi \wedge \psi))$	$HS, 4, 5$

7 $((K_a\varphi \wedge K_a\psi) \rightarrow (K_a\psi \rightarrow K_a(\varphi \wedge \psi))) \rightarrow$
$((K_a\varphi \wedge K_a\psi) \rightarrow K_a(\varphi \wedge \psi))$ — $Prop$
8 $(K_a\varphi \wedge K_a\psi) \rightarrow K_a(\varphi \wedge \psi)$ — $MP, 6, 7$

Answer to Exercise 2.37 For the first four items, see Exercise 2.1.2.1 in [148], and for the fifth item, consult Exercise 2.1.2.3 in the same reference. Finally, for the last item, for the 'only if' direction, use Theorem 2.38. Here we give a proof of the 'if' part. Assume $B' \subseteq B$. Note that we then immediately have $E_B\varphi \rightarrow E_{B'}\varphi(*)$, by definition of everybody knows, and propositional steps.

1	$C_B\varphi \rightarrow E_BC_B\varphi$	$mix, Prop, MP$
2	$E_BC_B\varphi \rightarrow E_{B'}C_B\varphi$	$(*)$
3	$C_B\varphi \rightarrow E_{B'}C_B\varphi$	$(1, 2, HS)$
4	$C_{B'}(C_B\varphi \rightarrow E_{B'}C_B\varphi)$	$3, necessitation$
5	$C_{B'}(C_B\varphi \rightarrow E_{B'}C_B\varphi) \rightarrow (C_B\varphi \rightarrow C_{B'}C_B\varphi)$	$induction for\ C_{B'}$
6	$C_B\varphi \rightarrow C_{B'}C_B\varphi$	$MP, 4, 5$
7	$C_B\varphi \rightarrow \varphi$	$mix, Prop, MP$
8	$C_{B'}(C_B\varphi \rightarrow \varphi)$	$7, necessitation$
9	$C_{B'}C_B\varphi \rightarrow C_{B'}\varphi$	$8, mix, distribution, MP$
10	$C_B\varphi \rightarrow C_{B'}\varphi$	$6, 9, HS$

Answer to Exercise 2.41 Note that **KD45** is an extension of **K**, so we can use the properties of Exercise 2.18.

1	$B(\varphi \wedge \neg B\varphi) \rightarrow (B\varphi \wedge B\neg B\varphi)$	K'', Exercise 2.18
2	$B\varphi \rightarrow BB\varphi$	$Axiom\ 4$
3	$(B\varphi \rightarrow BB\varphi) \rightarrow ((B\varphi \wedge B\neg B\varphi) \rightarrow (BB\varphi \wedge B\neg B\varphi))$	$Prop$
4	$(B\varphi \wedge B\neg B\varphi) \rightarrow (BB\varphi \wedge B\neg B\varphi))$	$2, 3, MP$
5	$B(\varphi \wedge \neg B\varphi) \rightarrow (BB\varphi \wedge B\neg B\varphi)$	$HS, 1, 4$
6	$(BB\varphi \wedge B\neg B\varphi) \rightarrow B(B\varphi \wedge \neg B\varphi)$	Exercise 2.18.4
7	$B(\varphi \wedge \neg B\varphi) \rightarrow B(B\varphi \wedge \neg B\varphi)$	$HS, 5, 6$
8	$(B\varphi \wedge \neg B\varphi) \rightarrow \bot$	$Prop$
9	$B(B\varphi \wedge \neg B\varphi) \rightarrow B\bot$	8, Exercise 2.18.2
10	$\neg B\bot \rightarrow \neg B(B\varphi \wedge \neg B\varphi)$	$9, Prop$
11	$\neg B(B\varphi \wedge \neg B\varphi)$	$MP, 10, D$

Answers to Exercises from Chapter 3

Answer to Exercise 3.8

1. Suppose $\oplus$ satisfies $(\mathcal{K} \oplus 1), (\mathcal{K} \oplus 2)$ and $(\mathcal{K} \oplus 3)$, and also $(\mathcal{K} \oplus min)^{\{1,2,3\}}$. We show that is also satisfies $(\mathcal{K} \oplus 4)$. Suppose $\mathcal{K}$ is a belief set and $\varphi \in \mathcal{K}$. By $(\mathcal{K} \oplus 3)$ we know that $\mathcal{K} \subseteq \mathcal{K} \oplus \varphi$. Now, if the

other direction does not hold, we can show that we are be able to find a smaller candidate for the expansion of $\mathcal{K}$ with φ. To be more precise, suppose $\mathcal{K} \oplus \varphi \not\subseteq \mathcal{K}$. Let $\mathcal{K} \oplus' \varphi = \mathcal{K}$, and for all other φ and $\mathcal{K}$, we let $\oplus'$ be equal to $\oplus$. It is easy to check that $\oplus'$ verifies $(\mathcal{K} \oplus 1)$ (we assumed that $\mathcal{K}$ is a belief set), $(\mathcal{K} \oplus 2)$ (we assume the antecedent of $(\mathcal{K} \oplus 4)$, i.e. $\varphi \in \mathcal{K}$) and $(\mathcal{K} \oplus 3)$ (we even have put $\mathcal{K}$ *equal* to $\mathcal{K} \oplus' \varphi$). We have $(\mathcal{K} \oplus' \varphi) = \mathcal{K} \subset \mathcal{K} \oplus \varphi$: contradicting the fact that $\oplus$ give the smallest set satisfying the first three postulates!.
2. Suppose $\mathcal{K} \subseteq \mathcal{H}$ but at the same time $\mathcal{K} \oplus \varphi \not\subseteq \mathcal{H} \oplus \varphi$, for a given $\mathcal{K}, \mathcal{H}$ and φ. Then for some ψ we have $\psi \in \mathcal{K} \oplus \varphi$, but $\psi \notin \mathcal{H} \oplus \varphi$. Now define $\oplus'$ by $\mathcal{K} \oplus' \varphi = (\mathcal{K} \oplus \varphi) \cap (\mathcal{H} \oplus \varphi)$ (and, for all 'other' $\mathcal{K}, \mathcal{H}$ and φ, we can define $\oplus'$ to equal $\oplus$). Since the intersection of two belief sets is a belief set, $\oplus'$ satisfies postulate $(\mathcal{K} \oplus 1)$. Postulate $(\mathcal{K} \oplus 2)$ also holds for it, since φ is an element of both $\mathcal{K} \oplus \varphi$ and $\mathcal{H} \oplus \varphi$. On top of this, $\oplus'$ satisfies $(\mathcal{K} \oplus 3)$: $\mathcal{K} \subseteq (\mathcal{K} \oplus \varphi) \cap (\mathcal{H} \oplus \varphi) = \mathcal{K} \oplus' \varphi$. Hence, $\oplus'$ satisfies the postulates $(\mathcal{K} \oplus 1), (\mathcal{K} \oplus 2)$ and $(\mathcal{K} \oplus 3)$. But since $(\mathcal{K} \oplus' \varphi) \subseteq (\mathcal{K} \oplus \varphi)$, and moreover $\mathcal{K} \oplus \varphi$ is not the smallest set satisfying $(\mathcal{K} \oplus 1), (\mathcal{K} \oplus 2)$ and $(\mathcal{K} \oplus 3)$. □

Answer to Exercise 3.9 This is done by an easy case-distinction:

$\varphi \in \mathcal{K}$ In this case, the property to be proven follows directly from $(\mathcal{K} \ominus 5)$.
$\varphi \notin \mathcal{K}$ Now, by $(\mathcal{K} \ominus 3)$, $\mathcal{K} \ominus \varphi = \mathcal{K}$, and, by $(\mathcal{K} \circledast 3)$, we also have $\mathcal{K} \subseteq \mathcal{K} \oplus \varphi$. Together this gives the desired $\mathcal{K} \subseteq (\mathcal{K} \ominus \varphi) \oplus \varphi$. □

Answer to Exercise 3.10 The $\subseteq$-direction is immediate from $(\mathcal{K} \ominus 2)$. For the other direction, we use $(\mathcal{K} \ominus 5)$: Since $\mathcal{K}$ is a belief base, we know that $\top \in \mathcal{K}$. So, by the postulate just referred to, we have $\mathcal{K} \subseteq (\mathcal{K} \ominus \top) \oplus \top$. Since, by $(\mathcal{K} \ominus 1)$, the set $\mathcal{K} \ominus \top$ is also a belief set, we have $\top \in (\mathcal{K} \ominus \top)$ and hence, by the postulate $(\mathcal{K} \oplus 4)$, we derive $(\mathcal{K} \ominus \top) \oplus \top = \mathcal{K} \ominus \top$, giving us $\mathcal{K} \subseteq (\mathcal{K} \ominus \top) \oplus \top = \mathcal{K} \oplus \top$.

Note that only the postulates $(\mathcal{K} \ominus 1)(\mathcal{K} \ominus 2)$ and $(\mathcal{K} \ominus 5)$ for contraction are needed, with the rather weak postulate $(\mathcal{K} \oplus 4)$ for expansion. □

Answer to Exercise 3.26 We first show the hint. Suppose that $\mathcal{K}' \in (\mathcal{K} \bot (\varphi \wedge \psi))$. This implies that:

1. $\mathcal{K}' \subseteq \mathcal{K}$
2. $\mathcal{K}' \not\vdash \varphi \wedge \psi$
3. for any $\gamma \in \mathcal{K} \setminus \mathcal{K}'$, we have $\gamma \rightarrow (\varphi \wedge \psi) \in \mathcal{K}'$.

In order to show that $\mathcal{K}' \in (\mathcal{K} \bot \varphi) \cup (\mathcal{K} \bot \psi)$, notice, by item 2 above, that either $\mathcal{K}' \not\vdash \varphi$, or $\mathcal{K}' \not\vdash \psi$. Suppose, without lack of generality, that the first holds (*). Then we have:

1. $\mathcal{K}' \subseteq \mathcal{K}$ (immediately from item 1 above)
2. $\mathcal{K}' \not\vdash \varphi$ (from (*))

3. for any $\gamma \in \mathcal{K} \setminus \mathcal{K}'$, we have $\gamma \rightarrow \varphi \in \mathcal{K}'$ (immediately from item 3 above and the fact that $\mathcal{K}'$ is a belief set).

In other words, we have $\mathcal{K}' \in (\mathcal{K} \bot \varphi)$, as required.

To prove the main claim, we have to show that, for any φ and ψ,

$$(\mathcal{K} \ominus \varphi \cap \mathcal{K} \ominus \psi) \subseteq \mathcal{K} \ominus (\varphi \wedge \psi) \tag{A.2}$$

In case we have one of the three situations in which $\vdash \varphi$ or $\vdash \psi$ or $\vdash \varphi \wedge \psi$, (A.2) follows immediately. This is seen as follows: if $\vdash \varphi \wedge \psi$, all three sets $\mathcal{K} \ominus \cdot$ in equation (A.2) are equal to $\mathcal{K}$, due to Exercise 3.20, and hence the equation is trivially true. If only $\vdash \varphi$, we have to show $\mathcal{K} \ominus \psi \subseteq \mathcal{K} \ominus (\varphi \wedge \psi)$. But this is obvious, since $\vdash \psi \leftrightarrow (\varphi \wedge \psi)$, so that we can apply Exercise 3.20 once more.

So, now we may assume $\not\vdash \varphi$ and $\not\vdash \psi$. Using the definition of contractions, showing that (A.2) holds is then equivalent to showing

$$\bigcap S(\mathcal{K} \bot \varphi) \cap \bigcap S(\mathcal{K} \bot \psi) \subseteq \bigcap S(\mathcal{K} \bot (\varphi \wedge \psi)) \tag{A.3}$$

Now, let $\mathcal{K}'$ be a belief set occurring in the left hand side of (A.3). This means that $\mathcal{K}'$ fails to imply φ, it fails to imply ψ, it is $\leq$-best among $\mathcal{K} \bot \varphi$ and also $\leq$-best among $\mathcal{K} \bot \psi$. Then, obviously, $\mathcal{K}'$ fails to imply $\varphi \wedge \psi$. Is $\mathcal{K}'$ also $\leq$-best among $\mathcal{K} \bot (\varphi \wedge \psi)$? Suppose not. This would mean there is a $\mathcal{K}'' \in (\mathcal{K} \bot (\varphi \wedge \psi))$, such that $\mathcal{K}'' \not\leq \mathcal{K}'$. But then, by the hint just proven, also $\mathcal{K}'' \in (\mathcal{K} \bot \varphi)$ or $\mathcal{K}'' \in (\mathcal{K} \bot \psi)$. But then, $\mathcal{K}'$ cannot be $\leq$-best in both $\mathcal{K} \bot \varphi$ and $\mathcal{K} \bot \psi$. □

Answer to Exercise 3.8

1. Suppose $\oplus$ satisfies $(\mathcal{K} \oplus 1), (\mathcal{K} \oplus 2)$ and $(\mathcal{K} \oplus 3)$, and also $(\mathcal{K} \oplus min)^{\{1,2,3\}}$. We show that is also satisfies $(\mathcal{K} \oplus 4)$. Suppose $\mathcal{K}$ is a belief set and $\varphi \in \mathcal{K}$. By $(\mathcal{K} \oplus 3)$ we know that $\mathcal{K} \subseteq \mathcal{K} \oplus \varphi$. Now, if the other direction does not hold, we can show that we are be able to find a smaller candidate for the expansion of $\mathcal{K}$ with φ. To be more precise, suppose $\mathcal{K} \oplus \varphi \not\subseteq \mathcal{K}$. Let $\mathcal{K} \oplus' \varphi = \mathcal{K}$, and for all other φ and $\mathcal{K}$, we let $\oplus'$ be equal to $\oplus$. It is easy to check that $\oplus'$ verifies $(\mathcal{K} \oplus 1)$ (we assumed that $\mathcal{K}$ is a belief set), $(\mathcal{K} \oplus 2)$ (we assume the antecedent of $(\mathcal{K} \oplus 4)$, i.e. $\varphi \in \mathcal{K}$) and $(\mathcal{K} \oplus 3)$ (we even have put $\mathcal{K}$ *equal* to $\mathcal{K} \oplus' \varphi$). We have $(\mathcal{K} \oplus' \varphi) = \mathcal{K} \subset \mathcal{K} \oplus \varphi$: contradicting the fact that $\oplus$ give the smallest set satisfying the first three postulates!.
2. Suppose $\mathcal{K} \subseteq \mathcal{H}$ but at the same time $\mathcal{K} \oplus \varphi \not\subseteq \mathcal{H} \oplus \varphi$, for a given $\mathcal{K}, \mathcal{H}$ and φ. Then for some ψ we have $\psi \in \mathcal{K} \oplus \varphi$, but $\psi \notin \mathcal{H} \oplus \varphi$. Now define $\oplus'$ by $\mathcal{K} \oplus' \varphi = (\mathcal{K} \oplus \varphi) \cap (\mathcal{H} \oplus \varphi)$ (and, for all 'other' $\mathcal{K}, \mathcal{H}$ and φ, we can define $\oplus'$ to equal $\oplus$). Since the intersection of two belief sets is a belief set, $\oplus'$ satisfies postulate $(\mathcal{K} \oplus 1)$. Postulate $(\mathcal{K} \oplus 2)$ also holds for it, since φ is an element of both $\mathcal{K} \oplus \varphi$ and $\mathcal{H} \oplus \varphi$. On top of this, $\oplus'$ satisfies $(\mathcal{K} \oplus 3)$: $\mathcal{K} \subseteq (\mathcal{K} \oplus \varphi) \cap (\mathcal{H} \oplus \varphi) = \mathcal{K} \oplus' \varphi$. Hence, $\oplus'$ satisfies the

postulates $(\mathcal{K} \oplus 1), (\mathcal{K} \oplus 2)$ and $(\mathcal{K} \oplus 3)$. But since $(\mathcal{K} \oplus' \varphi) \subseteq (\mathcal{K} \oplus \varphi)$, and moreover $\mathcal{K} \oplus \varphi$ is not the smallest set satisfying $(\mathcal{K} \oplus 1), (\mathcal{K} \oplus 2)$ and $(\mathcal{K} \oplus 3)$. □

Answers to Exercises from Chapter 4

Answer to Exercise 4.9 We show that $Hexa, 012 \models [\neg 1_a]\hat{K}_a K_b 0_a$:

We have that $Hexa, 012 \models [\neg 1_a]\hat{K}_a K_b 0_a$ iff ($Hexa, 012 \models \neg 1_a$ implies $Hexa|\neg 1_a, 012 \models \hat{K}_a K_b 0_a$). The premiss is satisfied as before. For the conclusion, $Hexa|\neg 1_a, 012 \models \hat{K}_a K_b 0_a$ iff there is a state s such that $012 \sim_a s$ and $Hexa|\neg 1_a, s \models K_b 0_a$. State $021 = s$ satisfies that: $012 \sim_a 021$ and $Hexa|\neg 1_a, 021 \models K_b 0_a$. The last is, because for all states, if $021 \sim_b s$, then $Hexa|\neg 1_a, s \models 0_a$. The only $\sim_b$-accessible state from 021 in $Hexa|\neg 1_a$ is 021 itself, and $021 \in V_{0_a} = \{012, 021\}$.

The other parts of this exercise are left to the reader. □

Answer to Exercise 4.15 For example, $Hexa, 012 \models [\neg 0_a]1_a$ but $Hexa, 012 \not\models \langle \neg 0_a \rangle 1_a$. For the first, we have that by definition

$$Hexa, 012 \models [\neg 0_a]1_a \text{ iff } (Hexa, 012 \models \neg 0_a \text{ implies } Hexa|\neg 0_a, 012 \models 1_a)$$

This is true because $Hexa, 012 \not\models \neg 0_a$ (i.e., 'box'-type modal operators are satisfied if there are no accessible worlds at all). For the second, we have that by definition

$$Hexa, 012 \models \langle \neg 0_a \rangle 1_a \text{ iff } (Hexa, 012 \models \neg 0_a \text{ and } Hexa|\neg 0_a, 012 \models 1_a)$$

This is false, because $Hexa, 012 \not\models \neg 0_a$ and therefore the conjunction is false (i.e., for 'diamond'-type modal operators to be satisfied there must at least be an accessible world — the announcement must be executable). □

Answer to Exercise 4.16 We do Proposition 4.13. We only need to prove one more equivalence:

$M, s \models \varphi \rightarrow \langle \varphi \rangle \psi$
$\Leftrightarrow$
$M, s \models \varphi$ implies $M, s \models \langle \varphi \rangle \psi$
$\Leftrightarrow$
$M, s \models \varphi$ implies ($M, s \models \varphi$ and $M|\varphi, s \models \psi$)
$\Leftrightarrow$ propositional
$M, s \models \varphi$ implies $M|\varphi, s \models \psi$
$\Leftrightarrow$
$M, s \models [\varphi]\psi$
□

Answer to Exercise 4.23 We prove that $[\varphi](\psi \rightarrow \chi) \leftrightarrow ([\varphi]\psi \rightarrow [\varphi]\chi)$. The direction $[\varphi](\psi \rightarrow \chi) \rightarrow ([\varphi]\psi \rightarrow [\varphi]\chi)$ will be obvious. For the other direction, let M and s be arbitrary and assume $M, s \models [\varphi]\psi \rightarrow [\varphi]\chi$. To prove that $M, s \models [\varphi](\psi \rightarrow \chi)$, we assume that $M, s \models \varphi$ and have to prove that $M|\varphi, s \models \psi \rightarrow \chi$. Therefore, suppose that $M|\varphi, s \models \psi$. If $M|\varphi, s \models \psi$ then $M, s \models [\varphi]\psi$. Using our assumption $M, s \models [\varphi]\psi \rightarrow [\varphi]\chi$, it follows that $M, s \models [\varphi]\chi$. From that and $M, s \models \varphi$ follows $M|\varphi, s \models \chi$. Therefore $M|\varphi, s \models \psi \rightarrow \chi$. Done. □

Answer to Exercise 4.25 Let M and s be arbitrary. Then we have:

$M, s \models \langle\varphi\rangle\neg\psi$
$\Leftrightarrow$
$M, s \models \varphi$ and $M|\varphi, s \models \neg\psi$
$\Leftrightarrow$ propositional
$M, s \models \varphi$ and ($M, s \models \varphi$ implies $M|\varphi, s \models \neg\psi$)
$\Leftrightarrow$
$M, s \models \varphi$ and $M, s \models [\varphi]\neg\psi$
$\Leftrightarrow$
$M, s \models \varphi \wedge [\varphi]\neg\psi$
$\Leftrightarrow$ duality
$M, s \models \varphi \wedge \neg\langle\varphi\rangle\psi$
□

Answer to Exercise 4.35 φ may be successful but not $\neg\varphi$:

For example $\neg(p \wedge \neg K_a p)$ is successful, but its negation $p \wedge \neg K_a p$ is—as we already know—unsuccessful. That $\neg(p \wedge \neg K_a p)$ is successful can be shown directly, but it also suffices to observe that $\neg(p \wedge \neg K_a p)$ is equivalent to $\neg p \vee K_a p$, and that that formula is in the language fragment that is preserved under taking arbitrary submodels, and therefore a fortiori in the unique submodel resulting from its announcement. See Proposition 4.37, later.

φ and ψ may be successful but not $[\varphi]\psi$:

Consider a model M with $\{s, t\}$ as the set of possible worlds. There is only one accessibility relation $\sim_a = \{(s, s), (s, t,), (t, s), (t, t)\}$ and only one propositional variable p, which is only true in t, i.e. $V_p = \{t\}$. We take the epistemic state (M, s). Now consider the formula $[\neg p \rightarrow K_a\neg p]\bot$. The subformulas $\neg p \rightarrow K_a\neg p$ and $\bot$ are both successful. However: $M, s \models \langle[\neg p \rightarrow K_a\neg p]\bot\rangle\neg[\neg p \rightarrow K_a\neg p]\bot$. This can be seen as follows. The formula $\neg p \rightarrow K_a\neg p$ is true in t, but false in s. Therefore $[p \rightarrow K_a p]\bot$ is trivially true in s. It is obviously false in t. So M restricted to this formula consists of s only. In this model $\neg p \rightarrow K_a\neg p$ is true. Therefore $\langle\neg p \rightarrow K_a\neg p\rangle\top$, which is equivalent to $[\neg p \rightarrow K_a\neg p]\bot$, is true there as well.

An example where φ and ψ are successful but not $\varphi \rightarrow \psi$ is left to the reader.□

Answer to Exercise 4.48 We can assume $\vdash \psi \leftrightarrow \chi$ throughout. We show that $\vdash \varphi(p/\psi) \leftrightarrow \varphi(p/\chi)$ by induction on φ.

If $\varphi = p$, then $\vdash p(p/\psi) \leftrightarrow p(p/\chi)$ equals $\vdash \psi \leftrightarrow \chi$ which was assumed.

If $\varphi = q \neq p$, then the substitution results in $\vdash q \leftrightarrow q$ which is a tautology.

If $\varphi = \neg\varphi$, then $\vdash (\neg\varphi)(p/\psi) \leftrightarrow (-\varphi)(p/\chi)$ becomes $\vdash \neg\varphi(p/\psi) \leftrightarrow \neg\varphi(p/\chi)$ and, for one direction of the equivalence, we use an instance of the tautology 'contraposition', the induction hypothesis, and modus ponens:

1	$(\varphi(p/\chi) \rightarrow \varphi(p/\psi)) \rightarrow (\neg\varphi(p/\psi) \rightarrow \neg\varphi(p/\chi))$	tautology
2	$\varphi(p/\chi) \rightarrow \varphi(p/\psi)$	induction hypothesis
3	$\neg\varphi(p/\psi) \rightarrow \neg\varphi(p/\chi)$	1,2, modus ponens

If $\varphi = \varphi_1 \wedge \varphi_2$, then we have to show $\vdash (\varphi_1 \wedge \varphi_2)(p/\chi) \leftrightarrow (\varphi_1 \wedge \varphi_2)(p/\psi)$, which is by definition $\vdash \varphi_1(p/\chi) \wedge \varphi_2(p/\chi) \leftrightarrow \varphi_1(p/\psi) \wedge \varphi_2(p/\psi)$, and our induction hypotheses are $\vdash \varphi_1(p/\chi) \leftrightarrow \varphi_1(p/\psi)$ and $\vdash \varphi_2(p/\chi) \leftrightarrow \varphi_2(p/\psi)$. This can be achieved by simple propositional reasoning.

If $\varphi = K_a\varphi$ and if $\varphi = [\varphi_1]\varphi_2$, we use necessitation. Details are left to the reader. □

Answer to Exercise 4.49 We show that $\vdash (\varphi \rightarrow [\varphi]\psi) \leftrightarrow [\varphi]\psi$ by induction on ψ. Simple steps have not been justified in the derivations, e.g., we often use Proposition 4.46 without reference. In (only) the case p we explicitly repeat the right side of the equivalence. Alternatively, one can make derivations with assumptions, but such are avoided in our minimal treatment of Hilbert-style axiomatics.

Case p:

1 $[\varphi]p \leftrightarrow [\varphi]p$
2 $(\varphi \rightarrow p) \leftrightarrow [\varphi]p$
3 $(\varphi \rightarrow (\varphi \rightarrow p)) \leftrightarrow [\varphi]p$
4 $(\varphi \rightarrow [\varphi]p) \leftrightarrow [\varphi]p$

Case $\psi \wedge \chi$:

1	$[\varphi](\psi \wedge \chi) \leftrightarrow [\varphi](\psi \wedge \chi)$	
2	$[\varphi]\psi \wedge [\varphi]\chi \leftrightarrow \dots$	announcement and conjunction
3	$(\varphi \rightarrow [\varphi]\psi) \wedge (\varphi \rightarrow [\varphi]\chi)$	induction
4	$\varphi \rightarrow ([\varphi]\psi \wedge [\varphi]\chi)$	propositional
5	$\varphi \rightarrow [\varphi](\psi \wedge \chi)$	announcement and conjunction

Case $\neg\psi$ (induction hypothesis is not used):

1	$[\varphi]\neg\psi$	
2	$\varphi \rightarrow \neg[\varphi]\psi$	announcement and negation
3	$\varphi \rightarrow (\varphi \rightarrow \neg[\varphi]\psi)$	propositional
4	$\varphi \rightarrow [\varphi]\neg\psi$	

Case $K_a\psi$ (induction hypothesis not used):

1 $[\varphi]K_a\psi$

2 $\varphi \rightarrow K_a[\varphi]\psi$
3 $\varphi \rightarrow \varphi \rightarrow K_a[\varphi]\psi$
4 $\varphi \rightarrow [\varphi]K_a\psi$
Case $[\psi]\chi$:
1 $[\varphi][\psi]\chi$
2 $[\varphi \wedge [\varphi]\psi]\chi$ announcement composition
3 $(\varphi \wedge [\varphi]\psi) \rightarrow [\varphi \wedge [\varphi]\psi]\chi$ induction
4 $\varphi \rightarrow [\varphi]\psi \rightarrow [\varphi \wedge [\varphi]\psi]\chi$ propositional
5 $\varphi \rightarrow \varphi \rightarrow [\varphi]\psi \rightarrow [\varphi \wedge [\varphi]\psi]\chi$ propositional
6 $\varphi \rightarrow [\varphi][\psi]\chi$ similar to 1–4

Answer to Exercise 4.50 We use the equivalence of $\varphi \rightarrow \psi$ and $\neg(\varphi \wedge \neg\psi)$. As for other items of the proof of Proposition 4.46, the proof consists of a sequence of equivalences, and to improve readability we delete the right hand side. Line numbering and justifications are omitted — most steps are propositional.

$[\varphi](\psi \rightarrow \chi) \leftrightarrow [\varphi](\psi \rightarrow \chi)$
$[\varphi]\neg(\psi \wedge \neg\chi) \leftrightarrow \ldots$
$[\varphi]\neg(\psi \wedge \neg\chi)$
$\varphi \rightarrow \neg[\varphi](\psi \wedge \neg\chi)$
$\varphi \rightarrow \neg([\varphi]\psi \wedge [\varphi]\neg\chi)$
$\varphi \rightarrow \neg([\varphi]\psi \wedge (\varphi \rightarrow \neg[\varphi]\chi))$
$\varphi \rightarrow (\neg[\varphi]\psi \vee (\varphi \wedge [\varphi]\chi))$
$\varphi \rightarrow ((\neg[\varphi]\psi \vee [\varphi]\chi) \wedge (\neg[\varphi]\psi \vee \varphi))$
$\varphi \rightarrow (([\varphi]\psi \rightarrow [\varphi]\chi) \wedge ([\varphi]\psi \rightarrow \varphi))$
$(\varphi \rightarrow [\varphi]\psi \rightarrow [\varphi]\chi) \wedge (\varphi \rightarrow [\varphi]\psi \rightarrow \varphi)$
$\varphi \rightarrow [\varphi]\psi \rightarrow [\varphi]\chi$
$[\varphi]\psi \rightarrow \varphi \rightarrow [\varphi]\chi$
$[\varphi]\psi \rightarrow [\varphi]\chi$
□

Answer to Exercise 4.55 Proof of $\vdash C_B(\varphi \rightarrow E_B\varphi) \rightarrow \varphi \rightarrow C_B\varphi$. We outline the derivation as follows:

First, note that a propositionally equivalent form of the induction axiom is $C_B(\varphi \rightarrow E_B\varphi) \wedge \varphi \rightarrow C_B\varphi$. Next, for $\varphi = \top$ the rule for announcement and common knowledge becomes: from $\chi \rightarrow \psi$ and $\chi \rightarrow E_B\chi$ follows $\chi \rightarrow C_B\psi$. This we will now apply in the following form: from $C_B(\varphi \rightarrow E_B\varphi) \wedge \varphi \rightarrow \varphi$ and $C_B(\varphi \rightarrow E_B\varphi) \wedge \varphi \rightarrow E_B(C_B(\varphi \rightarrow E_B\varphi) \wedge \varphi)$ follows $C_B(\varphi \rightarrow E_B\varphi) \wedge \varphi \rightarrow C_B\varphi$. From the two premises of this conclusion, the first one, $C_B(\varphi \rightarrow E_B\varphi) \wedge \varphi \rightarrow \varphi$, is a tautology. The second can be derived from $C_B(\varphi \rightarrow E_B\varphi) \wedge \varphi \rightarrow E_BC_B(\varphi \rightarrow E_B\varphi)$ (i) and $C_B(\varphi \rightarrow E_B\varphi) \wedge \varphi \rightarrow E_B\varphi$ (ii). Formula scheme (i) can also be written as $C_B(\varphi \rightarrow E_B\varphi) \rightarrow \varphi \rightarrow E_BC_B(\varphi \rightarrow E_B\varphi)$ which is a weakening of $C_B(\varphi \rightarrow E_B\varphi) \rightarrow E_BC_B(\varphi \rightarrow E_B\varphi)$ which makes it clear that this is an instance of 'use of common knowledge'. Whereas (ii) can also be written as $C_B(\varphi \rightarrow E_B\varphi) \rightarrow \varphi \rightarrow E_B\varphi$ which makes it another instance of 'use of common knowledge'. □

Answer to Exercise 4.57 We prove the generalisation of 'partial functionality' ($\vdash (\varphi \rightarrow [\varphi]\psi) \leftrightarrow [\varphi]\psi$). 'Substitution of equals' is left to the reader. 'Announcement and implication' did not require induction so remains valid as a matter of course.

We (only) need to add a case $C_A\psi$ to the proof. For the case $\psi = C_A\psi$ from the inductive proof of $\vdash (\varphi \rightarrow [\varphi]\psi) \leftrightarrow [\varphi]\psi$, we have to derive $\vdash (\varphi \rightarrow [\varphi]C_A\psi) \leftrightarrow [\varphi]C_A\psi$. The direction $\vdash [\varphi]C_A\psi \rightarrow (\varphi \rightarrow [\varphi]C_A\psi)$ is trivial.

We derive $\vdash (\varphi \rightarrow [\varphi]C_A\psi) \rightarrow [\varphi]C_A\psi$ by an application of the rule for announcement and common knowledge, namely, from $\vdash (\varphi \rightarrow [\varphi]C_A\psi) \rightarrow [\varphi]\psi$ and $\vdash (\varphi \rightarrow [\varphi]C_A\psi) \wedge \varphi \rightarrow E_A(\varphi \rightarrow [\varphi]C_A\psi)$.

$\vdash (\varphi \rightarrow [\varphi]C_A\psi) \rightarrow [\varphi]\psi$:

Use that by inductive hypothesis, $\vdash [\varphi]\psi \leftrightarrow (\varphi \rightarrow [\varphi]\psi)$, and observe that $\vdash (\varphi \rightarrow [\varphi]C_A\psi) \rightarrow (\varphi \rightarrow [\varphi]\psi)$ follows propositionally from $\vdash [\varphi]C_A\psi \rightarrow [\varphi]\psi$, which follows from 'use of common knowledge', 'necessitation for announcement' ($[\varphi]$), 'distribution of $[\varphi]$ over $\rightarrow$', and modus ponens.

$\vdash (\varphi \rightarrow [\varphi]C_A\psi) \wedge \varphi \rightarrow E_A(\varphi \rightarrow [\varphi]C_A\psi)$:

1	$C_A\psi \leftrightarrow E_AC_A\psi$	
2	$[\varphi]C_A\psi \leftrightarrow [\varphi]E_AC_A\psi$	necessitation and distribution, and propositional
3	$[\varphi]E_AC_A\psi \leftrightarrow (\varphi \rightarrow E_A[\varphi]C_A\psi)$	announcement and knowledge
4	$(\varphi \rightarrow E_A[\varphi]C_A\psi) \rightarrow (\varphi \rightarrow E_A(\varphi \rightarrow [\varphi]C_A\psi)$	propositional
5	$[\varphi]C_A\psi \rightarrow (\varphi \rightarrow E_A(\varphi \rightarrow [\varphi]C_A\psi)$	2–4, propositional
6	$([\varphi]C_A\psi \wedge \varphi) \rightarrow E_A(\varphi \rightarrow [\varphi]C_A\psi)$	propositional
7	$(\varphi \rightarrow [\varphi]C_A\psi) \wedge \varphi \rightarrow E_A(\varphi \rightarrow [\varphi]C_A\psi)$	

Answer to Exercise 4.72 We explain in detail why (Anne announces: "I have one of $\{012, 034, 056, 135, 246\}$," and Bill announces "Cath has card 6") is a solution. Let π ($= 012_a \vee 034_a \vee 056_a \vee 135_a \vee 246_a$) be Anne's announcement. We have to show that all of the following hold. Note that the common knowledge requirements are translated into *model* requirements of the commonly known formula:

$\mathit{Russian}, 012.345.6 \models K_a\pi$	*i*
$\mathit{Russian}\|K_a\pi \models \mathsf{cignorant}$	*ii*
$\mathit{Russian}\|K_a\pi, 012.345.6 \models K_b6_c$	*iii*
$\mathit{Russian}\|K_a\pi\|K_b6_c \models \mathsf{cignorant} \wedge \mathsf{bknowsas} \wedge \mathsf{aknowsbs}$	*iv*

We can now prove these requirements by checking their combinatorial equivalents in the model:

- Hand 012 is in $\{012, 034, 056, 135, 246\}$. Therefore i holds.
- If c holds 0, the remaining hands are $\{135, 246\}$. Each of $1, 2, ..., 6$ both occurs in at least one of $\{135, 246\}$ and is absent in at least one of those (1 occurs in 135 and is absent in 246, 2 occurs in 246 and is absent in 135, etc.). If c holds 1, the remaining hands are $\{034, 056, 246\}$. Each of $0, 2, ..., 6$ both occurs in at least one of $\{034, 056, 246\}$ and is absent in at least one of those (0 occurs in 034 and is absent in 246, ...), etc. for c holding 2, ..., 6. Therefore ii holds.
- From $\{012, 034, 056, 135, 246\}$, Bill can remove any hand that contains either 3, 4, or 5. This leaves only hand 012. In deal 012.345.6 Cath actually holds 6. Therefore iii holds.
- After both communications, the following deals are still possible:

$$\{012.345.6, 034.125.6, 135.024.6\}.$$

They are all different for Anne and for Bill, therefore bknowsas and aknowsbs hold. They are all the same for Cath. Each of $0, 1, ..., 5$ both occurs in at least one of $\{012, 034, 135\}$ and is absent in at least one of those. Therefore iv holds. □

Answers to Exercises from Chapter 5

Answer to Exercise 5.16 A side effect of the first action is that b learns that a learns p. But the knowledge b obtained after $L_{ab}?q$ is exactly the same as what he obtained after $L_{ab}L_{ab}?q$, so there should not be that side effect. □

Answer to Exercise 5.26 A simple counterexample is the non-deterministic action $(L_a?p \cup L_b?p)$. We have that $gr(L_a?p \cup L_b?p) = gr(L_a?p) \cap gr(L_b?p) = \emptyset$, but of course, for given (M, s) and (M', s') such that $(M, s)[\![L_a?p \cup L_b?p]\!](M', s')$, it is not the case that $gr(M', s') = \emptyset$. □

Answer to Exercise 5.29 By induction on α. We only show one direction of the crucial case 'learning': Suppose $(M, s) \models \langle L_B\alpha \rangle \top$. Let (M', s') be such that $(M, s)[\![L_B\alpha]\!](M', s')$. From the definition of action interpretation follows $(M, s)[\![\alpha]\!]s'$. Therefore $(M, s) \models \langle \alpha \rangle \top$. By induction, $(M, s) \models \mathsf{pre}(\alpha)$, By definition $\mathsf{pre}(L_B\alpha) = \mathsf{pre}(\alpha)$. Therefore $(M, s) \models \mathsf{pre}(L_B\alpha)$. □

Answer to Exercise 5.39 We now compute the interpretation of the show action in detail, to give one more example of the semantics of epistemic actions. We will refer repeatedly to Definition 5.13 on page 116. We first apply the clause for 'learning' in that definition. To interpret show $= L_{abc}(!L_{ab}?0_a \cup L_{ab}?1_a \cup L_{ab}?2_a)$ in $(Hexa, 012)$, we interpret the type $L_{ab}?0_a \cup L_{ab}?1_a \cup L_{ab}?2_a$ of the action bound by L_{abc} in any state of the domain of $Hexa$ that is $\{a, b, c\}$-accessible from state 012. Specifically: we interpret $L_{ab}?0_a \cup L_{ab}?1_a \cup$

$L_{ab}?2_a$ in all states of *Hexa*. The resulting states will make up the domain of $(Hexa, 012)[\![\mathsf{show}]\!]$. We then compute access on that domain.

Action $L_{ab}?0_a \cup L_{ab}?1_a \cup L_{ab}?2_a$ has a nonempty interpretation in *any* state of *Hexa*. By applying clause $\cup$ in Definition 5.13, $L_{ab}?0_a \cup L_{ab}?1_a \cup L_{ab}?2_a$ can be interpreted in $(Hexa, 012)$ because $L_{ab}?0_a$ can be interpreted in that state. Similarly, $L_{ab}?0_a \cup L_{ab}?1_a \cup L_{ab}?2_a$ can be interpreted in $(Hexa, 201)$ because $L_{ab}?2_a$ can be interpreted in that state. We compute the first.

Again, we apply clause 'learning' in the definition. To interpret $L_{ab}?0_a$ in $(Hexa, 012)$, we interpret $?0_a$ in any state of *Hexa* that is $\{a, b\}$-accessible from 012, i.e., in all states of *Hexa*. The interpretation is not empty when Anne holds 0, i.e., in $(Hexa, 012)$ and in $(Hexa, 021)$. We compute the first.

We now apply clause 'test' ('$?\varphi$') of the definition. State $(Hexa, 012)[\![?0_a]\!]$ is the restriction of *Hexa* to states where 0_a holds, i.e., 012 and 021, with empty access, and with point 012. Figure A.2 pictures the result.

Having unravelled the interpretation of show to that of its action constituents, we can now compute access for the so far incomplete other stages of the interpretation. The epistemic state $(Hexa, 012)[\![?0_a]\!]$ is one of the factual states of the domain of $(Hexa, 012)[\![L_{ab}?0_a]\!]$. This is visualised in Figure A.2 by linking the large box containing $(Hexa, 012)[\![?0_a]\!]$ with the small box

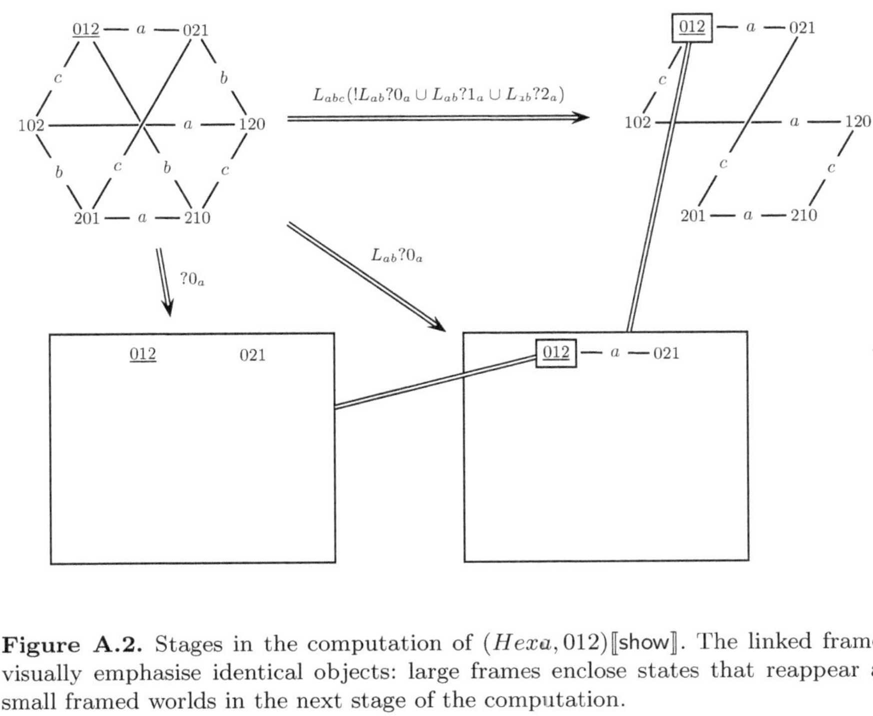

Figure A.2. Stages in the computation of $(Hexa, 012)[\![\mathsf{show}]\!]$. The linked frames visually emphasise identical objects: large frames enclose states that reappear as small framed worlds in the next stage of the computation.

containing an underlined 012. The epistemic state $(\mathit{Hexa}, 012)[\![?0_a]\!]$ is also the point of the epistemic state $(\mathit{Hexa}, 012)[\![L_{ab}?0_a]\!]$. The other factual state of that epistemic state is $(\mathit{Hexa}, 021)[\![?0_a]\!]$. As Anne does not occur in (the group of) either of these, and as their origins under the interpretation of $?0_a$ are the same to Anne—$012 \sim_a 021$ in *Hexa*—we may conclude that $(\mathit{Hexa}, 012)[\![?0_a]\!] \sim_a (\mathit{Hexa}, 021)[\![?0_a]\!]$ in $(\mathit{Hexa}, 012)[\![L_{ab}?0_a]\!]$. For the same reason, both states are reflexive for both Anne and Bill in $(\mathit{Hexa}, 012)[\![L_{ab}?0_a]\!]$. Access for Bill is different: $(\mathit{Hexa}, 012)[\![?0_a]\!] \not\sim_b (\mathit{Hexa}, 021)[\![?0_a]\!]$, because in $012 \not\sim_b 021$ in *Hexa*. In other words: even though Bill does not occur either in the groups of epistemic states $(\mathit{Hexa}, 012)[\![?0_a]\!]$ and $(\mathit{Hexa}, 021)[\![?0_a]\!]$, he can tell them apart in $(\mathit{Hexa}, 012)[\![L_{ab}?0_a]\!]$, because he already could tell deal 012 apart from deal 021 (in 012 he holds card 1, whereas in 021 he holds card 2). The valuation of atoms does not change as a result of action execution. Therefore state $(\mathit{Hexa}, 012)[\![?0_a]\!]$ is named 012 again, and state $(\mathit{Hexa}, 021)[\![?0_a]\!]$ is named 021 again, in Figure A.2 that pictures the result. Indeed, these names were convenient mnemonic devices 'showing' what facts are true in a state.

Similarly to the computation of $(\mathit{Hexa}, 012)[\![L_{ab}?0_a]\!]$, compute the five other epistemic states where Anne and Bill learn Anne's card. These six together form the domain of $(\mathit{Hexa}, 012)[\![\mathsf{show}]\!]$. We compute access for the players on this domain in some typical cases. Again, reflexivity trivially follows for all states. Concerning Anne, we have that $(\mathit{Hexa}, 012)[\![L_{ab}?0_a]\!] \sim_a (\mathit{Hexa}, 021)[\![L_{ab}?0_a]\!]$ as factual states, because $012 \sim_a 021$ and also, as epistemic states, $(\mathit{Hexa}, 012)[\![L_{ab}?0_a]\!] \sim_a (\mathit{Hexa}, 021)[\![L_{ab}?0_a]\!]$. The two epistemic states in the latter are the same for Anne, because the points of these states are the same for Anne (here we have applied Definition 5.12 in the domain of the model underlying epistemic state $(\mathit{Hexa}, 012)[\![L_{ab}?0_a]\!]$). Note that from "$(\mathit{Hexa}, 012)[\![L_{ab}?0_a]\!] \sim_a (\mathit{Hexa}, 021)[\![L_{ab}?0_a]\!]$ as epistemic states" and the fact that a is in the group of both epistemic states, already follows that $012 \sim_a 021$. The first condition in the clause for computing access is superfluous when the agent occurs in the epistemic states that are being compared.

Concerning Cath, we have $(\mathit{Hexa}, 012)[\![L_{ab}?0_a]\!] \sim_c (\mathit{Hexa}, 102)[\![L_{ab}?1_a]\!]$, because $c \notin \{a, b\}$ (so that they are, as epistemic states, the same for Cath) and $012 \sim_c 102$ in *Hexa*. In this case, unlike the access we just computed for Anne, the condition $012 \sim_c 102$ is essential.

Concerning Bill, we have that $(\mathit{Hexa}, 012)[\![L_{ab}?0_a]\!] \not\sim_b (\mathit{Hexa}, 210)[\![L_{ab}?2_a]\!]$ as factual states, because Bill occurs in both and $(\mathit{Hexa}, 012)[\![L_{ab}?0_a]\!] \not\sim_b (\mathit{Hexa}, 210)[\![L_{ab}?2_a]\!]$ as epistemic states. The last is, because we cannot by $(\sim_b)$ shifting the point of the latter find an epistemic state that is bisimilar to the former. This is obvious, as the underlying models of $(\mathit{Hexa}, 012)[\![L_{ab}?0_a]\!]$ and $(\mathit{Hexa}, 210)[\![L_{ab}?2_a]\!]$ have a different structure.

Again, the valuation of atoms in the factual states of the resulting epistemic state $(\mathit{Hexa}, 012)[\![\mathsf{show}]\!]$ does not change. Therefore, factual state $(\mathit{Hexa}, 012)[\![L_{ab}?0_a]\!]$ is named 012 again in Figure A.2, etc. The point of $(\mathit{Hexa}, 012)[\![\mathsf{show}]\!]$ is $(\mathit{Hexa}, 012)[\![L_{ab}?0_a]\!]$, because the unique epistemic state such that $(\mathit{Hexa}, 012)[\![L_{ab}?0_a \cup L_{ab}?1_a \cup L_{ab}?2_a]\!]$ is $(\mathit{Hexa}, 012)[\![L_{ab}?0_a]\!]$ (see

Definition 5.13 again: the point of an epistemic state that is the result of executing $L_B\alpha$ is an epistemic state that is the result of executing α). We have now completed the interpretation. Figure A.2 pictures the result.

In any world of the resulting model, Bill knows the deal of cards. Anne does not know the cards of Bill and Cath, although Anne knows that Bill knows it. Cath also knows that Bill knows the deal of cards. □

Answer to Exercise 5.42 A counterexample to the first is the first minimal sequence, where agent 1 makes the same call twice to agents over 4. A counterexample to the second is, e.g., call 14 in the sequence starting with $12, 34, 13, 24, 14, \ldots$. □

Answers to Exercises from Chapter 6

Answer to Exercise 6.4 Let φ_n and $\boldsymbol{\alpha}_n$ be the set of formulas and actions, respectively, constructed at step n of the inductive construction in Definition 6.3. The first steps of the inductive construction deliver the following—in $\boldsymbol{\alpha}_2$ the expression (F, s) stands for an arbitrary finite pointed frame.

$$\begin{aligned}
\varphi_0 &= \emptyset \\
\boldsymbol{\alpha}_0 &= \emptyset \\
\varphi_1 &= \{p\} \\
\boldsymbol{\alpha}_1 &= \emptyset \\
\varphi_2 &= \{p, \neg p, p \wedge p, K_a p, K_b p, C_a p, C_b p, C_{ab} p\} \\
\boldsymbol{\alpha}_2 &= \{(\langle F, \mathsf{pre}\rangle, \mathsf{s}) \mid \mathsf{pre}(\mathsf{s}') = p \text{ for all } \mathsf{s}' \in \mathcal{D}(F)\}
\end{aligned}$$

The set of action models constructed in $\boldsymbol{\alpha}_2$ is already infinite, as there are an infinite number of action frames. Note that at this stage as preconditions are only formulas allowed that have already been constructed in φ_1, in other words, only p. After stages φ_2 and $\boldsymbol{\alpha}_2$, matters get out of hand quickly. For example, φ_3 contains an infinite number of expressions $[\langle F, \mathsf{pre}\rangle, \mathsf{s}]\varphi$ with φ one of the eight formulas in φ_2, and $(\langle F, \mathsf{pre}\rangle, \mathsf{s})$ one of the infinitely many action models constructed in step $\boldsymbol{\alpha}_2$. Set $\boldsymbol{\alpha}_3$ is the first where preconditions $\neg p$ are allowed, because $\neg p \in \varphi_2$. This is indeed the level where we find the required epistemic action (Read, p), as the pointed frame np—b—$\underline{\mathsf{p}}$ is one of the (F, s) used in the inductive construction. □

Answer to Exercise 6.14 We show that $[\mathsf{pub}(\varphi)]\psi$ is equivalent to $[\varphi]\psi$. The remaining two items are left to the reader.

The action model $\mathsf{pub}(\varphi)$ is formally $(\langle\{\mathsf{pub}\}, \sim, \mathsf{pre}\rangle, \mathsf{pub})$ such that $\sim_a = \{(\mathsf{pub}, \mathsf{pub})\}$ for all $a \in A$, and $\mathsf{pre}(\mathsf{pub}) = \varphi$: it consists of a single state pub, that is publicly accessible, and with precondition φ. For convenience in this proof, we name the model $\langle\{\mathsf{pub}\}, \sim, \mathsf{pre}\rangle$: Pub. Let (M, s) be an arbitrary epistemic model. Either $M, s \not\models \varphi$, in which case both $M, s \models [\mathsf{pub}(\varphi)]\psi$ and

$M, s \models [\varphi]\psi$ by definition, or $M, s \models \varphi$. The model $M \otimes \mathsf{Pub}$ is constructed as follows:

Domain: Its domain consists of all pairs (t, pub) such that $M, t \models \varphi$. Note that, modulo naming of states, this is the set $[\![\varphi]\!]_M$—the set of all φ-states in M.

Access: For an arbitrary agent a, access $\sim_a$ is defined as $(s, \mathsf{pub}) \sim_a (s', \mathsf{pub})$ iff $s \sim_a s'$ and $\mathsf{pub} \sim_a \mathsf{pub}$. As $\mathsf{pub} \sim_a \mathsf{pub}$ is true, we have that $(s, \mathsf{pub}) \sim_a (s', \mathsf{pub})$ iff $s \sim_a s'$. In other words: access between states in the model $M \otimes \mathsf{Pub}$ is simply the restriction of access in M to the domain $[\![\varphi]\!]_M$.

Valuation: The valuation in $M \otimes \mathsf{Pub}$ remains unchanged, i.e., $s \in V_p$ iff $(s, \mathsf{pub}) \in V_p$.

Together this describes the model $M|\varphi$ as in public announcement logic. The truth definition

$$M, s \models [\mathsf{pub}(\varphi)]\psi \text{ iff for all } M', s' \colon (M, s)[\![\mathsf{pub}(\varphi)]\!](M', s') \text{ implies } M', s' \models \psi$$

is in this case

$$M, s \models [\mathsf{pub}(\varphi)]\psi \text{ iff } M, s \models \varphi \text{ implies } M \otimes \mathsf{Pub}, (s, \mathsf{pub}) \models \psi$$

We have just shown that this computes to

$$M, s \models \varphi \text{ implies } M|\varphi, (s, \mathsf{pub}) \models \psi$$

In other words, as the names of states are irrelevant

$$M, s \models \varphi \text{ implies } M|\varphi, s \models \psi$$

The last defines

$$M, s \models [\varphi]\psi \ .$$

□

Answer to Exercise 6.18 Let the agents be Anne, Bill, and Cath, and the cards 0, 1, and 2, and the actual card deal 012 (Anne holds 0, Bill holds 1, Cath holds 2).

- Anne says that she holds card 0: singleton action model with universal access for a, b, c and precondition 0_a.
- Anne shows card 0 to Bill: three-point action model with universal access for c and identity for a and b, preconditions 0_a, 1_a, and 2_a (for Anne holding 0, 1, and 2, respectively), and point 0_a.
- Following a request from Bill to tell him a card she does not hold, Anne whispers into Bill's ear that she does not hold card 2: as the previous description, but now with preconditions $\neg 0_a$, $\neg 1_a$, and $\neg 2_a$ (for Anne *not* holding 0, 1, and 2, respectively), and point $\neg 2_a$. □

Answer to Exercise 6.39 We provide a derivation of the second item.

1	$[\mathsf{Read}, \mathsf{np}]\neg p \leftrightarrow (\neg p \rightarrow \neg[\mathsf{Read}, \mathsf{np}]p)$	action and negation
2	$[\mathsf{Read}, \mathsf{np}]p \leftrightarrow (\neg p \rightarrow p)$	$\mathsf{pre}(\mathsf{np}) = \neg p$, atomic permanence
3	$(\neg p \rightarrow p) \leftrightarrow p$	tautology
4	$[\mathsf{Read}, \mathsf{np}]p \leftrightarrow p$	2, 3, propositional
5	$\neg p \rightarrow \neg[\mathsf{Read}, \mathsf{np}]p$	4, propositional
6	$[\mathsf{Read}, \mathsf{np}]\neg p$	1, 5, propositional
7	$K_a[\mathsf{Read}, \mathsf{np}]\neg p$	6, necessitation for K_a
8	$\neg p \rightarrow K_a[\mathsf{Read}, \mathsf{np}]\neg p$	7, weakening
9	$[\mathsf{Read}, \mathsf{np}]K_a\neg p \leftrightarrow (\neg p \rightarrow K_a[\mathsf{Read}, \mathsf{np}]\neg p)$	action and knowledge
10	$[\mathsf{Read}, \mathsf{np}]K_a\neg p$	8, 9, propositional
11	$[\mathsf{Read}, \mathsf{np}](K_a p \vee K_a\neg p)$	10, taut. $\varphi \rightarrow (\psi \vee \varphi)$, nec., prop. steps
12	$[\mathsf{Read}, \mathsf{p}]K_a p$	Example 6.38
13	$[\mathsf{Read}, \mathsf{p}](K_a p \vee K_a\neg p)$	12, taut. $\varphi \rightarrow (\varphi \vee \psi)$, nec., prop. steps
14	$[\mathsf{Read}, \mathsf{p}](K_a p \vee K_a\neg p) \wedge [\mathsf{Read}, \mathsf{np}](K_a p \vee K_a\neg p)$	11, 13, propositional
15	$[\mathsf{Read}](K_a p \vee K_a\neg p)$	14, non-determinism, propositional

In the last step, note that action model Read is defined as non-deterministic choice $(\mathsf{Read}, \mathsf{p}) \cup (\mathsf{Read}, \mathsf{np})$. □

Answer to Exercise 6.41 We give the descriptions in $\mathcal{L}_!^{\mathrm{act}}$ of the four actions given the restriction to 0...5. In all cases, the description for the general case cannot be made because it would be of infinite length. Or, in other words, because the domain of the corresponding action state is infinite. Action descriptions are constrained to have finite domains. (Allowing only a finite subset of a possibly infinite domain to be named, does not help either in this case.) Below, let i_a stand for 'Agent a is being told the natural number i; below, we give the types of action, the points will be obvious.

$$L_{ab}(\bigcup_{i=0..5}?(i_a \wedge i_b))$$
$$L_{ab}(\bigcup_{i=0..4}?(i_a \wedge (i+1)_b) \cup \bigcup_{i=1..5}?(i_a \wedge (i-1)_b))$$
$$L_{ab}(!L_a?4_a \cup \bigcup_{i=0,1,2,3,5} L_a?i_a)$$
$$L_{ab}(!L_b?3_b \cup \bigcup_{i=0,1,2,4,5} L_b?i_b)$$

The corresponding action models consist of: 25, 10, 6, and 6 points, respectively. Obviously, all these models are of infinite size in the general case. □

Answers to Exercises from Chapter 7

Answer to Exercise 7.15

1. Suppose $\varphi \in \Phi$. Suppose $\Gamma \vdash \varphi$. Since Γ is consistent, so is $\Gamma \cup \{\varphi\}$. Since Γ is also maximal in Φ, it must be the case that $\varphi \in \Gamma$.
2. Suppose $\neg\varphi \in \Phi$. Therefore $\varphi \in \Phi$. From left to right. Suppose that $\varphi \in \Gamma$. By consistency $\neg\varphi \notin \Gamma$.

From right to left. Suppose that $\neg\varphi \notin \Gamma$. By maximality it must then be the case that $\Gamma \cup \{\neg\varphi\}$ is inconsistent. Therefore $\Gamma \vdash \varphi$. By 1 of this lemma $\varphi \in \Gamma$.

3. Suppose $(\varphi \wedge \psi) \in \Phi$. From left to right. Suppose $(\varphi \wedge \psi) \in \Gamma$. Then $\Gamma \vdash \varphi$ and $\Gamma \vdash \psi$. Since Φ is closed under subformulas, also $\varphi \in \Phi$ and $\psi \in \Phi$. Therefore, by 1 of this lemma $\varphi \in \Gamma$ and $\psi \in \Gamma$.
   From right to left. Suppose $\varphi \in \Gamma$ and $\psi \in \Gamma$. Therefore $\Gamma \vdash (\varphi \wedge \psi)$. Therefore by 1 of this lemma $(\varphi \wedge \psi) \in \Gamma$.
4. Suppose that $\underline{\Gamma} \wedge \hat{K}_a\underline{\Delta}$ is consistent. Suppose that it is not the case that $\Gamma \sim_a^c \Delta$. Therefore, there is a formula φ such that
   a) $K_a\varphi \in \Gamma$ but $K_a\varphi \notin \Delta$, or
   b) $K_a\varphi \notin \Gamma$ but $K_a\varphi \in \Delta$.
   We proceed by these cases
   a) By 2 of this lemma and the fact that Φ is closed under single negations, $\neg K_a\varphi \in \Delta$. However, by positive introspection $\Gamma \vdash K_aK_a\varphi$. Note that $K_aK_a\varphi \wedge \hat{K}_a\neg K_a\varphi$ is inconsistent. However $\vdash \hat{K}_a\underline{\Delta} \rightarrow \hat{K}_a\neg K_a\varphi$. Therefore $\underline{\Gamma} \wedge \hat{K}_a\underline{\Delta}$ is inconsistent, contradicting our initial assumption.
   b) By 2 of this lemma and the fact that Φ is closed under single negations, $\neg K_a\varphi \in \Gamma$. However, $\vdash \hat{K}_a\underline{\Delta} \rightarrow \hat{K}_aK_a\varphi$ and $\vdash \hat{K}_aK_a\varphi \rightarrow K_a\varphi$. Therefore $\underline{\Gamma} \wedge \hat{K}_a\underline{\Delta}$ is inconsistent, contradicting our initial assumption. □

   In both cases we are led to a contradiction. Therefore $\Gamma \sim_a^c \Delta$.
5. From right to left is trivial by the truth axiom.
   From left to right. Suppose that $\{K_a\varphi \mid K_a\varphi \in \Gamma\} \vdash \psi$. Therefore $\vdash \bigwedge\{K_a\varphi \mid K_a\varphi \in \Gamma\} \rightarrow \psi$. By necessitation and distribution $\vdash \bigwedge\{K_aK_a\varphi \mid K_a\varphi \in \Gamma\} \rightarrow K_a\psi$. By positive introspection $\{K_a\varphi \mid K_a\varphi \in \Gamma\} \vdash \bigwedge\{K_aK_a\varphi \mid K_a\varphi \in \Gamma\}$. Therefore $\{K_a\varphi \mid K_a\varphi \in \Gamma\} \vdash K_a\varphi$.

Answer to Exercise 7.16 Suppose that $\bigvee\{\underline{\Gamma} \mid \Gamma \text{ is maximal consistent in } cl(\varphi)\}$ is not a tautology, i.e., that $\neg\bigvee\{\underline{\Gamma} \mid \Gamma \text{ is maximal consistent in } cl(\varphi)\}$ is consistent. Therefore $\bigwedge\{\neg\underline{\Gamma} \mid \Gamma \text{ is maximal consistent in } cl(\varphi)\}$ is consistent. Therefore $\bigwedge\{\bigvee\{\neg\varphi \mid \varphi \in \Gamma\} \mid \Gamma \text{ is maximal consistent in } cl(\varphi)\}$ is consistent. Therefore, for every maximal consistent Γ in $cl(\varphi)$ there is a formula $\varphi_\Gamma \in \Gamma$ such that $\{\neg\varphi_\Gamma \mid \Gamma \text{ is maximal consistent in } cl(\varphi)\}$ is consistent. Therefore, by the Lindenbaum Lemma (and the law of double negation) there is a maximal consistent set in $cl(\varphi)$ that is inconsistent with every maximal consistent set in $cl(\varphi)$. That is a contradiction. Therefore $\vdash \bigvee\{\underline{\Gamma} \mid \Gamma \text{ is maximal consistent in } cl(\varphi)\}$. □

Answer to Exercise 7.23

1. By induction on ψ.
   Base case If ψ is a propositional variable, its complexity is 1 and it is its only subformula.

Induction hypothesis $c(\psi) \geq c(\varphi)$ if $\varphi \in Sub(\psi)$ and $c(\chi) \geq c(\varphi)$ if $\varphi \in Sub(\chi)$.

Induction step We proceed by cases

negation Suppose that φ is a subformula of $\neg\psi$. Then φ is either $\neg\psi$ or a subformula of ψ. In the former case, we simply observe that the complexity of every formula is greater than or equal to its own complexity. In the latter case, the complexity of $\neg\psi$ equals $1+c(\psi)$. Therefore, if φ is a subformula of ψ it follows immediately from the induction hypothesis that $c(\psi) \geq c(\varphi)$.

conjunction Suppose that φ is a subformula of $\psi \wedge \chi$. Then φ is either $\psi \wedge \chi$ or it is a subformula of ψ or χ. Again in the former case, the complexity of every formula is greater than or equal to its own complexity. In the latter case the complexity of $\psi \wedge \chi$ equals $1 + \max(c(\varphi), c(\psi))$. Simple arithmetic and the induction hypothesis gives us that $c(\psi \wedge \chi) \geq c(\varphi)$.

individual epistemic operator This is completely analogous to the case for negation.

common knowledge This is also completely analogous to the case for negation.

public announcement Suppose that φ is a subformula of $[\psi]\chi$. Then φ is either $[\psi]\chi$ or it is a subformula of ψ or χ. Again, in the former case, the complexity of every formula is greater than or equal to its own complexity. In the latter case, the complexity of $[\psi]\chi$ equals $(4 + c(\psi)) \cdot c(\chi)$. Simple arithmetic and the induction hypothesis gives us that $c([\psi]\chi) \geq c(\varphi)$.

2. $$\begin{aligned} c([\varphi]p) &= (4 + c(\varphi)) \cdot 1 \\ &= 4 + c(\varphi) \end{aligned}$$
and
$$\begin{aligned} c(\varphi \rightarrow p) &= c(\neg(\varphi \wedge \neg p)) \\ &= 1 + c(\varphi \wedge \neg p) \\ &= 2 + \max(c(\varphi), 2) \end{aligned}$$
The latter equals $2 + c(\varphi)$ or 3. Both are less than $4 + c(\varphi)$.
3. $$\begin{aligned} c([\varphi]\neg\psi) &= (4 + c(\varphi)) \cdot (1 + c(\psi)) \\ &= 4 + c(\varphi) + 4 \cdot c(\psi) + c(\varphi) \cdot c(\psi) \end{aligned}$$
and
$$\begin{aligned} c(\varphi \rightarrow \neg[\varphi]\psi) &= c(\neg(\varphi \wedge \neg\neg[\varphi]\psi)) \\ &= 1 + c(\varphi \wedge \neg\neg[\varphi]\psi) \\ &= 2 + \max(c(\varphi), 2 + ((4 + c(\varphi)) \cdot c(\psi))) \\ &= 2 + \max(c(\varphi), 2 + 4 \cdot c(\psi) + c(\varphi) \cdot c(\psi)) \end{aligned}$$
The latter equals $2 + c(\varphi)$ or $4 + 4 \cdot c(\psi) + c(\varphi) \cdot c(\psi)$. Both are less than $4 + c(\varphi) + 4 \cdot c(\psi) + c(\varphi) \cdot c(\psi)$.
4. Assume, without loss of generality, that $c(\psi) \geq c(\chi)$. Then
$$\begin{aligned} c([\varphi](\psi \wedge \chi)) &= (4 + c(\varphi)) \cdot (1 + \max(c(\psi), c(\chi))) \\ &= 4 + c(\varphi) + 4 \cdot \max(c(\psi), c(\chi)) + c(\varphi) \cdot \max(c(\psi), c(\chi)) \\ &= 4 + c(\varphi) + 4 \cdot c(\psi) + c(\varphi) \cdot c(\psi) \end{aligned}$$

and

$$\begin{aligned} c([\varphi]\psi \wedge [\varphi]\chi) &= 1 + \max((4 + c(\varphi)) \cdot c(\psi), (4 + c(\varphi)) \cdot c(\chi)) \\ &= 1 + ((4 + c(\varphi)) \cdot c(\psi)) \\ &= 1 + 4 \cdot c(\psi) + c(\varphi) \cdot c(\psi) \end{aligned}$$

The latter is less than the former

5. This case is completely analogous to the case for negation.
6. $$\begin{aligned} c([\varphi][\psi]\chi) &= (4 + c(\varphi)) \cdot (4 + c(\psi)) \cdot c(\chi) \\ &= (16 + 4 \cdot c(\varphi) + 4 \cdot c(\psi) + c(\varphi) \cdot c(\psi)) \cdot c(\chi) \end{aligned}$$

   and

   $$\begin{aligned} c([\varphi \wedge [\varphi]\psi]\chi) &= (4 + (1 + \max(c(\varphi), (4 + c(\varphi)) \cdot c(\psi)))) \cdot c(\chi) \\ &= (5 + ((4 + c(\varphi)) \cdot c(\psi))) \cdot c(\chi) \\ &= (5 + 4 \cdot c(\psi) + c(\varphi) \cdot c(\psi)) \cdot c(\chi) \end{aligned}$$

   The latter is less than the former. □

Answers to Exercises from Chapter 8

Answer to Exercise 8.23 From left to right. Suppose that $(M, s) \equiv_{\mathcal{L}_K} (M', s')$. Suppose that there is an n such that duplicator does not have a winning strategy for the n-round $\mathcal{L}_K$-game on (M, s) and (M', s'). By Theorem 8.21, there is a formula φ of depth at most n such that $(M, s) \models \varphi$ and $(M', s') \not\models \varphi$. This contradicts the initial assumption.

From right to left. Suppose that for all $n \in \mathbb{N}$ duplicator has a winning strategy for the n-round $\mathcal{L}_K$-game on (M, s) and (M', s'). Suppose that $(M, s) \not\equiv_{\mathcal{L}_K} (M', s')$. Therefore there is some formula φ such that $(M, s) \models \varphi$ and $(M', s') \not\models \varphi$. But according to the assumption duplicator has a winning strategy for the $d(\varphi)$-round $\mathcal{L}_K$-game on (M, s) and (M', s'). By Theorem 8.21, it should be the case that $(M, s) \models \varphi$ iff $(M', s') \models \varphi$, which contradicts our earlier conclusion. □

Answer to Exercise 8.25 Let t and t' be such that duplicator responds with t' if spoiler chooses t or duplicator responds with t' if spoiler chooses t. We have to show these states satisfy the atoms, forth, and back conditions.

The atoms condition follows straightforwardly. Since the strategy is a winning strategy for duplicator, the states must agree on atomic properties.

For the forth condition, suppose that there is a state u such that $t \sim_a u$. Then also $s \sim_a u$, because it is an *S5* relation. Therefore duplicator also has some response when spoiler chooses u. Let the response be u'. Of course $s' \sim'_a u'$, and therefore $t' \sim'_a u'$, and also (u, u') are in the bisimulation relation.

The case for the back condition is analogous to the case for the forth condition. □

Answer to Exercise 8.28 We show that the universal relation $S \times S'$ is a bisimulation. Given that $V = V' = \emptyset$, it follows immediately that any pair of states linked in this relation have the same atomic properties.

For the forth condition, take two states $s \in S$ and $s' \in S'$. Suppose that $s \sim_a t$. Given that the relations are *S5*, there is a t' such that $s' \sim'_a t'$. By definition (t, t') are in the universal relation.

The back case is analogous to the forth case. □

Answer to Exercise 8.42 We have to show that $\mathcal{L}_K(\{a\}) \preceq \mathcal{L}_{KC}(\{a\})$, and that $\mathcal{L}_K(\{a\}) \succeq \mathcal{L}_{KC}(\{a\})$. For the first it suffices to observe that $\mathcal{L}_K(\{a\})$ is a sublanguage of $\mathcal{L}_{KC}(\{a\})$. For the second take a formula $\varphi \in \mathcal{L}_{KC}(\{a\})$. Now replace every occurrence of C_a in φ with K_a. This yields a formula $\varphi' \in \mathcal{L}_K(\{a\})$. It follows that $\varphi \equiv \varphi'$ from the fact that in *S5* it is the case that $K_a\varphi \leftrightarrow C_a\varphi$, because $\sim_a = \sim_{\{a\}}$. □

Answer to Exercise 8.43 The formula $C_{ab}\neg K_a p$ is true in state 0 in all models $Spine(n)$, if n is odd, and false if n is even.

There is no such formula in $\mathcal{L}_K$. Suppose there is such a formula φ. Let $d(\varphi) = n$. It follows from Theorem 8.32 that $(Spine(n), 0) \equiv_{\mathcal{L}_K^n} (Spine(n+1), 0)$, which contradicts the assumption. □

Answer to Exercise 8.55 We have to show that $\mathcal{L}^-_{KC\otimes} \preceq \mathcal{L}_{KC\otimes}$ and that $\mathcal{L}_{KC\otimes} \preceq \mathcal{L}^-_{KC\otimes}$. The former is trivial, because $\mathcal{L}^-_{KC\otimes}$ is a sublanguage of $\mathcal{L}_{KC\otimes}$. For the latter we have to show that for every formula $\varphi \in \mathcal{L}_{KC\otimes}$, there is an equivalent formula $\psi \in \mathcal{L}^-_{KC\otimes}$ We prove this by induction on the number of $\cup$ operators in φ.

Base case If the number of $\cup$ operators is 0, then φ is already a formula in $\mathcal{L}^-_{KC\otimes}$.

Induction hypothesis For every $\varphi \in \mathcal{L}_{KC\otimes}$ it holds that if the number of $\cup$ operators in φ is less than or equal to i, then there is a formula $\psi \in \mathcal{L}^-_{KC\otimes}$ which is equivalent to it.

Induction step Suppose that the number of $\cup$ operators in φ is $i+1$. Take a subformula of φ of the form $[\alpha \cup \alpha']\chi$. This formula is equivalent to $[\alpha]\chi \wedge [\alpha']\chi$. The number of occurrences of $\cup$ in $[\alpha]\chi$ is less than $i+1$. Therefore, by the induction hypothesis, there is a formula $\xi \in \mathcal{L}^-_{KC\otimes}$, which is equivalent to it. The same holds for $[\alpha']\chi$, where we find an $\xi' \in \mathcal{L}^-_{KC\otimes}$. So $[\alpha \cup \alpha']\chi$ is equivalent to $\xi \wedge \xi'$ which is in $\mathcal{L}^-_{KC\otimes}$. If we substitute $\xi \wedge \xi$ for $[\alpha \cup \alpha']\chi$ in φ, we obtain a formula with less than $i+1$ occurrences of $\cup$. Therefore the induction hypothesis applies, and therefore there is some formula $\psi \in \mathcal{L}^-_{KC\otimes}$ which is equivalent to φ. □

References

1. M.H. Albert, R.E.L. Aldred, M.D. Atkinson, H.P. van Ditmarsch, and C.C. Handley. Safe communication for card players by combinatorial designs for two-step protocols. *Australasian Journal of Combinatorics*, 33:33–46, 2005.
2. L. Alberucci and G. Jäger. About cut elimination for logics of common knowledge. *Annals of Pure and Applied Logic*, 133(1-3):73–99, 2005.
3. C.E. Alchourrón, P. Gärdenfors, and D. Makinson. On the logic of theory change: partial meet contraction and revision functions. *Journal of Symbolic Logic*, 50:510–530, 1985.
4. G. Aucher. *A combined system for update logic and belief revision*. Master's thesis, ILLC, University of Amsterdam, Amsterdam, 2003.
5. R.J. Aumann. Agreeing to disagree. *Annals of Statistics*, 4(6):1236–1239, 1976.
6. R.J. Aumann. Interactive epistemology I: Knowledge. *International Journal of Game Theory*, 28:263–300, 1999.
7. R.J. Aumann and A. Brandenburger. Epistemic conditions for Nash equilibrium. *Econometrica*, 63(5):1161–1180, 1995.
8. P. Balbiani and D. Vakarelov. PDL with intersection of programs: a complete axiomatization. *Journal of Applied Non-Classical Logics*, 13:231–276, 2003.
9. A. Baltag. A logic of epistemic actions. In W. van der Hoek, J.J. Meyer, and C. Witteveen, editors, *(Electronic) Proceedings of the ESSLLI 1999 workshop on Foundations and Applications of Collective Agent-Based Systems*. Utrecht University, 1999.
10. A. Baltag and L.S. Moss. Logics for epistemic programs. *Synthese*, 139: 165–224, 2004. Knowledge, Rationality & Action 1–60.
11. A. Baltag, L.S. Moss, and S. Solecki. The logic of common knowledge, public announcements, and private suspicions. In I. Gilboa, editor, *Proceedings of the 7th conference on theoretical aspects of rationality and knowledge (TARK 98)*, pages 43–56. 1998.
12. A. Baltag, L.S. Moss, and S. Solecki. The logic of public announcements, common knowledge, and private suspicions. Technical Report SEN-R9922, CWI, Amsterdam, 1999.
13. K.A. Bartlett, R.A. Scantlebury, and P.T. Wilkinson. A note on reliable full-duplex transmission over half-duplex links. *Communications of the ACM*, 12:260–261, 1969.

14. J. Barwise. Scenes and other situations. *Journal of Philosophy*, 78(7):369–397, 1981.
15. J. Barwise and L.S. Moss. *Vicious Circles: on the mathematics of non-wellfounded phenomena*, volume 60 of *CSLI Lecture Notes*. CSLI Publications, Stanford, 1996.
16. J. Barwise and J. Perry. *Situations and Attitudes*. The MIT Press, Cambridge, Massachusetts, 1983.
17. M. Ben-Air, J.Y. Halpern, and A. Pnueli. Deterministic propositional dynamic logic: finite models, complexity, and completeness. *Journal of Computer and System Science*, 25(3):249–263, 1982.
18. J. van Benthem. *Modal Correspondence Theory*. Ph.D. thesis, University of Amsterdam, 1976.
19. J. van Benthem. Semantic parallels in natural language and computation. In H.D. Ebbinghaus, J. Fernandez-Prida, M. Garrido, D. Lascar, and M.R. Artalejo, editors, *Logic Colloquium '87*. North-Holland, Amsterdam, 1989.
20. J. van Benthem. Logic and the flow of information. In D. Prawitz, B. Skyrms, and D. Westerståhl, editors, *Proceedings of the 9th International Congress of Logic, Methodology and Philosophy of Science*, volume 134 of *Studies in logic and the foundations of mathematics*. Elevier, Amsterdam, 1994. Also available as: Report LP-91-10, ILLC, University of Amsterdam.
21. J. van Benthem. *Exploring Logical Dynamics*. CSLI Publications, Stanford, 1996.
22. J. van Benthem. Update as relativization. ILLC, University of Amsterdam, 1999. Manuscript.
23. J. van Benthem. One is a lonely number: on the logic of communication. Technical report, ILLC, University of Amsterdam, 2002. Report PP-2002-27 (material presented at the Logic Colloquium 2002).
24. J. van Benthem. Conditional probability meets update logic. *Journal of Logic, Language and Information*, 12(4):409–421, 2003.
25. J. van Benthem, J. van Eijck, and B. Kooi. Common knowledge in update logics. In R. van der Meyden, editor, *Theoretical aspects of rationality and knowledge: proceeding of the tenth conference (TARK 2005)*, pages 253–261. 2005.
26. J. van Benthem, J. van Eijck, and B. Kooi. Logics of communication and change, 2006. Accepted for publication.
27. J. van Benthem and F. Liu. Dynamic logic of preference upgrade. Technical report, University of Amsterdam, 2005. Report PP-2005-29.
28. P. Berman, J.Y. Halpern, and J. Tiuryn. On the power of nondeterminism in dynamic logic. In M. Nielsen and E.M. Schmidt, editors, *Automata, Languages and Programming, 9th Colloquium*, volume 140 of *Lecture Notes in Computer Science*, pages 12–16. Springer-Verlag, Berlin, 1982.
29. P. Blackburn, M. de Rijke, and Y. Venema. *Modal Logic*, volume 53 of *Cambridge Tracts in Theoretical Computer Science*. Cambridge University Press, Cambridge, 2001.
30. I. Boh. *Epistemic logic in the later Middle Ages*. Routledge, London, 1993.
31. B. Bollobás, editor. *Littlewood's Miscellany*. Cambrdige University Press, 1986.
32. M.E. Bratman. *Intention, Plans, and Practical Reason*. Harvard University Press, Cambridge, Massachusetts, 1987.

33. B.P. de Bruin. *Explaining Games – On the Logic of Game Theoretic Explanations*. Ph.D. thesis, University of Amsterdam, 2004. ILLC Dissertation Series DS-2004-03.
34. R. Carnap. Modalities and quantification. *The Journal of Symbolic Logic*, 11(2):33–64, 1946.
35. K.M. Chandy and J. Misra. How processes learn. In *PODC '85: Proceedings of the fourth annual ACM symposium on Principles of distributed computing*, pages 204–214. ACM Press, New York, NY, USA, 1985. ISBN 0-89791-168-7.
36. J. Copeland. The genesis of possible world semantics. *The Journal of Philosophical Logic*, 31(2):99–137, 2002.
37. T.M. Cover and J.A. Thomas. *Elements of Information Theory*. Wiley Series in Telecommunications. John Wiley & Sons Inc, New York, 1991.
38. A. Dabrowski, L.S. Moss, and R. Parikh. Topological reasoning and the logic of knowledge. *Annals of Pure and Applied Logic*, 78:73–110, 1996.
39. C.V. Damásio and L.M. Pereira. A survey of paraconsistent semantics of logic programs. In D. Gabbay and P. Smets, editors, *Handbook of Defeasible Reasoning and Uncertainty Management Systems*, pages 241–320. Kluwer Academic Publishers, Dordrecht, 1998.
40. A. Darwiche and J. Pearl. On the logic of iterated belief revision. *Artificial Intelligence*, 89(1-2):1–29, 1997.
41. R. Demolombe. Belief change: from situation calculus to modal logic. *Journal of Applied Non-Classical Logics*, 13(2):187–198, 2003.
42. H.P. van Ditmarsch. The logic of knowledge games: showing a card. In E. Postma and M. Gyssens, editors, *Proceedings of BNAIC 99*, pages 35–42. Maastricht University, 1999.
43. H.P. van Ditmarsch. *Knowledge games*. Ph.D. thesis, University of Groningen, 2000. ILLC Dissertation Series DS-2000-06.
44. H.P. van Ditmarsch. Knowledge games. *Bulletin of Economic Research*, 53(4):249–273, 2001.
45. H.P. van Ditmarsch. The semantics of concurrent knowledge actions. In M. Pauly and G. Sandu, editors, *ESSLLI 2001 workshop on Logic and Games*. 2001.
46. H.P. van Ditmarsch. Descriptions of game actions. *Journal of Logic, Language and Information*, 11:349–365, 2002.
47. H.P. van Ditmarsch. The russian cards problem. *Studia Logica*, 75:31–62, 2003.
48. H.P. van Ditmarsch. Prolegomena to dynamic logic for belief revision. *Synthese (Knowledge, Rationality & Action)*, 147:229–275, 2005.
49. H.P. van Ditmarsch, W. van der Hoek, and B. Kooi. Concurrent dynamic epistemic logic. In Hendricks et al. [96], pages 45–82.
50. H.P. van Ditmarsch, W. van der Hoek, R. van der Meyden, and J. Ruan. Model checking russian cards. *Electronic Notes in Theoretical Computer Science*, 149:790–795, 2006.
51. H.P. van Ditmarsch and B. Kooi. The secret of my success. *Synthese*, 151(2):201–232, 2006.
52. H.P. van Ditmarsch, J. Ruan, and R. Verbrugge. Model checking sum and product. In S. Zhang and R. Jarvis, editors, *Proceedings of the 18th Australian Joint Conference on Artificial Intelligence (AI 2005)*, volume 3809 of *Lecture Notes in Artificial Intelligence*, pages 790–795. Springer-Verlag, Berlin, 2005.

53. H.C. Doets. *Completeness and Definability, applications of the Ehrenfeucht game in second-order and intensional logic.* Ph.D. thesis, University of Amsterdam, 1987.
54. J. Doyle. *A Truth Maintenance System*, volume 12. Elsevier, Amsterdam, 1979.
55. D. Dubois and H. Prade. *Possibility Theory: An Approach to the Computerized Processing of Uncertainty*. Plenum Press, New York, 1988.
56. P. Economou. Sharing beliefs about actions: A parallel composition operator for epistemic programs. In H.P. van Ditmarsch and A. Herzig, editors, *Proceedings of the ESSLLI 2005 workshop Belief Revision and Dynamic Logic*. 2005. Available on `http://www.irit.fr/~Andreas.Herzig/Esslli05/`.
57. J. van Eijck. DEMO: a system for dynamic epistemic modeling. `http://homepages.cwi.nl/~jve/demo`.
58. J. van Eijck. Dynamic epistemic modelling. Technical report, Centrum voor Wiskunde en Informatica, Amsterdam, 2004. CWI Report SEN-E0424.
59. J. van Eijck and J. Ruan. Action emulation, 2005. Manuscript.
60. P. van Emde Boas, J. Groenendijk, and M. Stokhof. The Conway paradox: Its solution in an epistemic framework. In J. Groenendijk, T.M.V. Janssen, and M. Stokhof, editors, *Truth, Interpretation and Information: Selected Papers from the Third Amsterdam Colloquium*, pages 159–182. Foris Publications, Dordrecht, 1984.
61. R. Fagin and J. Halpern. A formal model of knowledge, action and communication in distributed systems. In *Proceedings of the fourth annual ACM symposium on Principles of distributed computing*, pages 224–236. 1985.
62. R. Fagin, J.Y. Halpern, Y. Moses, and M.Y. Vardi. *Reasoning about Knowledge*. The MIT Press, Cambridge, Massachusetts, 1995.
63. R. Fagin, J.Y. Halpern, Y. Moses, and M.Y. Vardi. Knowledge-based programs. *Distributed Computing*, 10(4):199–225, 1997.
64. M.J. Fischer. The consensus problem in unreliable distributed systems. Technical Report RR-273, Yale University, 1989.
65. M. Forti and F. Honsell. Set theory with free construction principles, 1983. Serie IV, X(3).
66. H. Freudenthal. (formulation of the sum-and-product problem). *Nieuw Archief voor Wiskunde*, 3(17):152, 1969.
67. H. Freudenthal. (solution of the sum-and-product problem). *Nieuw Archief voor Wiskunde*, 3(18):102–106, 1970.
68. A. Fuhrmann and M. Morreau, editors. *The Logic of Theory Change, Workshop, Konstanz, FRG, October 13-15, 1989, Proceedings*, volume 465 of *Lecture Notes in Computer Science*. Springer-Verlag, Berlin, 1991.
69. P. Gammie and R. van der Meyden. MCK: Model checking the logic of knowledge. In R. Alur and D. Peled, editors, *Proceedings of the 16th International conference on Computer Aided Verification (CAV 2004)*, pages 479–483. Springer-Verlag, Berlin, 2004.
70. G. Gamow and M. Stern. *Puzzle-Math*. Macmillan, London, 1958.
71. P. Gärdenfors. *Knowledge in Flux*. The MIT Press, Cambridge, Massachusetts, 1988.
72. M. Gardner. Mathematical games. *Scientific American*, 241:20–24, December 1979. Also addressed in the March (page 24) and May (pages 20–21) issues of volume 242, 1980.

73. M. Gelfond. Logic programming and reasoning with incomplete information. *Annals of Math and AI*, 12:98–116, 1994.
74. K. Georgatos. Knowledge on treelike spaces. *Studia Logica*, 59:271–231, 1997.
75. J.D. Gerbrandy. *Bisimulations on Planet Kripke*. Ph.D. thesis, University of Amsterdam, 1998. ILLC Dissertation Series DS-1999-01.
76. J.D. Gerbrandy. The surprise examination in dynamic epistemic logic. *Synthese*, 2006. To appear.
77. J.D. Gerbrandy and W. Groeneveld. Reasoning about information change. *Journal of Logic, Language, and Information*, 6:147–169, 1997.
78. E.L. Gettier. Is justified true belief knowledge. *Analysis*, 23:121–123, 1963. Text is available at `http://www.ditext.com/gettier/gettier.html`.
79. R. Goldblatt. *Logics of Time and Computation*, volume 7 of *CSLI Lecture Notes*. CSLI Publications, Stanford, second edition, 1992.
80. S. Gottwald. *A Treatise on Many-Valued Logics*. Methuen and Co, London, 2001.
81. J. Groenendijk and M. Stokhof. Dynamic predicate logic. *Linguistics and Philosophy*, 14(1):39–100, 1991.
82. W. Groeneveld. *Logical investigations into dynamic semantics*. Ph.D. thesis, University of Amsterdam, 1995. ILLC Dissertation Series DS-1995-18.
83. A.J. Grove. Two modellings for theory change. *Journal of Philosophical Logic*, 17:157–170, 1988.
84. J.Y. Halpern. A note on knowledge-based programs and specifications. *Distributed Computing*, 13(3):145–153, 2000.
85. J.Y. Halpern. *Reasoning about Uncertainty*. The MIT Press, Cambridge, Massachusetts, 2003.
86. J.Y. Halpern and R. Fagin. Modelling knowledge and action in distributed systems. *Distributed Computing*, 3:159–179, 1989.
87. J.Y. Halpern, R. van der Meyden, and M.Y. Vardi. Complete axiomatizations for reasoning about knowledge and time. *SIAM Journal on Computing*, 33(3):674–703, 2004.
88. J.Y. Halpern and Y. Moses. Knowledge and common knowledge in a distributed environment. In *Proceedings of the 3rd ACM Symposium on Principles of Distributed Computing (PODS)*, pages 50–61. 1984. A newer version appeared in the *Journal of the ACM*, vol. 37:3, 1990, pp. 549–587.
89. J.Y. Halpern and Y. Moses. A guide to completeness and complexity for modal logics of knowledge and belief. *Artificial Intelligence*, 54:319–379, 1992.
90. J.Y. Halpern and J.H. Reif. The propositional dynamic logic of deterministic, well-structured progams. *Theoretical Computer Science*, 27(1-2):127–165, 1983.
91. J.Y. Halpern and L.D. Zuck. A little knowledge goes a long way: Simple knowledge-based derivations and correctness proofs for a family of protocols. In *Proceedings of the sixth annual ACM Symposium on Principles of distributed computing*, pages 268–280. 1987.
92. D. Harel. Dynamic logic. In D. Gabbay and F. Guenthner, editors, *Handbook of Philosophical Logic*, volume II, pages 497–604. Kluwer Academic Publishers, Dordrecht, 1984.
93. D. Harel, D. Kozen, and J. Tiuryn. *Dynamic Logic*. The MIT Press, Cambridge, Massachusetts, 2000. Foundations of Computing Series.
94. W. Harper. Rational conceptual change. In *Proceedings of the Meeting of the Philosophy of Scienee Association*, pages 462–494. 1975.

95. B. Heinemann. Revisiting knowledge and time from a topological point of view. In G. Grahne, editor, *Sixth Scandinavian Conference on Artificial Intelligence (SCAI)*, volume 40, pages 40–51. IOS Press, Amsterdam, 1997.
96. V.F. Hendricks, K.F. Jørgensen, and S.A. Pedersen, editors. *Knowledge Contributors*, volume 322 of *Synthese Library*. Kluwer Academic Publishers, Dordrecht, 2003.
97. A. Heuerding, G. Jäger, M. Schwendimann, and M. Seyfried. A logics workbench. *AI Communications*, 9(2):53–58, 1996.
98. J. Hintikka. Modality as referential multiplicity. *Ajatus*, 20:49–64, 1957.
99. J. Hintikka. *Knowledge and Belief, An Introduction to the Logic of the Two Notions*. Cornell University Press, Ithaca, New York, 1962. Republished in 2005 by King's College, London.
100. J. Hintikka. Reasoning about knowledge in philosophy. In J.Y. Halpern, editor, *Proceedings of the 1986 Conference on Theoretical Aspects of Reasoning About Knowledge*, pages 63–80. Morgan Kaufmann Publishers, San Francisco, 1986.
101. J. Hintikka. A second generation epistemic logic and its general significance. In Hendricks et al. [96], pages 33–55.
102. W. van der Hoek. Systems for knowledge and beliefs. *Journal of Logic and Computation*, 3(2):173–195, 1993.
103. W. van der Hoek and M. de Rijke. Interleaved contractions. In L.S. Moss, J. Ginzburg, and M.D. Rijke, editors, *Logic, Language and Computation*, volume 2, pages 106–127. CSLI Publications, Stanford, 1999.
104. W. van der Hoek and R. Verbrugge. Epistemic logic: a survey. In L.A. Petrosjan and V.V. Mazalov, editors, *Game theory and applications*, volume 8, pages 53–94. 2002.
105. W. van der Hoek and M. Wooldridge. Towards a logic of rational agency. *Logic Journal of the IGPL*, 11(2):133–158, 2003.
106. W.v.d. Hoek and J.J.C. Meyer. Making some issues of implicit knowledge explicit. *International Journal of Foundations of Computer Science*, 3(2):193–224, 1992.
107. G.E. Hughes and M.J. Cresswell. *A New Introduction to Modal Logic*. Routledge, London, 1996.
108. C.A.J. Hurkens. Spreading gossip efficiently. *Nieuw Archief voor Wiskunde*, 5/1(2):208–210, 2000.
109. I.M. Isaacs. The impossible problem revisited again. *The Mathematical Intelligencer*, 17(4):4–6, 1995.
110. J. Jaspars. *Calculi for Constructive Communication*. Ph.D. thesis, University of Tilburg, 1994. ILLC Dissertation Series DS-1994-4, ITK Dissertation Series 1994-1.
111. M. Kaneko, T. Nagashima, N. Suzuki, and Y. Tanaka. A map of common knowledge logics. *Studia Logica*, 71(1):57–86, 2002.
112. H. Katsuno and A. Mendelzon. On the difference between updating a knowledge base and revising it. In *Proceedings of the Second International Conference on Principles of Knowledge Representation and Reasoning*, pages 387–394. 1991.
113. A.N. Kolmogorov. *Foundations of the Theory of Probability*. Chelsea Publishing Company, New York, second edition, 1956. Translation edited by N. Morrison with an added bibliography by A.T. Bharucha-Reid.
114. B. Kooi. *Knowledge, Chance, and Change*. Ph.D. thesis, University of Groningen, 2003. ILLC Dissertation Series DS-2003-01.

115. B. Kooi. Probabilistic dynamic epistemic logic. *Journal of Logic, Language and Information*, 12(4):381–408, 2003.
116. B. Kooi and J. van Benthem. Reduction axioms for epistemic actions. In R. Schmidt, I. Pratt-Hartmann, M. Reynolds, and H. Wansing, editors, *AiML-2004: Advances in Modal Logic*, Department of Computer Science, University of Manchester, Technical report series, UMCS-04-9-1, pages 197–211. 2004.
117. D. Kozen and R. Parikh. An elementary proof of the completeness of PDL. *Theoretical Computer Science*, 14:113–118, 1981.
118. M. Kracht. *Tools and techniques in modal logic*, volume 142 of *Studies in logic and the foundations of mathematics*. Elsevier, Amsterdam, 1999.
119. S. Kraus and D. Lehmann. Knowledge, belief and time. *Theoretical Computer Science*, 58:155–174, 1988.
120. S. Kripke. A completeness theorem in modal logic. *Journal of Symbolic Logic*, 24:1–14, 1959.
121. S. Kripke. Semantical analysis of modal logic. *Zeitschrift für Mathematische Logik und Grundlagen der Mathematik*, 9:67–96, 1963.
122. R. Kurki-Suonio. Towards programming with knowledge expressions. In *Proceedings of the 13th ACM SIGACT-SIGPLAN symposium on Principles of programming languages*, pages 140–149. 1986.
123. F. Landman. *Towards a Theory of Information*. Ph.D. thesis, University of Amsterdam, 1986.
124. Y. Lespérance, H.J. Levesque, F. Lin, and R.B. Scherl. Ability and knowing how in the situation calculus. *Studia Logica*, 66(1):165–186, 2000.
125. H.J. Levesque and G. Lakemeyer. *The logic of knowledge bases*. The MIT Press, Cambridge, Massachusetts, 2000.
126. H.J. Levesque, R. Reiter, Y. Lespérance, F. Lin, and R.B. Scherl. GOLOG: A logic programming language for dynamic domains. *Journal of Logic Programming*, 31(1-3):59–83, 1997.
127. I. Levi. *The Entherprise of Knowledge*. The MIT Press, Cambridge, Massachusetts, 1980.
128. D. Lewis. *Convention — A Philosophical Study*. Harvard University Press, Cambridge, Massachusetts, 1969.
129. D. Lewis. *Counterfactuals*. Blackwell, Oxford, 1973.
130. M. Li and P.M.B. Vitányi. *An introduction to Kolmogorov complexity and its applications*. Graduate texts in computer science. Springer-Verlag, Berlin, second edition, 1993.
131. B. van Linder, W. van der Hoek, and J.J.C. Meyer. Actions that make you change your mind. In A. Laux and H. Wansing, editors, *Knowledge and Belief in Philosophy and Artificial Intelligence*, pages 103–146. Akademie Verlag, Berlin, 1995.
132. S. Lindström and W. Rabinowicz. Belief change for introspective agents, 1999. `http://www.lucs.lu.se/spinning/`.
133. S. Lindström and W. Rabinowicz. DDL unlimited: dynamic doxastic logic for introspective agents. *Erkenntnis*, 50:353–385, 1999.
134. L. Lismont and P. Mongin. Strong completeness theorems for weak logics of common belief. *Journal of Philosophical Logic*, 32(2):115–137, 2003.
135. J.E. Littlewood. *A Mathematician's Miscellany*. Methuen and company, 1953.
136. Logic and the foundations of game and decision theory (LOFT). `http://www.econ.ucdavis.edu/faculty/bonanno/loft.html`.

137. A.R. Lomuscio and M.D. Ryan. An algorithmic approach to knowledge evolution. *Artificial Intelligence for Engineering Design, Analysis and Manufacturing (AIEDAM)*, 13(2), 1999. Special issue on Temporal Logic in Engineering.
138. C. Lutz. Complexity and succinctness of public announcement logic. In P. Stone and G. Weiss, editors, *Proceedings AAMAS'06*, pages 137–144. ACM Press, 2006.
139. K.S. Makarychev and Y.S. Makarychev. The importance of being formal. *Mathematical Intelligencer*, 23(1):41–42, 2001.
140. G.J. Massey. *Understanding Symbolic Logic*. Harper & Row, New York, 1970.
141. J. McCarthy. Formalization of two puzzles involving knowledge. In V. Lifschitz, editor, *Formalizing Common Sense: Papers by John McCarthy*, Ablex series in artificial intelligence. Ablex Publishing Corporation, Norwood, New Jersey, 1990. Original manuscript dated 1978–1981.
142. J. McCarthy and P.J. Hayes. Some philosophical problems from the standpoint of artificial intelligence. In B. Meltzer and D. Michie, editors, *Machine Intelligence 4*, pages 463–502. Edinburgh University Press, 1969.
143. R. van der Meyden. Axioms for knowledge and time in distributed systems with perfect recall. In *Proceedings of the Ninth Annual IEEE Symposium on Logic in Computer Science (LICS-94)*, pages 448–457. Paris, July 1994.
144. R. van der Meyden. Mutual belief revision. In J. Doyle, E. Sandewall, and P. Torasso, editors, *Proceedings of the 4th international conference on principles of knowledge representation and reasoning (KR)*, pages 595–606. Morgan Kaufmann Publishers, San Francisco, 1994.
145. R. van der Meyden. Finite state implementations of knowledge-based programs. In *Proceedings of the conference on Foundations of Software Technology and Theoretical Computer Science*, volume 1180 of *Lecture Notes in Computer Science*, pages 262–273. 1996.
146. R. van der Meyden. Common knowledge and update in finite environments. *Information and Computation*, 140(2):115–157, 1998.
147. R. van der Meyden and K. Su. Symbolic model checking the knowledge of the dining cryptographers. In *17th IEEE Computer Security Foundations Workshop*, pages 280–291. 2004.
148. J.J.C. Meyer and W. van der Hoek. *Epistemic Logic for AI and Computer Science*, volume 41 of *Cambridge Tracts in Theoretical Computer Science*. Cambridge University Press, Cambridge, 1995.
149. J.S. Miller and L.S. Moss. The undecidability of iterated modal relativization. *Studia Logica*, 79(3):373–407, 2005.
150. R. Milner. An algebraic definition of simulation between programs. In *Proceedings of the 2nd International Joint Conference on Artificial Intelligence*, pages 481–489. William Kaufman, Los Altos, 1971.
151. G.E. Moore. A reply to my critics. In P.A. Schilpp, editor, *The Philosophy of G.E. Moore*, volume 4 of *The Library of Living Philosophers*, pages 535–677. Northwestern University, Evanston, Illinois, 1942.
152. R.C. Moore. Reasoning about knowledge and action. In *Proceedings of the Fifth International Joint Conference on Artificial Intelligence (IJCAI-77)*. Cambridge, Massachusetts, 1977.
153. R.C. Moore. Possible-worlds semantics for autoepistemic logic. In *Proceedings of the Non-Monotonic Reasoning Workshop*, pages 344–354. 1984.

154. Y.O. Moses, D. Dolev, and J.Y. Halpern. Cheating husbands and other stories: a case study in knowledge, action, and communication. *Distributed Computing*, 1(3):167–176, 1986.
155. L.S. Moss and R. Parikh. Topological reasoning and the logic of knowledge. In Y. Moses, editor, *Proceedings of TARK IV*, pages 95–105. Morgan Kaufmann Publishers, San Francisco, 1992.
156. R. Muskens, J. van Benthem, and A. Visser. Dynamics. In J. van Benthem and A. ter Meulen, editors, *Handbook of Logic and Language*, chapter 10, pages 587–648. Elsevier, Amsterdam, 1997.
157. J. von Neumann and O. Morgenstern. *Theory of Games and Economic Behavior*. Princeton University Press, Princeton, 1944.
158. M.J. Osborne and A. Rubinstein. *A Course in Game Theory*. MIT Press, Cambridge, Massachusetts, 1994.
159. E. Pacuit and R. Parikh. The logic of communication graphs. In J. Leite, A. Omicini, P. Torroni, and P. Yolum, editors, *Declarative Agent Languages and Technologies II: Second International Workshop, DALT 2004, New York, NY, USA, July 19, 2004, Revised Selected Papers*, volume 3476 of *Lecture Notes in Computer Science*, pages 256–269. Springer-Verlag, Berlin, 2005.
160. G. Panti. Solution of a number theoretic problem involving knowledge. *International Journal of Foundations of Computational Science*, 2(4):419–424, 1991.
161. R. Parikh. The completeness of propositional dynamic logic. In *Proceedings of the 7th Symposium on Mathematical Foundations of Computer Science*, volume 64 of *Lecture Notes in Artificial Intelligence*, pages 403–415. Springer-Verlag, Berlin, 1987.
162. R. Parikh. Finite and infinite dialogues. In *Proceedings of a Workshop on Logic from Computer Science*, MSRI publications, pages 481–498. Springer-Verlag, Berlin, 1991.
163. R. Parikh. Monotonic and nonmonotonic logics of knowledge. *Fundamenta Informaticae*, 15(3-4):255–274, 1991.
164. R. Parikh and R. Ramanujam. Distributed processing and the logic of knowledge. In *Logic of Programs*, volume 193 of *Lecture Notes in Computer Science*, pages 256–268. Springer-Verlag, Berlin, 1985. A newer version appeared in *Journal of Logic, Language and Information*, vol. 12, 2003, pp. 453–467.
165. D. Park. Concurrency on automata and infinite sequences. In P. Deusen, editor, *Conference on Theoretical Computer Science*, volume 104 of *Lecture Notes in Computer Science*, pages 167–183. Springer-Verlag, Berlin, 1981.
166. M. Pease, R. Shostack, and L. Lamport. Reaching agreement in the presence of faults. *Journal of the ACM*, 27:228–234, 1980.
167. D. Peleg. Concurrent dynamic logic. *Journal of the ACM*, 34(2):450–479, 1987.
168. J.A. Plaza. Logics of public communications. In M.L. Emrich, M.S. Pfeifer, M. Hadzikadic, and Z.W. Ras, editors, *Proceedings of the 4th International Symposium on Methodologies for Intelligent Systems*, pages 201–216. 1989.
169. V.R. Pratt. A near-optimal method for reasoning about action. *Journal of computer and system sciences*, 20:231–254, 1980.
170. F. Raimondi and A. Lomuscio. Verification of multiagent systems via ordered binary decision diagrams: An algorithm and its implementation. In *Proceedings of the Third International Joint Conference on Autonomous Agents and Multi-Agent Systems (AAMAS 04)*, pages 630–637. IEEE Computer Society, 2004.

171. F. Raimondi and A. Lomuscio. Automatic verification of multi-agent systems by model checking via OBDDs. *Journal of Applied Logic*, 2005. To appear in Special issue on Logic-based agent verification.
172. A.S. Rao and M.P. Georgeff. Modeling rational agents within a BDI-architecture. In R. Fikes and E. Sandewall, editors, *Proceedings of Knowledge Representation and Reasoning (KR&R-91)*, pages 473–484. Morgan Kaufmann Publishers, San Francisco, April 1991.
173. R. Reiter. *Knowledge in Action. Logical Foundations for Specifying and Implementing Dynamical Systems*. The MIT Press, Cambridge, Massachusetts, 2001.
174. G.R. Renardel de Lavalette. Memories and knowledge games. In J. Gerbrandy, M. Marx, M. de Rijke, and Y. Venema, editors, *JFAK. Essays Dedicated to Johan van Benthem on the Occasion of his 50th Birthday*. Amsterdam University Press, Amsterdam, 1999.
175. G.R. Renardel de Lavalette. Changing modalities. *Journal of Logic and Computation*, 14(2):253–278, 2004.
176. M. de Rijke. Meeting some neighbours. In J. van Eijck and A. Visser, editors, *Logic and information flow*, pages 170–195. The MIT Press, Cambridge, Massachusetts, 1994.
177. S. Russell and P. Norvig. *Artificial Intelligence: A Modern Approach*. Prentice-Hall, New Jersey, second edition, 2003.
178. M. Ryan, P.Y. Schobbens, and O. Rodrigues. Counterfactuals and updates as inverse modalities. In Y. Shoham, editor, *TARK'96: Proceedings of the 6th conference on Theoretical aspects of rationality and knowledge*, pages 163–173. Morgan Kaufmann Publishers, San Francisco, 1996.
179. L. Sallows. The impossible problem. *The Mathematical Intelligencer*, 17(1): 27–33, 1995.
180. D. Sangiorgi. Bisimulation: from the origins to today. In *Proceedings of the 19th Symposium on Logic in Computer Science (LICS'04)*, pages 298–302. 2004.
181. S. Sardiña. *Deliberation in Agent Programming Languages*. Ph.D. thesis, University of Toronto, 2005.
182. K. Segerberg. The basic dynamic doxastic logic of AGM. In *The Goldblatt Variations*, volume 1, pages 76–107. Uppsala Prints and Preprints in Philosophy, 1991.
183. K. Segerberg. Belief revision from the point of view of doxastic logic. *Bulletin of the IGPL*, 3:535–553, 1995.
184. K. Segerberg. Default logic as dynamic doxastic logic. *Erkenntnis*, 50:333–352, 1999.
185. K. Segerberg. Two traditions in the logic of belief: bringing them together. In H.J. Ohlbach and U. Reyle, editors, *Logic, Language, and Reasoning*, pages 135–147. Kluwer Academic Publishers, Dordrecht, 1999.
186. C.E. Shannon. A mathematical theory of communication. *Bell Systems Technical Journal*, 27:379–423, 623–656, 1948.
187. F. Stulp and R. Verbrugge. A knowledge-based algorithm for the internet protocol TCP. *Bulletin of Economic Research*, 54(1):69–94, 2002.
188. Theoretical aspects of rationality and knowledge (TARK). `http://www.tark.org`.
189. G. van Tilburg. Doe wel en zie niet om (do well and don't look back). *Katholieke Illustratie (Catholic Illustrated Journal)*, 90(32):47, 1956. Breinbrouwsel 137 ('Brain Brew' 137).

190. M.Y. Vardi. Implementing knowledge-based programs. In *Proceedings of the 6th Conference on Theoretical Aspects of Rationality and Knowledge (TARK 1996)*, pages 15–30. Morgan Kaufmann Publishers, San Francisco, 1996.
191. F. Veltman. Defaults in update semantics. *Journal of Philosophical Logic*, 25: 221–226, 1996.
192. S. Vickers. *Topology via logic*, volume 5 of *Cambridge Tracts in Computer Science*. Cambridge University Press, Cambridge, 1989.
193. M. Wajsberg. Ein erweiterter klassenkalkül. *Monatshefte für Mathematik*, 40: 113–126, 1933.
194. M. Wooldridge and N.R. Jennings. Intelligent agents: Theory and practice. *The Knowledge Engineering Review*, 10(2):115–152, 1995.
195. G.H. von Wright. *An Essay in Modal Logic*. North Holland, Amsterdam, 1951.
196. L. Zadeh. Knowledge representation in fuzzy logic. *IEEE Transactions on Knowledge and Data Engineering*, 1:89–100, 1989.

Index

SYNTHESE LIBRARY

1. J. M. Bochénski, *A Precis of Mathematical Logic*. Translated from French and German by O. Bird. 1959 ISBN 90-277-0073-7
2. P. Guiraud, *Problèmes et méthodes de la statistique linguistique*. 1959 ISBN 90-277-0025-7
3. H. Freudenthal (ed.), *The Concept and the Role of the Model in Mathematics and Natural and Social Sciences*. 1961 ISBN 90-277-0017-6
4. E. W. Beth, *Formal Methods*. An Introduction to Symbolic Logic and to the Study of Effective Operations in Arithmetic and Logic. 1962 ISBN 90-277-0069-9
5. B. H. Kazemier and D. Vuysje (eds.), *Logic and Language*. Studies dedicated to Professor Rudolf Carnap on the Occasion of His 70th Birthday. 1962 ISBN 90-277-0019-2
6. M. W. Wartofsky (ed.), *Proceedings of the Boston Colloquium for the Philosophy of Science, 1961–1962*. [Boston Studies in the Philosophy of Science, Vol. I] 1963 ISBN 90-277-0021-4
7. A. A. Zinov'ev, *Philosophical Problems of Many-valued Logic*. A revised edition, edited and translated (from Russian) by G. Küng and D.D. Comey. 1963 ISBN 90-277-0091-5
8. G. Gurvitch, *The Spectrum of Social Time*. Translated from French and edited by M. Korenbaum and P. Bosserman. 1964 ISBN 90-277-0006-0
9. P. Lorenzen, *Formal Logic*. Translated from German by F.J. Crosson. 1965 ISBN 90-277-0080-X
10. R. S. Cohen and M. W. Wartofsky (eds.), *Proceedings of the Boston Colloquium for the Philosophy of Science, 1962–1964*. In Honor of Philipp Frank. [Boston Studies in the Philosophy of Science, Vol. II] 1965 ISBN 90-277-9004-0
11. E. W. Beth, *Mathematical Thought*. An Introduction to the Philosophy of Mathematics. 1965 ISBN 90-277-0070-2
12. E. W. Beth and J. Piaget, *Mathematical Epistemology and Psychology*. Translated from French by W. Mays. 1966 ISBN 90-277-0071-0
13. G. Küng, *Ontology and the Logistic Analysis of Language*. An Enquiry into the Contemporary Views on Universals. Revised ed., translated from German. 1967 ISBN 90-277-0028-1
14. R. S. Cohen and M. W. Wartofsky (eds.), *Proceedings of the Boston Colloquium for the Philosophy of Sciences, 1964–1966*. In Memory of Norwood Russell Hanson. [Boston Studies in the Philosophy of Science, Vol. III] 1967 ISBN 90-277-0013-3
15. C. D. Broad, *Induction, Probability, and Causation*. Selected Papers. 1968 ISBN 90-277-0012-5
16. G. Patzig, *Aristotle's Theory of the Syllogism*. A Logical-philosophical Study of *Book A* of the *Prior Analytics*. Translated from German by J. Barnes. 1968 ISBN 90-277-0030-3
17. N. Rescher, *Topics in Philosophical Logic*. 1968 ISBN 90-277-0084-2
18. R. S. Cohen and M. W. Wartofsky (eds.), *Proceedings of the Boston Colloquium for the Philosophy of Science, 1966–1968, Part I*. [Boston Studies in the Philosophy of Science, Vol. IV] 1969 ISBN 90-277-0014-1
19. R. S. Cohen and M. W. Wartofsky (eds.), *Proceedings of the Boston Colloquium for the Philosophy of Science, 1966–1968, Part II*. [Boston Studies in the Philosophy of Science, Vol. V] 1969 ISBN 90-277-0015-X
20. J. W. Davis, D. J. Hockney and W. K. Wilson (eds.), *Philosophical Logic*. 1969 ISBN 90-277-0075-3
21. D. Davidson and J. Hintikka (eds.), *Words and Objections*. Essays on the Work of W. V. Quine. 1969, rev. ed. 1975 ISBN 90-277-0074-5; Pb 90-277-0602-6
22. P. Suppes, *Studies in the Methodology and Foundations of Science. Selected Papers from 1951 to 1969*. 1969 ISBN 90-277-0020-6
23. J. Hintikka, *Models for Modalities*. Selected Essays. 1969 ISBN 90-277-0078-8; Pb 90-277-0598-4

24. N. Rescher *et al.* (eds.), *Essays in Honor of Carl G. Hempel.* A Tribute on the Occasion of His 65th Birthday. 1969 ISBN 90-277-0085-0
25. P. V. Tavanec (ed.), *Problems of the Logic of Scientific Knowledge.* Translated from Russian. 1970 ISBN 90-277-0087-7
26. M. Swain (ed.), *Induction, Acceptance, and Rational Belief.* 1970 ISBN 90-277-0086-9
27. R. S. Cohen and R. J. Seeger (eds.), *Ernst Mach: Physicist and Philosopher.* [Boston Studies in the Philosophy of Science, Vol. VI]. 1970 ISBN 90-277-0016-8
28. J. Hintikka and P. Suppes, *Information and Inference.* 1970 ISBN 90-277-0155-5
29. K. Lambert, *Philosophical Problems in Logic.* Some Recent Developments. 1970 ISBN 90-277-0079-6
30. R. A. Eberle, *Nominalistic Systems.* 1970 ISBN 90-277-0161-X
31. P. Weingartner and G. Zecha (eds.), *Induction, Physics, and Ethics.* 1970 ISBN 90-277-0158-X
32. E. W. Beth, *Aspects of Modern Logic.* Translated from Dutch. 1970 ISBN 90-277-0173-3
33. R. Hilpinen (ed.), *Deontic Logic.* Introductory and Systematic Readings. 1971 *See also* No. 152. ISBN Pb (1981 rev.) 90-277-1302-2
34. J.-L. Krivine, *Introduction to Axiomatic Set Theory.* Translated from French. 1971 ISBN 90-277-0169-5; Pb 90-277-0411-2
35. J. D. Sneed, *The Logical Structure of Mathematical Physics.* 2nd rev. ed., 1979 ISBN 90-277-1056-2; Pb 90-277-1059-7
36. C. R. Kordig, *The Justification of Scientific Change.* 1971 ISBN 90-277-0181-4; Pb 90-277-0475-9
37. M. Čapek, *Bergson and Modern Physics.* A Reinterpretation and Re-evaluation. [Boston Studies in the Philosophy of Science, Vol. VII] 1971 ISBN 90-277-0186-5
38. N. R. Hanson, *What I Do Not Believe, and Other Essays.* Ed. by S. Toulmin and H. Woolf. 1971 ISBN 90-277-0191-1
39. R. C. Buck and R. S. Cohen (eds.), *PSA 1970.* Proceedings of the Second Biennial Meeting of the Philosophy of Science Association, Boston, Fall 1970. In Memory of Rudolf Carnap. [Boston Studies in the Philosophy of Science, Vol. VIII] 1971 ISBN 90-277-0187-3; Pb 90-277-0309-4
40. D. Davidson and G. Harman (eds.), *Semantics of Natural Language.* 1972 ISBN 90-277-0304-3; Pb 90-277-0310-8
41. Y. Bar-Hillel (ed.), *Pragmatics of Natural Languages.* 1971 ISBN 90-277-0194-6; Pb 90-277-0599-2
42. S. Stenlund, *Combinators, γ Terms and Proof Theory.* 1972 ISBN 90-277-0305-1
43. M. Strauss, *Modern Physics and Its Philosophy.* Selected Paper in the Logic, History, and Philosophy of Science. 1972 ISBN 90-277-0230-6
44. M. Bunge, *Method, Model and Matter.* 1973 ISBN 90-277-0252-7
45. M. Bunge, *Philosophy of Physics.* 1973 ISBN 90-277-0253-5
46. A. A. Zinov'ev, *Foundations of the Logical Theory of Scientific Knowledge (Complex Logic).* Revised and enlarged English edition with an appendix by G. A. Smirnov, E. A. Sidorenka, A. M. Fedina and L. A. Bobrova. [Boston Studies in the Philosophy of Science, Vol. IX] 1973 ISBN 90-277-0193-8; Pb 90-277-0324-8
47. L. Tondl, *Scientific Procedures.* A Contribution concerning the Methodological Problems of Scientific Concepts and Scientific Explanation. Translated from Czech by D. Short. Edited by R.S. Cohen and M.W. Wartofsky. [Boston Studies in the Philosophy of Science, Vol. X] 1973 ISBN 90-277-0147-4; Pb 90-277-0323-X
48. N. R. Hanson, *Constellations and Conjectures.* 1973 ISBN 90-277-0192-X

49. K. J. J. Hintikka, J. M. E. Moravcsik and P. Suppes (eds.), *Approaches to Natural Language.* 1973 ISBN 90-277-0220-9; Pb 90-277-0233-0
50. M. Bunge (ed.), *Exact Philosophy.* Problems, Tools and Goals. 1973 ISBN 90-277-0251-9
51. R. J. Bogdan and I. Niiniluoto (eds.), *Logic, Language and Probability.* 1973 ISBN 90-277-0312-4
52. G. Pearce and P. Maynard (eds.), *Conceptual Change.* 1973 ISBN 90-277-0287-X; Pb 90-277-0339-6
53. I. Niiniluoto and R. Tuomela, *Theoretical Concepts and Hypothetico-inductive Inference.* 1973 ISBN 90-277-0343-4
54. R. Fraissé, *Course of Mathematical Logic* – Volume 1: *Relation and Logical Formula.* Translated from French. 1973 ISBN 90-277-0268-3; Pb 90-277-0403-1
    (For *Volume 2* see under No. 69).
55. A. Grünbaum, *Philosophical Problems of Space and Time.* Edited by R.S. Cohen and M.W. Wartofsky. 2nd enlarged ed. [Boston Studies in the Philosophy of Science, Vol. XII] 1973 ISBN 90-277-0357-4; Pb 90-277-0358-2
56. P. Suppes (ed.), *Space, Time and Geometry.* 1973 ISBN 90-277-0386-8; Pb 90-277-0442-2
57. H. Kelsen, *Essays in Legal and Moral Philosophy.* Selected and introduced by O. Weinberger. Translated from German by P. Heath. 1973 ISBN 90-277-0388-4
58. R. J. Seeger and R. S. Cohen (eds.), *Philosophical Foundations of Science.* [Boston Studies in the Philosophy of Science, Vol. XI] 1974 ISBN 90-277-0390-6; Pb 90-277-0376-0
59. R. S. Cohen and M. W. Wartofsky (eds.), *Logical and Epistemological Studies in Contemporary Physics.* [Boston Studies in the Philosophy of Science, Vol. XIII] 1973 ISBN 90-277-0391-4; Pb 90-277-0377-9
60. R. S. Cohen and M. W. Wartofsky (eds.), *Methodological and Historical Essays in the Natural and Social Sciences. Proceedings of the Boston Colloquium for the Philosophy of Science, 1969–1972.* [Boston Studies in the Philosophy of Science, Vol. XIV] 1974 ISBN 90-277-0392-2; Pb 90-277-0378-7
61. R. S. Cohen, J. J. Stachel and M. W. Wartofsky (eds.), *For Dirk Struik. Scientific, Historical and Political Essays.* [Boston Studies in the Philosophy of Science, Vol. XV] 1974 ISBN 90-277-0393-0; Pb 90-277-0379-5
62. K. Ajdukiewicz, *Pragmatic Logic.* Translated from Polish by O. Wojtasiewicz. 1974 ISBN 90-277-0326-4
63. S. Stenlund (ed.), *Logical Theory and Semantic Analysis.* Essays dedicated to Stig Kanger on His 50th Birthday. 1974 ISBN 90-277-0438-4
64. K. F. Schaffner and R. S. Cohen (eds.), *PSA 1972. Proceedings of the Third Biennial Meeting of the Philosophy of Science Association.* [Boston Studies in the Philosophy of Science, Vol. XX] 1974 ISBN 90-277-0408-2; Pb 90-277-0409-0
65. H. E. Kyburg, Jr., *The Logical Foundations of Statistical Inference.* 1974 ISBN 90-277-0330-2; Pb 90-277-0430-9
66. M. Grene, *The Understanding of Nature.* Essays in the Philosophy of Biology. [Boston Studies in the Philosophy of Science, Vol. XXIII] 1974 ISBN 90-277-0462-7; Pb 90-277-0463-5
67. J. M. Broekman, *Structuralism: Moscow, Prague, Paris.* Translated from German. 1974 ISBN 90-277-0478-3
68. N. Geschwind, *Selected Papers on Language and the Brain.* [Boston Studies in the Philosophy of Science, Vol. XVI] 1974 ISBN 90-277-0262-4; Pb 90-277-0263-2
69. R. Fraissé, *Course of Mathematical Logic* – Volume 2: *Model Theory.* Translated from French. 1974 ISBN 90-277-0269-1; Pb 90-277-0510-0
    (For *Volume 1* see under No. 54)

70. A. Grzegorczyk, *An Outline of Mathematical Logic.* Fundamental Results and Notions explained with all Details. Translated from Polish. 1974 ISBN 90-277-0359-0; Pb 90-277-0447-3
71. F. von Kutschera, *Philosophy of Language.* 1975 ISBN 90-277-0591-7
72. J. Manninen and R. Tuomela (eds.), *Essays on Explanation and Understanding.* Studies in the Foundations of Humanities and Social Sciences. 1976 ISBN 90-277-0592-5
73. J. Hintikka (ed.), *Rudolf Carnap, Logical Empiricist.* Materials and Perspectives. 1975 ISBN 90-277-0583-6
74. M. Čapek (ed.), *The Concepts of Space and Time.* Their Structure and Their Development. [Boston Studies in the Philosophy of Science, Vol. XXII] 1976 ISBN 90-277-0355-8; Pb 90-277-0375-2
75. J. Hintikka and U. Remes, *The Method of Analysis.* Its Geometrical Origin and Its General Significance. [Boston Studies in the Philosophy of Science, Vol. XXV] 1974 ISBN 90-277-0532-1; Pb 90-277-0543-7
76. J. E. Murdoch and E. D. Sylla (eds.), *The Cultural Context of Medieval Learning.* [Boston Studies in the Philosophy of Science, Vol. XXVI] 1975 ISBN 90-277-0560-7; Pb 90-277-0587-9
77. S. Amsterdamski, *Between Experience and Metaphysics.* Philosophical Problems of the Evolution of Science. [Boston Studies in the Philosophy of Science, Vol. XXXV] 1975 ISBN 90-277-0568-2; Pb 90-277-0580-1
78. P. Suppes (ed.), *Logic and Probability in Quantum Mechanics.* 1976 ISBN 90-277-0570-4; Pb 90-277-1200-X
79. H. von Helmholtz: *Epistemological Writings. The Paul Hertz / Moritz Schlick Centenary Edition of 1921 with Notes and Commentary by the Editors.* Newly translated from German by M. F. Lowe. Edited, with an Introduction and Bibliography, by R. S. Cohen and Y. Elkana. [Boston Studies in the Philosophy of Science, Vol. XXXVII] 1975 ISBN 90-277-0290-X; Pb 90-277-0582-8
80. J. Agassi, *Science in Flux.* [Boston Studies in the Philosophy of Science, Vol. XXVIII] 1975 ISBN 90-277-0584-4; Pb 90-277-0612-2
81. S. G. Harding (ed.), *Can Theories Be Refuted?* Essays on the Duhem-Quine Thesis. 1976 ISBN 90-277-0629-8; Pb 90-277-0630-1
82. S. Nowak, *Methodology of Sociological Research.* General Problems. 1977 ISBN 90-277-0486-4
83. J. Piaget, J.-B. Grize, A. Szeminśska and V. Bang, *Epistemology and Psychology of Functions.* Translated from French. 1977 ISBN 90-277-0804-5
84. M. Grene and E. Mendelsohn (eds.), *Topics in the Philosophy of Biology.* [Boston Studies in the Philosophy of Science, Vol. XXVII] 1976 ISBN 90-277-0595-X; Pb 90-277-0596-8
85. E. Fischbein, *The Intuitive Sources of Probabilistic Thinking in Children.* 1975 ISBN 90-277-0626-3; Pb 90-277-1190-9
86. E. W. Adams, *The Logic of Conditionals.* An Application of Probability to Deductive Logic. 1975 ISBN 90-277-0631-X
87. M. Przełęcki and R. Wójcicki (eds.), *Twenty-Five Years of Logical Methodology in Poland.* Translated from Polish. 1976 ISBN 90-277-0601-8
88. J. Topolski, *The Methodology of History.* Translated from Polish by O. Wojtasiewicz. 1976 ISBN 90-277-0550-X
89. A. Kasher (ed.), *Language in Focus: Foundations, Methods and Systems.* Essays dedicated to Yehoshua Bar-Hillel. [Boston Studies in the Philosophy of Science, Vol. XLIII] 1976 ISBN 90-277-0644-1; Pb 90-277-0645-X

90. J. Hintikka, *The Intentions of Intentionality and Other New Models for Modalities.* 1975 ISBN 90-277-0633-6; Pb 90-277-0634-4
91. W. Stegmüller, *Collected Papers on Epistemology, Philosophy of Science and History of Philosophy.* 2 Volumes. 1977 Set ISBN 90-277-0767-7
92. D. M. Gabbay, *Investigations in Modal and Tense Logics with Applications to Problems in Philosophy and Linguistics.* 1976 ISBN 90-277-0656-5
93. R. J. Bogdan, *Local Induction.* 1976 ISBN 90-277-0649-2
94. S. Nowak, *Understanding and Prediction.* Essays in the Methodology of Social and Behavioral Theories. 1976 ISBN 90-277-0558-5; Pb 90-277-1199-2
95. P. Mittelstaedt, *Philosophical Problems of Modern Physics.* [Boston Studies in the Philosophy of Science, Vol. XVIII] 1976 ISBN 90-277-0285-3; Pb 90-277-0506-2
96. G. Holton and W. A. Blanpied (eds.), *Science and Its Public: The Changing Relationship.* [Boston Studies in the Philosophy of Science, Vol. XXXIII] 1976 ISBN 90-277-0657-3; Pb 90-277-0658-1
97. M. Brand and D. Walton (eds.), *Action Theory.* 1976 ISBN 90-277-0671-9
98. P. Gochet, *Outline of a Nominalist Theory of Propositions.* An Essay in the Theory of Meaning and in the Philosophy of Logic. 1980 ISBN 90-277-1031-7
99. R. S. Cohen, P. K. Feyerabend, and M. W. Wartofsky (eds.), *Essays in Memory of Imre Lakatos.* [Boston Studies in the Philosophy of Science, Vol. XXXIX] 1976 ISBN 90-277-0654-9; Pb 90-277-0655-7
100. R. S. Cohen and J. J. Stachel (eds.), *Selected Papers of Léon Rosenfield.* [Boston Studies in the Philosophy of Science, Vol. XXI] 1979 ISBN 90-277-0651-4; Pb 90-277-0652-2
101. R. S. Cohen, C. A. Hooker, A. C. Michalos and J. W. van Evra (eds.), *PSA 1974. Proceedings of the 1974 Biennial Meeting of the Philosophy of Science Association.* [Boston Studies in the Philosophy of Science, Vol. XXXII] 1976 ISBN 90-277-0647-6; Pb 90-277-0648-4
102. Y. Fried and J. Agassi, *Paranoia.* A Study in Diagnosis. [Boston Studies in the Philosophy of Science, Vol. L] 1976 ISBN 90-277-0704-9; Pb 90-277-0705-7
103. M. Przełęcki, K. Szaniawski and R. Wójcicki (eds.), *Formal Methods in the Methodology of Empirical Sciences.* 1976 ISBN 90-277-0698-0
104. J. M. Vickers, *Belief and Probability.* 1976 ISBN 90-277-0744-8
105. K. H. Wolff, *Surrender and Catch.* Experience and Inquiry Today. [Boston Studies in the Philosophy of Science, Vol. LI] 1976 ISBN 90-277-0758-8; Pb 90-277-0765-0
106. K. Kosík, *Dialectics of the Concrete.* A Study on Problems of Man and World. [Boston Studies in the Philosophy of Science, Vol. LII] 1976 ISBN 90-277-0761-8; Pb 90-277-0764-2
107. N. Goodman, *The Structure of Appearance.* 3rd ed. with an Introduction by G. Hellman. [Boston Studies in the Philosophy of Science, Vol. LIII] 1977 ISBN 90-277-0773-1; Pb 90-277-0774-X
108. K. Ajdukiewicz, *The Scientific World-Perspective and Other Essays, 1931-1963.* Translated from Polish. Edited and with an Introduction by J. Giedymin. 1978 ISBN 90-277-0527-5
109. R. L. Causey, *Unity of Science.* 1977 ISBN 90-277-0779-0
110. R. E. Grandy, *Advanced Logic for Applications.* 1977 ISBN 90-277-0781-2
111. R. P. McArthur, *Tense Logic.* 1976 ISBN 90-277-0697-2
112. L. Lindahl, *Position and Change.* A Study in Law and Logic. Translated from Swedish by P. Needham. 1977 ISBN 90-277-0787-1
113. R. Tuomela, *Dispositions.* 1978 ISBN 90-277-0810-X
114. H. A. Simon, *Models of Discovery and Other Topics in the Methods of Science.* [Boston Studies in the Philosophy of Science, Vol. LIV] 1977 ISBN 90-277-0812-6; Pb 90-277-0858-4

115. R. D. Rosenkrantz, *Inference, Method and Decision.* Towards a Bayesian Philosophy of Science. 1977 ISBN 90-277-0817-7; Pb 90-277-0818-5
116. R. Tuomela, *Human Action and Its Explanation.* A Study on the Philosophical Foundations of Psychology. 1977 ISBN 90-277-0824-X
117. M. Lazerowitz, *The Language of Philosophy.* Freud and Wittgenstein. [Boston Studies in the Philosophy of Science, Vol. LV] 1977 ISBN 90-277-0826-6; Pb 90-277-0862-2
118. Not published 119. J. Pelc (ed.), *Semiotics in Poland, 1894–1969.* Translated from Polish. 1979 ISBN 90-277-0811-8
120. I. Pörn, *Action Theory and Social Science.* Some Formal Models. 1977 ISBN 90-277-0846-0
121. J. Margolis, *Persons and Mind.* The Prospects of Nonreductive Materialism. [Boston Studies in the Philosophy of Science, Vol. LVII] 1977 ISBN 90-277-0854-1; Pb 90-277-0863-0
122. J. Hintikka, I. Niiniluoto, and E. Saarinen (eds.), *Essays on Mathematical and Philosophical Logic.* 1979 ISBN 90-277-0879-7
123. T. A. F. Kuipers, *Studies in Inductive Probability and Rational Expectation.* 1978 ISBN 90-277-0882-7
124. E. Saarinen, R. Hilpinen, I. Niiniluoto and M. P. Hintikka (eds.), *Essays in Honour of Jaakko Hintikka on the Occasion of His 50th Birthday.* 1979 ISBN 90-277-0916-5
125. G. Radnitzky and G. Andersson (eds.), *Progress and Rationality in Science.* [Boston Studies in the Philosophy of Science, Vol. LVIII] 1978 ISBN 90-277-0921-1; Pb 90-277-0922-X
126. P. Mittelstaedt, *Quantum Logic.* 1978 ISBN 90-277-0925-4
127. K. A. Bowen, *Model Theory for Modal Logic.* Kripke Models for Modal Predicate Calculi. 1979 ISBN 90-277-0929-7
128. H. A. Bursen, *Dismantling the Memory Machine.* A Philosophical Investigation of Machine Theories of Memory. 1978 ISBN 90-277-0933-5
129. M. W. Wartofsky, *Models.* Representation and the Scientific Understanding. [Boston Studies in the Philosophy of Science, Vol. XLVIII] 1979 ISBN 90-277-0736-7; Pb 90-277-0947-5
130. D. Ihde, *Technics and Praxis.* A Philosophy of Technology. [Boston Studies in the Philosophy of Science, Vol. XXIV] 1979 ISBN 90-277-0953-X; Pb 90-277-0954-8
131. J. J. Wiatr (ed.), *Polish Essays in the Methodology of the Social Sciences.* [Boston Studies in the Philosophy of Science, Vol. XXIX] 1979 ISBN 90-277-0723-5; Pb 90-277-0956-4
132. W. C. Salmon (ed.), *Hans Reichenbach: Logical Empiricist.* 1979 ISBN 90-277-0958-0
133. P. Bieri, R.-P. Horstmann and L. Krüger (eds.), *Transcendental Arguments in Science.* Essays in Epistemology. 1979 ISBN 90-277-0963-7; Pb 90-277-0964-5
134. M. Marković and G. Petrović (eds.), *Praxis.* Yugoslav Essays in the Philosophy and Methodology of the Social Sciences. [Boston Studies in the Philosophy of Science, Vol. XXXVI] 1979 ISBN 90-277-0727-8; Pb 90-277-0968-8
135. R. Wójcicki, *Topics in the Formal Methodology of Empirical Sciences.* Translated from Polish. 1979 ISBN 90-277-1004-X
136. G. Radnitzky and G. Andersson (eds.), *The Structure and Development of Science.* [Boston Studies in the Philosophy of Science, Vol. LIX] 1979 ISBN 90-277-0994-7; Pb 90-277-0995-5
137. J. C. Webb, *Mechanism, Mentalism and Metamathematics.* An Essay on Finitism. 1980 ISBN 90-277-1046-5
138. D. F. Gustafson and B. L. Tapscott (eds.), *Body, Mind and Method.* Essays in Honor of Virgil C. Aldrich. 1979 ISBN 90-277-1013-9
139. L. Nowak, *The Structure of Idealization.* Towards a Systematic Interpretation of the Marxian Idea of Science. 1980 ISBN 90-277-1014-7

140. C. Perelman, *The New Rhetoric and the Humanities.* Essays on Rhetoric and Its Applications. Translated from French and German. With an Introduction by H. Zyskind. 1979 ISBN 90-277-1018-X; Pb 90-277-1019-8
141. W. Rabinowicz, *Universalizability.* A Study in Morals and Metaphysics. 1979 ISBN 90-277-1020-2
142. C. Perelman, *Justice, Law and Argument.* Essays on Moral and Legal Reasoning. Translated from French and German. With an Introduction by H.J. Berman. 1980 ISBN 90-277-1089-9; Pb 90-277-1090-2
143. S. Kanger and S. Öhman (eds.), *Philosophy and Grammar.* Papers on the Occasion of the Quincentennial of Uppsala University. 1981 ISBN 90-277-1091-0
144. T. Pawlowski, *Concept Formation in the Humanities and the Social Sciences.* 1980 ISBN 90-277-1096-1
145. J. Hintikka, D. Gruender and E. Agazzi (eds.), *Theory Change, Ancient Axiomatics and Galileo's Methodology.* Proceedings of the 1978 Pisa Conference on the History and Philosophy of Science, Volume I. 1981 ISBN 90-277-1126-7
146. J. Hintikka, D. Gruender and E. Agazzi (eds.), *Probabilistic Thinking, Thermodynamics, and the Interaction of the History and Philosophy of Science.* Proceedings of the 1978 Pisa Conference on the History and Philosophy of Science, Volume II. 1981 ISBN 90-277-1127-5
147. U. Mönnich (ed.), *Aspects of Philosophical Logic.* Some Logical Forays into Central Notions of Linguistics and Philosophy. 1981 ISBN 90-277-1201-8
148. D. M. Gabbay, *Semantical Investigations in Heyting's Intuitionistic Logic.* 1981 ISBN 90-277-1202-6
149. E. Agazzi (ed.), *Modern Logic – A Survey.* Historical, Philosophical, and Mathematical Aspects of Modern Logic and Its Applications. 1981 ISBN 90-277-1137-2
150. A. F. Parker-Rhodes, *The Theory of Indistinguishables.* A Search for Explanatory Principles below the Level of Physics. 1981 ISBN 90-277-1214-X
151. J. C. Pitt, *Pictures, Images, and Conceptual Change.* An Analysis of Wilfrid Sellars' Philosophy of Science. 1981 ISBN 90-277-1276-X; Pb 90-277-1277-8
152. R. Hilpinen (ed.), *New Studies in Deontic Logic.* Norms, Actions, and the Foundations of Ethics. 1981 ISBN 90-277-1278-6; Pb 90-277-1346-4
153. C. Dilworth, *Scientific Progress.* A Study Concerning the Nature of the Relation between Successive Scientific Theories. 3rd rev. ed., 1994 ISBN 0-7923-2487-0; Pb 0-7923-2488-9
154. D. Woodruff Smith and R. McIntyre, *Husserl and Intentionality.* A Study of Mind, Meaning, and Language. 1982 ISBN 90-277-1392-8; Pb 90-277-1730-3
155. R. J. Nelson, *The Logic of Mind.* 2nd. ed., 1989 ISBN 90-277-2819-4; Pb 90-277-2822-4
156. J. F. A. K. van Benthem, *The Logic of Time.* A Model-Theoretic Investigation into the Varieties of Temporal Ontology, and Temporal Discourse. 1983; 2nd ed., 1991 ISBN 0-7923-1081-0
157. R. Swinburne (ed.), *Space, Time and Causality.* 1983 ISBN 90-277-1437-1
158. E. T. Jaynes, *Papers on Probability, Statistics and Statistical Physics.* Ed. by R. D. Rozenkrantz. 1983 ISBN 90-277-1448-7; Pb (1989) 0-7923-0213-3
159. T. Chapman, *Time: A Philosophical Analysis.* 1982 ISBN 90-277-1465-7
160. E. N. Zalta, *Abstract Objects.* An Introduction to Axiomatic Metaphysics. 1983 ISBN 90-277-1474-6
161. S. Harding and M. B. Hintikka (eds.), *Discovering Reality.* Feminist Perspectives on Epistemology, Metaphysics, Methodology, and Philosophy of Science. 1983 ISBN 90-277-1496-7; Pb 90-277-1538-6
162. M. A. Stewart (ed.), *Law, Morality and Rights.* 1983 ISBN 90-277-1519-X

163. D. Mayr and G. Süssmann (eds.), *Space, Time, and Mechanics.* Basic Structures of a Physical Theory. 1983 ISBN 90-277-1525-4
164. D. Gabbay and F. Guenthner (eds.), *Handbook of Philosophical Logic.* Vol. I: Elements of Classical Logic. 1983 ISBN 90-277-1542-4
165. D. Gabbay and F. Guenthner (eds.), *Handbook of Philosophical Logic.* Vol. II: Extensions of Classical Logic. 1984 ISBN 90-277-1604-8
166. D. Gabbay and F. Guenthner (eds.), *Handbook of Philosophical Logic.* Vol. III: Alternative to Classical Logic. 1986 ISBN 90-277-1605-6
167. D. Gabbay and F. Guenthner (eds.), *Handbook of Philosophical Logic.* Vol. IV: Topics in the Philosophy of Language. 1989 ISBN 90-277-1606-4
168. A. J. I. Jones, *Communication and Meaning.* An Essay in Applied Modal Logic. 1983 ISBN 90-277-1543-2
169. M. Fitting, *Proof Methods for Modal and Intuitionistic Logics.* 1983 ISBN 90-277-1573-4
170. J. Margolis, *Culture and Cultural Entities.* Toward a New Unity of Science. 1984 ISBN 90-277-1574-2
171. R. Tuomela, *A Theory of Social Action.* 1984 ISBN 90-277-1703-6
172. J. J. E. Gracia, E. Rabossi, E. Villanueva and M. Dascal (eds.), *Philosophical Analysis in Latin America.* 1984 ISBN 90-277-1749-4
173. P. Ziff, *Epistemic Analysis.* A Coherence Theory of Knowledge. 1984 ISBN 90-277-1751-7
174. P. Ziff, *Antiaesthetics.* An Appreciation of the Cow with the Subtile Nose. 1984 ISBN 90-277-1773-7
175. W. Balzer, D. A. Pearce, and H.-J. Schmidt (eds.), *Reduction in Science.* Structure, Examples, Philosophical Problems. 1984 ISBN 90-277-1811-3
176. A. Peczenik, L. Lindahl and B. van Roermund (eds.), *Theory of Legal Science.* Proceedings of the Conference on Legal Theory and Philosophy of Science (Lund, Sweden, December 1983). 1984 ISBN 90-277-1834-2
177. I. Niiniluoto, *Is Science Progressive?* 1984 ISBN 90-277-1835-0
178. B. K. Matilal and J. L. Shaw (eds.), *Analytical Philosophy in Comparative Perspective.* Exploratory Essays in Current Theories and Classical Indian Theories of Meaning and Reference. 1985 ISBN 90-277-1870-9
179. P. Kroes, *Time: Its Structure and Role in Physical Theories.* 1985 ISBN 90-277-1894-6
180. J. H. Fetzer, *Sociobiology and Epistemology.* 1985 ISBN 90-277-2005-3; Pb 90-277-2006-1
181. L. Haaparanta and J. Hintikka (eds.), *Frege Synthesized.* Essays on the Philosophical and Foundational Work of Gottlob Frege. 1986 ISBN 90-277-2126-2
182. M. Detlefsen, *Hilbert's Program.* An Essay on Mathematical Instrumentalism. 1986 ISBN 90-277-2151-3
183. J. L. Golden and J. J. Pilotta (eds.), *Practical Reasoning in Human Affairs.* Studies in Honor of Chaim Perelman. 1986 ISBN 90-277-2255-2
184. H. Zandvoort, *Models of Scientific Development and the Case of Nuclear Magnetic Resonance.* 1986 ISBN 90-277-2351-6
185. I. Niiniluoto, *Truthlikeness.* 1987 ISBN 90-277-2354-0
186. W. Balzer, C. U. Moulines and J. D. Sneed, *An Architectonic for Science.* The Structuralist Program. 1987 ISBN 90-277-2403-2
187. D. Pearce, *Roads to Commensurability.* 1987 ISBN 90-277-2414-8
188. L. M. Vaina (ed.), *Matters of Intelligence.* Conceptual Structures in Cognitive Neuroscience. 1987 ISBN 90-277-2460-1

189. H. Siegel, *Relativism Refuted*. A Critique of Contemporary Epistemological Relativism. 1987 ISBN 90-277-2469-5
190. W. Callebaut and R. Pinxten, *Evolutionary Epistemology*. A Multiparadigm Program, with a Complete Evolutionary Epistemology Bibliograph. 1987 ISBN 90-277-2582-9
191. J. Kmita, *Problems in Historical Epistemology*. 1988 ISBN 90-277-2199-8
192. J. H. Fetzer (ed.), *Probability and Causality*. Essays in Honor of Wesley C. Salmon, with an Annotated Bibliography. 1988 ISBN 90-277-2607-8; Pb 1-5560-8052-2
193. A. Donovan, L. Laudan and R. Laudan (eds.), *Scrutinizing Science*. Empirical Studies of Scientific Change. 1988 ISBN 90-277-2608-6
194. H.R. Otto and J.A. Tuedio (eds.), *Perspectives on Mind*. 1988 ISBN 90-277-2640-X
195. D. Batens and J.P. van Bendegem (eds.), *Theory and Experiment*. Recent Insights and New Perspectives on Their Relation. 1988 ISBN 90-277-2645-0
196. J. Österberg, *Self and Others*. A Study of Ethical Egoism. 1988 ISBN 90-277-2648-5
197. D.H. Helman (ed.), *Analogical Reasoning*. Perspectives of Artificial Intelligence, Cognitive Science, and Philosophy. 1988 ISBN 90-277-2711-2
198. J. Woleński, *Logic and Philosophy in the Lvov-Warsaw School*. 1989 ISBN 90-277-2749-X
199. R. Wójcicki, *Theory of Logical Calculi*. Basic Theory of Consequence Operations. 1988 ISBN 90-277-2785-6
200. J. Hintikka and M.B. Hintikka, *The Logic of Epistemology and the Epistemology of Logic*. Selected Essays. 1989 ISBN 0-7923-0040-8; Pb 0-7923-0041-6
201. E. Agazzi (ed.), *Probability in the Sciences*. 1988 ISBN 90-277-2808-9
202. M. Meyer (ed.), *From Metaphysics to Rhetoric*. 1989 ISBN 90-277-2814-3
203. R.L. Tieszen, *Mathematical Intuition*. Phenomenology and Mathematical Knowledge. 1989 ISBN 0-7923-0131-5
204. A. Melnick, *Space, Time, and Thought in Kant*. 1989 ISBN 0-7923-0135-8
205. D.W. Smith, *The Circle of Acquaintance*. Perception, Consciousness, and Empathy. 1989 ISBN 0-7923-0252-4
206. M.H. Salmon (ed.), *The Philosophy of Logical Mechanism*. Essays in Honor of Arthur W. Burks. With his Responses, and with a Bibliography of Burk's Work. 1990 ISBN 0-7923-0325-3
207. M. Kusch, *Language as Calculus vs. Language as Universal Medium*. A Study in Husserl, Heidegger, and Gadamer. 1989 ISBN 0-7923-0333-4
208. T.C. Meyering, *Historical Roots of Cognitive Science*. The Rise of a Cognitive Theory of Perception from Antiquity to the Nineteenth Century. 1989 ISBN 0-7923-0349-0
209. P. Kosso, *Observability and Observation in Physical Science*. 1989 ISBN 0-7923-0389-X
210. J. Kmita, *Essays on the Theory of Scientific Cognition*. 1990 ISBN 0-7923-0441-1
211. W. Sieg (ed.), *Acting and Reflecting*. The Interdisciplinary Turn in Philosophy. 1990 ISBN 0-7923-0512-4
212. J. Karpiński, *Causality in Sociological Research*. 1990 ISBN 0-7923-0546-9
213. H.A. Lewis (ed.), *Peter Geach: Philosophical Encounters*. 1991 ISBN 0-7923-0823-9
214. M. Ter Hark, *Beyond the Inner and the Outer*. Wittgenstein's Philosophy of Psychology. 1990 ISBN 0-7923-0850-6
215. M. Gosselin, *Nominalism and Contemporary Nominalism*. Ontological and Epistemological Implications of the Work of W.V.O. Quine and of N. Goodman. 1990 ISBN 0-7923-0904-9
216. J.H. Fetzer, D. Shatz and G. Schlesinger (eds.), *Definitions and Definability*. Philosophical Perspectives. 1991 ISBN 0-7923-1046-2
217. E. Agazzi and A. Cordero (eds.), *Philosophy and the Origin and Evolution of the Universe*. 1991 ISBN 0-7923-1322-4

218. M. Kusch, *Foucault's Strata and Fields.* An Investigation into Archaeological and Genealogical Science Studies. 1991 ISBN 0-7923-1462-X
219. C.J. Posy, *Kant's Philosophy of Mathematics.* Modern Essays. 1992 ISBN 0-7923-1495-6
220. G. Van de Vijver, *New Perspectives on Cybernetics.* Self-Organization, Autonomy and Connectionism. 1992 ISBN 0-7923-1519-7
221. J.C. Nyíri, *Tradition and Individuality.* Essays. 1992 ISBN 0-7923-1566-9
222. R. Howell, *Kant's Transcendental Deduction.* An Analysis of Main Themes in His Critical Philosophy. 1992 ISBN 0-7923-1571-5
223. A. García de la Sienra, *The Logical Foundations of the Marxian Theory of Value.* 1992 ISBN 0-7923-1778-5
224. D.S. Shwayder, *Statement and Referent.* An Inquiry into the Foundations of Our Conceptual Order. 1992 ISBN 0-7923-1803-X
225. M. Rosen, *Problems of the Hegelian Dialectic.* Dialectic Reconstructed as a Logic of Human Reality. 1993 ISBN 0-7923-2047-6
226. P. Suppes, *Models and Methods in the Philosophy of Science: Selected Essays.* 1993 ISBN 0-7923-2211-8
227. R. M. Dancy (ed.), *Kant and Critique: New Essays in Honor of W. H. Werkmeister.* 1993 ISBN 0-7923-2244-4
228. J. Woleński (ed.), *Philosophical Logic in Poland.* 1993 ISBN 0-7923-2293-2
229. M. De Rijke (ed.), *Diamonds and Defaults.* Studies in Pure and Applied Intensional Logic. 1993 ISBN 0-7923-2342-4
230. B.K. Matilal and A. Chakrabarti (eds.), *Knowing from Words.* Western and Indian Philosophical Analysis of Understanding and Testimony. 1994 ISBN 0-7923-2345-9
231. S.A. Kleiner, *The Logic of Discovery.* A Theory of the Rationality of Scientific Research. 1993 ISBN 0-7923-2371-8
232. R. Festa, *Optimum Inductive Methods.* A Study in Inductive Probability, Bayesian Statistics, and Verisimilitude. 1993 ISBN 0-7923-2460-9
233. P. Humphreys (ed.), *Patrick Suppes: Scientific Philosopher.* Vol. 1: Probability and Probabilistic Causality. 1994 ISBN 0-7923-2552-4
234. P. Humphreys (ed.), *Patrick Suppes: Scientific Philosopher.* Vol. 2: Philosophy of Physics, Theory Structure, and Measurement Theory. 1994 ISBN 0-7923-2553-2
235. P. Humphreys (ed.), *Patrick Suppes: Scientific Philosopher.* Vol. 3: Language, Logic, and Psychology. 1994 ISBN 0-7923-2862-0
Set ISBN (Vols 233–235) 0-7923-2554-0
236. D. Prawitz and D. Westerståhl (eds.), *Logic and Philosophy of Science in Uppsala.* Papers from the 9th International Congress of Logic, Methodology, and Philosophy of Science. 1994 ISBN 0-7923-2702-0
237. L. Haaparanta (ed.), *Mind, Meaning and Mathematics.* Essays on the Philosophical Views of Husserl and Frege. 1994 ISBN 0-7923-2703-9
238. J. Hintikka (ed.), *Aspects of Metaphor.* 1994 ISBN 0-7923-2786-1
239. B. McGuinness and G. Oliveri (eds.), *The Philosophy of Michael Dummett.* With Replies from Michael Dummett. 1994 ISBN 0-7923-2804-3
240. D. Jamieson (ed.), *Language, Mind, and Art.* Essays in Appreciation and Analysis, In Honor of Paul Ziff. 1994 ISBN 0-7923-2810-8
241. G. Preyer, F. Siebelt and A. Ulfig (eds.), *Language, Mind and Epistemology.* On Donald Davidson's Philosophy. 1994 ISBN 0-7923-2811-6
242. P. Ehrlich (ed.), *Real Numbers, Generalizations of the Reals, and Theories of Continua.* 1994 ISBN 0-7923-2689-X

243. G. Debrock and M. Hulswit (eds.), *Living Doubt.* Essays concerning the epistemology of Charles Sanders Peirce. 1994 ISBN 0-7923-2898-1
244. J. Srzednicki, *To Know or Not to Know.* Beyond Realism and Anti-Realism. 1994 ISBN 0-7923-2909-0
245. R. Egidi (ed.), *Wittgenstein: Mind and Language.* 1995 ISBN 0-7923-3171-0
246. A. Hyslop, *Other Minds.* 1995 ISBN 0-7923-3245-8
247. L. Pólos and M. Masuch (eds.), *Applied Logic: How, What and Why.* Logical Approaches to Natural Language. 1995 ISBN 0-7923-3432-9
248. M. Krynicki, M. Mostowski and L.M. Szczerba (eds.), *Quantifiers: Logics, Models and Computation.* Volume One: Surveys. 1995 ISBN 0-7923-3448-5
249. M. Krynicki, M. Mostowski and L.M. Szczerba (eds.), *Quantifiers: Logics, Models and Computation.* Volume Two: Contributions. 1995 ISBN 0-7923-3449-3
Set ISBN (Vols 248 + 249) 0-7923-3450-7
250. R.A. Watson, *Representational Ideas from Plato to Patricia Churchland.* 1995 ISBN 0-7923-3453-1
251. J. Hintikka (ed.), *From Dedekind to Gödel.* Essays on the Development of the Foundations of Mathematics. 1995 ISBN 0-7923-3484-1
252. A. Wiśniewski, *The Posing of Questions.* Logical Foundations of Erotetic Inferences. 1995 ISBN 0-7923-3637-2
253. J. Peregrin, *Doing Worlds with Words.* Formal Semantics without Formal Metaphysics. 1995 ISBN 0-7923-3742-5
254. I.A. Kieseppä, *Truthlikeness for Multidimensional, Quantitative Cognitive Problems.* 1996 ISBN 0-7923-4005-1
255. P. Hugly and C. Sayward: *Intensionality and Truth.* An Essay on the Philosophy of A.N. Prior. 1996 ISBN 0-7923-4119-8
256. L. Hankinson Nelson and J. Nelson (eds.): *Feminism, Science, and the Philosophy of Science.* 1997 ISBN 0-7923-4162-7
257. P.I. Bystrov and V.N. Sadovsky (eds.): *Philosophical Logic and Logical Philosophy.* Essays in Honour of Vladimir A. Smirnov. 1996 ISBN 0-7923-4270-4
258. Å.E. Andersson and N-E. Sahlin (eds.): *The Complexity of Creativity.* 1996 ISBN 0-7923-4346-8
259. M.L. Dalla Chiara, K. Doets, D. Mundici and J. van Benthem (eds.): *Logic and Scientific Methods.* Volume One of the Tenth International Congress of Logic, Methodology and Philosophy of Science, Florence, August 1995. 1997 ISBN 0-7923-4383-2
260. M.L. Dalla Chiara, K. Doets, D. Mundici and J. van Benthem (eds.): *Structures and Norms in Science.* Volume Two of the Tenth International Congress of Logic, Methodology and Philosophy of Science, Florence, August 1995. 1997 ISBN 0-7923-4384-0
Set ISBN (Vols 259 + 260) 0-7923-4385-9
261. A. Chakrabarti: *Denying Existence.* The Logic, Epistemology and Pragmatics of Negative Existentials and Fictional Discourse. 1997 ISBN 0-7923-4388-3
262. A. Biletzki: *Talking Wolves.* Thomas Hobbes on the Language of Politics and the Politics of Language. 1997 ISBN 0-7923-4425-1
263. D. Nute (ed.): *Defeasible Deontic Logic.* 1997 ISBN 0-7923-4630-0
264. U. Meixner: *Axiomatic Formal Ontology.* 1997 ISBN 0-7923-4747-X
265. I. Brinck: *The Indexical 'I'.* The First Person in Thought and Language. 1997 ISBN 0-7923-4741-2
266. G. Hölmström-Hintikka and R. Tuomela (eds.): *Contemporary Action Theory.* Volume 1: Individual Action. 1997 ISBN 0-7923-4753-6; Set: 0-7923-4754-4

267. G. Hölmström-Hintikka and R. Tuomela (eds.): *Contemporary Action Theory.* Volume 2: Social Action. 1997 ISBN 0-7923-4752-8; Set: 0-7923-4754-4
268. B.-C. Park: *Phenomenological Aspects of Wittgenstein's Philosophy.* 1998 ISBN 0-7923-4813-3
269. J. Paśniczek: *The Logic of Intentional Objects.* A Meinongian Version of Classical Logic. 1998 Hb ISBN 0-7923-4880-X; Pb ISBN 0-7923-5578-4
270. P.W. Humphreys and J.H. Fetzer (eds.): *The New Theory of Reference.* Kripke, Marcus, and Its Origins. 1998 ISBN 0-7923-4898-2
271. K. Szaniawski, A. Chmielewski and J. Woleński (eds.): *On Science, Inference, Information and Decision Making.* Selected Essays in the Philosophy of Science. 1998 ISBN 0-7923-4922-9
272. G.H. von Wright: *In the Shadow of Descartes.* Essays in the Philosophy of Mind. 1998 ISBN 0-7923-4992-X
273. K. Kijania-Placek and J. Woleński (eds.): *The Lvov–Warsaw School and Contemporary Philosophy.* 1998 ISBN 0-7923-5105-3
274. D. Dedrick: *Naming the Rainbow.* Colour Language, Colour Science, and Culture. 1998 ISBN 0-7923-5239-4
275. L. Albertazzi (ed.): *Shapes of Forms.* From Gestalt Psychology and Phenomenology to Ontology and Mathematics. 1999 ISBN 0-7923-5246-7
276. P. Fletcher: *Truth, Proof and Infinity.* A Theory of Constructions and Constructive Reasoning. 1998 ISBN 0-7923-5262-9
277. M. Fitting and R.L. Mendelsohn (eds.): *First-Order Modal Logic.* 1998 Hb ISBN 0-7923-5334-X; Pb ISBN 0-7923-5335-8
278. J.N. Mohanty: *Logic, Truth and the Modalities from a Phenomenological Perspective.* 1999 ISBN 0-7923-5550-4
279. T. Placek: *Mathematical Intiutionism and Intersubjectivity.* A Critical Exposition of Arguments for Intuitionism. 1999 ISBN 0-7923-5630-6
280. A. Cantini, E. Casari and P. Minari (eds.): *Logic and Foundations of Mathematics.* 1999 ISBN 0-7923-5659-4 set ISBN 0-7923-5867-8
281. M.L. Dalla Chiara, R. Giuntini and F. Laudisa (eds.): *Language, Quantum, Music.* 1999 ISBN 0-7923-5727-2; set ISBN 0-7923-5867-8
282. R. Egidi (ed.): *In Search of a New Humanism.* The Philosophy of Georg Hendrik von Wright. 1999 ISBN 0-7923-5810-4
283. F. Vollmer: *Agent Causality.* 1999 ISBN 0-7923-5848-1
284. J. Peregrin (ed.): *Truth and Its Nature (if Any).* 1999 ISBN 0-7923-5865-1
285. M. De Caro (ed.): *Interpretations and Causes.* New Perspectives on Donald Davidson's Philosophy. 1999 ISBN 0-7923-5869-4
286. R. Murawski: *Recursive Functions and Metamathematics.* Problems of Completeness and Decidability, Gödel's Theorems. 1999 ISBN 0-7923-5904-6
287. T.A.F. Kuipers: *From Instrumentalism to Constructive Realism.* On Some Relations between Confirmation, Empirical Progress, and Truth Approximation. 2000 ISBN 0-7923-6086-9
288. G. Holmström-Hintikka (ed.): *Medieval Philosophy and Modern Times.* 2000 ISBN 0-7923-6102-4
289. E. Grosholz and H. Breger (eds.): *The Growth of Mathematical Knowledge.* 2000 ISBN 0-7923-6151-2

290. G. Sommaruga: *History and Philosophy of Constructive Type Theory*. 2000 ISBN 0-7923-6180-6
291. J. Gasser (ed.): *A Boole Anthology*. Recent and Classical Studies in the Logic of George Boole. 2000 ISBN 0-7923-6380-9
292. V.F. Hendricks, S.A. Pedersen and K.F. Jørgensen (eds.): *Proof Theory*. History and Philosophical Significance. 2000 ISBN 0-7923-6544-5
293. W.L. Craig: *The Tensed Theory of Time*. A Critical Examination. 2000 ISBN 0-7923-6634-4
294. W.L. Craig: *The Tenseless Theory of Time*. A Critical Examination. 2000 ISBN 0-7923-6635-2
295. L. Albertazzi (ed.): *The Dawn of Cognitive Science*. Early European Contributors. 2001 ISBN 0-7923-6799-5
296. G. Forrai: *Reference, Truth and Conceptual Schemes*. A Defense of Internal Realism. 2001 ISBN 0-7923-6885-1
297. V.F. Hendricks, S.A. Pedersen and K.F. Jørgensen (eds.): *Probability Theory*. Philosophy, Recent History and Relations to Science. 2001 ISBN 0-7923-6952-1
298. M. Esfeld: *Holism in Philosophy of Mind and Philosophy of Physics*. 2001 ISBN 0-7923-7003-1
299. E.C. Steinhart: *The Logic of Metaphor*. Analogous Parts of Possible Worlds. 2001 ISBN 0-7923-7004-X
300. P. Gärdenfors: *The Dynamics of Thought*. 2005 ISBN 1-4020-3398-2
301. T.A.F. Kuipers: *Structures in Science Heuristic Patterns Based on Cognitive Structures*. An Advanced Textbook in Neo-Classical Philosophy of Science. 2001 ISBN 0-7923-7117-8
302. G. Hon and S.S. Rakover (eds.): *Explanation*. Theoretical Approaches and Applications. 2001 ISBN 1-4020-0017-0
303. G. Holmström-Hintikka, S. Lindström and R. Sliwinski (eds.): *Collected Papers of Stig Kanger with Essays on his Life and Work*. Vol. I. 2001 ISBN 1-4020-0021-9; Pb ISBN 1-4020-0022-7
304. G. Holmström-Hintikka, S. Lindström and R. Sliwinski (eds.): *Collected Papers of Stig Kanger with Essays on his Life and Work*. Vol. II. 2001 ISBN 1-4020-0111-8; Pb ISBN 1-4020-0112-6
305. C.A. Anderson and M. Zelëny (eds.): *Logic, Meaning and Computation*. Essays in Memory of Alonzo Church. 2001 ISBN 1-4020-0141-X
306. P. Schuster, U. Berger and H. Osswald (eds.): *Reuniting the Antipodes – Constructive and Nonstandard Views of the Continuum*. 2001 ISBN 1-4020-0152-5
307. S.D. Zwart: *Refined Verisimilitude*. 2001 ISBN 1-4020-0268-8
308. A.-S. Maurin: *If Tropes*. 2002 ISBN 1-4020-0656-X
309. H. Eilstein (ed.): *A Collection of Polish Works on Philosophical Problems of Time and Spacetime*. 2002 ISBN 1-4020-0670-5
310. Y. Gauthier: *Internal Logic*. Foundations of Mathematics from Kronecker to Hilbert. 2002 ISBN 1-4020-0689-6
311. E. Ruttkamp: *A Model-Theoretic Realist Interpretation of Science*. 2002 ISBN 1-4020-0729-9
312. V. Rantala: *Explanatory Translation*. Beyond the Kuhnian Model of Conceptual Change. 2002 ISBN 1-4020-0827-9
313. L. Decock: *Trading Ontology for Ideology*. 2002 ISBN 1-4020-0865-1

314. O. Ezra: *The Withdrawal of Rights*. Rights from a Different Perspective. 2002 ISBN 1-4020-0886-4
315. P. Gärdenfors, J. Woleński and K. Kijania-Placek: *In the Scope of Logic, Methodology and Philosophy of Science*. Volume One of the 11th International Congress of Logic, Methodology and Philosophy of Science, Cracow, August 1999. 2002 ISBN 1-4020-0929-1; Pb 1-4020-0931-3
316. P. Gärdenfors, J. Woleński and K. Kijania-Placek: *In the Scope of Logic, Methodology and Philosophy of Science*. Volume Two of the 11th International Congress of Logic, Methodology and Philosophy of Science, Cracow, August 1999. 2002 ISBN 1-4020-0930-5; Pb 1-4020-0931-3
317. M.A. Changizi: *The Brain from 25,000 Feet*. High Level Explorations of Brain Complexity, Perception, Induction and Vagueness. 2003 ISBN 1-4020-1176-8
318. D.O. Dahlstrom (ed.): *Husserl's* Logical Investigations. 2003 ISBN 1-4020-1325-6
319. A. Biletzki: *(Over)Interpreting Wittgenstein*. 2003 ISBN Hb 1-4020-1326-4; Pb 1-4020-1327-2
320. A. Rojszczak, J. Cachro and G. Kurczewski (eds.): *Philosophical Dimensions of Logic and Science*. Selected Contributed Papers from the 11th International Congress of Logic, Methodology, and Philosophy of Science, Kraków, 1999. 2003 ISBN 1-4020-1645-X
321. M. Sintonen, P. Ylikoski and K. Miller (eds.): *Realism in Action*. Essays in the Philosophy of the Social Sciences. 2003 ISBN 1-4020-1667-0
322. V.F. Hendricks, K.F. Jørgensen and S.A. Pedersen (eds.): *Knowledge Contributors*. 2003 ISBN Hb 1-4020-1747-2; Pb 1-4020-1748-0
323. J. Hintikka, T. Czarnecki, K. Kijania-Placek, T. Placek and A. Rojszczak † (eds.): *Philosophy and Logic In Search of the Polish Tradition*. Essays in Honour of Jan Woleński on the Occasion of his 60th Birthday. 2003 ISBN 1-4020-1721-9
324. L.M. Vaina, S.A. Beardsley and S.K. Rushton (eds.): *Optic Flow and Beyond*. 2004 ISBN 1-4020-2091-0
325. D. Kolak (ed.): *I Am You*. The Metaphysical Foundations of Global Ethics. 2004 ISBN 1-4020-2999-3
326. V. Stepin: *Theoretical Knowledge*. 2005 ISBN 1-4020-3045-2
327. P. Mancosu, K.F. Jørgensen and S.A. Pedersen (eds.): *Visualization, Explanation and Reasoning Styles in Mathematics*. 2005 ISBN 1-4020-3334-6
328. A. Rojszczak (author) and J. Wolenski (ed.): *From the Act of Judging to the Sentence*. The Problem of Truth Bearers from Bolzano to Tarski. 2005 ISBN 1-4020-3396-6
329. A. Pietarinen: *Signs of Logic*. Peircean Themes on the Philosophy of Language, Games, and Communication. 2005 ISBN 1-4020-3728-7
330. A. Aliseda: *Abductive Reasoning*. Logical Investigations into Discovery and Explanation. 2005 ISBN 1-4020-3906-9
331. B. Feltz, M. Crommelinck and P. Goujon (eds.): *Self-organization and Emergence in Life Sciences*. 2005 ISBN 1-4020-3916-6
332. R. van Rooij (ed.): *Attitudes and Changing Contexts*. 2006 ISBN 1-4020-4176-1
333. L. Albertazzi: *Immanent Realism*. An Introduction to Brentano. 2006 ISBN 1-4020-4201-9
334. A. Keupink and S. Shieh (eds.): *The Limits of Logical Empiricism*. Selected Papers of Arthur Pap. 2006 ISBN 1-4020-4298-1
335. M. van Atten: *Brouwer meets Husserl*. On the Phenomenology of Choice Sequences. 2006 ISBN 1-4020-5086-0
336. F. Stjernfelt (ed.): *Diagrammatology*. An Investigation on the Borderlines of Phenomenology, Ontology, and Semiotics. 2007 ISBN 978-1-4020-5651-2
337. H. van Ditmarsch, W. van der Hoek and B. Kooi (eds.): *Dynamic Epistemic Logic*. 2007 ISBN 978-1-4020-5838-1

Previous volumes are still available.